Comparative Politics

Continuity and breakdown in the contemporary world

PAUL W. ZAGORSKI
Pittsburg State University

Routledge
Taylor & Francis Group

LONDON AND NEW YORK

First published 2009
by Routledge
2 Park Square, Milton Park, Abingdon, Oxon OX14 4RN

Simultaneously published in the USA and Canada
by Routledge
270 Madison Avenue, New York, NY 10016

*Routledge is an imprint of the Taylor & Francis Group,
an informa business*

© 2009 Paul W. Zagorski

Typeset in GaramondThree by Keyword Group Ltd
Printed and bound in the United States by Edwards Brothers, Inc.

British Library Cataloguing in Publication Data
A catalogue record for this book is available from the British Library

Library of Congress Cataloging-in-Publication Data
Zagorski, Paul W.
Comparative politics : continuity and breakdown in the contemporary
world / Paul W. Zagorski.
   p. cm.
   Includes bibliographical references.
      1. Comparative government. 2. Comparative government–Case studies.
      I. Title.
   JF51.Z33 2009
   320.6–dc22   2008034148

ISBN10: 0-415-77728-3 (hbk)
ISBN10: 0-415-77729-1 (pbk)
ISBN10: 0-203-88247-4 (ebk)

ISBN13: 978-0-415-77728-5 (hbk)
ISBN13: 978-0-415-77729-2 (pbk)
ISBN13: 978-0-203-88247-4 (ebk)

Comparative Politics

Comparative Politics: Continuity and breakdown in the contemporary world is an exciting new core text for introduction to comparative politics courses, focusing on the dynamics of politics: modernization, revolution, coups, and democratization.

Unlike other texts, *Comparative Politics* integrates thematic and extensive country-specific material in each chapter, striking a unique balance between discussing a wide range of countries and civilizations in detail, whilst using shorter focused textboxes to clearly illustrate key thematic points.

Key features and benefits include:

- Explanation of core concepts such as state, nation, regime, legitimacy, modernization, globalization, revolution, and mass movements.
- Introduction of key theoretical approaches such as institutionalism, structural functionalism, political culture, political economy, and game theory.
- Detailed coverage of democratization, advanced democracies, developing countries, and communist and post-communist states.
- A range of perspectives to present a nuanced view of the discipline and contemporary political developments.
- Case studies of individual countries including Germany, the United States, Russia, Iran, Saudi Arabia, Iraq, Nigeria, Zaire/Congo, South Africa, Brazil, Argentina, Peru, Pakistan, India, Japan, Indonesia, Taiwan, and the People's Republic of China.
- Country-focused textboxes giving a chronology of key developments, including the United Kingdom, France, Afghanistan, and Kosovo.

Extensively illustrated throughout with maps, photographs, tables, and explanatory boxes, *Comparative Politics* is an innovative core text, and essential reading for all students of comparative politics.

Paul W. Zagorski is Professor of Political Science and Coordinator of the International Studies Program at Pittsburg State University in Pittsburg, Kansas, USA.

Contents

CONTENTS

Illustrations

ILLUSTRATIONS

Maps

Boxes

Tables

Acknowledgements

Thanks are due to the anonymous reviews and my students whose comments on the earlier versions of the manuscript helped improve this text. The background information for many of the case studies can be found in the Area Study series published online by the Library of Congress (www.loc.gov). I have tried as much as possible to rely on the judgments of specialists in the appropriate areas in preparing the tables and maps in this text. Most are noted in the citations. Polity IV time-series data were particularly useful in rating regimes as democratic or authoritarian. Also, I would like to thank my friend and chair, Dr. Mike Kelley, whose patience in serving as a sounding board I deeply appreciate. Finally, special recognition and thanks are do to my colleague, Dr. Kyun Joong Kim, and his student assistant, Matt Butterworth. It is Dr. Kim's tireless assistance and mastery of the Geographic Information System that produced the maps in this text. As always, the ultimate responsibility for the judgments (and misjudgments) herein is solely my own.

Introduction

The train of regulated thoughts is of two kinds. One, when of an effect, we seek the cause or means that produced it ... The other is, when imagining anything whatsoever, we seek all the possible effects that can by it be produced.

(Thomas Hobbes, *Leviathan*, 1651)

In this chapter

We explore the aims and methods of comparative politics. As a branch of political science, comparative politics attempts to explain the political world. Specifically, comparative politics focuses on how political systems across the world are organized, how they affect the lives of their citizens, and how they change. Specifically as a scientific enterprise, comparative politics aspires to give a rigorous and systematic account of these matters, but its ability to predict is far less than that of the natural sciences. While the natural sciences have changed dramatically over the centuries, the physical world that they study continues to be governed by the same principles. The same cannot be said for comparative politics. Political systems and our study of them have both evolved dramatically over time. Despite that progress, political scientists who study comparative politics have not been able to settle on a single understanding of their discipline or the sort of agreed upon repertoire of methods for advancing it that, by and large, characterize the natural sciences. Instead, a variety of theories and methods exist. These approaches can be seen as mutually inconsistent and in conflict with one another, but this text, along with many practitioners of the discipline, treats these alternatives as useful components of our intellectual toolkit for understanding the contemporary political world.

What is comparative politics?

Despite the old adage, ignorance is not really bliss. Quite the contrary, what we are ignorant of can hurt us, and what we are unaware of we may be unable to enjoy or profit from. More than ever before, the world is a source of trade, travel, and employment for all of us. The world and its peoples can add to our prosperity and personal growth, but the world beyond our national borders is also a source of danger. What other countries do and how they are organized politically affect us both positively and negatively. Similar democratic values and institutions in Europe and Japan dispose these countries to cooperation and friendly relations with Americans personally and the United States government. Rising Asian stock markets offer the prospects of a prosperous retirement for our parents and grandparents, but falling Asian stock markets threaten these same prospects. A terrorist attack in Nigeria drives up world oil prices. Controlling illegal immigration and drugs requires that the countries from and through which these immigrants and drugs come – e.g., Mexico, South and Central America for the United States, or North Africa and the Balkans for Western Europe – adopt policies that promote economic growth and equity for their own citizens. Islamist radicals, primarily from Saudi Arabia, strike at their own government by destroying New York's World Trade Center and attacking the Pentagon on September 11, 2001. The resulting struggle against terrorist organizations requires creating a stable and effective government in Afghanistan and involves the United States and its allies more deeply than previously with the Islamic world. In short, other countries' domestic politics do affect us. Ignorance is not a viable option.

Of all the academic courses an undergraduate can take, comparative politics is one of the most useful for improving understanding of the international opportunities and pitfalls that we face as individuals and as a nation. **Comparative politics** is the study of political systems around the globe. It investigates not only the governmental institutions responsible for making binding legal decisions but also the formal and informal political arrangements and attitudes that undergird them. It raises and attempts to answer questions about why some countries are stable and prosperous while others are not, why different sorts of governments predominate in certain regions and not others, and why and how certain individuals or groups are able to exercise influence over public policy rather than others. This text is designed as an introduction to the study of comparative politics. It combines theory with concrete discussions of particular cases of signal importance.

Explaining the present and anticipating the future

In ancient times science or theory was seen as an end in itself. It was good for human beings to know the truth and contemplate the world and the way it worked regardless of the fact that their knowledge of it could not be used either to alter the world or to make everyday life better. The practical arts – what today we call "technology" – had the useful as their proper end. It was this latter branch of knowledge that would help people make things and so make the world a better place in which to live. Yet even in ancient times, philosophers recognized that there was an in-between sort of knowledge – knowledge that was true, just as the most abstruse discoveries of contemporary nuclear physics are true, but also comprehensible and useful to ordinary people in the way that nuclear physics is not. From the beginning political science and comparative politics were seen as just this in-between sort of knowledge. They could tell us important things about how the political world works and what we need to do to be successful politically, or at least they could advise us on what we need to do to minimize our chances of contributing to social or political disasters.

However, there are serious questions about how successful comparative politics is or can be in providing guidance or in explaining and predicting events. Will comparative politics ever have the predictive power of, say, astronomy, which has the capacity to predict celestial events with great precision far into the future? In his classic science fiction trilogy, *The Foundation*, Isaac Asimov describes a social scientist who was able to do just that – to predict the course of galactic history centuries in advance and take steps to alter its course. Asimov's hero, Heri Seldon, did not rely on powers of clairvoyance or hunches, he was a true scientist armed with mathematical equations and scientific laws. The fictional Seldon achieved what the real Thomas Hobbes, an important figure in the history of philosophy and political science and the source of the epigraph at the head of this chapter, speculated about – a fully developed science of politics.

Hobbes (and Seldon) saw not only science but also all rational activity as directed toward discovering the relationship between causes and effects. Hobbes was, if anything, more demanding than Asimov's Seldon. While Asimov portrays Seldon as having a science that made predictions about the general course of history, not about specific individuals, Hobbes thought that in principle even discrete events could be predicted. A strong wind slams a door shut – the noise for the slamming door startles a sleeping cat – the suddenly-excited cat jumps on a table – the cat's jump overturns the table, sending a lighted kerosene lamp crashing to the floor – the flame from the lamp starts a fire and burns down the barn in which the cat, the lamp, and the table stood. Hobbes was a determinist. A **determinist** believes that all events have causes; they are neither matters of chance nor choice. Hobbes believed that working backwards, we see causal connections: the gust of wind caused the barn to burn down. If our knowledge were precise enough, Hobbes thought we could reason forward as well. In theory if we understood completely the laws that govern the world and the precise location of things within it, we could accurately predict the future. Knowing the strength of the wind, the positions of the door, the table and the lamp, and knowing the general laws that determine a cat's reaction to outside stimuli, the heat produced by burning kerosene, and the ignition point of the material on the barn's floor, we could have predicted the fire before it happened. The fire was not really a chance event. We simply lacked sufficient knowledge of the underlying causes to predict it. That the fire would occur was unknown, but not inherently unknowable (Hobbes 1950: 18–19, 67–8).

In many respects the natural sciences seem to validate Hobbes's deterministic worldview. Natural scientists have been successful at both predicting and controlling nature. In part, natural scientists have been so because they have advantages that those of us interested in acquiring political knowledge do not have. They can conduct controlled experiments where they can limit the number of potential causes. By dropping objects in a vacuum, the physicist can demonstrate that all objects, regardless of their weight, fall at the same rate of acceleration. Friction with the atmosphere and the varying effects of objects' aerodynamic can be eliminated. Or natural scientists can make precise observations at times and places where they are relatively sure that extraneous factors will not influence the outcome. Astronomers can go to remote locations where the instruments are relatively unaffected by the effects of human civilization on the atmosphere. Biologists can seek out relatively pristine environments to observe and catalogue animal behavior.

In contrast, politics is messy, and Hobbes himself despaired of actually reaching the level of knowledge required for truly accurate prediction. In the political world, a wide variety of possible causes are often present, and it is often difficult to sort them out. Even similar events, such as national elections within a particular country, are not exact replications of one another. Different, sometimes unknown, factors operate in each iteration. Yet some contemporary social scientists remain optimistic. George Homans, in almost Hobbesian fashion, argues that the actions of groups can be explained from the general psychological laws governing individual behavior. He, like Hobbes, believes choice is only an illusion and that individual actions are completely determined, but unlike Hobbes, he believes we already have the basic tools and discoveries required for developing the full range of social sciences (Homans 1967: 103–5; Hobbes 1950: 47–8). Thus, if Homans is correct, the messiness of politics simply makes political prediction much more difficult than predictions about the natural world. Perfecting comparative politics as a science may take time, but with enough effort, comparative politics could yet achieve the rigor and predictive ability of the natural sciences.

Others – ordinary people, poets such as William Shakespeare, and even some scientists – are not so sure. The determinist view stands in sharp contrast to another perhaps more common view, namely that somehow we humans are masters of our own fate. The important part of the world is not its material element and the deterministic laws that govern matter. The behavior, of air, doors, burning kerosene, and even cats, may be subject to physical or psychological laws, but human choice is not. And the important element in the political world we are trying to explain involves human choice. Thus, in politics big causes sometimes account for relatively little. We can all pull ourselves up by our own bootstraps despite the odds. Shakespeare's play, *Julius Caesar*, gives an example of and an object lesson about this point of view. Cassius, a politician plotting Caesar's assassination, tells a prospective coconspirator, Marcus Brutus, that they have the power to control events. "The fault, dear Brutus," he admonishes, "is not in our stars, but in ourselves"(Act I, Scene II). If Cassius, Brutus, and the others but act, they and not Caesar will control Rome! Human beings, not fate, decide. Yet Cassius's optimism about his ability to control events miscarries. Although the conspirators succeed in assassinating Caesar, they are eventually defeated in the Battle of Philippi by Caesar's allies and die by their own hands. Nonetheless, if Cassius and the "voluntarists" like him are correct, a rigorous approach to comparative politics would be all but impossible. Individuals control events, and there is no predicting what individual human beings may want to do and may be capable of accomplishing.

Hobbes and Cassius represent two incompatible extremes. A more balanced view of humans' capacities to control events is presented in the play by Brutus himself. "There is a tide in the affairs of men," he tells his colleague, "when taken at its height, leads on to fortune; omitted, all the voyage of their life is bound in shallows and in miseries" (Act IV, Scene III). In other words, we are often the prey of forces greater than ourselves. But there are some times when these forces may temporarily balance one another and, in fact, open the opportunity for us to affect our own destiny in a decisive manner. Human beings control events, but only at the margins – the tide must be at its height. If Brutus is right about the way human choice can alter the world, we will never, even in principle, be able to predict political outcomes with complete confidence. There will always be at least a degree of uncertainty since human choice will affect the results. It is not a matter of knowing too few facts or possessing an inadequate theory. With all the facts and the best possible theory, we still could not make predictions with absolute assurance because human beings themselves are unpredictable, and human beings make a difference. Yet, if Brutus is right that grand forces have a decisive role in shaping our destiny (or the viable choices actually available to us), then we still ought to be able to predict or at least anticipate events to some degree. Brutus's middle view on freedom and determinism seems to be a safe bet. Comparative politics' success and the success of the social sciences generally appear to be much more than a matter of dumb luck. We can explain why events happened, and we can get some realistic sense of the way things are likely to evolve in the future.

For practical purposes and for the foreseeable future at least, we can safely ignore Hobbes's and Homans's notion of complete determinism. Students of comparative politics – both those of us who make our livelihoods studying and teaching it as well as those of us who will take only one introductory course – are, in fact, in possession of less than complete and perfectly accurate information. And small events, apparently caused by human choice or sheer chance, can have immense consequence. If Napoleon had not been fatigued and retired to his tent at a critical juncture of the Battle of Waterloo, the fight might have evolved much differently and much of Europe might today be a French empire. Or if Yuri Andropov had been in good health, he might not have died so soon after his selection as Soviet leader and his successor, Mikhail Gorbachev, might never have become General Secretary of the Soviet Communist Party. The collapse of the Soviet Union in 1991 at the end of a prolonged crisis that was in large measure brought on by Gorbachev's attempts at reform might never have occurred. And consequently the Soviet Communist Party and the Soviet Union might have survived. Could a Hobbesian science of politics have predicted either of these two events, let alone their consequences? We shall probably never know.

Comparative politics as a science of politics

What is clear is that we do not today have such a deterministic science of politics. Hobbes's, Homans's, and Asimov's vision of social science remains science fiction and probably always will. However, we do possess a variety of techniques that allow us to understand the political world and draw some general conclusions about causes and effects in a way that fits the middle position expressed by Shakespeare's hero, Marcus Brutus. Comparativists are able to generalize successfully because they recognize that their conclusions must be based on evidence. To acquire this evidence and come to these conclusions, they have a variety of facts, methods, findings, and theories at their disposal. Over time, the body of facts increases. And theories, findings, and methods are refined through research and debate. **Facts** are discrete bits of information. They constitute the building blocks upon which generalizations rest. They are pieces of evidence the existence of which can be verified by all knowledgeable observers. The names and biographies of individuals holding particular offices or engaged in the political process, the constitutional texts that describe the powers and tenure of these offices, collective or individual opinions, the actions taken by particular individuals and groups – all count as facts, or as things capable of factual determination. Facts are critical, but facts don't speak for themselves. Nor are the readily available facts sufficient to permit us to draw conclusions about many questions of interest to us in comparative politics.

Theories, generalizations or sets of generalizations that define basic terms and propose explanations of how the world or a part of it works, are necessary adjuncts to facts. All facts are not created equal. Theories tell us what facts are most important. Theories purport to tell us how politics works by making predictions about events or statements about relationships in the political world. These predictions and statements are **hypotheses** that, in turn, can be tested against the facts. The better tested the theory and the more capable it is of making useful predictions, the more likely it is that practitioners of comparative politics will accept it into the core of the discipline. This acceptance is always a matter of degree. In politics even the soundest generalizations admit of exceptions, and a set of facts may support different theories. Thus, comparativists disagree among themselves about which theories are well founded or the most important. Comparative politics relies on methods. **Methods** are the systematic ways we acquire facts that would not otherwise be readily available. They constitute the ways we do political research. We may study legal texts, examine political history or the contemporary record of events, interview participants in political events or consult their memoirs, construct and administer opinion surveys, collect and analyze statistics on the government, economy and society. Where accurate data are available, political scientists can use statistical tools to assess the relative importance of various causes over a number of different cases. Methods give us facts. A systematic analysis of the facts gives us **findings**; these are statements about relationships of different sets of facts that can serve to build, undermine, or support theories.

In other words, there are a variety of methods that practitioners of comparative politics find useful. On the macro level, the statistical data from a wide variety of countries can be used to test broad generalization, such as the hypothesis that rich countries are more likely than poor countries to become and remain democratic. Alternately, investigators can examine specific regions, countries, or institutions within individual countries in an attempt to gain a more fine-grained understanding of how politics operates. The use of parallel cases can be a valuable tool that can help tease out relationships. In short, facts, whatever the method of collection, cannot substitute for theory. Facts and theory work in tandem.

Anyone expecting to find in today's comparative politics something that matches the success of the version of social science described in Asimov's *Foundation* novels is bound to be disappointed. Perhaps the feature of contemporary comparative politics that most undermines its scientific aspirations is that there is no single overarching theory that satisfies all the discipline's practitioners and into which all the methods and findings of the discipline conveniently fit. Despite the fact that the discipline has been around since at least the time of the ancient Greeks, comparative politics does not have a general theoretical overview that guides all practitioners the way that evolution unifies biological research or the common mathematical/mechanistic focus unifies physics. Instead, there are a variety of theories that help explain different aspects of politics. And practitioners of comparative politics assign different value or relevance to each of its components. In the final analysis, however, diversity and disagreement about some of the basics has its compensations. Individually, the methods and theories available have considerable limitations. Collectively they provide a repertoire of tools practitioners can use to address important questions faced by policy-makers and citizens. They allow us to anticipate rather than exactly predict the future.

Institutionalism and neo-institutionalism

In the late nineteenth and early twentieth centuries, comparative politics focused on legal institutions – the branches of the government and associated bodies. **Institutions** are long-standing patterns of behavior that have a strong normative component. Members of institutions not only can be expected to conform to these established patterns; as members, they are morally obliged to do so. **Institutionalism** is the approach to comparative politics that focuses on the *formal legal rules* that direct how the government, the various parts of it, and related entities such as political parties, are supposed to work. Institutionalism is particularly important where politics is actually structured by legal rules and where these legal rules are well respected, e.g., in modern democracies that respect the rule of law. In these countries, competitors for power generally respect electoral outcomes, and officeholders normally abide by the legal limits placed upon them. Since the legal rules and their consequences are well known, we can anticipate what politicians, political parties, and interest groups are likely to do and how politics is likely to evolve. However, traditional institutionalism can take us only so far. Power holders make decisions and strike deals that are allowed but not determined by institutional norms. Moreover, the utility of this version of institutionalism is further circumscribed by the fact that not all countries have written constitutions and not all of those that have such constitutions actually follow them. In addition, even some countries that adhere to written constitutions suffer violent constitutional change. In short, legal rules explain only one aspect of politics.

As a consequence, institutionalism has evolved over the past several decades to provide useful analyses even of countries where the rule of law is not well respected. This new approach to institutions is called "neo-institutionalism." **Neo-institutionalism** is the approach to comparative politics that investigates the informal rules that govern institutions, the evolution of institutions, and the strategies politicians and others use to take advantage of institutional rules. In investigating informal rules, neo-institutionalism takes a sociological rather than a primarily legal approach. Even countries where the rule of law is poorly respected have governmental institutions that endure and have considerable effect on the way politics is conducted. Governmental bureaucracies, court systems, and the armed forces are such institutions. The rules that govern these institutions may be unwritten or informal, but they are rules nonetheless. How these institutions recruit and train their members, how they govern themselves, how efficient they are, how they protect their own interests, the power they have in the political process, and how they have evolved over time are all subject to rigorous neo-institutionalist analysis. If analysts know enough about how these particular institutions within a given country work, they can make intelligent guesses about the likelihood of coups d'etat, political collapse, and the course of governmental policy. In addition, neo-institutionalism includes the historical study of how legal institutions develop and the manner in which people involved in institutions use them for their own objectives (see "Rational choice and game theory" below).

Structural–functionalism

Like neo-institutionalism, the structural/functional approach also borrows heavily from sociology. It too transcended the narrow focus of the original version of institutionalism and became the most comprehensive, most generally accepted comparative theory in the second half of the twentieth century. It takes a comprehensive view of politics within a country in all its aspects. **Structural–functionalism** is the approach to comparative politics that considers "political systems" in the broadest sense: the formal and informal power arrangements that comprise a political system and the functions they must carry out for the system to survive. The elements of this definition need to be further unpacked. First of all, structures are the rough equivalent of institutions spoken of earlier, but an understanding of formally organized institutions established in legal documents has to be supplemented by a grasp of other political and even social institutions that were not so officially and formally organized. Without a broader consideration of other structural elements, the political system as a whole cannot be understood. In other words, the analysis of governmental structures (institutions) has to be supplemented by a discussion of other *structures* – political parties, interest groups, the media, social movements, voluntary organizations, etc. – to get a more well-rounded understanding of the way politics works in any particular country. More critical still, structural–functionalism recognizes that structures are important only because they carry out certain necessary functions essential for the maintenance of the political system – acquiring resources, providing for the legitimacy of officials and their decisions, articulating and aggregating different interests, making policy decisions expeditiously, and implementing those decisions efficiently.

Structural–functionalism sees through the legalisms that often obscure how things really work. It allows for nuanced comparisons across countries. Structures that appear quite dissimilar may have the same function. Structural–functionalism also prompts us to see the big picture and take the long view. Structural–functionalists often address change as "development" – a gradual process by which less articulated structures become more complex and efficient or even more democratic. However, while structural–functionalism's attention to the big picture allows the student of politics to recognize how in general a system may be failing, it provides only a limited account of the mechanisms that can account for this failure.

Political culture and political socialization

Political culture is the set of basic political attitudes that characterize a country's population or some of its subgroups. A study of political culture provides a necessary adjunct and corrective to structural–functionalism's universalistic implications. Political culture can be studied in various ways. National character studies take a broad historical and anthropological approach. But political scientists are more likely to investigate political culture by means of opinion surveys. Political culture is important because basic political attitudes such as tolerance or intolerance, views of political authority, or trust or lack of trust of fellow citizens affect the nature of politics profoundly. Political culture also affects how and if institutional structures will be copied from abroad, and how they will function in their new environment. In its broadest sense, political culture might be said to include political skills as well as attitudes, but since the classic studies of political culture have been based on opinion surveys, political scientists normally speak of political culture in terms of attitudes alone. However, neither basic political attitudes nor skills change quickly. Hence, the focus is implied continuity. Political culture has a companion approach, political socialization. While the study of political culture focuses on complexes of attitudes and their likely effects, **political socialization** is the branch of comparative politics that examines the formal and informal mechanisms by which these attitudes are inculcated. Schools, churches, the mass media, civic groups, other formal organizations, families, and peer groups socialize their members in distinctive ways, both intentionally and unintentionally. The study of political socialization explores the methods by which cultures are reinforced or altered. It focuses on the process as much as the product.

Political economy

Economics as the branch of social science examines how the production of goods and services is organized. It critiques policies and provides advice about how the system of production can be made more efficient via the type of protection the government extends to property, its tax laws and other regulations, the management of the banking and financial systems, and the way the government itself spends money. The economists' advice is almost always of an "all other things being equal" variety. For purposes of analysis, economists assume that their advice can be applied without the need for side deals to induce important economic and political actors to accept it. Political economy studies the intersection of economics and politics. Economists may think about maximizing the society's overall wealth, but the politicians, who actually make policy, are more interested in their own share of that wealth and the share of the group they represent. Thus, political side deals must be made to make specific economic policies acceptable. **Political economy** is the approach to comparative politics that investigates both a country's overall economic policies and the set of interests that back them. In other words, it is concerned with both the policies and the process that produced them. Political economy can help explain both stability and breakdown. When policies are tolerably efficient and satisfy all key constituencies, both policy stability and political stability are likely to ensue. However, if economic policies fail significantly on either count for a considerable period of time, there will be a political price to pay. Orthodox Marxists foresee economic failure and political breakdown as the inevitable consequences of economic laws. Other students of political economy tend to be more agnostic. Policy failure and political breakdown are always possibilities, but they have to be investigated on a more ad hoc basis than Marxists normally opt for. A significant number of countries have had successful economic policies and political stability for extended periods of time.

Rational choice and game theory

Human beings are rational, or at least some of them are rational some of the time. Thus, it is fruitful to study the political choices people make to make the best use of their limited resources. Examining individuals, groups, and their leaders in terms of the choices they make is at the core of rational choice theory. **Rational choice** is the approach to political analysis that examines how decision-makers can make efficient use of means to obtain their ends. Although they were not based on a formal rational choice analysis, the "checks and balances" of the United States Constitution, where officeholders are supposed to use the rights of the office to block the actions of others and advance their own interests, were designed on the basis of implicit rational-choice assumptions (Madison 1961: 56–65, 347–53). In its contemporary iteration, the rational choice approach can be highly formalistic. It assumes individuals are rational, that ends and means can be accurately articulated, and that risks and opportunities can be correctly assessed. For example, rational choice theorists can devise formulas for when and under what conditions a prime minister should call new elections (and put her own tenure at risk) even before she is obliged to do so by constitutional mandate. The assumptions rational choice theory makes are not necessarily heroic although reason certainly does not drive all political events.

Sometimes rational, we as individuals can make choices without reference to what others may do, but in other instances the likely reaction of others to frustrate or further our ends is the key to making a rational decision in the first place. Game theory takes up this interactive problem. **Game theory**, in the strict sense of the term, is a branch of mathematics that developed during the mid-twentieth century. It is a highly systematic approach to the sometimes complex interrelationships between individual choices and payoffs when individuals or groups compete with one another or when they try to cooperate but cannot coordinate their actions. Game theory can establish a payoff matrix, players, and can use this matrix to evaluate the best strategy for each competing player to follow. The simple

Table I.1   Rock–paper–scissors

	B chooses rock	B chooses paper	B chooses scissors
A chooses rock	0,0	0,1	1,0
A chooses paper	1,0	0,0	0,1
A chooses scissors	0,1	1,0	0,0

game of "rock–paper–scissors" can serve as an example. Since paper covers rock, rock breaks scissors, and scissors cut paper, the payoff matrix for the game would look something like Table I.1 describing the payoffs for two players, A and B. (The first number in each cell is A's payoff, and the second number is B's.)

The payoffs are the result of the basic rules of the game, and the matrix tells us explicitly what we probably recognized intuitively already: there is no one best choice for either A or B to make. The most we can say is that, if the game is to be played a number of times, it is in the interest of a player not to fall into a predictable pattern that his opponent can recognize and exploit. In short, analysis of the matrix clarifies the nature of the game and the strategies that rational players ought to follow. "Rock–paper–scissors" is a highly artificial game. It has no apparent real-world applications. But game theoretical analysis has had many practical successes. It can handle games that are much more complex and mirror situations found in the real world. When individuals or groups are in competition with one another or at least choose independently of one another, where the possible choices they can make are known, and where the consequences of these interacting choices are predictable, then a situation is susceptible to game-theoretical analysis.

An example of applying game theory to politics can be found in *Radicals, Reformers, and Reactionaries* by Youssef Cohen (Cohen 1994). In explaining the political dynamics that led to military coups in Latin America during the 1960s and 1970s, Cohen analyzes the alternatives faced by leftwing and rightwing moderates, both of whom valued democracy but whose preferences for policies differed profoundly. The moderates on each side had the choice of cooperating with each other or the extremists on their own side who oppose a democratic solution. Cohen produces a payoff matrix which, simplified, looks like that of Table I.2.

When run only once, rock–paper–scissors has no solution – that is, there is no best strategy that would at least minimize the chance of a loss. Cohen's matrix does have such a solution. What the matrix tells us is if

Table I.2 Radicals, reformers, and reactionaries

	Moderate right abandons extreme right and works with moderate left	Moderate right supports extreme right
Moderate left abandons extreme left and works with moderate right	Reforms passed, no regime breakdown	Only marginal reforms
Moderate left supports extreme left	Radical reform	Democracy breaks down

Source: Adapted from Cohen 1994: 67

both groups of moderates simultaneously back away from their maximum demands, they will get a result that is at least second best for each. However, opting for a second-best outcome has its own risks. If the moderates on the other side do not sincerely cooperate, however, the cooperative moderates get what is for them the worst possible outcome. Since there is no way to guarantee that the other side's moderates will sincerely carry though on any pledges of cooperation, the game theoretic solution is for each group of moderates to make the choice that avoids the worst possible outcome. This leads to noncooperation between the moderates and the breakdown of democracy, which neither particularly wanted.

Game theory shows us that although people involved in politics may be rational and try to maximize the good for themselves, they do not always get what they intend. More than that, it tells us why this is the case. Political scientists have applied game theory to the study of conflict-ridden periods in a particular country's national politics (e.g., Cohen), coalition formation in parliamentary governments, and electoral strategy in two-party democracies. Even beyond the formal applications that game theory and rational choice provide, their focus upon political actors and political actors' strategic choices provides a fruitful way to approach comparative politics.

A synthetic approach

Many contemporary comparative politics texts are organized along structure-by-structure and function-by-function lines. Other texts focus holistically on different regime types. Still others discuss countries individually and show how their institutions operate as a whole. This text does something a little different and somewhat more eclectic. It uses a variety of theoretical approaches to shed light on a single theme, continuity and breakdown in the contemporary world. Each chapter is structured around a basic issue of comparative politics and uses one or more short case studies occasionally along with shorter country-focused boxes to illustrate the thematic points. The text focuses on the dynamics of politics: political actors, their interests and strategies, as well as the causes of continuity and breakdown of regimes. The first two chapters examine the themes of continuity and breakdown in general, and, in the process, explain core concepts such as state, nation, regime, legitimacy, modernization, revolution, and mass movements. These concepts and approaches are then applied and developed further in the discussion of specific sorts of regimes and breakdowns in the next ten chapters. While covering the traditional topics of comparative politics, the text gives pride of place to issues that have emerged over the past several decades. Democratization, semi-authoritarian and semi-democratic regimes receive systematic treatment. The armed forces and the varying political roles they play are discussed. The final two chapters discuss globalization and the future of democracy.

Reprise: why study comparative politics?

Even a cursory inspection of the political panorama of the early twenty-first century makes the importance of addressing political continuity and breakdown obvious. Citizens and policy-makers have in many ways been overtaken by events. Comparative politics needs to account for the collapse of apparently stable communist states, the consolidation of democracies in countries once beset by military dictatorships, and the rise of Islamic revolutionary movements. Not inconsequentially, comparative politics also needs to account for the persistence of regimes, such as absolute monarchies, that seem to be obsolete throwbacks to the past. And, perhaps most importantly, comparative politics needs to anticipate where the unprecedented changes of the last several decades are leading us. Thus, although comparative politics explains how political systems work, today more than ever, it must also account for how and why they break down and what's likely to emerge when they do. In short, the study of comparative politics is worthwhile for a variety of reasons. It provides students with the wherewithal to anticipate where they and the world around them are heading and what they can do about it. An understanding of comparative politics makes the world less bewildering and more intriguing. Moreover, studying comparative politics gives an additional bonus. It provides another chance to look at one's own country and some of the political and social practices that are taken for granted in a new light. Comparative politics shows institutions and practices that work both better and worse than our own. It provides new ideas and insights.

Questions for further consideration

1　How do comparative politics and the rest of the social sciences compare with the natural sciences in terms of their subject matter? Their methods? How significant are the ways in which they are different? What sorts of problems interfere with arriving at exact and accurate predictions in the social sciences?

2　Can any scientific or comparative politics theory be a "fact"? Why not? Does this make theory unimportant? Why not?

3　Which of the basic theoretical approaches discussed in the Introduction focus on individuals and individual choices? Which focus on groups or systems as a whole? What are the general implications of either approach?

Further reading

Martin Hollis, *The Philosophy of Social Science: An Introduction*. Cambridge: Cambridge University Press, 1994. Discusses how social scientists attempt to take a rigorous (scientific) approach to the study of society. Although comparative politics is not its primary focus the issues raised will help the student understand the importance of the methodological and theoretical choices comparativists make.

George Homans, *The Nature of Social Science*. New York: Harcourt, Brace and World, 1967. A classic statement of the determinist approach to social science.

Kenneth R. Hoover, *The Elements of Social Scientific Thinking* (4th edn). New York: St. Martin's Press, 1988. A basic text on quantitative methods in political science.

Peter Mair, "Comparative Politics: An Overview," in R. Goodin and H.D. Klingemann (eds), *A New Handbook of Political Science*. Oxford: Oxford University Press, 1996. A short overview of comparative politics today.

Bernard Susser, *Approaches to the Study of Politics*. New York: Macmillan Publishing Co., 1992. Provides a detailed discussion of the theoretical approaches described in the Introduction.

1 Continuity and breakdown

A man never steps in the same river twice. He's not the same man.
And it's not the same river.

(Heraclitus, sixth century BC)

In this chapter

We examine some of the basic concepts of comparative politics, including those that will be most pivotal in the rest of the text. Comparative politics wrestles with the issues of the change and continuity of political systems or regimes, the basic political structures that define the political order in self-governing, independent countries. This text and this chapter take a synthetic approach to explain why and how important individuals and groups act to enhance or preserve their power, and the consequences their actions have for preserving or undermining the political system. The text draws on the various approaches outlined in the text's Introduction. Structural–functionalism informs the text's overall framework: a regime thrives when it possesses certain basic functional supports. Political culture plays a key role in understanding the regime support of legitimacy. Political economy is important in understanding another support, the effectiveness of governmental administration. And the notion of strategic calculation derived from game theory is critical for understanding how governments and oppositions act. The chapter concludes with two case studies, one on the fall of the Weimar Republic in Germany in the 1930s and the other on the 1964 Brazilian coup. These case studies illustrate how the political strategies followed by individuals and groups can have dramatic consequences for the political system.

Introduction

Change is a constant in both the natural and human worlds, but not all changes are the same. Human beings may age slowly and imperceptibly, but they may also die sudden and violent deaths. The water in a river may flow on placidly, subtly altering the position of the pebbles in its bed, but rivers also suffer cataclysmic five-hundred-year floods that change their course dramatically forever. The range of changes in the political world is not much different. In countries such as France, Great Britain, and Japan, for nearly half a century at least, individual politicians and parties gain and lose office on a regular basis; laws are passed after open debate, and mass protests, when they occur, are largely peaceful. Yet nothing very violent or dramatic occurs. Political life there seems to resemble a slowly flowing river. But in countries such as Iran in 1979, the Soviet Union in 1991, Congo in 1997, and Afghanistan for much of the last quarter century, revolution, rebellion, or coups d'etat were the norm. One group of politicians threw out another with dramatic consequences for the entire country. Neither continuity nor improvement is guaranteed. This chapter introduces some of the concepts and theories of comparative politics that shed light on why in some countries and in some periods, change is generally incremental and peacefully accommodated and in other countries or other periods it is quite the opposite. We leave the issues of improvement or deterioration of political conditions to later chapters.

Politics and power

The most basic political concept is that of **political power** – the ability of one person or group to impose its will on another. The struggle for power is seemingly ubiquitous. "I put it down as a general inclination of all mankind," Thomas Hobbes wrote, "a perpetual and restless desire of power after power that ceases only in death" (Hobbes 1950: 79). Hobbes had a bleak view of human nature. Politics is about power, and no one is ever satisfied. Power may come in many forms: physical force, legal authority, wealth, reputation, even knowledge. Once we achieve power, we may seek many different ends, but, in the final analysis, power is politics' coin of the realm, and the struggle for power breeds conflict. This thought, not original with Hobbes, has been echoed many times since he published *Leviathan* in 1651. Harold Lasswell, a twentieth-century political scientist, put it not quite so starkly when he said that politics was the process that determines who gets what, when and how (Lasswell 1936).

Almost everyone who understands the realities of power politics, Hobbes included, wishes to moderate or avoid the worst aspects of a naked struggle for power. Hobbes called the most extreme version of this naked struggle for power the "**state of nature**." In the state of nature there was no government to enforce order and no agreement about basic moral principles that ought to govern political affairs. In the state of nature,

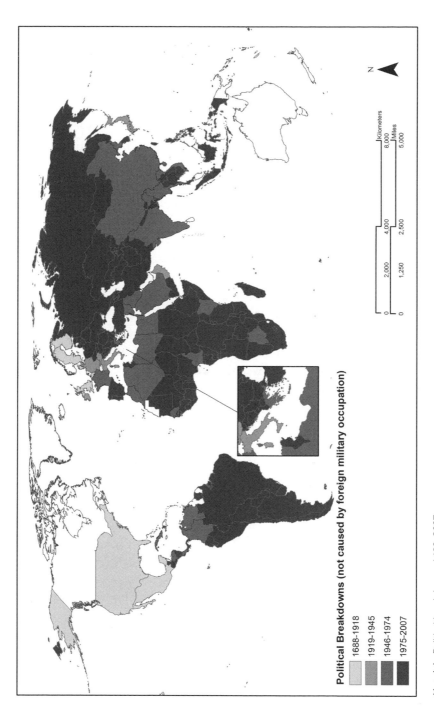

Political Breakdowns (not caused by foreign military occupation)

- 1688–1918
- 1919–1945
- 1946–1974
- 1975–2007

Map 1.1 Political breakdowns, 1688–2007

Source: Environmental Systems Research Institute (ESRI) map data

human beings are trapped in a war of all against all. And life is "solitary, poor, nasty, brutish, and short." To escape the state of nature, Hobbes believed that human beings would – and should – accept any arrangement that provided for settled, predictable government. He called this collective recognition of the individual or group in ultimate command the "**social contract**." This individual or group with moral authority and the physical capacity to command Hobbes called the "sovereign." This coupling of moral and physical power was the essence of political power. Once they made the social contract, either by explicit or by implicit agreement, human beings were obliged by morality and self-interest to keep it. The evils of the state of nature were so great, Hobbes believed, that anyone or any group capable of imposing peace ought to be granted the moral authority to do so (Hobbes 1950: 108–18).

Today most historians and political scientists do not believe that anything resembling Hobbes's state of nature or social contract ever existed. Nonetheless, whether or not a person is prepared to take Hobbes's account literally, it gives some sense of how and why politics becomes the orderly process implied by Lasswell's definition. And whatever we think about Hobbes's claim that people have a moral obligation to obey any government whatsoever so long as it has effective power, his analysis underscores some important psychological facts. In politics, moral authority and physical power do go hand in hand. One cannot exist indefinitely without the other. Rule by force alone is not likely to endure, and the moral authority of government unsupported by physical force is likely to be flouted and ultimately break down. The social contract is meant to guarantee peace and public order, but Hobbes, Lasswell, and most others who have explored the issue of power and politics have recognized that the consensus that lies behind any political order does not abolish the struggle for power; it only channels it. The underlying struggle for power goes on.

Political actors

The struggle for power is conducted by **political actors** – individuals and groups exercising a degree, however limited, of political power. Political actors have interests and objectives that they attempt to defend or realize. To do so, they employ the resources they have at their disposal. In other words, they make strategic choices. Political actors' strategies can change over time as they learn from experience, acquire new resources, or the underlying situation changes. There is a vast difference among political actors, their interests, objectives, resources, and strategies. Some are active and exercise a great deal of power; others are largely passive. In some ages, vast numbers of people, such as the serfs of the Middle Ages, were more the objects of the power of others than actors who actually exercised power themselves. Until recently, women lacked political power. But when they became politically mobilized, even formerly powerless groups can become significant political actors. Women first gained political rights, and in the past several decades have used their power to shape policy and assume roles of direct leadership in many countries. Both groups and individuals count as political actors: Prime Minister Gordon Brown and Senator Harry Reid count as political actors. As are the Democratic Party, the Trades Union Congress, the American Nursing Association, industrial workers, small farmers, and even so-called "soccer moms" and "NASCAR dads" even though they have differing degrees of organization and unity of purpose.

Some actors are members of the **elite** – those who have significant influence over the political process in their own right; others are non-elite actors. Some actors are individuals; other actors are **mass actors**, who often compensate for their lack of significant direct influence over the political process and limited individual power by their numbers. Some groups are formally organized; some are not. When mobilized into a mass movement, mass actors can have a great impact on public policy and even on the way the political order itself is structured. However, such mobilization requires the continuing commitment of large numbers of people to act collectively for a single purpose. It also requires sufficient direction so that the movement's efforts are focused rather than dissipated. These capacities are quite difficult to sustain over time. Thus, to endure, mass movements often rely on formal organizations. More often than not, a significant number of such organizations help organize, animate, and direct the energies of the movement's members. Mass movements, however spontaneous they may be, also generate a cadre of leaders. The organizations generated or bolstered by mass movements and the leaders whose careers they further often remain important even after the mass movement itself loses its dynamism. For example, the US civil rights movement of the 1950s and 1960s was dependent upon organizations like the National Association for the Advancement of Colored People (NAACP), the Student Nonviolence Coordinating Committee, and the Southern Christian Leadership Conference, and leaders such as Dr. Martin Luther King, Jesse Jackson, and Stokely Carmichael to give it a sense of purpose and direct its energies. Though some organizations have faded, many of the organizations and the successors of King and the leaders of his generation are around today. The civil rights movement is not unique. Mass movements elsewhere are not much different in principle although their aims range from reform to revolution and their methods from peaceful protest to mass violence. They too often generate organizations that survive.

Different political actors have different sorts of power. The power of some may be primarily physical, for example, wealth or military power. That of others may be psychological, for example, popularity, prestige, or moral authority. A mobilized mass movement may have power of both sorts. Not all types of power are equally valuable in all circumstances. Military command may be the key to acquiring political power in countries where civilian authority is weak, but in consolidated liberal democracies, military command rarely permits the officer holding it to seize control of the government. At best his military achievements can win him popularity, which, in turn, may help him win office. Different actors have different aims. Some actually seek political power for themselves; others are satisfied to influence the governmental process. Some, such as revolutionaries, seek complete and unrestricted power to issue commands and are unwilling to share it. For others, such as most political actors in liberal democracies, having a share of power is sufficient. Still others are satisfied with a smaller share still; they simply want to be left alone. Like small farmers in early nineteenth-century America, they seek very little positive from government beyond the protection of their persons and the small amount of property they possess. Some actors' objectives and use of power imply that they see themselves in a kind of Hobbesian state of nature. They rely heavily on coercion and feel relatively unconstrained by conventional moral norms of evenhandedness and the avoidance of excessive violence. At other times, most actors abide by what Hobbes called the social contract. They recognize the moral authority of the political system and govern their struggle for power accordingly. Situations of the second sort are capable of attaining stability or continuity. Governments can successfully accommodate changes, even incremental changes in their own structure. Like Heraclitus's man or Heraclitus's river, they are never exactly the same from one year to the next, but from a common sense perspective, they continue on. However, when powerful actors act as if they are in the state of nature, political breakdown is likely to ensue. Such breakdown often entails chaos, violence, and the destruction of wealth. Much of the remainder of this chapter will be devoted specifically to breakdown, but we will turn to situations characterized by stability or continuity first.

Regimes

Hobbes's social contract establishes a "**regime**," "**form of government**," or "**political system**" – a system of government that is supposed to have

Plate 1.1 Aristotle. Founder of political science and comparative politics.

sufficient moral authority and physical power to secure its continuance
even as individual leaders leave office. This text uses the three terms
interchangeably although some authors use "regime" to the ruling elite.
In the text's usage, a regime is clearly different from a government – the
set of people who exercise day-to-day political power. Governments can
frequently change in an orderly and almost predictable fashion, as when
popular elections produce a new president or prime minister or when an
absolute monarch is replaced by his hereditary successor. Such changes of
personnel do not constitute a change in regime since the system of
government remains intact.

Classifying regimes I: Aristotle

Regimes define the basic legal rules for gaining and exercising political power. Regimes differ from one another in a variety of ways. It is often useful to classify regimes because classification aids comparison, but classification is as much art as science. Regime types are handy terms that allow comparative politics to make rough and ready distinctions and assessments of how a particular regime works. In reality regime types bleed into one another. Actual regimes may change slowly, and after a long period they may be quite different from what they were when they began. In other words, actual regimes may change their form without anyone ever making a conscious choice to do so. Aristotle, who founded comparative politics in the fourth century BC, recognized these subtleties, but space permits only the barest outline of what he wrote. Basically Aristotle classified regimes by the number of rulers and the way that they conducted themselves as rulers (see Table 1.1). In terms of the number of rulers, he put regimes into three basic categories. Where one ruled, the regime was a monarchy. When relatively few ruled, the regime was an aristocracy or oligarchy. Where many ruled, the regime was a democracy. In addition each of these three classes was subdivided into two in terms of whether the rulers looked after their own interest only or were concerned with the good of the whole. Aristotle noted that the regimes that ruled in everyone's interest shared power to a limited degree with the non-ruling class and followed the rule of law – two hallmarks of what is known as "**constitutionalism.**" He also argued that such regimes were less subject to breakdown than those in which rulers governed solely in their own interest because they gave almost everyone a stake in the system.

Classifying regimes II: Robert Dahl

Modern regimes are much different from the small city states Aristotle analyzed, and contemporary political scientists have had to take this into account. One of the most influential contemporary regime typologies is that crafted by Robert Dahl. Dahl avoids most of the traditional terms used by Aristotle, preferring more analytic terms that directly refer to

Table 1.1 Aristotle's typology of regimes

Number of rulers/purpose	Rulers' good	Common good
One (monarchy)	Tyranny	Kingship
Few	Oligarchy	Aristocracy
Many (democracy)	Mob rule	Constitutional government

Table 1.2   Robert Dahl's political typology

Liberalization/inclusiveness	Least inclusive	Most inclusive
Most liberal	Competitive oligarchies	Polyarchies
Least liberal	Closed hegemonies	Inclusive hegemonies

breadth and inclusiveness of the ruling elite and rights of participation on the one hand, and the nature of the decision-making process on the other (see Table 1.2). In regard to the right to participate, political systems can be more closed or more inclusive. Closed systems involve no sharing of power beyond a small number of people or limited number of groups, while open systems expand access. For example, in the early Middle Ages a small elite composed of the king and landed aristocracy had a monopoly of power, and the mass of the population was composed of virtually rightless serfs. The system was closed. Only later did the system become more inclusive when citizens of the towns gained the right to participate in government. Systems can also be more hegemonic or more liberal. Hegemonic systems restrict the rights of even the elite to speak out while competitive or liberal systems permit members of ruling groups to voice their objections to existing policy or form groups to advance their views. For example, communist systems have traditionally been hegemonic. Public statements announce decisions, but these statements do not tell the public who, if anyone, advocated a different policy. In contrast, nineteenth-century constitutional monarchies restricted political participation but followed the rule of law and supported some right to freedom of speech and press.

Regimes that we would normally call liberal democracies Dahl terms "**polyarchies**" (from the Greek words for "many" and "rule"). Unlike the democracies Aristotle described, in polyarchies, citizens do not rule directly; elites do. But different elites (political parties and candidates) compete for office in a system in which the general public has an important say. Regimes that fall into the other three broad classes most commentators would normally term "**authoritarian**" since they are illiberal and violate the rule of law to some degree or restrict access to political power narrowly. The most extreme of closed hegemonies is what commentators term a "**totalitarian**" system, where a single party controls political power, and citizens are even passively hostile to the regime at their peril. Totalitarian regimes see nothing, no matter how private and insignificant, as beyond the legitimate scope of their control. Totalitarian regimes try to transform society and its members according to the regime's own blueprint of what the good society and the good human being ought to be (Dahl 1971: 4–10).

Even more than Aristotle, Dahl's typology is fluid. In fact, Dahl's scheme is really a two-dimensional matrix where regimes can become more or less liberal and more or less inclusive simultaneously. These changes may be gradual or abrupt. Many regimes have a degree of both inclusiveness and competitiveness without being sufficiently inclusive or competitive to be classified as polyarchies or true liberal democracies. And that is precisely the point of Dahl's scheme. Both liberal rights and participation can be a matter of degree. In fact, Freedom House, a research group, has for decades ranked the countries of the world according to liberal rights and political rights (Freedom House 2008). Dahl developed his schema to encourage us to think about paths and prospect for democratic change. We shall explore some of these paths in future chapters.

Economics and politics

Regimes, which distribute political power, are closely related to economic systems, which distribute economic power, primarily wealth. This connection was recognized as far back as Aristotle. Differences in wealth and different abilities to acquire it are one of the most durable bases for the formation of groups. These differences create classes that often see the political order as a means of either defending their share of wealth and economic power or as a means of rectifying or even completely overturning what they see as an unfair division of economic resources. Furthermore, class divisions may reinforce other differences based on religion, ethnicity, and geography. Although virtually all those who have studied the subject seriously recognized the importance of economics to politics, they have come to quite divergent judgments about exactly how the relationship between the two works.

It's easy to imagine that, all things being equal, growing economic scarcity tends to intensify conflict while increasing prosperity can provide the resources to mitigate it, but the relationship between prosperity and political stability is not nearly so straightforward or uniformly positive. Sometimes the increased economic importance or wealth of a hitherto politically subservient class can give that class the resources and self-confidence to overturn the established political order. This is precisely what Karl Marx, writing in the mid-nineteenth century, saw as the general pattern of history. He argued that not only were classes necessarily antagonistic to one another but also, in the long run, this conflict would lead to a violent change in the regime precisely because economic change would undermine the old ruling class. Changes in the way goods and services were produced led to the rise of new classes. Economic change, he believed, occurred faster than political change and occurred in ways that political authorities could not fully control. As new classes became more pivotal for the functioning of the economy, those who held political power would resist ceding to the new class its due share of political influence until they were forced to do so. Gradual but significant economic change would eventually lead to dramatic and violent political change. Such changes, he believed, were responsible for the political rise of the middle class and the overthrow of absolute monarchy in eighteenth-century Europe. And he also thought economic change would ultimately lead to a communist revolution by the working class as well. In short, Marx believed that economics determined politics. Classes were the most important groups in politics, and classes were necessarily in conflict with one another (Marx 1977). Marx's perspective helped shape the views of scholars and revolutionaries from his own day to the present.

Marx stressed the inevitability of conflict. However, others, even some Marxists (Bernstein 1963), were much more sanguine about the possibility of avoiding violence and attaining some division of economic power and wealth mutually acceptable to divergent classes. Aristotle believed that political stability was possible if both the rich and the poor had a common stake in the preservation of the political system (*Politics*: 1307a 7–15). While Marx foresaw conflict between two principal class adversaries that encompassed most of the wealth, power, and population of a society, James Madison, the "Father of the US Constitution," thought that the differences in economic condition and interest were much more fine-grained than that. In large complex societies, there were likely to be a great number of separate and contrary interests. Madison further argued that a modicum of justice and stability could be attained in a democracy if there were a variety of interests competing with one anther. So long as no one unified interest comprised a majority of citizens or held a majority of the positions of power, the majorities required to set policies could only be brought together by compromise and persuasion. And hence, the worst forms of injustice could be avoided (Madison 1961: 56–65).

Neither the Marxist nor the more moderate views of class conflict describe every situation adequately. In some cases, even Marxists would admit that class conflict can be mitigated and violent revolution postponed, maybe indefinitely. By the same token, some economic conditions and class conflict seem incapable of peaceful, mutually acceptable policy solutions. Rich and poor may be unable or unwilling to compromise, or the divisions of economic interest within society may not be as numerous or as balanced as the sort of situation Madison envisioned.

In any event, economics may provide the context, but the continuity of a regime – its ability to avoid breakdown – is dependent upon a variety of factors, some systemic and some related to specific decisions made by individual political actors that are not purely economic.

Factors promoting continuity

Regimes that have survived and flourished generally have certain basic capacities to keep opposition to the regime in check. First, successful regimes are favored by psychological factors. If potential opponents of a regime are to overthrow it, they must be confident enough to take action to bring it down. If they believe that opposition is futile or that opposition to the regime is actually immoral, they are unlikely to take the action necessary to bring it down. Second, successful regimes can "deliver the goods." Even if, all things being equal, potential opponents would rather see the regime replaced, they may, in fact, grant it their grudging support so long as it provides some of the basic things they want – security of person and economic prosperity. In the final analysis, regimes that survive can rely on force. Even if the opposition really wishes to overthrow the regime, it may be unable to do so, if the regime commands instruments of violence and uses them effectively to intimidate the society at large and destroy those it cannot intimidate. In short, the continuity of a regime – its ability to adapt successfully to changing circumstances – depends upon a variety of factors. Four of the most fundamental factors that promote regime continuity are described below.

Legitimacy

Nothing succeeds like success, or as Hobbes put it, "Reputation of power is power" (Hobbes 1950: 69). Success brings prestige to the person, the group, and institutions associated with it. Prestige, when it arouses admiration, is "soft power." Those who possess it can often get what they want without monetary cost or the undesirable side effects associated with outright coercion. Prestige is a form of psychological power although the exercise of physical power may be needed to create and maintain it. Leaders, governments, and regimes of high prestige are more likely to survive than those without it. Regimes need a particular sort of prestige more than any other – moral authority. This moral authority is their **legitimacy**. In psychological or behavioral terms, legitimacy is simply the subjects' assent to the government's right to rule. Without this residual moral support from its subjects, regimes are potentially in serious peril. Problems may become crises, and crises may lead to the collapse of the system. In pre-modern societies, regimes claimed legitimacy on the basis of tradition (time-hallowed practice) or the personal authority of a leader. In contrast, modern regimes are grounded on abstract principles – democracy, nationalism, or religion. If a regime is to remain legitimate in the long term, the principle grounding it must maintain its credibility. Yet, there is no magic formula for establishing legitimacy. Legitimacy depends on the peculiarities of time, place, and culture. For example, the tsarist regime in Russia collapsed in 1917 only after two and a half years of ruinous war. Another absolutist monarchy, that of the shah of Iran, fell in 1979 undermined by only an economic recession. Governments can use the techniques of political socialization to enhance regime legitimacy. The mass rallies and overt propaganda of Nazi and communist regimes are examples of heavy-handed use of these techniques. However, the study of a country's history that highlights national heroes and its national achievements, civics courses in schools, the building of national monuments, celebration of patriotic holidays, and the display of patriotic symbols are all means of enhancing a regime's legitimacy as well.

Governmental efficacy

Regimes can break down when governments are unable to address pressing problems. An example of this phenomenon can be found in the first case study at the end of this chapter. During the 1920s and 1930s, the government of Weimar Germany alternately made bad choices and deadlocked in facing problems such as the hyperinflation and the growth of a violent opposition movement. The ability of the government to reach decisions critical to the continuity of the regime is known as **governmental efficacy** (Linz 1978: 20–3). This efficacy is the product of a properly organized constitution and a political elite committed to solving the regime's problems. An efficacious constitutional organization and the skill of the political elite in using it are important since real problems require real solutions. Decisions must be made in a timely manner. The interests of elite and mass actors whose opposition could create further difficulties must be taken into account. Potential opponents must be either placated or coerced.

Constitutions, whether written or unwritten, are often a key to governmental efficacy. When they fulfill their purpose, constitutions provide rules and procedures to determine who rules, and what specific powers the ruler or rulers have. In addition, they provide sufficient power to solve problems that threaten the continuity of the regime. Constitutional rules go beyond the written document entitled "constitution" (where such a document exists). They include a host of other supporting laws, rules, and practices that are essential for resolving the sort of succession and jurisdictional disputes just mentioned. Today almost all regimes have a written document titled "constitution" or "basic law," but some of these documents serve ceremonial purposes only. They are ignored whenever the ruling elite find it convenient to do so. Such nominal or **facade constitutions** cannot effectively settle disputes over who rules and what the powers of the rulers are since the procedures prescribed by the constitution can do no more than ratify decisions already made by other means and in other forums. Even so, in such systems, there may be informal procedures for choosing leaders and apportioning power. In such situations, the real constitution is not the same as its nominal constitution.

State effectiveness

To assure their continuity, regimes require state effectiveness. **State effectiveness** is the ability of the permanent administrative part of the government – the state – to impose law and order, provide the government with resources, and assure that the resource base upon which the government draws will be protected and cultivated. The familiar term "state" means something quite different in the context of comparative politics than it usually does in US politics. In comparative politics the term has two related meanings, neither of which is equivalent to the normal use of the word in the context of US government. In US government we speak of California, Florida, and Kansas as states. In the US context, states are territories with autonomous governments operating under the US constitution and the government of the United States. In comparative politics, we would speak of the United States, *as a whole*, as a state. The attributes of **statehood** are: territory, population/citizens, and a government that has sovereignty – the ultimate legal say about what goes on in its territory. California, Florida, and Kansas are not states in this sense since they do not have sovereignty; under the Constitution that authority belongs to the government of the United States. In comparative politics, the term "**state**" also means the permanent part of the governmental administration responsible for implementing the decisions of the policy-making part of the government. The personnel who staff the state are called "bureaucrats" or "civil servants." They normally remain in office even when higher-ranking governmental officials in the executive and legislature are replaced.

If governments are to succeed in putting their policies into effect, they must be supported by an effective state (governmental administration). The state's bureaucracy provides for the maintenance of law and order, including the settlement of private disputes, and provides resources needed by the government. Moreover, the state must be able to extract resources while at the same time protecting its resource base and maintaining at least the passive acquiescence of the population. Even in antiquity, governments needed to be concerned about the erosion of their tax base. Production was primarily agricultural, and governments extracted wealth from the peasantry. The erosion of rural productive capacity over time was endemic in most large empires for a variety of reasons. Excessive taxation often destroyed the independent peasantry. The appropriation of formerly peasant lands in the hands of the privileged, who were exempt from taxation, put these resources beyond the reach of the state. The decay of the state's resource base led to the erosion of state power, sometimes provoking further unsustainable exactions. The "extraction–coercion cycle" (Finer 1997: 19–20), as one political scientist termed it, was difficult to maintain. In modern times, industry is the most important resources base of the most powerful states. Industrial societies are more concerned about the rate of growth of the resource base than its erosion. Nonetheless, the problem of cultivating and protecting the state's economic base remains. States face a further requirement. They must manage public policy in ways that do not undermine the regime's legitimacy. In democratic regimes and sometimes in non-democratic regimes as well, this requires the state to promote the wellbeing of the people.

Coercive capacity

Regimes also require the ability to defend themselves against internal and external enemies. The security services, i.e., the state's political police and internal intelligence establishment, are key players here. It is their task to nip subversion in the bud. The more authoritarian the system, the greater and more intrusive is the surveillance and repression exercised by the security services on a routine basis, but in times of national emergency even liberal states will increase the everyday power of these services. Authoritarian governments sometimes masquerade as democracies by declaring national emergencies almost continuously and by using the pretext of national emergency to repress their political opponents.

Regimes also have to solve the problem of defense against external enemies. Few are so favorably situated that they can do without a military, and even those that do without a full-fledged armed forces have a constabulary force that is midway between ordinary police and regular armed forces. The armed forces provide security against foreign enemies, and they are also responsible for suppressing internal revolts should they occur. In this regard, civilian regimes have to balance two sometimes conflicting aims. On the one hand, the armed forces have to be sufficiently powerful to deter aggression or undue influence by other states, and they have to be powerful enough to prevent rebellion within the state's own territory. On the other hand, they must be loyal to the regime and under the control of government. Throughout history, a variety of regimes have had armed forces that failed to meet one or both of these criteria. The failure to meet either can be fatal. Weak government legitimacy, unclear or unenforced constitutional rules, and weakness in the state may lead to a military seizure of power or an unhealthy increase in the political influence of the armed forces. When political systems slide in that direction, they suffer from **praetorianism**, the political condition in which brute force and the threat of force are substituted for negotiation, persuasion, and the rule of law. Praetorianism obviously entails the militarization of politics, but it also promotes the politicization of the military. Sacrificing military competence for the sake of loyalty can be ultimately a bad bargain as the technical incompetence of the Iraqi army in the 1980s war against Iran and in both the 1991 and 2003 wars against the United States and its allies demonstrated. Yet, praetorianism, once it arises, is not easy to correct.

Factors promoting breakdown

There is an old saying that successful families are successful for the same reasons but fail for a multitude of different causes. The same might be said of regimes. The sources of a regime's strength – its legitimacy, governmental efficacy, state effectiveness, and coercive capacity – may vary in their particulars depending on time and place, but all successful regimes have all of them. Regime breakdown can be brought about by a variety of causes. Quite often these causative factors reinforce one another. But even when several of the causes are present, the mix is often quite distinctive.

Technological change

Politics is a competitive business. Ruling elites must hold their own against actual and potential domestic opponents, and they must defend the territorial integrity of their states. A political elite may wish to maintain complete stability, avoiding any real change in the way it does things, but that may not be a live option. Adopting new military technology and new techniques is frequently a matter of necessity, but changes in military technology can have profound political repercussions. For example, in ancient Greece, the dominant type of regime shifted from kingship and aristocracy to limited democracy and then to radical democracy and back to kingship again as military technology and organization changed. In the heroic age that the poet Homer describes, armored warriors on horseback and horse-drawn chariots ruled the battlefield. Only the aristocracy could afford such equipment, and their military dominance empowered them to deny political rights to most of the population. As heavily armored foot soldiers became the dominant force, middle-class farmers and artisans could afford the equipment necessary to serve as effective soldiers. The close-ordered formations and tactics of these hoplite infantry not only marginalized the aristocratic cavalry militarily, they eventually marginalized them politically as well. Even later, maritime cities, such as Athens, developed navies that became pivotal for military operations in island-studded Greece, and the poor citizens who pulled the oars on the warships became politically enfranchised. However, the democratic era could not last. The greater size and wealth of the kingdom of Macedonia allowed Philip, Alexander the Great, and their successors to recruit subjects and hire mercenaries, forging a powerful combined-arms military establishment that outclassed competitors and brought the aristocratic cavalry back into the forefront. This larger and more professional force was able to overwhelm the largely amateur armies of the popularly governed Greek cities. Kings and their aristocratic retainers were literally and figuratively back in the saddle.

Not all technological change is military. In our own times, new communications technologies have posed a threat to authoritarian governments who regularly attempted to control information and build legitimacy through pro-regime propaganda. This was much easier to do when there were a few large media that could be easily controlled. However, over the past several decades communications technology has changed. A spontaneous popular resistance movement used cell phones and other means of electronic communication to help thwart a military coup in Guatemala in 1993. The People's Republic of China (PRC) has been uneasy about the subversive potential of the Internet, whose economic benefits it cannot afford to be without. Whether the PRC will succeed in its attempt to shear the Internet and satellite broadcasting of their subversive potential is still an open question. As noted above, Karl Marx had an elaborate technologically driven explanation of political change. He saw new technologies and ways of producing wealth giving rise to new classes, and the rise of new classes ultimately leading to political revolution.

New political actors

New technologies and other factors often create new actors or empower and increase the importance of old ones. Yet they may not tell the entire story. In medieval Europe, for instance, changes in military technology were only part of a more complex and much longer process that undermined existing regimes. In the Middle Ages, the expense of castles, battle horses, and armor, as well as the lengthy training required to be a knight, excluded all but the landed aristocracy from military service, but the development of inexpensive firearms and cannon changed the equation. Kings who could afford to raise and arm forces with these new weapons began to consolidate their power, taking it away from their aristocratic underlings. However, change involved more than military technology. The spread of law and order, the growth of towns, and trade increased the size and importance of the middle class. This process took centuries. In contrast, during the nineteenth century, the rapid growth of the industrial working class increased their power much more rapidly and led to demands for inclusion. New actors continue to emerge. Mass immigration, both internal and external, has changed the shape of politics in many countries and continues to do so today. Movements on behalf of civil rights for minorities and, in some cases, disenfranchised majorities including women have challenged the political status quo in various countries across the globe. Today's new actors include mass movements, parties, interest groups, and individual leaders. Existing regimes will have to accommodate or repress these new actors, but their very presence itself means that politics cannot continue unaltered.

Ideological change

Ideas shape the world. Philosophical and scientific ideas direct the way we study nature and influence our ability to discover its laws and control natural forces. Philosophical ideas about politics translated into the practical and generally accessible language of political ideologies shape the way politics is conducted. Ideologies are formulated to appeal to particular political actors, to identify good and evil, to spell out a course of action, and to energize mass movements and political parties. Ideologies can reinforce or undermine the legitimacy of regimes, and they can mobilize support for or resistance to them. Nationalism and democracy shaped and reshaped politics in the nineteenth and twentieth centuries, and they still do today. Communism and fascism, now essentially defunct, caused immense upheavals in the twentieth century. The roster of important ideologies continues to change. Human rights and political Islam are two of the most potent world-makers today. The former began to energize political movements after the Second World War. The latter gained significant momentum in the last quarter of the twentieth century. As with new actors, regimes ignore new ideologies at their peril.

External pressure

In modern times no regime is an island – in the figurative sense. Even geographically isolated island nations have found themselves part of the international scene. Physical barriers that before could be used to keep new ideologies, new technologies, and new actors at bay are no longer effective. In fact, the last major civilization to maintain its splendid isolation from foreign pressure was Japan. But its isolation ended in the 1850s and 1860s. Whether ruling elites like it or not, they and the regimes they control are part of a larger world. Global interconnectedness had its origins in medieval Europe. Foreign pressure was a fact of life for European monarchs of that era although this "foreign" pressure might have come from no further away than the neighboring duchy or county. As monarchs were able to expand their territory and consolidate their power, the ongoing struggle among them required that regimes innovate or see their power wither. During that same era Islamic and Chinese civilizations were not subject to the same intense competition. But eventually the Europeans' overseas expansion pressed in upon them and much of the rest of the globe too. Countries outside of Europe were forced to adopt new techniques or succumb in much the same way that the principalities in Europe had.

Today formal empires have largely disappeared, but economic, military, diplomatic, and migration pressures are no less intense. Not only do regimes have to adopt new ideas and new ways of doing things, foreign actors become domestic actors in one another's domestic politics. Multinational corporations, governments, and **multilateral organizations** (organizations composed of many governments) demand trade and investment opportunities. Foreign actors are interested in matters beyond economics. Their agendas include human rights, religion, changes in government and administration, to name a few. Foreign actors lobby, contribute to political parties, provide funding to private groups, and train domestic individuals and groups. Pressure is today and always has been something of a two-way street. The United States may be the world's most powerful country, but it is also on the receiving end of external pressure. US citizens with foreign connections lobby on behalf of the countries from which they and their families came; the European Union (EU) prevents mergers of US firms by suing the firms in EU courts. Competition from foreign producers puts some US citizens out of work.

No ruling elite can act in complete isolation. If it does not copy techniques and ideas developed abroad, its opposition is likely to. Even if it does not ally itself with political actors outside the country, the opposition is likely to anyway. The People's Democratic Republic of Korea (North Korea) was for much of the late twentieth century the most isolated medium-sized state in the world. It carried most appropriately the country's traditional sobriquet, "the hermit kingdom." Its isolation produced economic collapse, mass starvation, and ultimately multilateral diplomatic pressure to change its military and foreign policies – an object lesson that regimes, no matter how hard they try, cannot escape external pressure.

The dynamics of regime breakdown

Although politics is a struggle for power, in most countries most of the time, the struggle is moderated by the basic rules that lie at the heart of the established regime. In the most favorable circumstances, the regime has both moral authority and physical force on its side. The breakdown of the regime is not in prospect. At other times, significant political actors may wish, under some conditions at least, to see the regime overthrown, and the ability of the regime to contain or destroy the opposition may be limited. Ruling elites normally try to act before a crisis actually threatens the regime itself. They are not always able to do so. Breakdowns don't happen at random. Juan Linz describes as interconnected the failures that lead to regime breakdown (Linz 1978: 14–49). While Linz refers specifically to democratic breakdown, his general framework applies to other regimes as well. Regimes may suffer from weak legitimacy. Regimes may suffer from lack of state effectiveness, the ability of the system to mobilize resources to address problems. And, finally, a regime may suffer from lack of efficacy, the ability to address the ongoing problems that beset it. Such problems individually weaken the system, and worsen one another in turn. They can provide those who oppose the regime with an opportunity to overthrow it.

The ruling elite and the opposition

Opposition to the ruling elite can come in various forms. Not all opposition is opposition to the regime itself. In fact, opponents may be part of a *loyal* opposition – opposing the government of the day and its policies but not the system as such. In effect, the loyal opposition presents itself as an alternative governing elite ready to take over by lawful means. The term "loyal opposition" originated in nineteenth-century Britain, when opponents of the government wanted to profess both their loyalty to the queen and the constitution and simultaneously to express their opposition to the policies backed by her majesty's government. In labeling themselves a "loyal opposition," the opposition presented itself as an alternative set of government personnel with distinctive policies, and avoided being identified as a band of subversives bent on overthrowing the system. The loyal opposition ran candidates and even elected majorities to the legislature, and so was able to move from being the opposition party to being the party of government. Modern democracies tolerate – indeed they depend upon – the existence of loyal oppositions. Without a loyal opposition, voters would have no real alternative to the government in power. Yet many other types of regimes neither encourage nor even officially tolerate opposition, even opposition of the loyal sort. Totalitarian systems consider all opposition by its very nature disloyal. That tendency is common in other authoritarian systems as well. Thus, the opposition strategies discussed here, including even loyal opposition, may not always be available to opposition political actors in an authoritarian regime.

A political actor opposed to the system root and branch, be it an authoritarian or a democratic system, constitutes a *disloyal* opposition. For example, from the time they were first organized, the Nazi Party wanted to overthrow Weimar's democracy and establish a totalitarian regime. They used their power under the democratic constitution to undermine and eventually destroy the regime itself. An anti-regime political actor, however, may also be part of the *semi-loyal* opposition. Such an actor's loyalty to the system is real but provisional. So long as its basic policy preferences are respected, it is loyal to the system, but when its interests are seriously compromised, it seeks to overthrow the system. Semi-loyal oppositions may follow a less extreme version of the disloyal opposition's dual strategy, but they position themselves to overthrow the system only in extreme circumstances. This happened in Latin America during the decades of the 1960s and 1970s. In these coups rightwing civilian extremists were often able to make a common cause with hardliners in the military who feared the weakness or the progressive character of civilian governments. In almost all cases, those who overthrew the system had participated in it either by contesting elections legally or by serving as apparently loyal military servants of the established government. Disorder, government deadlock, and a rising tide of unsolved problems had provided the semi-loyal opposition with its opportunity and excuse to act.

The ruling elite normally have an array of tactics open to them when they confront opposition to the system. **Repression** – punishing members of the opposition and making its actions and organizations illegal – is often an option, but for some elites repression may not be the preferred option. Real democrats can use it only in extreme cases. And since the 1980s, democracy has had high prestige. Thus, appearing to be democratic has been an important part of many elites' strategies, and hence open repression carries a cost. This is especially true when external watchdogs such as multilateral bodies, such as the Organization for Security and Cooperation in Europe (OSCE), and highly respected private groups, such as Amnesty International, are able to sound the alarm when a government uses a false pretext to claim harsh action against its opponents is justified. However, ruling elites unwilling to engage in repression have other alternatives. These are accommodationist strategies – strategies aimed at giving in partially to the demands of opponents to placate them. These strategies were of two general sorts. They take the paths that Dahl indicates authoritarian regimes follow when they become less hegemonic and less closed. **Liberalization** is the strategy of granting legal rights to opposition political actors and those allied to them. Thus, property rights, rights of free association, religion and the press might be extended and protected by effective legal guarantees. Liberalization can take place without granting rights to participate in the process of government itself. Expanding *political* rights (the rights to effectively participate in the government directly and vote for officeholders) constitutes **democratization**. In nineteenth-century Europe, the ruling elites in authoritarian regimes adopted a strategy of liberalization before eventually being compelled to follow a democratization strategy (Rustow 1999: 14–41). In the late twentieth century, however, dominant political actors were often forced to follow both paths almost simultaneously, as the ruling elite in the Soviet Union did during the late 1980s.

Revolution

Regimes break down in various ways. One of these is revolution. Revolution is the stuff of melodrama. Not only is the nature of the regime transformed, but people's lives are altered dramatically as well as their being caught up in the revolutionary process. **Revolutions** are participatory events; they involve mass movements and, most often, extensive violence. They are driven by ideologies and counter-elites who see the mass violence as the opportunity for establishing a new and better political order. Revolutions must be distinguished from rebellions, on the one hand, and coups d'etat, on the other. Just like revolutions, **rebellions** make good melodrama. They too involve mass movements and violence, but unlike revolutions they do not lead to a change in regime. Throughout human history, regimes have suffered from rebellion. When people are pushed to the brink – when they see their families starving while others are well fed, when fundamental long-established obligations are ignored by the elite – in short when ordinary people see no other way out, they rebel. Rebellions, even when they succeed in their immediate objectives, rarely have a long-term impact, however. Members of the elite may be massacred, property destroyed, and resources seized for the benefit of the rebels. Still, because the rebels have no alternative plan for a governmental system or clear ideas about how to reorganize society, the aftermath of successful rebellion is likely to be chaos rather than a new order. Eventually, old patterns reemerge. Like a forest swept by fire growing back, politics after a rebellion ultimately returns to the status quo ante. Thus, the ultimate failure of rebellions to produce regime change has little to do with the size of their mass backing or their level of violence. Rather, the failure has everything to do with rebellions' lack of ideologies or political programs aimed at remaking the existing structures of government and society as well as the lack of a new leadership that wants to put these ideologies into effect.

Revolutions, in short, are rebellions with an ideological focus led by an ideologically driven counter-elite that seeks to create an entirely new political order. Revolutionary leaders have political ideas about the nature and cause of pre-revolutionary injustice. The leaders of revolutions, and possibly even a substantial number of their followers, have a clear idea about what they want to achieve. Thus, revolutionary leaders can do more than simply expel or execute the old governing class. They can begin constructing new structures of power – new regimes. Whether or not they actually achieve what they expect to is beside the point. For the dramatist, it is the chaos, the human hope and human suffering that make revolutions interesting. For the student of comparative politics, the role of ideas and the attempt to transform political and social structures, if anything, hold even greater interest. Chapters 5 and 6 will explore the theory of revolution and discuss some specific cases.

Coups d'etat

Coups d'etat, like revolutions and rebellions, are the stuff of drama, but in this case, the story is one of plots and conspiracies. Like revolutions, coups usually aim at regime change, but unlike either a revolution or a rebellion, they are not mass movements and often involve little violence. The **coup** is etymologically a "blow to the state" (a seizure of power) by a small, armed group. Most often, this small armed group is part of the government army since in most circumstances it is only such a group that would have the wherewithal to stage a coup. For a coup to be successful, the coup-makers must force the government's leaders to cede power.

At the same time they must persuade others who might intervene to protect the existing government that such intervention is pointless. Those members of the armed forces not involved in the coup and the population at large, whose active and widespread resistance could cause the coup to fail, must acquiesce to the seizure of power. Secrecy of planning and speed of execution are essential for a coup. Key personalities and installations must be seized simultaneously to short-circuit any effective defense of the existing government. Only when times are desperate or when coups have become an almost normal part of the political process, can coup-makers dispense with the actual physical seizure of government officials and property. In such cases, a polite visit by the senior armed forces commander may suffice. Although coups may be made in the name of broad social class or on behalf of the people at large, coups do not require the active support of either. More often than not, protestations of national or class interests by coup-makers are merely pro forma.

A coup d'etat involves the removal of the old government by violence or by the explicit or implicit threat of violence. At the minimum a coup replaces the leading officials of the old government, or most of them, by illegal means. A coup may usher in a completely new regime or simply change the officeholders of the existing regime. While a coup could provoke a revolution or take place while a revolution is underway, coups generally avoid mass upheavals and mass violence (see Table 1.3).

An abrupt change in regime, be it a revolution or a coup, is likely to lead to continued instability. The fall of an established regime puts its moral and legal rules into question, and there is likely to be no agreed upon replacement for them. Revolutions, especially, but coups, to a degree, are normally based on an opposition coalition. It is easier for the opposition to agree to overthrow the old regime than it is for them to agree on what should replace it. Different political actors in the coalition are likely to have different preferences; some may have radically different preferences. With legal and moral rules unsettled, decisions are often made on the basis of force, and praetorianism prevails.

Table 1.3   Violent breakdowns

	Rebellion	Revolution	Coup d'etat
Mass involvement	Yes	Yes	No
Extensive violence	Yes	Yes	No
Ideologically motivated	No	Yes	Possibly
Aims at regime change	No	Yes	Possibly

Subversion in democracies

In democracies, breakdowns become probable when pro-democratic elites are unable to coalesce behind common strategies that address underlying challenges to democratic continuity. The democracy may fall by coup d'etat, but it may also fall by means of a more subtle process – subversion from within. Pro-democratic political parties may be too busy with political maneuvers designed to remove one another from office by legal means to address the serious economic problems or the menace extremist parties bent on overthrowing the system. In such circumstances, disloyal oppositions may follow a dual strategy of participating in the system to block reforms by using constitutional means while at the same time mobilizing outside forces against the regime itself. This was the situation that confronted democratic politicians in the Weimar Republic. They faced unprecedented economic problems in the shape of hyperinflation and debilitating reparations payments from the First World War. Meanwhile, the Nazis and the communists were able to take advantage of democratic tolerance of opposition to undermine the system. The German case was not unique even in that era. Much of Central Europe and Italy suffered from similar problems to Germany's. Democratic breakdowns were also endemic in much of Latin America throughout much of the twentieth century.

Radical reform of authoritarian states

Individuals or groups with democratic convictions living under authoritarianism may constitute a disloyal or semi-loyal opposition. If they are unable to change the regime by direct action – a coup d'etat or a revolution – they may seek radical reform from within. Ultimately, radical reformers want what amounts to regime change, although some may profess their basic loyalty to the existing regime's principles. Reformers can exercise influence in two basic ways: voice and exit (Hirschman 1970). **Voice** can be exercised in several ways. Informal groups not officially recognized by the government can engage in public protests, circulation of materials hostile to the regime, and other individual or group actions. Those exercising this sort of voice often argue that they wish to act within the system and reform it although they wish to reform the system in ways unacceptable to the political elite who dominates it. Some seeking voice may be members of the ruling elite; they might be able to take a reform position within the regime's councils. This strategy was used by reformist members of the communist parties of Eastern and Central Europe, who were able to shape policies during the 1980s. **Exit** is the option of ceasing to be a member of the ruling party or officially sanctioned organizations

Plate 1.2 Hitler reviewing an SA parade. The SA was a party militia used to bully opponents.

or, even more radically, physically pulling up stakes and leaving the country. Physical exit may weaken the system to the extent that it deprives the regime of economically valuable workers, but it normally weakens remaining opposition actors as well. Many opponents of the Castro government in Cuba have followed the exit strategy since the early 1960s. They were able to criticize the regime from outside, but their inability to shape events on the island itself has been clear.

Gradual and negotiated transitions

Gradual transitions may occur over a period of decades and are the result of the dominant political actors consistently pursuing an accommodationist strategy. Gradual regime change of this last sort can have positive consequences for the continuity of the regime. The constitutional evolution of Great Britain briefly described in Box 2.1 of the next chapter is an instance of this. Over a period of several centuries the British political elite gradually liberalized and democratized, eventually turning a mixed regime in which the monarch and aristocracy predominated into a "crowned democracy" – a liberal democracy with the ceremonial trappings of a monarchy. At other times much less gradual transitions are negotiated and include an explicit or implicit agreement designed to provide certain guarantees to the outgoing governmental elite. A wave of transitions occurred in the 1980s in Latin America as military governments gave up power. Chile and Uruguay had negotiated transitions that preserved some of the changes imposed by the outgoing military governments and provided for amnesties for military officers who were accused of human rights abuses. Brazil had a similar transition with the agreement being implicit rather than formally negotiated. And in Argentina the military regime was forced out, and no agreement was struck although the process took a year and a half. Beginning in 1989 with the fall of the Berlin Wall, communist regimes in Europe were also replaced. Here the transitions were usually more abrupt with little in the way of formal agreements. Especially in the states that were once part of the old Soviet Union, members of the old political elite often reemerged as "democratic" politicians controlling the new governments. Changes like these in the communist and noncommunist world are examined in Chapters 9 and 10.

Failed states

Gradual political change may also entail growing disorder and the government's loss of resources, the decline in state effectiveness, and the erosion of the regime's legitimacy. In short, political change may resemble decay. People with the requisite loyalties and skills may not be available to fill offices essential for the regime's continuance. Resources necessary to pay these officials may be exhausted. Normally, the dominant political actors follow a strategy designed to preserve the system, but the dominant political actor may, in fact, choose methods of ruling and acquiring personal wealth that actually undermine the system in the long run. This can lead to the emergence of a "**failed state**" – a political system unable to carry out the basic functions of government, such as maintaining law and order, and protecting the state's territorial integrity. A case study in Chapter 11 examines state failure in Zaire during the last several decades of the twentieth century. The state continues to exist as a legal entity, but it is more a legal fiction than a functioning government. Other paths to state failure include coups, insurgency, and civil war.

Summary

There are a wide variety of ways that regimes break down: revolution, coup d'etat, subversion, radical reform, gradual or negotiated transition, and state failure. The opposition to the regime that results in breakdown can arise from a variety of sources and take a variety of paths. New actors, new ideologies, changes in technology, and foreign pressure may all play a role. Yet, all regimes that fail lack one or more of the basic capacities to survive and adapt to changing circumstances. They are deficient in legitimacy, efficacy, or effectiveness; they are all unable to deal with disloyal or semi-loyal oppositions. The ruling elite may lack the resources to address problems either by repressing the opposition or accommodating it; the ruling elite may be unable to agree among themselves on a workable strategy to counter threats to the regime. Ultimately, if crises are serious or prolonged, the regime may collapse.

CASE STUDY: THE DEMISE OF THE WEIMAR REPUBLIC (1919–33)

The collapse of the interwar Weimar Republic of Germany represents a classic twentieth-century example of democratic breakdown. The Weimar regime had to face a disloyal and semi-loyal opposition, unprecedented foreign pressure, and economic disintegration. Its legitimacy was challenged from the outset. Political parties and the constitutional structures they worked through hampered the system's overall ability to address efficaciously the immense problems the system faced. And the state itself was ridden with oppositionists. The Weimar Republic's collapse is an object lesson about what can go wrong in liberal democracies. Perhaps most importantly, the collapse of democracy in Germany in 1933 and the rise of Adolf Hitler to power demonstrate the earth-shattering consequences domestic politics in one country can have on others.

Germany's interwar democratic constitution was written at Weimar in 1919 shortly after the end of the First World War. A socialist government had come to power when the imperial regime collapsed at the end of the war. And they continued to be the dominant party during the first several years of the post-war period. By 1919 Germany's Social Democratic Party (SPD) was radical and Marxist only in theory. It had made its peace with constitutionalism, democracy, and capitalism even before the outbreak of the war. Radicals had left the party during the war in protest over mainline socialist support for the German war effort. However, democrats who came to power under the Weimar constitution had received a poisoned chalice. The new regime was immediately prey to disloyal and semi-loyal opposition groups. Nationalists created the "stab in the back myth" that blamed the SPD for the loss of the war. And the German General Staff, the elite of the German army, did its best to reinforce that belief despite the fact they had considered continued war hopeless. The peace treaty that Germany was forced to sign at Versailles was punitive. Germany had to be demilitarized, and it lost considerable territory – some symbolically significant land in the West as well as much larger stretches in the East (see Map 1.2.). The new government was required to pay indemnities. And the country was forced to admit "war guilt": Germany and its allies alone were held responsible for the First World War and its terrible consequences.

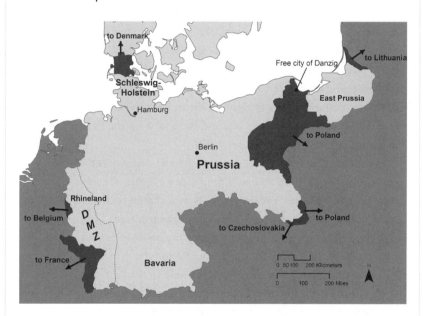

Map 1.2 Territory lost by Germany under the Versailles Treaty
Source: Environmental Systems Research Institute (ESRI) map data
Note: The demilitarized zone (DMZ) in the Rhineland

The republic labored under an additional burden. The SPD and the General Staff had struck an unprincipled bargain that secured its continuance and undermined the legitimacy of the new democracy. Under the previous regime, they had sworn their loyalty to the kaiser, but their real loyalty was to their own particular version of the German nation. At the advent of the revolution that led to the creation of the Weimar Republic, the General Staff had promised to support the new government if the government would suppress the radical socialists, known as Spartacists, who were prepared to press the revolution further toward a Marxist workers' state. In return for its support, the SPD had also promised to guarantee the continued existence of the General Staff and its role within the German military and German state. The General Staff's position was critical to the way politics developed in the new democracy. The military in general and the General Staff in particular were ardent nationalists eager to see the country rearm and regain territory lost in the war. Their loyalty to the democratic government was provisional at best. What the General Staff really wanted was a blank check from the democrats to do what they saw fit in matters of defense. In fact, the armed forces were able to begin a program for rearmament almost at once albeit on a small scale. They struck a deal with the Bolshevik government in Russia, another international pariah state at the time, to train their forces on Soviet territory far from the prying eyes of allied military observers supervising German disarmament. Politically the General Staff supported ultra-nationalist politicians eager to see a rearmed and aggressive Germany regain its former position on the world stage. Even though the General Staff quickly assumed a position as a semi-loyal opposition to the governing democrats, democratic politicians did virtually nothing to keep the institution in check. The business elite, the bureaucracy, and the courts by and large aligned themselves with the position of the military.

The constitution itself established procedures that worked effectively enough when times were relatively pacific, but in times of crisis its provisions invited abuse. Executive power was shared between the president and chancellor. The chancellor (prime minister), normally the more powerful of the two, required a majority confidence vote by the lower house of the legislature, the Reichstag, to remain in office. In fact, the chancellor and cabinet were jointly responsible to the Reichstag. At the same time, the popularly elected president assumed a position in some ways similar to the kaiser under the German Empire although with diminished powers and prestige. The president appointed the chancellor and the cabinet. He could dissolve the cabinet. The president himself could also constitutionally assume emergency power in times of a crisis without the consent of either the cabinet or the Reichstag. When the pro-regime parties lost control of the Reichstag in the early 1920s, it was difficult to form coherent or long-lived governments (i.e., cabinets). The situation was further exacerbated by the 1923 allied occupation of the heavily industrial Ruhr meant to pressure Germany into making its reparation payments. The government called for a general work stoppage in the Ruhr and intentionally inflated the currency by over a million percent to frustrate the occupation. Inflation, already high, created a disaster that led to strikes, street violence, and rumors of a coup. One coup attempt in which Adolf Hitler participated failed. In short, semi-loyal and disloyal oppositions gained in popularity, and the allied powers played into their hands by undermining Germany's democratic government.

Adolf Hitler and the National Socialist German Workers' Party (Nazi Party) he joined and later dominated were well situated to exploit the growing chaos. The Nazis were a disloyal opposition. They began by undermining the system and then overthrew it. The Nazi Party followed a dual strategy of participating in elections and winning seats in the Reichstag and then using their position to block progress by using constitutional means. At the same time the Nazis formed paramilitary forces to intimidate their opponents. From the beginning, the Nazis wanted to overthrow Weimar's democracy and establish a totalitarian regime. The communist party on the extreme left had similar aims and used similar tactics, but it was much less of a threat. Nazi ideology attacked the legitimacy of the Weimar and provided an alternative justification for a new regime. Nazi ideology stressed German nationalism and the supposed superiority of the Aryan race, a group that included Germans and related peoples. A pseudo-science backed up Nazi claims that Aryans were physically, intellectually, and morally superior to all other peoples. The Nazis sought racial purity and saw enemies within as the source of the supposed weakness and treason that had led to the loss of the First World War. According to their ideology the worst of these internal enemies were the Jews, who had wormed their way into German business and finance, created radical leftist movements, and even infiltrated the German state. The Jews thus served as a scapegoat, and they became frequent targets for rhetorical and physical abuse by the Nazi Party. The Nazis, as with many parties on the right, considered parliamentary democracy a corrupt and corrupting form of government. It gave political power to money-grubbing politicians who were willing to sacrifice the country's interest to line their own pockets and flatter their own egos. Germany required a strong state with a new ruling elite composed of those who were naturally superior. The Nazi Party considered itself the vanguard of this new aristocracy. It had to take strong measures to transform a state and society that were already deeply corrupt. Once reconstructed, the state would require total obedience. Democratic consent was neither sought nor required. The Fuhrer (Leader) Principle was all the sanction that was required. The Fuhrer Principle meant that those who were superior had the right and obligation to command. The highest and most absolute of leaders was *the* Fuhrer, Adolf Hitler himself.

Hitler and the Nazis had emerged from a welter of ultra-rightwing competitors for a variety of reasons. Hitler's oratory and single-mindedness, patronage from industrialists and financiers, and the party's propaganda and organizational skills all helped set them apart. Thus, it was the Nazis who managed to mobilize ex-soldiers, members of the economically stricken middle class, and small farmers into a mass movement to overthrow the system. No coup d'etat or revolution was needed. The Nazis were able to take over from within by competing in elections and using their power in the streets to magnify their power within the halls of the Reichstag. The financial crash of 1929 and the Great Depression that followed bolstered Nazi prospects. In 1932 the Nazis became the largest party in the Reichstag, and the president was compelled to allow a moderate conservative to serve as chancellor and rule by decree. Frenzied maneuvering followed. By January the next year Hitler had been chosen chancellor and used his power to undercut the other parties in his original coalition and quickly make himself absolute dictator under the auspices of the Nazi Party.

The Weimar Republic suffered from manifold weaknesses. Its legitimacy was questioned from the start; it lacked the state capacity to control Nazi and other party militias or to solve the economic problems faced by the country, and loyal democrats were unable to unite to form an effective government that might have saved democracy. At the same time the regime was beset with a welter of disloyal and semi-loyal opponents, some of whom like the General Staff were deeply ensconced in the structure of the state.

CASE STUDY: THE BRAZILIAN COUP OF 1964

Brazil represents an alternative case to the collapse of democracy in Germany. Germany was an advanced industrial country. Brazil, in contrast, was a developing country. By 1964 it had attained a degree of economic and social development, but challenges persisted. Brazil was neither as modern economically nor as institutionally developed as wealthier countries. The per capita wealth of society was less. The inequality of income and education was greater. And the effectiveness of state administration was less. The Brazil of that era shares many similarities with other developing countries today. Nonetheless, Brazil shared some similarities with Weimar Germany as well. As in Germany, the armed forces were an institution of high prestige and significant political influence. As in Germany, the military played the role of a semi-loyal opposition, but in the Brazilian case it proclaimed a democratic as well as a nationalist vocation. In practice, however, the armed forces commitment to democracy was considerably less than advertised. They intervened repeatedly to undermine governments and occasionally overthrow them outright. Brazil had had a hard time establishing effective institutions and universally accepted legal norms. Its legitimacy was weak, and state effectiveness was limited. This led to bouts of instability.

Brazil became independent from Portugal in 1822, when the Emperor of Brazil declared its independence from the Kingdom of Portugal. It was a tactical move that preserved the dynasty's control of both countries. Brazil's republican history began in 1889. In that year, the emperor was overthrown by a coalition of military officers and landowners. Landowners were angered by the emperor's abolition of slavery the previous year and desired greater regional autonomy. A federal republic was established. Thus, although the change of government seems like a move in the direction of democracy, vested economic interests were behind the constitutional change. These vested interests were, in many ways, less concerned with the rights of the poorest Brazilians than the Emperor had been. When the franchise expanded and the regime became more democratic, they would become part of the semi-loyal opposition, more concerned about the protection of their own privileges than the defense of democracy. However, for nearly half a century, vested political and economic interests dominated the scene. A clear and dramatic break with the old order did not occur until 1930 just as a global Great Depression was beginning. In that year, the "New Republic" was founded under the leadership of Getúlio Vargas. Supported by elements of the armed forces, Vargas came to power after a contested election. He remained in office, in one guise or another, until he was forced out by military pressure in 1946. By that year the army had again taken a conservative turn. During his time in office Vargas swept away the old boss-ridden political system, strengthened the state and promoted national patriotism, and incorporated the working class and other popular sectors into the political order. The Vargas era led to the rapid economic, social, and political modernization of the country. Brazil became more industrialized; labor attained more rights, and Brazil began to become a player on the international stage. Yet, many of the old practices as well as class and regional divisions remained important. The job of modernization and building democracy was only partly completed.

In 1951 Vargas was elected president again. This new term occurred in the midst of the cold war, and his program aimed at extending popular reforms and caused significant unease among the military, the upper class, and the United States. In 1954 under pressure from the armed forces to resign, Vargas committed suicide, but no outright political breakdown occurred. As the decade wore on, the Brazilian and international situations became more fraught. In 1959 Fidel Castro came to power in Cuba as a result of the Cuban Revolution. Castro claimed to be fighting for the restoration of the progressive 1940 constitution and headed a broadly based popular coalition. In power, however, Castro took a radical path and declared that he was and always had been a communist. The Cuban Revolution sent shockwaves throughout all of Latin America and raised serious concerns in the United States. How could the region modernize and democratize without simultaneously promoting the sort of mass movements that brought communism to power in Cuba? The Brazil military had not been standing idly by watching these developments. Throughout the 1950s, the army's Superior War College (Escola Superior de Guerra – ESG), among others, had been considering just such questions. And they had developed their own Doctrine of National Security and Development. The doctrine was an analysis of the profound internal problems facing Brazil and a set of new military roles that would involve the institution deeply in the development and policing of the country. It did not specifically call for a military coup, but provided a critique of what civilian governments had been doing and carried the implicit claim that the armed forces could do things better (see Chapter 8).

In 1961 Jânio Quadros was elected president, setting the stage for regime breakdown. A maverick, Quadros resigned in a dispute with congress over reform. His resignation put João Goulart, his vice-president and running mate, into the presidency. Goulart, much more radical than Quadros, was visiting communist China at the time of his predecessor's resignation. The military and congress at first tried to force Goulart to resign, and, failing at that, they attempted to curtail his powers. But Goulart was able to reconfirm his full presidential powers in a plebiscite. Under pressure from the landed, business, and military elites, Goulart moved to the left to consolidate radical and mass support. Rural activists increasingly mobilized agricultural workers. Strikes and land seizures multiplied. Mass demonstrations by right and left created an aura of crisis. The situation did reach a crisis in early 1964. A military coup removed Goulart from power. The armed forces claimed the president was preparing for a revolutionary dictatorship. In addition, they were upset by his neglect of the armed forces' budget and his apparent support for military mutineers. Although Goulart was removed from office, congress remained in operation throughout much of the period of military rule that followed, but the military banned certain political activities and organizations, censored the media, and exiled and imprisoned opponents. Military intelligence focused on domestic affairs and established for itself and the military government freedom of action unrestricted by the principles of due process of law. A series of military presidents succeeded one another on an orderly basis for over two decades. The set of expanded military roles presaged by the Doctrine of National Security and Development had become a reality. The military regime remained in power until 1985 when mass protests, economic problems, and international pressure finally forced it from office.

In Brazil the breakdown of democracy occurred on a number of levels. The armed forces functioned as a semi-loyal opposition unwilling to support the government if the government followed policies with which the military seriously disagreed. Government institutions and political leaders were unable to reach a compromise over policies that would satisfy the disenfranchised and at the same time prove acceptable to the economic elite. Groups on the right and the left had at best a provisional loyalty to democracy, and did not see it as an unquestionably legitimate system. Some of these were semi-loyal oppositionist; others were disloyal. And the political leadership's ability to address problems was undercut by the fact that the Brazilian state was relatively weak and inefficient, and the economy was in the process of development. In short, while Weimar Germany suffered from a crisis precipitated primarily by unique events such as the loss of the First World War and the Great Depression, Brazil's problems were much more systemic. Regime breakdown occurred in 1889, 1930, 1946, and 1964 in the face of similar problems and similar political actors. In fact, the last of these breakdowns was provoked in part by the armed forces' desire to address these underlying problems once and for all. Brazil is not unique. Other developing countries suffer from the same sort of systemic problems, have restive armed forces and face military coups, and, at the best of times, are more subject to the threat of breakdown than their more developed counterparts.

Conclusion

This chapter has explored the concept of political change. It began by noting how politics is a matter of power and that power is often exercised by or with the assistance of groups. It further pointed out that not all individuals or groups are equal in their power. Most often the struggle for power takes place within regimes and the rules they prescribe. To be effective, regimes must have both physical force as well as moral authority at their command. Further, they must have a structure that allows them to make effective decisions in a timely manner and to acquire the resources and put their decisions into effect. New technologies, new political actors, new ideologies, and external pressures can undermine a regime's equilibrium. In such cases oppositions of various sorts may succeed in taking power. The trajectories of how this occurs are varied, ranging from violent revolution to negotiated transition. Some countries, such as Germany, have been subject to regime breakdowns that led to a new stable political order replacing the old one. Other countries, such as Brazil, have been subject to periodic breakdowns because of ongoing systemic problems. Brazil and countries like it have struggled with internal and external pressures throughout their history, finding it difficult to consolidate a system that had all the requisites for maintaining continuity. Change is unavoidable, but breakdown is not. In theory, at any rate, regimes may adapt and persist indefinitely although indefinite continuity seems to fly in the face of historical experience. As a class, liberal democracies once consolidated in advanced industrial societies appear to be quite stable. As we shall see in the next chapter, this stability has been a hard-fought historical achievement, and significant policy challenges face these societies today. For most other regimes, the challenges appear to be even more daunting. Chapter 2 will explore how a variety of countries have achieved requisites for continuity and successful adaptation – legitimacy, efficacy, and effectiveness – via state building, the development of nationalism, and democracy. This process, known as "modernization," has been of global importance. But not all countries have modernized successfully or in the same way.

Questions for further consideration

1　Legitimacy, state effectiveness, and governmental efficacy are intertwined. Consider in concrete terms how these sorts of interconnections can play out. For example, how do the sorts of problems that Weimar Germany or Brazil faced fall under these major categories?

2　The armed forces play a key role in sustaining the state. What sorts of characteristics can develop in the military that can undermine this role?

3　Consolidated regimes do not have very powerful disloyal or semi-loyal oppositions. Why not? What could cause such oppositions to develop?

4   What sorts of new ideologies, technologies, and political actors have
    recently come on the political stage in a country with which you are
    familiar? What challenges do they pose for the political system?
5   What sorts of political risks do authoritarian regimes run in trying to
    repress their oppositions? In trying to accommodate them?

Further reading

Robert A. Dahl, *Polyarchy: Participation and Opposition*. New Haven, CT:
    Yale University Press, 1971. Explains the basic requisites of democracy
    (polyarchy) and democratization.
Albert O. Hirschman, *Exit, Voice, and Loyalty: Responses to Decline in Firms,
    Organizations, and States*. Boston, MA: Harvard University Press, 1970.
    Develops the basic concepts of "voice" and "exit."
Juan J. Linz, *The Breakdown of Democratic Regimes: Crisis, Breakdown and
    Reequilibration*. Baltimore, MD: Johns Hopkins University Press, 1978.
    Explains the relationship between legitimacy, state effectiveness,
    governmental efficacy and breakdown.
James Madison, *Federalist*, No. 10, 1961. A classic statement on the
    importance of economics in politics with a view to how stability can be
    maintained and interests reconciled.
Karl Marx and Friedrich Engels, *The Communist Manifesto*, first published
    in 1848. The classic statement of why economic conflicts lead to
    revolution.

2 Nation, state, "democracy"

How the breakdown of the traditional order led to the modern world

We hold these truths to be self-evident, that all men are created equal, that they are endowed by their creator with certain unalienable rights, that among these rights are life, liberty, and the pursuit of happiness – that to secure these rights, governments are instituted among men deriving their just powers from the consent of the governed.

(Thomas Jefferson, *The Declaration of Independence*)

Whatever happens we have got
The Maxim gun, and they have not.

(Hilaire Belloc)

In this chapter

We explore the process of modernization – both the indigenous development of the phenomenon in the West as well as imported development that occurred sometimes forcibly in much of the rest of the world. Modern political systems are based on a sense of nationalism, an effective bureaucratically rational state administration, and a belief in active citizenship rather than merely passive obedience. These characteristics did not develop all at once. Nor was their development smooth and painless. In fact, many states today are not yet fully modern. They still retain, or many of their people still retain, one foot in the traditional agricultural world that existed before modernization began. In Europe, modernity developed over centuries and was transplanted overseas by massive European settlement. Across the non-European world,

European colonialism either forcibly transplanted elements of modernity to its colonies or impelled local regimes to adapt modern practices if they were to remain independent. This partial and forced modernization left unintended consequences when the colonialists were forced out, in most cases just after the Second World War. These consequences as well as how the modernization process itself works and where it is leading us continue to be hotly debated. The key to understanding the modernization process is a global approach typical of structural–functionalism. But political culture and political economy help explain how a political system works at any point in time. So too appreciation of the rational strategies typical of game theory helps us understand why the key political actors in the modernization process do what they do. The chapter includes case studies of Western Europe, Japan, and India.

Introduction

Most people take modern governments and national loyalty for granted. And most regimes claim that they are democratic or somehow rest on the consent of the people they govern even when such claims appear to be transparent lies. But nationalism, an effective state administration, and the appeal of democracy should not be taken lightly. Even where the principles Jefferson enunciated in the *Declaration* have been substantially realized, the road to their realization has frequently been violent and riddled with conflict. In the developing world, the change has often been even more wrenching. There the road to the creation of modern states and nations has involved the use of force that Belloc's couplet both celebrates and mocks. Early Maxim machineguns in the hands of nineteenth- and early twentieth-century imperialists helped European states create empires because more militarily backward societies could not successfully resist modern armies. And it was out of these colonial entities that many contemporary developing countries emerged. In both the developing and developed worlds, revolutions, mass protests, and other forms of coercion forced ruling elites to abandon power or change their methods of rule. In short, the sorts of political actors and strategies discussed in the last chapter are not simply applicable to contemporary politics; these concepts also provide the key to understanding the emergence of the modern world. More than that, an understanding of how the modern world emerged can in turn provide a key to contemporary politics because many of the political conflicts that brought it about continue. This chapter has three main parts. The first contrasts the ways in which traditional and modern regimes attempt to guarantee their legitimacy, and organize their states, governmental structures, and armed forces. The second part is a case study that describes how these modern institutions arose in the West focusing on the political conflicts that helped bring them about. The third major section focuses on how often incomplete modernization was transferred to the world.

Modern and traditional societies

Until about five hundred years ago, the world's economies were based on subsistence agriculture. Most of its peoples lived in villages. Authority was based on tradition, which meant that one's social status was ascribed (inherited) and the pace of social and economic change was slow. The sacred, natural, and political worlds were merged. Political leaders were often religious leaders, and natural events were often seen as omens or retribution for the actions taken by political leaders. Age gave experience, and since things did not change rapidly, age conferred wisdom and respect as well (Chirot 1994: 14–56). It is true that many pre-modern societies had great cities, high culture, and a highly educated scientific and literary class long before the modern era. Ancient China, the ancient Middle East, and parts of the Americas are conspicuous examples. Yet these high civilizational achievements rested on a traditional, largely agricultural, resource base, and they did little to unsettle the way of life of the ordinary person, which remained agricultural, rural, and tradition driven. Most of the time, ordinary people, individually or collectively, were not and could not envision themselves as political actors. In contrast, modernity is associated with urbanization, modern industry, the emergence of the modern middle and industrial working classes, modern science and technology, and mass literacy. Under modern conditions, people generally have greater opportunities to improve their status over that of their parents. The ordinary man or woman in the street is affected by and, to some degree, shares the way of life enjoyed by the elite. People experience and sometimes seek out change. And while some people may be apathetic, most realize, at least in theory, that they can or ought to have an effect on the way their societies are governed. As Chapter 1 indicated, there are four basic supports for any political regime: legitimacy, governmental efficacy, state effectiveness, and force. These supports can be mutually reinforcing or, when they are not organized or functioning properly, mutually enfeebling. Each of these supports functions differently in a traditional and in a modern setting.

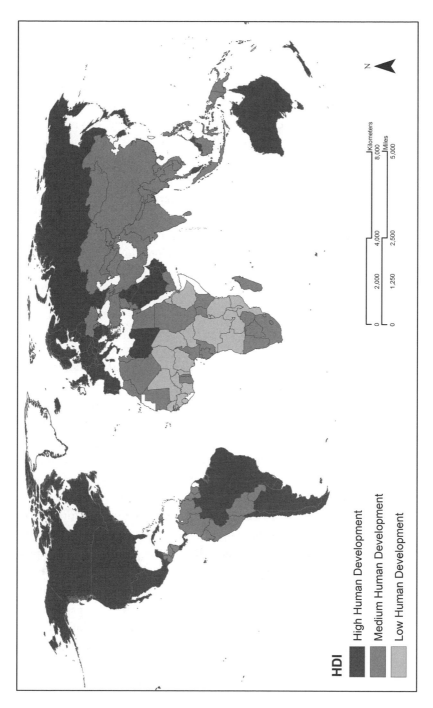

Map 2.1 Level of development (Human Development Index)

Source: Environmental Systems Research Institute (ESRI) map data. Data: UNDP

Legitimacy

Legitimacy, the moral authority of the regime, is perhaps the most basic support a regime can have. Its presence makes all the other operations of the political system just that much easier while weak or absent legitimacy can render even the most common operations of the government hard to perform. **Traditional authority** was the sort of authority that had undergirded various sorts of regimes from the simplest and earliest of human societies to absolute monarchies that survive into the twentieth century and even today. Traditional rulers confirmed their authority by appealing to the sacredness of time-honored practices. Traditional authority was both personalistic and patrimonial. **Personalism** is the practice of basing authority primarily on the person of the ruler rather than the formal office he or she holds. In fact, the ruler claims office because of his or her personal status. The "big man" in a village gains his position because of his personal talents and achievements. Alternately, in hereditary monarchies, a claimant to the throne bases his or her claim to rule on being the legitimate heir to the previous ruler (Weber 1964: 328–9).

Modern concepts of legitimacy are quite different from traditional ones. Modern governments rest on ideas rather than sheer force of habit or the personal authority of a particular individual or family. In the West, where modernity first took root, a number of developments undermined the sacredness of traditional practices. The Renaissance of the fifteenth and sixteenth centuries investigated ancient authorities with a critical eye, and used them as a source of new ideas, not as restraints upon the possibility of original inquiries. Science ceased to be a primarily bookish pursuit, and scientists actually began to examine the world, to make detailed empirical observations, to experiment. The Protestant Reformation, which began in the sixteenth century, provided another shock to intellectual foundations of traditional society in the West. It recast the idea of the Christian community. Even in its earliest phase, the Reformation provided an opportunity for princes to break free from ecclesiastical control and assume power over their own national churches. Radical versions of Protestantism asserted the right of individuals to interpret scripture for themselves.

The Enlightenment of the seventeenth and eighteenth centuries gave the ongoing discussion of rights and popular consent a new twist. The Enlightenment was characterized by a belief in reason both as a means of discovering the truth and as a means for organizing society. Although many Enlightenment thinkers defended the concept of enlightened absolutism, others paved the way for changes that would undermine royal absolutism or abolish it altogether. The Enlightenment gave rise to theories that asserted that human beings were asocial by nature and that society and government could come about only by agreement among its members. According to John Locke, one of the most influential proponents of this notion, human beings once lived in a "state of nature," bound only by "the law of nature." The purpose of government, he argued, was to enforce the law of nature and protect natural rights (Locke 1963: 307–99). Locke's theory provided moral justification for individualism and revolution. It helped inspire both the American "Declaration of Independence" and the French "Declaration of the Rights of Man and the Citizen." Locke was willing to accept monarchy if only provisionally. Others rejected monarchy altogether. Thomas Paine put it quite bluntly: "All hereditary government is in its nature tyranny" (Paine 1961: 407). In sum, the intellectual ferment produced by Renaissance, Reformation, and the Enlightenment undercut the legitimacy of traditional authority. No longer could regimes rely only on tradition; they needed to defend their right to rule by rational argument.

Governmental efficacy

Governmental structures and practices usually conform in significant measure to the principle of legitimacy that undergirds them, but whatever the structure and principles, governmental efficacy requires that the ruling elite be able to placate, incorporate, or repress all other important political actors. It also demands that they do so consistently and predictably. Thus, governmental efficacy is directly dependent upon the binding procedures that define who gets into office and the powers possessed by that office – in other words the regime's constitution. Constitutional principles made some traditional rulers **absolute** – legally and morally unlimited in what they could command. But even so, tradition limited as well as empowered them. Rulers had to make use of the institutions they inherited to get things done. The Russian tsar could not rule without the Russian Orthodox Church although he was its head. The emperor of China needed the mandarins (scholar-bureaucrats) if he was to have an effective governmental staff and get his decisions implemented throughout the country.

In contrast to absolutism, many traditional states embodied the principles of constitutionalism (limited government) and the rule of law, but they had a different conception of these principles than modern states do. The modern concept assumes that rules are made by legislatures and are subject to change. The older conception of constitutionalism and the rule of law relied on the sanctity of traditional practices and norms, and explicit agreements between rulers and their principal subjects. Even the ruler could not licitly breach these norms or agreements. This conception of constitutionalism created privileged classes and made reform and adaptation to changing circumstances difficult. A ruler's failure to observe traditional limits might lead to a rebellion by subjects powerful enough to carry it out. Rebellion might, in turn, lead to civil war or an embarrassing climbdown. King John of England, for example, was forced to accede to the demands of his barons at Runnymede in 1215 and to issue the Magna Carta.

Modern constitutionalism is quite different. Whether supported by tradition or not, privileges (special rights granted to specific individuals) are inherently suspect. According to modern conceptions, the rule of law means that laws are general rules meant to bind everyone, even those who made them, and rights should be equal for everyone. Thus, the modern rule of law demands the independence of the judiciary and legislative checks on the executive lest general laws are enforced in a biased manner. Modern concepts of constitutionalism and the rule of law are based upon modern concepts of legitimacy. Government is ultimately responsible to the people, and it must recognize the moral equality of all its citizens. In addition, systems embodying a modern conception of constitutionalism and the rule of law are more adaptable than those based on the inviolability of existing practices and rules.

State effectiveness

An effective state enforces internal law and order, defends the state's territory against outside incursions, and extracts sufficient resources from society for its own operation without eroding that same resource base. Traditional systems of administration were **patrimonial**. Patrimonial rulers did not distinguish clearly between their own private interests and the interests of their states or domains, nor was the distinction between the ruler's private purse and the public treasury clearly spelled out. Patrimonial rulers relied on personal and family connections to solidify their rule and appointed officials from the ranks of those personally connected to them. Max Weber used "**sultanism**" as the term to describe the extreme form of patrimonialism. Patrimonialism stands in stark contrast to the practices deemed acceptable in systems where modern legal rules provide the norm. The modern state is governed by **legal–rational** principles. Under legal–rational authority, subjects or citizens obey the law because it embodies principles of absolute value, as Weber put it (1964: 124). They obey rules rather than persons. The rules are sanctioned by the fact that they have been imposed via a formally acceptable procedure – i.e., they have been made by legally constituted authorities acting within their legal powers. The Weberian concept of rational–legal authority embodies the modern understanding of the bureaucrat as a functionary. It distinguishes clearly between the person of the official and the office that the official holds. Civil servants in modern governments are given defined responsibilities and directions. There is a difference between the right to make a rule and the responsibility of enforcing it. The modern civil servant has only the latter. Modern rational–legal authority or bureaucratic rationality allows the state to hire competent experts and hold them accountable.

Coercive capacity

Defense is a key function of the state. A state unable to defend itself against foreign invasion is unlikely to survive. A regime that cannot keep internal order and face down rebels is likely to suffer governmental or regime change. Thus the state's armed forces are pivotal for regime survival and political continuity. As noted in Chapter 1, even those few states that do not have official armed forces have a low-level military force, normally called a constabulary force, to police their borders and keep internal order. If they are to carry out their role effectively, the armed forces must be both competent and loyal. Neither criterion should be taken for granted. Most traditional societies assure themselves of the loyalty of the armed forces by placing only members of the ruling elite in command of the military. In fact, sometimes only members of the elite are allowed to serve in the ranks as well. The aristocratic officer class in eighteenth-century Europe is an example of such a method of control. Premodern democracies often found it convenient to have all citizens serve in the armed forces. In the contemporary era with its instantaneous electronic communications, mass armies, and constantly changing military technologies, armed forces require professional leadership. Simply putting members of politically reliable classes in charge will not suffice. The armed forces would be loyal but largely incompetent. In the present era, regimes must transcend traditional methods to develop a military that is both competent and loyal.

Summary

Modern societies differ radically from traditional societies, but modern forms did not fall from the sky, nor were they adopted all at once. The process of modernization has a Darwinian aspect about it. Political actors organized along modern lines and using modern techniques have advantages over those organized on a more traditional basis.

Modern societies have clear advantages in the struggle for power and survival against those organized along traditional lines in the competition for survival between them. Thus, once modernization took hold in one part of the globe, it proved impossible for other societies to hold back the tide. It was a matter of survival. Modernization is in many respects an ongoing and open-ended process.

CASE STUDY: THE RISE OF STATE, NATION, AND DEMOCRACY IN WESTERN EUROPE

During the mid-twentieth century, many political scientists saw the centuries-long process of modernization in Europe as paradigmatic. What was achieved there would ultimately be accomplished elsewhere, even in what was known as the "developing world" (Apter 1996: 380–3). Today practitioners of comparative politics generally take a more nuanced view; Europe does not represent the inevitable end point of development. Still, even if Western Europe cannot serve as a paradigm of what must occur elsewhere, it illustrates many of the dynamics of the process – the interplay of the aims and strategies of political actors as they attempt to develop or adapt new ideas and ways of doing things. Technological, social, and ideological changes interacted with one another, and once it is clearly under way, political actors could not abort it. The European case also reveals that conscious choices often produce unintended consequences. Kings, determined to increase their power, in the long run created opposition to the principle of monarchy itself. Coupled with knowledge of how modernity was spread to the rest of the world, the topic of the next major section, the reader will gain an understanding of what may lie ahead. This understanding is not a roadmap by any stretch of the imagination but a problematic – a set of interrelated problems and issues – entailed when political systems and political actors grapple with survival and advancement in the contemporary world.

Medieval political actors

The impetus for modernization could have begun in a variety of places. Five hundred years ago, three civilizations possessed the wealth, population, and territory, as well as the scientific and technological sophistication to begin moving from an agricultural, tradition based, rural society to the more dynamic industrial one – China, the Ottoman Empire, and the warring states of Europe. Yet it was in Europe alone that self-sustaining modernization began. Unlike the Emperor of China or the Turkish Sultan, any European king had competitors close at hand. Unlike the Emperor or Sultan, European kings could not simply stand pat and survive. European monarchs could ill afford to be outclassed by their neighbors in military technology, wealth, and in the administrative system needed to acquire and manage them. Thus, once modernization had begun, political competition made it self-sustaining.

Medieval kingdoms were ramshackle affairs first established when barbarian invaders overran the Roman Empire. The system under which they were governed, known as feudalism, diffused rather than centralized power. The diffusion of power had originally been the result of necessity rather than choice. With the decay of communication and transportation systems, the decline in literacy, economic decline, and pervasive physical insecurity, rulers and their subjects could not afford to be choosy. Order had to be established by means of any rough and ready system that worked. And in such a context, feudalism worked. Under feudalism, a hierarchy composed largely of the nobility exercised economic, political, and military power. At the apex of this hierarchy sat the king, who nominally ruled the whole society. But the king's control of his individual subjects and the resources they produced was tenuous at best. He had few ways to affect the lives of most individual subjects directly. The king had to rule through his immediate vassals or tenants-in-chief, the major noblemen. The tenants-in-chief held their offices or fiefs directly from the king. The fief-holder had the right to control the resources of the territories of the fief, the duty and right to dispense justice, to collect taxes, and to provide military forces for the king. The tenants-in-chief, in turn, further carved up much of their fiefs into smaller fiefs. They did this for the same basic reason that forced the king to break up his realm into fiefs in the first place – given the conditions of the times, no one could control large territories directly. And these smaller fiefs were often subdivided as well. Monarchs also had to contend with the power and influence of the Catholic church. The church, through the pope, could refuse to sanction the election of a Holy Roman Emperor, the nominal ruler of the German-speaking world. The pope could also put the emperor or any other Catholic monarch under a papal ban, forbidding the celebration of the sacraments in his realm until the monarch acceded to the pope's decisions about the proper role of civil and religious authority. This was more than a matter of ritual. It was a powerful tool of compulsion since people who could not receive the sacraments risked eternal damnation in the fires of hell! However, the more typical and more troubling form of authority and influence, in so far as kings were concerned, was that which was exercised by the church on a day-to-day basis.

The church was granted specific lands that churchmen, as royal vassals, ruled in the same manner as did their civil counterparts.

From the point of view of efficient centralized control, feudalism had two chief drawbacks. First, as a typical patrimonial system, feudalism was based on personal loyalty, but that bond was often unreliable. Important nobles often aspired to the throne. It was not hard to find a pretext to absolve oneself from loyalty and to serve as a cause for war. But perhaps even more debilitating for royal power was that feudal obligations were fixed by tradition. The vassal owed his lord a certain number of soldiers for a certain period of time and a fixed amount of produce. Neither the amount nor the quality of these feudal dues could be altered unilaterally. And what was useful and reasonable in one age turned out to be insufficient in another. Under the strict rubric of the feudal system, the resources available to the king at the center did not increase automatically as the wealth of the society increased, nor did his ability to impose his will on his subjects (Bloc 1961).

Monarchical aims and the creation of the state

Many kings wanted to increase their personal power and the power of their governments. Royal strategies normally operated on a variety of levels. They strengthened powers legally by gaining consent piecemeal to changes in the constitutional structure. And since existing rules, be they written or unwritten, were often ambiguous, part of the work could be done by reinterpretation. At other times it was necessary to venture into new territory. General statutes were promulgated and charters issued to particular groups. Monarchs also attempted to bypass the nobility and higher clergy in gaining and sharing resources. To do this they established a set of officials largely independent of the church and the nobility to collect taxes, serve as judges, and provide a permanent military force. Members of the middle class (see below) increasingly filled positions in this royal bureaucracy. Few had any special axe to grind as would a nobleman or many members of the clergy. Apologists for monarchy presented the king as the representative of God and the embodiment of the nation. Increasingly kings argued that they were only responsible to God and to no other earthly figure.

The methods used by centralizing monarchs were far superior to older methods. With this rudimentary modern state, the monarch could collect taxes – and in real money! – and did not have to rely on feudal payments in kind. With money, a king could hire himself a professional army, or, at least, add a professional component to his feudal array. Professional troops could be brought into the field in the numbers and at the times the king chose. Professional troops could be trained and equipped with the latest arms – artillery and firearms. With a trained corps of judicial officials, the king's law and the king's peace could be imposed throughout the realm, and not checked and sidetracked by the local nobility. Such organization was superior in terms of efficiency and power to its feudal predecessor. The church and the nobility saw the basis of the strength eroded. Despite their efforts to push back, eventually the role of the pope and the church was diminished as was the nobility's. By the sixteenth century, the Protestant Reformation put many churches under national control. And in Catholic countries, popes normally signed concordats (legal agreements) that ceded to the king the authority over appointments he most sought in exchanges for the preservation of church lands and church control of education and family law. Even so, some Catholic monarchs took it upon themselves to unilaterally divest the church of much of its property. The practice would expand as republican governments eventually replaced monarchies in the nineteenth century. In short, successful monarchs created the rudiments of a modern state. A monarch who commanded a proto-modern state could more easily take advantages of his domain's resources and control his traditional domestic political competitors (Diamond, J. 1997: 265–92).

The emergence of new actors and ideologies

Successful monarchs managed to create something like the prototype modern state, but the political strategy that created the state had unintended consequences as well. The creation of the state and the centralization of royal power also promoted economic and social change that gave increasing prominence to actors and ideas that had been marginal in the medieval epoch. In the seventeenth and eighteenth centuries the rise of absolute monarchs such as the "Sun King," Louis XIV of France, heralded the end of the medieval constitution and the beginning of a new era in which absolute monarchs controlling states competed with one another for power and glory. Monarchs had changed the legal rules so decisively and the de facto power of weaker political players strengthened so much that a new system had emerged. Key among these was the middle class.

The middle class

During the high Middle Ages, the middle class had been a subordinate political actor within the feudal system. Initially it was the loyal ally of the crown, but as time progressed it became a semi-loyal and then, in some cases, a disloyal opposition. Under the feudal system, towns and guilds had

Plate 2.1   The Hall of Mirrors in Louis XIV's Versailles palace. Louis's architecture and statecraft were imitated by lesser European monarchs.

charters from the local lord or king himself guaranteeing their rights, but despite their chartered rights, the townspeople (burghers or bourgeoisie) could not counterbalance the economic, social, or political importance of the feudal nobility, who controlled much of what the serfs, the peasant cultivators who comprised the bulk of the society, produced. As time passed, however, conditions changed. As the king and the feudal nobility successfully imposed law and order internally and kept foreign invaders at bay, they created conditions ripe for an increase in trade. Technical improvements in farming, as well, provided the basis for an agricultural surplus. With the rise in economic activity, the position of the bourgeoisie was strengthened relative to their feudal overlords. The nobility held the land for which they received fixed rents in kind. Their wealth had not increased as rapidly as that of the towns. Merchants and manufacturers provided the arms and luxury goods the nobility wanted. Moneylenders, developing into bankers, had the liquid wealth that the nobility needed to undertake crusades to the Holy Land or to meet other expenses. It was the commercial activities of the middle class that could provide cash payment of taxes rather than the typical feudal payment-in-kind. Members of the middle class could also serve as functionaries in the royal bureaucracy. Much more than the hereditary nobility or papal appointees, they were likely to be loyal servants of the crown. Yet, the middle class was more than simply a cash cow or source of governmental administrators. Individually and as a class, they had their own interests. All in all, as time progressed and modernization of the state and economy increased, the bourgeoisie's ability to resist feudal impositions increased. Ultimately they would be able to resist the king himself.

Capitalism

Along with the growth of the middle class and its political influence came the development of the economic system that typified middle-class directed production – capitalism. The middle class was engaged in commerce, money-lending (later banking), and manufacture (originally making things by hand). The economy of the towns was based on private property and cash transactions while most agricultural land was incorporated into the feudal system of land tenure that gave the holder the right to use it in exchange for service or a share in the crop. Although the economy of the towns was more dynamic than the economy of the countryside, the urban cash economy was legally only a specially chartered sector of the overall feudal system. Only gradually had the towns and commercial people been able to expand the scope of their activities. Ultimately, the abolition of feudal rights and the emancipation of the serfs helped unchain economic activity further. Trade increased, invention was better rewarded, and bourgeois rather than feudal property rights became the norm. The economy of the towns, owned and managed by the middle class, had laid the physical, legal, and cultural foundation for the rise of modern industrial production that became the premier economy of the modern era. State formation and economic growth, in turn, fostered nationalism.

Nationalism

Although the two terms are often used interchangeably in ordinary speech, states are different from nations. States are organizations, institutions, legally recognized entities. Nations, in contrast, are states of mind. Nations entail community, loyalty, and a sense of belonging. A common ancestry, language, or religion may provide a seedbed for the rise of national consciousness, but they are neither necessary nor sufficient conditions for its emergence. A **nation** is a broadly based community that, in some way or other, has the ultimate claim to its members' loyalty, and which aspires to complete or partial self-government. It may have religious overtones, but the national community is not quintessentially religious. Membership in the community is primarily ascribed: one is born into it, but at the same time, most members freely and gladly recognize their obligations to the community. Membership in the nation is their primary or one of their primary sources of identity. Unlike a clan or village, the members of the nation cannot all know each other. The nation is much too large and amorphous. Yet, fellow nationals feel an instinctive sense of comradeship when they meet for the first time. We tend to take nations and nationalism for granted, but it is important to note that nations are made not born (Anderson 1983).

In Europe, state-formation began while the mass of the population had little sense of nationalism. The serf, the townsman, or the knight was loyal to his immediate superior, to his family, guild, or corporation. Ultimately he may have owed fealty to the king, but the king was for the most part a remote figure. And given the feudal status of the monarchy, that loyalty was essentially personal. State-formation and political centralization as well as the growth of commerce, however, provided a physical basis upon which a sense of nationalism could grow. More trade, better communications, a common set of rules applying to all the king's subjects helped engender a sense of community that went beyond loyalties that were merely local, and at the same time were more limited in scope than loyalty to the church, the transnational community of all Christians that imbued the consciousness of the Middle Ages. As literacy increased, and writers began to use the vernacular in place of Latin, there were additional reasons for individuals to feel themselves members of a community that was more than local and less than universal in scope.

Revolution

Eventually, monarchs became victims of their own success. The great French Revolution began in 1789, when the Estates General, an old feudal institution that had not met for a century, was called to grant King Louis XVI additional power that he believed he needed to face a financial crisis. Instead of acceding to royal demands, the middle class (the Third Estate) as well as progressive members of the nobility and clergy rebelled, demanding a wholesale transformation of royal absolutism. The Revolution changed everything, and eventually spread to much of the rest of Europe. Citizens, now no longer subjects, owed their loyalty to the nation, the community, not to the person of the king. And when the new French Republic faced an array of other states attempting to reestablish the monarchy by force of arms, it was French nationalism that saved the republic.

The old French army had largely dissolved with the Revolution. Many officers had fled when the king was arrested. In 1792 the National Assembly of the new French Republic called for volunteers en masse.

The nation responded enthusiastically. Revolutionary and later Napoleonic armies were several times the size of their royal predecessors. The ordinary soldiers were motivated by patriotism, not fear. Once they were seasoned and trained, revolutionary armies were able to do much more than simply defend the republic. They were able to conquer or threaten much of monarchical Europe. The French nation became a nation-in-arms and established a new-style mass national army. Along with the expansion of French military power came French ideas. Republicanism and the rights of man shook the foundations of the established order. So too did French nationalism. French nationalism helped spark the growth of German, Italian, and Russian nationalism, among others. Nationalism grew even among peoples who were politically subject to powerful empires where political independence was a distant dream. Music, literature, history, philosophy, and religion often fostered a growing sense of national identity that later would give rise to political demands.

The consolidation of liberal democracy

When Napoleon Bonaparte declared himself Emperor in 1804, the dynamism and democratic ethos of the French Revolution of 1789 faded. Much of what remained was further rolled back with his defeat and the restoration of the monarchy in 1815, but the reversal was not permanent. Conditions would not allow a full and permanent restoration of the old order. Portions of the old elite's dogged resistance to fundamental change eventually provoked fresh revolutions. The revolutionary coalition stressed two fundamental principles: popular rule and freedom. Backed by large elements of the middle and working classes, emerging political elites struggled against the absolute monarchies to expand popular liberties and the right of the people to control the government. They assailed the very religious and legal principles that undergirded absolute monarchy. They argued that governments that pretended to base their authority on tradition, even tradition supposedly sanctioned by divine fiat, were illegitimate. In 1830, 1848, and 1871, France, still Europe's leading power, was shaken by revolution.

In the long run, monarchists, the nobility, and other elite actors who followed an accommodationist strategy fared much better than did their hardline counterparts. Accommodationists opted to give in to gradual reform, allowed the old dominant actors to preserve much of their wealth and a considerable influence over the political process. Great Britain is the archetype of such a successful accommodationist strategy. From 1688 on, the British elite realized that the no-holds-barred defense of royal absolutism was a losing cause (see Box 2.1). The traditional elite of France, on the other hand, followed the opposite strategy. The Bourbons, the dynastic family of France, were said to have forgotten nothing and learned nothing. Good at keeping grudges but bad at learning from their mistakes, they became politically irrelevant by the turn of the twentieth century (see Box 2.2). In short, the heirs to the eighteenth-century revolutionaries, either in principle or in practice, eventually won the day across most of Western Europe. In the end, repression led to breakdown. Accommodation led to continuity although, in the end, there too the system was fundamentally altered.

BOX 2.1
BRITISH CONSTITUTIONAL DEVELOPMENT: ACCOMMODATION

Overview

For much of its early history, Great Britain followed a pattern typical of development of European feudal societies. In the 1600s it suffered two revolutions and was known for its political turbulence. But by the eighteenth and nineteenth centuries, it had become a quintessential example of the development of democracy via gradual political change. The ruling elite after 1688 followed the accommodationist strategy.

1066 William the Norman and his barons from France defeat the English King Harold and lays claim to the English throne. William's French nobles displace the Anglo-Saxon nobility. William and his successors attempt to centralize the kingdom to the extent that the times and existing methods allow.

1215 Faced with a rebellion of his barons, King John accedes to Magna Carta, recognizing the rights of the nobility. The document becomes an important part of the country's constitutional tradition and is used as a precedent for guaranteeing the rights of other subjects.

1534 King Henry VIII confiscates church lands and declares himself head of the church of England. To reinforce his claims he has the actions sanctioned by parliament (the House of Lords and House of Commons). Henry consolidates royal power, but also gives parliament a role in the process.

1603 When Queen Elizabeth (daughter of Henry) dies childless, the throne passes to James I (James VI of Scotland). James, a defender of divine-right absolutism, attempts to govern without the consent of parliament and meets considerable resistance.

1649 Charles I, son of James and also a believer in divine-right absolutism, is executed after a civil war in which parliamentary forces defeat the royalists. A dictatorship is established under the military head of the parliamentary forces, Oliver Cromwell. After Cromwell's death, the monarchy is restored.

1688 Faced with a rebellion and foreign invasion brought on by his absolutist claims and his attempts to reestablish Catholicism as the official religion of England, James II flees to France. William and Mary of Holland and later George I from Hanover assume the throne. The new Hanoverian dynasty agrees to rule the country as limited, constitutional monarchs, setting the pattern for political accommodation that will follow.

Eighteenth-century constitutional model

In 1704 Scotland is united to England, creating the United Kingdom. The "king in parliament" is sovereign. King, lords, and commons share equal power over legislation. The assent of each is necessary for a bill to become law. The functional separation between the executive (the king and his ministers) and the legislature (the House of Lords and House of Commons) plus the fact that each branch was chosen separately from the other made the English constitution the historical model for the separation of powers. It is used (along with more democratic elements) by the framers of the American constitution.

BOX 2.2
FRENCH CONSTITUTIONAL DEVELOPMENT: ABSOLUTIST INTRANSIGENCE

Overview

After a prolonged period of turmoil as the Middle Ages came to a close, King Louis XIV, the "Sun King," stabilized French politics in the mid-seventeenth century and created an absolutist state that was the envy of monarchs across Europe. Royalists thereafter were generally unwilling to accommodate demands of the middle class, let alone the working class. Thus, from the late eighteenth to the mid-twentieth century,

France presented a picture of political turmoil once again, as monarchists contended with republicans and Bonapartists, and later democrats with communists and the fascist-inclined political right. Only the inception of the Fifth Republic in 1958 seemed to establish a stable and broadly based consensus for the liberal democratic order.

987 The establishment of the Capetian dynasty centered on Paris. As most medieval monarchs, the Capetian kings have to contend with rebellious nobles as they attempt to extend the territorial reach of their power beyond their original domain.

1302 The Estates General is formed. Three houses – the clergy, nobility, and the towns – are brought together to grant taxes to the king. The assembly is meant to serve as a national substitute for similar negotiations conducted at the local or provincial level.

1338–1453 The Hundred Years' War between the kings of England and the kings of France. The kings of England, who are also dukes of Normandy on the French mainland, claim the right to the French throne. For more than a century, English expeditions in conjunction with local allies attempt to enforce this claim and extend the territory under English rule. The French finally succeed in expelling the English from continental France.

1562–98 The wars of religion between Catholics and Calvinists divide the nobility and set groups of nobles against the French king. However, royal power is strengthened as astute monarchs and their ministers play one faction against the other. At the end of the period, the Edict of Nantes gives equal rights to Catholics and Huguenots (Calvinists). However, the Huguenots do not disappear as an armed political faction until the failure of a revolt over thirty years later.

1643 A child of five, Louis XIV ascends to the throne. By the time he dies seventy-two years later, he has consolidated the French state around himself, converting the rebellious feudal nobility into a court nobility dependent upon royal favor. Head of the dominant European power, Louis exhausts the French treasury with expansionist efforts in Europe and overseas, ultimately gaining very little in the process. Although the French state is supposed to be centralized and rationally organized, it remains honeycombed with privileged groups and inefficiencies.

1789 Confronting a financial crisis, Louis XVI summons the Estates General, which has not met for a century. The third estate composed of the middle class demands that the three orders meet together and cast individual votes. The third estate assumes the title of "National Assembly" and meets separately, inviting the other two to join it. The first republic is formed. Thus begins a period of revolutionary turmoil punctuated by the trial and execution of the king, the flight of the nobility, and international war.

1804 Napoleon Bonaparte, a revolutionary general and executive of the republican government, declares himself emperor. The First Empire lasts until 1815 when an international coalition finally defeats Napoleon and restores the monarchy.

1830 A dispute between King Charles X and the Chamber of Deputies leads to the king's dissolution of the chamber and a series of harsh decrees. A moderate, Louis Philippe, Duke of Orléans, is offered the throne, to save the cause of constitutional monarchy. The new king disillusions the radicals with his moderate policies.

1848 An economic depression, agitation over electoral reform, and the emergence of the socialist movement leads to revolution. The second republic is established. Louis Napoleon, nephew of Napoleon Bonaparte, is elected president.

1852 Louis Napoleon becomes emperor under the Second Empire, assuming the title of Napoleon III. The powers of the emperor are extended over time in the face of revolutionary agitation. In 1870 the emperor is captured in Sedan during the Franco-Prussian War, and the Second Empire comes to an end.

1871 The Prussians and their allies besiege Paris. At a constituent assembly the monarchists, while having the initiative, are unable to prevail, and the third republic is established. Under the third republic a multi-party system prevails, power gravitates into the hands of the National Assembly. Weak executives are the norm. The third republic comes to an end in 1940 during the Second World War, when the German army occupies much of France.

1946 The fourth republic was established, modeled after the later phases of the third republic. Mired in colonial wars, the republic collapsed in 1958 after a military coup.

1958 The fifth republic is established with a strong executive presidency tailor-made for Charles de Gaulle the Free French resistance leader during the Second World War. The constitution of the fifth republic, as amended, endures to this day.

Yet, there were significant divisions within the anti-absolutist camp that created conflict once absolutism was defeated. The most significant dispute was over which principle — rule by the people or individual freedom — should take priority in establishing a government. Liberals stressed freedom and distrusted government – even governments controlled by the people. The majority, they feared, would violate the rights of the minority, specifically their right to property. Thus, liberals feared the extension of the franchise and devoted much intellectual energy into trying to limit majority rule without violating the principle of government by consent. In Britain, for example, John Stuart Mill suggested multiple votes for electors based on their level of education (Mill 1958: 154–71, 138–9). Even in the United States where much of the population owned at least some property, fear of the majoritarian principle led the framers of the constitution to adopt the mechanism of indirect election for at least some officeholders. In contrast, radical democrats argued for majority rule. So-called "social democrats" considered political democracy too limited; they wanted not only equal votes but equal wealth for all. As it turned out, liberal and social democratic fears were both exaggerated. James Madison's eighteenth-century analysis of factions turned out to be substantially correct. A large and complex country would produce a multiplicity of factions. To gain a majority, any self-interested group would have to persuade others of the justice of their cause or at least bargain with them. Moderation would be the norm in policy-making, not radical action directed against the few (Madison 1961: 56–65). As the worst social consequences of the Industrial Revolution faded, the Madisonian perspective became more plausible. The working class gained the vote and property rights remained secure. Dankwart Rustow argues that process that led to the establishment of liberal democracy may have varied country by country but that there were common threads. Liberal democracy was the result of a grand bargain made either essentially in a single stage or over a protracted period of time. National consolidation preceded the making of the bargain, and many times the elites who made the democratic bargain did not have democracy as an aim. Rather, its provisions that entrench core democratic principles were preferable to the political deadlock that preceded it (Rustow 1999: 25–31).

As a consequence, in the twentieth century, the communists were the only substantial political party that maintained the original social democratic position. These factors allowed the various other strands of progressive theory to coalesce into **liberal democracy** – a regime that recognizes majority rule and protections for civil rights and civil liberties. By the end of the twentieth century, liberal democracy became one of the most generally accepted systems of government in the world. Monarchs in the developed world, if they survived at all, came to hold largely ceremonial powers. In sum, absolutists had overplayed their hand and had become politically irrelevant.

> Accommodationists among the old elite had eventually given up so much
> that the old order they wished to preserve was unrecognizably altered.

A question: does modernization entail democratization?

Questions about the implication of the European experience abound.
Among the most important is whether modernization entails
democratization. **Democratization**, in the sense that it is used here, is the
process of initiating and consolidating the growth of
liberal democratic institutions and practices similar to those of the West.
Democratization in Western Europe included the expansion of the right
to vote, the creation of mass-based political parties, and the protection of
individual rights and liberties under modern conceptions of the rule of
law. On its face, few relationships are better established than that between
state effectiveness and economic development, on the one hand, and
democracy, on the other (Lipset 1959: 29–63). Modern states require a
large middle class. The state cannot staff a modern bureaucracy; modern
economies cannot develop and flourish, and even modern armed forces
cannot function without a cadre of literate competent individuals capable
of thinking on their own and making independent decisions, i.e., the
middle class. It stands to reason that while it is possible to organize the
middle class in such a way that it lacks effective political power, once the
charm of tradition, the allure of benefits, and the debilitating effects of
fear dissipate, it is difficult to prevent middle-class individuals from
demanding their share of political power. What is true of the middle class
is also true of the industrial working class once it attains a sufficient level
of organization and wealth. All other things being equal, they too become
reluctant to endure political exclusion.

Although the European case illustrates the interaction of ideology,
technology, and new classes that gives rise to modern forms of politics, it
cannot provide anything like an exact template for what modernization
entails. Many non-European countries today are in vastly different
circumstances. Barrington Moore cites a variety of cases, some of them
European, in which modernization did not entail democratization. There
can be no democracy without an independent middle class, but social and
political contingencies can keep such a middle class from coming to the
fore politically. From the 1920s to the mid-1940s, fascists came to power
in many European countries. Japan and Germany in the 1930s testify to
the fact that cutting-edge modern societies can even be antidemocratic. It
is conceivable that the sharp twists and turns of French political

development could have landed the country in a different political location. Nationalism, the modern state, industry, and a trained and educated populace are essential parts of modernity. The development of democracy along with them is more problematic (Moore 1993). In short, an "it stands to reason" sort of argument must always be tested against the available evidence. Since the evidence is inconclusive, the issue continues to be debated. There is even disagreement about the term "democracy" itself.

Forced modernization: the politics of colonialism and its consequences

Domestic politics is rarely conducted in a vacuum, especially today. International politics affects domestic politics, sometimes with a vengeance. The previous case study examined how the modernization process has affected politics. It focused on Europe. This section takes the analysis a step further both conceptually and geographically. It examines **colonialism**, the practice of subjugating weaker states and unorganized territories to the legally recognized sovereign political control of an outside power. Colonialism imposed partial modernization on many countries, and it induced others to modernize in self-defense. Today colonialism (or imperialism) is virtually dead, but its aftereffects live on in terms of the incomplete modernization that it initiated. All over the world, domestic politics takes place within state structures; nationalism is a major political force, and calls for democracy play an important part in the political process. Yet, in many instances traditional practices and some largely traditional political actors continue to play an important role.

The initial impulse toward colonial expansion came from Europe, but it could have been otherwise. From 1403 to 1433 the government of imperial China dispatched a series of naval expeditions through the South Sea that may have circumnavigated Africa and probed much of the globe. These expeditions, motivated by grand military and commercial designs, involved hundreds of ocean-going junks, but at the end of the period court intrigue brought this program of overseas expansion to an end before it could bear any enduring fruit. The great ships were dry-docked and later burned, and an imperial decree restricted the Chinese to their own coastal waters. Had China continued with its expeditions, had it built upon its leadership in the new technologies of the day (iron-making, the clock, the compass, and gunpowder), and had the emperors of the late Ming and Manchu dynasties followed the example of their more innovative predecessors, modern history might have had a Sino-centric focus. As it turned out, successful initiatives for overseas expansion came from other sources, the contentious and emerging nation-states of Western Europe. In search of new trade routes to the Far East, the Portuguese by 1487 rounded the Cape of Good Hope at the southern tip of Africa and eleven years later reached India. Spain and Holland quickly followed, and later France and England entered the race as well. European governments expanded the territory they controlled far beyond their metropolitan core and sent out administrators and settlers to form colonies. At its height, colonialism affected virtually every corner of the globe. In the fifteenth century, the luxury trade with the Far East, and the gold, silver and agricultural wealth of the New World attracted Europeans. By the turn of the twentieth century, virtually the entire world was caught up in colonialism, either as imperial or would-be imperial powers, victims, or wholly or partially successful resisters of the colonial expansion of others. As a region, only Latin America was largely outside the system, having escaped direct colonial control almost a century earlier, but even Latin American countries found themselves as objects of economic domination by Europe and the United States, a condition sometimes termed "semi-colonialism."

Strategies of imperial expansion

Imperial expansion was seldom a straightforward process. Even in the heyday of the use of direct force, it was rarely a clear-cut matter of "us versus them" where a united group of locals resisted a united imperialist power. Colonial politics often included a crazy-quilt cast of political actors with interests that often converged and diverged in complex ways. Some of the citizens of imperial powers promoted the enterprise; others resisted it. In the target countries too attitudes varied. Some resisted while others cooperated with the outsiders. Even among those who chose to resist, strategies were different. During the colonial era, international politics was clearly power politics. Superior technology and organization, especially in the military realm, often conferred decisive advantages. Before the industrial age, European superiority in sailing vessels, navigation aids, firearms, and cannon, as well as modern state organization, allowed Europeans to penetrate other parts of the world. Industrialization that began in the nineteenth century further enhanced the advantages of technologically more advanced countries (Headrick 1981). Yet, despite their technological superiority, imperial powers could rarely mount a full-scale military invasion of target countries from the outset. Without overwhelming force, imperialists needed entrance strategies to insinuate themselves into local politics. They had to justify the creation of a colonial enclave or, at the minimum, a role within

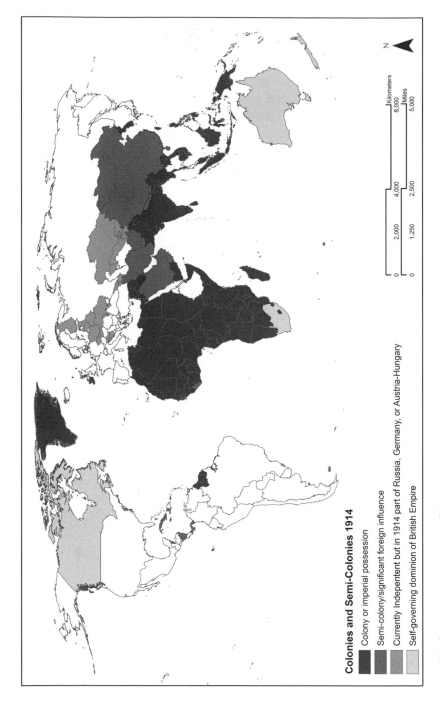

Map 2.2 Colonies and semi-colonies, 1914

Source: Environmental Systems Research Institute (ESRI) map data

Colonies and Semi-Colonies 1914

Colony or imperial possession

Semi-colony/significant foreign influence

Currently Independent but in 1914 part of Russia, Germany, or Austria-Hungary

Self-governing dominion of British Empire

local politics. Entrance strategies were varied and often combined a multiplicity of aspects. Imperialists came as traders, missionaries, explorers, or diplomats. They could present themselves as purveyors of new technologies, oftentimes military, that offered a decisive edge to the local government against its rivals or vice versa. They could offer their services as advisors to the government, capable of interpreting strange languages, laws and customs that now confronted the locals.

Establishing full colonial control was often a gradual process. Initially imperialists might make relatively modest demands for such concessions as exclusive or partial control of a limited territory, or special trading privileges. Initial demands were often followed by others as the local power found itself increasingly unable to refuse imperialist exactions. Imperial powers invented the principle of extraterritoriality that gave subjects of the imperial power special status and protection within the foreign state. For instance, by the end of the nineteenth century, European powers and Japan had established special privileges for themselves in much of coastal China. In some cases this status extended to local groups, usually local Christians as well, making them a potential fifth column for further imperial expansion. Once full colonial control was established, imperial powers could use their status as sovereigns over the territory to modify local laws as they chose. If the local government bent but did not break, conquest strategies were required. Imperial powers could normally rely on their technological and organizational superiority. But outsiders most often lacked numbers. They could normally overcome this by recruiting local allies. The dominant political actors locally often had competitors anxious to find allies who would help them change the system to their advantage. Thus, imperialists frequently adopted a "divide and conquer" strategy. They befriended weaker political actors, thus gaining a certain legitimacy as well as valuable, if unwitting, support for the initial stages of their project. Imperialists would, as convenient, make use of the sort of traditional principles that had long since lost relevance in their own homelands, sometimes assuming traditional titles and insinuating themselves into the local elite. As their penetration of the country progressed, imperialists also recruited locals to work directly for them. The British, for example, identified certain peoples as "martial races" and employed them heavily in private armies run by trading companies and later in the imperial armed forces themselves. They used other ethnic groups whom they regarded as particularly suited for administrative duties. Sometimes imperial takeover did occur as the result of a full-scale invasion. For instance, France assaulted Algeria in 1830 to avenge a supposed insult to the French ambassador and collect a longstanding debt. And the United States used the sinking of the battleship *Maine*, as a pretext to seize what remained of the Spanish Empire. But even an initial massive use of force could not remove the need to deal with disparate local actors.

Resistance strategies

Many local rulers or their opponents originally thought they could manipulate outsiders, using the newcomers' wealth, technology, and military prowess for their own advantage and excluding foreigners when they became too dangerous. Few succeeded. In most cases, once the ruling elite in the target countries realized what the thrust of the outsiders' policies was, resistance was often ineffectual. By then colonial incursions were usually well advanced, and imperialists had co-opted locals as their allies. Locals too often worked for foreign firms, governments, and households. By the nineteenth century the ruling elite of some target countries chose a strategy of adopting modern methods at least selectively to counter imperial threats. The advocates of this strategy were known as "westernizers." In nineteenth-century Russia, China, and the Ottoman Empire, some key governmental advisers recommended such a policy. The western methods that were the most obviously useful were military. Possession of modern firearms, gunboats, railroads, and communications could give the target country a fighting chance, as it were. But reorganization of the military and its recruitment methods were needed as well. This entailed policy changes that tended to disrupt local politics further, promoting the rise of new political actors, such as a military officer corps not affiliated with the old political elite. Military modernization also tended to encourage changes beyond the narrow military sphere. No modern military organization would be content to rely completely on foreigners for equipment and supplies. A local industrial base was desirable if not absolutely necessary. Industrialization, in turn, required patronizing other new political actors, modern commercial and industrial elites. Furthermore, when individuals went abroad to study military science or western science and technology, they often returned with western ideas about society and government as well, further undermining the hold of traditional local elites. Westernization thus proved to be an additional source of instability.

Some local elites and their supporters chose a path that stressed local strengths and refused to adopt foreign ways at all. The Boxers of late nineteenth-century China were, perhaps, the most well known example of such a strategy. The foreigners were devils, but local culture and technology (even magic) were superior. Violent resistance was imperative. Such extreme strategies could not work in the end, but other less extreme nativist strategies were viable. Elements of modern technology could be grafted into local practice, even while local culture was seen as morally superior to its outside competitors. Slavophiles, Islamists, Confucian modernizers and others supported this sort of strategy in a variety of milieux. The approach toward westernization is still common even in the post-colonial era.

The long-term results of the struggle against imperialism were varied. In the fifteenth, sixteenth, and seventeenth centuries, most of the native peoples of the Americas fell under the colonial yoke. Even powerful empires, the Aztec Empire in present-day Mexico and the Incan Empire in the Andean region of South America, were quickly conquered. Massive European settlement followed. Even in those parts of the Americas with a large native population, Europeans remained the dominant political actors even after independence (Chasteen 2006: 25–116). Massive European settlement marginalized the native population in Australia and New Zealand. Tropical diseases prevented Europeans from establishing more than limited coastal colonization in Africa early on in the imperial era. Nonetheless, European powers established way stations on the coast along the route to Asia and set up trading posts for the capture and purchase of slaves and the acquisition of local products. With the discovery of quinine, which provided protection against malaria, and the lure of Africa's newly discovered wealth in rubber, ivory, and minerals, European incursions subdued most of the continent by the end of the nineteenth century. Much of South and Southeast Asia also fell to expanding European empires.

A few countries in the Middle East and East Asia succeeded or partially succeeded in adopting European technologies and methods critical for their survival. They followed the route of modernization by adaptation. The most successful of these was Japan (see the case study below). China and the Ottoman Empire came under increasing European pressure throughout the nineteenth century. They were torn between westernizers and advocates of retaining traditional ways as the best way to counter European moves. Neither China nor the Ottomans (Lewis 2002: 31–58) quite succumbed, but neither managed to successfully adapt to the changing political environment as Japan did. Both lost territory and were forced to grant rights of extraterritoriality to European powers.

Colonial governance

When a territory came under full imperial rule, the imperial power could follow one of several governing strategies. In the few cases where settlement was so extensive it displaced the local population, the colony could be governed as a distant province of the mother country or as the property of a private company or individual under a royal charter. In colonies where the local population remained large and foreign settlers relatively few, colonial governance strategies were of two basic sorts (Smith 1982: 31–58). Perhaps the easier to adopt was **indirect rule**. Indirect rule left much of the local power structure in place. Local chiefs, headmen, even nobles or kings could remain in power, provided they performed the necessary services for their imperial overlords. Taxes, troops, the imposition of law and order, access to land and other resources coveted by imperialists were required of these underlings if they were to retain their status. Most of the locals still felt themselves bound by their traditional allegiance to their local leaders, but now these local leaders were in the service of foreigners rather than independent. The imperial government also required a veto power over the choice of local leaders, lest someone unwilling to cooperate with the imperial system gained power.

When the situation required it, the imperial powers imposed **direct rule**. Direct rule entailed the replacement of the local elite and the establishment of a western-style system of administration from top to bottom. Locals might find their way into the system, but they would have to assimilate western ways. In other words, they would have to adopt European dress, culture, language, and norms. They would be, in effect, brown, black, or yellow-skinned westerners. The Japanese too, when they had embarked on their own imperial enterprise at the turn of the twentieth century, used assimilated locals in the administration of their colonies. The assimilation strategy was aimed at a small number of locals and was never meant to undercut imperial power. Even so, assimilated locals might be granted admission to the imperial home country and its institutions, becoming lower-ranking government officials, lawyers, clergy, and other professionals.India (see the case study below) provides a good example of how imperial conquest and governance strategies worked.

Support for and opposition to imperialism

In the beginning of overseas expansion, imperialists held the initiative. They could create facts on the ground overseas and demand that governments back home support them. Governments, not wishing to squander opportunities or abandon their nationals in the breach, often backed these imperialist initiatives. Imperialists justified their project in both self-interested and altruistic terms. For the religious, they represented fertile mission fields. For others, colonies promised wealth, prestige, and military advantage. In point of fact, those who controlled or hoped to control the mines, plantations, and other natural wealth of colonies represented a powerful set of interests that profited mightily from the colonial enterprise. The nature of that economic enterprise differed from era to era and country to country, but its essence was virtually always the same: the extraction of wealth from the colonial area and the use of colonies as markets for the imperial metropole. Colonies were to be kept economically dependent on the imperial power. The fully modern part of the empire was the center while the colonies were generally economically backward except for the modern enclaves developed and controlled by imperial interests.

Imperial powers saw themselves as racially or at least culturally superior to the locals. Thus, colonial rule was for the locals' own good. "Take up the white man's burden," Rudyard Kipling wrote – as if colonialism were simply an exercise in service to one's fellow human beings. Others were not so sure of the real benefits of the imperial project. To those citizens of the imperial power not engaged personally or psychologically in the enterprise, imperial expansion often seemed like a wasteful adventure and a distraction. Some senior politicians and government officials, members of the middle class, and clergymen opposed imperialism in whole or in part. Imperial expansion, after all, entailed financial costs to the government, placed their country at odds with other countries with which they might otherwise be natural allies, and threatened to precipitate unnecessary wars. On the whole, however, anti-imperialist motivations were ideological or moral. The barbarities often committed against native peoples undermined the moral principles that the imperial power claimed to support. From the very first decades of Spanish colonialism, some of Spain's Catholic clergy protested the colonists' treatment of the Indians. At the turn of the twentieth century, opposing King Leopold's brutal treatment of Africans became an international cause célèbre (Hochschild 1998: 195–259). Still other citizens in the imperial power could be moved by either imperialist or anti-imperialist appeals. A hundred years ago, the working class and working-class political parties, for instance, were torn two ways: in the direction of patriotism and imperialism, on the one hand, and in the direction of international solidarity and anti-imperialism, on the other. It was not until the mid-twentieth century that anti-colonial movements in the colonies and the mother countries gained the upper hand.

Unintended consequences of colonialism

Colonialism was originally intended to secure the power and prestige of the imperial power and the prosperity and advancement of its nationals at the expense of local subject peoples. The independence of the colonies was not something imperialists had planned for. At the turn of the twentieth century, it seemed that the "white man's burden" would last indefinitely. As late as the 1940s, Prime Minister Winston Churchill remarked that Britain was not fighting a world war simply to give away its empire (Churchill 1996: 91). Be that as it may, Britain did, and so did France, the United States, the Netherlands, Belgium, and others – either willingly or unwillingly. However, the forced and partial modernization promoted by colonialism left newly independent states with a variety of problems that proved difficult to address.

Competing principles of authority

Europe and countries where European modernization was transplanted by large-scale European settlement often developed a broadly shared view of the world. Governmental authority rested on consent, not tradition, and religion was largely a private matter. However, few former colonies had had an indigenous equivalent to the Renaissance, Reformation, and Enlightenment that had shaped these views in the West. Nonetheless, colonialism had helped undermine the moral authority of traditional rulers and rules, and had introduced the western intellectual tradition. In concrete terms, colonialism had changed local educational systems. It either replaced traditional rulers or compelled them to collaborate, thus undercutting their moral authority. Yet in most ex-colonies, traditional leaders still survived. Meanwhile, liberation struggles had also conferred moral authority on a new set of leaders. Those who had led those struggles, especially when one leader stood out among the rest, could often claim the sort of charismatic authority that many founding fathers have historically exercised. And the ideas of democracy, equality, and freedom, ideas that had had their origins in the West, also came into the mix. Many liberation movements that had led the struggle against colonialism had appealed convincingly to these principles. But so too did disloyal or semi-loyal oppositions to newly independent governments.

Weak sense of nationalism

Indigenous modernization tended to foster nationalism, and in the mid-twentieth century the nationalisms that had developed frequently coincided with the boundaries of existing states. In contrast, in ex-colonies the situation was often much different. Especially in Africa and much of the Middle East, the territorial configuration of new states was often the result of the interests of imperial powers which had established the colonies in the first place. Ethnic groups had been torn asunder or lumped with others with which they had no historic connections. Nationalism or patriotism is a powerful force. But nationalism can have strikingly different effects depending on how nationalists conceive of their country. When the country the nationalist identifies with coincides with the territory and population controlled by the state, it generally reinforces the stability of the system. In ex-colonies, however, state-centered nationalism was often only skin deep, and when the dominant nationalism is not state-centered, nationalism promotes instability. This discrepancy can manifest itself in several ways. Many new states and even some old ones are composed of diverse national groups whose basic loyalty is to their own subgroup within the state rather than to the state as a whole. This phenomenon is called "**ethnic nationalism.**" On the other hand, a subgroup within the state or the citizens of the state as a whole may feel loyalty to a national group a large part of whom live outside the state's boundaries. In this case their loyalty is a species of **pan-nationalism**. In some new states, any sort of nationalism was weak. Elites might be nationalistic, but the mass of the population might feel little sense of community with the rest of their fellow citizens. Nations like France have had centuries to promote a sense of national feeling among Normans, Bretons, and Parisians. The new states of Africa have rarely been that fortunate. In many such new states, older ties of family, village, clan, and ethnic group may overwhelm any sentiment of possessing a common nationality.

State ineffectiveness

Countries that had the luxury of indigenous modernization usually developed efficient states with an economic base sufficient to support a variety of costly state programs that the government and its citizens consider important. Few ex-colonies find themselves in this situation. Instead, ex-colonies generally possessed what Gunnar Myrdal called a "soft state" (Myrdal 1968: 66–7). Soft states are states that aspire to be modern in their structure and practices but fail to do so. People see the state as the enemy and seek to avoid complying with its norms. This failure can arise from a variety of causes. Bureaucratic rationality and the rule of law can only be implemented successfully if bureaucratic and judicial institutions have the proper material and psychological support. In many new states and in some old ones, as well, this support is lacking. And without adequate support, traditional practices can regularly trump modern administrative norms.

In many states, revenues fall far short of what is required to meet expenditures. As a result, capital investment projects – e.g., building roads, schools, clinics, dams and irrigation systems – are often curtailed. So, too, is maintenance. Along with the general limit on outlays often comes a squeeze on the salaries of public servants. Civil servants can easily find themselves in a position where they are unable to support their families on the income they receive from their full-time state jobs. A number of options are possible: moonlighting, even during what are supposed to be regular office hours; accepting "tips" or personal "fees" for what are supposed to be free services or have their charges fixed by regulation; becoming a fixer, for a fee of course, to guide clients through the bureaucratic maze that must be negotiated to secure their legal entitlements. In many ex-colonial countries, such practices are almost expected. These practices are encouraged by the fact that in modernizing societies, loyalties to family, clan, and village remain strong and are likely to override equal enforcement of laws and regulations. There is, in fact, a clash of cultures. Should a state functionary ignore his moral obligations to family and clan members and old associates and instead favor complete strangers just because the written rules say he should? How can these established moral obligations be cast aside?

The dangers of such systematic corruption are often compounded by a number of other factors. Over-hiring by politicians is an attractive way for them to give their friends and supporters an income. Over-regulation creates the need for more forms, bureaucrats, and time to negotiate the system. Inflation robs the salary of officials of its purchasing power. (Politicians and senior officials do a much better job of protecting their own incomes than they do at protecting the incomes of their subordinates.) Overall, a variety of causes may sap morale and put the individual bureaucrat's back to the wall. When such conditions occur, it is no wonder that the rule of law and bureaucratic probity suffer. More serious still is the large-scale corruption that often flourishes. In short, in a soft state, administration tends to revert to its default position – patrimonialism, administering the state on the basis of personal and family connection rather than adherence to rule. Actually it is more accurate to label these soft state practices "**neo-patrimonialism**," i.e., patrimonialism in a nominally modern setting. The soft state and neo-patrimonialism promote disrespect for law and authority and tend to undermine civic mindedness.

A weak middle class

The middle class is the linchpin of democratic stability. It provides the administrators, professionals, and entrepreneurs indispensable for the proper functioning of the economy and the state. In addition it provides the foundation of civil society, the wide range of voluntary groups that nurture active citizenship and so make the formal structures of democracy actually work. The middle class, with something to lose from radical change, provides a reservoir of support for existing regimes that are attentive to its interests. In many ex-colonies, the middle class is small and lacks confidence. This should come as no surprise. A long history of independent development is often necessary to produce a large and self-confident middle class. In many colonies, locals were excluded from positions of responsibility and denied opportunities for education and advancement. In the Belgian Congo, for instance, no native Congolese had made it into the officer corps even at the time of independence. Lacking a middle class, ex-colonies can run into serious difficulties.

Summary

The complex of problems reviewed above helps generate an additional one – praetorianism. Governments require the ability to defend themselves against internal and external enemies. They need military force. Yet, soft states with governments of uncertain authority invite a military takeover or an increase in the political role of the military beyond what would be tolerable in well-run polities. Both are manifestations of **praetorianism** discussed in Chapter 1, the political condition in which brute force and the threat of force are substituted for negotiation, persuasion, and law. The problem of praetorianism is not easily fixed. Sacrificing military competence for the sake of loyalty is ultimately a bad bargain that can put a country at risk from foreign invasion or domestic rebellion. Although military intervention is a problem in itself, it is also a symptom of other serious deep-seated problems.

In sum, although outright colonialism has disappeared, its effects live on. The forced and partial modernization that was the byproduct of colonialism complicates the domestic politics of ex-colonies. And even though imperial powers have withdrawn from direct political control, economic, political, and diplomatic influence remains, sometimes to the detriment of the former colony. Imported and local factors, and direct force, have, over time, created a complicated political playing field in many former colonies. Political breakdowns – be they revolutions, coups d'etat, and other forms of political rupture – are an ever-present possibility.

CASE STUDY: JAPAN

Japan represents a signal success story of a target of imperialism first resisting outsiders and eventually becoming modern and powerful enough to join them as an equal in the international arena. On its journey from target of imperialism to practitioner of imperialism, Japan adopted a number of strategies. First, the government selectively made use of would-be European colonizers to strengthen its hand in an ongoing civil war. Then, once the civil war was won, the government shut out Europeans almost entirely. Finally, several centuries later, faced by a new imperial threat from both Europeans and Americans, the government embarked on a program of modernization and partial westernization. The twists and turns of the Japanese experience illustrate many of the perils and responses of other targets of imperial ambition although few others were able to emulate Japan's success. When confronting outsiders, Japan had an advantage that most others did not have. The uniformity of Japanese language and culture and the accession of the first Japanese emperor several centuries before the birth of Christ gave the Japanese a sense of their own unique national identity. This incipient sense of nationalism made the imperialist strategy of divide-and-conquer harder to apply.

When Europeans arrived, Japan was divided among feuding noblemen, but all these noblemen recognized themselves as Japanese and pledged nominal loyalty to the emperor of Japan. Then, in decisive battle in AD 1600, Tokugawa Ieyasu defeated rival noblemen ending a long-running civil war. He proceeded to consolidate his power within a system that was reminiscent of European feudalism. Ieyasu founded the Tokugawa Shogunate, which perfected feudal methods of control. At that time of Ieyasu's victory, the nobility, or *samurai*, were a military caste, who owed military service and loyalty to their respective lords. The major noblemen, or *daimyo*, each controlled large tracts of the country, and subinfeudated their holdings to lesser nobility just as their counterparts were doing in medieval Europe. Tokugawa's achievement was to bring a degree of centralized rationality into the chaos inherent in such a system. He strengthened the position of shogun, which he officially assumed in 1603. The shogun was, in theory, the deputy of the emperor, but it was the shogun that held the real power. Under the Tokugawa Shogunate, which lasted until 1868, the *daimyo* were kept in check in a variety of ways. One of the most important of these was the requirement that the *daimyo* spend every other year in the shogun's court, and members of his household had to be there at other times. This increased the expenses that had to be borne by the great noblemen, and provided the shogun with hostages to assure the *daimyo's* good behavior. Japanese feudalism had an additional advantage over the European variety. In the Japanese system there were clear lines of authority. The shogun was no one else's vassal, nor did any vassal or *samurai* owe allegiance to more than one lord.

Ieyasu had originally made use of European arms and European advisers to strengthen his armies during the civil war, but when he had defeated his adversaries, he reversed course. The Tokugawa Shogunate brought a

Plate 2.2 Samurai military regalia.

period of stability to Japan by isolating the country from an outside world that threatened to undermine the traditional order. These threats had come in a variety of forms. Christian missionaries and traders had arrived in Japan during the sixteenth century, spreading foreign ideas and practices that threatened the power and prestige of the military aristocracy, the dominance of indigenous religious practices, and the ability of the government to control its own people. European-introduced firearms were especially destabilizing. They allowed a commoner, with a few months' training and armed at modest expense, to kill an armored nobleman, who had trained for years in the military arts and could only be equipped at great expense. The shogunate saw to it that such foreign contacts and practices were abolished or severely curtailed. Local production of modern firearms was discontinued. For more than two and one-half centuries this isolationist policy provided a formula for political and social stability. Under the shogunate, traditional society remained intact, and the forces of modernization were held at bay.

In 1853, however, Commodore Matthew Perry of the United States Navy arrived in Tokyo Bay in command of four modern warships. Perry delivered a letter from the President of the United States, demanding that Japan open relations with America. Increased pressure from the United States and European powers followed. The Japanese political establishment was divided between those who wanted to resist and follow the traditional policy, and those who saw that modernization was necessary. In 1868, a palace coup removed the shogun, abolished the shogunate itself, and placed the emperor in direct command. The emperor, in turn, promised the creation of a deliberative assembly. The Meiji Restoration had begun, but the "restoration" was far from a conservative or reactionary undertaking, the term served as a cultural facade for a rapid and thoroughgoing state sponsored modernization.

The real power under the Emperor Meiji was exercised by a group of modernizing noblemen, who recognized that Japan would have to change radically or it would become a colony or protectorate of foreign powers. The new government abolished fiefs, and in their place it established prefectures. The government also established a centralized bureaucracy, a conscript army, a postal service, and a ministry of education. The country industrialized. The government promoted the adoption of western practices in culture, science, philosophy, and education. In 1877 an armed revolt by disaffected noblemen was put down by a conscript army composed of commoners, demonstrating the superiority of modern over traditional forces. In 1889, a new constitution established a bicameral assembly, whose upper house was based on birth and merit and whose lower house was elected on the basis of a restricted franchise (about 10 percent of the population). The power of the emperor to issue decrees, declare war, and make treaties was preserved. In 1919 the assembly debated universal suffrage, but the reform it eventually passed merely doubled the size of the electorate to three million, and the right to vote still remained far from universal. Agricultural and industrial laborers, by and large, did not possess the right to vote. Still, by that time, the personal power of the emperor over public affairs had waned considerably.

Rapid modernization allowed Japan to become one of the world's great powers. In 1910 it took Korea as a colony, defeating both the Chinese (in 1895) and the Russians (in 1905) in the process. The peace settlements of the First World War gave Japan control of former German colonies in the Pacific and Germany's zone of influence in northwest China. Japan had an empire of its own. Between the two world wars, a struggle ensued between westernizers and liberals, on the one hand, and conservatives and the military, on the other. Japan's imperial policy, the ability of the armed forces to avoid civilian control, and the still largely conservative and agricultural nature of the country strengthened the hand of conservatives and militarists. As a result, the military, the big industrialists, and the landlord class were able to dominate politics for their mutual benefit. More moderate politicians were cowed by violence and intimidation. Thus, militarism, authoritarianism, and nationalism increased during the 1930s. In 1932 Japan established a protectorate in Manchuria under the name of Manchukuo. And several years later, invaded China proper. By the end of 1941, Japan was at war with the United States and Britain.

The defeat of Japan in the Second World War ushered in another stage of Japanese political development. The country had been devastated almost completely even before the dropping of two atomic bombs at the end of the war. Japan fell under US occupation. The United States used its influence as an occupying power to reshape the Japanese economy and society and to establish a new constitution. Occupation authorities broke up the major industrial conglomerates or *zaibatsu* and carried out land reform. The old landlord class was shorn of its power, and the influence of the industrialists was curtailed. An even more telling blow to the old militarist coalition was a constitutional provision that forbade Japan's involvement in aggressive war and officially abolished the armed forces. The effect of the prohibition on keeping military forces was as much psychological as physical. Japan has professional land, sea, and air "Self-Defense Forces" that for all intents and purposes are an army, navy, and air force. These forces, however, have little capacity to project military power beyond Japan proper and the adjacent sea lanes. More importantly the "no war" clause of the constitution and the country's horrendous experiences during the Second World War has ingrained anti-militarism deeply into the Japanese psyche. In addition, the constitution clearly established a liberal democratic system along parliamentary lines. The emperor remained untouched after he had renounced his claim to divinity. And he serves as a de facto head of state. Most of the changes imposed by the occupying forces have taken deep root.

Both under the Meiji Restoration and under allied occupation, Japan adapted western practices successfully even though in many ways its culture and history were much different from that of the West. There had been no Renaissance, Reformation, or Enlightenment. Japan accepted ideas it found attractive and which seemed to work. Despite changes, the country's language, culture, and many social conventions remain firmly in place after a century and a half of often wrenching interaction with the West. The Japanese remain group-oriented and consensus-seeking; they avoid direct confrontation if possible. The Japanese political style reflects these traits. But Japan has managed to reconcile social deference with democratic governance. The Japanese experience demonstrates that western and non-western hybrids are not only possible but potentially highly successful. Even liberal democracy seems to be more than an accident of western history, nontransferable to other parts of the world.

CASE STUDY: INDIA

If Japan represents the relatively rare instance where a target of imperialism turned the tables on outsiders, India was a more typical victim. Ethnically and religiously heterogeneous, India had been a prey to many invaders over the centuries. When Europeans arrived at the turn of the sixteenth century, the country was politically divided. The newcomers were able to play upon these divisions to insinuate themselves into local politics and ultimately bring all of India under colonial control. The Indian experience illustrates how imperialists were able to use the divide-and-conquer strategy successfully. It illustrates some of the typical factions that often beset the imperial power itself, as well as the methods of direct and indirect methods of rule. Indians followed a variety of strategies to resist the outsiders but in the end failed. Eventually some of the most assimilated Indians emerged as leaders of the independence struggle. However, independent India, unlike Japan, suffered from problems typical of forced modernization.

Before the advent of European colonial powers, India was a quintessentially traditional society. One of the wealthiest areas of India was the Mogul Empire. The empire was controlled by a Muslim dynasty, but the mass of its subjects were Hindus. The Moguls were an offshoot of Genghis Khan, the thirteenth-century Mogul conqueror. Their dynasty was established in the early sixteenth century. The Mogul emperor presided over a welter of landed aristocrats of Muslim and non-Muslim origins. And the empire was only loosely integrated. Hinduism remained the dominant religion. Hinduism meticulously divided and subdivided its adherents into four main castes and hundreds of sub-castes. One's caste was inherited from one's parents, and determined not only status but occupation. The caste system, as Hinduism itself, had evolved over four millennia into a remarkably durable and nuanced order. Individuals were not permitted to rise from one caste to another, but the belief in reincarnation, with higher or lower *rebirth* dependent on one's conduct in past lives, helped sanction the system. Non-Hindus, of which Muslims were the most numerous, fell outside the caste system. As in other traditional societies, the life of the individual was centered on the village, where subsistence agriculture was the major economic activity. The elite lived off the agricultural surplus produced by the peasantry.

India faced European imperialism early in the Age of Discovery. In 1498 Vasco da Gama, the Portuguese explorer, reached Malabar in southwest India. The Portuguese sought military outposts from which to extend and protect their trading activities. The Portuguese erected forts and defeated local rulers, eventually establishing their headquarters in Goa. Though Portugal had been able to get the jump on other European powers because of effective leadership and an efficient state, it lacked the size and overall power to maintain its dominance in either Asia or the newly discovered Americas. Hence, the Portuguese were followed later by the Dutch, French, and British, who established similar enclaves and eventually displaced Portugal from some of its most lucrative outposts in Asia.

Though wealthy and extensive, the Mogul Empire that controlled the North of India was relatively weak. It had never had the degree of centralization and sense of unity the Tokugawa Shogunate introduced in Japan. By 1700 the empire was further weakened by internal revolts and lack of efficient central control. It thus provided additional opportunities for Europeans to expand their influence. In 1717 the English East India Company took advantage of the opportunity the Mogul weakness offered. It secured an exemption from taxation and won concessions from the Mogul emperor in consideration for gifts and medical services. The company had arrived over a hundred years earlier to conduct trade, but now became a more active instrument of imperial policy. The British, of course, were not alone. In 1744 French and British forces came into conflict. Each power supported a rival Indian prince as a means of extending its power and influence in the subcontinent. In time French-backed forces were defeated. The French equivalent of the English East India Company was dissolved in 1769. By 1764 the English East India Company had become the official ruler of Bengal, a rich province in eastern India from which the company gradually extended its power into neighboring territories. The company was both a commercial concern and a government. Reactions back home were mixed. Many thought the company and its commercial interests were too influential in determining British policy. Thus, in 1784 Parliament in London passed an act establishing "dual control" that made directors of the company responsible to the British government for their activities. The measure was an attempt to curtail the company's expansionist activities. Nonetheless, the company's control continued to expand. Difficulties between the company and the government continued as well. In response, in 1858 parliament passed the Government of India Act, transferring governmental control of Indian territory from the East India Company to the British government. The crown inherited a hodgepodge of arrangements. In some areas, the British ruled directly. In others, they ruled through local princes. Eventually a Royal Indian Army and Royal Indian Civil Service were created. These institutions were modeled after their counterparts in the mother country. Senior and middle-ranking officials were recruited in Britain primarily from the same classes that provided the personnel for similar British posts at home.

British subjects from the mother country became landlords, traders, administrators, military officers, and professionals under the British raj (rule) in India. Especially where Britain ruled directly, the locals were in a clearly inferior position. British landlords were more interested in export crops, such as cotton, than crops for local consumption. Indian agriculture became tied to the world economy. British neglect of local interests led to periodic famines. A modern British education became essential for the local elite and aspiring members of the Indian middle class. Many Anglicized Indians became impatient with British rule, however. And an independence movement after decades of organization and protest finally compelled the British to leave the subcontinent in 1947.

Today India is an independent country and a functioning democracy, but its governance suffers from many of the problems typical of former colonies. It has a sector that is modern in terms of education, profession, and outlook; a large traditional sector; and other sectors somewhere in between. It is desperately poor, riven by deep religious, linguistic, and social divisions, and before independence it had no history of democratic governance. Freedom House, a leading foundation that evaluates the status of democracy in the world, lists the country as "free" today. Yet, as recently as 1998, it gave India a "partly free" rating. Despite recognizing the most recent election as "the fairest in India's history," Freedom House noted that the rule of law and civil liberties were not adequately protected (Karatnycky 1998: 278–82). Especially troubling were widespread human rights violations by security forces in a number of rebellious territories, most notably Kashmir. On the whole, Indian political development must be considered at least a partial success, but present-day India illustrates most of the unfortunate carryovers from the colonial era that affect many other ex-colonies as well. The colonial government was more concerned with extracting wealth and assuring its home-country's place in the world than in addressing long-term local problems and promoting well-rounded modernization.

Together Japan and India represent two different experiences in confronting colonialism. The Japanese were successful in two quite different eras. In the first, the Tokugawa elites were able to take advantage of outsiders and then exclude them, allowing continuity to be reestablished after a protracted civil war. Two and one-half centuries later, the Meiji elite was able to abandon the traditional system and engineer the development of a modern society. India was not so fortunate. Internally divided, it was penetrated and exploited by outsiders. India was denied the sort of relatively smooth transition to modernity that Japan was able to engineer for itself. India fell under the colonial yoke and suffered many of the typical long-term consequences associated with colonialism.

Conclusion

The breakdown of the traditional order in the West led to the formation of states that today are supported by a strong sense of nationalism and governed by liberal-democratic principles. The process by which this occurred took centuries and involved conflict among an evolving set of political actors. The next two chapters will examine why consolidated liberal democracies have been able to flourish. Later chapters address issues that are especially pertinent to the "developing world," whose states, sense of nationalism, and democracy (where it exists at all) are often quite fragile. In the developing world traditional practices often still play an important role. The clash of norms and weakness of modern institutions set the stage for various sorts of breakdowns and various sorts of efforts aimed at constructing a stable political order. Much of the core of this book (Chapters 5 through 12) explores these issues, but first we take up liberal democratic institutions and their requisites.

Questions for further consideration

1   Is modernization equivalent to westernization? Why is westernization likely to be controversial in much of the world?

2   Consider modernization from the perspective of the ruling elite of a developing society today. Which aspects of modernization would likely appear most attractive? Which would likely appear least attractive? Why?

3   Why does modernization often favor the rise of democracy? Would
    democratization be likely if middle-class interests ran counter to the basic
    interest of the broad masses of the remainder of society? Explain.
4   Rulers resisting colonial incursions often failed to do so successfully. What
    might be some of the primary factors accounting for this failure? How
    could Japan manage to resist successfully?
5   Colonial policy created a modern imperial core and a periphery that
    served the economic interest of the core imperial states. Has this survived
    today? In what way?
6   How do the typical features of the post-colonial world help account for
    the rise of praetorianism there? What would it take to solve the problem
    of praetorianism?

Further reading

Marc Bloc, *Feudal Society*, trans. by L.A. Manyon. Chicago, IL: University
    of Chicago Press, 1961. A classic description of European feudalism.
Daniel Chirot, *How Societies Change*. Thousand Oaks, CA: Sage, 1994.
    A short, readable description of the modernization process.
Jared Diamond, *Guns, Germs, and Steel: The Fates of Human Societies*.
    New York: W.W. Norton, 1997. A discussion of the geographic and
    environmental factors that shaped human development.
Adam Hochschild, *King Leopold's Ghost: A Story of Greed, Terror, and
    Heroism in Colonial Africa*. New York: Houghton Mifflin, 1998.
    A riveting account of atrocities of colonialism in the Congo and the
    opposition it spurred.
Seymour Martin Lipset, "Economic Development and Democracy"
    (29–63) in *Political Man: The Social Bases of Politics*. Garden City, NY:
    Doubleday, 1959. A classic essay that describes the correlation between
    level of economic development and democracy.
Barrington Moore, Jr., "The Democratic Route to Modern Society"
    (413–32) in *Social Origins of Dictatorship and Democracy: Lord and Peasant
    in the Making of the Modern World*. Boston, MA: Beacon Press, 1993.
    Argues that democracy is only one of several paths to modernity.
Max Weber, *The Theory of Social and Economic Organization*. New York: Free
    Press, 1964. The seminal text that developed many of the key concepts
    pivotal for understanding traditional and modern societies and the
    modernization process.

The requisites of democratic continuity

No one pretends that democracy is perfect or all-wise. Indeed, it has been said that democracy is the worst form of government except all those other forms that have been tried from time to time.

(Winston Churchill)

In this chapter

We examine some of the most important social, legal, and economic requisites for stable democracy. Democracy can be defined in either minimalist or more expansive terms. This chapter takes the extensive view that democracy includes effective participation, the protection of basic personal liberties, as well as a broad distribution of social and economic benefits. Underlying all of the requisites for democratic continuity is the need to keep the representative institutions that are central to modern democracy truly responsive to the will of the people. In approaching this issue, the chapter concentrates heavily on democratic political culture and how people are socialized into it. But it also discusses certain institutions, such as the rule of law, and the policy consensus buttresses successful democracies. The chapter concludes with two contrasting case studies: one on the United States, the other on modern India.

Introduction

As an old 1980s pop song had it, "Everybody wants to rule the world." On its face, absolute power seems an appealing prospect. Vested with absolute power we could do what we think is just or simply advantageous.

But, as Churchill implies, that sort of arrangement, in the final analysis, is not really desirable. Absolute government by one individual disadvantages and often oppresses the rest. If given the choice and knowledge of the consequences, few people would willingly participate in a political system that concedes unchecked power to someone else. Perhaps even less desirable is a political system in which many individuals continue to strive obstinately for absolute power. Because of these considerations, democracy emerges as the worst form of government *except for all the rest*. In a democracy each individual is compelled to share power with others and voluntarily accept restraints on his or her own conduct. The ability of individuals to get everything they want is curtailed. Even their ability to insure that justice, as they see it, is done is strictly limited, but absolute government or the ceaseless struggle for absolute power is worse still. Modern liberal democracy is based on tolerance, consent, freedom of association, the rule of law, and an equitable division of benefits and responsibilities. Liberal democracy provides a modicum of personal security, freedom, and influence over collective decisions to every citizen. No one gets to rule in an absolute manner, but no one is enslaved by others either. In short, liberal democracy follows Aristotle's maxim, cited in Chapter 1, that to assure their continuity, regimes should give every class of citizen a stake in the regime. Thus, once consolidated, liberal democracies usually endure since they provide a method by which new groups can put forward their demands and be accommodated. This chapter examines the requisites for democratic continuity – the basic social and economic conditions, basic public attitudes, basic legal guarantees, and the skills citizens should have if democracies are to function well. These factors shape political actors and allow them to interact in a manner conducive to democratic continuity. Chapter 4 will investigate the various sorts of governmental and political structures that democratic polities have used to institutionalize their politics.

What is liberal democracy?

Liberal democracy is the modern system of representative government that embodies the principle of popular rule while protecting individual rights. In an operational sense, liberal democracy can be characterized in either minimalist procedural terms or in more expansive terms. The first approach sees the central feature of democracy as the "selection of leaders through competitive elections by the people they govern" (Huntington 1991: 6). But not everyone thinks that this definition is sufficient. For example, Morton Halperin, Joseph Siegle, and Michael Weinstein define

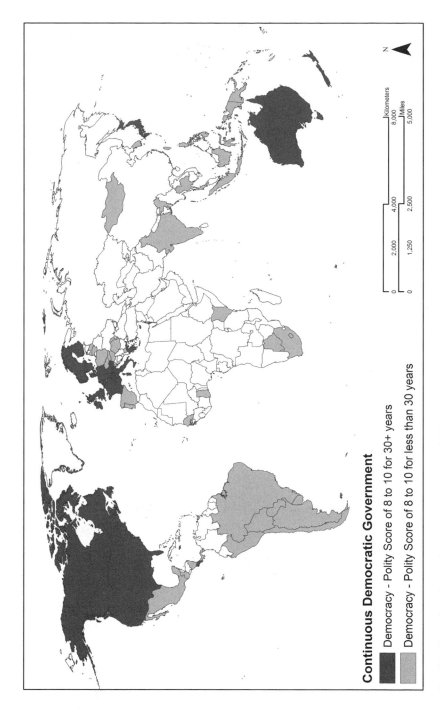

Map 3.1 Years of continuous democratic government to 2004

Source: Environmental Systems Research Institute (ESRI) map data. Data: Polity IV

Note: Polity IV ratings range from +10 (most democratic) to −10 (most authoritarian)

Continuous Democratic Government

Democracy - Polity Score of 8 to 10 for 30+ years

Democracy - Polity Score of 8 to 10 for less than 30 years

democracy in terms of free and fair elections, a shared distribution of power among governmental bodies, citizen participation in politics, and a "high degree of basic political freedoms, civil liberties, and political rights" (Siegle and Weinstein 2005: 9). Specifically, these basic civil liberties are described in the United Nations' *Universal Declaration of Human Rights* as follows. All persons are "free and equal in dignity and rights." "Everyone has the right to life, liberty and security of person" (Article 3), and cannot be held in slavery (Article 4) or subject to torture, or cruel or inhuman punishment (Article 5). All people are entitled to equal protection of the law (Article 7). When charged with a criminal offense, the accused has certain rights of due process: trial before a fair and independent tribunal (Article 10), presumption of innocence, and the prohibition of ex post facto laws (Article 11). All have the right to privacy (Article 12) and freedom of movement (Article 13). Individuals have the right to own property (Article 17), freedom of religion (Article 18), and freedom of the press (Article 19). These are basic liberal rights and have a history that extends back to the seventeenth century. **Liberal rights**, in sum, are those basic limits on government that protect the citizen from the arbitrary power of state functionaries.

Both the first conceptualization of democracy that singles out political rights and the second that adds civil liberties to the list of democracy's defining features have their uses. Yet, they do not address the need to provide all citizens with the sort of stake that Aristotle recognized was necessary for any stable regime. As Anatole France put it over a hundred years ago, "[The poor] have to labor in the face of the majestic equality of the law, which forbids the rich as well as the poor to sleep under bridges, to beg in the streets, and to steal bread." The right to vote and civil liberties are not enough. Alone they did not encapsulate democratic ideas or assure democracy's continuity. Increasingly by the turn of the twentieth century, the goal of an equitable distribution of the wealth and advantages of society become broadly accepted. This third element of economic rights speaks to the need of building support for democracy and fleshes out democracy's definition (Sen 1999). For example, the UN Declaration's Article 23 says that everyone has a right to work in favorable conditions at wages sufficient for the family to live in dignity. The Declaration further speaks of the right to join labor unions, the need to limit hours of work (Article 24), social security, unemployment insurance, and healthcare (Article 25), cultural rights (Article 27), and the equality and rights of women (Articles 23 and 25). Thus, the full definition becomes: democracy is a system of government that includes broad rights of political participation, liberal rights, as well as social and economic rights.

Breakdown and continuity in liberal democracies

Liberal democracies survive and flourish when they effectively
guarantee the three sets of rights just described. Liberal democracies
break down for some of the same reasons other regimes do. They may lack
legitimacy; the government may not be able to make efficacious
decisions; the state may be ineffective, or the armed forces may be disloyal
or incompetent. Failures in these areas may provide opportunities for
disloyal or semi-loyal oppositions to undermine and overthrow the
system, such as the democratic breakdowns described in the case studies
in Chapter 1 demonstrate. But democracy may also break down because
their adherence to democratic principles erodes or because they are
unable to consolidate democratic practices and procedures in the
first place.

In authentic democracies, the people rule. But citizen consent must be
informed consent. Achieving this norm cannot be taken for granted. Unless
real debate occurs, consent is unlikely to be informed consent. Some
regimes have elections, but allow no real debate or citizen choice and thus
there is no real consent. For example, elections in communist states and
many other authoritarian regimes often appear to be democratic. There is
a universal franchise, and frequently there is a high rate of voter turnout as
well. Sometimes opposition candidates and parties even appear on the
ballot. However, in these systems the ruling elite organizes the process in
such a way that there is no effective competition between real alternative
slates of candidates. Voters have no ability to elect the opposition even
when it is on the ballot because the opposition is denied the ability to
compete effectively and is denied access to the media or right to campaign
publicly. Real debate or choice may also be stifled by popular attitudes.
Citizens may, in fact, rally around authoritarian rulers and be intolerant of
the opposition for reasons of ethnicity, religion, or ideology. Yet, good
democratic citizens must not only tolerate, they must even encourage
loyal opposition. If political opposition does not exist, the regime cannot
be democratic.

Modern liberal democracies must also overcome what is called the
"agency problem." The **agency problem** is the situation that occurs when
an individual or group (a **principal**) delegates to someone else (an **agent**)
the authority to do something in the principal's name. For example,
someone becomes a principal by authorizing a friend to sell her car, and
the friend becomes the principal's agent. When the delegation of
authority is clearly circumscribed and where established laws govern how
it is to function, the agency problem is minimal – the agent does what the
principal wants and is subject to effective sanctions if she does not act in

accordance with the principal's wishes. In the direct democracies of antiquity, where citizens came together and deliberated in common, they might be deceived by persuasive orators or misled by their own ignorance or prejudgments, but the agency problem was nonexistent simply because there were no agents, only principals.

In contrast to ancient democracies, modern liberal democracies are based on representation. Seldom, if ever, do most people show up in person to make decisions over policy directly. Even referenda that allow citizens to cast ballots on specific policy issues or constitutional changes, common today in Switzerland and some US states, do not really replicate the ancient system. As a result, few individuals are political actors in their own right. The most important political actors in modern liberal democracies are frequently collective actors: interest groups, political parties, or social movements. Citizens have to work through them to have their say. This difference in structure between ancient direct democracy and modern representative democracy has important implications. The people's representatives, be they governmental officials or officers in organizations that are not directly part of the government, are never frictionless transmitters of how the public really thinks or feels. Representative systems in practice never work perfectly; people never have an equal say and equal access to decision-makers, and officeholders have their own collective interest distinct from the interests of those they represent. This was the point Robert Dahl made in labeling what we commonly call liberal democracies "polyarchies" instead of "democracies" (Dahl 1971: 1–9).

Modern democratic citizens must often examine and attempt to influence a welter of agents and would-be agents who hope to or actually do act in their name. Various political parties, trade groups, labor unions, and citizens' groups may claim to be the agents of voters, their members, or the public at large. Citizens must decide whether each of these actually deserve their support. Worse still, citizens in some countries new to democracy may be confronted with a lack of potential agents – no one may speak for their interests. Such groups may have to be constructed and controlled from the ground up. Thus, in modern societies there are barriers to effective participation that did not exist in ancient times. Ancient democratic citizens only had to show up at the appointed place at the appointed time to effectively exercise their democratic rights. Distance, the frequency of meetings, and the lack of leisure time were the major barriers to having one's voice heard. In modern democracies, citizens are relieved of the burdens of direct participation, but they must have additional skills and knowledge to participate in the political process effectively.

If it is to be truly democratic, representative democracy must embody the principles of responsiveness, transparency, and accountability. Each of these principles can be understood in a variety of ways; some of these understandings are complementary, others in tension with one another. This tension is perhaps clearest in regard to **responsiveness**, the principle that the elected representatives are the agents of the electors (the principals) that elected them. There are three different approaches to responsiveness that embody different conceptions of what the principal–agent relationship ought to be in a democracy. In the earliest period of representative institutions, responsiveness meant that elected officials were supposed to look after the public good, and voters were to choose public officials on the basis of the candidates' character and credentials. The representative's view on public policy was supposed to be of secondary interest to the electors; the representative's superior knowledge and civic virtue were the principal determinants of how he would vote on specific issues. This was the outlook of early British parliamentarians such as Edmund Burke (Burke 1774) and the view of many of the founding generation of the United States.

In revolutionary France after the overthrow of the monarchy in 1789 and in the United States by the 1830s, responsiveness took a more democratic twist. The representative was supposed to express the opinions and feelings of the electorate. Voters now inquired about how a candidate was likely to vote on issues once elected to office. In short, good character, knowledge, and concern about the public interest were not sufficient for representatives to be considered responsive to the public; representatives had to reflect public opinion as well. This shift in standards frequently had little to do with formal institutional changes; it was, rather, a shift in public attitudes. These two views of responsiveness are not exhaustive, however. Nineteenth- and some twentieth-century radicals objected to the principle of representation altogether because they claimed political elites could not adequately represent the interests of non-elite members of the general public, who were demographically different from their supposed representatives. These early critiques are in fact echoed in institutional adaptations today. Affirmative action in representation – i.e., party or governmental efforts to assure the presence of women, ethnic minorities, and others among decision-makers – has become increasingly acceptable. Globally, such efforts include reserved seats in legislatures, a system of representation designed to have a national minority make up a majority within certain districts, quotas within party councils or lists of party candidates.

Transparency is the principle that the public must be aware of what their agents are doing. Transparency has three aspects. First, official secrecy must be kept to a minimum. Second, rules governing the conduct of public business must be publicly known and adhered to. If the public business is not conducted openly or rules are violated, corruption and favoritism are the likely results. Third, transparency means that it must be clear to the public who is responsible for decisions. Decisions made in secret obviously violate this standard. But so too do decisions made by a process so complicated and confusing that it is not readily apparent who is really responsible for the outcome. When different political actors can each credibly blame the other or claim credit for a policy, something is amiss as far as transparency is concerned. For example, if a bill that the public favors fails to pass, the public should be aware who was responsible for killing it. Transparency is important because without it responsiveness is largely hollow and accountability is impossible.

Accountability is the third principle designed to solve the agency problem. It means that, in a democracy, citizens must have the ability to reward and punish officeholders for good or bad conduct and successful or unsuccessful policies. Accountability entails individual accountability for criminal conduct in extreme circumstances, but it also entails citizens' ability to reelect or refuse to reelect officials because of their decisions on public policy. This second element of accountability is political accountability, and it applies not only to individuals but to political parties.

In sum, democratic continuity today requires certain capacities and attitudes on the part of the citizenry as well as certain structural attributes in the political system and the society at large. There must be real public debate of issues, and citizens must understand that debate well enough to vote in their own interest intelligently. Citizens must have a basic commitment to democratic values; they must tolerate those who have interests and opinions contrary to their own. Finally, citizens must have the capacity and knowledge to function in an organizationally complex world. Even though they are unfamiliar with the term, "agency problem," people often recognize it intuitively and respond with cynicism about all political and organizational claims, become apathetic, and do nothing. This is an inappropriate response in a democracy. While a healthy skepticism about partisan claims is warranted, citizens must find positive ways of using the system for their own purposes and for their own vision of the public good. These citizen skills and attitudes and societal characteristics constitute a demanding list of requirements. Hence, consolidated democracies have been relatively scarce until recent times. Yet, how these requirements can be met has been increasingly well understood. It is to this issue that we turn next.

Maintaining democratic participation

Research has confirmed what common sense would seem to indicate, namely, that societies where wealth and income are high and widely distributed have an easier time in maintaining democracy than other societies do. Individual citizens and society as a whole are more likely to have the resources and attitudes that promote democratic continuity. In a famous essay, Seymour Martin Lipset set down what he termed the "requisites" for democracy (Lipset 1959: 27–63). He noted that these requisites were not absolute requirements for democratic success, but there was a high degree of correlation between them and democratic success. Specifically, there is close correlation between high levels of per capita income, a political culture that values equality, equality of opportunity, capitalism, high rates of literacy, participation in voluntary association, on the one hand, and consolidated democracy, on the other. On the whole, countries with over $10,000 GDP per capita (in 2008 dollars) successfully consolidated liberal democracy once they have been able to make the transition to it. And, generally speaking, the lower the GDP per capita, the more difficult it is to consolidate democracy (Przeworski *et al.* 1996: 39–55).

Middle-class individuals with decent incomes have something at stake in maintaining a democratic system. In addition they have the skills and experience to make complex organizations work for them and circumvent some of the worst effects of the agency problem. Conversely, where resources are scarce and inequitably distributed, democracy is hard to establish and consolidate. Under conditions of scarcity, the struggle for political power often is more intense than it otherwise would be. In poor countries most citizens are likely to be ill informed and uneducated. They may not only lack the ability to participate in public debate over sensitive political issues; they may also see that debate as psychologically threatening. They may be inclined to simply follow a strong personalistic leader or local notable without carefully thinking through their own personal or the public interest. Finally, in poor societies citizens are likely to find few organizations that effectively represent their interests that they can join and participate in. These organizations are pivotal to making democracy function well.

Civil society and government

The large and varied assemblage of organizations that in successful democracies stands between the state and the political order, on the one hand, the individual citizen and family, on the other, is known as **civil society**. The organizations that comprise civil society, such as churches, labor unions, professional associations, business groups, and civic clubs, do more than simply stand on a sort of middle ground; they serve as active intermediates between the people and government. In that capacity they are often referred to as "interest groups," groups that articulate the interest and views of their members before government officials and before the public generally. While the groups of civil society are part of the agency problem since they propose to speak for their members but can never do so perfectly, they are also part of the solution to the agency problem that arises between citizens and their government. In modern societies, the state is a complex and imposing organization with considerable power over people's lives. An ordinary citizen faced with this behemoth can feel completely powerless. However, interest groups have the resources and access to authorities that individuals lack. They can lobby, mobilize voters, initiate court cases, and provide alternatives to government-provided services. But such groups can only function effectively if citizens themselves have certain attitudes and skills.

Alexis de Tocqueville and the "art of association"

The set of skills that enables middle-class individuals and others to establish and maintain civil society goes by various names. Perhaps the earliest formulation is the "art of association." This term comes from the nineteenth-century French political theorist and politician, Alexis de Tocqueville. And it is Tocqueville's discussion that provides much of the intellectual backdrop for contemporary views on how individuals influence government via their participation in civil society. Tocqueville came to the United States in the 1830s to study how democracy functioned and to apply the lessons he learned to Europe generally and his native France in particular. His book, *Democracy in America*, took a grand historical sweep that covered much of the same ground explored in the European case study in Chapter 2. For seven hundred years, since the formation of stable monarchies in Europe, Tocqueville argued, social conditions had been moving with an ever-increasing velocity in the direction of equality of conditions. Medieval society was based upon inherited status and rank. At their height, inequalities had been so stark, inbred, and continually reinforced that members of different classes seemed to be almost members of different species. The aristocratic principle that guided medieval society had provided wealth and independence for the nobility and subordinated all lower ranks to them. However, over time things changed dramatically. The increase of commerce, the centralization of government, the rise of commercial and administrative classes, the growth of knowledge and science had inexorably undermined the aristocratic form of society. Any attempt to reconstruct society upon the aristocratic principle, Tocqueville believed, was foredoomed in the long run, since its social basis had already been fatally eroded. Governmental power had become more and more concentrated. Most of the older political actors had lost their legitimacy and their virtual monopoly on wealth. As a consequence, they had lost any effective capability to check the government and the individual holding supreme executive power. Only two alternative lines of development were possible Tocqueville asserted, despotism (what Dahl called "closed hegemony") and democracy. But democracy required relatively weak individuals to band together to become effective political actors who could themselves check and control the government. To do this they had to possess an art of association.

Tocqueville saw the Europe of his day as teetering on the brink of despotism, but he was much more optimistic about the United States. By the 1830s, American democracy was in full flower. However, Americans were individualistic and change-oriented, and it was just these sorts of characteristics that seemed to undermine community, at least as it had been understood in the Old World. There, community rested on stability, unity, and a sense of purpose based on the traditions and traditional loyalties antithetical to individualism and change. But in America individualism did not overwhelm a sense of community, nor did the constant restlessness of America produce anarchy. Least of all did it allow a despotic government to dominate society. Americans constantly formed all sorts of organizations: churches, charities, clubs, and impromptu groupings to carry out pressing tasks of the moment, such as raising a barn or harvesting a sick neighbor's crops. Even religion had cut itself free from government control in the United States while in most European countries there was a governmentally established church. This complex of non-state organizations that today political scientists call "civil society" was critical for democracy. It was a stratum of society more complex and inclusive than the merely familial and less complex and authoritative than the political and governmental.

These intermediary sorts of organizations gave each individual a sense of how he was personally dependent on the community, and how community effort could help all. It gave Americans what Tocqueville called a sense of "self-interest rightly understood" – self-interest enlarged beyond immediate self-absorbed concerns. At the same time civil society was independent of the state. The government did not organize and could not control it. Civil society organizations allowed individuals to band together and act without the government. It gave them the capacity to collectively influence the government as well. Although a solitary individual would be virtually powerless confronting the state, civil society provide

Plate 3.1 A barn raising near Toronto, Canada, at the turn of the twentieth century. Community barn raising was an expression of the 'art of association' that Tocqueville celebrated. Published with the permission of the City of Toronto Archives.

a sphere where individuals could act collectively and still have a sense of their individual importance. Tocqueville concluded that for democracy to function effectively, ordinary members of society had to possess the art of association – the capacity to organize themselves into groups *without* government direction to meet objectives that members of the group see as important. Without such a capacity, participation would be a mere formality at best, and democratic forms would enslave rather than liberate citizens.

Civic culture

Contemporary social scientists, using more rigorous, less impressionistic methods have generally confirmed and refined Tocqueville's theories about democracy and the art of association. In their 1963 study, *The Civic Culture*, Gabriel Almond and Sidney Verba examined basic attitudes about government and politics in five countries. They were interested in examining **political culture** – broadly shared political attitudes and beliefs that characterized people's approach to politics and their own political role within society. While these attitudes and beliefs might shape what individuals think about particular political figures or issues, they were more basic than that. They determined the citizen's orientation toward politics as a whole. Almond and Verba's empirical study was based on survey research and classified political cultures into three basic patterns. In short, *The Civic Culture* explored attitudes that underlay the behavior Tocqueville observed in America better than a century earlier. A **parochial political culture** has no specific roles or role expectations; its focus is local. Individuals had local ties and associations, but these are not overtly political. In contrast, a **subject political culture** had institutionalized specific roles and role expectations. A government official or political figure has a specific status that differed from others, and he or she is expected to conform to that status and the responsibilities associated with it. Ordinary citizens are tied to the political system more overtly than under a parochial political culture. They too have a specific status and role, but they are largely passive; they are expected to be loyal and obey the authorities. In a **participant political culture**, the ordinary citizen's role is more than mere passive loyalty. Citizens are supposed to take an active role in shaping the outcomes of the political process. These orientations are, in actuality, something like pure types; no society manifests them in their pure form. What Almond and Verba termed the **civic culture** was a combination of all three traits where participation in politics is instrumental and rational; i.e., it is oriented toward the achievement of specific goals. In a civic culture the citizen balances active participation with more passive political roles. They may voice adherence to norms of active participation, but in practice they often fall short of the participatory norms. In effect, most citizens are satisfied to cede decision-making to those professionally active in government and politics most of the time. On balance, a civic culture maintains democratic continuity in non-crisis circumstances. It does not overload the system with citizen demands (Almond and Verba 1963: 17–21, 31–2, 481–7). In sum, Almond and Verba take a less idealized view of democratic politics than Tocqueville. For them, democracy works because citizens are willing to let certain elites act as their agents. Ordinary citizens are just informed enough and participant enough to prevent agents from abusing their trust.

Social capital

Other contemporary political scientists have further developed and modified some of Tocqueville's insights about the democratic art of association. In his analysis of politics and society in a southern Italian village, Edward Banfield (Banfield 1958) found some of the very pathologies Tocqueville feared would be common if individuals lacked the art of association and an expansive concept of self-interest. He labeled the phenomenon he discovered "amoral familialism." Individuals' sense of community and self-interest rarely went beyond their immediate family. They had little sense of moral obligation to anyone beyond that narrow group. Relations with those outside were limited and focused on the acquisition of immediate benefits for the individual and the family. As a consequence, politics and government were riddled with corruption, the public administration was shot through with inefficiencies, and democracy was seriously flawed.

In later comparative research involving different regions in Italy (Putnam *et al.* 1993), Robert Putnam found many of the same things that Banfield had. The North of Italy stood in stark contrast to the South. The former had an active and flourishing civic life that the later lacked. Putnam referred to the skills and habits of civic participation as "**social capital.**" He found that the North's social capital, the skills of its citizens, the networks they had created and participated in enhanced democratic participation, administrative efficiency, governmental probity, and economic growth. The South, on the other hand, languished. Putnam showed that this difference in social capital endowments could be traced back to nineteenth-century social and political patterns. In his studies of the United States (Putnam 2000), Putnam also discovered differences in social capital, this time primarily differences over time. The generation that reached adulthood during World War II was a generation of civically committed joiners compared to the generations that followed. Putnam noted that participation rates in almost all sorts of organizations declined. Included among them are political organizations. Voting rates too have been in persistent decline. Americans have become so individualistic, they are less and less inclined to even join bowling leagues; instead they go bowling alone. To use Tocqueville's term, Americans seem to be forgetting the art of association.

Summary: interest groups versus patron–client networks

Civil society in modern democracies differs from traditional social relationships. In societies influenced by traditional norms, associations among individuals and families are often hierarchical and follow a "patron–client" pattern. Just as amoral familialism described earlier betokens a lack of social capital, so too does the widespread existence of **patron–client** relationships or clientelism. Under such a relationship a high-status, more powerful and wealthier individual or family (the patron) forms an association with weaker, lower-status, and poorer individuals and families (the clients). These relationships may be between landlord and tenant, moneylender and borrower, or employer and laborer. These relationships are unequal. The clients as a group never bargain with their common patron collectively, but deal with him or her individually or as heads of their families. Although often at root economic, obligations are reciprocal, general, and ongoing. The patron is expected to be concerned about the overall welfare of the client and the client's family. In turn, the client is expected to honor the patron and follow his or her directions in spheres beyond the mere economic. If violence breaks out between patrons, the clients are expected to support their respective patrons. If clients have the right to vote, they are expected to follow the political lead of their patron.

In contrast to clientelism, democratic interest groups are essentially associations among equals, for common, though limited, purposes. Labor unions, professional associations, civic clubs, political parties, neighborhood associations, follow the modern model. Individuals are free to join or leave such associations or form new ones. Leaders are normally elected and responsible to the membership. In short, when they function correctly, they operate according to the principles of grassroots democracy – open meetings, majority voting, and free discussion. Such organizations are both schools for democracy as well as mechanisms for influencing the democratic process.

Interest groups can be configured in different ways. In some liberal democracies corporatism is the norm. **Interest group corporatism** has three defining characteristics: "tripartite concertation, relatively few and relatively large interest groups, and the prominence of peak associations" (Lijphart 1999: 37–8). Tripartite concertation is the practice of large business associations, labor federations, and government leaders getting together to resolve major policy issues. Typically these issues include wage agreements as well as other economic issues that involve concessions from all three parties. If an industry is under pressure, for example, an agreement may include business assurances to refrain from layoffs, union pledges to accept wage concessions, and government provision of loans or tax advantages. Other democracies are closer to the pluralist model. **Interest group pluralism** is a system in which a large number of interest groups compete with one another to influence government policy, each trying to get its own way (Lijphart 1999: 16–17). For instance, an industry may pressure government for subsidies and tax advantages but make no countervailing concessions to labor about such things as employment or pension guarantees. James Madison laid out the pluralist model over two hundred years ago. "In a free government," he wrote, "the security for civil rights must be the same as for religious rights. It consists in the one case in the multiplicity of interests, and in the other, in the multiplicity of sects" (Madison 1961: 351–2). Both the corporatist and pluralist model are approximations of actual patterns in real democracies. The legal right of association essential to democracy transcends both of them.

Clientelism can sometimes infect even nominally democratic and participatory organizations even when such legal protections exist. Turn of the twentieth-century urban political machines in the United States have their contemporary echo in political parties, labor unions, and peasant associations in many developing countries. The ruling party of Mexico for decades, for example, successfully used such associations to cement the ruling elite's political control. Patron–client relations represent a kind of default political and social condition. If the mass of the population is poor, uneducated, and effectively denied legal rights, individuals fall back on whatever protection is available to them and their families. Powerful individuals can provide the limited protection and security the prospective clients lack while the prospective clients can provide the powerful with labor, gratitude, and social support. The existence of democratic interest groups, in contrast, requires citizens who possess social capital or the art of association. They must treat one another as equals. Not surprisingly, the growth of interests groups normally goes hand in hand with economic prosperity and social equity.

The protection of liberal rights

While democracy requires popular participation, *liberal* democracy entails an additional principle – the protection of liberal rights. The protection of these rights is critical for several reasons. First, without freedom of the press and association, elections cannot be counted upon to represent the informed will of the people even though everyone votes and all the votes are honestly counted. Second, overcoming the agency problem requires the existence of intermediate associations between the government and the citizen. Where these intermediate organizations do not have the right to exist, citizens have a difficult time influencing the conduct of the governmental elites who are supposed to represent them. Third and just as important is the fact that the protection of individual rights constitutes the moral basis of liberal democracy. Modern democracy differs substantially from its ancient predecessors not simply because it is representative in nature. Ancient democracies did not recognize any protected rights, nor did they aspire to universal citizenship.
The democracies of antiquity were, in effect, private clubs of limited membership where the majority of full members had the final say.
The majority treated nonmembers and the minority any way it chose.
In contrast, liberal democracy is meant to guarantee each person's human rights regardless of what the majority or the public at large might think.
Individual rights are universal and meant to be independent of
human whim.

The rule of law

Modern concepts of liberal rights are incorporated in the notion of "the rule of law" or "due process of law." But, as Woodrow Wilson wrote a century ago, "There never was such a government" as "a government of laws and not of men." All governments are "governments of men." Laws can change, and they are changed by human beings. The central principle "is that an officer is an officer only so long as he acts within his power" (Wilson 2002: 17, 19). Laws may change, but the executive branch must enforce the law as written, not invent it as it goes along. As a procedural minimum, the rule of law requires that standing rules (laws promulgated in advance of the trial or legal action involved) be applied by unbiased judges to individual cases that are brought before them. In short, all must know the law in advance, and the law must be enforced evenhandedly. Under arbitrary governments individuals lack these protections. Even when an arbitrary government may have rules, they are not applied as written or are not applied in the same manner to everyone. Thus, citizens suffer not only from the injustices found in the law; they also suffer from an additional insecurity: even the laws themselves are not respected in practice.

The judiciary is the key institution in enforcing the rule of law. Even Thomas Hobbes, who emphasized power as the core element of politics, argued that the appointment of fair-minded judges was essential for running even an absolutist state properly (Hobbes 1950: 130). In a democracy it is even more important that the judiciary be unbiased and independent of political pressures. Thus, judges should be chosen for their professional qualifications and judicial temperament rather than on the basis of their political connections alone. Least of all should they be chosen on the basis of how they would treat particular criminal defendants or parties in civil suits. And, once appointed, they should not be swayed either by the government of the day or public opinion. There are a variety of mechanisms that have been employed to try to assure judicial professionalism, independence, and lack of bias. Some democracies treat the judges as just another branch, albeit a highly specialized branch, of the civil service. Judges are recruited from a select group of law school graduates and enter a special career track. They are promoted on the basis of established rules, and the judiciary itself remains largely self-governing. Other methods include appointment by the executive and confirmation by the legislature, and popular election. Often political appointment and election are hedged about by restrictions, and really amount to hybrid methods in which professional qualifications are meant to play a major role. For the highest judicial offices, the executive, for example, may be required to choose nominees from a short list submitted to him by the judiciary itself. Popular election may apply only to sitting judges who have been appointed to office for their first term. The public would then get a yes/no choice on retention. Judicial tenure, whether for a term of years or life, is guaranteed. A judge is not to be removed from office except for misconduct or incompetence.

Judicial review, the power of the courts to review executive actions when those actions affect the legal rights of individuals, is a core element of the definition of the rule of law. In democracies, limits, whether imposed on the discretion of executive officials by statute, the constitution, treaty, or decree, are enforceable by the courts. Yet, judicial review has sometimes been expanded since the law itself may be unlawful! For example, laws that hold Jews, the mentally impaired, homosexuals, or other carefully defined classes of people subject to incarceration or death (e.g., Nazi Germany's Nuremberg laws) are of themselves violations of the rule of law. No matter how evenhandedly they are enforced, they violate basic human rights. Democratic theory holds that the law must respect the dignity and moral integrity of persons. The practical problem is how to protect individuals against violations of their rights by the legislature. To solve this problem some democratic constitutions extend judicial review to legislation.

However, while judicial review of executive action is essential to the rule of law, judicial review of legislation is optional since it brings along with it unavoidable problems. Democracies have tried a range of approaches toward judicial review of legislation, none of which is completely satisfactory. At one extreme is the US practice: rights are entrenched in the constitution and any court may rule on the constitutionality of any law any time it is challenged in a case. At the other extreme, all legislation is exempt from review by the judiciary. For example, in Great Britain (the United Kingdom or UK), the constitution and existing statutes are amended by the same method – an act of parliament. Thus, under British practice any legislation that differs from the constitution as previously understood is seen as amending the constitution. The courts give the law full effect. This practice is defended by appealing to the principle of majority rule or in Great Britain "parliamentary sovereignty."

There is no right answer about how to define the judiciary's role constitutionally. The record of both extremes has been mixed. The United States congress and the president have often been able to ignore important rights by claiming that a national emergency existed and the courts often accepted these claims. In addition, the United States has allowed slavery, racial discrimination, mass internments of citizens and non-citizens alike, and wars of extinction against groups of Native Americans. In short, the judicial branch is often weak compared to the legislature and the executive especially in a highly charged political climate. At other times, however, when public opinion is more divided, courts may be able to impose their own preferences on the other two branches. American practice has given US courts, especially the Supreme Court, significant political influence throughout US history. The court helped bring on the Civil War with its infamous *Dred Scott* decision in which it declared blacks had no legal or human rights, and that slavery had to be permitted anywhere in the territories despite legislation to the contrary passed by congress. The uneven results of US judicial review help explain why other democracies have chosen a different path.

However, British experience too has been less than salutary. One might expect that the United Kingdom, civilized, humane, largely untroubled by domestic turbulence during most of a century, would be a good test of how well basic rights could be protected under a system of legislative sovereignty. By and large the record has been favorable, but there are disturbing aspects. The violence in Northern Ireland provoked legislation that permitted preventive detention; parliament has altered some of the fundamental rights of accused parties, and the UK's official secrets act has hampered the public's right to know by restricting the freedom of the press. Britain, however, has by treaty subjected itself to the European Human Rights Covenant and European Union law. These treaties have been enforced by international courts, and the UK has accepted their rulings.

In fact, the experience overall of Pan-European judicial institutions has been encouraging. The courts of the European Union (EU) and the European Human Rights Court have had at least a slightly better track record than judicial protection of rights during the much longer and more turbulent history of the United States. These recently created bodies have been able to secure the compliance of national governments despite the fact that most Europeans consider the EU and pan-European institutions remote and unresponsive. Recognition and protection of individual rights is dependent, in large measure, on the political culture of the country. If people are committed in principle to the rule of law, serious violations of these rights are more likely to be of limited scope or short duration even when popular passions occasionally tolerate or even demand those violations. In sum, while democracy requires popular rule, liberal democracy goes even further. It holds that individual rights are sacrosanct, and that neither the executive, the legislature, nor even the majority itself may violate them. Providing the right sort of protection for individual rights is difficult in practice, but inviolable rights remain fundamental to the liberal democratic ideal.

The right of association

Social capital is necessary if liberal democracies are to function effectively. Without the proper habits and outlook referred to by the term "social capital," the ability of the people to compel the government to represent its interests and to hold the government accountable will be circumscribed. But social capital does not develop or operate in a legal vacuum or where societal norms are hostile to the formation of independent groups. Liberal democratic constitutions provide the legal space for groups to form individuals to participate in them. The right of association is the legal guarantee of the existence of social, economic, and political organizations beyond the government's direct control. The right of association is essential for liberal democracy since democracy entails structured political competition, not simply between politicians but between organizations – political parties and interest groups – as well. In a democratic society citizens must be free to join or form political parties, trade unions, churches, professional and civic organizations, as well as a host of other groups. And the media must be free from undue government interference. Only then can these groups monitor the performance of the government and assure its responsiveness to public opinion.

Protection of cultural and group rights

Liberal rights as traditionally understood protect the rights of individuals, treating all equally before the law. Yet many countries have a variety of long-standing social groups based on religion, language, and ethnicity that have required a special recognition of their identity because the mechanism of purely individual rights has proven insufficient to assure basic fairness. Often divisions of ethnicity and religion are mutually reinforcing. Thomas Jefferson put the problem of securing minority rights under a system of majority rule bluntly: "[T]he will of the majority is in all cases to prevail, that will, to be rightful, must be reasonable... the minority possess their equal rights, which equal laws must protect, and to violate which would be repression" (Jefferson 1944: 322). Protection against majority repression is especially important where social divisions and a history of injustice based upon them exists. Where such problems exist, the concept of group or cultural rights comes into play. In many countries, the specific recognition of cultural rights, such as the recognition of more than one national language, the right of parents to educate their children in their own native tongue, and the right to publish, broadcast, and speak in a minority language in public, are all important. The protection of minorities in some situations may require additional means. In India, for example, tribal peoples, lower-caste

Hindus, and Hindus that fall outside the caste system have historically suffered discrimination. Thus, Indians made affirmative action part of the Indian constitution. In addition, crimes against women, such as widow-burning, have been a long-standing historical injustice. They too are specifically outlawed.

Some democracies provide protections for minorities that are embedded in the structure of government and the political system itself. In many countries, ethnic and religious minorities have a traditional homeland where they are, in fact, the majority. In such cases, regional autonomy can help secure the protection of their rights. Electoral systems can be crafted to insure the representation of minorities and minority points of view. The executive can be structured in such a way that minorities have their due influence. The Swiss have even developed a collective presidency to give due weight to the various ethnic groups in Swiss society. In Nigeria, to win the election a presidential candidate must receive a minimum percentage of votes for states across the country, and parties cannot have regional, ethnic, or religious identities as part of their official title. Constitutions with structured arrangements such as these have been dubbed "**consociational**" or "**consensus government**." They are likely to find favor where deeply seated ethnic and religious divisions exist or, as in the United States, where there is a historical distaste for centralized power. In contrast, some constitutions enhance the ability of the majority to act quickly and with relatively little check from minorities. Such constitutional arrangements are termed "**majoritarian**" (Lijphart 1999: 1–47).

No existing liberal democracy fully adheres to liberal rights norms. Nonetheless, the success and ultimately the continuity of liberal democracy depend on the rule of law, and right of association, and cultural differences being respected and promoted just as that success depends upon adherence to the norms of responsiveness, transparency, accountability. If a supposed liberal democracy repeatedly and seriously fails to follow these principles, that democracy becomes not simply worst except for all the others, it becomes just one of the others. And the consensus underlying it is likely to erode or vanish entirely. But democratic continuity also depends upon the ability to promote an even broader consensus.

Economic and social rights

Liberal democracy has been successful in part because it has been able to promote the right of political participation as well as civil liberties. Yet, in the contemporary world, a democratic system of government is unlikely to remain legitimate indefinitely if it does not promote the basic aspirations of its citizens for full human development and the good life. While representation and the rule of law are issues of constitutional scope, promoting prosperity and social equity are matters primarily of policy. The right to work at a fair wage, in safe conditions, with adequate provisions for leisure, means little in the abstract if the economy faces mass unemployment and stagnation or worse. Liberal democracies in developed countries have been successful since the mid-twentieth century because they have found a policy mix that has promoted a generalized prosperity. This mix has involved capitalism, government regulation and transfer payments, and a degree of government ownership of productive property. In fact, there have been a variety of policy mixes that have been successful in promoting generalized prosperity, each with a slightly different balance between government and the private sector. Each successful democracy has a set of policies that constitutes a consensus that the public and major interest groups support. Contemporary commentators have borrowed the Enlightenment term, "social contract," to describe this underlying consensus. Although today all versions of this social consensus face challenges from within and without, they continue to prove durable. Each involves a slightly different position on the role of the state as well as a different mix of economic and social policies. It is to the role of the state in the economy that we now turn.

The state and welfare policy

In theoretical terms, liberal democratic countries have three basic options on the economic role they assign the state. The most limited of these is the **liberal state**. The liberal state takes its name from the old nineteenth-century liberals, who believed the functions of government should be strictly limited. The policy followed by the liberal state is often termed "laissez-faire." The state, of course, has to provide for the country's defense. Beyond defense the liberal state, as with other states, must provide the legal basis for a sound economy: establishing property rights, enforcing these rights as well as contracts, and providing a sound money supply. The liberal state provides security for the free exchange of goods and services as well as the basic protection of individuals against direct physical injury from others. Any state achieves these ends through its legal system. It is the law that defines the rights of property, individual, corporate, or communal. The law specifies what is necessary for a legally binding contract, which, in turn, defines the rights and obligations of individuals and legally recognized associations. The state through its judiciary enforces contracts and property rights. Without the state and the legal structure it supports, modern economies could not function efficiently. The state also provides another key foundation for a modern economy, the money supply. Without a universally accepted medium of exchange that holds its value over an extended period of time, modern commerce could not flourish. But even the liberal state, in the contemporary era, does more than simply mint coins out of precious metal. The state not only guarantees the medium of exchange; it attempts to smooth out the booms and busts of the unregulated business cycle. Since the liberal state is not the employer of last resort and does not involve itself in extensive welfare functions, it is via fiscal (budgetary) and monetary policy (controlling the availability of money in the economy) that the contemporary version of the liberal state undertakes this function. The control of monetary policy normally devolves to an autonomous state institution, known generically as the central bank. By controlling interest rates and private banks' reserve requirements, by buying and selling government bonds, the central bank can stimulate or contract business activity. Even the liberal state has to provide for certain basic public services – roads, highways, and airports – or it has to provide the basic legal assistance such as securing rights of way that allow for the private sector to provide them. Very few modern states restrict themselves to only the activities that define the liberal state. Rather, the liberal state is a kind of intellectual benchmark. If a state cannot perform the activities characteristic of the liberal state adequately, it falls into decay.

The second sort of state, the **welfare state**, is typical of modern liberal democracies. All liberal democracies have adopted at least some of the functions of the welfare state. In effect, the welfare state is the liberal state *plus*. The modern welfare state carries out the functions of the liberal state: it provides security to persons and property; it provides the basis for a sound market economy; it guarantees civil liberties and due process of law. The "plus" involves additional legal guarantees and entitlements that advance economic and social rights to education, income, healthcare, and state-supported retirement. Advocates of the welfare state argue that formal equality before the law and market forces are insufficient to guarantee everyone's economic and social rights. The workings of the market are too haphazard to protect the less fortunate. The solution, for defenders of the welfare state, is positive government intervention. One major instrument of the welfare state about which all its proponents agree is the use of income transfers. The government's ability to tax and spend can be used to support economic and social rights. Income can be transferred from one class to another and from one generation to another. To help accomplish this, taxation is progressive. Those with higher incomes pay higher rates of tax. Access to education, healthcare, childcare, and income protection is universally guaranteed. Monetary and fiscal policy is used to promote full employment and high wages, even at some risk of inflation.

The welfare state may adopt socialist principles of ownership. Almost all states own certain parts of the country's basic economic infrastructure. However, socialism asserts that the "commanding heights of the economy" ought to be owned by the government as well and be managed with the common benefit of all citizens. When these principles are widely applied, the third variety of state exists, the (western) **socialist state**. Under socialism, the state owns utilities and major industries, but only firms of monopoly or near monopoly status and those that are strategically important for the development of the economy need be owned by the state. Airlines, the rail system, steel, chemicals, communications, the major banks are all candidates for nationalization. Government ownership allows the state itself to determine levels and types of investment, and to provide employment. In addition, government ownership assures that the public interest and national sovereignty are respected when business decisions are made. The socialist state is different from communist-style "state socialism" that will be described in Chapter 5. Under state socialism, markets disappear entirely and the state owns all the means of production. While the western version of socialism is compatible with liberal democracy and freedom of association, communist-style socialism has proven not to be.

For more than half a century, a broad consensus has prevailed in most liberal democracies that some sort of welfare state is the most desirable option. Parties, politicians, and policy experts may argue about the extent and management of social programs, but few are willing to argue that the narrow liberal version of state power should be accepted. Socialist principles of ownership have generally been superseded on pragmatic grounds. If private ownership, markets, and government regulation can together produce greater efficiencies than state ownership of major industries, why maintain such ownership? Even though consensus about the general relations between the state and the economy has existed in industrialized liberal democracies for some time, there are significant differences about how that general relationship should work in detail. Each of the three major models described below has its own advantages and offsetting disadvantages (Dore *et al.* 1999: 102–20).

The Anglo-American model

With the paring back of the welfare state and widespread privatizations in the 1980s, the United Kingdom found itself, along with the

United States, as the leading representative of "**shareholder capitalism**." Shareholder capitalism (the Anglo-American model) combines elements of the liberal state with the welfare state, but the model takes its basic inspiration from the norms of the liberal state. Hence, state ownership of the means of production is limited. Private firms normally own even utilities and natural resources, not to mention steel, chemical, and automobile manufacturers, as well as railroads and airlines, which are otherwise often in state hands. Markets determine wages, prices, and the allocation of resources. Hence, regulation in these areas is minimal. Minimum wage laws exist, but they are held at rather low levels compared to the average wage. Today unionization, while protected, is in no way encouraged and often unofficially discouraged. Managers and stockholders are free to run companies largely as they see fit. Workers are not normally granted a voice on corporate boards. Mergers and buyouts are generally permitted. Firms are free to close or open operations with little interference from the government. In short, in this contemporary version of laissez-faire (minimal government regulation), corporations via their owners and management do pretty much what they wish to enhance their profits. The competition between interest groups means that the Anglo-American model promotes interest-group pluralism. The argument for a largely laissez-faire set of policies is that they are efficient. They allow for rapid adjustments to changes in technology and consumer demands. They allow for what economic theorist Joseph Schumpeter called "creative destruction" (Schumpeter 1975: 82–5) typical of capitalism's development.

The harsh edges of shareholder capitalism are softened by a variety of policies not strictly consonant with a liberal state. The state provides old-age pensions; health insurance or healthcare for either all or part of the population; unemployment insurance, and some retraining. In addition, the state regulates pollution, as well as product and worker safety. It provides a measure of assistance to the destitute. Education at the secondary and primary levels is free; higher education is subsidized. The state also provides direct and indirect subsidies to encourage private home ownership. The state provides highways, regulates transportation and communication. The government controls the economy indirectly through fiscal (i.e., taxes and central government budgets) and monetary policy. Fiscal policy is in the hands of the executive and legislature. Monetary policy is the province of a largely autonomous central bank. Fiscal policy controls the balance between expenditures and revenues to promote economic growth or control inflationary pressure. Monetary policy addresses the same issues, via such mechanisms as controlling the money supply. Both monetary and fiscal policies are supposed to balance the need to control inflation with the requirement of promoting full employment.

The Anglo-American model involves some typical tradeoffs. It aims at rapid economic adjustment more than stability, and economic growth rather than equitable income distribution. When the model is successful, it achieves relatively low unemployment (i.e., rapid job creation), usually at the cost of the loss of some older, higher-paying jobs. The winners in such a system are likely to be the younger and the better educated who are more able to adjust to rapid change. The less educated and the middle-aged normally do not do so well. They are generally less flexible and less likely to be able to move in search of a job. And when they are forced to change jobs, they often are forced to change careers too, trading a more lucrative occupation for one that is less well paid. The unskilled suffer from an addition disadvantage, the globalization of the economy. When production moves across frontiers, economic theory holds that it moves in the direction where the requisite resources are plentiful. Thus, low-skilled manufacturing jobs are often lost in the developed world, as firms import labor-intensive products manufactured overseas by their subsidiaries or subcontractors. At the turn of the twenty-first century, the Anglo-American model seemed to be doing better than its major competitors, reversing a position that it held a decade earlier. Generally, policy debates within the countries following this model have not challenged the model directly. The right has argued for less regulation and a smaller government budget, while admitting the need for what they call the "social safety net" – i.e., means-tested welfare rather than universal welfare payments. And the left has generally argued for retaining or expanding the role of the state to compensate for the model's social inequities.

The social market

Another major version of social and economic policy that has made for the popularity and success of liberal democracy is the **social market** model. The terminology "social market" applies most particularly to the Federal Republic of Germany, but most of the countries of Western Europe incorporate many of the features of this model. Indeed, the social charter of the twenty-seven-member European Union has promoted that uniformity. While the Anglo-American model is the stockholder model, the social market model is one version of the **stakeholder** model. It embraces the practice of interest group corporatism by promoting bargaining and consensus among those who hold stakes in a company – owners, managers, employees, customers, and local communities – to

Map 3.2 The European Union
Source: Environmental Systems Research Institute (ESRI) map data

moderate the effect of markets. In this model organized labor plays a
major role in the economy and in individual firms. Employees and union
representatives sit on firms' governing boards. Unions are protected and
unionization encouraged. The social market functions within a welfare
state. Thus, the state plays a major role in the economy beyond that of
economic and fiscal policy, and providing universal rather than
means-tested welfare payments to all rather than just to those in need. The
provision or guarantee of pensions, healthcare, education to the university
level, maternity leave, job-training, generous long-term unemployment
compensation, holidays are seen as the proper role of the state. By law,
minimum wages are kept high relative to the average wage. Entry into
professions and occupations is often carefully regulated and requires
special training beyond what would be the case in a more market-oriented
model. The adversarial relationship between the state (and its officials)
and the private sector typical of the Anglo-American model is largely
absent. Many important firms are state-owned at least in part.

Public sector managers, high-level bureaucrats, and directors of private
firms often come from the same social class and often the same
universities. The state often takes a directive role in the economy via an
industrial policy – a policy that channels state subsidies, tax benefits, and
research grants into economic growth areas, and cushions industries and
their employees who are hard hit by economic change. The social market
encourages interest-group corporatism. The goal is to limit economic

shocks, retain employment, and keep viable firms viable. In other words, individuals and firms are not at the mercy of an unregulated market, but each bargains with the other through their organized representatives while the government buffers some of the market's harsher effects.

Just like the Anglo-American model, the social market also produces relative winners and losers. In the best of times, the social market produces rapid growth along with social equity. It minimizes the possibility for the growth of an underclass of the poorly educated and unemployed. Generous social benefits stimulate the development of a middle-class society. However, in times of economic slowdown, adjustment can be slow. As stakeholders, current employees are much better protected than they would be under a stockholder model. Jobs, salaries, benefits are retained. At the same time, the young and first-time job-seekers are at a disadvantage. Wages tend to be higher than in the Anglo-American model, but unemployment is often higher and more persistent. In the adjustment–stability tradeoff, the social market leans in the direction of stability. As far as the growth–equity tradeoff is concerned, the model aims at equity. At the same time, long-term growth appears to be no worse than the Anglo-American model although the latter may rebound more quickly from recessions. Unemployment and slow growth produced a challenge for the social market model through much of the 1990s.

The Japanese model

Until the early 1990s, Japan's mix of social and economic policies seemed clearly superior to both its Anglo-American and European counterparts. Japan beat almost all of them in terms of high rates of GDP growth, low unemployment, and low inflation. Until the 1990s, the model seemed to promise limitless potential. A more balanced view now seems to be in order about both its strengths and its weaknesses. Japan has followed a kind of hybrid of the welfare state and state-supported capitalism. The state has played a major role in the economy, which has remained largely capitalistic. Though Japan has maintained a modest welfare state, generally the state takes care of firms, and firms take care of their employees. The success of the Japanese model rests on the state, primarily through the Ministry of Finance (MoF) and Ministry of International Trade and Industry (MITI), picking and backing promising industrial sectors. This procedure is generally similar to that followed by the social market model, but the Japanese have been generally more meticulous, detailed and successful in their ability to decide which sectors would be engines of overall growth in the future. As a consequence, the Japanese economy successfully switched from textiles and other labor-intensive manufacture, to steel and shipbuilding, to electronics and automobiles, to computers and services.

Japan's growth has been export-led. Its most efficient firms beat the competition worldwide. And the state encourages exports in a variety of ways. On the other hand, Japan's least efficient enterprises are often not much better than those of the developing world. The least efficient are protected from competition by a variety of measures that help close off Japan's domestic markets to foreign competition. As a result, the growth in the most dynamic sectors of the economy indirectly subsidizes the economy's backward sectors, such as agriculture and retailing. The most dynamic Japanese firms are grouped into *keiretsu*, loosely organized alliances composed of companies that are held together by cross-stockholding (each one holding shares in the others) and ongoing business dealings. Member firms buy from and sell to one another, and borrow from the bank associated with their *keiretsu*. Employees in the major companies have a job for life. Promotion is based on seniority rather than merit until one reaches the highest levels. As in the social market, outright layoffs are avoided. Economic downturns cause a decline in new hiring. Firms often create subsidiaries, even in unrelated industries, rather than turn employees out on the street. Outright layoffs usually occur only among subcontractors. The Japanese model has provided the country with a fast-growing GDP and workers with high incomes. Workers receive substantial bonuses that varied as the company's profits rise or decline. As might be expected, the Japanese model inspires loyalty and dedication from employees.

As with the other two models, the Japanese model produces relative winners and losers. The best off are salaried employees of major companies. Farmers and small retailers are propped up by a variety of policies, but hardly prosper. Women, by and large, have their advancement cut off by a glass ceiling that has often been so low that it left them virtually in the basement. Salaried employees have been almost exclusively male; "office ladies" were supposed to leave paid employment early, and take up raising a family full time. Consumers, as a group, are not well served by the system. Japanese personal income is high, but prices in Japan are among the highest in the world. Japanese products often sell more cheaply overseas than they do in their country of origin. Japanese agricultural products are of high quality, but of even higher price. The Japanese model makes some of the same tradeoffs as the social market model, but until the 1990s, Japan had been even more successful in reconciling the demands of stable jobs and economic adjustment. During that decade, however, conditions changed. With the economic slowdown that struck Japan in the early 1990s, openings for college graduates were limited. The recession that began during the last several years of the decade put more pressure on the model. Even major companies began pressuring their unneeded employees to resign. Japan's manufacturing base, as the United States', began to shift overseas. A banking crisis, a governmental budget deficit, and a rapidly graying population posed a set of problems which Japan had not faced together in the past. Nonetheless, the model retains high appeal. Versions of it have been adopted by South Korea and the Republic of China (Taiwan) as well as other Southeast Asian nations. The People's Republic of China too has tried to copy some of the salient features of the Japanese model.

Summary

Despite their past successes, each of these three models faces challenges in the twenty-first century. All have had to balance economic growth with equity. None has discovered how to do it effectively in the face of changing global conditions. The jury is still out as to which model does the best job. Worse still, the likely verdict shifts over time. In the 1990s, the Japanese model seemed to be far and away the best. Measured in terms of employment, growth, and inflation, the Japanese economy outperformed both Europe and the United States. Japanese leaders regularly lectured Americans about the need to lower the US budget and trade deficits and to educate and train its citizenry. Europe, while not performing so well as Japan, still outperformed the United States and seemed to have fewer structural problems. At the turn of the twenty-first century, Japan's real estate and stock markets had lost much of their value. And Japanese and outsiders both spoke of the preceding prosperity as the "bubble economy." It was the turn of the US, which was doing the best or at least the least bad of the three, to lecture the Japanese on the need to open their markets and allowing highly indebted firms and insolvent banks to fail. Europeans were in no mood to lecture anyone, suffering as they were from low growth and high unemployment. However, the apparent superiority of the Anglo-American model may be only temporary. The US suffered its own stock market and mortgage bubbles, and its trade and budget deficits continue and may worsen, potentially setting the stage for a devaluation of the dollar. In 2007 a crisis began in the financial sector. Furthermore, while the American economy has grown, so too has income inequality. The economic security of the middle and working classes may also be undermined by the weakening position of private pension funds, the increased cost of higher education, and increasing burdens placed on the Medicare system that provides healthcare for retired Americans. In short, defenders of none of the three systems can afford to feel complacent. Nor are demographics on their side. The aging of the population in all three will put additional burdens on government budgets and make the growth with equity that is necessary to maintain the middle class and social support for democracy more difficult to sustain.

CASE STUDY: DEMOCRACY IN AMERICA

So far this chapter has treated democracy as largely a finished product with only policy issues left to be addressed, but democracy is a process as well as a form of government. Democratic countries have been successful because they have been able to adjust to new political actors, new technologies and new ideas, and to cope with external pressures. Even more, they have been successful because they have been able to improve the quality of their democracy over time. Much can be learned from seeing how democratic countries adjusted in the past. At least from Tocqueville's time, the United States has been seen as the leading exemplar of the democratic movement. Yet even then, adherence to the democratic standard was far from perfect. Most glaringly, slavery was not only tolerated but defended by national and some state laws, and women were denied the right to vote. This case study examines democratic development in the United States, the expansion of legal rights, and how Tocqueville's art of association and governmental institutions evolved.

It was the nineteenth-century United States, the country that had departed most clearly from the pattern of traditional society, where liberal democracy first took root. In the United States traditional society barely existed at all, and most citizens had a stake in the system and the skills to participate in politics – two fundamental social requisites for democracy. The country had a strong middle class (largely in the guise of small, independent farmers) since virtually the inception of colonization. The New England colonies in particular were settled by people of middle-class origins: small farmers, merchants, religious dissenters. Both the importance of commerce in these colonies and the nature of the land, which was generally unsuited to large-scale plantation-style agriculture, preserved and enhanced the colonies' middle-class character. Self-government flourished. Only the slave-holding South bore much of a resemblance to traditional society and the authoritarian traditions of the mother country. Yet even there republican institutions were the norm. Americans inherited from the British a respect for the rule of law and a tradition of independent legal institutions. The colonial yoke was relatively light. London was far away, and for much of the colonial period the British government followed a policy of benign neglect, allowing the colonists to manage their own commercial and governmental affairs. Elected assemblies dominated colonial governments. Only the governor was a royal official or a representative appointed by the colony's proprietor. While property qualifications limited the right to vote, their effect upon democratic governance was limited. Most families farmed their own land, and most heads of households could vote. The distribution of wealth and power was strikingly egalitarian in comparison to most of the societies of Europe. Before and after independence the United States lacked the aristocratic class typical of Europe. Families of wealth and power resembled England's landed gentry, not the great families of the English aristocracy.

Unlike the revolution soon to follow in France, the American Revolution (1776–83) was much more of a political than a social movement. Tories (British sympathizers) were expelled and their property confiscated, but most of the social institutions of the country were left largely untouched. Few drastic changes were needed in the constitutions of the local (state) governments to reflect the new realities. The major alteration was the substitution of elected for appointed governors. Even the central government, such as it was, was a successor to the informal cooperative arrangement that had developed among the states before the revolution. It was not until 1787 that nationalist politicians produced a constitution that strengthened the central government considerably. The wealthy were able to dominate the political scene more by their prestige and connections than by a stranglehold on the country's wealth or the exclusion of the mass of the population from the right to vote. Thus, it is not surprising that the new constitution was largely democratic.

The constitution's framers took the model of British government, with which they were intimately familiar and which many of them thought was the best form of government on earth, and democratized it. Much of the structure and some of the details were copied almost directly from the British constitution of the day. There were three branches of government: executive, legislative, and judicial. Neither could remove nor select the other (with the partial exception of the judiciary, which was appointed by the executive and confirmed by the upper house of the legislature, the senate). The legislature (congress) itself was divided into two virtually equal houses. The assent of the executive was required for a bill to become law. Bills raising taxes had to originate in the lower house. The executive (the president) held most foreign policy powers. Other provisions of the document were clear departures from the British model. The president was indirectly elected by the people and for a fixed term. During his term he was removable only by impeachment. The executive did not have an absolute veto as did the British king. The president's veto was subject to legislative override by two-thirds of both houses of congress. So, too, key decisions on treaties, war, and appointments required legislative assent. Both houses of the legislature were elected, directly or indirectly, by the people. Unlike Britain, class power could not be preserved and exercised via hereditary control of two of the three branches of the government.

The influence of wealth was largely indirect. Staggered elections and long terms prevented the popular majority from sweeping all officeholders aside frequently or easily. Indirect elections and large districts were meant to advantage members of the elite over their poorer and less distinguished fellow citizens. State governments were denied the right to abrogate debts or in other ways "impair the obligation of contracts." In a glaring violation of natural rights principles, slavery was not only allowed but protected. And women's suffrage was an issue whose time had not yet come. The framers of the constitution took a dim view of political parties, which reminded them of the Whigs and Tories of the revolutionary era, two ideologically distinct and warring factions that had fought on opposite sides of the revolution. The framers preferred that the people, by and large, choose men of wealth and character to run the new nation's affairs at their own discretion, hence the reliance on indirect election for the president and members of the senate. In sum, the constitution provided the structure for a national government that despite its flaws was the most democratic of its time. It also provided a government that was liberal in character, since it limited the powers of government in several ways. First, the central government had only certain enumerated powers. It could not claim sovereignty outside these designated spheres. Second, almost immediately after the government went into operation, a bill of rights was attached, explicitly listing rights the government was required to respect. Both limits received judicial enforcement.

The federal constitution provided an enduring political context within which political and social evolution occurred. Amendments eventually abolished slavery, provided federal guarantees for civil rights, expanded the right to vote to all races and both sexes, and abolished the indirect election of senators. Yet, the basic structure of government remained. Changes in governmental institutions grew up under its auspices. Political parties arose despite the distaste for them expressed by many of the framers. By 1801 the Republican Party (the modern-day Democrats) were firmly in power, and government by the "great and the good" was beginning to pass from the scene. The parties helped turn the presidential selection process, originally meant to give the elite the real choice, into something approximating direct popular election. Civil society became more diverse and democratic. By 1828 a westerner without the family prestige of previous presidents was elected to office. Andrew Jackson ushered in a further democratization of the system. Ordinary citizens with their muddy boots tramped into the presidential mansion, the White House, during the inauguration. "To the victor belong the spoils," Jackson proclaimed and established the "spoils system" in place of appointing well-educated and well-connected individuals to the civil service. Anyone with a grade-school education, he believed, ought to be able to do almost any government job. Significant restrictions on the universal male franchise were fast disappearing.

It was during the Jacksonian era that Tocqueville traveled to the United States and wrote his famous *Democracy in America*. He was more impressed by social conditions than he was by the federal system of government itself. It was the fact that Americans removed from the state the function of organizing and mobilizing society that was the key to America's democratic success. There was no state religion, but religion prospered. There was no titled social elite or intrusive state, but Americans constantly organized themselves voluntarily for successful community projects. The country might lack a steady hand at the governmental tiller, but even though policy-making might be erratic, unlike the monarchies of Europe, the country possessed the capability of correcting a faulty course quickly. Americans' respect for law, their "civic religion" (i.e., the social responsibility required by all the major faiths), and their restless spirit of improvement made the country a viable democracy. And, Tocqueville believed, these same features made the United States the likely model of societies of the future.

Both America's optimism and its democratic vocation met a significant challenge in the Civil War. Seventy years before, the constitution had swept the slavery issue under the rug. Although the actual terms "slave" and "slavery" were not used, the constitution provided protection for the slave trade, gave slave-holding states extra votes in the House of Representatives, and mandated a national fugitive slave law. The framers had hoped that the institution of slavery and the issue of how to deal with it would disappear on their own. But the cotton gin had made cotton king and made slavery a highly profitable institution. Defenders of the institution abandoned the natural rights and human equality of the Declaration of Independence and clung to the notion that the constitution was a limited contract for limited purposes that was meant to protect slavery forever. The North won the war against the slave-holding South, and as a consequence the institution was doomed. The defeat of the South produced not only the emancipation of the slaves (via the thirteenth amendment to the constitution) but the strengthening of national consciousness and national power. The post-war fourteenth and fifteenth amendments provided the basis for federal enforcement of civil rights, voting rights, and property rights although, in many cases, this expansion of power was not immediate. In short, the old consensus that accepted slavery as necessary broke down, and it was replaced by one that reaffirmed the principles of the Declaration of Independence. Yet, any real attempt to create a new consensus behind policies that supported social and economic equality for Blacks died in 1877 when federal intervention in Southern politics ended. That new consensus had to wait.

Industrialization, large-scale immigration, the continued oppression of African Americans, and the anti-alcohol, farmers', laborers', and women's movements drastically altered the shape of society the constitution was meant to govern. By the 1930s the "New Deal" of President Franklin Roosevelt altered the shape of federal policy and established a new social consensus. The federal budget and regulatory role expanded immensely, and the states and federal government began to cooperate on a range of activities from the building of highways to aid to the indigent. Popular programs such as Social Security providing old-age pensions cemented in place a new view of the government's proper role in the contemporary era. Finally in the 1960s effective federal civil rights protections were extended to African Americans. The new consensus ushered in by the "New Deal" involved a radical updating of practices Tocqueville had observed a century earlier. Interest group pluralism became a dominant political motif with business, labor, professional, and other groups contending for influence over policy-making at the national level. The American middle class's participation in politics has basically followed the norms of a civic culture; most Americans' direct involvement is limited. They seem to prefer letting the professionals handle most decisions. In fact, the long-term decline in voter turnout at least until the 2004 cycle has been a concern for those interested in the health of American democracy. Judicial review, used primarily to support property rights in the late nineteenth and early twentieth centuries, provided support for racial equality and women's rights. Thus, the courts gave these important social rights a constitutional status.

The United States has been able to expand the economic and social activities of the central government without substantially altering the actual powers of the central government beyond the explicit permission to levy an income tax. Thus, an eighteenth-century document that existed before the computer, the airplane, the automobile, even the steam engine continues to be used to address twenty-first-century problems, but the constitution is both flexible and restrictive. The fact that it is difficult to change and the fact that US courts exercise judicial review over laws passed by the legislature have shaped American policy debates. Debates are often framed in constitutional rather than pragmatic terms. States' rights and other constitutional principles are appealed to selectively as it suits the interests of a particular participant. The actual authority of institutions can be extended or contracted, but the institutions themselves, once sanctioned by the constitution, have been virtually impossible to replace. The US experience has served as a guide, both negative and positive for other democracies. Except for Latin America, most democracies have decided to avoid the US constitution's formal separation of powers. Most federal systems today are much more specific about the powers that reside in the local and national governments. One civil war because of lack of constitutional specificity is enough. But basically Tocqueville was right. Democracy on a large scale could be made to work, and in this respect, for all its imperfections, the United States showed the way.

CASE STUDY: DEMOCRACY IN INDIA

India represents a history of democratic development almost the polar opposite of that of the United States. A poor country with an entrenched caste system, it nonetheless was able to establish a functioning, if flawed, democracy. Bucking the extremist revolutionary tide, the Indian independence struggle represented a largely nonviolent, pluralistic model of political struggle. The Indian National Congress, the organization that headed the movement, became Congress Party with all the prestige that a successful independence struggle bestowed. It governed India as the dominant party for nearly thirty years. By and large, Congress Party maintained the pluralistic outlook of its older incarnation as did the Indian state. As most other countries with a colonial past, India had an essentially negative colonial legacy. As we noted in the case study of the previous chapter, Britain ruled India for the advantage of its British subjects and the British Empire as a whole, not specifically to benefit Indians. Local industries were undercut by British manufactures. Land was used for export agriculture instead of providing food for the local population even when famine raged. The British government resisted demands for autonomy and independence as long as it could. Yet, the period of British rule did provide the country with a more modern and more competent state administration and judiciary than many other former colonies inherited. And, although the British resisted the independence movement, the British raj was not as repressive as many other colonial regimes of the period.

The struggle for self-rule was actually part of a process that helped build Indian institutions and reshape Indian political culture. The independence movement officially began in 1885 with the formation of the Indian National Congress. The congress was formed to fight pro-British discrimination, advance the rights of native Indians, and work for autonomy. The congress was a multi-communal, multi-caste grouping that attempted to unite all Indians under a common sense of national purpose. It espoused secular and democratic principles. In effect, it represented a major step in the formation of a modern democratic national consciousness. Furthermore, its organizing advanced the process of developing the social capital necessary for a functioning democracy. However, the British did not see the Indian National Congress in such positive terms. Congress's and other nationalists' demands were met by stiffening British resistance and repression. But the outbreak of the First World War in 1914 seemed to promise an opportunity for compromise. Most nationalists cooperated with the war effort, hoping to win British concessions on self-rule. Their hopes were dashed. The British were unwilling to make significant concessions. And the end of the war brought even greater British repression. The situation between the two world wars provided no decisive breakthroughs. Congress and Indian nationalists continued to press for greater freedom while the British continued to resist. An unfortunate consequence of this dynamic was the development of a political culture in which the state was considered the enemy, and the ignoring of state exactions a patriotic response. This attitude would be detrimental to Indian democracy once the country attained independence.

The most dramatic example of British repression during the interwar period occurred in 1919. In an attempt to terrorize the population into submission General Reginald Dyer ordered his troops to fire on unarmed civilians. The "Amritsar massacre" left 379 dead and 1,200 wounded. The massacre backfired and produced a backlash in Britain itself. The British parliament passed the Government of India Act that provided for reforms. Locally elected representatives were to constitute 70 percent of an Indian legislature, but important matters were reserved to the governor and appointed officials. However, the concessions failed to meet Indian demands. Under the moral leadership of Mohandas K. Gandhi, congress undertook widespread campaigns of civil disobedience demanding greater self-governance. Civil disobedience required protesters to violate the laws they objected to, knowing that they would be punished. The willingness of masses of people to sacrifice for their beliefs was meant to prick the consciences of those in power and provoke a change of policy. Such campaigns became a staple of Indian protests. The techniques were later adopted by others, including the US civil rights movement.

Plate 3.2 Mohandas Gandhi and his wife Kasturba, a political activist in her own right. Photo of statues by Saad Akhtar.

The situation improved somewhat in 1928 when an all-parties conference adopted the Nehru report, calling for Britain to give Indian dominion status under a representative government. The report included a model constitution. Yet the improvement was temporary. Muslim representatives accepted the report although they were troubled by the lack of specific protections for minorities. The British, however, refused to negotiate further, and a political stalemate ensued. In 1929, the congress declared the Nehru report had lapsed. The British government and the congress remained at loggerheads as limited British concessions failed to meet congress's demands. The British continued to argue that despite its secular stance, congress was predominantly Hindu, and that India, a federated entity within the British Empire, was composed of Muslim and other religious minorities as well as monarchical states that were still nominally under their traditional rulers. The Hindu–Muslim split became more evident in 1937. Pursuant to the Government of India Act of 1935, elections were held for provincial assemblies, and congress won majorities in six of the eleven provinces and pluralities in three. The Muslim League saw the result as a threat to the interests of its constituents.

When the Second World War began in 1939, the British-controlled government of India declared war on Germany and joined the war effort. Three years later, congress rejected the British offer of autonomy for India with the right of secession if congress agreed to support the war effort. They were suspicious of British intentions, remembering their experience with the British during the First World War. Instead, congress demanded immediate independence. Key leaders of congress were arrested and interned for the duration of the war. In 1945, the British government renewed the 1942 autonomy offer, but again congress rejected it and demanded that Britain leave India altogether. In elections to the central legislative assembly that followed, congress and the Muslim League won the largest number of seats. But the rift between the two continued. As the post-war era dawned, it became clear that European colonialism would not survive. Unlike some of its imperial counterparts, Britain undertook serious negotiations that would lead to full independence. In 1947 after negotiations between Britain, congress, and the Muslim League failed to reach a mutually satisfactory agreement, the independence of India and the Muslim-majority state of Pakistan went into effect. Independence was followed by a massive transfer of populations. Millions of Hindus moved from what was to become Pakistan, and millions of Muslims moved from Hindu-dominated India. Relations between the two newly sovereign states were extremely difficult. War quickly broke out over the Muslim-majority territory of Jammu and Kashmir. No mutually recognized border in the region was ever settled. And more wars followed over the decades.

From its long-established colonial predecessor, independent India inherited a military establishment committed to civilian control of the armed forces, a competent civil service, and a well-regarded judiciary although the last two have decayed over time. The Indian constitution provides for a secular democracy based on a federal system and a two-house parliament. Traditional practices that oppressed women and members of interior castes were outlawed. The state was supposed to remain neutral in matters of religion, but the principles of democracy, human rights, and tolerance and mutual respect were difficult to inculcate into social practice. The Indian social consensus involves a set of policies that are socialist. The Indian government owns many industries directly, and it provides extensive protection from foreign competition to the private sector. In addition, the government provides extensive subsidies to agriculture. These policies have changed somewhat since the 1990s, but a strong government role in the economic and a commitment to policies promoting economic equity are basic to Indian politics. Today the Indian middle class numbers in the hundreds of millions, but given the fact that the country's population exceeds one billion, it is not the dominant sector. Thus, the limited existence of a civic culture and the persistence of traditional social practices should not be surprising. Even such extreme practices as widow-burning have continued in some places. Inter-communal animosity and rioting remained a persistently recurring problem. Still, India was a country governed by an elected government with elections that were generally fair and free especially when compared to other developing countries. As a nation, India's commitment to democracy and human rights – even when those rights are often in danger – is unquestioned.

Conclusion

Modern democracy aims to defend and instantiate the full range of human rights, not just in some distant utopian future but in the present. That being said, no democracy is or can be perfect. Thus, the practice of democratic politics requires tolerance, a sense of community, adequate social capital, and a willingness to participate in politics, social equity, and the rule of law. Democracies survive and flourish when citizens know how to use the political process to serve their interests and the public good, while, at the same time, limiting their demands and the methods they are willing to use to influence that process. Democracies flourish when virtually all citizens have a stake in preserving the system. Countries as diverse as the United States and India have managed to sustain functioning democracies. Yet, democracy can most easily thrive when its citizens are prosperous and educated. For a democracy to survive, its institutions must be flexible enough to accommodate changing circumstances. As the next chapter will show, there is no one-size-fits-all institutional model. Institutional choices are important and include tradeoffs. No one system can assure quick and effective decision-making and still protect all minority interests. No one system assures that all major ideological points of view are represented by viable parties and, at the same time, provides for single-party government. No one system can maximize majority control at both the national and local levels. However, even though institutions vary, all liberal democracies rest on the same ethical basis – rights of participation, liberal rights, and social and economic rights.

Questions for further consideration

1   Rights of participation, liberal rights, and a consensus on economic and social policy play major roles in sustaining democracy. Consider what a regime based on any one or any two of these principles without the others might look like.

2   Tocqueville was unfamiliar with the term "civic culture." If surveys similar to those in our day had been taken in the 1830s, what might they have found? Explain why you think this would have been the case given Tocqueville's impressionistic description of the United States in his era.

3   Consider the agency problem. Give some concrete instances of how it manifests itself in terms of situations you are aware of.

4   The rule of law is essential for the protection of liberal democratic rights. How might it be undermined? How might it be reinforced?

5   Consider the differences between interest group pluralism and interest group corporatism. Which would you personally prefer? Why?

6   Political economy plays a significant role in sustaining democracy. How do the three models described in this chapter compare with one another? How do they relate to the role of sustaining democracy?

Further reading

Ronald Dore, William Lazonick, and Mary O'Sullivan, "Varieties of Capitalism in the Twentieth Century," *Oxford Review of Economic Policy*, 15, 4 (1999), 102–20. A good summary of the political economy of modern democracies.

Arend Lijphart, *Patterns of Democracy: Government Forms and Performance in Thirty-six Countries*. New Haven, CT: Yale University Press, 1999. The first two chapters of the book provide an analysis of the differences between majoritarian and consensus democracy.

Adam Przeworski, Michael Alvarez, José Antonio Cheibub, and Fernando Limongi, "What Makes Democracies Endure?," *Journal of Democracy*, 7, 1 (1996), 39–55. An analysis of the economic, social, international, and institutional arrangements that help sustain democracy.

Robert D. Putnam, Robert Leonardi, and Raffaella Y. Nanetti, *Making Democracy Work: Civic Traditions in Modern Italy*. Princeton, NJ: Princeton University Press, 1993. Develops the concept of "social capital" and examines two very different traditions in Italy.

Alexis de Tocqueville, *Democracy in America*. New Rochelle, NY: Arlington House, n.d. The classic work on the cultural basis of modern democracy.

4 Democratic institutions

The devil's in the detail.

(Anonymous)

In this chapter

The discussion of democracy continues. Taking an institutional and neo-institutional perspective, the chapter focuses on the choices about institutional arrangements that democracies have to make and the consequences of these choices. Political parties are an essential part of modern liberal democracy, and they follow a variety of organizational models and adhere to a wide range of political principles. Individuals decide which political party to support, but liberal democracies have to decide via public policy on their electoral systems. And the electoral rules they establish can have a profound effect on the number of competitive political parties and the ideological character of these parties. Democracies must also structure legislative–executive relations. Here there are two polar alternatives as well as a range of choices in between. The parliamentary alternative, characteristic of most European states, makes the executive responsible to the legislature, which selects and normally removes it. In contrast, the presidential alternative makes the two branches independent of one another. Central–local government relations are also a pivotal part of any constitutional system. A range of choices exists in this area as well. On one extreme, the central government has complete power and can reconstruct or abolish local authorities as it chooses. On the other extreme, local governments have the preponderance of power and the weak central government can act only with their cooperation. All the alternatives for electoral systems, legislative–executive relations, and intergovernmental relations are democratic, and each involves tradeoffs in terms of responsiveness, efficiency, and the full representation of local interests. After exploring these issues, the chapter concludes with a case study of the contemporary democratic institutions in the Federal Republic of Germany.

Introduction

Successful democracies are almost invariably supported by a political culture that stresses tolerance and civic involvement. Successful democracies respect the rule of law and the right of association. Democracies thrive when the society is prosperous and wealth is equitably distributed. However, these background conditions tell only part of the story. As with every other form of government, liberal democracies require well-crafted political and governmental institutions to thrive. There are always tradeoffs to be considered in designing institutions: rapid response to majority opinion versus the protection of minority interests; control by local versus control by national majorities; single-party government versus an array of competitive parties that represent all major ideological preferences of the population. The specific nature of these tradeoffs will become clearer as we examine some key democratic institutions: political parties, ideologies, electoral systems, legislative–executive relations, and central government–local government relations.

Political parties

A **political party** is an organization, united on the basis of some principle, with the purpose of nominating and electing candidates to office. Political parties are important institutions in all contemporary liberal democracies. They aggregate interests found in civil society by attracting the support of interest groups and individual voters. They articulate policy options and put them before the public. They can be held accountable by the electorate for their governmental failures and successes. Large-scale democracy is virtually impossible without them. Although political parties have evolved gradually over time, some contemporary parties retain the organizational principles typical of earlier eras (Krouwel 2006: 252–8).

The earliest form of political party organization is the cadre party. **Cadre parties** are parties with a small, weak, or nonexistent central organization to manage party affairs and help determine policy. They grew up as associations of like-minded politicians as early as the eighteenth century. The key and sometimes the only members of cadre parties are the political leaders of the party themselves. These leaders are socially, economically, or politically prominent before joining the party. The party is really an association of leaders that allows them to present a common front to the electorate. But these parties are more than just ad hoc coalitions between politicians, meant to be dissolved, as circumstances require. Cadre parties, if successful, can exist for an extended period. Although the cadre party is composed of members of the established elite, these individuals must rely on and often draw substantial support from outside their own class. So-called "local notables" – members of socially prominent families in rural areas – often draw a significant number of votes from the areas in which their families have been long established. Old ties, social deference, and a tradition of leadership can have a strong pull in areas where social and economic changes have been relatively slow-paced. In other areas, the candidate's stature along with the party's ideology and program work in much the same way as they would for any party's candidate. In short, the cadre party's lack of an official mass membership does not necessarily mean that it lacks popular appeal.

Taxi parties (also known as "couch" or "phone-booth" parties), however, are a different matter. Taxi parties are cadre parties writ small. The term, "taxi party," came into use during the 1990s to describe the parties that emerged in many post-communist states. The word, "taxi," was used to describe these parties because they had striking similarities to the means of conveyance of the same name. First, all the members of a taxi party could fit into a single taxi cab. Second, members joined the party for the same reason that patrons share a cab – for personal convenience. And third, as one rider in a taxi leaves when he reaches his destination, and another can easily get in, so too the membership of these parties is not stable. Politicians join and leave them, sometimes with mind-numbing frequency. And the taxi party, like the taxicab, lacks a consistent political orientation. Taxi parties are a blight on democracy since they vitiate the rationale for having parties in the first place. Where they exist, they usually exist in great profusion. And the parties themselves do not stand for much. Hence, they are likely to confuse voters and frustrate voters' attempts to hold politicians accountable. Although the term "taxi party" was developed to describe Eastern Europe, it can also be used appropriately to apply to parties in other countries with a completely different history. Where parties are weak and numerous, and where politicians can easily change parties without paying a political penalty, taxi parties can emerge. The Brazilian political system has many of them. The fact that Brazil's major party, though numerically dominant, is extremely weak and fragmented only exacerbates the problem.

Nineteenth-century radical socialists invented the mass party to make the revolution, but the mass party turned out to be such an effective form of organization that other political movements adopted that structure as well. **Mass parties** are based on a commitment to principle, and they derive much of their strength from a mass membership whose interests and point of view they represent. Originally mass parties took a firm stand on sometimes extreme ideological principles and had a clear class basis. Mass parties have a number of strengths. They have a large number of adherents, who can be expected to vote for the party on a regular basis. For much the same reason, mass parties find it relatively easy to mobilize campaign workers and collect significant funds to support the party from their membership fees. Mass parties have well-established procedures for choosing party officials and nominating candidates. They have a permanent organization to run the party's operations and help determine the party's stand on a variety of political issues. Parties of this sort normally require elected officials to support party decisions, and to work to change these decisions within the confines of the party and as prescribed by party rules. If an officeholder is regularly unable to support the party's positions, he or she ought to leave and join another party more closely aligned with their preferences. Traditional mass parties have, by and large, evolved into catch-all parties. **Catch-all parties** have many of the same organizational principles as mass parties, but they aim at a multi-class, multi-interest group appeal. Hence, ideology is more muted than it would be in a traditional mass party, and catch-all parties are more ready to participate in government and compromise so as to strengthen their appeal.

Mass parties also gave birth – albeit indirectly – to another type of party organization, the vanguard party. The communist party was the prototypical vanguard party, a form of organization that was adopted by other extremists of both the left and right. The organizational principles behind the vanguard party were developed by Vladimir Ilyich Lenin in the early twentieth century. While other radical socialists had or aspired to have mass parties, Lenin thought that such organizations were too reform-oriented and too open organizationally to make a revolution, especially in a society subject to periodic repression. In place of the mass party, Lenin proposed the vanguard party as the appropriate organization for Marxist revolutionaries (Lenin 1902). The hallmarks of a **vanguard party** (also known as "cell-based devotee parties") are selective membership criteria, tight discipline, a utopian ideology, and top-down decision-making. Charismatic leaders often head these parties. While vanguard parties may function in democracies, they are not designed with democracy in mind. Quite the reverse! They normally constitute a disloyal opposition as the Nazis were under Weimar. The ideological basis of these elite parties is the strident opposition to liberal democracy in principle. These parties can choose from a repertoire of tactics, some legal, some illegal, some nonviolent, some violent, to further their overall goal. Vanguard parties, even when their membership expands to rival mass parties in size, keep their elite characteristics. Discipline and loyalty are never sacrificed for the sake of numbers. Like socialist mass parties in the nineteenth and twentieth centuries, they can have a wide array of affiliated organizations, divided along the lines of age, sex, occupation, or avocational interest. In power, or when circumstances otherwise permit it, youth groups provide a mechanism for indoctrinating future party members and a pool of potential applicants from which the party can choose the best.

Parties require more than organization to compete effectively within a given democratic system. To compete successfully, a party must attract supporters. This ability is influenced by a variety of factors, some of them highly idiosyncratic such as the personalities of party leaders. The discussion here will focus on more general factors, electoral systems, and party ideologies. We turn to ideologies first.

Political ideologies

Parties compete for support in a several ways. Parties often provide tangible benefits for their supporters – jobs for party activists, government contracts for financial contributors, and various sorts of immediate aid for ordinary party voters such as a pair of shoes or a small cash bribe. Parties, in short, often serve as patronage networks. But most parties claim to stand for something beyond the delivery of patronage. They espouse principles and programs that are supposed to distinguish them from their opponents. From this perspective, people support parties not for any direct immediate benefit to themselves alone, but to change or defend certain public policies. Supporters benefit from the policies a party advocates, but they do so as members of the general public through the mechanism of public policy, not as insiders with special access to those who wield power. In short, parties compete with one another by assuming a particular ideological coloration and cultivating a certain sector of the electorate. An **ideology** is a comprehensive and relatively coherent set of political ideas that describe the proper purposes and methods of government, evaluate institutions and policies, and serve to mobilize a mass following for the purpose of political action. Modern ideologies began to develop during the Enlightenment of the eighteenth century when education and literacy expanded, and when members of the middle class, at least, were no longer willing to leave political decisions to their "betters." Ideologies can be arrayed along a conventional left–right axis. Rightwing ideologies normally stress, order, hierarchy, and the power of the state. Leftwing ideologies stress equality, solidarity, and community although some leftwing ideologies, such as communism, stress the power of the state as well. The political center is characterized by a commitment to individualism and liberty. Centrists are skeptical of the right's emphasis on the power of the state or the left's willingness to impose obligations upon the individual in the name of the community. However, many latter-day adherents to the centrist position have recognized an extensive role for the state in promoting economic growth and in distributing the benefits (Baradat 2003).

Parties of the political center

Parties of the center have a variety of labels: "Liberal," "Democratic," "Liberal Democratic," "Christian Democrat," and "Center," to name a few. To add to the confusion, not all parties that bear one of these labels are actually centrist parties. The Liberal Democratic Party of Japan, for instance, is actually a conservative party, and the Liberal Democrats of Russia are neo-fascist! Centrist parties compete for the allegiances of middle-income voters. They were initially focused on mobilizing and recruiting the middle class as narrowly defined – individuals engaged in trade and manufacturing, professionals, as well as many involved in large-scale commercial agriculture. As blue-collar workers became more prosperous and white-collar occupations proliferated, center parties have tried to attract these individuals as potential constituents as well. Center parties promise to protect private property while extending the benefits of economic growth broadly, by state action if need be.

Liberals

Parties of the center first arose in the seventeenth century as proponents of reform espoused liberal principles. One version of liberalism, natural rights liberalism, stresses what we today would call civil liberties. Natural right liberals thought that individuals, by the mere fact that they were rational, had a moral claim to certain basic rights: life, liberty, and property. Government was necessary, but government's role should be limited to the protection of those rights. Even the majority under a democratic government was obliged to recognize that these rights were absolute and inalienable. This version of liberalism has its origins in John Locke's *Second Treatise of Government*, and its consequences can be seen in the US Declaration of Independence.

Another version of liberalism has a different theoretical emphasis, but it has much the same policy implications. Economic liberalism is concerned about the overall prosperity of society rather than individual rights per se. But it too takes issue with the power of the state. The state had traditionally played a major role in the economy, granting monopolies, regulating prices, attempting to restrict and channel foreign commerce. Economic liberals, beginning with Adam Smith in the late eighteenth century, saw these state interventions as counterproductive. The free exchange of goods and services between buyers and sellers in a

Plate 4.1 Adam Smith.

largely unregulated market, he argued, would maximize overall prosperity by making the most efficient use of the wealth and contributions of each of the society's members. The role of the government was to protect property, enforce contracts and provide a stable money supply and certain basic services, such as defense that private individuals could not provide for themselves (Smith n.d.: 1, 293–571). A later version of liberalism, utilitarianism, also sprang from this school. The utilitarians argued that the only proper standard for individual morality or public policy was the "greatest happiness for the greatest number" (Bentham 1948: 1–7).

By the twentieth century, some liberals began to soften their emphasis on markets and advocate a role for the state in securing the economic welfare of those less well off. Minimum wage laws, health and safety legislation, government social insurance became part of this version of the liberal program. Called "social liberals," these liberals include leftwing Democrats in the United States and the Liberal Democrats of the United Kingdom. Today liberals defended the primacy of non-economic values – freedom of expression and personal development, and the right to make lifestyle choices, even choices offensive to the majority of society. Liberals are open to the sorts of post-industrial values described in Chapter 13. By the end of the twentieth century, so-called "neo-liberals" came onto the scene. They took the opposite position on the tenets of classical liberals from the social liberals, emphasizing free markets and guarantees for the freedom for international trade and investment.

Christian Democrats

Another potent centrist ideology is Christian Democracy. Christian Democracy is sometimes difficult to place on the conventional political spectrum with any precision. In its various versions, Christian Democratic parties have occupied a position from the moderate right to the extreme left. Christian Democracy combines conservatism in morality with a commitment to economic, social, and political reform. European Christian Democratic parties and most Latin American parties find themselves on the moderate right. A few Latin American parties have been found on the extreme left. The history of the Christian Democratic movement has its intellectual roots in the last decade of the nineteenth century when Pope Leo XIII issued an encyclical letter entitled *Rerum Novarum* (*Of New Things*). The letter, addressed to the Catholic Church and the public in general, took up the issue of social justice in the modern world. Historically, the Catholic Church had taught and preached about issues of justice, but its teachings had little direct relevance to the issues of the industrial age. In fact the church had been a conservative or even a reactionary political force through much of the modern era. The church's natural constituents had been the more traditional sectors of society, but with the growth of modern industry, the working class was becoming an increasingly large part of society, and its problems could not be ignored. *Rerum Novarum* and the social encyclicals that followed in the same vein rejected key parts of the then current versions of both liberalism and socialism while agreeing with some principles from each. On the side of the liberals and against the socialists, the church taught that the right to own property, even productive property, was a fundamental human right. On the side of socialism and against liberalism, the church taught that justice demanded that workers' rights be respected. Workers had a right to organize, the right to a living wage, and decent working conditions. And it was the government's responsibility to defend these rights. The early encyclicals especially recommended corporatist forms of interest-group representation.

These Catholic social teachings became the basis of Christian Democratic ideology when Christian Democratic parties were formed in the post-Second World War era. Christian Democrats thus support social welfare legislation, workers' rights, and the co-determination of business decisions by labor and management. The expression, "social market economy," sums up this set of policies. It has clear similarities to the economic aims pursued by social democrats (see below). However, on such issues as law and order, obscenity, abortion, divorce, and state support for religion, Christian Democrats take a more conservative line than their social democratic colleagues. Christian Democratic parties played the dominant role in the Federal Republic of Germany and Italy for decades, and they have played an important role in other European states with significant Catholic populations. Christian Democratic parties exist in Latin America as well. Christian Democrats are non-confessional – i.e., they are not organized so as to include only Catholics, nor do they defend Church interests as such. But although Protestants and others are members, Catholics remain their core supporters.

Parties of the left

Parties of the left normally have names such as "Socialist," "Social Democrat," "Labor," "Communist," or "Green" although these monikers do not exhaust the list. The political left rose to prominence in the late nineteenth century as the industrial working class grew in numbers and self-confidence. Originally the left's natural constituency was this same industrial working class although over time it has expanded to a significant degree.

Socialists

In the late nineteenth century, socialists espoused the liberation and full enfranchisement of the working class. Socialists believed that existing social, economic, and political relations needed to be destroyed root and branch. They saw no hope for reforming the old order. Nineteenth-century socialists often called themselves "social democrats" to indicate that they were not simply political democrats. They believed that political democracy was incomplete and manipulative. It had to be replaced by social democracy. To be truly free and equal, people had to have truly equal rights, including equal rights to use property. This equality could only arrive with a new form of society that held property in common and allowed all to participate directly in the making of decisions. Ultimately, capitalism and representative democracy had to be replaced by full communism – a society in which industry was fully developed and the community managed it collectively and had free use of its products. In short, throughout much of the nineteenth century, socialism was the most radical of doctrines that preached revolution as the only solution to the injustices of the status quo. Although Karl Marx was not the only socialist theoretician, by the end of the century he had become the most influential. And many of the basic ideas that found their way into Marx's writings had their origins or echoes elsewhere.

Socialist parties at that time were anti-system parties. They functioned, in theory at least, as a disloyal opposition. They worked to increase their strength and influence by legal means, electing members to the legislature and organizing labor unions and affiliated groups, but they espoused revolution. However, by the turn of the twentieth century, socialist parties, like the world around them, had changed considerably. While the mainstream of the movement adhered to radical ideology even while participating in conventional politics, one group of socialists, known as "**revisionists**," rejected the radicals' dogmatism. They argued that experience showed that under capitalism and representative government, the working class could make significant concrete gains. They asserted that the end of socialism (full communism) was nothing since it could never be achieved. Rather, they said, the movement (socialist parties and labor unions, laws to protect workers' rights, social security) was everything (Bernstein 1963). By the middle of the twentieth century, socialists in the West had accepted the revisionist position. In the contemporary setting, socialists advocate state ownership of the major industries and support an extensive welfare state, but they support liberal democracy as the means by which these goals are to be achieved. And socialists have little appetite for nationalizing small and medium-sized businesses; they are content to leave them in private hands.

Social Democrats

In the last two decades of the twentieth century, some European socialist parties moved even more decidedly to the center. The earlier revisionists had laid aside the doctrine of revolution and accepted liberal democracy and state ownership of the "commanding heights" of the economy – major industries and natural monopolies – instead. However, by the end of the twentieth century, even the commitment to state ownership seemed excessively dogmatic. Many socialist parties moved in the direction of social democracy (in the late twentieth-century sense of the term) – an extensive welfare state with medical care, pensions, childcare, and free education for all but very limited state ownership even of major industries. In other words, latter-day social democrats accept a large role for the government in assuring equality of opportunity and result but a more limited role for the government in actually managing the economy than do their (revisionist) socialist compatriots. This change was necessitated by the fact that the socialists' program had often seemed dated and out of touch with middle-class voters, an important constituency for almost all parties. Thus, socialists in Britain, Germany, and elsewhere began to speak of a "**third way**" between old-style socialism and full-bore, free-market capitalism of a neo-liberal variety.

Greens

The 1970s saw the emergence of an entirely new party, the Greens. The Greens had their immediate origins in the counterculture movement of the 1960s that rejected capitalism, conventional politics, and the pollution and social dislocations of the modern industrial age. The Greens fit into the radical left of the political spectrum. They were designed as part of the "**new left**" because they rejected the old left's reliance on the state and representative institutions. In a way, they attempted to recapture the anti-state radicalism of many nineteenth-century socialists. The party first came into its own in Germany in the 1970s when it won seats in the national legislature. The party had a radical democratic ideology that echoed anarchist ideas of an earlier era; it espoused "participatory democracy" (direct democracy) as the only way of attaining the democratic ideal of harmony and community control. Today, however, the German Greens are a mainline pro-environment party. They have come to accept, as did their radical predecessors, the necessity of representative democracy and a permanent party bureaucracy, things against which they had earlier rebelled. By the turn of the twenty-first century, the Greens had made their presence felt in a number of European countries.

Communists

Communism, or Marxism–Leninism, grew out of the late nineteenth-century socialist movement. While socialism began to move toward the center at the turn of the twentieth century, communism emerged to its left. Initially, communism's basic disagreement with radical socialism was over means, not ends. Like the nineteenth-century socialists, communists believed that full communism was both desirable and historically inevitable. But they also believed that large parties without strict membership standards would impede rather than further the revolution. Communists supported the idea that their party ought to be a vanguard party that served the interests of the working class without being controlled directly by them. Communists also espoused the dictatorship of the proletariat: once in power, the party would never leave office voluntarily, at least not until full communism was established. Communists supported the principle of "**proletarian internationalism**." Under principles of the Communist (Third) International or Comintern, established in Moscow in early 1918 just after the Bolshevik Revolution, all communists were supposed to follow the International's direction. In the end, that meant supporting the foreign policy of the Soviet Union. Even after the Comintern was disbanded in 1943, the principle of proletarian internationalism lived on.

Other radical leftwing movements such as the anarchists were quite influential at one time, but they eventually became marginal as far as their capacity for mobilizing masses of people was concerned. Anarchists advocated something like full communism but by radically different means than communists espoused. The state would have to be destroyed, and anarchy (literally "no-rule") would arise. Out of this condition, true freedom and the cooperative administration of resources by the community would emerge. Anarchism had a violent and a nonviolent wing. It had echoes in some of the radical movements of the 1960s and 1970s.

Euro-communism and beyond

A sea change overtook the communist movement in the 1970s. Increasingly, important non-ruling communist parties in Europe began to assert their independence from the Communist Party of the Soviet Union (CPSU) and the ideological orthodoxy it endorsed. The communist parties of Italy and Spain, and, to a much more limited degree, the French Communist Party, one by one, dropped central tenets of Marxism–Leninism. Proletarian internationalism was the first to go since as far back as the Hitler–Stalin Pact of 1939, CPSU leadership of the international communist movement had been nakedly self-serving. The Italians and Spanish also began to criticize the concept of "**the dictatorship of the proletariat**," i.e., unchecked rule by the communist party and the repression of the opposition. For the Communist Party of Italy (CPI) especially, the abandonment of this notion seemed critical. The communists were the second largest party in Italy, providing good government in the cities that they controlled, and they were willing as well to abide by the decisions of municipal elections. Nonetheless, some Italians still harbored doubts: were the communists really good democrats, or were they just playing the game to get into power nationally? Once ensconced in the national government, would they revert to the party's traditional anti-democratic position? The formal abandonment of the dictatorship of the proletariat was a necessary step to reassuring the country. The dictatorship of the proletariat, the CPI came to argue, was necessary in Russia under specific historical circumstance, but it was inappropriate and counterproductive in contemporary Italy. **Democratic centralism**, the organizational principle that permitted the party leadership to dominate decision-making in the party, was also passé.

It too was rejected. And where the CPI led, the Spaniards and other Western European parties followed. By the time the Soviet Union collapsed, most western communist parties were ready to follow the Italian road. Many, like the Italians, changed their name as well. As a consequence, communist parties today range from groupings barely distinguishable from social democrats to hardliners supporting almost all the basic principles of orthodox Marxism–Leninism.

Parties of the right

Today parties of the right normally wear the label "Conservative," "National" or "Nationalist," or "Popular," although more idiosyncratic names also exist. These parties defend tradition, law and order, and are generally in favor of the status quo (or a prior status quo, real or imagined). Rightist parties are generally friendly toward state power, especially when that power is used to enhance national security, the security of property, and the furtherance of traditional (often religious) norms. Parties of the right attempt to mobilize the traditional elite, rural voters, and those disaffected with equality, and those threatened by rapid political, social, and economic change. In addition, rightwing parties appeal to nationalism and patriotism as opposed to narrower sub-national, or broader transnational loyalties. Rightwing political parties generally fall within well-recognized classifications: conservative, reactionary, and fascist (or neo-fascist). Each bears a certain ideological kinship to the others, but each also differs considerably from its rightwing compatriots.

Conservatives

Parties of the moderate right usually espouse a conservative ideology. Conservatism first arose as a response to liberalism. While liberalism and most other ideologies propose universal, rational principles for political action, conservatism from its origins has been skeptical of the rationalist approach. The hallmarks of conservatism are caution and defense of the status quo. Conservatives defend the state's role in enforcing law and order as well as social norms, and they have historically defended a substantial state role in the economy. The intellectual founder of conservatism, Edmund Burke, reacted against revolution and liberal rationalism precisely because he believed that any systematic and thoroughgoing attempt to apply rational principles to politics was mistaken. Yet, Burke admitted that political change was necessary. "A state without the means of some change," he wrote, "is without the means for its own conservation" (Burke n.d.: 33). Still, change needed to be gradual and organic. It needed to preserve the time-tested institutions of the past, and to refrain from upsetting the established social order. Change, he further asserted, is not necessarily reform. Society was a compact between generations, a community that endured through the ages. If that community was to endure, hereditary property and privilege needed to be protected. Rank and order had to be preserved. People had to feel secure in their status, be it high or low.

When Burke first enunciated his version of conservatism, he needed to rally few beyond the privileged sectors of society, intellectuals, and others who were deeply distrustful of change to have a political effect. No democrat, Burke in the 1790s defended the British monarchy, which then still had substantial power, and aristocratic privilege. He attacked the French Revolution and explicitly rejected the concepts of human equality, natural rights, and government by consent. By the end of the nineteenth century, his conservative successors were forced to backtrack considerably. As the temper of the times became more democratic and popular pressure from the lower classes increased, conservatism needed a mass base to survive politically. Thus, conservatives in Britain sponsored a reform bill that extended the franchise to sections of the working class. Conservatives acceded to the diminution of monarchical and aristocratic power. Both were actions that would have appalled Burke. Nonetheless, the defense of tradition, its adaptation rather than its abandonment, remain the hallmark of conservative thought and politics, even after conservatives had been forced to make strategic retreats. Conservatives retain their emphasis on the community rather than the individual. While they recognize human rights in practice, they reject the rationalism and one-size-fits-all notions often associated with the concept. Conservatism outside the United States still retains these basic attitudes although in the last two decades of the twentieth century many European conservatives have advocated reducing the state's role in the economy and encouraging the development of the free market.

Reactionaries

Today people generally use the term "reactionary" as a reproach. During the early nineteenth century, it was merely a description of a particular political ideology to the right of conservatism. Reactionaries, like conservatives, rose to the challenge of revolution. But while conservatives were willing to bend with the prevailing winds to preserve as much as they could of the old order, reactionaries were unwilling to make such compromises. Conservatives generally attempted to adapt tradition to changing circumstances as Burke had said they must, but reactionaries asserted that the old regime had to be defended in its entirety against both revolutionaries and reformers, or reestablished in its entirety after a revolution. Reactionaries appealed to religion and nostalgia for the past. Their potential for a mass base was limited, and they met repeated failure in the nineteenth century. The peasantry, who might well be expected to support rightwing movements, had other parties and ideologies from which to choose. The monarchists' power at the 1871 constituent assembly in France represented their last, best chance to refashion politics decisively in a major European country. After that, reaction was clearly on the wane. After the First World War, it was not reaction that became the dominant extreme rightwing ideology, but fascism.

Fascists

In liberal democracies, fascist parties constitute a disloyal opposition, trying to overthrow the system while at the same time working within it to garner strength. Fascism was one of the main ideological competitors with liberal democracy and communism from the 1920s to the 1940s. Under the right circumstances, it could garner a much larger mass base than reaction ever could. In the face of lost wars, stymied war aims, depression, and social disruption, fascism offered the prospect of a new order that appealed to many of the newly disadvantaged. It promised law and order, discipline, national power, civic virtue, and prosperity. While the working class was the natural constituency of the communists and socialists, the lower middle class was the natural mass constituency of the fascists. The events of the 1920s and 1930s had brought disaster to many in the lower middle class. Fascism provided an explanation. It was not the nation or its people that were to blame, but dark conspiratorial forces, enemies within the gates. Communists, socialists, liberals, Jews, international bankers had united their efforts to bring the nation down. The lower middle class was looking for a way to reaffirm their old status and improve their economic condition. Patriotic, they wanted to see their nation powerful and internationally respected and to rectify the unjust treatment it had received in the recent past. Fascism promised a way to achieve these goals. It provided a sense of belonging and empowerment: mass rallies and patriotic displays. It restored a sense of order. Law enforcement was strengthened; "social undesirables" and dissidents were rounded up. The nation's military power grew, and displays of military force were later matched by political and territorial gains.

Fascists despised the communists as anti-nationalist, but fascists, especially the Nazis, adapted communist methods of party organization because they were effective. An elite organization, with members totally committed to the ideology and willing to follow any order from the leadership, was a splendid revolutionary – or counterrevolutionary – tool. Such an organization could act clandestinely to subvert the established order, and, at the same time, it could organize the masses through various associated organizations and campaign effectively in elections. Fascists, like communists, followed a flexible political strategy and used a variety of tactics. The lodestar was gaining power. And, like the communists, once they had attained power, they would not voluntarily relinquish it. It was the defeat of the fascist powers in the Second World War that clearly demonstrated their corruption and intellectual bankruptcy. Today fascism in its extreme form is a spent force, but the extreme rightwing parties in democracies have at times adopted fascist themes and tactics: ultra-nationalism, scapegoating minorities and immigrants, appeals to the recently psychologically uprooted in times of stress, and emphasis upon the imposition of law and order using harsh means. While such appeals have relatively little resonance in prosperous times, in periods of rapid social and economic change they can have considerable effect. For instance, the National Front in France and the Freedom Party of Austria have had a major influence on their countries' politics.

Summary

In industrial democracies the growth of the middle class after the Second World War and a prolonged period of prosperity lessened the attractiveness of parties taking radical approaches. The left's hostility toward capitalism mellowed, and the mainline right's suspicion of democracy and human rights moderated as well. The last two decades of the twentieth century saw the continued migration of political parties toward the center. Parties of the radical left modified their ideologies and often changed their names. The most successful non-governing communist party, the Communist Party of Italy, became explicitly Euro-communist and later changed its symbols and name to the Party of the Democratic Left and merged with other leftwing parties. The Green Party of Germany moderated its position to the point that its radical, anti-capitalist, and direct-democracy roots are now difficult to detect. A social democratic orientation has become the most common ideological posture of most so-called socialist parties today. And conservatives have taken on a more market-friendly guise. Only on the extreme right has the trend been reversed. Neo-fascist groups that play on the same themes as the original fascists without explicitly adopting fascist ideology have had an effect in long-established democracies, winning office themselves or pulling more modern conservatives further to the right.

Electoral systems

In democracies, politicians and activists are normally free to form a
party based on any ideology they please. Yet few countries have all or
even most of the parties just discussed. The limitation of political choice
occurs for a variety of reasons. Sometimes it is the result of specific
exclusions. For example, Germany bans Nazi and communist parties.
Most restrictions are more subtle and are due to the way the electoral
system operates.

Electoral systems determine who wins office. They award the office
of chief executive and allocate legislative seats on the basis of specific
formulas based on popular votes. Different formulas have drastically
different effects. They can promote the growth of two main parties, a few
big parties, or a welter of small parties. In addition, they can promote or
detract from the representative's responsiveness to constituents in a
specific geographical region. They can help promote responsiveness,
transparency, and accountability. But there are tradeoffs. For reasons of
simplicity, we will focus on systems for electing the legislature, but some
of these systems could be used for the direct election of a chief executive
as well. Let us begin by considering the hypothetical distribution of
votes in Table 4.1. The table represents a country with only five districts
and with five political parties on the ballot. The number of districts is
unrealistically small, but simplifies our example sufficiently to make it
manageable. We will find that the electoral system for translating votes
into seats makes a profound difference on which and to what degree
different parties gain seats in the legislature (Farrell 2001; Sartori 1997:
3–79; Soudriette and Ellis 2006).

Single-member district/plurality election

Single-member district/plurality election (SMD/PE), also called the
"first-past-the-post" system, is the system used in the United States,
United Kingdom, Canada, India, and the English-speaking Caribbean,

Table 4.1 Votes (thousands)

District/party	1	2	3	4	5	Total
A	101	90	76	75	40	382
B	59	60	74	85	65	343
C	30	35	30	35	20	150
D	10	15	20	5	5	55
E	0	0	0	0	70	70
Total	200	200	200	200	200	1,000

but it is not widely used in the rest of the democratic world.
Single-member district/plurality election works in the following
manner. As the name implies, under SMD/PE each district has one
legislative seat. Voters vote within their district for one candidate and one
candidate only. The candidate who receives the most votes (the plurality)
wins the district. This system produces straightforward results. Unless
there is a tie or contested election, there is no need for a runoff. The
winner need only receive more votes than any other candidate; he or she
does not need a majority. Since there is only one candidate elected per
district, the results are unambiguous: one candidate/party wins, all the
others lose. In our example, party A, the party that took the most votes
nationally, received only 38 percent of the vote (382,000 out of 1,000,000
votes), yet it won 60 percent of the seats. According to electoral rules of
SMD/PE, the allocation of seats in the legislature would be as follows:
party A, 60 percent of the seats; party B, 20 percent; and party E,
20 percent (see Table 4.2).

SMD/PE tends to produce the following sorts of results. It normally
gives the winning party a disproportionately large share of seats in the
legislature. The example exaggerates the effect somewhat, but it is not
unusual in the United Kingdom for the winning party to take around
45 percent of the votes and gain a three-fifths majority in the House of
Commons. In India, for much of the first thirty years of independence,
there were similar disproportionate results. This "over-representation" of
the winning party can promote efficient government and political
transparency. With a clear majority in the legislature, party A, in this
hypothetical example, cannot blame any of its colleagues for the failure to
pass bills or for badly crafted legislation. Party A is in control, and the
public has the right to hold them accountable. For those who like clear
lines of responsibility and efficient government, the first-past-the-post
system would seem to be highly desirable. On the other hand, this
electoral system seems to discriminate against minority political views.
Parties that do not win districts get no seats. Parties C and D, with 15 and
6.5 percent of the overall vote respectively, are frozen out of the legislature.

Table 4.2 Distribution of seats in legislature (%)

Electoral system/party	SMD/PE	PR	SMD/ME
A	60	38	20 + ?
B	20	34	?
C	0	15	?
D	0	6	?
E	20	7	?

Of the minority parties, only party E does well under SMD/PE. It wins one district, but takes no votes elsewhere. Such a phenomenon is far from unusual. For example, the Scottish National Party runs candidates and is organized only in Scotland, and wins seats there in British elections. Similar regional parties exist in India in great profusion. Generally, however, SMD/PE discourages third parties. Voters normally wish to vote for candidates who have a chance of gaining office, and politicians running for office normally like to have a chance of winning. Unless strong regional or historical loyalties keep third and fourth parties in the game, SMD/PE tends to produce a system dominated by two major parties. In a **two-party system** either one or the other of two main parties controls a majority of seats in each house of the legislature and the executive branch. In fact, the same party might control all of these institutions. Where a two-party system exists, the two parties (and the legislature they dominate) will tend to support SMD/PE and other mechanisms that tend to protect two-party dominance. The two parties will each try to capture a majority of the vote since that is the only way they can be assured of winning pluralities in a majority of districts. The two parties each tend to become catch-all parties composed of a great number of factions and interests. Such a catch-all party often differs from its major competitor only in matter of degree since both need to be close to where the majority of voters are in order to win elections.

Proportional representation

The first-past-the-post and two-party dominance strike many people as unfair. Efficiency and political transparency that SMD/PE promotes are only two virtues of democratic government. They are not the only virtues, and perhaps they are not even the most important virtues. Why, critics of SMD/PE ask, should minority party views be excluded from the legislature? Such exclusion can undermine protections for minority rights and needlessly limit the alternatives available in political debate. Proportional representation (PR) overcomes these problems.

Proportional representation (PR) assigns seats in a legislative body according to the percentage of the overall vote each party wins. In pure closed-list PR systems, such as Israel's, the entire country consists of one legislative district. Voters cast their votes for a party. The percentage of popular votes translates directly into the percentage of seats each party receives. In the simplest of systems considered here, 10 percent of the popular vote entitles a party to 10 percent of the seats in the legislature. Since each party has filed a **party list**, a slate of candidates listed in order of priority, the appropriate number of names is taken from the top of the list. These individuals then serve in the legislature.

Most PR systems are more complex, however. Seats are assigned to districts, and quotas determine how many votes it takes to win a seat. Once the quotas for winning seats are established, the determination of who will sit in the legislature is simple. The quotas can be set to give larger parties a more than proportionate advantage. The party list itself can be organized in a variety of ways. The simplest is closed-list PR. Under **closed-list PR**, voters vote for a party, and in doing so vote for its party list. The party itself establishes the list, and, as a consequence, the party leadership usually has a disproportionate share of safe positions on the ballot. Under the closed-list system, there is no way for the voter to vote for the party but against the wishes of the party leadership as expressed in priorities established by the party list. The established party leaders have the dominant influence over the party, and they can use their ability to control the list to punish or reward party colleagues. The perceived unfairness of this practice has led to the adoption of other variations of PR to overcome this problem. Various versions of open-list PR have been used to avoid the dominance by party leaders inherent in the closed-list system. Under an open-list system, the party leadership's control over who gets elected is curtailed. Voters are allowed to vote for a candidate and not simply for the party. A candidate's personal vote can allow him or her to jump ahead of candidates higher on the list and secure a seat. The exact number of votes required to do this depends on the rules of the particular electoral system. Depending on these rules, it may be very difficult or relatively easy to buck the party leadership. Other variants of PR allow parties to run multiple lists. This has the effect of strengthening and giving official recognition to factions within parties. Extreme open-list (and, to a certain extent, multi-list) systems can personalize the election and weaken party discipline. Candidates may campaign more for themselves than for the party.

PR promotes a **multiparty system** – a system in which more than two parties have a significant role to play in the legislature. It encourages like-minded activists and politicians to form a minor party rather than joining an established one so long as that party would be assured of winning the minimum number of votes to gain seats in the legislature. Thus, in multiparty systems, parties can often afford to be "niche marketers," appealing to a specific minority of voters who share all or almost all the major views of the party. If we examine Table 4.2 again, we find using the pure PR formula that no party controls a majority. In a legislature of 100 seats, parties D and E would have 6 and 7 respectively, and could have important bargaining power.

Maybe too much bargaining power! In parliamentary systems, where the legislature elects and removes the chief executive at pleasure, small parties can have a disproportionate influence on policy. For example, in Israel over a period of decades Orthodox Jewish parties that had little interest in most other areas of policy used their bargaining power to get what they did want – funding for their schools, exemption from military conscription, and the enforcement of strict religious rules over a largely secular Israeli population. Since potential chief executives needed their votes to get elected and stay in office, candidates from the larger parties were willing to give in to Orthodox demands. Because of these sorts of drawbacks, few countries follow a pure PR system. Most countries assign seats to districts as noted earlier. The larger the number of seats per district, the more the results will resemble pure PR. The fewer the number of seats, the closer they come to resemble SMD/PE. Some PR systems use a cutoff rule, so that parties have to take a minimum percentage of popular votes to qualify for any seats at all even though they would otherwise qualify.

Other systems are similar to open-list PR. Irish, Maltese, and some Australian elections use the **single transferable vote (STV)**. STV requires voters to rank order their preferences for candidates on the ballot. A quota of votes is calculated that determines who will be elected on the first tally of ballots. Anyone who attains or exceeds this quota is elected. The surplus votes of winning candidates are distributed to their voters' second choice. When no more candidates can be elected by distributing winners' surplus votes, the candidate with the lowest number of top preferences is eliminated, and the process begins again, this time distributing the votes of the eliminated candidates. Under STV, factions of a party get seats in proportion to the strength of the faction, and candidates can gain support by providing local services to their constituents.

Single-member district/majority election

The first-past-the-post and nationwide PR systems are the two extremes. They have advantages and disadvantages opposite to each other. And even though it is not possible to gain the full advantages of both, many constitution-makers and political scientists believe it desirable to strike some kind of a balance. The supposed minority under-representation of SMD/PE need not drive us to the opposite potentially deadlocked and instability-wracked model of pure PR. There are, in fact, a number of alternatives besides modifications to the pure PR formula. **Single-member district/majority election (SMD/ME)** is one of them.

The candidate who gets the majority (more than half) of the votes in a district wins the district. On its face, there may seem to be little difference between SMD/ME and first-past-the-post SMD/PE. Indeed, the procedural differences seem to be slight. The former requires that the winning candidate gets the majority (more than half the votes); the latter requires that the winning candidate simply gets the plurality – i.e., more votes than his or her competitors. Majority winners always have the plurality. Quite often, where SMD/PE election has successfully promoted a two-party system, the winner there has the majority as well. But the difference between a majority and plurality requirement does make a considerable difference. First-past-the-post promotes a two-party system. SMD/ME has no such effect. In fact, it can encourage the growth of third and fourth parties.

It works in this way. If no candidate gains a majority in an SMD/ME district, there has to be a runoff election. In the simplest version of the system, all but the top two vote-getters in each district are stricken from the ballot. In our example, Party A wins one district, and four out of the five parties (A, B, C, and E) have candidates in the second round necessary in four districts. And unless we knew the ideological proclivities of the parties, it would be impossible to estimate how voters might allocate their second-round ballots. The runoff requirement is the key to understanding why politicians and activists could find it advantageous to form third and fourth parties in SMD/ME systems. To see how this works, consider an entirely different example. Suppose that in a particular district the Beer Drinkers Party normally takes 55 percent of the votes and the Prohibitionists normally take 45 percent. Thus, in an SMD/PE system, the Beer Drinkers always win if they stick together and normal voting patterns prevail. But what happens if the Lite-Beer Drinkers who favor the complete abolition of taxes on alcohol were to split from the Beer Drinkers, who would allow such taxes, and form their own party? If the new Lite-Beer Drinkers Party takes as little as 11 percent of the vote, the Prohibitionists win: Lite-Beer Drinkers, 11 percent; Beer Drinkers, 44 percent; and Prohibitionists, 45 percent. The Beer Drinkers (original and lite) both lose. In a SMD/ME system, the likely result would be different. With 45 percent of the vote, the Prohibitionists do not have a majority, and a runoff would be required. In this case, the Lite-Beer Drinkers would in all probability come to their senses and in the runoff vote for the lesser of two evils – the original Beer Drinkers candidate – rather than risking losing the right to drink altogether. Unlike the first-past-the-post system, third parties under SMD/ME do not force voters to risk throwing their vote away by expressing their first preference.

In other words, SMD/ME involves nothing like the party-unity premium or party-split penalty of SMD/PE. Factions of an existing party have little need to stay in the same party, provided their voters vote for the candidate nominated by larger party in the second round. Hence a political faction is free to test the political waters by forming its own party or running its own independent candidate. Maybe the Lite-Beer Drinkers will take more votes as the original Beer Drinkers in a first round; then the original party's voters will have to vote for them. Even if Lite Beer does not take more votes, by running separately in a general election the party can demonstrate to its former colleagues just how much public support it does have. And if this support is as little as 5–10 percent, it may induce the Beer Drinkers Party to compromise and move closer to Lite-Beer Drinker positions. In short, under SMD/ME, factions can split off from existing major parties or run their own candidates without risking the disastrous consequences typical of the first-past-the-post system.

Election of a chief executive by majority vote, a common method used by democracies with executive presidents, also tends to favor the development of a multiparty system. The logic is very much the same as SMD/ME is with legislatures. As in the legislative example, the Beer Drinkers would lose little in splitting their vote in a presidential election's first round, provided they united behind the top vote-getting anti-prohibitionist candidate for the second. In addition, SMD/ME can be modified so that the second round does not actually require an absolute majority. In the revised system, all candidates receiving a minimum percentage of the vote are permitted to run in the second round, and in that round the plurality vote-getter wins.

Alternative vote

The **alternative vote** (AV), or "instant runoff," is a system that has similar consequences to SMD/ME. As with SMD/ME, a majority is required to win, and there is only one seat per district. However, AV avoids the need for a second round election by having voters indicate their order of preference for each candidate. The first orders of preference are counted, and if one candidate receives the majority of these, he or she is declared the winner. But if no such result occurs, a second count is required. This time the candidate who received the lowest number of first preferences is eliminated from the tabulation. Voters who listed that candidate as their first choice now have their second choices tallied in the new tabulation. If a candidate receives the majority this time, he or she is declared the winner. If not, the candidate with the least number of votes in the second tally is eliminated, and the voters who preferred that candidate have their votes assigned to the candidate they next favored. The elimination and tallying continue until one candidate receives the majority. Thus, AV has multiple rounds of vote tallying without multiple elections. It saves the time and cost of a second election, but it does not allow for a second, shorter campaign.

Other systems

There are some electoral formulas, involving multi-member districts that purposely skew the results, either assigning a premium to the winning party or a premium to the losing party. Perhaps the most controversial is Chile's binomial system that assigned a premium to coming in second. According to the rules, the party or coalition that wins the district receives one seat. If it carries the district with two-thirds of the vote, it receives the second seat. If not, the second place finisher gains the seat. This provision is arguably anti-democratic. It was crafted under the military dictatorship to guarantee its partisans, always likely to be numerically weaker, a disproportionate share of the seats in the national legislature.

Another system, important because of one of the countries that used it, Japan, has some peculiar consequences. The system, the single nontransferable vote (SNTV), was used in Japan until 1994; it is used today in Jordan, Vanuatu, the Pitcairn Islands, Afghanistan, and for some seats in Taiwan. It provides for multi-member districts. Each voter casts one nontransferable vote, not for a party but for a specific candidate. There is no shifting of excess votes between members of the same party. This system can have a number of odd – even perverse – consequences. In Japan, party candidates campaigned against one another. Intense identification with the candidate is important since voters had to write in the name of the person for whom they wish to vote. Large amounts of money for personal gifts to constituents were often a necessity to be elected. Parties that nominate too many candidates relative to the strength of the party vote in the district are likely to be penalized by diluting their party's vote among too many candidates. Parties that nominate too few candidates for their strength in the district would be penalized by electing fewer candidates than they could have. The system helped provoke a crisis in Japan, and was changed in an electoral reform in 1994.

Summary

Different electoral systems tend to promote or reinforce different sorts of party systems. SMD/PE has a strong tendency to limit the number of competitive national parties to two. Two is normally the upper limit, rather than the minimum. For example, in the first three decades of Indian independence, the Congress Party was the only significant national party. But as the Indian and British experience attests, SMD/PE can support a variety of regional parties, provided that these parties can actually carry districts in their home regions. PR systems allow more than two parties to be competitive. Depending on the exact nature of rules and the heterogeneity of the country, competitive parties can be quite numerous. SMD/ME also supports the multiparty system, but the number of competitive parties in it is likely to be significantly less than under extreme forms of PR. While constitution-makers could choose an electoral system based on their and the public's theoretical preferences, more often than not, party and electoral systems evolve side by side. Once parties become entrenched, they are unlikely to permit a radical change in the system that works to their disadvantage. Parties and party politicians who have developed successful strategies for using one electoral system will be extremely reluctant to change the rules in such a way that they are forced to develop new and untested strategies. Thus, once established, electoral and party systems tend to endure.

Executive–legislative relations

Electoral laws provide the rules that determine how parties and politicians get elected to office, but once they are elected to office, these same parties and politicians have to govern. To do this they have to follow a different set of rules. How politics is conducted within governments depends, in large measure, on the way in which legislatures and executives are structured and the constitutional relationship they have to one another. There are two basic methods of choosing the executive and legislature: presidential and parliamentary systems (Sartori 1997: 83–194).

Presidentialism

Most Americans are familiar with the presidential or separation of power system since that is the organizational principle of the United States constitution. The hallmark of the presidential system is the selection of the chief executive and the legislature independently of one another. Except in extreme circumstances, such as impeachment, the one has no direct role in removing or selecting the other. Even when the elections of the two branches are held simultaneously, the voters are forced to make separate choices for the executive and the legislature. The chief executive, normally with the title of "president," may be elected directly by popular vote or via some indirect method or weighing formula

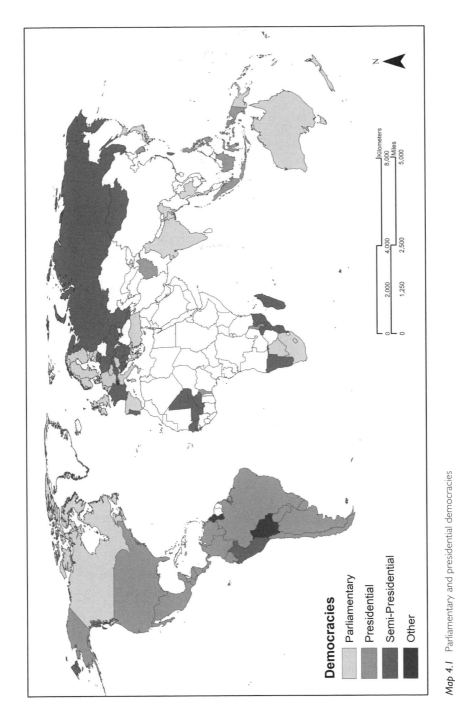

Map 4.1 Parliamentary and presidential democracies

Source: Environmental Systems Research Insitute (ESRI) map data. Data: Shugart (2006)

Note: Democracies are defined as states having a democracy score of 6 or better in the Polity IV data for 2004. Polity IV ratings range from +0 (most democratic) to −10 (most authoritarian)

Democracies

Parliamentary

Presidential

Semi-Presidential

Other

(such as the US electoral college) and has a fixed term of office.
The legislature too has a fixed term in office. The president is not
removable except by impeachment, and then only for serious breaches of
the public trust. Eligibility for reelection varies widely. In some systems,
presidents may serve only one term in office, and they are never eligible to
run again. Other systems limit the president to two terms, or render
incumbents ineligible until they have been out of office for a specified
period. In Latin America, which accounts for a large share of presidential
systems, limits on reelection are the result of earlier experience where
incumbency allowed sitting presidents to win reelection repeatedly
because of their control of patronage and their influence over the
voting-counting authorities. Only recently have a number of Latin
American states begun to modify their no-incumbency rule.

In a presidential system, the legislature (often called "congress") may
be unicameral (one-house) or bicameral (two-houses). The two houses or
chambers in bicameral legislatures typically have roughly equal power.
Unicameral legislatures generally have more power vis-à-vis the executive
because the president cannot play the game of divide and conquer.
Outside the United States, legislatures rarely have the degree of expertise
and elaborate committee system found in the US congress. This tends to
make party politics and patronage rather than the crafting of legislation
and detailed oversight of the executive the primary motivating factor in
the legislature.

Under presidentialism, presidents are granted specific powers by the
constitution, as is the legislature. However, this separation should not
be overstated. Most politicians seek executive power to enact policies
they and their constituents favor. Rarely does the executive branch
possess sufficient power to enact these policies without legislation.
Legislative majorities themselves are also dependent on the executive
since the president usually wields a veto that makes legislative
majorities sufficiently large to act consistently against the president's
will difficult to muster. Thus, while executive and legislature are formally
independent of one another and secure in office until their respective
terms expire, this independence only allows them to remain players
in the governmental game. To obtain their particular objective, each must
strike a deal, persuade, or browbeat the other into seeing things its way.
The nature of the party system can have an important effect on the
president's ability or lack of ability to persuade the legislature. And the
nature of presidential elections, in turn, can have an important effect on
the party system. If a two-party system obtains, presidents can more easily
count on their fellow party members in the legislature for support. This
party support can be a decided advantage when the presidency and the

legislature are both controlled by the same party. Even so, the president's ability to persuade depends upon the unity of his party and his influence with the country at large. Multiparty legislatures constitute a different sort of problem. Presidents may feel compelled to secure ongoing cooperation from the legislature by including members of opposition parties in their cabinet with the explicit or implicit promise of legislature support.

To gain better control of the policy-making process, presidents sometimes seek delegated powers from the legislature. The request for wholesale delegation of powers is more likely to be successful early in a new president's term when he or she is seen as having a popular mandate. Once this early "honeymoon" period ends, presidents are much less likely to get the legislature to concede such dominance. However, presidents may be delegated emergency powers to face a specific economic, military, or political crisis. In addition, some Latin American constitutions once allowed presidents to declare emergencies themselves, putting into play a number of special circumstances: the suspension of civil liberties and the power to rule by decree. These emergency powers have been frequently abused. There are other provisions, in some constitutions, that allow the president to legislate by decree in more limited emergencies. The promulgation of such an emergency decree gives the legislature only a limited amount of time to amend or abrogate it. Again, such provisions have frequently been subject to abuse. In short, the business of running the government under presidentialism is a shifting affair involving bargaining, appeals to the public and threats to block the other branch's initiative. Often it produces no clear-cut decision or a compromise decision which all sides claim credit for if it is popular or which all sides deny responsibility for if it turns out to be unpopular. However, presidentialism is capable of producing other results as well.

Presidentialism, especially where the powers of the president are great and legislature's weak, can lead to executive dominance. At other times, in weak democracies, presidentialism leads to deadlock or vulnerability to coups d'etat. In fact deadlock between the legislature and executive may help induce coups. When stymied by the legislature, the president may claim the right to act independently. Such an expansion of executive power is bound to cause a legislative and public outcry. It is in this context that the armed forces often lead a coup, overthrowing the government (legislature and executive – and sometimes the courts as well). Brazil's 1964 coup described in the second case study in Chapter 1 is a good example of how this happens. Critics blame the problem of recurrent coups sometimes found in countries using presidential systems on the winner-take-all character of presidentialism (Linz and Valenzuela 1994).

Parliamentary government

Most consolidated democracies have parliamentary systems. Under a parliamentary system, the legislature (i.e., parliament) chooses the chief executive (the prime minister or premier). The prime minister, in turn, is responsible for choosing the cabinet, i.e., the senior officials of the executive branch. Collectively prime minister and cabinet are known as the "government." At its pleasure, the legislature can remove the prime minister via a vote of no confidence. **A no confidence vote** when passed by the majority is a vote taken by the legislature that requires that the government resigns and paves the way for the formation of a new government without the need to hold new elections. However, the legislature is also dependent on the executive. Commonly, the prime minister (usually acting through a constitutional intermediary) can **dissolve parliament**, i.e., call new elections. In parliamentary systems, the constitution requires a new election be held within a certain time after the last election even if there is no other reason to dissolve parliament. Some constitutions do not allow the prime minister to dissolve parliament for reasons of political expediency. In some countries, such as Sweden, regular elections fall on fixed dates, even if the legislature has been dissolved and new elections held in the intervening period. Parliaments can be unicameral or bicameral. More often than not, the lower house in bicameral systems is considerably more important than the upper house, but whether or not they are equal or nearly equal in other ways, it is the lower house that, with rare exceptions, chooses the executive on its own.

Parliamentary systems promote cooperation rather than antagonism between executive and legislature. Parliamentary government also puts a premium on party discipline. Without disciplined parties, it is hard to form a government or keep it in office. Even so, prime ministers face the ongoing task of keeping the government's supporters together. The leader of a one-party government faces the task of party management. Various factions of the party must be satisfied. Prime ministers or opposition party leaders who try to domineer over their party risk finding themselves out of office or removed as leader. A successful governing strategy must satisfy party factions by taking these factions' positions into account in submitting legislation. Success also means satisfying the ambitions of the factional leaders. As with presidential systems, the cabinet is composed primarily of ministers (US = secretaries), who head ministries (US = departments), as well as some others (ministers without portfolio). And as with presidential systems, these positions are in the gift of the chief executive. Moreover, prime ministers and presidents often choose cabinet officials for the same set of reasons: their competence, agreement with the chief executive on policy matters, friendship with the chief executive, or because they help the chief executive build political support. Using a cabinet appointment to build political support in the legislature is often a minor consideration for presidents. For prime ministers, on the other hand, political support from the legislature is paramount. Thus, using appointments to satisfy the leaders of the party's factions normally assumes priority over other motives. Prime ministers who let the other motives assume priority are often accused of acting presidentially, not as a complement within a parliamentary system. Few prime ministers stray far in this direction. And when they do, as did Britain's Margaret Thatcher in 1990, they risk being removed by their party.

The strategy of coalition management in multi-party governments follows the same sort of rules as party management in one-party governments. However, here the players are other parties and their leaders instead of the majority party's factions. Managing a coalition is almost always a trickier affair than managing a majority party. Party members are loyal primarily to their party rather than the government. With majority-party governments, there is, of course, no distinction. But with multiparty governments, the difference is critical. When a prospective prime minister puts together a government/cabinet in the first place, he or she must balance several important factors. First, the prospective government must try to get support from a majority of members of parliament (MPs). Governments with less than majority support tend to be weak and incapable of taking far-reaching initiatives. Second, a perspective government should have the smallest number of parties commensurate with obtaining a comfortable majority in parliament. All other things being equal, the greater the number of parties in the coalition, the harder the coalition is to manage and the more widely cabinet positions must be distributed to form it in the first place. Finally, the parties in the coalition should be as ideologically compatible as possible since they will not be able to put many proposals before parliament if they do not share some basic policy preferences.

The prime minister is a partisan, political official. He or she is the **head of government**. However, parliamentary systems also have another executive official who holds primarily ceremonial powers: the **head of state**. (In presidential systems, the two functions are combined in a single official, the president.) "Head of state" is the generic term for the office. In monarchies, the position is filled by a king, queen, or similar official with royal or noble rank. The office is hereditary. In republics, the head of state has the title "president." Presidents are elected, normally by the legislature or some other group of officeholders.

Heads of state represent the country at important international events where pomp and ceremony rather than policy-making or negotiation are the order of the day. They are often the officials constitutionally responsible for dissolving the lower house of the legislature or promulgating laws. Their functions are primarily non-discretionary. They do not make policy. Policy is the responsibility of the government. That is why monarchs can serve as heads of state for what are really liberal democracies. Heads of state who step too far beyond their limited role risk provoking a constitutional crisis.

In parliamentary systems, the lower house is almost always the only body responsible for appointing and removing the government. Some upper houses do play a considerable role in the legislative process, however. Some specifically represent states, provinces, or major territorial subdivisions of the country. Others, specifically the old British House of Lords, historically represented a different class than the lower house. And, as is typical for second houses, their purpose is to take a second and different look at legislative proposals presented by the government. The ability of upper houses to play a coequal or nearly coequal role varies. Hereditary or appointed houses do not have the democratic credentials to have a full share of legislative power. Thus, the House of Lords in the United Kingdom has what amounts to a suspending (delaying) veto only. On the other hand, the German *Bundesrat*, elected by the governments of the German states, has equal power with the *Bundestag*, the lower house, over legislation in specified areas, including legislation affecting the states. Japan's House of Councillors, the upper house, is chosen by the people. It must assent to bills passed by the House of Representatives if they are to become law. The Australian Senate can withhold, if it wishes, its assent from the government's budget bill. Thus, these upper houses can thwart the will of the government and the lower house in some constitutional settings. In these cases, they make legislative negotiation over bills a task above and beyond party or coalition management. Only in Italy is the parity of upper and lower houses complete; there the assent of the upper house is required to form a government.

Semi-presidentialism

The hallmark of presidentialism is a single strong executive elected by a mechanism in which the legislature has no role. However, the president has no power to dissolve congress or call new elections. The hallmark of the parliamentary system is the ability of the parliament to approve and remove the chief executive (prime minister) from office at its pleasure. Additionally, in parliamentary systems the prime minister often has the de facto power to dissolve the lower house of parliament and call new elections. Most constitutions establish a form of government that falls clearly into one category or the other, but some do not. The most famous contemporary example of semi-presidential systems is the constitution of the Fifth Republic of France. The French Fifth Republic was established in 1958 after a prolonged constitution crisis undermined the Fourth Republic.

The Fifth Republic's constitution was tailored for Charles de Gaulle, the Second World War head of the Free French government in exile. De Gaulle's status as a war hero had catapulted him into politics under the Fourth Republic, but he eventually withdrew from active participation. However, he was in 1958 the figure the country could rally around. The constitution of the Fifth Republic provided for a strong president (de Gaulle) in addition to a prime minister. The president was elected for a seven-year term (changed to five years in 2000) and is not removable from office by the legislature. As amended, the constitution provides for direct popular election of the president by majority vote of the people. However, the president, although officially the head of state, is far from just a figurehead. The president has the power to dissolve the National Assembly (the lower house) once during his term of office. The president promulgates laws and decrees, presides over the cabinet and designates the prime minister and other members of the cabinet. The actual language of the constitution makes it unclear how far the president's powers actually extend. The president's designee for prime minister and other ministers have to receive majority approval of the National Assembly although it is understood the president has a free choice in making the selection of the prime minister. By refusing his assent, the president can block laws or decrees, but he can do so only temporarily.

Under de Gaulle's leadership and that of his immediate successors, constitutional ambiguities did not matter since conservative majorities controlled both houses of parliament. The president was able to follow the strategy of dominating and bargaining with the dominant coalition in the lower house since he was, in effect, its leading member. In these circumstances, the French president had most of the advantages of a president in a presidential system and a parliamentary prime minister. The actual premier was, in effect, the president's right-hand man (or woman), serving at the president's pleasure and implementing the president's program. A quarter century after the founding of the Fifth Republic, however, an anomaly occurred. A socialist held the presidency while a rightwing majority dominated the National Assembly. This "cohabitation" as it was called did not provoke the constitutional crisis that some had feared. Instead, the strategy of accommodation has evolved.

Table 4.3 Separation of powers versus parliamentary systems

	Separation of powers	Two-party parliamentary system	Multi-party parliamentary system
Legislature chooses executive	No	Yes	Yes
Encourages unified disciplined parties	No	Yes	Yes
Main legislative check on executive	Legislature may veto or substantially modify government bills	Majority party may remove leader by majority vote	Legislature may remove executive by majority vote
Primary locus of bargaining/interest aggregation	Forming legislative coalition to pass a bill	Establishing a party program	Forming a coalition government

The coincidence of the president's and National Assembly's five-year terms (both were elected in 2002) is likely to reduce the need for cohabitation, allowing future presidents to follow a course similar to that of Charles de Gaulle.

The semi-presidential system is not unique to France. New democracies in the former Soviet Union and Central Europe have adopted versions of semi-presidential systems as have many former French colonies in Africa.

Summary

The constitutional power of executives and legislatures matters. In every democracy bargaining and checks and balances occur, but they occur in different ways in different systems. Party systems also have a considerable effect on how governments run. Parliamentary systems put a premium on party discipline and unity, which is absent in other systems. Table 4.3 compares some of the major differences between presidential systems, parliamentary systems with two parties, and parliamentary systems with more than two effective parties.

Central–local government relations

Most countries have both central governments as well as local governments. The relationship between these levels is known as **intergovernmental relations**. The division of authority between the levels can take various forms. Almost always, the central government takes care of certain matters directly: defense, foreign affairs, and the currency. Other matters can be shared with local governments or be run by local governments exclusively. Local matters often include policing, public services, schools, and local streets and roads. Either or both levels of government may undertake a variety of regulatory matters as well as the provision for economic infrastructure, such as airports, highways, and power-generation. The relationship between the central government (sometimes known as national) and local government (state, provincial, departmental, etc.) is an important one affecting the way politics is conducted as well as the quality of the services provided. The constitutional relationship between central and local government can range from unitary to confederal. At the **unitary** end of the spectrum, the central government is sovereign. Under a purely unitary system, the central government is constitutionally authorized to create and staff local governments as it sees fit. In theory, a unitary system allows the central government to delegate considerable power to the local governments it creates and have these governments popularly elected. In practice, however, the central government is more likely to keep most power in its own hands and restrict local autonomy.

On the other end of the continuum, confederal systems make the local governments sovereign. In **confederal systems/confederations**, local governments are sovereign. Local governments delegate some authority to the central government, but most important powers and the capacity to act upon the population directly remain in the hands of the local governments. Since they are sovereign, local governments may retain the power unilaterally to withdraw from the confederation. Most important central government decisions are a matter of consensus or unanimity. And important decisions of the central government, such as the raising of troops or the collection of taxes, are implemented primarily through agencies directly responsible to the local governments. Until recently, true confederations were largely historical relics. The US Articles of Confederation (1781–8), the medieval Swiss confederation, and various political leagues in ancient Greece were confederations. Confederalism today has made a comeback in the guise of the European Union (EU) and other similar though less successful systems. The EU grew out the European Coal and Steel Community of the early 1950s. It was an attempt to integrate the economies of key Western European countries. Although some statesmen of the period had advocated a federal Europe, the EU and its earlier embodiments entailed integration on a functional basis. Instead of a comprehensive government, functionalists argued that common policies ought to be made covering special policy (functional) areas – tariffs, labor standards, immigration, etc. Functionalism allowed the scope of confederal authority to expand as member governments recognized the need for further coordination (Calleo 2001: 135–51). Other confederal arrangements are still in their infancy. The Association of Southeast Asian

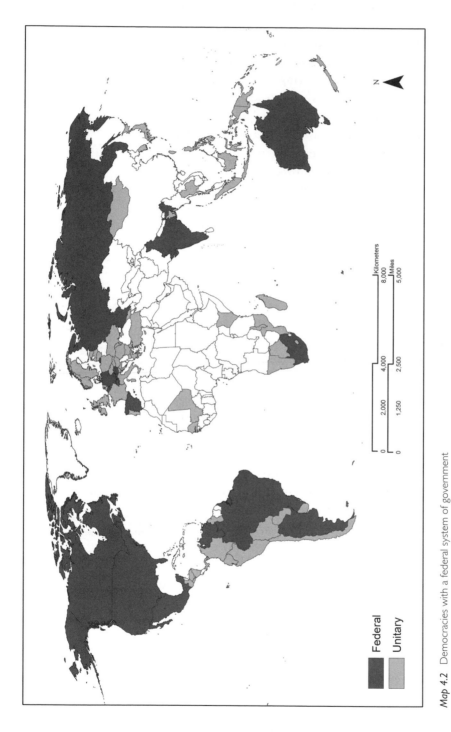

Map 4.2 Democracies with a federal system of government

Source: Environmental Systems Research Institute (ESRI) map data. Data: Hueglin and Fenna (2006)

Note: Democracies are defined as states having a democracy score of 6 or better in the Polity IV data for 2004. Polity IV ratings range from +10 (most democratic) to −10 (most authoritarian)

Nations (ASEAN) and the Common Market of the South (Mercosur) that includes most of the southernmost countries of South America are, perhaps, the most advanced.

Between unitary and confederal government, stands **federalism**. Under federalism, people delegate powers directly to two different levels of government. Both the powers granted and the integrity of each level of government is guaranteed by the constitution. Federalism offers a range of options for structures as well as the actual division of powers. But any division of powers includes three basic classifications: those powers that belong to the central government exclusively; those that are exclusively local, and those that are concurrent. **Concurrent powers** are those powers exercised by both levels of government. Most modern federal constitutions define the powers that fall into each category more precisely than does the Constitution of the United States. The American Civil War as well as the intrusive and controversial use of judicial review against the power of the government in the United States has served as object lessons for later constitution-writers. Many modern federal systems assume a greater degree of consensus between central and local governments than does the US Constitution. American federal institutions were based on mutual suspicion, a suspicion that often turned out to be well grounded. Thus, the US Constitution established **dual federalism** (also known as "competitive federalism") – complete court and tax systems on both the central (federal) and the local levels. Today many modern federal systems anticipate cooperation between the various levels of government and provide a more functional allocation of responsibilities. A single court system is sometimes used for both federal and local cases, and a single tax-collection system can be used to collect taxes for all levels of government. Where coordinated institutions prevail, the system is dubbed "**cooperative federalism**" or "administrative federalism." Under such a system typically local governments fill in the details and administer national legislation. However, where sharp differences exist between regions because of ethnic, linguistic, or religious differences competitive federalism with its characteristic antagonisms is likely to prevail either in theory or in practice (Elazar 1987).

Federalism has worked efficiently enough to allow for the evolution of quasi-federal features in unitary systems. In the 1980s, the French government undertook reforms that represented a major departure from historical precedents. The powers and structure of local governments were upgraded and the chief executive elected locally, instead of being appointed from Paris. In 1998, the new Labour government in Britain began to devolve power to regional governments in Scotland and Wales. Thus, federal systems and federal-like practices have offered politicians a range of possibilities in the contemporary world. A well-established, efficient and popularly supported system of intergovernmental relations can enhance the viability of democracy. It can allow for ethnic or religious groups with a clear territorial base to have a significant degree of autonomy while still preserving the integrity of the state. However, a federal solution is not always available. The majority at the national level may view demands for federal autonomy as the first step down a slippery slope to full independence, and the minority in question may see decentralization as insufficient.

CASE STUDY: GERMAN DEMOCRATIC INSTITUTIONS

German political experience in the last half of the twentieth century shows that institutions matter. Today Germany serves as an example of a successful transition from extreme authoritarianism to democracy, but as late as the 1960s, political scientists were not so sure that such a transition would actually be consolidated. Two of the most respected wrote: "Though the formal political institutions of democracy exist in Germany and though there is a well-developed political infrastructure ... the underlying set of political attitudes that would regulate the operation of these institutions in a democratic direction is missing" (Almond and Verba 1963: 496). German political culture and history seemed hopelessly authoritarian, and more importantly seemed to trump Germany's new constitutional arrangements. Modern Germany's one major experiment with democracy, the pre-Second World War Weimar Republic, led to the Nazi Third Reich. Yet, since the Second World War German democracy has been remarkably stable. While German prosperity and the international environment have much to do with this success, the design of German political and governmental institutions and statesmanlike decisions by German political leaders have also played a major role. The political structures of contemporary Germany have been well crafted to overcome many of the institutional flaws that the Nazis were able to take advantage of.

Germany is a federal system as the official title of the state, the Federal Republic of Germany (FRG), indicates. It is composed of sixteen *Länder* or states with substantial powers of local governance. *Länder* boundaries do not conform with any precision to the historical division of the county. No state has the disproportionate share of territory that Prussia had in the past. In fact, Prussia has been broken up into separate *Länder*, and its name has disappeared from the political map. Germany has a cooperative federal system, in which the central government decides many matters of broad policy and the states administer them. However, significant powers are assigned to the *Länder*, including education, law enforcement, religion, and cultural affairs. *Länder* governments are parliamentary in form, as is the central government. Germany is a republic whose head of state is a president elected for a five-year term by a special meeting of all members of the *Bundestag* (see below) plus an equal number of members chosen by the *Länder*. The president's duties are largely ceremonial. And although the constitution is unclear, tradition indicates he has the affirmative duty to sign legislation rather than using his refusal to sign as a de facto veto. The German Basic Law, which serves as the state's constitution, thus avoids the pitfall of a president with extensive emergency powers who might subvert the system as was the case under the Weimar Republic described in the first case study in Chapter 1.

The central government is a bicameral parliamentary system. The *Bundesrat*, the upper house, is chosen by the *Länder*, and the *Bundestag*, the lower house, is chosen by direct popular election. Unlike the US Senate, the size of a *Land's* population determines the size of its delegation in the *Bundesrat*. Those above seven million have six seats. Those between two and six million have four seats. And *Länder* with less than two million people have two seats. The *Bundesrat* works mainly through committees. The Basic Law requires its assent only on legislation in stipulated policy areas although presently this amounts to 60 percent of legislation. When the opposition controls *Länder* with sufficient votes to control the chamber, the *Bundesrat* can exercise a considerable check on the government. The *Bundestag* functions as a typical parliamentary lower house. It is elected for a four-year term. Parties are strong and disciplined.

Germany's parliamentary institutions have several distinctive features that set them apart. The German constitution gives the chancellor (prime minister) considerable power to run the government, which gave rise to the term "chancellor democracy" to describe the system. The Weimar Republic experienced government instability and prolonged periods of political maneuvering following the dismissal of the chancellor by a no confidence vote. It was easier for opponents of the government to agree to cashier it than it was to form a new one. Germany's Basic Law today provides for a "constructive no-confidence vote" that is meant to solve that problem. The *constructive vote of no-confidence* provision requires the *Bundestag* to name a new chancellor at the same time as it dismisses the old. Such a vote has been tried only twice and only succeeded once. The chancellor may attach a no-confidence resolution to ordinary legislature to gauge support in the legislature. If the no-confidence motion passes, the chancellor may ask the president to call new elections, but the chancellor cannot dissolve the *Bundestag* simply to time elections for partisan advantage. These provisions have helped the country avoid the governmental paralysis typical of the late Weimar period when the country had only weak chancellors or no chancellor at all for extended periods.

The German electoral system for the *Bundestag* is a combination of PR and SMD/PE in which the PR element predominates. It is called the "Mixed Member Proportional" (MMP) system. Approximately half of the members of the German *Bundestag*, the lower house of the national legislature, are chosen by SMD/PE. The rest are chosen by PR. Each voter has two votes: one the voter casts in the district race, the other is a straight party vote. Parties that win at least three districts outright or have a minimum of 5 percent of the PR vote receive seats according to the PR formula. The formula works in this way. The number of seats each party has won in the district races and initial PR distribution is tallied. That tally is compared to the proportion of seats that the party would be due according to its share of the PR vote (provided it has won three district seats or 5 percent of the PR vote). Extra PR seats are given to parties until the balance in the *Bundestag* reflects the party distribution in the corrected PR vote. The requirement of winning districts outright or 5 percent of the PR vote have excluded splinter parties from the national legislature. Thus, unlike the Weimar Republic, the FRG has never had a fascist or fascist-like group represented in the national legislature. The system has the virtues of limited PR plus district-by-district representation that provide a specific legislative point of access for constituents with local problems and grievances.

The German party system gave birth to two main and two minor national parties that have played important roles in forming the government: the Christian Democrats, the Social Democrats (SPD), the Free Democrats, and the Greens. Every government has included either the Christian Democrats or the SPD. For a short period in the 1970s and again after 2005, a grand coalition of both major parties governed the country. In all other periods either the Free Democrats or the Greens served as coalition partners for one of the large parties. The Christian Democrats are actually a federation of two parties. The Christian Social Union (CSU), the more conservative of the two, exists only in Bavaria. And the larger Christian Democratic Union (CDU) is organized in the rest of Germany. The CDU/CSU is the heir to the old Catholic Center Party,

Plate 4.2 Typical German ballot. Note the two columns. Each voter votes once for an individual candidate (left column) and once for a party (right column). Courtesy of German Embassy, Washington, DC.

originally formed to protect Catholic interests against government persecution sponsored by Chancellor Otto von Bismarck in the late nineteenth century. After the Second World War, it broadened its appeal to become the mainline conservative reform party, backing a social market version of the welfare state. The Social Democratic Party was originally the most important radical Marxist party in Europe. The SPD moderated its position through the first half of the twentieth century as did most socialist parties. In 1959 its Bad Godesberg dropped its references to Marxist ideology and asserted that private property would be defended and the central planning and the market would be balanced with one another. In short, the major parties have become moderate catch-all parties.

The minor parties too have been generally loyal to the system. The Free Democrats are the successor of an array of liberal parties that functioned in Germany in earlier eras. Until the rise of the Greens, they served as the natural kingmaker in the system. To the left of the CDU/CSU on civil liberties and to the right of the SPD on economic matters, the Free Democrats were seen by much of the public as natural balancers. However, the fact that they remained perilously close to the 5 percent cutoff meant that they had to tread carefully and responsibly lest voters saw them as mere opportunists and transfer their PR vote to other parties. By the 1970s, the Greens had taken over the radical left portion of the political spectrum once occupied by the socialists. Radical environmentalists, they believed that the environment had to be saved and economic growth stopped. They opposed war, nuclear weapons, and the armed forces. However, success changed the Greens. Once they began to win seats in the legislature, divisions within the party became apparent. The "*fundis*," or fundamentalists, wanted the party to continue to hold fast to its original principles. They argued that party members should not join the cabinet, and that representatives should resign after two years so that their elected substitutes could finish out the balance of the term. The "*realos*" or realists thought compromise was necessary. Better to gain some reforms than to throw away the chance for progress altogether, they argued. In the course of the 1980s and 1990s, the German Greens' radicalism waned. They began to serve as cabinet ministers at state level, and in 1998 they joined the federal cabinet as part of a coalition government with the Social Democrats. The party's anti-militarism also lessened with the end of the cold war as did its demands for participatory democracy. With the unification of formerly communist East Germany with the FRG in 1990, the (ex-communist) Party of Democratic Socialism (PDS) emerged on the political scene. It has inherited the old communist party's organization and membership, but it is more a representative of eastern interests than a strong ideological counterweight to the main parties. In mid-2007 it merged with former members of the SPD to form a leftwing opposition party, the Left Party. From time to time, neo-fascist parties have emerged that occasionally received enough votes to gain seats in some *Länder* legislatures. They have campaigned against immigrants and immigration, especially Germany's large Turkish minority. However, none has managed to surmount the 5-percent barrier to gain seats in the *Bundestag*.

The Basic Law is enforced by the Constitutional Court, which has managed to escape the sort of political controversy that has from time to time swirled about the US Supreme Court. The Constitutional Court's judges are appointed for nonrenewable twelve-year terms, half by each house of the legislature. Judges reach decisions by a two-thirds vote. Review of a law may be requested by various governmental officials even before it is passed. The Constitutional Court does not hear ordinary cases. All but one *Land* have their own constitutional courts.

The combination of federalism, a strong parliamentary government, moderate PR, a party system dominated by centrist parties, and the effective enforcement of constitutional dictates has served Germany well. The country has achieved economic prosperity, consolidated a popular welfare state, avoided governmental deadlock, advanced human rights, and promoted the legitimacy of liberal democracy. The crises and ultimate disaster of the Weimar period have been avoided. Germany's electoral system has even been copied, albeit with modifications, by Russia, Italy, Bolivia, Venezuela, Lesotho, and Japan when they reformed their own systems. Versions are also used for UK regional parliaments and New Zealand among others.

Conclusion

Institutions can make a difference. Properly regulated and motivated political parties can present clear and reasonable alternatives to voters. Executives and legislatures can work together to formulate and pass legislation that address important societal problems. Federal and sometimes even unitary structures can be used to diffuse power and authority to regions of the country providing a sense of local control and even forestalling regional demands for full independence. Yet, institutions do not come about automatically; they are a product of foresight and political bargaining. Moreover, institutions cannot work without other factors. The proper political culture and good leadership are especially important. It is easy to copy provisions from the constitutions' legislation of other countries. It is not always so easy to get borrowed institutions to function the same way they did in their original homelands. Yet, the design or reform of institutions to meet a country's specific needs is a key element in the success of liberal democracies.

Questions for further consideration

1 Within democracies, which political ideologies tend to be anti-system ideologies typical of a disloyal opposition? Why is this so?

2 Why, as democracies become more well established, have political parties moved toward the ideological center?

3 What advantages and disadvantages are the various sorts of party organizations likely to have in terms of mobilizing votes, rapidly reorganizing, and winning elections?

4 Under which sort of system is the government likely to have the easiest time passing sweeping legislation: presidentialism, multi-party parliamentary government, single-party parliamentary government? Why?

5 What are the advantages and disadvantages of the various sorts of electoral systems?

6 Why might a country establish a federal system of government? Why might it choose to establish or retain a unitary system of government?

Further reading

Thomas O. Hueglin and Alan Fenna, *Comparative Federalism*. Toronto: Broadview Press, 2006. A systematic discussion of democratic federalism across the globe.

Arend Lijphart, *Patterns of Democracy: Government Forms and Performance in Thirty-six Countries*. New Haven, CT: Yale University Press, 1999. A wide-ranging discussion of democratic institutions contrasting those which promote effective government by the majority and those that promote consensus building.

Giovanni Sartori, *Comparative Constitutional Engineering: An Inquiry into Structures, Incentives and Outcomes*. New York: New York University Press, 1997. Detailed discussion of the consequences of electoral systems and various versions of presidentialism and parliamentarism.

Ronald L. Watts, *Comparing Federal Systems* (2nd edn). Montreal: McGill-Queen's University Press, 1999. A short exposition of some of the differences in federal systems.

5 Revolution

Breakdown in the face of mass movements

Workers of all countries unite! You have nothing to lose but your chains.
(*The Communist Manifesto*)

Power tends to corrupt, and absolute power corrupts absolutely.
(Lord Acton)

In this chapter

We turn to the most cataclysmic sort of breakdown – revolution. True revolutions are relatively infrequent, but they can reverberate around the globe for decades. Revolutions occur because regimes fail on a variety of levels, losing legitimacy, governmental efficacy, and state effectiveness, even including at times the loyalty and effectiveness of their armed forces. This chapter examines the failure of each of these functional regime supports in turn. Using the comparative approach pioneered by historian Crane Brinton and the strategic perspective inspired by game theory, the chapter examines how revolutionary actors and their opponents operate. In addition, it summarizes one of the most important revolutionary ideologies of the twentieth century, Marxism–Leninism, and concludes with case studies of the Russian and Chinese Revolutions.

Introduction

To be viable, politics in liberal democracies must be conducted with tolerance and respect for the rule of law. All major political actors must make fundamental concessions that benefit other political actors. They must play by rules of a constrained and civilized "political game."
In contrast, revolutionary politics, especially in its early phases, is a blood sport played for the highest stakes. In these phases there is no consensus

about what constitutes a legitimate regime. Politics follows the rules of Hobbes's state of nature (see Chapter 1). To justify the sort of violence that frequently accompanies revolutions, modern revolutionaries hold forth the prospect of complete human liberation and a free, non-exploitative society. Such an aim is certainly attractive in principle, but most people shy away from the practical consequences of real revolution. Most people prefer the devil they know (i.e., what security and predictability they have in the existing regime) to the devil they don't know (i.e., the uncertain prospects for revolutionary violence). In short, revolutions require the right preconditions to succeed. They occur in countries where deep-seated and long-standing injustices have eroded the legitimacy of the regime and where a multiplicity of other problems has undercut the regime's ability to respond to them and govern effectively. Moreover, revolutions can only begin in earnest when the status quo has been disrupted by a crisis that demonstrates the government's inability to govern effectively. This chapter explores the dynamics of revolution – breakdown, seizure of power, radicalization, and denouement. It investigates the Bolshevik Revolution of 1917, the classic twentieth-century revolution, and its aftermath as well as the communist revolution in China. Each has had a worldwide impact. The subsequent chapter will explore more contemporary revolutionary movements – national liberation struggles and Islamist revolutionary movements.

The elements of revolutionary breakdown

A **revolution** is a change of regime brought about by a mass movement; it entails not only a change in the form of government but also transformation of the state, the military, and most often the class structure of society. By the time revolutions occur, regime breakdown has been profound and has developed on a variety of fronts. The four basic supports for regime continuity have eroded significantly. First, legitimacy, the functional support that sustains popular loyalty to the system in the face of unpopular rulers and serious policy setbacks, has been undermined. Second, in revolutionary situations state capacity is seriously undermined. The government is often unable to finance its budget or enforce law and order. As matters worsen, the de jure power of the government is often replaced by the de facto power of groups or individuals within society. Third, in the face of mounting problems, political efficacy declines. The governing elite become divided or deadlocked. In a crisis it may suffer from opportunistic defections as factions within it become part of the disloyal opposition. Finally, the armed forces become disloyal or factionalized. Or they may lose their capacity to defend the regime

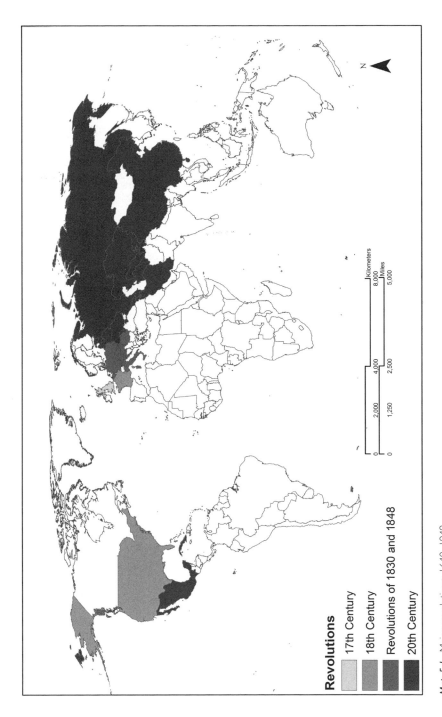

Map 5.1 Major revolutions, 1640–1949

Source: Environmental Systems Research Institute (ESRI) map data

Revolutions

- 17th Century
- 18th Century
- Revolutions of 1830 and 1848
- 20th Century

effectively because of battlefield defeat. Scholars disagree about which sort of regime failure is most critical to the outbreak of revolution; the next three sections consider each of these failures in turn.

Relative deprivation and the loss of legitimacy

Legitimacy rests on belief or political culture. In his seminal study, *Why Men Rebel*, Ted Gurr explains how popular attitudes can come to support revolutionary change (Gurr 1970: 37–91). He argues that people rebel for psychological rather than economic reasons. It is relative deprivation, not absolute deprivation, that causes rebellion and revolution by destroying the legitimacy of the **old regime** (the generic term used to describe existing regimes ripe for revolution). **Absolute deprivation** is the shortage of the basic necessities – food, clothing, shelter, and leisure time – required to lead a decent life. In traditional societies, absolute deprivation was endemic. Most of the people were illiterate, overburdened by work, and politically powerless. Yet, until their survival and the survival of their families were at stake, they did not rebel. Traditional societies were generally stable because, relative to their expectations, the poor and powerless were not deprived. They expected no more out of life than what generations of their forebears had had. They did not suffer from **relative deprivation**, i.e., the *perceived* discrepancy between what individuals think they can attain and what they believe they are entitled to. In traditional societies, this discrepancy is largely absent, but it is likely to develop as societies modernize, and sometimes it develops with a vengeance. The dramatic increase in what people expect out of life and what they expect from their government has been termed the "**revolution of rising expectations**."

Why the revolution of rising expectation occurs is easy to see. When technologies change, when people move geographically and socially, new experiences lead to changed expectations. The old order no longer appears to have the finality of a fact of nature or to be sanctioned by the will of God. Even so, modernizing societies can remain relatively stable as long as the individuals believe that they and their families are making progress. When relative deprivation is on the wane, individuals have little reason to rebel against the existing order. James C. Davies has even argued that the size of the gap between expectations and actual capacity can remain constant without significant problems so long as the gap is modest and actual capacity to meet expectations is growing. Revolution occurs when the gap suddenly increases: when expectations grow but actual capacity to achieve what one rightfully expects diminishes. When graphed, the growth and sudden decrease in capacity looks like a reverse "J" curve.

When progress is reversed, the resulting relative deprivation can have a revolutionary effect. For example, American colonists rebelled against British taxation and increased British control in the 1770s not because British exactions amounted to much but because they reversed the course of colonial fiscal and governmental autonomy (Davies 1962: 5–19).

Decline in state capacity

Others see the precipitous decline in state capacity as the essential element of breakdown. Theda Skocpol argues that revolutions can be best understood in terms of the underlying class antagonisms. The six societies she focuses on had large peasant sectors and a noble, landlord, or administrative class that drew their income from control of the land and domination of the peasantry. However, Skocpol explains the occurrence or nonoccurrence of revolution across these societies in terms of a key institution, the state and specifically state capacity (Skocpol 1979). **State capacity** is the ability of the state, the permanent administrative structure of the government, to do its job effectively. This text has considered state capacity under two separate heads both of which are relevant to Skocpol's analysis – the civil administration that collects taxes, enforces law and order, and executes governmental policy generally (state effectiveness); and the armed portion of the state, the military. The serious deficiencies in state capacity allow a revolutionary situation to develop and then get out of hand. Even illegitimate governments may be able to remain in power indefinitely if they deliver security and prosperity to the population and selectively use repression to control disloyal or semi-loyal oppositions. Even if prosperity and personal security are lacking, the populace may be unable to revolt if the regime is effective enough in its use of repression.

The state's capacity to provide security and prosperity can be undercut in a variety of ways. Because of an inefficient tax system and high or unforeseen expenditures, revenues may be inadequate, and the state may be unable to finance its own operations. If the shortfall could be remedied by a marginal increase in the rate of taxation, the shortfall might be only temporary. The problems would be cyclical, and the government could work its way through them without facing the prospect of breakdown. But in a pre-revolutionary situation, the problems are often structural. Whole classes of persons or property may be exempt from taxation, and they may guard that privilege jealously. The administrative system for collecting taxes may be honeycombed with inefficiencies and personnel who contribute to these inefficiencies may be entrenched in their positions. These sorts of structural problems require the government to make hard choices. It can allow state functions to atrophy or it can attempt to raise more revenue. The attempt to raise more money may, in turn, cause a rupture among the ruling elite or place the society under such pressure that it is ripe for rebellion. Neither bodes well for the stability of the government.

The state may be unable to enforce law and order. One of the basic functions of the state is to define and protect the rights to property and to settle property disputes as they arise. If the state is too weak or inefficient to do this, it risks ceding de facto authority to a host of private local groups strong enough to act in their own interest. The state must also protect people's lives and provide for their personal security. As with property, the failure to protect persons risks the practical loss of authority and power to non-state groups. The state's military capacity may also be seriously deficient. Defeat in war can be a clear indication of the deficiency. Yet, if defeat is simply a matter of poor leadership, inadequate training, improper equipment, or simply bad luck, it probably does not presage a revolutionary upheaval. On the other hand, specific inadequacies may be symptomatic of deeper structural problems. Leadership may be vested in a class of people unable or unwilling to change. The training of the troops may be a byproduct or the leadership structure and entrenched recruitment practices. The continued use of traditional weaponry may be the result of the predilections of the established military class. Even the purchasing modern weaponry and establishing of modern military schools may not fix the problem unless entrenched practices and privileges of established military elites are rectified.

Many state deficiencies may be only latent until a serious crisis occurs. Defeat in a foreign war, a foreign invasion, famine, or other natural disasters may put pressure on the state that it cannot respond to adequately. When that happens, non-state actors begin to usurp state functions. In effect, a system of **dual power** develops. Moreover, serious state failures in the face of calamitous events can destroy the old regime's legitimacy. Masses of people are unwilling to support the old system even when they had been previously inclined to do so. Revolutionaries can use the old regime's loss of legitimacy and expand the system of dual power to first undermine and then overthrow the old regime.

Lack of governmental efficacy and the emergence of a revolutionary crisis

Charles Tilly takes an essentially structural approach to revolution, explaining the dynamics of breakdown from the perspective of elites who control the government and mass actors who desire change (Tilly 1978). Tilly's explanation of the social dynamics of revolution dovetails nicely

with the notion that governmental efficacy is a key element in assuring
the continuity of any regime. The government (what Tilly calls the
"polity"), the people actually in charge of decision-making, play a key role
in maintaining the political system. They must address the pressing
problems the political system faces. But sometimes governments do not
address the pressing issues that society as a whole wants solved. Worse,
sometimes governments are so internally divided they cannot reach
decisions at all. It is important to remember that no regime, even Dahl's
closed hegemony (Chapter 1), is composed of a single homogeneous cadre
of insiders. A regime and its government, in fact, can be viewed as a
coalition of insiders, elite groups or individuals who share in the major
benefits and decision-making authority of the regime. The elite may
include high-ranking governmental and party officials, titled noblemen,
senior military officers, large industrialists, or large landowners. The
character of the elite depends on the particular regime involved.

In well-run authoritarian systems, elites need to pay minimal attention
to the demands and interests of groups outside the elite circle. A coalition
of elites decides upon policy and reaps the benefits. However, when the
system of intra-elite bargaining breaks down, when an authoritarian
regime is under pressure from below, ruptures may develop among elite
groups. Members of these groups may defect from the ruling coalition.
Some groups or individuals may attempt to build a new coalition with
hitherto non-elite groups to insure their own survival or freedom of
action. New actors emerge as groups within society mobilize.
Mobilization occurs as individuals who share common demographical
characteristics or interests begin to recognize them and act in common.
Mobilization can entail the formation of informal or formal groups, or
engaging in collective actions such as demonstrations and strikes. When
they reach sufficient intensity and duration, such mass mobilizations
become the basic stuff of revolution. They destabilize the government and
make it impossible for the old regime to continue unaltered.

Revolution occurs as risk and cost calculations of elite and non-elite
groups begin to tilt against the old regime. Non-elite outsiders calculate
the risks of mobilization are less than remaining passive. Elite insider
groups begin to defect as the relative cost of doing so decreases. These
effects can snowball leading to the outbreak of revolution. At the core of
this process is the inability of the ruling elite to manage its own affairs
and respond to external pressures that need to be managed before they get
out of control. There is an additional implication in this: reform of a
repressive regime can be dangerous. As an authoritarian regime liberalizes
and attempts to buy mass support, it may unwittingly make mass
mobilization directed against it easier. "Men must either be caressed or

annihilated," the Renaissance Italian political theorist Niccolò Machiavelli cautioned (Machiavelli 1940: 9). His advice certainly seems to apply to modern authoritarian regimes. No time is so dangerous or potentially unstable as when a bad regime starts to reform.

Summary

Revolutionaries, both masses and elites, can overthrow the old regime only if it is undermined from within. Scholars have pointed to three sources of the old regime's decay: loss of legitimacy, erosion of state capacity, and lack of governmental efficacy. Weakness in one area may further erode the regime's capacity in the others. This can leave an authoritarian system confronted by a hostile emerging new class and a revolutionary vanguard (an emerging counter-elite) ripe for revolution.

The revolutionary vanguard's pivotal role

The strategy and role of the revolutionary vanguard, the counter-elite that winds up leading a revolution, requires further elaboration since it is the presence of such leadership that turns revolts in true revolutions. The vanguard not only marshals mass discontent to overthrow the old regime; it provides the core of a new ruling elite. And its ideology shapes new structures of power.

The nature of revolutionary vanguard

Successful revolutions lead to real, permanent institutional and social change. A new class assumes power. To do so, it must have the capability of acting and organizing. Revolutions need a cadre of leaders with a vision of a new political order and how to bring it about. True revolution is a relatively modern phenomenon. Until philosophers or religious thinkers provided a comprehensive critique of the existing order and a vision of what might replace it, true revolutions were next to impossible. However, with the advent of that critique, rebellion can become revolution. In other words, revolution has both the energy of a mass revolt and the conscious direction provided by a comprehensive theory of politics and political change. In effect, revolutions are revolts with ideological leadership.

Thus, the pivotal actor in revolution is the cadre of leaders, the revolutionary vanguard or simply the vanguard; it arises during the first phase of any revolutionary process. The **vanguard** (cf. Lenin 1902) is the set of people that provides the leadership that distinguishes a revolution from a mere revolt. Vanguards consist of the most radical elements of the rising new class and defectors from the old governing class that champion radical change. The vanguard opposes the old regime, i.e. the status quo, root and branch, and constitutes the disloyal opposition to the old regime. Members of the vanguard are extremists. They serve as the catalyst for revolution; they provide new ideas and standards by articulating an ideological position that directly challenges the old regime's legitimacy and fitness to rule. And it mobilizes new political actors that were hitherto largely passive in the face of official power. The vanguard can be almost entirely informal, such as the committees of correspondence were during the American Revolution, or it may be a disciplined and centrally directed elite party, such as Lenin's Bolsheviks in Russia. Whether or not revolutionary leaders are tightly organized and provide detailed direction to a mass movement, they serve as its inspiration and possess moral authority because of their courage and foresight.

The vanguard may be unified or divided organizationally, but its members are distinguishable from the loyal opposition, the reformers who are basically satisfied with the old regime provided it makes some fundamental changes. Reformers are prone to compromise; the vanguard drives the revolution forward. Reformers mute differences between those factions supporting the old regime and those seeking to overthrow it. The vanguard attempts to exaggerate them, to polarize the situation. It casts issues in black-and-white terms. The struggle to overthrow the existing old regime is a struggle of good versus evil in which there can be no neutrals. The vanguard's élan, self-confidence, and competence must be the polar opposite of what they hope to find in the forces defending the old regime. Before the revolution, to the eyes of the old regime's establishment, the vanguard often appears as nothing much more than a hopelessly quixotic grouping of ne'er-do-wells. To rise above this, the vanguard needs an ideology accurate and sophisticated enough to guide them about how to take advantage of popular discontents. At the same time, this ideology must also be simple and appealing enough to rally the new class and the general population to the cause of the revolution.

Mobilizing the discontented

Beyond ideology, revolutionaries need organizational principles as well as strategies and tactics that will allow their organization to make use of its ideology to exploit the old regime's weaknesses and mobilize the population against it. By the same token, they must outmaneuver mere reformers who are willing to accept the existing system provided that certain key elements of it are changed. The vanguard must mobilize a mass base. It is the people en masse enraged at the injustices they have suffered that provide the energy to overthrow the old regime and build a new one. Yet, the loyalty of a mass base cannot be taken for granted; it must be cultivated just as parties in the democracies cultivate particular constituencies. The vanguard presents itself as its constituency's representative, not in the legal but in the moral sense. "We're on your side; we act for your interests," is the message they must send. Furthermore, this message must be credible. If it is to be so, the vanguard must develop themes that resonate with their would-be constituency. And the message must be sincere. This does not mean that the vanguard's ideology is immediately comprehensible to their constituents. The vanguard is expected to be more sophisticated and farsighted, but the vanguard must believe that they are acting in the interest of their would-be constituents, and their would-be constituents must come to believe it too.

The vanguard's first task is to undermine the old regime and establish its own credibility. It must do this before it can hope to replace the old regime physically. This requires the use of persuasion. And persuasion requires propaganda (the systematic propagation of political ideas). At some point, however, mere persuasion will not be enough. At some point, the propaganda of the word must be matched by the "**propaganda of the deed.**" The term is usually associated with terrorism and is used to refer to an act of political violence – an assassination, an act of sabotage, or some other act that undermines the prestige of the government. But in the broader sense propaganda of the deed is any action that allows the vanguard to put its money where its mouth is, as it were. Mass demonstrations, strikes, success in elections, or any other set of actions that demonstrates the vanguard is an important political actor will serve. Propaganda of the deed shows that revolutionaries are a force to be reckoned with and unmasks the government as weak and oppressive.

Ultimately the vanguard must command sufficient force to topple the government. Methods of actually seizing power have varied. Until midway through the twentieth century, revolutionaries seized power in the capital. An armed uprising led by a radical vanguard was the normal mechanism. However, as early as 1895, Friedrich Engels, the close associate of Karl Marx, doubted the viability of such an approach in the future (Engels 1895). Modern firearms, he argued, would doom any revolt by a poorly armed populace. Moreover, capital cities had been redesigned to provide for broad thoroughfares that made it impossible for rebels to barricade the streets and hold out against government forces. The Russian Revolution of 1917 was, in fact, one of the few major twentieth-century revolutions in which the decisive military action occurred in the capital. The communist revolutions in China and Vietnam, and the Cuban Revolution, followed a different pattern. Revolutionaries began the military struggle that would bring them to power in the countryside. Would-be leftist revolutionaries since then have often been attracted to this later model. But whatever the military means and strategy chosen, the old regime and other contenders have to be driven from the field – usually militarily.

The classical theory of revolutionary development

Revolutionaries often believe that the emergence of a perfect society is possible or even historically inevitable. In his analysis of the English Revolution of the 1640s, and the later American, French and Russian Revolutions, the noted historian, Crane Brinton (Brinton 1965), took a contrary view. In these four revolutions, he observed a revolutionary cycle in which the results were far from utopian or even optimal. Brinton divided the revolutionary process into four phases. The first phase of revolution takes place before the seizure of power and the revolution proper. In fact, it may be underway decades in advance of the seizure of power. The first phase involves the breakdown of the old regime. Over time the old regime increasingly loses legitimacy and demonstrates its own incompetence. Elite individuals defect intellectually if not politically, developing theories that are at odds with the old regime's principles and practices. The old regime is faced with a worsening set of structural problems but does not recognize them, or recognizing them, it is unable to deal with them. A crisis develops and events spin out of control. Military defeat, a financial crisis, or mass mobilizations confront the ruling elite with a difficult decision. They falter. Leaders and movements already latent now become active, taking de facto power into their own hands and demanding recognition as the legitimate government. Unable to deal with the challenge, the old regime collapses or is defeated militarily. The initial phase of the revolution ends with the fall of the old regime.

In the second phase, the moderates (reformers who constituted the loyal opposition to the old regime) take over, and the struggle between them and the radicals (the true revolutionaries) begins. Once the old regime breaks down, the moderates become revolutionary leaders who have modest expectations for revolutionary change and are willing to make compromises with members of the old establishment. In the case of Brinton's four revolutions, these included leaders who favored constitutional monarchy or a republican government of limited powers. The radicals, on the other hand, have an almost utopian vision of the future, and they want to establish a new status quo that will end the vices of the past once and for all. The moderates are ill-equipped to govern in the midst of the chaotic situation they have inherited. Diehard defenders

Plate 5.1 Delacroix's *Liberty Leading the People*, a celebration of the revolution of 1830 in France.

of the old regime refuse to compromise. State capacity, already eroded, collapses almost completely. The radicals and mass movements continue to press for more thoroughgoing change. The situation is one of dual power. The moderates control the government and a much-diminished state while the radicals control the streets as well as assemblies and committees that exercise de facto power in much of the country.

In the end, the moderates are outmaneuvered. They lose legitimacy, lack effective state and military support, and often cannot reach efficacious decisions within the government. The radicals either vote them out, compel them to resign, or remove them by force of arms.

When the radicals take over, the third phase of the revolution that Brinton labels the "reign of terror and virtue" begins. In this third phase, the revolutionary vanguard composed of leaders pushing for radical change gets its opportunity to change society according to its vision. The new government casts aside the moderates' half-measures. Constitutional checks on the government disappear. The radical government destroys the old social and political structures and creates new ones. The new regime's enemies are arrested and many executed. Even the trivial formalities associated with the old regime often change. "Citizen" or "comrade" replaces "Mister" or "Madam." The old established religion – in some cases religion itself – comes under attack. In Russia and France even the calendar was changed. But as the third phase advances, the revolution begins to eat its own children. Radical factions fall out with one another. Accustomed to using extreme rhetoric and extreme measures, the victors charge their fellow radicals with treason, purge them from the government, and often execute them. The violent infighting continues until a victorious faction decides that the internecine violence must end. The end of terror sets the stage for the last revolutionary phase.

The fourth and final phase Brinton called the "Thermidorean reaction." The name is taken from the month of the new French revolutionary calendar when a group of radicals overthrew Robespierre, the principal radical leader. Robespierre's radical opponents had not intended to usher in moderation, but that was what happened. The government's reliance on violence diminishes and groups demobilize. By and large, the society finds some kind of normalcy. The new post-revolutionary status quo winds up with many of the features of the old regime that the vanguard wished to expunge. Inequality, injustice, and the abuse of power remained although in an altered form. In short, the revolutions Brinton analyzed moved from right to left, then slightly back to the right again. The revolutionary process he described is one of raw power both physical and psychological.

Some implications

Things have not changed much since Brinton first developed his theory. Although most revolutionaries are never able to get their revolutions off the ground, many successful revolutions do follow the pattern laid out by Brinton, including the more recent revolutions that we consider in the next chapter. If there is a change over time, more recent revolutionaries have been more self-conscious about their choice of strategies and tactics than their pre-twentieth-century predecessors. Success in making a revolution still requires the skillful combination of persuasion and brute force and an ability to recognize opportunities. The clumsy or exclusive application of either force or persuasion is likely to lead to defeat. This is true both for the old regime as well as the revolutionary vanguard, but established governments have a margin for error that the vanguard normally lacks. And, in the end, the radicals' utopian designs are frustrated.

Today many societies today find themselves beset with would-be revolutionaries with a variety of often conflicting utopian visions. For well-organized regimes with adequate functional support, these revolutionary groups are usually little more than a nuisance. Yet, where these institutional supports are weak or nonexistent, revolutionary agitation and even revolutionary violence may constitute a real threat. Even so, weak regimes may face a prolonged period of instability rather than outright revolutionary change. Revolutionary challenges may, in fact, lead to other political developments, such as the growth of authoritarianism, coups d'etat, or even state failure. Hence, the dynamics of revolutionary phase I are important in their own right regardless of whether an outright revolution ensues.

Communism: the twentieth century's revolutionary paradigm

Communism – or Marxism–Leninism – was the quintessential revolutionary ideology of the twentieth century. Today the revolutionary communist parties in Nepal, India, and Colombia that are leading insurgencies against established governments are tiny remnants of the once-powerful movement that shook the globe. Yet, the theory and practice of communist revolution and communist government still shape politics in much of the world. Twentieth-century communists used the theories of Karl Marx to explain what they believed were the deterministic laws of history. They relied on Vladimir Ilyich Lenin, the founder of the first modern communist party, for many organizational principles and for the strategy and tactics of making revolutions.

Communist theory: Karl Marx and revolution

While contemporary social scientists attempt to take a dispassionate view of revolution, Karl Marx (1818–1883), the German philosopher and economist, asserted that the point of philosophy was not to understand the world but to change it (Marx 1969: 15). He presented a concrete theory of how and why revolutions occur that was calculated to inspire revolutionaries by explaining the weakness of their enemies, the justice of their cause, and the inevitability of their victory. Marx's influence was considerable throughout the twentieth century and remains so even today. Marx recognized that new ideologies, new political actors, and new technologies were all part of the revolutionary process. However, he put the primacy on new technologies as the underlying cause. Any given technology required a particular form of social organization, a class system, to support it. Slaves, for example, could work in plantation agriculture, but slavery was ill-suited to an industrial society. The dominant classes that controlled the means of production in each society always developed ideas – political, religious, philosophical, and cultural – that supported their position. As technology changed, new classes emerged and became important. As this change advanced, the new class became more self-confident and developed ideas of its own that supported its own interests. But the old elite would use all means at their disposal to cling to power and attempted to thwart the new class's rise to political power. Eventually the vital new class would have to use violence to force the decrepit old ruling class aside. Thus, social and political transformation almost always involved revolutionary upheavals.

Taking the long view, Marx looked forward to a communist revolution that would empower the industrial working class and produce a society of freedom, abundance, and equity that relied on free consent rather than force. This society, called "communism," would be the final stage of human history. Ultimately all human beings would live in a global communist society. All the means of production would be owned in common. And all instruments of repression – the military, police, courts, and prisons – would disappear. Marx thought that the communist revolution would occur in the most advanced industrial (capitalist) societies and spread outward from there. At the time he was writing, these societies did seem ripe for revolution. The first hundred years of the Industrial Revolution produced immense inequalities and intense human suffering. It seemed that the newly formed industrial working class, legally powerless and in misery under the rules of the old regime, was at the end of its tether and ripe for revolution, which Marx believed his own theories would help bring about.

Marx supported his conclusions about the inevitability of a communist revolution and communist society on the basis of an elaborate and comprehensive theory. Marx's influence on his contemporaries and later revolutionaries was enormous because his ideology seemed to explain everything in a well-integrated, systematic way that appealed both to intellectuals who would form a revolutionary vanguard and the working class and other dispossessed classes who would have to form the mass base of a communist revolutionary movement. Marx borrowed ideas freely from others, but wove them into a coherent system all his own. Marx's ideology had three major elements: scientific materialism, the dialectic, and economic determinism. The theoretical principle of **materialism** propounded by Marx asserted that matter was the only thing in the universe. Everything else – thought, human culture, spirit – was simply the product of material forces. According to Marx, materialism was a fundamental principle of science. Science did not prove materialism was true. Rather, no one could develop any truly scientific theory without first accepting materialism as a bedrock philosophical principle. Marx's scientific materialism often sounds strange to those familiar with the contemporary philosophy of science, where materialism is not normally treated as a metaphysical first principle as it was with Marx, but merely a methodological starting point. According to the common contemporary view, natural science investigates the material world because that's its subject matter, not necessarily because matter is the only thing that exists (Popper 2002: 3–16). Marx, in contrast, was dogmatic about his materialism. God, the soul, any purely spiritual substance did not really exist. To entertain the possibility that such substances might exist was to be unscientific. In other words, Marx's "science" was atheistic.

Marx saw freedom as the end of all human action. People were always struggling to control their own destiny. True freedom, however, was multifaceted. Slavery, of course, was incompatible with freedom. So too was despotic government, or any system in which decisions were made contrary to the will and interests of any of its members. But freedom also entailed the ability to make effective choices. People who were denied the physical resources to lead a decent life were not truly free regardless of their official legal or political status. Finally, freedom required knowledge and virtue, or, as Marx put it, a correct "**consciousness**." People could not be free if they were enslaved to ignorance, superstition, or physical or psychological addictions. Marx believed that, the march toward freedom was a historical process that moved by fits and starts. He called this process the **dialectic**. History was divided into stages. In each historical stage or epoch, there was a primary class conflict, or **principal contradiction**: for example, master versus slave in antiquity, or lord versus serf in the Middle Ages. The power of the oppressed class in each stage eventually grew until the oppressed overthrew the old regime and created a new society in their own image, but the new society too was founded on a contradiction and would be replaced in another revolution until the complete freedom for all was implemented and there were no classes.

Economic laws governed the march of history. Once discovered, these laws would accurately predict which classes would grow weaker and which more powerful as a society developed economically. The notion that general movement of human history could be formulated in terms of economic laws is called "**economic determinism**." For Marx, **capitalism** – the economic system based on private property and free markets – was the next to last stage of human history. Although Marx discussed the whole historical dialectic in general throughout his writings, he explained specifically how the capitalist system worked in his monumental work, *Das Kapital*. In it he laid out what he claimed to be the scientific laws that explained how capitalism's collapse would occur. With the collapse of capitalism, the stage would be set for the communist revolution and the rise of a non-exploitative society. These laws were not only logically consistent and similar to those of pro-capitalist economists of the day, but in Marx's time they seemed to accord with observable facts, as Marx himself painstakingly pointed out.

Capitalism had replaced the old economic order of feudalism. It had immensely increased the productive capacity of human beings, spurred the development of science and technology, and laid the material groundwork for communism. According to Marx, the secret of capitalism's early success, as well as its ultimate collapse, was the form of property known as "**capital**." Capital is a dynamic, two-sided entity. Capital is productive property – land, tools, buildings, machinery, in fact, any object that can be put to use in producing goods for sale. And capital is also money, or at least amounts of money sufficiently large to allow its possessor (the capitalist) to purchase enough productive property to engage in a successful business enterprise. Capital (money) is used to buy productive property and labor. Capitalism works in this way. The capitalist uses productive property plus the labor of others to generate commodities (goods for sale). These commodities are then sold, generating more capital (money). Successful enterprises generate profit (what Marx called "**surplus value**"), which constitutes an increase in the capitalist's capital. Marx saw capitalism as an incalculable improvement over earlier forms of production, which depended upon nature's reproductive cycle. Capitalist production is largely independent of that cycle and adds to the wealth and productive power of society much more quickly than other forms of production. Thus, it enhances human capacity to conquer nature, and so provides the material basis for future human liberation.

However, in its day-to-day workings, as seen in the laws of capitalist accumulation, capitalism is much less admirable. As capitalism develops, the need for capital increases; the number of capitalists grows fewer and fewer; the number of workers grows greater and greater; profits decline; economic crises worsen, and industrial workers (the class to which almost everyone eventually belongs) barely survive at the subsistence level (Marx 1965: 1, 564–712). In effect, in the long run capitalism was doomed to collapse under its own weight. At some point, in desperation the workers would rise up and overthrow it. Marx's early followers saw the economic crises of the late nineteenth century as a confirmation of Marx's theory. Latter-day adherents saw the First World War, the Great Depression of the 1930s, the Second World War, the Vietnam War, among others, as heralding the final death throes of capitalism. The collapse of the Soviet Union and European Communist states has dampened the ardor of present-day Marxists, however.

Lenin and revolution

If Marx provided the grand theories that inspired many modern revolutionaries, it was Vladimir Ilyich Lenin (1870–1924) who provided the practical advice about how to make a revolution. Lenin and the communist party he founded were dedicated to "seizing the day" – making use of opportunities as they presented themselves. Lenin was a dogmatic Marxist. He was unwilling to change any of Marx's analysis in the slightest. Yet, in many ways he modified Marx substantially, setting the stage for the creation of an elite-run repressive state that Marx would have detested.

The vanguard party

The vanguard party appeared in Chapter 4 as a distinctive – and undemocratic – form of party organization. The concept of the vanguard party is perhaps Lenin's greatest contribution to revolutionary practice. His principle of a closed, self-perpetuating elite guiding a broad mass movement has been adopted by other revolutionaries as well as counter-revolutionaries. Marx had seen the industrial working class (the proletariat) as the real protagonist, the chief political actor, of the final stage of world history. Yet, even he recognized that leadership was necessary. In the *Communist Manifesto*, Marx and Friedrich Engels had written:

> The Communists ... are ... the most advanced and resolute section of the working class parties of every country ... they have over the great mass of the proletariat the advantage of a clear understanding of the line of march, the conditions, and the ultimate general results of the proletarian movement.
>
> (Marx 1977: 231)

Marx did not write much more about the proper structure of the party, but for Lenin this was enough. Lenin used Marx's brief description to establish the theory of the "**vanguard party**," a party that would in fact control rather than lead the working class and the entire society.

Following the lead of Marx and Engels, Lenin argued that a true communist party had two major features. First, its members would have to be thoroughly dedicated to the party's goals. Members would have to be willing to sacrifice everything else – careers, families, their own identities, their lives – if required to do so by the party. They would have to be, to use Lenin's own words, "professional revolutionaries." And second, the party would be the most theoretically advanced section of the proletarian movement. Party members would have to have a solid intellectual grasp of communist theory. They would have to be revolutionary intellectuals. For Lenin, "working-class consciousness" was the scientific understanding of the world as Karl Marx had elaborated it and as he, Lenin, had added to it. The party for Lenin was the true repository of that working-class consciousness. In short, Lenin replaced the working class with the communist party as the force directing the revolutionary process. The working class was to be led (in reality manipulated and controlled) by the party. The party could establish and maintain the link its members had to one another and provide for unity of action by adhering to a centralized yet flexible organizational structure. In 1902, when Lenin first sketched out this structure, he envisioned a central committee composed of about a dozen members, who would serve as the party's high command. The central committee would decide on the course of action that was to be followed by the rest of the party organization. In pre-revolutionary Russia, the rest of the party organization was composed of agents in the principal towns and districts of the country. Their identity as members of the Bolshevik Party (the name Lenin's group assumed after 1903) would usually not be known.

The party was small in size, but it would lead the masses since no revolution was possible unless the masses supported it. However, the party would not be subject to direction by ordinary workers, who, by and large, lacked a scientific understanding of society and history. These ordinary workers usually had what Lenin termed "trade union consciousness" at most. They saw no further than the need for a strike against specific employers to improve their pay and working conditions. It was the duty of the party's agents to follow the party line, to carry out agitation and propaganda, and, by so doing, to provide direction to the working-class movement. Propaganda consisted of efforts to publicize the party's position on matters without having that position necessarily identified as the position of the party. Agitation was organizing for action – local or general strikes, protests, etc. In short, agents were to educate the workers and mobilize them and others behind the party and its positions. The agents were to follow the orders they received; it was not their function, as agents, to deliberate about whether those orders were sound. Agents often worked through front organizations – unions, student groups, and professional associations – either formed by others or by the party itself. These organizations had, or aspired to have, a mass base. Thus, the party would have the best of both worlds. It would be an elite organization with working-class consciousness and totally dedicated members. At the same time, it would have a mass following (Lenin 1902).

In theory the central committee was under the direction of the party congress, an intermittent body that met to establish the party program, set the overall party line, and chose members of the central committee. All the members of the party would, in theory, choose this party congress. In practice, in pre-revolutionary Russia, representative party congresses were impossible to hold. When party congresses met, they were forced to meet outside the country. Hence, for all practical purposes, it was the central committee that directed the party. This form of organization was quite effective in tsarist Russia, where the secret police were often bent on tracking down and arresting Bolsheviks. When the situation permitted revolutionary action, the Bolshevik Party, despite its small size (around 5,000, the smallest of the major revolutionary groups), was able to act in a disciplined and coordinated manner. Lenin's Bolshevik Party explicitly became the model for all parties that joined the Third (Communist) International that was formed in 1918, almost immediately after the Bolshevik Revolution in Russia.

The multi-staged revolution

Originally, the communist party's constituency was the proletariat. Marx had been clear on this point. No other class could serve as the vehicle for human liberation; his analysis of capitalism had demonstrated that. The change of setting for revolution from the most advanced capitalist countries to economically backward Russia where Lenin wished to make a revolution created problems. How could communists make a communist revolution in a country where the proletariat was small in size and immature in development and where there had been no "bourgeois-democratic [i.e., capitalist] revolution"? Lenin's solution was to rely in part on the peasantry. Normally dismissed by Marxists as the "reserve army of reaction," Lenin saw Russian peasants as a revolutionary force. They were at odds with the old order, desiring land and power that that order denied them. And they constituted a majority of the population in turn-of-the-century Russia. Only after the bourgeois-democratic revolution that gave them control of land, Lenin argued, would the peasantry assume a reactionary character.

To take advantage of peasant opposition to the old regime, Lenin proposed a two-stage strategy for coming to power. Stage one would be the bourgeois-democratic revolution made by the proletariat and the peasantry and led by the party. That revolution would establish the **"revolutionary dictatorship of the proletariat and the peasantry,"** the equivalent to the bourgeois republic that was that revolution's normal outcome. But once the bourgeois democratic revolution succeeded, the party and the workers would abandon the peasantry. Peasants wanted their own privately held land. They had no desire to see the advent of true communism and the emergence of a classless society. Hence, a second revolution was necessary: the true communist revolution. This second revolution would not require another violent seizure of power. Already in power, all the party would need to do was shift course and expel any peasant representatives from the government. This would usher in the "**dictatorship of the proletariat,**" again, under the control of the communist party (Lenin 1935).

Lenin's flexibility in choosing allies served the communist party well. In Russia, the Bolsheviks seized power in the center after having undermined the provisional government and having backed peasant demands, and after that it fought a civil war to consolidate power. In China over thirty years latter, the Chinese party won its revolution after having mobilized the peasantry during a twenty-year struggle against the Nationalist government. The Chinese went further than Lenin, actually recruiting the peasantry into the communist party itself. Communist parties in Southeast Asia followed strategies similar to the Chinese. This led Asian communists and parties that adopted this approach to speak of the "toiling masses" or the "workers and peasants" as the group for which they were the vanguard instead of simply the "industrial working class." Although it blurred the theoretical clarity of Marx's original analysis, this shift was almost pure gain. It allowed the party to speak to and sometimes for masses of dissatisfied people in virtually every country across the globe.

CASE STUDY: THE RUSSIAN REVOLUTION

For much of the twentieth century, communist revolutions threatened to engulf large portions of the world. The Bolshevik Revolution in November 1917 set the stage for what was to follow. Alone among radicals, Lenin and the Bolsheviks managed to make and consolidate revolutionary power in the aftermath of the First World War. This gave them immense prestige. Radical socialist parties joined Lenin's Third (Communist) International or Comintern in droves. The Comintern had strict rules requiring membership and parties had to follow the principles of organization laid down by Lenin exactly. It also required strict loyalty to its party line that coincided with that of Russia's Soviet government. Thus, the revolution in Russia influenced other countries' politics both directly and indirectly.

Phase I: the breakdown

Lenin's analysis summarized above proved essentially correct. Pre-revolutionary Russia was a backward capitalist society that had not had a bourgeois-democratic revolution that would sweep aside the old tsarist regime and lay the groundwork for full capitalist development and later communism. Instead, the tsar, a traditional autocrat, was head of both state and church and wielded effective power over the government. The Russian government realized that it had to modernize both its economy and state, but had only achieved limited success. Until virtually the end, it remained divided between westernizers who wanted to embrace the political, social, and economic principles of the West, and Slavophiles who wanted only limited changes in traditional practices. In the end, this indecision and vacillation in policy would prove fatal. The tsarist regime had bought itself time by making its peace with local and international capitalists, encouraging industrialization and foreign investment, and suppressing radical labor and peasant movements. Lenin's Bolsheviks were just one of a host of groups who wanted substantial change in the old regime. One of the most important of these, the Social Revolutionaries (SRs), divided into various factions and worked among the peasantry. The Marxists (Social Democrats) had two major camps. The more moderate Marxists (Mensheviks) worked among the working class as Marx prescribed but had a more open form of organization typical of Marxist mass parties in Western Europe. Lenin's Bolsheviks were the smallest of all the major revolutionary groups. The Bolsheviks saw this period as an opportunity for the party to strengthen itself while it awaited the crisis of the old regime to mature. Moderate constitutional monarchists and republicans also sought change, although they wanted much less radical changes than did the SRs and Marxists.

Russia's defeat in the 1904–5 Russo-Japanese War led to an aborted revolution. The tsar retained most of his power but was forced to share some legislative power with a Duma elected on the basis of a restricted franchise. Russia's entry in World War I, however, set the stage for the old regime's ultimate collapse. Military and administrative incompetence led to two and a half years of military disasters and famine. By March of 1917, civil order had broken down. Solders and sailors had seized control of their units and purged or executed their officers. Workers had seized control of factories. And peasants had seized land. Local soviets – de facto governments – controlled much of the country. The tsar attempted to resign in favor of the crown prince, but support for tsarism had come to an end. The old regime had suffered a severe deflation in legitimacy, state capacity, and its ability to make effective autonomous decisions. Tsar Nicholas II abdicated, and the Provisional Government based on the old Duma assumed power. In sum, the tsarist regime had failed on all levels. It had lost its legitimacy to a welter of competing ideologies; it had failed to adequately modernize its state and army. As cascading defeats in war collapsed the military, the tsarist elite could not hit upon an acceptable political solution to mounting popular pressure. Finally, the once-loyal opposition took the lead in a new revolutionary government.

Phase II: March 1917 – the moderates come to power

The Provisional Government made two fateful errors. It decided to continue the disastrous war even though the war was the proximate cause of the old regime's collapse. And it decided to postpone consideration of the land question until a constituent assembly could be elected. In addition, the Provisional Government faced a situation of dual power. While they nominally constituted the government, considerable power was in the hands of local soviets. For much of the war Lenin and most of the central committee had been in exile in Switzerland. German intelligence, knowing Lenin and the Bolsheviks' anti-war views, decided to spirit him into Russia so that his agitation could undermine the Provisional Government's war effort. Upon his arrival, Lenin followed a modified two-stage revolution strategy. Although a capitalist government was already in place, the peasantry remained potential allies of the Bolsheviks since the land issue was still not settled.

The Bolsheviks used the slogan, "Peace, Land, Bread!" to undermine the Provisional Government. They urged "All power to the Soviets!" to further erode the Provisional Government's legitimacy. Without the support of an effective state or army, beset by radical agitation and dual power, the Provisional Government was unable to act. The Bolshevik Revolution took place in November 1917. The revolution was really a coup d'etat against the seat of the Provisional Government in the tsar's Winter Palace in Petrograd (St. Petersburg). The coup was followed by a protracted multisided civil war that gave the Bolsheviks effective control of the whole country by the early 1920s. The Constituent Assembly that was supposed to solve Russia's problems never met. The Bolsheviks either infiltrated or disbanded the soviets once dual power had ceased to serve their purposes. The dictatorship of the proletariat had begun.

Phase III: rule of the Bolsheviks and the rise of totalitarianism

Even as the First World War drew to a close, Lenin himself continued to think that communism would evolve out of workers' committees (Lenin 1965: 46–7), and a world revolution that would rebound to Russia's benefit seemed a live possibility. The reality was to be far different. Lenin did not intend to create a tyranny, but his and the Bolsheviks' cold-blooded realism about power played him false. The disciplined vanguard party and the political chaos that had helped bring it to power produced a uniquely modern form of dictatorship known as totalitarianism. Totalitarian dictatorships would arise later in other communist countries and Nazi

Germany as well. Totalitarianism has six defining characteristics (Friedrich and Berzezinski 1965). First, the regime and its ruling party have an official millennialist (utopian) ideology. Second, the means of mass communication are under party control. Third, the ruling party exercises control over all means of force, including the armed forces, and it forces their members to accept its ideology. Fourth, there is a dictatorial leader with a personality cult. Fifth, the party exercises complete control over the economy. And sixth, the dictator and the party rule by the systematic use of terror. Above all, it is a mobilization regime; it is not satisfied with passive obedience but requires active and enthusiastic participation of the population in the process of social transformation (Linz 2000: 73–4, 83–7).

It is instructive to see how these characteristics emerged after the Russian Revolution. Perhaps, the key to its emergence was communist ideology itself. Communist ideology was by its very nature millennialist. It foresaw the creation of communism, a worldwide stateless society that provided complete human freedom to all human beings. Full communism required a highly advanced economic base and the emergence of the "new communist man" – actually both men and women with an intense overriding commitment to the common good of the whole society. The task of morally transforming the human race seems beyond the reach of any political party in even the best of circumstances. Yet, communists were committed to try, casting aside the rule of law, freedom of association, and any other barrier that stood in the way of their attempt to transform society materially and spiritually.

For Lenin, the Communist Party, the name the Bolshevik Party assumed after seizing power, was supposed to be the soul as well as the eyes and ears of the revolution. The party was to serve as the vehicle to mobilize the population and transform society. It is to serve as the moral leaven of the revolutionary regime. It was present in all parts of the government and all social organizations to assure that enemies of the new order could not function there. When moral suasion failed, brute force was used. Marx and Lenin had recognized that dictatorship was a necessary phase of the revolution. As time progressed, the party established a wide range of governmental institutions to regularize its rule. But it never truly ceded power to these legally prescribed, nominally popularly elected institutions. Elections and legislative assemblies, at all levels, were just for show. Fully consolidated communist regimes had **facade constitutions**, documents that prescribed how elections were to be conducted and how policy was to be made and implemented, but the communist party retained real power, making decisions behind closed doors. One institution, however, did function as advertised – the secret police. Beset by enemies, real or supposed, the party perfected rather than gave up the heavy-handed repression of their old-regime predecessors. To do otherwise would be to concede that the full communism was simply an unrealizable utopia.

In retrospect, it is not surprising that a dictatorial figure should emerge in such a political environment. Dictators had emerged during the English and French Revolutions where military leaders had simply seized power. However, in Russia, Joseph Stalin's dictatorship grew out of a perversion of party rules, allowing him to claim that he was true to communist principles even as he exercised arbitrary power. His use of the party as an instrument of his dictatorship helped perpetuate his rule. The party rules prescribed "**democratic centralism,**" which was supposed to provide not only for top-down decision-making but collective leadership and intra-party democracy as well. The rules made the All-Union Party Congress (generally similar to a national party convention in the United States) the supreme authority in party affairs at least nominally. However, once a vote was taken, everyone was duty-bound, as a good communist, to carry it out (see Figure 5.1). After the revolution, Stalin had been put in charge of the Orgburo (Organization Bureau) that was responsible for recruiting new members into the now governing, revolutionary party. This pivotal role allowed him to build personal support among masses of new members and pack the party congress. Once he had defeated his opponents, he was to label any opposition an "anti-party group." Members of such groups were eventually expelled from the party, and many received the severest sanction. Since the party congress met only once every five years for a brief period and opposition was forbidden to organize, actual power devolved to the central committee and the politburo, the latter of which could be called into session at virtually any time. Stalin's control was so complete, he was able to ignore both of these as he chose (Fainsod 1967: 31–208).

After Stalin had consolidated power, he was able to magnify his personal importance via a personality cult. Old colleagues were demoted, expelled from the party, tried for treason, and executed. Their accomplishments were attributed to Stalin instead. Stalin was glorified as one of the three most important figures in communist history. Marxism–Leninism, during the period of Stalin's dominance, became Marxism–Leninism–Stalinism although his contributions to the ideology were minimal. Stalin led the Soviet Union from 1927 to 1953, and his cult was mimicked by others, including Mao Zedong, Chairman of the People's Republic of China from 1949 to 1976.

Even Kim Jong-Il, the current head of North Korea and a second-generation leader, has managed to inherit part of his late father's personality cult.

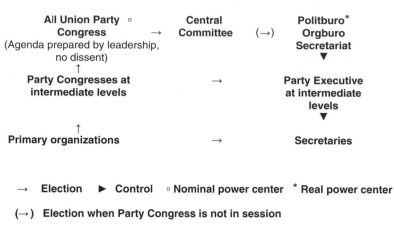

All Union Party ▫	→	Central Committee	(→)	Politburo*
Congress				Orgburo
(Agenda prepared by leadership, no dissent)				Secretariat ▼
↑				
Party Congresses at intermediate levels	→			Party Executive at intermediate levels ▼
↑				
Primary organizations	→			Secretaries

→ **Election** ▶ **Control** ▫ **Nominal power center** * **Real power center**

(→) **Election when Party Congress is not in session**

Figure 5.1 Organization of the Communist Party of the Soviet Union

Threatened by real and imagined enemies within and without, Stalin adopted terror as a strategy of governance. Historically, tyrannical dictators had often been in a precarious position, holding absolute power and unchecked by the rule of law, they were, nonetheless, surrounded by hidden enemies. Absolute tyrannical power generated hatred and fear. Few tyrants of ancient Greece died in their beds. Roman emperors as well often feared assassination by members of their inner circle. To survive, the tyrant had to assure that his secret enemies' fear overbalanced their hatred of him, and he had to ensure those with the motive to remove him were never able to unite and act upon their desires. The tyrants of old had spies and bodyguards to keep their opponents off balance and strike before any real threat could develop, but such methods often proved unreliable. Stalin, however, had the secret police, an organization that had precursors under the tsars and under Lenin. Unlike the slapdash methods of ancient tyrants, the secret police were numerous and effectively organized, keeping tabs on individuals to a degree unknown in prior dictatorships. During the worst periods of Communist totalitarianism, Stalin's Soviet Union in the 1930s and Mao Zedong's China during the mid-1950s and mid-1960s, tens of millions of people died as a result of executions, forced labor, and planned and unplanned famines; many more were imprisoned or displaced. The secret police itself had to be kept off guard or its leader might seize power. Thus, its leadership too was subject to purges and summary executions.

The building of communism required that all material and human resources be mobilized for the task. Marx had said that the rule in the final stage of communism would be "From each according to his ability; to each according to his need." But there would be a time after the working class had seized control, when rules for determining wages and investment similar to those of capitalism might be appropriate. In this earlier phase of communism – socialism – the rule would be "From each according to his ability; to each according to his work" (Marx 1977: 568–9). In 1927 Stalin's "Socialist Offensive" initiated what would become the orthodox method of communist economic management, state socialism. **State socialism** (or simply "socialism" in communist parlance) had two main principles. First, all productive property – all mines, factories, apartments, utilities, communications and transportation systems – are owned by the state. And second, the entire economy is centrally planned. In communist states, planning was the province of the state planning agency, and the typical planning period was five years. The state-planning agency not only produced a five-year plan, but updated it annually, via one-year plans, throughout the five-year period. Thus, the step-by-step process of implementing the plan could be revised annually to account for shortfalls of over-fulfillment of targets. Centralized planning was supposed to overcome what communists saw as the irrationality and anarchy of capitalist production and to prevent the rise of a new capitalist class. Stalin got what he desired, absolute control over the country and the party along with personal security. He exercised virtually unchecked power from 1927 to 1953. But Stalin's personality cult and state terror helped delegitimize communism as a governmental system and created a culture of fear quite opposed to what would be required for the full communism Marxism–Leninism had promised. Stalin's prolonged period of rule and his demise set the stage for emergence of the final revolutionary phase.

Phase IV: Russia's Thermidorean reaction – the rule of Khrushchev

Of Stalin's colleagues in the politburo (the party's steering committee composed of senior leaders) at the time of Lenin's death in 1924, only V.M. Molotov survived him. Most of the rest had met a violent and humiliating end. Thus, after Stalin's death there was little enthusiasm among the politburo for continuing the totalitarian system that Stalin had consolidated. The leadership itself sought to establish more regularized procedures of governance, and new informal rules that would guarantee their physical survival at least. Only one member of the top leadership was violently purged, Lavrenti Beria, the head of the secret police. Beria was the only politburo member with the resources and direct control of the secret police's regular military formations that would allow him to seize power immediately and become Stalin's successor. After eliminating Beria, the others abided by a pact to keep their political disagreements peaceful. Losers forced from office were granted a comfortable, if obscure, retirement. The first secretary (now general secretary) of the post that Stalin had held would have to abide by the party's rules and function as a first among equals with his politburo colleagues as the rules indicated. Thus, politics in the post-totalitarian era involved bargaining among senior level officials representing important party and state bureaucracies. The general secretary would not ignore his politburo colleagues but would instead be bound by their decisions. The politburo, as the rules specified, could remove the general secretary if his performance was unsatisfactory. Politics seemed to settle into a more stable, less violent status quo, but some leaders, at least, were eager to repair the damage done to the party by Stalin.

Plate 5.2 Stalin's personality cult gets a "two-fer." The stamp celebrates Stalin and the Stalin prize medal.

At the time of Stalin's death, the Soviet Union was a military and diplomatic superpower, and in terms of the sheer size of the Soviet economy, an economic superpower as well. Soviet prestige was high internationally, and the Soviet political and economic model appeared to be a success. Radicals in newly independent ex-colonies in Asia and Africa rushed to adapt it to local circumstances. But Stalin had used the idealism of millions upon millions of loyal communists and others and sucked many of them dry. During his lifetime, Stalin had been heralded as a veritable oracle of communist dogma, but he had, in fact, committed terrible crimes and inexcusable blunders. He had millions of loyal party members executed. His interference in military strategy prolonged and nearly lost the Second World War for the Soviet Union. Stalin had made himself a dictator over the party and damaged the country by his paranoia and megalomania. These were not the charges of an anticommunist firebrand, but the analysis of General Secretary Nikita Khrushchev at the twentieth party congress in 1956. Khrushchev criticized Stalin, not the party, Stalin's errors, not Marxism–Leninism as an ideology. Khrushchev gave some hope to those who advocated "socialism with a human face." These advocates argued that socialism ought to be cleansed of its Stalinist barbarities – its purges, personality cults, internal repression – and that socialism's productive potential should be used to promote the full flowering of human potential that Marx had promised would eventually follow the communist revolution.

Khrushchev went further and tried to resurrect the idealism that motivated communism during the first years of the revolution. Under his initiative the party adopted a new *Program of the Communist Party of the Soviet Union*, only the third such program that the party had ever adopted. It was for that very reason a historic document. The program proclaimed itself to be the program for a new era, the era of the building of communist society. By 1970, the program predicted, the Soviet Union would surpass the productive capacity of the United States, the most productive country in the world, on both a per capita and absolute basis. By 1980, the Soviet Union would establish the economic basis for full communism! Labor would be fully emancipated. The only thing that could prevent the withering away of the state, which also typified full communism, was the continued existence of the capitalist enemy (CPSU 1961: 61–2). In other words, the program promised a timetable for full communism, something no previous program had ever done. Still, many of the old political structures and rules remained largely unaffected by the Khrushchev program. The expanded party hierarchy, the secret police, the military, government ministries established under Stalin or before remained largely intact. Yet, instead of being mere instruments for the dictator, they took on a life of their own. No subsequent Soviet leader was strong enough to ignore them as the totalitarian dictator had been.

This post-totalitarian system had a number of features that show its totalitarian origins. Communist ideology and party control remained. Every unit in the armed forces, all levels of government, and each economic enterprise had their own associated party organization, responsible to its own separate hierarchy. Party activists were to supervise their counterparts, who were also party members. Moreover, the legal system was still constituted so as to assure everyone was subject to party oversight and ultimately party control. There could be no political space or private institutions from which the class enemies of the proletariat could undermine the transition to full communism. Even so, party rule came to be more predictable and mass terror disappeared. Party, state, and economy had established structures that made radical change difficult to bring about. In the Soviet Union, at any rate, political decisions were made largely by consensus with the politburo.

The optimism of the Khrushchev program did not survive for long after Khrushchev's fall in 1964. Until the party published another program during the 1970s, the party program, as a document, disappeared from view. By the time that the fourth program was issued, the credibility of Marxism–Leninism as a science and the reputation of the Soviet Union as a dynamic progressive society had been seriously undermined. The Soviet economy never came close to meeting the Khrushchev projections. Soviet economic growth rates actually diminished throughout the 1960s, 1970s, and 1980s. The Soviet Union remained a superpower, but its ideological credibility along with its economic reputation was severely dented.

Khrushchev's speech and the de-Stalinization campaign that followed burst the bubble of Marxist–Leninist "scientific" infallibility and set off shockwaves throughout the communist movement. Foreign communist parties were increasingly unwilling to accept the Soviet line uncritically. A number of ruling and non-ruling parties tried to exercise a degree of independence. Most notably, the communist government of Hungary had announced its intention to withdraw from the Warsaw Pact. A Soviet invasion had followed. Euro-communism developed in Western Europe. After Stalin, communism suffered from a legitimacy deficit. Its cause was simple: communism had over-promised and under-delivered. Stalin's Great Socialist Offensive, in the late 1920s, inspired a mass mobilization of human and natural resources to modernize the country dramatically and provide the foundation for full communism. But full communism never arrived.

Instead, Soviet life was governed according to a drab work-a-day procedure, where inequities and alienation persisted. Soviet jokes captured this malaise. "We pretend to work," one put it, "and they pretend to pay us." Another joke mocked Soviet ideological orthodoxy. "What is capitalism?" it began. The answer: "The exploitation of man by man." "What is socialism?" "Socialism", the response went, "is just the opposite." In short, Soviet citizens became cynical about communist ideology and its promises. Other communist states suffered from similar problems.

The demise of Khrushchev brought on a prolonged period of stagnation. The established bureaucratic interests of government and party dominated the politburo. The armed forces, the foreign ministry, the party's permanent bureaucracy, heavy (i.e., raw materials and producers' goods) industry were in charge. The leadership continued to age as few retired voluntarily or were forced to do so. Decisions were largely made by consensus rather than a simple majority vote, which meant few radical decisions were made at all. Meanwhile, the Soviet Union's and other communist states' problems grew. But the genie of opposition was out of the bottle. Dissent still unauthorized and punished slowly began to grow. What Russians termed "samizdat" (self-publishing) of essays, plays, stories, and histories by typewriter using carbon paper increased. Underground religious activity increased, as did Russian and Central European dissidents' contacts in the West. The communists' revolutionary momentum had ended.

CASE STUDY: THE CHINESE REVOLUTION AND ITS AFTERMATH

China followed a revolutionary pattern quite different from that of Russia's or previous revolutions. Instead of beginning with a seizure of power in the capital city, Chinese communists built a rural base and used control of the countryside to overwhelm their opponents' urban strongholds. The Chinese pattern was followed successfully in Southeast Asia and attempted elsewhere as well. As the following chronology indicates the Chinese model, dubbed "**protracted people's war**," can be both long in duration and can include many unexpected twists and turns.

Phase I: the breakdown of imperial authority

For millennia imperial China had been not only one of the world's leading states but one of the world's leading civilizations. The Chinese regime was headed by the emperor, an absolute monarch, who ruled through an extensive network of scholar–bureaucrats (Mandarins). The Mandarins were in principle a meritocracy, obtaining their positions by passing examinations in the Confucian classics that served as the moral and theoretical foundation of the regime. When all functioned well, the system provided peace and security for both the elite and the masses of peasants that made up the bulk of the population. However, things rarely worked in practice as they ought to in theory; China was subject to the dynastic cycle. Because of their power in the state, Mandarins were able to use their influence to gain land and other forms of wealth, and because passing the imperial examination required extensive study and private tutoring, only the sons of the rich could become Mandarins. Times of peace and prosperity meant an increase in population and a press on scarce land. At the same time, the Mandarin class was accumulating land and renting it to landless peasants often at exorbitant rates. Social disruption often followed. A wealthy but weakened China provided a tempting target for foreign invaders and rebels. Thus, after a period of chaos, the dynasty would fall, and the "mandate of heaven" as the right to rule was termed would pass to a new dynasty that would suppress disorder and reestablish the old system on its old foundations. So effective was the Chinese system of government and so appealing was Chinese civilization that foreign conquerors adopted Chinese manner and methods of governing once they had entrenched themselves in power.

This cycle endured for millennia, but the nineteenth century represented a unique challenge. European powers and later Japan were pressing to divide the country into their own colonial spheres of influence. China had to modernize in its own self-defense as had nineteenth-century Japan (see Chapter 2), but the ruling elite lacked the decisiveness to follow through with the necessary measures. It was internally divided about tradition and modernization as was the Russian elite during the same period. However, China's situation was much more dire since it was much less modern than Russia and open to the imperial expansion that Russia avoided. In a course of less than a century China suffered a mass rebellion that may have cost the lives of 30 million people, lost wars to Britain, a grand European coalition, and Japan. China was forced to cede sovereignty over Taiwan, de facto control over many of its richest provinces, and spheres of influence in many of its borderlands including Korea. These "unequal treaties" became a cause of resentment to the present day. Phase I came to an end in 1911 when the Chinese emperor was overthrown by a revolt that began in Hankow. The general sent to crush the rebels, Yuan Shikai, joined the revolt instead. Yuan became premier and later president and eventually schemed to make himself emperor. Meanwhile, the true revolutionary leader, Sun Yatsen, and his Guomintang (KMT or Nationalist Party), were sidelined by Yuan's power play.

Phase II: the rule of the moderates

Yuan Shikai and the republic that followed after his death were unable to gain effective control over the country. By 1920 a civil war had begun among local military leaders, and Japanese influence also increased as a result of its post-First World War accession to formerly German concessions in China. In 1924, aided by the Communist International or Comintern (founded in 1918), the KMT reorganized as a Marxist–Leninist party. The Comintern also aided the Chinese Communist Party (CCP) and supported an alliance between the KMT and CCP. The Comintern viewed the KMT as the representative of the "national [patriotic] bourgeoisie" and a grand alliance with them as the only way to successfully make a communist revolution in a semi-colonial country. The Whampoa Military Academy was established to provide both parties with armed forces loyal to them. Officers trained at Whampoa were soon put to good use. In 1926 Jiang Kaishek, who replaced Sun as KMT leader upon the latter's death the previous year, led the Northern Expedition from Canton to Hunan to Hankow. In the offensive, KMT troops, aided by communists in the enemy's rear, met with great success.

However, in 1927 Jiang and KMT conservatives broke with the communists. The communists reacted by staging an urban revolt that failed, and the party was soon on the brink of extermination. The traditional revolutionary road to power, a mass revolt in the capital, had failed. However, Mao Zedong and other radical CCP leaders survived the debacle. During the period that others were working in urban areas and serving as allies to the KMT, Mao and his associates had been backing a peasant revolt that the rest of the party leadership and the Comintern had rejected. Mao and the survivors were now in a position to lead the party in a peasant-based **protracted people's war** against the KMT. This style of warfare was based on a flexible strategy beginning with political agitation and armed propaganda in selected rural villages, advancing toward guerrilla war, and then to a mobile war based on larger and larger units. The strategy was one of attrition. Not until the enemy was severely weakened did the strategy call for full-scale "positional" combat and an assault on the cities. In short, the strategy was the direct opposite of the usual one followed by successful revolutionaries that seized the capital first and then suppressed resistance in the hinterland. Protracted people's war (Mao 1962: 71–115) would serve as a model for later communist and noncommunist revolutions in the century. It was uniquely suited to countries that were largely rural and where the mass base for the revolution was other than in major cities. Yet protracted people's war meant that moderates would remain in power for an extended period as the radicals mobilized politically and militarily to overthrow them. In practice, Protracted people's war involved a series of ups and down for the CCP, the most dramatic of which was the Long March that lasted from October 1934 to October 1935 and traversed 8,000 miles (see Map 5.2).

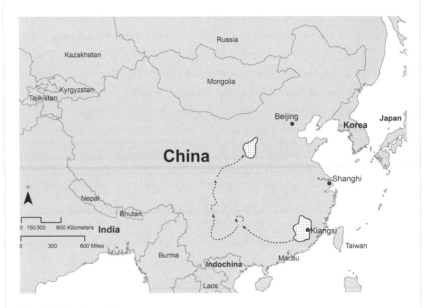

Map 5.2 The Long March
Source: Environmental Systems Research Institute (ESRI) map data. Data: The United States Military Academy's Department of History

The beginning of the civil war between the CCP and KMT plunged the country further into chaos. This was compounded by the 1931 Japanese occupation of Manchuria that resulted in the establishment of the puppet state of Manchukuo, which became independent of China. The increase in Japanese pressure on China culminated in the invasion of China proper in 1937. A three-sided war, Japan-versus-KMT-versus-CCP, followed, although the KMT and CCP were nominally allied against Japan. With the defeat of Japan in the Second World War, the civil war between the CCP and the KMT was renewed in earnest as attempts to mediate the differences between the two parties failed. Following the strategy Mao had developed two decades earlier, the CCP successfully forced the KMT and its Republic of China (ROC) government from the mainland to Taiwan in 1949 when the People's Republic of China (PRC) was proclaimed.

Phase III: Mao's reign of terror and virtue

Victory in the civil war and the struggle against Japanese occupation during the Second World War had given the CCP considerable legitimacy as the embodiment of Chinese nationalism and the spearhead of the forces of progressive social and economic reform. The CCP, under the chairmanship of Mao Zedong, embarked on two great attempts to revolutionize the state and the economy during the "Great Leap Forward" (1958–9) and the first phase of the "Great Proletarian Cultural Revolution" (1966–9). Mao's efforts were concerted attempts to advance full communism in China, and to do so in ways that avoided what he considered to be the pitfalls inherent in Soviet state socialism. Both Mao's critique of Soviet methods and the failure of the mass campaigns he led demonstrate some of the inherent problems of communist ideology. Since the formation of the Comintern in 1918, the Communist Party of the Soviet Union (CPSU) had been the lode star for other communist parties, providing guidance on party organization, revolutionary strategy, and the building of communism. Since the CPSU was the vanguard party of the first and most important state within the communist world, its leadership had been accepted virtually without question by fraternal communist parties. However, the relationship between the Soviet and Chinese parties was less than exemplary. The Chinese communists had departed from the Soviet line in a variety of ways, even before their revolution succeeded in 1949. Most critically, Mao rejected Soviet concepts of party, state, and economic development. Mao's own novel interpretation of Marxist–Leninist theory would have a profound effect on the development of the People's Republic of China.

Mao did not agree with the methods used in Soviet-style socialism to bring economic development or the "new communist man." In theory there was an equal emphasis on both the material and moral transformation of society, but, in actual Soviet practice, building the material requisites for full communism had pride of place. While the theory of full communism implied participatory administration of society rather than the hierarchical and technical administration of society by a specialized cadre of experts, Soviet socialism entailed the latter rather than the former. To create the new communist man, the CPSU used methods of socialization available in any society, noncommunist as well as communist: public education, the mass media, the arts, military service, elections, and the participation in public celebrations. But the Soviet state was not in a process of withering away, as was supposed to happen as full communism approached. The state, as a set of specialized administrative organs, was strong and intrusive. The Soviet Union used many of the same bureaucratic methods of the states and firms of the capitalist world, and it added other bureaucratic and technical controls as well. The Soviet state had taken what Mao termed the "capitalist road" of development. And since the Soviet state was following essentially capitalist methods, it would produce an essentially capitalist result.

Mao proposed a more participatory system of economic management that combined the task of building the moral and material prerequisites of communism. Relying on the sort of methods that had allowed the party to triumph in its popular struggle against the KMT and the Japanese, he used mass campaigns to mobilize resources for economic ends. Many CCP and government cadres had been trained in the Soviet Union and were admirers of Soviet methods. Mao was not. The mass campaign was his alternate development model. Instead of setting detailed targets for every branch of the entire economy, the mass campaign was more simple and straightforward. A limited number of key targets would be set. For example, instead of a detailed plan for steel production that broke down production by type, and specified the sources of raw materials, targets for each enterprise and the uses to which the steel was to be put, the mass campaign set a simple overall target for steel production, period. Then that target was subdivided by region, province, commune and village by the appropriate cadre and the people mobilized to fulfill or over-fulfill the target. In the war against the KMT and Japan, the party had relied on the enthusiasm, hard work, and the common sense of the masses, and it had triumphed. Mao believed the same methods would produce rapid economic development.

Mass campaigns, ideological as well as economic, had been a standard feature of political life throughout most of the history of the People's Republic, but, in 1958, Mao overcame opposition among the party's leadership and put his ideas into practice in a major way. The party announced a massive campaign to promote the formation of communes, rural agricultural cooperatives under government control that would employ the principle of equal distribution of benefits to all its members. Peasant preferences for family ownership were ignored. The commune, composed of tens of thousands of members, was to be centrally directed by local cadres. The principle that even Marx had recognized would guide socialism, "From each according to his ability, to each according to his work" (Marx 1970: 13–30), was held to be inappropriate. Each would have an equal share. During the same period, China launched another mass campaign to raise steel production to a level surpassing that of Great Britain. Disdaining typical Soviet methods, the campaign did not involve elaborate multiyear plans. Rather, it set a national target and relied upon lower-level authorities to apportion responsibility to local governments down to the commune level to fulfill their assigned part of the overall national target. These two hallmark campaigns of the Great Leap were unmitigated disasters. During the chaos of the communization campaign, tens of millions died, largely as a result of famine. Steel production rose, but the rise was more of symbolic than practical value. Pressed to produce more steel, cadres used whatever production facilities were available, no matter how outdated or how poor the quality of the output. Scrap steel was retrieved from every possible quarter. Even track from old unused railroad sidings were torn up and thrown into the blast furnaces. The results were as one might expect: steel production was often poor and sometimes only of scrap quality. The disasters of the Great Leap led to a premature halt in the program and an effective reduction of Mao Zedong's control over the government. Since he was the paramount hero of the revolution, he remained as party and state chairman, but his role, like that of many Chinese emperors before him, became largely honorific. And so the situation remained for almost ten years.

By the mid-1960s, the PRC was twenty-five years old. The generation of leaders who had made the revolution, including Mao himself, were growing old. Within the foreseeable future, a new generation of leaders would emerge. And China, a young country with a rapidly growing population, would have a government and a public without direct experience in the heroic revolutionary struggle. Soviet-trained leaders and their protégés had assumed control over state and party policy, and Mao Zedong had been pushed to the margins of the policy-making process. Chinese economic planning, although not as elaborate and detailed as that of the Soviet model, was made to conform, as far as possible, to the established state socialist model. Despite Mao's best efforts, the PRC seemed to be settling down into Soviet-style bureaucratic conformism. Mao wanted to cement his legacy lest the PRC lose its revolutionary dynamism. That opportunity came with student unrest in late 1965. Mao convinced the CCP Central Committee to issue a 16-point declaration attacking intellectuals and others who failed to show sufficient commitment and loyalty to communist ideals. This unleashed a fierce political struggle between those loyal to Mao's radical interpretation of communist principles and those committed to more moderate views. This struggle took place not only within the party leadership, but in the streets, factories, and schools as well. The struggle was known as the "Great Proletarian Cultural Revolution" (Esmein 1973). It lasted from 1966 to 1969 although it was not declared officially over until 1976.

The Cultural Revolution was an almost unprecedented event in the history of communist states. Most leadership struggles within communist regimes take place largely behind the scenes. Trials, firings, demotions, promotions, elections are all indicators of decisions already made. Public constitutional mechanisms do not decide disputes of personnel or policy. They register changes. Least of all, are leadership struggles decided in the streets. Yet, this is what happened during the Cultural Revolution. The Cultural Revolution involved direct action by the public in which Mao Zedong took the opportunity to settle scores with his ideological opponents within the party and to reset China on a revolutionary course that he hoped would outlive his personal leadership. He supported the student activists who dubbed themselves "Red Guards." Self-organized and not officially directed by the party, the Red Guards issued pronouncements redolent with revolutionary rhetoric and took direct action against professors and university administrators. Then they moved against factory directors and government officials. Their revolutionary slogans were endorsed by Mao, himself. "To rebel is justified!" "Down with those in authority taking the capitalist road!" Struggle sessions against capitalist-roaders led to verbal and at times physical abuse. The Red Guards sent many of the targets of their attacks to rural communes, so that they might "Learn from the people!" – another Red Guard slogan. Many leading party bureaucrats and a number of high-ranking state officials came under attack. But, by and large, Mao and the Red Guard limited their targets to the lower-level functionaries. The party, itself, was divided. Mao and his supporters were strong in the ideological, cultural, and propaganda arms while many of those who opposed Mao's radicalism dominated other sectors. The premier, Zhou Enlai, a Mao protégé, remained largely neutral in the struggle, trying to protect and retain as many of his subordinates as possible, but the state was purged significantly.

The military, the People's Liberation Army (PLA), played a pivotal role in the Cultural Revolution. Unlike many western armies, and even the Soviet Army after the Second World War, the PLA played a direct part in the economy in helping to direct and support mass campaigns and in deciding leadership and policy questions. The chaos created by the Cultural

Revolution provided the PLA leadership with an opportunity to expand its influence further. Most specifically, the Minister of Defense Marshal Lin Biao became a leading propagandist for Mao Zedong thought. The army published and distributed the "little red book," *Thoughts of Chairman Mao*, a collection of short homespun exhortations for revolutionary dedication and selfless effort. In effect, Lin made himself more Maoist than Mao. As the chaos brought about by the Red Guards moved from universities to primary and secondary schools, to factories and communes, the need for a stabilizing force became evident. The PLA was more than ready to fulfill that role. Revolutionary committees composed of the PLA, Red Guards, and so-called reformed cadres took over the administration from the old Red Guard-dominated groups. In most of these committees, the PLA came to play the leading role. Slogans like, "Struggle against those who wave the red flag against the red flag!" were meant to control Red Guard spontaneity. In early 1967, the Red Guards were officially abolished. The PLA became a dominant faction within the government. And the status of Marshal Lin Biao was second only to Mao Zedong, himself. Lin was, in fact, officially recognized as heir-apparent. But in 1971, the roof fell in. Accused of plotting a coup against Mao, Lin and his aircraft were shot down, fleeing to the Soviet Union.

However compelling Mao's critique of bureaucracy was, his notions of participatory administration miscarried in practice. In certain areas Mao's maxims of self-reliance and learning from the masses did make sense. For example, the "barefoot doctors" (really paramedics with rudimentary medical and nursing skills) brought some basic healthcare to rural areas. More administratively complex methods making use of more highly trained practitioners were, in fact, not appropriate for poor countries like China. Mao's efforts to promote industrial enterprises in rural communes were also well grounded. Seasonal agricultural cycles left much of the workforce unemployed for extended periods. Yet, mass campaigns proved to be no way to run the economy as a whole. By stressing ideological correctness rather than technical expertise on every level, Mao set the stage for an economic debacle of historic proportions. With Mao's physical decline and then his death in 1976, the PRC turned toward less heterodox methods of economic management.

Phase IV: China's Thermidor and Deng Xiaoping

In reality the Cultural Revolution helped pave the way for economic reform and political change, although not of the type that Mao Zedong had sought. The Cultural Revolution purged the state bureaucracy, loosened central control and put local cadres in a position where they had to innovate to survive. The economic reform began by Mao's successor, Deng Xiaoping, was based on a partial dismantling of the state socialist system. Beginning in 1978 with rural communes and then expanding to industrial enterprises in the coastal provinces, Deng tried to apply some of the techniques of capitalism in a socialist setting. By undermining centralized state institutions the Cultural Revolution had further strengthened de facto provincial and local autonomy. Provincial, municipal, and local authorities saw Deng's reforms as an opportunity to advance their personal and bureaucratic interests. The economy prospered. In addition, the advance of economic prosperity, the post-Mao era, saw political and policy stability.

Conclusion: the unintended consequences of revolution

Modern revolutionaries have often echoed Marx and Engels's call for unity and the creation of a new society. Yet, revolutions have produced a host of consequences that their leading promoters never intended. Not the least of these is arbitrary government. Lord Acton, who died in 1902 and whose famous maxim serves as an epigraph for this chapter, would not have been surprised. Absolute power turns out to be a blunt instrument. It can more easily destroy than create. By their own admission, even the communists, who provided the modern prototype of revolution, never completed the project of fully constructing a new society. The governments and societies they controlled never got beyond the construction phase. In the end popular disaffection with the vanguard's radical policies made the massive use of violence unsustainable. The vanguard had to find some way to live with a more moderate and stable status quo. And the vanguard's successors had to face challengers themselves. Despite all their disappointments, the importance of revolution and the revolutionary ideal should not be completely discounted. They can generate dedication among the vanguard and the public, inspire mass efforts at economic development, and legitimize governments, as did communism for over half a century. Although communism has lost its dynamism, other revolutionary ideals live on. Two of these are topics of the next chapter.

Questions for further consideration

1 Are the theories of Gurr, Skocpol, and Tilly contradictory or complementary? Defend your answer.

2 Revolutions have lifecycles; so too does their influence outside the country in which they occurred. What might help account for this?

3 How did the vanguards of revolutions you have studied in history courses differ from one another? For example, how did the vanguards of the American and various communist revolutions differ?

4 Are there would-be revolutionary counter-elites (revolutionary vanguards) in developed democracies? If so, what limits their ability to actually lead a revolution?

5 What sorts of societies today might be candidates for revolution? Why?

6 Consider the Russian and Chinese Revolutions? Do similar ideological justifications lead to similar consequences? Explain.

Further reading

Crane Brinton, *The Anatomy of Revolution*. New York: Random House, 1965. The seminal study on comparative revolutionary development.

Ted Robert Gurr, *Why Men Rebel*. Princeton, NJ: Princeton University Press, 1970. The classic exposition of relative deprivation.

Vladimir Ilyich Lenin, *What Is To Be Done?* Trans. J. Fineberg and G. Hanna. 1902. Online. Available HTTP: http://www.marxists.org/archive/lenin/works/1901/witbd/. Lenin's exposition of structure and role of the revolutionary vanguard party.

Theda Skocpol, *States and Social Revolutions: A Comparative Analysis of France, Russia, and China*. Cambridge: Cambridge University Press, 1979. The discussion of how the collapse of state capacity is responsible for revolution.

Charles Tilly, *From Mobilization to Revolution*. Menlo Park, CA: Addison-Wesley Publishing Co., 1978. The explanation of how governmental failure to act, popular mobilization, and the defection of key elites can lead to a revolutionary outbreak.

6 Revolutionary movements in the contemporary world

Colonial exploitation, poverty and endemic famine drive the native more and more to open, organized revolt. The necessity for an open and decisive breach is formed progressively and imperceptibly, and comes to be felt by the great majority of the people. Those tensions which hitherto were non-existent come into being. International events, the collapse of whole sections of colonial empires and the contradictions inherent in the colonial system strengthen and uphold the native's combativity while promoting and giving support to national consciousness.

(Franz Fanon, *The Wretched of the Earth*, 1963)

If laws are needed, Islam has established them all. There is no need … after establishing a government to sit down and draw up laws.

(Ayatollah Ruhollah Khomeini, 1900–89)

In this chapter

The discussion of revolutions continues, focusing on two types of late-twentieth-century revolutions that carry on directly to the present day. The first of these is wars of national liberation. The heyday of this form of struggle came in the first three decades after World War II when colonial peoples sought to throw off the colonial yoke. As local peoples gained independence, the number of these struggles diminished.

Yet, minority ethnic groups, often within newly independent states, sometimes make use of the same sort of struggle, claiming that the ethnic majority in fact practices a form of internal colonialism. A case study of the Algerian Revolution and a box summary of Kosovo's struggle for independence illustrate the earlier and later versions of this sort of revolutionary struggle. The second major form of revolutionary struggle is Islamic revolution. Islamism (political Islam) has a variety of forms, most of which are nonviolent. But the Islamist version of revolution has had a worldwide impact, beginning with the Iranian Revolution of 1979 (covered in a case study) and continuing with coups d'etat and terrorism inspired by Islamism. As in the previous chapter, a structural/functional analysis of where regimes are subject to breakdown, an analysis of political culture, and the analysis of political actors' strategic options undergird the discussion.

Introduction

Contrary to Karl Marx's expectation, revolutions have not occurred in the most advanced industrial societies. Regimes governing such societies have the economic resources and political structures likely to render revolutionary movements stillborn. Instead, as the analysis in the previous chapter suggests, regimes that govern societies with limited resources, that are in the throes of dramatic economic and social change, and that are without robust and effective governmental and state structures are the real candidates for revolutionary overthrow. In addition, regimes that govern such societies are further weakened by the fact that they are often hostage of international events and dependent upon foreign powers. In short, today revolutionary movements emerge and revolutions occur most frequently in the developing world. These contemporary revolutionary movements constitute an odd mix. On the one hand, some are essentially latter-day heirs to Marx and Lenin, looking forward to an essentially secular state with a utopian future. These movements first came to the fore in the post-Second World War era. Today many of the regimes they gave rise to are in their revolution's fourth phase. Some have even collapsed. When they were most numerous, these sorts of revolutionary movements were generally directed against overseas colonial powers. Today, they are primarily driven by ethnic nationalism and are directed against the multinational state of which they are a part. The second group, Islamist revolutionary movements represented by the epigraph from Ayatollah Khomeini, is of more recent vintage. Religious in ideology, it almost seems a throwback to an earlier era. The Iranian Revolution Khomeini headed triumphed in 1979 and spawned many imitators. Although the Iranian Revolution too is now in its fourth phase, Islamist revolutionary movements, on the whole, remain more dynamic than their secular counterparts. Islamists have even tried to co-opt ethnic nationalist struggles by giving ethnic divisions a religious coloration. This chapter will consider secular and Islamist movements in turn.

Wars of national liberation

National liberation is the freeing of subject peoples usually from foreign colonial rule. Colonial rule involved direct political control by an outside imperial power. Wars of national liberation came in two waves. The first occurred in the three decades that followed the Second World War. The scope and results of liberation movements in the post-Second World War were virtually unprecedented. Although the number of communist anti-colonial revolutions was limited (China and Vietnam stand out as spectacular exceptions), noncommunist national liberation struggles shaped politics in much of Asia and Africa in the second half of the twentieth century. The aftermath of these struggles continues to have a decided effect on the contemporary world. During this period, wars of national liberation were directed against imperial powers by their overseas subjects. Such wars came to an end in 1975 when Portugal decided to recognize its former colonies' independence.

However, the end of anti-colonial wars of national liberation did not spell the end of national liberation wars altogether. A second, smaller wave occurred in countries already liberated from imperial control. Second-wave national liberation struggles followed two basic patterns. The first sort consisted of liberation struggles organized by diehard radicals dissatisfied with the newly independent regime. When the old empires disappeared, these radicals often saw neo-colonialism as their underlying target. **Neo-colonialism** was direct economic but only indirect political control by a powerful foreign country over the dependent country (often its ex-colony). Radicals argued that neo-colonialism was just an updated version of old-fashioned imperialism. Foreign firms directly controlled much of the economy, and foreign governments indirectly controlled the important decisions of nominally independent and sovereign indigenous governments. Thus, radicals targeted their own national governments when they thought them insufficiently independent or revolutionary. An example of this is Laurent Kabila's successful revolt against Mobutu Sese Seku in 1997 (see the Zaire case study at the end of Chapter 11).

The second sort of latter-day national liberation movement is based on ethnic nationalism. **Ethnic nationalism** is nationalism that seeks to mobilize a minority community based in an identified territory within an existing state; its aim is to gain full statehood for that group and that territory. Ethnic nationalism has emerged in both the developed and

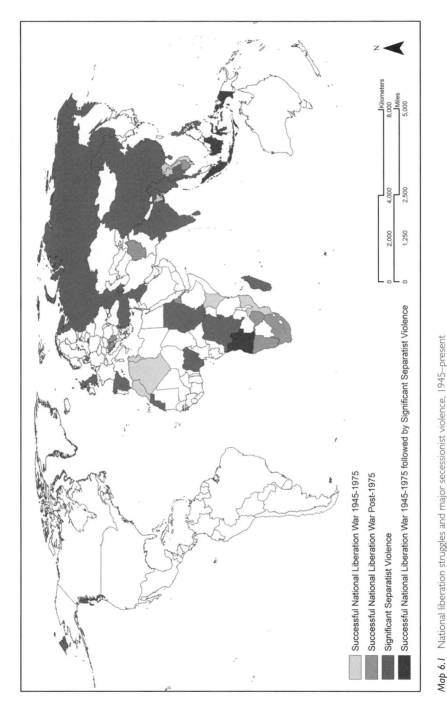

Map 6.1 National liberation struggles and major secessionist violence, 1945–present

Source: Environmental Systems Research Institute (ESRI) map data. Data: World Political Almanac (2001); Minorities at Risk Project (2005), College Park, MD, Centre for International Development and Conflict Management, retrieved from http://www.cidcm.umd.edu/mar, March 5, 2008

ex-colonial worlds. Nationalism among the East Timorese in Indonesia, the Basques in Spain, the Chechens and related groups in Russia, the Catholic Irish in the British province of Northern Ireland, and the Corsicans of France are all examples of ethnic nationalism. Sometimes the forced association of the minority and the majority in one state brought about by foreign conquest is quite old as it is in the European cases just cited. At other times it is a quite recent development. For example, Indonesia invaded East Timor in the 1970s, setting off a struggle between local nationalists and the Indonesian government.

As is the case with other sorts of revolutions, national liberation struggles often have their own moderates and radical vanguards. To a significant degree, the revolutionary cycle elaborated by Brinton and discussed in the last chapter also applies. But many revolutionary movements fail because of mistakes made by the would-be vanguard or lack of significant mass support. In other cases, moderates have been strong and clever enough to prevent the radicals from coming to power. Government repression or successful reform, foreign aid, or simple luck may also stop the revolutionary process in its tracks. Still, national liberation struggles have had a remarkable run of successes at least as far as overthrowing outright colonial control is concerned.

The nature of old (colonial) regime

The colonial powers had partially integrated their colonies into the global economic order. Colonies provided raw materials from their mines, plantations, and forests to the mother country. Colonies served as markets for goods manufactured from the metropolis as well. Foreign settlers and foreign firms took over the best lands, displacing native populations or forcing them to work for the colonizers, often as virtual slaves. Subsistence activities of the local population were disrupted. Their claims to ownership and personal freedom were largely ignored. As a result, local peoples found themselves strangers in their own country. The new economic activities introduced by the colonial powers were primarily extractive. Processing primary products and manufacturing were largely the province of the imperial power. Locals were used primarily for unskilled labor or as foremen. In colonial enterprises, the higher-level managers and those who reaped the profits from the enterprises were foreign expatriates, many of whom intended to return to the mother country. The sale of cheap manufactured goods from the mother country displaced local handicraft production. Local artisans could not compete with modern factories. Thus, although modernization of the local economy did occur, it was the sort of modernization that put the colony on the periphery of the modern economic world. In addition, in Africa for several hundred years even before the wholesale expansion of European colonies there, millions upon millions of human beings were exported as slaves. The slave trade helped provoke wars and undermined whole societies.

Colonialism, whether it lasted for centuries or only decades, also served to undermine the traditional social and political order. Colonization changed the patterns of government and administration. Local rulers were either replaced or co-opted by the colonial powers, and, as a consequence, lost much of their legitimacy. Often, new structures for enforcing law, collecting taxes, settling disputes and enforcing contracts were imposed. Moreover, these structures were established to benefit the colonizers, not the locals. Very often they were virtually inaccessible to the local population. Thus, the changes that occurred were haphazard. Old patrimonial patterns often remained in place for much of the population. Only too late and too occasionally did the colonial powers take steps to promote a smooth transition to independence. And often they actually tried to resist it. Even countries that were never formally colonized (e.g., Ethiopia and Thailand), or achieved early independence, as did most of Latin America in the early nineteenth century, felt the effects of the colonial heritage. The colonial connection did not end with formal independence; economic ties remained and were reinforced as the nineteenth century progressed. Foreign businessmen, bankers, and landowners supported by their governments dominated the local economy. Unsurprisingly, the history of colonialism often produced a radical backlash against it by peoples who had suffered from it. Dramatic revolts and brutal suppressions were often the stock and trade of establishing and maintaining a colony.

The old regime included a complex set of political actors. The principal political actors from the dominant power included the following groups. Settlers had a direct interest in maintaining the colonial system. Even if they had been there for generations, they were recent additions to the colony compared to the original population. They had retained their own culture, language, and religion. They had steadfastly refused to assimilate into local society in any meaningful way. As conquerors, they viewed themselves as being superior to the "natives." It was up to the locals to assimilate the "advanced" ways of their colonial overlords. The settlers, whether a fraction of 1 percent as in many African colonies, or up to 10 percent, as in Algeria, were a powerful group. They had ties with the colonial administration and the government of the mother country, and could often win the sympathy of the population of the imperial power back home. The colonial administration, by birth and by

official position, was sympathetic to the aims of the settlers –
with one difference. Administrators wanted to keep the task of
governing the territory as simple as possible. Hence, they might be more
inclined to consider compromise with local demands than the settlers
would. Home governments' interests were never the same as residents of
the colonies. The population of the imperial country could feel the
patriotic pride associated with empire. But the population and home
government had to bear the financial and sometimes part of the human
cost of fighting colonial wars. In the post-World War II era, colonialism
also entailed a moral and psychological cost as the principle of the
self-determination of peoples was increasingly seen as being of universal
applicability.

The vanguard and its base

The goal of national liberation is the expulsion of foreigners and the
creation of a new society that transcends the conflicts and antagonisms of
the present as well as bygone eras. **National liberation fronts** arose as
leaders began to sense that both the international and the domestic
climate had changed. These groupings were composed of locals from a
variety of backgrounds. Their leaders were often young and well educated,
thoroughly familiar with the ways of the imperial power, but they had
opted to reject assimilation. The front or at least the most radical within it
served as the vanguard of the revolutionary movement much as the
communist party served as a vanguard for social revolution elsewhere.
Though some of these fronts tried to copy communist organizational
methods especially after seizing power, few succeeded in producing
anything but a pale imitation of the communist party. The vanguard
envisioned a new society that would transcend the class, ethnic, and
cultural divisions of the old colonial society as well as the pre-colonial one.
However, as a practical matter, the people they wished to lead still
retained a loyalty to ethnicity, religion, and class. Furthermore,
colonialism had sharpened some of the old divisions and introduced new
ones of its own. Thus, the "unity" of the oppressed people the vanguard
spoke of glossed over important rifts.

Traditional leaders, heads of clans, tribal chiefs, religious leaders, and
even heads of the local dynasty were often pivotal figures in the national
liberation struggle. Often these leaders had been co-opted into the
colonial administration under the policy of indirect rule (see Chapter 2).
Even if they remained outside the colonial power structure and politically
passive, the passivity of many of them had been a sign that resistance to
imperial rule was not the preferred option for those who wanted to retain

their traditional ways. Some, however, were anxious to assert their people's independence from colonial rule. Yet, their vision of what sort of society and political system to create was decidedly different from that of radicals in the national liberation front. Assimilated or partially assimilated locals were another group that had to be reckoned with. Some were leaders or supporters of the front. But others were members of the colonial administration, the imperial armed forces, and the police. Still others were merchants working in the cash economy or employees of individual foreigners or foreign enterprises. These latter groups posed potential roadblocks to successfully forming a united front against the imperial power. The remainder of the local population was often only marginally connected to the modern economy and only had a minimum of modern education at best. Where a sense of nationalism had pre-dated colonialism, this minimally modern group could be sympathetic to the vanguard's aims. But where there was no preexisting nationalism to tap into, the vanguard's task was made more difficult. It had to create a new sense of national identity that would be stronger than clan, tribal, or ethnic identities. This often proved impossible except with people already connected to the modern economy.

Foreign influence and the demise of the colonial regime

Modern imperialism's origins date back to the European Age of Discovery. The beginning of the end for modern imperialism dates back to the First World War. At the end of the war, continental empires in Europe were broken up. Both Woodrow Wilson of the United States and Russia's Vladimir Ilyich Lenin had proclaimed the principle of the self-determination of peoples in general, but independence was slow in coming to many non-European nations. The victors in the First World War had refused to apply the principle of self-determination beyond Europe since many of them had extensive overseas colonial empires to protect. It was World War II that finally irretrievably undermined overseas colonialism. The Atlantic Charter, signed by the United States and Great Britain in 1941, promised self-determination to conquered peoples, putting de-colonization once again on the global agenda. Shortly thereafter, Japan's rapid defeat of European powers in Asia shattered the myth of the white man's invincibility. And the war itself put weapons into the hands of peoples seeking independence. Both the Japanese and their enemies raised local troops and armed local guerrillas. Both too appealed to aspirations for local self-rule.

   In sum, the Second World War put the colonial system in a state of crisis. The war destroyed much of the industrial base in continental

Europe and Japan. It undermined the power structure that had once exercised control over the colonies. It weakened the will and self-confidence of imperialists and strengthened organizations with an anti-imperialist agenda. The United States for reasons of its own opposed the continuation of colonialism, and the Soviet Union was even more opposed for both purely ideological as well as geo-strategic grounds to the continuance of European empires. The United Nations came on the scene with a commitment to self-determination, and if nothing else, it served as a forum in which spokesmen for oppressed peoples could voice their views. All in all, it proved impossible to put the genie of national self-determination back in its bottle in the post-war era. Those colonial powers that did not leave their overseas colonies voluntarily, most notably the French, the Dutch, and the Portuguese, often faced bitter wars of national liberation (Challand 1978).

Phase I: breakdown

National liberation fronts could draw from a repertoire of methods to defeat the colonial administration weakened by withdrawal of foreign support and colonial unrest. The set of methods actually chosen varied country by country. Given the proper motivation, mass protests could energize the opposition and demoralize proponents of imperial rule. In countries such as India, civil disobedience, actions in which large numbers of locals publicly refused to obey a symbolically important imperial exaction and suffered the legal consequences, were important for mobilizing local resistance and undermining imperial authority both in the colony and the imperial homeland. In a variety of countries, radicals sometimes undertook wars of national liberation that were the rough equivalent of Mao Zedong's protracted people's war (see Chapter 5).

Few national liberation movements, whatever the exact strategy and means they chose, were able to defeat the imperial power militarily in the field. And even when defeated militarily, imperialists could always have brought more forces into action. But that did not really matter. National liberation struggles were primarily psychological and moral. Both sides often used systematic political violence (terrorism) to advance their cause. Insurgent terrorism is, in large measure, political theater. It is meant to demonstrate that the oppressed are really powerful and that the seemingly powerful are really weak by inflicting unexpected damage on the dominant political actor or its supporters. Political violence is meant to provoke a reaction by the established authorities that will further strengthen the moral position of the rebels (Fanon 1963). It often did.

Terror often provoked counter-terror (state terrorism) by the government. State terror was often effective in decimating rebel military units and eradicating terrorist cells (small groups of terrorist operatives), but that was beside the point. The use of state terror further de-legitimized colonial authorities in the eyes of the local population and even among waverers in the imperial home country. Meanwhile it made the front's recruiting easier. Counter-terror thus added to the cost of maintaining colonial rule over an obviously unwilling population. As with mass protests and civil disobedience, political violence by the liberation front was meant to demonstrate to imperialists that the game was not worth the candle. The imperial power might be able to maintain its presence, but doing so would be physically and psychologically costly. And in fact, in the end imperial powers, regardless of the strategy they had followed, had to concede political if not military defeat.

Phase II: rule of the moderates

Imperial authorities, forced on the political defensive, could sometimes play one last card. A plebiscite, in which the population of the colony could voice a preference for continued association with the imperial power, albeit with significant autonomy, could save face for the imperial power and salvage a good share of its influence. In reality, such plebiscites rarely turned out as the imperial power had hoped. Many times imperial powers saw the handwriting on the wall, and decided to engineer a graceful exit, leaving nominally democratic institutions and local leaders amenable to the ex-imperial powers influence in place. Since they did not have deep roots or a supportive political culture, these democratic institutions often quickly withered. Incumbents were either overthrown or assumed dictatorial powers. In cases where a true multi-group front had secured liberation, the radicals within it frequently assumed power.

In large measure, the nature of the anti-colonial struggle often decisively shaped the form of regime that would rule the newly independent state. For example, in India (see the second case study in Chapter 3), the independence campaign was based largely on civil disobedience and mass protests, and a multi-party system dominated by the Congress Party followed. In other countries, where mass violence was an essential part of the strategy, the radical components of the national liberation movement were more likely to wind up in command of the newly independent state. In effect, just as in the classical revolutions discussed in the previous chapter, mass violence often resulted in dictatorship in the end. (For a comparison of revolutionary methods, see Table 6.1.)

Table 6.1   Primary means of liberation struggle: characteristics and results

	Civil disobedience/ mass protests	Classical revolution	Protracted people's war	Terrorism
Locus of struggle	Urban and rural	Urban	Rural	Urban and rural
Violence	None to limited	Yes	Yes	Yes
Mass support	Yes	Yes	Yes	Not required
Likely results	Multiparty politics possible	Authoritarianism likely	Authoritarianism likely	Authoritarianism likely

Phase III: rule of the radicals

The radicals had a vision of the future in which the nation transcends old divisions and animosities of class and ethnicity. They envisioned a vanguard party (in name or in fact) that mobilized society behind this vision. They saw political opponents as traitors to the nation. On the whole, Marxism–Leninism provided an attractive reservoir of ideas and political techniques for the radical vanguard. But, while many radical parties and movements adapted elements of Marxism–Leninism, they also incorporated distinctly indigenous elements into their ideologies and political organizations that made them more attractive in their own cultural milieu than orthodox communists generally were. Thus, radicals, in the developing world, often sought a "**third way**" between the intellectual perspectives of the capitalist and communist world (Sigmund 1972).

Nationalism

Adherents to national liberation movements and other developing-world radicals were nationalistic. The exploitation of their economies by colonial powers had been accompanied by a devaluing of local culture. The British spoke of the "white man's burden." The French had their "*mission civilisatrice*," their civilizing mission. In other words, they viewed the peoples of their colonies as backward, sometimes even savages. It was not simply that they lacked the technology or organization European colonials possessed; they were culturally or racially inferior. The "natives" who rose to positions of importance in the employ of colonial states or firms did so by adopting European ways and European culture. They could be accommodated, at least in limited numbers. The assertion of political and cultural nationalism was an assertion of collective and individual self-worth in the face of decades or centuries of the denial of that worth. Even when they borrowed ideas from elsewhere, radicals sought an indigenous basis for the institutions that they established. Nationalism required a variety of changes. Place names, even personal names, were changed. Independent governments strove to take control over the national economy, if possible, removing European influence. Nationalism had a great appeal among independence proponents of all stripes, but for the radicals it also entailed new institutions that would transcend the limitations implicit in European theories and practices.

One-party "democracy"

Radicals saw single-party regimes as consonant with their national tradition. They justified one-party rule in two different ways. More moderate leaders of newly independent states, especially in Africa, used an essentially pragmatic justification to defend their unwillingness to allow political competition. They argued that multi-party democracy was something their countries could ill afford in their current state of development. Political parties would reinforce traditional divisions and hostilities. And holding competitive elections was an expensive and time-consuming process. The pragmatists argued for **tutelary democracy** – i.e., a one-party system that would accustom people to elections, voting, and modern democratic procedures. The one-party system would some day be replaced by procedures more appropriate to liberal democratic practice: open elections, media freedom, and a multi-party system. According to this analysis, one-party rule was a temporary and necessary evil. The more radical, in contrast, believed that one-party rule was an unqualified good. Multi-party democracy was suspect. Radicals based their argument on national practices that had pre-dated the rise of the modern state. In traditional societies, decisions were not made by majority vote on the basis of alternatives presented by conflicting political parties; they were made on the basis of consensus. Partisan politics divides. It leads to clear winners and clear losers. The majority outvotes the minority, and on that basis the majority can govern solely in its own interest. Partisan democracy did not fit into a picture of a harmonious society, where all were concerned with the common good.

Radicals found the traditional model of consensus democracy, typical of village decision-making, more compelling. In a village or clan, the heads of families would often gather together to resolve collective problems in a mutually agreeable way. The elders discussed the issue at hand, considered all points of view, and came to a decision that was acceptable to all. The majority did not lord it over the minority. The good of the whole was of prime consideration. Radicals argued that one-party regimes applied the consensus principle on the level of the modern state. The ruling party represented the national interest. It served as a vanguard party in the way that the communist party did in communist states. One-party elections and various forums for popular participation allowed the people to express their will, and the party as the interpreter of that will put it into practice. This new version of democracy was given a variety of titles – e.g., African democracy, Arab democracy – depending on the locale. And, from the radical perspective, it was superior to liberal democracy. In effect, radicals often found an indigenous justification for communist-style one-party rule.

Socialism and the struggle against neo-colonialism

While many in the developing world in the post-World War II era supported moderate critiques of global capitalism (e.g., Cardoso and Faletto 1979; Prebisch 1950), radicals followed the Leninist line (Lenin n.d.). During the First World War Lenin had argued that capitalism had survived for longer than many Marxists had anticipated because of the globalization of his day, imperialism. The colonial expansion of capitalist states during the last several decades of the nineteenth century had taken pressure off capitalism. Since profit/surplus value could be extracted overseas, the capitalist class could afford to ease its oppression of the working class at home. Continued territorial expansion, economic growth, and an easing of exploitation lessened the prospects for an early revolution in advanced capitalist states. When he wrote *Imperialism: The Highest Stage of Capitalism*, Europe was in the midst of World War I, and Lenin saw that conflict as a confirmation of his theories. The world's major powers were tearing each other apart because colonial expansion could go no further. Lenin fully expected that that war would ultimately lead to world revolution in which the weakest and least prepared of the warring powers would probably begin the process. In that respect, he was, at least, partially correct. Revolution did occur in a failing state on capitalism's periphery, Russia, but it was not followed by an immediate world revolution as Lenin had anticipated.

Kwame Nkrumah, political theoretician and later president of Ghana, updated Lenin's theory with his own version that had broad currency among radicals. The title of Nkrumah's book, *Neo-colonialism: The Highest Stage of Imperialism*, played explicitly on the title of Lenin's famous analysis. Nkrumah argued that the arrival of political independence did not of itself guarantee true liberation. Rather, the former colonial powers kept their economic control even as they left formal political power in the hands of locals. However, it was economic power and the political leverage it generated that was the key for continuing to control the ex-colonies. This process Nkrumah dubbed "**neo-colonialism**." So long as the ex-colonies remained in the economic thrall of their former colonial masters, they would never be truly independent. The former mother country could even intervene directly to support its local protégés, who were willing to protect its interests. Hence, the newly independent states had to break both their political as well as their economic ties with the capitalist world. Radicals in power took this as a key objective (Nkrumah 1965).

The radicals' vision of economic development rejected both any connection with international capitalism as well as the establishment of domestic capitalism. Instead, their approach was based on state socialism and economic autonomy. These economic features were far preferable to capitalism. Capitalism entailed class exploitation. A just society had to transcend the class system. It had to foster community and social solidarity. As the radicals saw it, socialism not only fostered community; it resembled principles that had governed the community in the past. For instance, in traditional societies, land-tenure systems seldom resembled those of the capitalist West. Families often did not own the land that they worked; the community had granted them the temporary right to use it. This system of community ownership was similar to socialism, in which the state controlled productive property in the interests of the whole community. Thus, it made sense to radicals to speak of Arab socialism or African socialism as a local development. In many cases, there seemed to be little real difference between Arab or African socialism and its Soviet variant except that these non-Soviet versions were less well run. Bureaucratic formulas and development strategies were adapted from one to the other. In other cases, however, such as Tanzania, the ruling party made the attempt to run things differently. That country's villagization program attempted to couple true village ownership with adoption of modern agricultural practices. It too failed.

Phase IV: unfulfilled expectations

States newly freed from colonial control often produced improvement in the lives of their citizens, but the improvement was frequently uneven. Oftentimes basic healthcare improved and the young were educated, but young people often lacked opportunities commensurate with their education and what they had come to expect. Relative deprivation had paved the way for revolution. Yet, as the novelty of the new regimes wore off, the new regimes were caught in the same trap as the old regime. The post-colonial period ushered in an era of rising expectations. Rapid political change, the improvement in simple cheap communications like the transistor radio, foreign ideological propaganda sponsored by the two major cold-war rivals and their allies, and the regime's own ideology, all promoted the notion that rapid improvement was just around the corner. Such expectations were difficult to realize, and the sense of relative deprivation quickly grew in many societies, leading governments to seek ways of suppressing or redirecting popular dissatisfaction. One-party regimes or other dictatorships already had the mechanisms in place to prevent dissatisfaction from becoming dangerous to the ruling elite. They could rely upon the party (where it existed) and the political police, their control over society, economy and the mass media to mobilize society behind the regime. And as the expectations gap continued or worsened, these regimes came to rely more on the instruments of repression than the positive commitment of the population to the regime's ideals. Much like communist regimes, regimes formed by national liberation fronts lost much of their revolutionary dynamism, and often dedicated the lion's share of the political resources to reinforcing the one-party-dominated status quo.

With the 1990s, most one-party regimes based on national liberation ideologies had, at least officially, disappeared from the political scene. Africa especially saw a series of national conferences that included opposition leaders and paved the wave for a more open political system. In theory, these regimes have converted themselves into liberal democracies and market economies. Yet, all too often, as with many of the successor states of the former Soviet Union, these transitions suffered from their authoritarian legacy. We will take a more detailed look at the politics of some of these formerly revolutionary regimes in Chapters 11 and 12.

CASE STUDY: THE ALGERIAN REVOLUTION

The Algerian war was one of the twentieth century's most intense and most celebrated wars of national liberation. The history of colonial rule was a relatively long one. Algeria had become a target of French colonialists in the 1830s. By the mid-twentieth century, the French population (the colons) stood at over 10 percent of the population, and many French families had been there for generations. The French had adopted a policy of direct rule and treated Algeria as an integral part of France. The war pitted the large well-established settler population against the organized and intense mass of the local population committed to the settlers' expulsion. The war involved terrorism by the rebels, the colons, and the state and spurred hopes of a new society that would transcend class antagonisms. In the end, however, the new regime turned into a military dictatorship.

Breakdown

The duration and size of the colonial presence made the Algerian war of national liberation particularly violent and bitter. The colons controlled the proceeds of the revenue system that taxed the local population heavily. Early in the colonial period, the state had confiscated land that had supported Islamic charities and education, causing literacy to decrease substantially. By the 1890s the French had begun to offer French education to a limited number of local Algerians. Within several decades a French-educated class of Algerians developed, but it accounted for only a small fraction of the population. This group divided into assimilationists who wanted to be completely accepted as French (but on their own terms) and "integrationists" who sought a distinct Muslim identity.

Some 173,000 Algerians served in the French army during the First World War, and hundreds of thousands assisted the war effort working in France. This assistance led to only limited concessions to Algerians by the French government. After the war, the number of Muslims able to vote was expanded by 425,000, which many Algerians regarded as unsatisfactory. Thus, in 1926 the Star of North Africa was formed; the new organization called for Algerian independence. This organization was truly a united front consisting of a wide variety of groups; communists, educated Algerians, Algerian ex-soldiers who fought in the First World War, and Algerian workers in France were among its supporters. The movement was banned and went underground, but a variety of nationalist and Islamic movements developed to fill the void.

In the 1940s, the French government made several efforts to satisfy Algerian aspirations, but these initiatives failed in the face of growing Algerian nationalism and colon resistance. In 1943 Muslim leaders presented the Free French government in Algeria with the "Manifesto of the Algerian People" that demanded a new constitution that would guarantee the equality of Muslims. The government responded the next year with a reformist proposal that had been mooted a decade earlier. It was too little too late. Pressure for greater concessions continued. In 1945 French authorities violently suppressed Algerian protests. The French government claimed 1,500 were killed, but other estimates ran as high as 45,000. These events further polarized the situation, and the government responded with mass arrests. In 1947 the French National Assembly undertook another reform, granting Algeria a government with one house of the legislature controlled by the colons and the second by the Muslims. The statute also established municipal councils. When Muslims gained strength in municipal elections, the colons resorted to rigging the results to curtail their influence. Attempts to investigate the fraud were stymied. Another opportunity for conciliation had been missed.

Plate 6.1   A street in the Casbah, the old Arab quarter of Algiers and a seat of unrest during the war against the French.

Incited by these inadequate and miscarried reforms, Algerian radicals increased their agitation and began to prepare for a violent conflict. The Algerian National Liberation War began in 1954. A small group, the National Liberation Front (FLN), conducted the war by means of political violence and guerrilla warfare. The FLN operated both on the military and political level, building support among the Muslim population both in Algeria and France. Violence grew by a process of mutual escalation. The colons took the lead in urging the government to engage in repressive measures and often took matters into their own hands. The level of violence rose when a local FLN commander abandoned the policy of attacking only military targets and killed 123 civilians. The French responded by killing from ten to a hundred times that number of Algerian civilians. Then, as a matter of policy, the FLN began to direct some of its military attacks against French civilians. In their attempt to crush the insurgency, the French came to use state terror persistently themselves. The French army with its 400,000 troops was able to get the upper hand militarily forcing regular FLN units out of Algerian territory or into the Atlas Mountains. But the French were never able to crush the FLN. The external FLN, composed of politicians and military units outside the country, continued. And although the French destroyed the terrorist organization in Algiers, their massive use of state terror intensified popular resentment, and the war dragged on.

Rule of the moderates

In 1958 France's National Assembly passed the Algerian Reform Bill in one more attempt to win over moderate Algerians and keep the country as part of the French Union. But the bill failed to satisfy most Algerians, and the war continued. The continuing turmoil in Algeria helped produce the collapse of France's Fourth Republic. An army revolt in Algeria led to the accession of Charles de Gaulle, the leader of the Free French government during World War II, to power. The Fifth Republic, tailor-made for de Gaulle as executive president, was established. However, even de Gaulle was ultimately forced to recognize the inevitable. In 1961 unable to negotiate a compromise with the FLN that would keep some Algerian ties to France, the government under de Gaulle proposed the eventual recognition of Algerian independence. The plan was approved by 75 percent of French voters in a referendum, but the Algeria-based Secret Army Organization (OAS) tried to block the settlement. Nonetheless, an agreement was signed between France and Algeria the following year. The agreement led to another abortive army revolt and an assassination attempt on de Gaulle, but again the rightist rebels were unable to shake the government's resolve for a negotiated solution between France and Algeria. In 1962 in preparation for independence the FLN issued the Tripoli Program committing the organization to land reform, nationalization of industry, and a nonaligned foreign policy. The FLN formed a political bureau composed of senior leaders. However, deep fissures based on ideological and personal difference began to emerge within the FLN and independence movement as independence drew closer.

Reign of terror and virtue

The advent of independence meant the exit of the colons, who had held most administrative, managerial, and professional positions. A triumvirate representing the leaders of the army, party, and government, known as the Oujda Group, dominated the country, and the FLN followed through with its program of the economy and established a socialist state. Workers' self-management was put into effect. A variety of parties existed in the Algerian National Assembly, but contrary to the Tripoli Program, the FLN premier, Ahmed Ben Bella, one of the Oujda Group, began to consolidate power. He regarded the FLN as a vanguard party and sought to use it to mobilize the society for revolutionary change. The opposition was banned and the trade unions were incorporated under the FLN banner. In 1963 Ben Bella was elected president under a new constitution, and the country quickly became a one-party state. The phase-three rule of the radicals had begun. However, radical change did not produce either the intended results or political peace. Resistance in the country and internal troubles within the government multiplied.

Thermidorean reaction

In June 1965, Colonel Houari Boumediene, another member of the Oujda Group and the defense minister, replaced Ben Bella in a bloodless coup. The coup and the events that followed demonstrated unequivocally where real power lay. Boumediene's power base was the army, and he had led the coup to protect military interests. His regime shifted power from the FLN to the military and moved away from the radical socialism and workers' self-management of the Ben Bella era. Boumediene's regime brought into power a new technocratic class whose interests were allied to those of the armed forces. He ruled as president until he died in office in 1978. Chadli Bendjedid, whose power base was also the military, replaced Boumediene as president. The 1980s saw the liberalization of the economy. The reforms of the Algerian Revolution had achieved only mixed success. The country had urbanized, and the government had pushed industrialization. Public education had been expanded, but many of the educated youth had failed to find jobs because of a stagnant economy. Discontent between Arabs and Berbers also had grown as had Islamist opposition.

By the end of the decade, the regime realized it had to liberalize. In 1989 a new constitution was promulgated that allowed for other parties besides the FLN to compete in elections and civic groups not associated with it to form. As far as the military was concerned, the reform miscarried. Islamist radicals under the banner of the Islamic Salvation Front (FIS) won the municipal elections the following year. In 1991 the FIS won the first round of national legislative elections, and seemed poised to win the second round as well. In 1992 the government, controlled by the armed forces, cancelled the second round of parliamentary elections. The actions were followed by a prolonged period of political violence in which an estimated 150,000 people died. By 1999 with the election of Abdelaziz Bouteflika of the NLF as president, the political situation has at least been partially stabilized. The Islamic rebels have been suppressed, and parliamentary elections, from which the FIS was banned, were held in May 2007. The turnout in the elections, however, was only 35 percent. All in all, the armed forces have been able to continue to exercise indirect control over the political system, blocking decisions, parties, and candidates they do not wish to see succeed. Today no one accuses Algeria of being a radical revolutionary regime.

Ethnic nationalism and national liberation

Ethnic nationalism has never enjoyed the sort of international support that anti-colonial national liberation struggles once did. Ethnic nationalists demand secession from an existing state. They struggle against a government close to home, and, unlike national liberation struggles, the majority population tends to see ethnic nationalism as a threat to the very integrity of the country and its political ideals. The majority views the territory in question as an integral part of the country, not some far-off territory that can easily be cut loose when the going gets really tough. Furthermore, ethnic nationalism's threat to the territorial integrity of an existing state is a threat to the international system as well. Once ethnic nationalists are granted the right to secede in principle, there is no natural stopping point. There is no principled way of determining which groups can exercise the right of self-determination. Proposing as standards the size of the national group, the historicity of its claim, and viability of the future state as a way of resolving the issue all beg the question. It is not clear why any singly or all taken together should serve as justification for the formation a new independent state. Thus, while individual states may support ethnic nationalists abroad when they weaken states that are the adversaries, few states back self-determination for ethnic minorities as a universal principle. In this vein, it is worthwhile noting that the national liberation struggle in Algeria received much international support and attention while the national liberation movement in Kosovo (Box 6.1) languished for decades. In the latter, only an incipient human rights disaster brought concerted international attention to the province.

Ethnic nationalists, just as others seeking national liberation, vary in their radicalism and moderation. Radicals often vie with moderates to gain support of their ethnic constituency. Moderates often seek to bargain

BOX 6.1
NATIONAL LIBERATION STRUGGLE IN KOSOVO

Overview

Kosovo was until 2008 a part of Serbia. The struggle of the Muslim Kosovars against the ethnic Serbs has been long and ongoing. The Kosovo situation illustrates the contemporary mix of ethnic nationalism and Islam that is also present in Chechnya (part of Russia) and Palestine.

1389 In a decisive battle at the Field of Blackbirds, the Turkish Sultan Murad I defeats the Serbians and their allies led by Prince Lazar. Lazar is captured and Serbia becomes a vassal state of the Ottoman Turks. The province takes a central, if tragic, place in the annals of Serb history.

1830 With the empire in the process of decay, and after centuries of Turkish domination, the kingdom of Serbia gains full autonomy from the Ottomans.

1912 After a general Balkans war, Serbia reacquires Kosovo from the Turks. The kingdom initiates a policy of expelling Kosovars (ethnic Albanians), one of the few Balkan nationalities that has largely converted to Islam under Turkish occupation, as well as Turks for the territory. Serbia settles ethnic Serbs on the vacated lands.

1945 During the Second World War, Serbs and Albanians equipped partisan forces to fight against German occupation. At war's end, a short but violent civil war ensues between various factions. The Albanians attempt to establish their own state independent of greater Serbia (now Yugoslavia). The Yugoslav army suppresses the rebellion. Josef Broz Tito, the communist partisan leader and ultimate victor in the Yugoslav civil war, tries to create a sense of Yugoslav national consciousness that transcends the separate nationalism of Serb, Croat, Slovene, Albanian, and Macedonian. He is largely unsuccessful. Thousands of Albanian Muslims are deported to Turkey. Other Yugoslavs characterize the Muslim Albanians as "Turks."

1968 Despite policies aimed at making Kosovo ethnically Serbian, the Albanians still predominate. Kosovo is granted greater autonomy. The move does not placate the radicals. University students riot.

1971 With a new constitution preparing the way for the post-Tito era, the status of Kosovo is changed again. It becomes an autonomous province as part of the Yugoslav republic of Serbia.

1989 The Yugoslav Federation begins to break up into its constituent parts. Politicians in each republic play to the republic's majority ethnic group as former communists seek a way of retaining some degree of popular support and legitimacy. Slobodan Milosevic, the President of Serbia, rescinds Kosovo's autonomous status. Violence breaks out in the province. Twenty are left dead. Serbia later sends the armed forces into Kosovo.

1992 Ibrahim Rugova is elected president of a self proclaimed Kosovo Republic. Rugova is a moderate. Serbia remains in actual control, tolerating Rugova. Rural groups reject the policy, eventually forming the Kosovo Liberation Army (KLA). An armed insurgency develops.

1998 Serbian attempts to suppress the insurgency flounder. Serbian massacres of Kosovars raise western concerns.

1999 Serbian paramilitaries and international volunteers enter the province to support the Serbs. They begin a program of ethnic cleansing. The atrocities provoke international outrage and a North Atlantic Treaty Organization (NATO) bombing campaign of Serbia. Kosovo is occupied by a joint NATO/Russian force. Kosovo continues under United Nations administration, its final legal status unresolved.

2008 Kosovo declares independence. The United States, the United Kingdom, France, and Germany recognize the country's independence. Serbia and Russia, among others, refuse to do so.

with the government and are willing to settle for autonomy. Often radicals will settle for nothing less than full independence and will use extreme forms of political violence in an effort to bring it about. Radicals and moderates may work in tandem with one another; moderates participating in the political process while radicals make violent attacks against the authorities. At other times, moderates and radicals find themselves at loggerheads with the radicals willing to assassinate any moderate who "collaborates" with the existing government. Although relatively ethnic liberation movements have succeeded in gaining full independence, radical ethnic nationalism can have significant appeal once serious cases of relative deprivation are seen through an ethnic lens.

The dynamics of Islamic revolutionary movements

By the end of the twentieth century, many regimes that had had their origin in wars of national liberation had reached the fourth phase of the revolutionary process and themselves had begun to suffer from the sorts of problems that presage revolutionary breakdown. Other governments in the former colonial world were facing the same sort of malaise that aging revolutionary regimes were. Many of these were in the Muslim world, the belt of countries that runs across northern Africa (including parts of black Africa), the Middle East, Central, Northwest and Southeast Asia, into the

Indonesian archipelago (see Map 6.2). Unsurprisingly, Islam, or at least a political variant of it, became a fertile source of revolutionary movements. In fact, Islamic radicalism has become more influential than secular radicalism in almost all Muslim countries. Islamic radicalism, just like national liberation movements, sees itself as part of a worldwide movement against western imperialism although Islamic accounts of imperialism stress religious and cultural domination rather than economics. Muslims comprise a large and diverse community of well over a billion believers, and within this community there are significant theological (and ideological) divisions. Violent Islamic radicals are a relative handful of Muslims and are outside the Islamic mainstream. However, their influence far outstrips their numbers. They have mobilized politically in much of the Muslim world, and some elements of these movements have committed terrorist attacks in Muslim countries and the West (Fuller 2003: 2–65). They are the focus of this section.

Islam and Islamism

Committed liberal democrats in Islamic countries have opposed authoritarianism and corruption. However, their influence has often been limited, especially in the Muslim world's Arab heartland. Liberal democratic theory is attractive primarily to a segment of the educated elite and the middle class. It does not resonate well with the masses. Liberalism de-emphasizes the role of religion. Liberalism is clearly western, and, as such, it is associated with a civilization Muslims have struggled against virtually since Islam's inception. Liberalism rejects the communitarian perspective typical of radicals, traditionalists, and ordinary people in the Muslim world. Instead, liberal democracy stresses individual rights, political competition, and due process. It focuses on limitations of governmental power, and thus it does not directly address the problems of poverty and injustice from which the mass of society suffered. In short, liberals lack a mass base.

Islamic political movements, in contrast, have potentially a broad appeal. To many people in the West, these movement appear strange since to most westerners religion seems to be an interloper in politics, at best a throwback to the past. To westerners, Islamic political programs often seem to appeal to a narrow moralism that is intolerant of individual differences. Indeed, the western media have often treated Islam in this way. They have focused on traditional codes that severely curtailed women's rights; restrictions on popular and apparently innocent modes of entertainment; barbaric punishments not only for common crimes but for offenses against sexual morality as well. The West's image of the Islamic

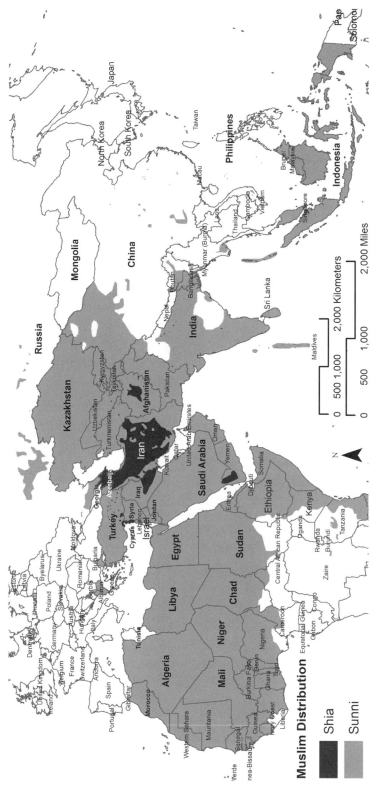

Map 6.2 Countries with Muslim majorities or significant Muslim minorities

Source: Environmental Systems Research Institute (ESRI) data and maps. CIA

Muslim Distribution

Shia

Sunni

political activist has become that of a violent, even a terroristic, bigot. Yet, this media-inspired image is at best a caricature, and at worst it represents the character assassination of an entire civilization. Religion often is compelled to play a political role, and it can often play it quite positively. It has served as a basis for political action in the West even in modern times. Catholicism and, to a more limited extent, Lutheranism had served as a rallying point for popular protest against communist states in Europe during the 1980s. Religion helped to undermine and overthrow these regimes as we shall see in later chapters. Radical leftist Catholics were a politically powerful force in Latin America from the 1960s through the 1980s. In all these countries, religion had the moral authority that the regime in power lacked. It had the organization and network of personal connections necessary if people were going to organize against a powerful state that had penetrated and controlled most other institutions. It should not be surprising that, for states with a large-majority Muslim population, Islam has come to play a substantial political role.

Political Islam (Islamism) is an offshoot of the religion of Islam, and the former cannot be understood without a basic appreciation of the latter. The religion of Islam rests on five pillars, fundamental principles that define the core of Muslim belief and practice. Christians and Jews as fellow members of the monotheistic Abrahamic faith tradition will recognize the five pillars' general tenor: a profession of faith, prayer, alms, fasting, and religious pilgrimage. The first pillar is bearing witness. This concerns the two-fold profession of faith: "There is no god but God" and "Muhammad is the messenger of God." The second pillar is daily prayer. Formal ritual prayer takes place five times a day, facing Mecca. Alms comes in the form of the yearly tithe or religious tax (*al-zakah* – the purification). Each believer is to pay 2.5 percent of his income and liquid assets. The fourth pillar, fasting, is observed during Ramadan, the ninth month of the Muslim calendar. No food, drink, or sex is allowed during the daylight hours. Since the Muslim calendar is a lunar calendar, Ramadan processes through the solar calendar, occurring during a slightly earlier period each year. When Ramadan occurs during the summer, the obligation is especially burdensome. The fifth pillar is pilgrimage to Mecca at least once in a lifetime for those who can afford it. The pilgrimage occurs during the twelfth month of the Muslim calendar. The pilgrimage has nine essential rituals associated with it. As is the case with other faiths, not all Muslims are equally observant of the faith's basic obligations. On the most basic level, the profession of faith defines who is and who is not a Muslim (Cornell 1999: 77–87).

Islam has social and political implications. It is a source of social idealism. It has always held out a standard of social justice. The rich are

not to oppress the poor, nor should the strong take advantage of
the weak. The law of God is superior to the law of human beings.
Rulers are responsible for abiding by it. Islam is more than a matter of
personal belief although it certainly is that. Belief in Islam makes the
individual Muslim a member of the *umma*, the Islamic community.
As part of the community, the member has rights and obligations, some of
which were strictly religious, relating to God alone, and others that
related to fellow Muslims. Ideally the *umma* is one people and ought to be
harmoniously governed as such, but conflicting interpretations concerning
Islam evolved within a generation or two after the Prophet Muhammad's
death. The Shia tradition holds that the Prophet's blood heirs should hold
political authority within the *umma* – i.e., serve as caliph. Although Shias
believe this line of authority has long since disappeared (its last
representative having gone into "occultation"), they also believe he will
reemerge in the end times. Shia ideas of religious authority were more
structured and hierarchical than the other major tradition, the *Sunna.*
The Sunni, the vast majority of Muslims, hold that the leaders of the
community should determine the line of succession to the caliphate; the
Prophet's blood heirs did not have a privileged position. Even though
today the issue of the caliphate is moot, over the centuries a multitude of
other doctrinal issues and practices have come to separate the two major
strains of Islam. However, both Sunni and Shia Islam have historically
seen a connection between secular and religious authority. States ruled by
Muslims were supposed to preserve this linkage. The Muslim ruler was
obliged to encourage the spread of Islam and protect members of the
umma. However, the state's advancement of Islam is primarily a matter of
moral suasion and the extension of certain privileges to Muslims that are
not available to non-Muslims. Thus, although early Muslim rulers
extended their kingdoms by conquest, conversion itself was not to be a
matter of force.

Anyone who professes the unity of God and the prophetic mission of
Muhammad is a Muslim. Muslim fundamentalists are a relatively small
subset of Muslims, but they play an important role in contemporary
radical Islamic political movements. Muslim fundamentalists share certain
characteristics with fundamentalists of other faiths, namely, "a discernible
pattern of religious militance by which self-styled 'true-believers' attempt
to arrest the erosion of religious identity, fortify the border of the religious
community, and create viable alternatives to secular institutions and
behaviors" (Almond *et al.* 2003: 17). In Islam the history of the
relationship between secular rulers and the law, and between religious
authorities and secular authorities, was a long and complicated one that
produced a variety of conflicting precedents. Muslim fundamentalists

regard none of these conflicting examples, other than that of Muhammad himself and his immediate successors, as definitive. Fundamentalists attempt to return to the authoritative origins of their faith; they view the traditions that have grown up around these sources as well as the contemporary religious establishment not as worthy guides but as heretical and corrupt. In their place fundamentalist Muslims adhere to a literal understanding of Islamic scripture, tradition, and the sayings of Muhammad (the *Koran*, the *Sunna*, and the *Hadith* respectively) and reject what traditional authorities say about them. Muslim fundamentalists (*salafis*) see the regimes under which they live as corrupt and unjust, and as such unworthy of the loyalty of believers. There are many Muslim fundamentalists who essentially want nothing to do with politics. Other fundamentalists are Islamists, proponents of political Islam.

Islamism or political Islam is the belief that the principles of Islam have to be applied systematically to politics in a way that corrects the corrupt practices of the recent past. As such it has no specific left–right ideological content. Just as there are fundamentalists who have no interest in politics, not all Islamists are fundamentalists. Moreover, many Islamists are reformers (Fuller 2003: 47–57). But regardless of their specific orientation, all Islamists see un-Islamic politics as a principal source of the problems troubling their societies, and they view politics, when guided by Islamic principles, as an essential engine for promoting religious and social reform. Some fundamentalist Islamists see violence as the principal mode of political action and advocate an Islamic revolution. Although they are a tiny minority, they are the ones that concern us here since they constitute a would-be revolutionary vanguard.

The vanguard

For Islamists of every stripe no state or nation can be the final focus of a true Muslim's political loyalty. Political authority and the authority of the state specifically must ultimately be subordinate to the moral commands of divine law, and those in power must look after the good of the whole Muslim community. This demand for social justice can serve as a very powerful rallying cry in a Muslim country governed by a corrupt and unpopular regime although it has been relatively infrequent until the current era. Traditionally, the Shiite clergy had been reluctant to engage in active politics; religious concerns always trumped secular ones, and the clergy did not see themselves as political leaders. The Sunni tradition without the formal clerical structure of the Shia seldom promoted political activism either. The ability of rulers to patronize and influence religious institutions led the leaders of these institutions to be generally accommodationist – willing to bend to the political will of secular leaders. They and others could cite the familiar maxim "A thousand years of tyranny is preferable to one day of anarchy." This changed in the twentieth century. However, the change in the Shiite position was presaged by the seventeenth-century Mullah Muhammad Bagher Majlesi, the chief mullah who opposed the Persian king on issues of public morality. Although Majlesi failed in his project, his actions established a precedent that would be used in the late twentieth century by the Ayatollah Ruhollah Khomeini and his followers (Molavi 2003). Under Khomeini's leadership, the clergy became the core of Islamist opposition to the secular government and led a revolution.

Islamists in Sunni Islam are much more informally organized and are generally not affiliated with the religious establishment. Nonetheless, like their Shiite counterparts they can make use of the institutional structure of the mosque. The history of contemporary Islamist political movements in the Sunni tradition goes back to the formation of the Muslim Brotherhood in Egypt during the 1920s. The Muslim Brothers were largely members of the rising middle class who sponsored charitable organizations and tried to bring about the end of corruption, prostitution, and western-style entertainments. Their broader political agenda included the establishment of an Islamist state. They pushed their agenda by a combination of peaceful and violent means. Banned in Egypt in 1954, many of its leaders fled to Saudi Arabia where their political activism encountered an extremely conservative version of Islam in Wahhabism, the official sect of the country. The amalgam of the Brotherhood's political activism and Wahhabism would influence one of the leading founders of al Qaeda, Osama bin Laden. The key figure in the early Brotherhood who elaborated methods of Islamist activism was Sayyid Qutb, executed in 1966 by the Egyptian government in its crackdown against the organization. Qutb's contributions to the Islamist movement were considerable. He introduced the concept of an Islamic "vanguard" that had a role similar to the Leninist vanguard in communist theory. Qutb asserted that the Muslim rulers of the current age in fact were not real Muslims at all but apostates who had given up the faith. Their rule was not true Islamic rule but was the same sort of godless impiety that had characterized government before the establishment of Islam by the Prophet Muhammad. Thus, it was the duty of good Muslims to replace them (Qutb n.d.). Qutb and those who followed his teachings came to believe that this could only be done by violence even though the Egyptian Brotherhood itself has accepted peaceful methods.

Contemporary Islamist radicals have taken the name "jihadis" and, in the process, have given a new twist both to traditional Islamic doctrines of holy war (jihad) and national liberation struggles. According to the common Islamic view, jihad has two meanings. The "greater jihad" is the personal struggle of every Muslim to live up to the standards of Islam. The "lesser jihad" is a holy war that requires military combat against an actual human enemy. Traditionally the lesser jihad is considered to be a communal obligation sanctioned by the political or religious leadership. Self-proclaimed jihadis turn the communal obligation into an individual one, claiming that Muslim lands are now occupied by foreigners or ruled by apostate Muslims. In this new situation, military jihad becomes an obligation on everyone capable of carrying it out and the sixth pillar of Islam (Gerges 2005: 3–4). National liberation is also given a religious coloration. Nationalism as such is anathema to Islamists since nothing, including the nation-state, should be placed above God. Yet, jihadis see liberating traditionally Muslim lands from apostates or foreign rule and uniting the *umma* under Islamic rule (i.e., reestablishing the caliphate that was abolished in 1924) as overriding religious obligations.

The Islamist vanguard's base

Islam provides the institutional network upon which Islamic political activists can draw. The mosque is more than a building, it is a social institution, perhaps the central institution for the entire community. It is the sort of institution that can be put to political uses. Friday prayers can provide opportunities for political sermons. The crowds they attracted can be mobilized for political protests afterwards. Islamic charities could help fill the social service void left by an inefficient and corrupt state. They provide opportunities to demonstrate the effectiveness of Islam and win converts to Islamists' political cause. They are a concrete demonstration of the fact that, as the Islamist slogan has it, "Islam is the solution!"

As is the case in all modern or modernizing societies, Muslim countries have a variety of groups and classes that can provide support for political movements. The French scholar, Gilles Kepel (Kepel 2002: 6–8, *passim*), explains that Islamism is particularly attractive to two large segments of society: largely unemployed or underemployed urban youth, and what he calls the "devout middle class." Both of these groups are deeply troubled by changes taking place in the Muslim world and form the natural constituency and recruiting ground for the Islamists. Most Islamic countries, as others in the developing world, have a predominantly young population. Many of their families have only recently migrated to urban areas because of the relatively greater opportunities there compared to the countryside. Much of the youth has been educated and prepared for work in the modern sector. However, the economy has rarely grown rapidly enough to provide adequate jobs for all of them. Thus, youth are keenly aware of inadequacies and injustices of the old regime that has promised them opportunities and failed to provide them. As many contemporary industrial societies with high urban crime rates can attest, the existence of a large number of young males without adequate prospects is a recipe for instability or disorder.

The devout middle class too finds the status quo deeply flawed. Their problem is not so much lack of economic opportunity as it is the psychological disorientation of the modernization process.
The modernizing of the economy has brought cultural change along with it. This cultural change, while welcome to some, has been shocking and even appalling to others. Those committed to a traditional view of their religion find the westernization that often comes along with economic modernization an affront to moral norms as most traditional Muslims understand them. Western forms of dress, entertainment, sexual mores, and alcohol use strike the traditionally devout as intolerable. To defend such practices by an appeal to the rights of individual choice is even more shocking, given the strong communitarian aspects of Islam.

Summary

In sum, Islam has become the natural idiom of protest. It has both moral force and is intelligible to all the relevant political actors, including the public at large. Even the old regime can ill afford to reject Islam in principle. Furthermore, Islam provides a rootedness with the past for which those in rapidly changing societies often yearn. Islam also seems to provide a basis for building a new and just order. Islamic parties, brotherhoods, conspiratorial societies, and loose Islamic movements that espoused this view became important political actors in the 1970s. Islamists hold a variety of sometimes conflicting political views. Some believe that violence is necessary for political change; others reject it. This difference has led to bitter and sometimes violent internal ideological or sectarian splits. Even small organizations have frequently fragmented into rival factions sometimes as zealous in fighting one another as they were in fighting the established authorities. However, whatever their state of organization, Islamists constitute a disloyal or semi-loyal opposition in most societies. Those willing to resort to violence often seek to become a revolutionary vanguard, especially when forcibly excluded from ordinary politics. In Iran they played just that role before the 1979 revolution. In Sudan Islamists used the armed forces to stage a coup d'etat. In Afghanistan (see Box 6.2) they formed a guerrilla group that seized power in a civil war.

CASE STUDY: THE ISLAMIC REVOLUTION IN IRAN

Although Islamists have cast a large shadow on the world stage especially since the events of September 11, 2001, there has been only one truly Islamist revolution – the Iranian Revolution of 1979. That revolution has followed the general pattern seen as long ago as the English Revolution of 1640. The old regime was delegitimized; moderates made a bid for power but were replaced by radicals, and the radicals themselves were eventually forced to retrench.

Phase I: breakdown

In many ways the Iranian monarchy seemed an unlikely candidate for revolution. Shah Muhammad Reza Pahlavi's rule had seemed unshakeable for decades. The shah's government had used increased oil revenues, a product of the 1973 Organization of Petroleum Exporting Countries (OPEC) oil boycott, to increase the size of his armed forces, making the country the region's leading power. The shah enjoyed the patronage of the United States, which under the Nixon Doctrine had sought regional allies to help support US interests across the globe. And as a consequence the United States sold Iran some of the most modern US military equipment available. Yet, despite the regime's advantages, the revolution triumphed and sent shockwaves throughout the region.

Shah Muhammad Reza Pahlavi had inherited the throne from his father in 1941. In the early 1950s, the shah had already embarked on a course that would eventually lead to political disaster. During that era, oil had become an issue for the country's nationalists. Much of Iran's oil wealth was controlled by the Anglo-Iranian Oil Company (AIOC) which held the major concessions on the extraction and export of the country's oil. Although the AIOC paid royalties to the Iranian government, it paid even more in taxes to the British government. Nationalists sought a better deal. Muhammad Mossadeq became the pivotal figure in the effort to retrieve Iran's oil from the foreign concessionaires. First, as head of the Majlis (national legislative) committee dealing with the issue and then as prime minister, he pressed for better terms from the AIOC. In the process, the Majlis nationalized the company. Pressure from the Majlis and popular demonstrations in support of his policies enhanced the status of Mossadeq and marginalized the shah. In 1953 the shah fled the country. Later that year, the US Central Intelligence Agency (CIA) along with the British orchestrated a coup that removed Mossadeq from office and restored the absolute power of the shah. Although Anglo-Iranian and other firms continued in business, ownership of Iran's oil remained in government hands (Meyer 2003: 70–6).

In 1963 the shah began the so-called "White Revolution." The proposal put to a popular vote in a plebiscite received a reported 99 percent support. It called for land reform, profit-sharing for industrial workers, nationalization of forests and pastureland, sale of government factories to finance land reform, voting rights for women, and a literacy corps. The revolution was meant to strengthen the shah's absolutism rather than democratize the country, however. In addition, many religious leaders opposed the extension of government power and the restriction of their own implicit in the reforms. A leading opponent was the Ayatollah Ruhollah Khomeini, a leader at the Shiite religious center of Qom. He was among those arrested as the shah's government cracked down on opponents of the reform. Khomeini's arrest sparked three days of rioting. The White Revolution never lived up to its advanced billing. Land reform led to the concentration of land into commercial farms and did not benefit the peasantry or rural labor while the lower and traditional middle classes of the cities fared little better. In 1971 the shah used the twenty-five-hundredth anniversary of the formation of the Persian Empire to try to legitimize the regime by celebrating the country's (and regime's) ancient roots. This focus on pre-Islamic Iranian history was also a slap at the religious establishment. Khomeini, then in exile, issued a statement condemning the celebration. The stress upon the non-Islamic foundations of the nation was not surprising. It had been a constant theme of the regime. Reza Shah, the shah's father, had been a militant secularist, centralizing state power at the expense of the clergy, attacking Islamic practices, and even prohibiting traditional dress. Thus, Muhammad Pahlavi was following an established pattern. However, the restoration of the site of the ancient capital and the lavish displays associated with the celebrations demonstrated how much the regime was out of touch with its own people. In short, the regime was both autocratic and antireligious; it was a combination that eventually produced a grand coalition among opposition forces.

Under the shah, the government followed a policy of state-promoted industrial growth. In five development plans, the government promoted the growth of commercial agriculture in the countryside. By the time of the revolution, however, much of the rural population were either smallholders or landless. Fifty percent of the rural population owned no land. In the cities, the government promoted the growth of large-scale industrial projects and major infrastructure construction. Rapid urbanization led

Plate 6.2 Ayatollah Khomeini, leader of the Iranian Revolution.

to the proliferation of slums as the population left the countryside to seek job opportunities in the cities. Economic and social inequality was considerable. Laborers lived in conditions of squalor as the rising new economic elite flaunted their wealth. The traditional traders, the bazaar merchants, profited little from the government's economic projects. The inflow of revenue from oil accelerated the government's modernization schemes in the 1960s and 1970s. The high levels of spending promoted government corruption and led to an overheated economy. In 1977 there was a sudden economic downturn brought about by the government's attempts to control inflation. The slowdown in GDP growth also brought a substantial increase in unemployment. Workers, who had had at least low incomes and some hope of progress, now saw even these limited gains reversed. The economic downturn helped destabilize the regime even further.

By the late 1970s, it was clear that the regime had to change. Yet, the shah faced the dilemma typical of authoritarian governments trying to reform. Too little reform would intensify popular protests and bring on a revolution. Too much reform would change the very nature of the regime, making a revolution largely superfluous. In the face of domestic and foreign pressure, the shah began to liberalize in early 1977. Some political prisoners were released. Laws allowing the military to arrest and try civilians were altered. Opponents of the regime, at home and abroad, began to speak out. Khomeini became an especially prominent figure. In January 1978 an article, inspired by the government, attacked Khomeini's piety and suggested he was actually a British agent. The slander backfired. Popular protests became widespread and accelerated. A coalition formed, composed of middle-class liberals, who had predominated in the previous protests, the Shiite clergy, bazaar merchants, and the urban lower class. During 1978 demonstrations took on an increasingly Islamist character. Tapes from Khomeini were played in mosques and widely circulated. Attempts by the government to conciliate the opposition came too late and were too feeble and erratic.

Phase II: rule of the moderates

By the end of the year, hoping to salvage something from the situation, the shah began talks with the moderate opposition. He did not gain much. Shapour Bakhtiar agreed to form a government only on the condition that the shah leave the country. By mid-January the shah left under the pretense of taking a short vacation. Khomeini returned to Iran in triumph and became the de facto head of the revolution. The stage was set for the radicalization. When Shah Muhammad Reza Pahlavi fled, formal power devolved upon a nominally parliamentary system of government that for over twenty years had really been an instrument of the shah. These institutions proved no match for power emanating from the streets. Prime Minister Bakhtiar proved too moderate for the Islamists. Although they had been only one element of the revolutionary coalition that also included bazaar merchants and middle-class reformers, they were quickly becoming the dominant one because of their ideology and superior organization. Bakhtiar was replaced in a month by Mehdi Bazargan, a person more acceptable to the radicals, but Bazargan too became a target of the radicals. Islamist clerics formed the Islamic Republican Party (IRP) to compete for power, and Ayatollah Khomeini established the Revolutionary Council to supervise the government. A Revolutionary Guard was established because of the military's supposed loyalty to the shah. Revolutionary committees policed neighborhoods. The clergy established revolutionary courts outside the normal judiciary. These bodies subjected many of the malefactors of the old regime to a summary trial. Despite government and international protests, many of the condemned were executed. A situation of dual power had developed.

At the same time, other groups were far from quiescent. Kurdish and Turkoman separatists in the North and Arab separatists in the South organized and demanded autonomy. Eventually, when their demands were rejected, violence erupted. The most serious rebellion occurred among the Kurds. Various groups across the political spectrum formed political parties to advance their interests and ideologies. Government employees, students, and workers took control of their institutions, demanding a greater say in their governance. In the climate of chaos, the revolution undertook social and economic transformation. Landowners, the business and industrial elite had their assets confiscated. Khomeini created the Foundation for the Disinherited, which took over the assets of the Pahlavi Foundation and other nationalized wealth. It became one of the leading conglomerates in the country. The Crusade for Reconstruction recruited young people for development projects. The organization quickly took over what hitherto had been state activities, constructing schools, clinics, and infrastructure projects. Islamic norms were strictly, if informally, enforced.

Phase III: rule of the radicals

In 1980 and 1981, the revolutionary process continued. The power struggle between radicals and moderates was played out against a backdrop of contested elections, assassinations, and other acts of political violence. The seizure of the American embassy and its employees, and a failed military rescue attempt by the United States aimed at freeing the captives, further radicalized the country. An international war (with Iraq) began in the fall of 1980, as Iran's old rival sought to take advantage of the country's internal turmoil. Purges of the military and civil service continued. The impeachment of the moderate president, Bani Sadr, in June 1981 gave control of the government to the clerics of the IRP. Political violence, including guerrilla insurgencies, intensified as did the regime's repression.

It was during this period that the originally unofficial power of religious authorities received official sanction and furthered the radicals' consolidation of power. The 1979 constitution (amended in 1989) formalized a dual-power relationship, in which religious authorities and the government each have power. The document states that Islamic law is superior to all other law, including the law of the state itself. A president is elected for a four-year term by popular vote. The president nominates a prime minister who must have the confidence of the legislature. The single-house legislature, the 270-seat Majlis, is also directly elected for a four-year term. However, real power remained in the hands of the religious establishment. The supreme religious jurist (*wali faqih*), originally Ayatollah Khomeini, currently Ayatollah Ali Hoseini Khamenei, is the key figure. The *faqih* appoints the head of the judiciary, declares war and makes peace, commands the armed forces, and ratifies the election of the president. The supreme leader is chosen by and acts in the name of the Assembly of Experts, who are themselves chosen from among the clergy by popular election. If the Supreme Court or two-thirds of the Majlis holds the president has violated the constitution, he can be dismissed by the *faqih*. A twelve-member Council of Guardians supervises the legislature and elections. Bills found to be un-Islamic by the Council and candidates not approved by it are disallowed. The *faqih* appoints six members of the Council and the judiciary the other six. The Revolutionary Guards and Crusade for Reconstruction are incorporated into the state as government ministries. The revolutionary courts too are incorporated into the regular judicial system. Little autonomy is granted the provinces. Under the Islamic Republic, Iran remains a highly unitary state. By early 1983 the government would brook no substantial opposition to the IRP. Yet, divisions within the Islamic establishment began to assume greater importance. Leaders differed among themselves over a variety of issues: over political liberalization versus the strict enforcement of Islamic law; over economic issues, such as privatization or nationalization, and the regulation of foreign trade; and over foreign policy issues. The end of the Iran–Iraq War in 1988, and the death of Khomeini the following year, brought an end to a turbulent epoch.

Phase IV: Thermidorean reaction

The 1990s saw the revolution enter its fourth phase. Elections have been held regularly for the presidency, the legislature, the Assembly of Experts, and local governments. After over some two decades in power, however, political Islam has discovered its limits. Serious economic and social problems continued to plague the country. Radicalism and enthusiasm for the revolution have waned. Significant disagreements about how to deal with them divided the political elite. The IRP was abolished and replaced by less formally organized factions. There has been an ongoing contest between various political currents within the Islamic leadership, encompassing a variety of policy questions. President Mohammed Khatami elected in 1997 and reelected in 2001 tried to liberalize social and political policies. But conservatives pushed back, and by the end of his term reformers were weaker than ever.

The Iranian revolution is not unique either in its causes or in its immediate consequences. In retrospect, despite its military power and international heft, the shah's out-of-touch authoritarian regime had been ripe for overhaul. Its nationalism had been pompous and self-serving. Its programs to aid the masses of the people had largely been a sham. In this respect the regime not only resembled its historical predecessors but many other authoritarian states in the region as well. The revolution and especially the role religion played in it sent shock waves throughout the region. Islam provided both a rallying cry to which the masses could respond, and an organization that could carry out agitation and propaganda effectively. More than its counterparts in other Muslim countries, the Islamic Republic has attempted to establish a constitutional system that would both give the people a direct role in choosing their leaders while preserving the theocratic character of the state. Yet, the regime has been facing stagnant economy and growing popular frustration that undermine the acceptability of this arrangement. In 2005 Iranian politics seemed to take another radical swing as a non-clerical radical with little national political experience, Mahmoud Ahmadinejad, was elected president. He has assumed an increasingly combative stance with the United States and other western powers, but has been unable to deliver the promised economic benefits to his primary constituency, the vast number of poor in the Islamic Republic. All in all, the Iranian Revolution followed the pattern that had been seen as typical of many other revolutions: growing chaos, the creation of multiple centers of power, the passing of power into the hands of the radicals, and finally the denouement. The revolution has matured. And although it has spawned no close copies, political Islam continues to be a force in the Muslim world.

Other Muslim states and movements

As the twenty-first century begins, political Islam is an important force in the Muslim world. Although today's handful of Islamist regimes are themselves under threat, political Islam has undermined the legitimacy of many other regimes. Like typical old regimes before them, the regimes threatened by Islamists have, in large measure, been the cause of their own problems. They have neither systematically nor successfully addressed issues of social justice even when their ideologies pledged that they would do so. They have provided very little political space for proponents of political Islam or any other opposition group, thus leaving violence and conspiracy as the only effective methods of resistance. In short, the rise of political Islam is the product of regime failure, and the consequence of Islam's role as a religious and social force.

Islamists in power and as power contenders

Today Islamists are in power in Sudan, and they were in power in Afghanistan until late 2001. In Sudan they came to power as the result of a coup, but regularized their rule by presidential and legislative elections in 1996. The government had a close relationship with the National Islamic Front, led by Hasan al-Turabi until Turabi was arrested in 2001 for signing an agreement with non-Muslim rebels in Sudan's South. Political parties are banned. The government has imposed Islamic law on all individuals living in the northern half of the country. A southern rebellion supported by Christians and adherents to traditional religions has sought the reversal or modification of this and other Islamist measures. The rebels struck a power-sharing bargain with the government in 2005.

In Afghanistan, a radical Islamist group, the Taliban, also came to power in most of the country during the late 1990s. By 1996, after a prolonged civil war that followed the Soviet Union's occupation of the country (1979–89), they had militarily pushed their opponents into remote areas in the northern part of the country. A radical, thoroughly fundamentalist Islamist group, the Taliban had been supported by the Pakistani national intelligence apparatus, which itself is influenced by currents of political Islam. Of all the important Islamist movements, the Taliban come the closest to the popular western caricature of political Islam. Essentially rural in background, they found the ways of Kabul and other cities difficult to fathom, and imposed their own notion of how a good Muslim should act. As a consequence, they closed down schools for girls, introduced stoning, amputation and other public punishments, and engaged in a running polemic with international aid agencies.

BOX 6.2
ISLAMIST REVOLUTION IN AFGHANISTAN

Overview

For centuries, a predominantly Muslim country, Afghanistan has always been a country difficult to govern. It has never had an effective centralized administration. Foreign invasion and internal turmoil since the 1970s gave Islamists the opportunity to seize power in key centers and rule for the better part of a decade.

1919 Afghanistan establishes its independence under King Amanullah (1919–29). Relations with major states are established. Previously, the country had been a prize in the "great game" played by Russia and Britain over Russian influence in the region and Russian access to the Indian Ocean.

1964 King Zahir Shah promulgates a constitution that allows for a representative assembly in which the king appoints one-third of the delegates, the people also elect one-third, and the remaining third are chosen by provincial assemblies. The king's reforms permit the growth of political parties, including the communist People's Democratic Party of Afghanistan (PDPA). In 1967 the party splits into two factions. The first, the Khalq (Masses), is led by Nur Muhammad Taraki and Hafizullah Amin. It receives the backing of elements with the armed forces. The other faction, Parcham (Banner), is headed by Babrak Karmal.

1973 With royal corruption and economic decline setting the stage, a former prime minister, Daoud, seizes power in a military coup. Daoud abolishes the monarchy and begins a series of reforms that meet with little success. Political turmoil grows.

1978 A reunified PDPA, supported by the Soviet Union, overthrows and assassinates Daoud. Nur Muhammad Taraki becomes prime minister. The PDPA attempts to revolutionize the country and is met with open resistance.

1979 An internal coup replaces Taraki with Hafizullah Amin. Unrest grows worse. The Soviet Union invades the country to stabilize the situation to its own advantage. It replaces Amin, who has refused to follow Soviet advice about how to quell the growing insurgency. The Soviets bring in Babrak Karmal, exiled leader of the Parcham faction, to serve as prime minister. The insurgency continues and worsens.

1985 The resistance to the Soviets and their Afghan allies continues to grow. Kabul, the capital, is shelled. The United States, Saudi Arabia, Pakistan, and others aid the Islamic mujihadeen rebels with equipment and advice.

1988 The Geneva accords provide for a Soviet withdrawal. Once Soviet forces leave, the civil war between ethnic and religious/ideological Afghan factions and the pro-Soviet Najibullah government continues. The Najibullah regime is overthrown in 1992 as rebels take the capital. Nonetheless, the civil war between the various factions continues.

1996 The newly emerged Taliban faction, supported directly by Pakistan, takes Kabul. Two years later they control 90 percent of the country.

> The Taliban impose a Draconian version of Islamic law in the territory under their sway.
>
> 2001 The United States allied with northern ethnic groups forces the Taliban from power. The Taliban had allied themselves with Osama bin Laden and his al Qaeda organization. They had provided him with sanctuary. He had provided them with fighters to continue the civil war.
>
> 2008 The Taliban, operating from across the Pakistan border, continue to lead an insurgency against the elected government and foreign occupying forces.

While actual Islamist seizures of power have been relatively few, Islamist movements have arisen in almost every country in the Middle East, North Africa, and Southeast Asia. The Islamic Salvation Front almost came to power in 1992 in Algeria, when they were on the brink of winning the second round of legislative elections. Rather than let that occur, the military intervened and outlawed the organization, provoking an Islamic insurgency with barbarities perpetrated by both the rebel and government sides. The unpopularity of the rebels was only surpassed by that of the government. But until the end of the decade, the generals seemed unable or unwilling to extract themselves from their predicament. In Egypt a variety of Islamist organizations have placed the government under attack for some two decades. In 1981, they succeeded in assassinating the president. Political violence provoked wholesale repression, but by the end of the 1990s, the government largely contained the violent opposition. Today the Muslim Brotherhood has accepted a nonviolent political role, but has been legally prevented from running official candidates under its own name. The reactions of the governments of Algeria and Egypt have been the most repressive, but other governments challenged by political Islam have tended to react with a relatively heavy hand as well. Perhaps, only in Lebanon have Islamists and others enjoyed considerable freedom to organize and contend for power. Even this degree of freedom is the result of Syrian occupation and an uneasy balance between factions following a protracted civil war.

Prospects

To build a revolutionary movement or to sustain a government, Islamists need to appeal to both the young, who tend to be radical, and the devout middle class, many of whom are basically conservative in the social and economic inclinations. This can be quite difficult. The rise of political Islam, while it led established regimes to reemphasize their religious roots, also led them to follow a policy of repression and diversion. Established regimes jailed the most dangerous advocates of Islamism or forced them into exile. In fact, during the 1980s the Afghan war against Soviet occupation provided a magnet for radicals that, happily for established regimes, especially Saudi Arabia, attracted many away from their home countries. This diversion strategy had divergent consequences. It weakened radicalism at home at least in the short run. However, these radicals (dubbed "international jihadis") would later become an army of Islamist soldiers of fortune, available for combat in such places as Bosnia, Algeria, Kosovo, and Chechnya, as well as in their own countries of origin.

Some latter-day jihadis without Afghan experience have also been attracted into terrorist networks organized against the United States and European democracies. These terrorists attack what they call the "far enemy," the West, only because western governments support the "near enemy" – apostate Muslim regimes in the Islamic heartland. Robert Pape (Pape 2005: 79–92) points out that Islamist-inspired suicide bombing campaigns and terrorism, also typical of secular national liberation struggles, have occurred in places where US troops have a significant presence or in historically independent Muslim areas incorporated into non-Muslim states. Even international terrorist attacks such as those in New York, Bali, Madrid, and London are seen by their perpetrators as part of this struggle against foreign occupation of Muslim lands. In short, the international jihadis attempt to tap into the same sort of mass base that secular wars of national liberation do, and have much the same political rationale.

The overall prospects for Islamism would seem to be good since the movement has plenty of popular discontent upon which to feed. Still, some of the force of political Islam has had time to play itself out. The Islamic Republic of Iran has existed long enough to be beset with its own dissatisfied youth and its own revolution of rising expectations. Furthermore, the tendency of Islamists to break into factions and fight with one another has undermined the bloody Islamic revolt in Algeria that raged through much of the 1990s. Sudan's Islamist regime too has been troubled by infighting. Terrorist attacks against civilian targets have produced revulsion among many ordinary Muslims. And repression has been effective against many violent radical movements in the Middle East. Still, it is as yet uncertain where the backlash against corruption, injustice, and foreign influence in the Muslim world is heading.

Conclusion

For much of the twentieth century, revolutionary movements seemed to be at high tide. Today the leading revolutions of the past century have advanced to a decrepit fourth phase, neither mobilizing social force inside nor inspiring imitators outside their countries. The Soviet Union, the product of the Russian Revolution, has disappeared entirely. Even many regimes formed by national liberation movements have reached their fourth stage. One branch of the revolutionary family remains dynamic – the Islamists. The actions of predatory governments of the Muslim world and the sometimes ham-handed response of the West must give Islamists hope despite their numerous tactical setbacks. Nonetheless, in most of the world the Islamists are only in the revolution's first stage.

Questions for further consideration

1 How do the classic revolutions discussed in Chapter 5 compare with wars of national liberation and Islamic revolutionaries discussed in this chapter?

2 Were all leaders of liberation movements radical? What conditions give radicals the upper hand?

3 How much does the news typically cover ethnic nationalist wars of liberation today? Why do you think this is so?

4 Who are the principal targets of Islamic revolutionaries? Why? How can these targets meet the challenge?

5 Was the Iranian Revolution successful? Explain.

6 Do you think the early twenty-first century more or less susceptible to revolution than earlier eras? Why or why not?

Further reading

Gérard Challand, *Revolution in the Third World*. New York: Penguin Books, 1978. A revolutionary intellectual's analysis of revolutions in developing countries in the era of anti-colonialism.

Forrest D. Colburn, *The Vogue of Revolution in Poor Countries*. Princeton, NJ: Princeton University Press, 1994. An analysis of revolutions in developing countries and what becomes of them.

Graham E. Fuller, *The Future of Political Islam*. New York: Palgrave Macmillan, 2003. A survey of the variety of ideas and tactics associated with Islamism today.

Gilles Kepel, *The War for Muslim Minds*. Cambridge, MA: Harvard University Press, 2004. A survey of Islamist radicalism, its global effects, and the way it has been fought.

William R. Polk, *Violent Politics: A History of Insurgency, Terrorism and Guerrilla War, from the American Revolution to Iraq*. New York: HarperCollins, 2007. A survey of the politics underlying revolutionary wars, mostly from the twentieth century.

Paul E. Sigmund (ed.), *The Ideologies of Developing Nations*. New York: Praeger Publishers, 1972. An anthology of the National Liberation ideologies.

The coup d'etat and its consequences
Breakdown engineered by elite actors

The chief foundations of all states ... are good laws and good arms.
[W]here there are good arms there must be good laws.

(Niccolò Machiavelli, *The Prince*, 1513)

In this chapter

The discussion of breakdown turns to the coup d'etat, the seizure of state power by an armed elite. Successful coups have occurred in a variety of political contexts. And coups have a variety of underlying causes, cultural, societal, and institutional. However, coups can be deterred by properly structuring civil–military relations to promote both the military's competence and loyalty to its civilian superiors. The chapter explores some of the underlying causes of coups, how coups are conducted, and the nature of modern military organizations with special reference to the officer corps. In discussing details of military institutions and civil–military relations, the chapter takes a neo-institutional approach. Political culture, structural functionalism, and political economy play important roles in explaining what sorts of countries are likely to be susceptible to coups. And game theory helps explain exactly when and how coups are likely to occur. The chapter concludes with two case studies on countries that have experienced a succession of coups – Nigeria and Pakistan.

Introduction

Mass movements and radical parties play the critical roles in revolutions. A revolution involves long-term social upheaval and aims at a thoroughgoing change in the regime. In contrast, a **coup d'etat** is a quick, sometimes bloodless seizure of power by armed elements (usually from the state's own military forces) who quickly remove incumbents from the seats of power and replace them with a government of their own choosing. The sorts of coups this chapter specifically examines are those led by senior or middle-ranking members of the armed forces (usually generals or colonels); they are seizures of power by a particular group of elite actors acting on their own behalf or on behalf of others. Although other sorts of coups occasionally occur, these have been the most numerous and most successful in modern times. While coups change the decision-makers at the top, they most often leave state structures intact even though state personnel may be subject to political purges. Sometimes coups have revolutionary objectives; sometimes they are status quo oriented. In either case, like revolutions, coups are high-stakes affairs. Like revolutions, they can only occur when politics is fundamentally unsettled or when the existing legal rules are contested by important political actors. Regardless of their ideological aims, the armed forces always intervene as patriots – at least as they themselves define the term. Successful coups frequently lead to a period of military rule of brief or extended duration. During the contemporary era successful coups have occurred in almost every major region of the developing world: the Americas, the Middle East, Africa, the Far East, and Southeast Asia. This chapter investigates the causes of coups, the military as a political actor, the dynamics of the coup d'etat, and manner in which civilian governmental authorities and the armed forces relate to one another. The next chapter will investigate long-term military rule.

The modern armed forces as a political actor

"Who shall guard the guardians?" is an age-old political question. The military must be both competent and loyal if the state and the public are to be safe. The officer corps is the key element for assuring both loyalty and military competence. Only rarely are others such as noncommissioned officers able to direct the armed forces in political interventions. Without good officers the best of troops are likely to be ineffective while with good officers, over time, even mediocre recruits can become effective soldiers. Until virtually the end of the nineteenth century, political authorities were often able to finesse the issue of combining loyalty with competence by allowing only those who were already politically well connected

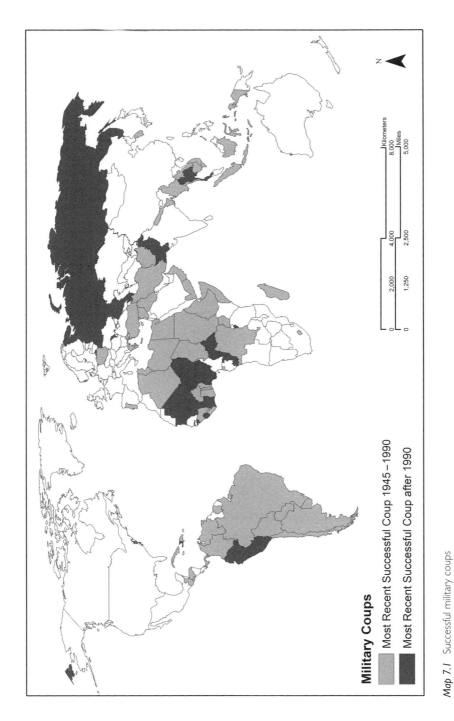

Map 7.1 Successful military coups

Source: Environmental Systems Research Institute (ESRI) map data. Data: O'Kane (1987); Department of State Background Notes

Military Coups

Most Recent Successful Coup 1945–1990

Most Recent Successful Coup after 1990

to become military officers. Officership was the vocation or avocation of the upper class, those most likely to be loyal to the established regime. Men in the ranks would follow someone of high status and personal authority. Since generals, who commanded armies in the field, could see the entire battlefield with their own eyes and the basic technology of war had evolved only slowly through the eighteenth and early nineteenth centuries, physical courage was often more important than mastery of the occupation's technical details for all but the senior-most military leaders.

The professional officer corps

Modern science and technology eventually changed all that. The Industrial Revolution had its effect on military as well as economic organization. The railroad and the telegraph, the machine gun and the repeating rifle, and greatly improved artillery altered the face of warfare. The logic of the situation was increasingly obvious. Commanders needed to coordinate the movement of troops they could not actually view in person. They needed to integrate a variety of new weapons and technologies into increasingly more complex military organizations and develop effective tactics for their use. Commanders themselves had to grapple with a welter of details. They needed technically competent subordinate commanders and well-trained staffs. Officership became ripe for professionalization (Huntington 1964: 7–10). As a result, military academies and war colleges were established and expanded. Exercises and war games were developed to test the application of new technologies. Instead of moving from civilian life into the armed forces at a military rank befitting one's social status, officers were promoted on the basis of seniority, education, and performance, just as any other professionally trained member of a state institution. States could not survive in the rough and tumble of international politics unless they had competent, modern military establishments. States that recruited officers on the basis of whom they knew rather than what they knew were doomed to military ineffectiveness. Thus, today the officer corps in almost every country is professional. And modern officers, be they full-time or reserve officers, are recruited, trained, and promoted under the rubric of professionalism (Huntington 1964: 30–58).

The military mentality

With professionalization, the social character of the officer corps changed. Professionalization meant that one had to earn a leadership position; he could not simply claim it by right of birth or by means of his political connections. Professionalization opened up a military career to the sons of the middle class, people with talent and ambition, willing to go through an arduous process of education, training, and service in often unattractive assignments and locales. By the same token, professionalization often made the armed forces less attractive to scions of the upper class. Other careers where access to privileged positions could be gained by personal connections beckoned. The change in the social composition of the officer corps had effects on the institution as a political actor. When the military leadership was drawn from the social and political elite, there was little chance that the interests of the military and a government, both run by that same elite, would diverge substantially. However, the modern officer corps, composed increasingly of middle-class professionals, is a different matter. Modern officers possess a distinct corporate identity and distinct interests that set them apart from the political class that rules the country. Furthermore, they have a distinctive worldview that sets them apart from other political actors as well. How people look at the world shapes how they act. And the military's worldview – its "military mentality" – is no exception. This mentality is less specific and often more subtle than a political ideology. It is the result of officers' education, training, and professional focus. It has several important elements (Huntington 1964: 59–79; Nordlinger 1977: 19–22, 53–60).

Patriotism

Military officers and military cadets are taught to be patriotic or nationalistic – "My country, right or wrong!" Only true patriots can be expected to sacrifice their lives for their country as soldiers are at times required to do. However, the notion that the military should be loyal to the nation is ambiguous and open to interpretation. The military can be loyal to the society, the state, the government of the day, or to all three. In consolidated regimes this ambiguity represents no great difficulty. The government of the day is seen as legitimate by the people, and the state – the permanent, professional administrative apparatus of government that includes the armed forces – dutifully carries out the government's orders. However, patriotism is a two-edged sword in situations where a government's legitimacy is eroded. In such cases nationalists inside and outside the military may claim the government itself has betrayed the country. They may come to believe that rebellion is a duty incumbent upon patriots. This was the position taken by some radical nationalists under Germany's Weimar Republic after the First World War. They were not only ready to remove the government but wanted to change the whole constitutional system, some by any means possible. Thus, nationalists may support the nation and the state, and rebel against the government of the day. Even the concept of nation can be given various sorts of ideological twists. Centrists tend to see the nation as the public, whose interests are expressed through the civic organizations and interest groups that comprise civil society. On the other hand, leftists may see the nation as the masses of people (especially the vast majority of the underprivileged) who make it up. Disenfranchised, often misled by the government and vested interests, the people require leadership. In contrast to both of the other two, rightists tend to see the nation as a historical entity distinct from public opinion and the actual people who currently comprise the nation. The rightists' nation is mystical, almost religious. Both the left and the right bring an ideological perspective to their concept of nation that makes the military or selected members of it better interpreters of what the nation needs than the actual majority of the national community. In short, the principle that military people should be patriotic and nationalistic establishes a problematic instead of solving a problem.

The ethic of self-sacrifice

Patriotism can call for self-sacrifice. Thus, military officers have to be more than simply skilled warriors; they have to possess the virtue of self-sacrifice as well. In the fourth century BC, Aristotle distinguished between the technical competence of the mercenary and the true courage of the citizen-soldier (*Nicomachean Ethics*: 1116b 5–24). The well-trained mercenary acts bravely, Aristotle noted, because he knows that resistance under attack is usually the best means of personal survival. He who breaks ranks and flees is likely to be cut down. The mercenary's action is a matter of calculation, not virtue. In fact, the mercenary will cut and run when that action actually does provide the best means of survival. True courage is another matter. The courageous citizen not only stands fast and obeys orders in situations where that happens to offer the best prospects for personal survival; he also steadfastly obeys orders and does his duty when doing so entails his own death. Adherence to the norm of self-sacrifice is no small matter. If officers' courage is to be reliable, they must be schooled in it. Models of heroism must be held up for daily admiration. Feelings of personal pride and national honor must be used to reinforce it. The conscious acceptance of the ethic of self-sacrifice often gives officers a sense of their own distinctiveness, even superiority to the rest of society.

Legalism

The military is taught to obey the law and obey its superiors. However, as with nationalism, obedience to the law is a malleable concept. Military officers are loyal servants of the state; they follow orders. But who has the right to issue orders? For most lower and middle-ranking officers, the answer to this question is straightforward. Their military superiors have the right to issue orders. And "due obedience" is a legal defense for obeying orders even if it turns out that superior officers themselves were acting illegally. The subordinates' responsibility is to obey, not to deliberate. For senior officers the concept of due obedience is trickier. Do the military commander-in-chief and other high-ranking individuals obey the law or their civilian superiors? They have sworn to defend the nation (and maybe its constitution). Is not obedience to these more important than loyalty to civilian authorities who are themselves acting against the constitution and the interests of the nation? Officers are even more inclined to answer "yes" than they otherwise would be when the constitution includes provisions that make the armed forces its guardians.

Realpolitik

More than any other branch of the state, the armed forces' business is power. They are professionally responsible for the defense of the state. If that defense should fall, they would be one of the primary recipients of blame. They are concerned with the direct military elements of power: the size, readiness, and discipline of the military forces themselves. To fulfill their responsibilities, the officer corps trains and plans as well as makes recommendations to and advises its civilian superiors. They are by their very profession both advocates of national power as well as alarmists. They are distrustful of other states' intentions, wary of the threats that those states pose, and advocates of the position that more military force is better than less. They may not actually advocate the use of force, but they advocate that the state have ample forces at its command should it need to use them. As a consequence of their mind-set, the armed forces can find themselves at odds with their civilian superiors over such issues as the size and configuration of the military budget, recruitment policies, and military salaries.

The professional role played by military officers is likely to make them proponents of realpolitik. **Realpolitik** is the view or practice of politics that stresses the centrality of power and downplays the importance of law and morality in international politics. Realpolitik stands in contrast to the liberal view more typical of most citizens in stable liberal democracies. Liberalism stresses the importance of morality and law in politics, both domestic and international. In contrast, advocates of realpolitik believe the liberal view is naive. States act internationally to increase their power. At its root, power is the ability to compel. The struggle for power is a zero-sum game – what one gains others must lose. Furthermore, the struggle for power is not governed by any mutually recognized set of moral rules. All other laws and moral rules must be subject to this one: the state must protect its territory and its subjects. If it fails to do so, it has failed to live up to its most basic obligation. While realpolitik was developed to explain state-to-state relations, it is an outlook that can influence the conduct of politics within states as well. Internal events can seriously weaken a state's ability to conduct its foreign policy successfully. And, in such situations, practitioners of realpolitik are likely to believe that they're justified in ignoring the demands of law and morality in domestic politics too.

Realpolitik also raises a set of issues, not part of the military's province in the narrowest sense. Concern for a nation's military power raises concerns about other elements of national power. In the modern era, military power relies upon economic power. Similarly, society itself can be a source of strength or weakness. A society that is orderly and disciplined, and united by a common sense of nationhood is strong. On the other hand, a society riven by social conflicts – be they ethnic, class, or religious in nature – is a society that is weak. When society is weak, the ability of the state to fight a war successfully or even its capacity and willingness to support the armed forces in time of peace may be open to question. Political movements and ideologies that attack militarism, stress class or international solidarity rather than nationalism, or appeal to ethnic nationalism, weaken state power. As a consequence, the military may find itself as an active participant in a political debate concerning issues that are not legitimately under its purview. In crisis situations, such non-military issues may serve as a goad to military intervention.

A technocratic outlook

Military officers have a technocratic orientation. By training and habit, they address problems head on, seeking the technically best and most feasible solution. They investigate alternates, give advice, and advocate their positions. However, the debate and advocacy concern technical matters, not matters of mere personal preference. Much like the discussion of engineering considerations for building a bridge, military debate about means is clearly circumscribed by what is technically the most feasible and efficient method of attaining the given objective. And once the commander makes his decision about a course of action, debate ceases, and it is the duty of the entire organization to implement that decision. The constant debate about ends and the continuous bargaining, compromise and revision of policy that typify politics are foreign to the military mind-set. In developing countries especially, military officers often have little respect for politicians who may be corrupt or prone to self-serving compromises, and they may well think that they could do better. In short, the armed forces are potentially a political actor even though that is not their professed vocation. Moreover, they are potentially a dominant one.

The issue of civilian control

Military professionalism is meant to provide good arms. Good laws must keep these good arms in their proper place. To put it another way: the military is most effective in securing the interests of the state when military leaders are chosen on the basis of their competence and experience and are allowed to structure the armed forces and conduct war according to their own best military judgment. This requires that they be granted a high degree of professional autonomy from political interference. In turn, lest politics be itself corrupted, military leaders must restrict their activity to their narrow professional sphere of preparing for and fighting wars. In short, if the military becomes politicized, its capability to make war suffers. Conversely, if politics becomes militarized, the rule of law and constitutionalism suffer. This functional division of responsibility between the military and their civilian superiors goes by a variety of names. Most often it is called "**objective civilian control**" (Huntington 1964: 94–7). This arrangement might also be referred to as the "**civil–military bargain**." Politicians should stay out of the business of the armed forces, and military officers should stay out of politics. There are, of course, many ways that this bargain can break down. Not the least of these is deciding the dividing line between what properly constitutes military and what constitutes political business. The dividing line is often fuzzy and subject to redefinition. Budgets are often a matter of dispute. Diplomatic maneuvers and other political decisions can affect the armed forces' ability to defend the country effectively. Senior-level military appointments with political and diplomatic responsibilities controlled by civilians can be a sensitive area. Conscription too can be a matter of contention. Still, in consolidated liberal democracies, despite all its vagaries the civil military bargain holds. In the matters just listed and in similar matters the civilians regularly make the final decisions, and the armed forces' leadership gives advice. Civilians are able to remain in charge because politicians, bureaucrats, and civilian experts have the necessary knowledge to engage in effective oversight of the armed forces, thereby policing the boundary between civilian and military business. Informed governmental oversight and public criticism prevent the armed forces from doing what they wish behind a shield of military secrecy and specialized technical knowledge.

In the final analysis, the civil–military bargain holds because political authorities have the moral force of public opinion and major political actors behind them when they come into conflict with military officers who are pushing the limits of their authority. In consolidated democracies political parties (including the opposition), the branches of the government, and the general public rally behind the civilian political leadership or at least deny any substantial support to recalcitrant military officers who try to usurp political power. A similar dynamic prevails in other consolidated civilian-controlled regimes that are not democratic although the composition of relevant political actors is different. In other words, the government is seen as legitimate and treated as such. And those who challenge it have gone beyond the pale. Regardless of their motives, regardless of friendship, regardless even of professional camaraderie, few of any seriousness would dare support them. This is not the case in countries beset by praetorianism. When the military is strong and political institutions and their legitimacy weak, the armed forces can become an important political actor. Weak, unpopular governments of contested legitimacy, social conflicts that threaten to erupt into outright violence, threats to the armed forces themselves can set the stage for direct military intervention into politics. The underlying problems that set the stage for this intervention are not easily solved. Thus, once they intervene, the armed forces are likely to remain a political actor. This political role can lead to the politicization of the armed forces as well. At the very least, it distracts them from their professional focus upon national defense and erodes their capability to perform that essential function. However, when brute force has the final say, the military has an advantage over many of its competitors, and may be tempted to use it.

Summary

In almost any situation the military is a potential military actor. It possesses a corporate identity and a specific outlook that defines its own interests as well as the national interest. Most critically, more than any other political actor it has the physical capability of seizing power against the will of others. Yet, in consolidated civilian regimes, its potential for direct intervention in politics is held in check. When the government is regarded as legitimate, disloyal military officers will find it difficult to find collaborators even within their own ranks. And should a military cabal form and try to seize power, other political actors and the general public will resist it. As a result, in consolidated civilian regimes, the armed forces cheerfully accept the civil–military bargain, gaining autonomy in exchange for withdrawal from politics. At worst, their role as a political actor resembles that of any other interest group. Their ethic of apolitical professionalism serves as a check on what they can do. An effort to shape policy that is seen as too aggressive by other political actors is likely to backfire. Yet, not all regimes are consolidated – i.e., regarded as legitimate by all important political actors. Where they are not, the armed forces' day-to-day influence can be disproportionate, and they can easily be drawn into the political fray. Coups can become endemic. Once drawn in, the military may find it difficult to fully extricate itself, even if it really wants to do so.

Underlying causes of breakdown

A revolutionary breakdown is massive; it involves the critical failure of most of the regime's key functional supports: legitimacy, governmental institutions, the state, and even the armed forces. The breakdown that precedes a coup is significant in scope but not as complete as that preceding a revolution. The coup itself and military rule – be that rule relatively permanent or intermittent – are consequence of praetorianism and serve to further deepen praetorianism. Earlier (in Chapters 1 and 2) praetorianism was defined as the process of settling political disputes by the appeal to force. By definition, praetorian systems are broken. In praetorian systems, institutional mechanisms, legal rules, and moral norms play a much more limited role than they do in stable systems where disputes are settled peacefully. In most praetorian systems, the armed forces control the preponderant force. It goes almost without saying, that countries in which praetorianism is the rule do not have the "good laws" of which Machiavelli spoke. Their laws are defective because they are more respected in the breach than in the observance. Nor, as Machiavelli warned, are these countries likely to have good arms either. If the laws are not well formulated or not obeyed, then military affairs suffer too. Without good laws, politics becomes militarized, and military affairs become politicized. It is the worst of both worlds. In sum, praetorianism is more than the simple fact of a military coup or a military government; it includes the complex of circumstances cultural, societal, and political that makes the use of direct force to settle political disagreements likely. This section examines three factors that promote praetorianism: authoritarian and militaristic political cultures, governmental institutional breakdown, and specific problems of economic development.

Political culture

Political culture is the set of strongly held attitudes and beliefs about politics that characterize a society or a distinct group within it. Political culture matters. When a democratic regime is supported by a civic culture, it is likely to endure. Citizens are tolerant of differences, respect the right to dissent, and seek to resolve political disagreements through public debate and honestly administered elections. Further, these countries are likely to possess the social capital necessary to make political authorities respond to what the public wishes. In contrast, when the legal rules embodied in a democratic constitution are not in accord with basic values and beliefs people have about politics, the legal rules remain provisional. Opponents of the government can easily become opponents of the system as well – i.e., members of the disloyal or semi-loyal opposition. In some countries, the political culture, while it may have some democratic elements, is strongly authoritarian. The public respects, even adulates, strong personalistic leaders regardless of their anti-democratic credentials and aspirations. It is intolerant of dissent and ready to obey. In such societies, liberal democracy is unlikely to be stable if it exists at all. Elections, political pluralism, free and open partisan competition and the rule of law can exist only intermittently and imperfectly when the times permit.

When a civic culture predominates, the public will tend to rally in support of democratic principles when there is the threat of a coup. Regardless of whether the public agrees with the government or not, almost all groups within the society recognize that liberal democratic and constitutional principles must be preserved. Governments must not be changed by force. In contrast, where an authoritarian political culture predominates, an attack upon duly constituted democratic authorities produces no such automatic rallying effect. The public is prone to support strong leadership regardless of its lack of democratic credentials and abandon the rule of law. Many political actors are only semi-loyal. Like much of the general public, they consider constitutionalism and democracy, if they exist, as instrumental rather than absolute goods. If democracy produces results favorable to a political actor, that actor will support it. If not, it will tolerate or even actively promote the overthrow of democracy. The general public too is likely to be indifferent to a coup when the democratic government is seen as weak, corrupt, or incompetent. Once a coup is successful, people will obey the new de facto government's dictates. Authoritarian political cultures are also likely to tolerate the rise of politicians and parties who wish to undermine democracy from within by abolishing democratic liberties and due process, especially when it is primarily minority parties, religions, and nationalities that seem to suffer from curtailing these democratic guarantees. Throughout the developing world, where military intervention is the most frequent and direct, authoritarian political cultures abound. In fact, personalism and patrimonialism are normal features of traditional or modernizing societies.

But cultures can be more than authoritarian; they can be specifically militaristic. Latin America is a clear example of this. The Iberian tradition that shaped contemporary Latin America stands in sharp contrast to the English tradition that shaped political development in much of North America and helps explain their divergent history of civil–military relations (Wiarda 1981). In the seventeenth century, England was the hotbed of revolution and revolutionary ideas. And the system England allowed its colonies to follow was more liberal and republican than the political practices followed back home. Many settlers in the English colonies were dissenters or people of commerce, not members of the titled nobility or their dependants. Participatory government took root in the English colonies, and control exercised by London was limited. Englishmen thought in terms of the "settlement" of North America.

In contrast, Spanish Americans speak of the "conquest" rather than the "settlement" of the New World. The conquest is a term reminiscent of the "re-conquest" – Spanish Christians' destruction of the Muslim kingdoms on the Iberian Peninsula, a centuries-long, military and religious crusade that ended in 1492, the year that Columbus sailed to America. While seventeenth-century England was the seed-bed of liberalism and radical ideas, Spain and Portugal continued to ground their political and social orders on Catholicism, the traditions of the military aristocracy, and absolutism. Some of the first fruits of Iberian culture to emerge in the independence period were the *caudillos*. Quintessential men-on-horseback, the *caudillos* embodied the personalism, militarism, and authoritarianism inherent in the Spanish tradition. In the crisis period of the independence wars, they were the ones who seized control of events, providing the model for later political leaders as well. Even with the professionalization of the Latin American armed forces, the figure of the *caudillo* was changed rather than eliminated. By the turn of the twentieth century, military leaders were more likely to be professional, academy-trained soldiers, who had worked their way up the officer ranks than amateur generals from the landed upper class, but the political culture still supported a political role for military leaders. In some cases, Latin American constitutions explicitly recognized the armed forces as a political balancer. Such legal provisions provided a justification for the armed forces' seizure of power. And, even where no such explicit constitutional justification existed, historical precedent and the social status of the military officer provided an ample justification for coups d'etat. A political deadlock or a contested policy often provided the pretext for a military coup or a less direct form of political intervention by the armed forces.

Although their modern history as independent states have been shorter lived than Latin America, much of the rest of the developing world also has cultural patterns that support military intervention. Many societies have a warrior tradition, where warrior princes played major historical roles. Even more tellingly, in many developing countries the existing armed forces are historically associated with the struggle for independence and the very formation of the state. Older states, such as those of Europe or even many of those in the western hemisphere, were established long before modern professional armies were created. But states that achieved their independence in the twentieth century are a different matter. Especially where the country fought a war of national liberation, the military often came to have immense prestige, and the national liberation army frequently became the new state's army. Even where wars of national liberation did not occur, the new state's armed forces have at times played a pivotal role in the formation or reformation of the state. Turkey stands as an outstanding instance of this phenomenon. The modern nation-state of Turkey emerged from the collapse of the Turkish Ottoman Empire after the First World War when a leading general and war hero, Mustafa Kamal ("Ataturk"), as head of the armed forces set the state of Turkey on its modern track, abolishing the caliphate and instituting a host of reforms. When the armed forces played such a pivotal role as they did in Turkey, they are often endowed with the prestige and self-confidence to play a continuing political role in state. The military institution can thus come to overshadow the rest of the state and its interests seem to be the interests of the nation as a whole. This sort of political culture makes it much easier than it otherwise would be for the military to seize power or intervene less directly in politics.

Institutional overload

Just as political culture can set the stage for military intervention, so too the stress the revolution of rising expectations places upon political institutions can promote coups. Scholars have often argued that modernization – economic growth, increased education, and the rise of the middle class – would be conducive to the development of democracy. In the long run, there is evidence for this. Yet, in the short run, modernization can also have the reverse effect. The "institutional overload" hypothesis (Huntington 1968: 1–92) describes how this happens and dovetails with the "revolution of rising expectations" phenomenon described in Chapter 5. Institutional overload is the result of a series of falling dominoes. The first of these dominoes is social mobilization. **Social mobilization** is the change from traditional to modern attitudes. In traditional society, the choices that individuals make are constrained by their lack of education and opportunities as well as by the expectations that the society as a whole places upon them. In traditional agrarian societies, an individual's role is ascribed. People are essentially born into their roles, and are supposed to fulfill their roles as society defines them. Modernization changes these traditional roles and expectations. As the society becomes more complex, as literacy and education increase, as people are able to move from place to place to seek new opportunities, individuals are likely to take on new roles and attitudes that break with the traditional patterns of fatalism and conformity. The degree of social mobilization refers to the degree to which the society, as a whole, is composed of individuals who have developed modern attitudes and expectations.

Once socially mobilized, people become at least potentially **socially mobile** – i.e., they can better their social and economic status. However, social mobility goes beyond a mere change of expectations; social mobility requires that people have real opportunities to meet their modern expectations. In short, individuals may be socially mobilized (i.e., modern in their expectations) but not socially mobile (i.e., they are unable to realize their expectations). When a system fails to deliver the social mobility its subjects expect, the result is social frustration. **Social frustration** is the collective dissatisfaction with the way society is run and with those that run it. Social frustration is likely to lead to **political mobilization**, an increase in political participation where the people are in fact free to participate. Political participation is channeled through political institutions. Political institutions allow political problems to be addressed in a regulated, systematic, and definitive manner. Politics entails competition over scarce resources. These resources may be tangible: land, money, and other physical assets that produce wealth. Or they may be intangible: prestige, power, status. Institutions can channel this competition and resolve these conflicts. Politics, while it involves competition between individuals, more importantly entails competition among groups. Individual leaders present themselves as representatives of groups and their interests. The unconstrained clash of individual and group interests leads to violence. Community and consensus can exist only to the degree that political institutions are sufficiently complex and responsive to resolve competing claims in a mutually satisfactory manner. Political institutions are the organizations and procedures inside and outside government for resolving disputes. Political institutionalization is the process by which these institutions are developed and become accepted by the society. The level of **institutionalization** refers to the complexity, adaptability, autonomy, and overall adequacy of the institutions themselves. In short, it includes both governmental efficacy and state effectiveness.

In the West, modernization ultimately promoted liberal democracy. The development of the economy led to an overall increase in wealth. Economic development also promoted the rise of the middle class and an increase in level of literacy and education of the society at large. The rise of a large and informed middle class helped promote the rule of law as the subjects of monarchies sought to limit the arbitrariness of royal power. The rise of the middle class eventually led to demands for greater public participation in the making of decisions, and culminated in demands for a universal franchise. Institutionalization grew apace. But as Chapter 2 noted, the road to liberal democracy was often a rocky one, marked by protests, revolutions, and reversals. Modernization and democratization, in effect, were not entirely peaceful processes in the past, nor are they peaceful processes in the contemporary world. Political instability will ensue unless certain key social, economic, and political processes are roughly synchronized with one another. Economic development must be sufficiently rapid to accommodate social mobilization, or social frustration will result. In other words, if people expect things to change for the better – i.e., if society has high levels of social mobilization – but the economy does not provide the opportunities they believe they have a right to, they will become frustrated. What they attain does not measure up to their perceived deserts.

When social frustration is high and the ability to rise within the society (social mobility) is low, people are likely to see political participation as a means of solving the problem. If the system is fair and open, and individuals are socially mobile, they can work within it to achieve their just deserts. But when the system is stacked in favor of those who do already hold wealth and power, then collective political action by the excluded is the proper means to resolve the problem. But as political participation grows, political institutionalization must be high to resolve the demands placed upon the political process. If it is not, instability will result. The process might be restated as follows:

Modernization →
Social mobilization (without adequate economic development) →
Social frustration (without adequate social mobility) →
Political participation (without adequate political institutionalization) →
Political instability

This line of falling dominoes could be stopped at a number of points. Greater economic development, greater opportunities for social mobility, or higher level of political institutionalization could all prevent the rise of political instability. Yet, these are not easily achieved. Outside of attempting to stop the modernization process outright – another forlorn hope – the only other place to intervene is at the level of participation. In short, modernization can lead to authoritarianism as those in power cut off avenues for political participation and so attempt to preserve their social and economic status. Political instability can induce the armed forces to intervene to save the nation either by defending the economic and social status quo or by decisively changing it.

The political economy of coups

Sometimes a political crisis may have economic roots much more specific than the general inability of the economy to deliver the opportunities that the society demands (O'Kane 1987: 41–62). Certain types of economic crises may actually subvert the general tendency of middle-class support for democracy. Where modernization has created a substantial middle class along with a well-organized industrial working class, roadblocks to economic development may create a situation in which the middle class is willing to tolerate coups and prolonged periods of military government. In 1973, Guillermo O'Donnell (O'Donnell 1979) attempted to explain just how situations of that character could arise.

The particular puzzle was Argentina and Brazil, newly industrialized countries in Latin America. Both seemed at or near the threshold where a large middle class would provide critical support for the consolidation of democratic institutions. But Argentina for decades had suffered from a succession of military governments, and Brazil in 1964 had had a coup that established a military government that would eventually last twenty-one years. O'Donnell argued that the peculiarities of economic development in these countries increased the likelihood of coups and rise of a particular sort of military regime. The industrialization that had occurred from the 1930s into the 1960s was based on substituting locally manufactured consumer products for those formerly imported. However, **import substitution industrialization (ISI)** as it was called had run into roadblocks. While ISI countries produced consumer goods they did not have the industrial base to create the producers' goods upon which consumer goods production itself depended. Machinery, heavy equipment, parts, and other essential industrial commodities still had to be imported. Their importation meant that ISI countries still depended on agriculture exports to support their industrial base, a dependency that ISI was supposed to solve. And as the 1960s wore on, it seemed clear from declining economic growth and erratic exports that drastic action was called for.

The only way to overcome the limits of ISI industrialization was to invest in the sort of heavy industry that would alleviate the need for industrial imports. With the need for industrial imports decisively curtailed, the countries' dependency on agricultural exports and their ever-fluctuating though generally downward revenue-generating potential would be sharply reduced as well. However, this "deepening" of industrial development required new sources of capital. The most obvious source of securing new capital was to squeeze workers' wages and benefits and to curtail employment. The money thus saved by firms could be reinvested in plant and equipment that would yield the necessary deepening of ISI. However, organized labor was bound to resist and make use of democratic institutions to counter the efforts to have its constituents pay for further industrial development. Middle-class managers, professionals, and service workers were more likely to see their interests aligned with further industrialization than with defending the gains of industrial workers. Furthermore, the crisis generated by the failures of ISI promoted all sorts of radical solutions and splinter groups.

The "solution" that Argentina, Brazil, and other South American countries came to was a coup that established a military regime backed by major domestic firms and foreign capital. These "bureaucratic-authoritarian" regimes were controlled by the armed forces and managed by civilian **technocrats**, experts principally in the fields of economics and finance and largely foreign trained, often in the United States. The basic rationale behind this arrangement was that politics – even democratic politics – should not get in the way of the government doing what was technically best for the long-term economic interests of the country. The bureaucratic-authoritarian option served as a kind of siren song to military officers and others fearful of the popular forces that democracy could unleash. Although O'Donnell developed his model to explain developments in major South American countries, it resonates as well with the sort of military-directed development regimes that arose in Asia.

Summary

Coups don't just happen. They have underlying causes. Developing countries more than developed are subject to the sort of systemic problems that can make coups d'etat seems attractive to some political actors and at least acceptable to others. Developed countries are less likely to have authoritarian or militaristic political cultures, governmental institutions that cannot address persistent social demands, or to face the sort of economic roadblocks that put democracy or any established regime under stress. Such stresses can lead to the military's intervention in politics.

How the armed forces intervene

The most dramatic form of military intervention is the coup d'etat, but coups are only part of the story. In many developing countries, the armed forces play a much wider role in state administration than they do in consolidated democracies. And they are often both willing and able to use the influence this position gives them to shape governmental policy. Still, the threat of a coup d'etat is often the most important tool of military influence. It has a chilling effect on some politicians while, at the same time, emboldening others who may even seek a military takeover. But before investigating the dynamics of the coup d'etat, we need to look at less dramatic methods of intervention first (Finer 1962).

Day-to-day intervention

The armed forces have a variety of advantages that other political actors lack. They often possess a mystique that few other organizations besides religious ones can equal. They have an ethic of obedience, discipline, and self-sacrifice. Their purpose is to defend the nation, not just the state and the government, and to do so in the most extreme and dangerous situations. Thus, the armed forces more than any other state organization can effectively cast their interests in terms of the good of the entire nation. They can present their budgetary and other requests as something more than the selfish demands of just another interest group. To sell the armed forces short, they can argue, is to sell the country short. The same sort of appeal can also be used to justify a coup d'etat. When a country is beset by corrupt and indecisive politics and has had little direct experience of military rule, the armed forces may seem to offer the prospect of a more efficient and more patriotic government. As with self-images generally, the military's view of itself may be hard to shake even in the face of contrary experience. And the armed forces are likely to retain its self-image even when the society at large no longer accepts it.

More than most other organizations, the military lacks transparency. The armed forces can often exclude outsiders, including their civilian superiors, from effective oversight and control, and they can wield considerable influence in even a legitimate government. Military technology and military organization are rather arcane subjects. A meaningful grasp of either is impossible without some understanding of military strategy. And military plans and capabilities are often intentionally and legitimately shrouded in secrecy since strengths or weaknesses might be effectively countered or exploited by potential adversaries. Thus, more than other sectors of the state, the armed forces can shield part of their budget and some of their activities from close inspection by the legislature and the general public by appealing to the national security requirement of secrecy. As a consequence, military activities may not receive the sort of scrutiny they deserve. A lack of transparency concerning military affairs exists, to some degree, in almost every society. In societies where military expertise is possessed by civilians and defense information is widely available and widely discussed, the armed forces become more transparent and subject to civilian control. However, where the civilian sector lacks that sort of competence, debate, when it exists, can take on an ideologically polarized character. In these circumstances, critics are prone to assail the institution as such instead of analyzing its policies. In the face of such criticism, the military is likely to respond by dismissing alternative positions as based on ill will, ignorance, or lack of patriotism. In such cases meaningful debate about defense matters may not occur at all. Effective civilian control over the armed forces is doubly difficult when the military has access to resources not provided by the government's budget or when fiscal controls are weak. It is common for the armed forces to own and manage defense industries, and sometime industries that have little to do with defense besides. Occasionally the armed forces' share of the budget is officially guaranteed. Such provisions can make military autonomy within the state more like virtual independence.

The armed forces can also be potent lobbyists. In consolidated liberal democracies, decisions about military affairs, as with other governmental decisions generally, have to be justified in a public forum and approved by either the legislature or the chief executive. However, because of the importance of their national defense mission, the armed forces have direct, often privileged, access to decision-makers that private interest groups or even other parts of the state administration often lack. In weak democracies and other systems where military influence predominates, even the degree of oversight typical of consolidated liberal democracies may be lacking. In weak democracies, deals are cut and pressure is applied within a relatively closed arena, rendering decision-makers less accountable to the public. The military is also likely to have an important domestic intelligence role. And the more closed the political arena and the more intrusive the military's domestic intelligence role, the more likely the armed forces will have the capability and willingness to blackmail politicians and other public figures. Nor is it uncommon for the minister of defense to be a military officer himself. Such an official is more likely to consider himself a representative of the institutional interests of the armed forces than a conduit for civilian control over them. And in some countries, military officers serve in the legislature.

In developing countries, where accountability is often weak, political decisions generally are likely to be based on naked personal and institutional interests, rather than the public good. And, in such an environment, the armed forces are usually more than capable of taking care of their own interests.

In developing countries, the armed forces may also run the airports, airlines, and perform border control. They may own key industries either directly or through their retirement funds. They may be called upon frequently to enforce law and order. From these positions of power, they can often exercise extraordinary influence over political and administrative decisions. When the armed forces can remove governments besides, governments are likely to play close attention to the military's institutional interests. They are unlikely to cut its budget, limit its functions, or curtail its autonomy. Beyond this, armed forces' concerns about a variety of policy matters are likely to receive respectful consideration. Armed forces' thinking on national security issues, national sovereignty, law and order, social issues, and economic security is likely to have considerable influence over their civilian colleagues. Senior officers are likely to fill important posts even within nominally civilian governments.

Day-to-day influence over policy may preclude the necessity of more overt interventions, and may make them easier when the senior military leadership believes they are required. If persuasion and verbal threats are insufficient to defend military interests, senior commanders have other means, short of direct intervention, for getting their way – a show of force. Troops or tanks may appear on the streets for no conceivable purpose; troops may be confined to barracks; commanders may order conspicuous preparations for military operations. Such overt threats may finally get the message through to recalcitrant politicians. Even if the government persists in its policies, such shows of force put the government on notice that the military is a force to be reckoned with.

Deciding on a coup: military factionalism

Although the armed forces can succeed as a political actor in many ways besides a coup d'etat, in political systems beset with praetorianism, coups remain the armed forces' ultimate sanction. However, the armed forces as a whole usually do not make coups; elements within them do. Despite the common mentality shared by almost all professional military officers, factions within the armed forces are common, as they are within other organizations, and these factions often play a considerable role in determining how the military institution acts politically: whether a coup occurs; how a military government, once established, is run, and how and when military rule is brought to a close. The various armed services – army, navy, air force, and sometimes a militarized police – not only serve as fraternal defenders of their common state and nation; they are rivals as well over such matters as status, defense planning, and budget allocations (Nordlinger 1977: 39–52). Rivalries between branches within the same service are often significant. For example, infantry versus armor, both versus artillery or engineers constitute important intra-service rifts within the army. Military intelligence, especially when it plays an important role in domestic intelligence gathering, is likely to develop as a distinct interest as well (e.g., Stepan 1988: 13–29). Once a military government is established, intelligence officers are more likely than their counterparts in other branches to resist turning political power back to civilians. Graduating classes from the nation's military academy may also serve as an important source of rivalry and cohesion. Unlike the United States, many countries graduate virtually all of their full-time officers from their military academy. Graduating classes tend to be relatively small and cohesive, and members look after each other's interests. In addition social divisions outside the armed forces may shape the factions within it. Economic class, regionalism, ethnicity, and religion can be important cleavages within society, and they can have an effect on the armed forces as well. If the officer corps is recruited predominantly from one class or social group, its members are likely to sympathize with their compatriots in the society at large, and could be disposed to act in their interests. On the other hand, if recruitment is more broadly based, the military is likely to be divided along lines that correspond to the fault lines of the larger society. Whether institutional factors or socially based factions in the armed forces are more important varies from country to country and from era to era.

The most important and perhaps the most typical division within militaries that have a history of intervention or are about to embark on intervention is between institutionalists and interventionists. This division at times may be loosely associated with differences between services, branches, ranks and graduating classes, but it is basically a disagreement about what is best for the military and the country. **Institutionalists** believe that the armed forces ought to obey their political superiors and refrain from initiating or threatening coups. They believe that such a mode of conduct is the best way to preserve the professionalism and integrity of the military institution. Institutionalist officers generally accept objective civilian control although they may have exaggerated ideas about how autonomous the armed forces should be. **Interventionists**, on the other hand, argue that the armed forces have a duty to intervene in politics at least under certain conditions. They often appeal to the will of the people, to the good of the nation, and to the integrity and good discipline of the armed forces themselves as justifications for intervention. They are prone to argue that the crisis of the moment renders appeals to institutionalist principles moot, however desirable these principles may be in theory. Interventionists differ from one another over the issue of what sorts of situations require military intervention.

Interventionists of whatever stripe can usually get the better of institutionalists when the survival or integrity of the armed forces themselves appears to be at stake. Military discipline is of paramount importance to military officers. Unless the officer corps can impose discipline within the ranks, the institution is doomed. The specter of the institution disintegrating underneath them can induce wavering officers to support political intervention. Thus, when governments pardon mutineers, allow radical political activity within the enlisted ranks, tolerate or even encourage the growth of parallel armed forces, they are likely to face concerted military resistance or even a coup d'etat. Officers are likely to see the politicization of the armed forces – using the armed forces for political purposes or making partisan loyalty a prerequisite for promotion – as almost as serious a threat as the breakdown of discipline. Politicization strikes at the heart of the armed forces' autonomy and professionalism. Even without other contributing causes, genuine attempts to politicize the armed forces may spark a serious military pushback, even a coup. Other institutional interests may also weigh considerably on the judgment of military officers when considering whether they should intervene in politics. Severe cuts in officers' salaries, the defense budget, or the size of the forces strengthen the hand of those arguing for intervention.

Leaders

Not all coups are alike. The most dramatic sort of coup, one that takes place before the military's intervention has become an almost normal part of the political process, might be called a "full-dress" coup. This sort of coup has a number of components (Luttwak 1968). Cooperation among any array of military units is normally necessary. Most often the coup's leader cannot simply command those in charge of units essential to the coup to take part. Frequently the coup's main leader and his primary collaborators are of equal rank. Even a senior commander working with those junior to him needs to persuade his subordinates. He has to convince his associates to do something that is both illegal and highly risky.

Coup-makers must be sure the prize is worth the risk. Moreover, in most coups the plotters must feel that their action has legitimacy even if that legitimacy is only in their own eyes. The leader needs negotiating ability, the trust of his associates, and charisma. He has to have a personal network of friends inside and sometimes outside the armed forces. The coup's actual leader need not be the public face of the coup. A figure known and respected by the public can be co-opted to play this role. Should the coup be successful, it can serve as a political launching pad for its leader who may be able to develop a power base independent of the armed forces.

Seizing power

In the strict sense of the word, a coup d'etat is the seizure of governmental power by a small, armed force, usually from the government's own military. Yet, not all coups actually involve conspiracies, secrecy, or even the movement of troops. Politicians accustomed to yielding to military demands may resign when given a simple ultimatum from a senior military commander to do so. However, all coups, even the most "normal" and bloodless, entail at least an implicit threat of force. The most violent and risky type of coup, what might be called the "full-dress" version (Nordlinger 1977: 63–107), assumes that the government will resist military efforts to replace it to the maximum extent possible. Thus, in this case, the actual use rather than the mere threat of military force is required. Full-dress coups often occur when the armed forces themselves are divided about the necessity or propriety of a coup. We focus on the full-dress coup in the following account of the coup's mechanics. Coups usually involve risk of serious personal retribution. Thus, important institutional, group, or personal interests must be at stake. Other military officers must be willing to accede to the coup-makers' actions, at least after the fact. The political situation in the country must be such that the general population will accept the coup. At a minimum, the coup-makers need the assurance that the general public will not turn out in the streets to support the existing government, and that important military units will not resist the coup.

The coup-makers need to be in direct command of the troops sufficient to carry out the mission. Troops will normally obey the orders of commanders whom they personally recognize and who, in fact, normally lead them in person. In most cases, this gives middle-ranking officers the key to the process. Commanders of the rank of major to colonel usually command hundreds or thousands of troops. With the right combination of units, they would have sufficient forces and forces in the proper position to execute a successful coup. In some cases, however, junior officers or even noncommissioned officers may be positioned to execute a coup. This is relatively rare, and is likely only where the military is relatively small. The army is normally the branch of the armed forces that provides key leaders and units since it possesses the sort of units most likely to be useful in executing the coup.

Military coups rarely come completely out of the blue without any perceivable cause or warning. Still, the watchwords of successful coup making are secrecy, surprise, and economy of force. The forces that execute the coup need not be excessively large. To overthrow the government, the coup-makers must command sufficient forces to seize senior government officials, the political leaders likely to resist the coup, as well as key transportation and communications hubs in the vicinity of central government offices. If other military forces do not intervene to defend the government against a coup, relatively few of the nation's military forces will be required. Thus, surprise is more important than marshaling all or nearly all the country's armed forces. And secrecy is usually more critical than obtaining the consent of all senior officers before the coup occurs. In crisis situations, the government is likely to suspect that a coup may be in the offing. The sort of prior conditions that lead to a coup are impossible to disguise. Rumors, true and false, often circulate that a coup is close at hand. This normally causes coup-makers little difficulty unless these rumors tip their hand about the details of the coup. Only if the government knows exactly who is plotting, or the actual timing of the coup and the military units that will be involved, can it react effectively to defend itself. To guarantee the element of surprise, coup-makers usually try to keep the number of people who are informed about their plans as small as possible. If at all possible, they use forces close to the capital to reduce the government's warning time to the bare minimum. In short, although political conditions and discontent within the armed forces may lead intelligent observers to suspect a coup is likely, the coup can still succeed if the timing, identity of participants, and the operational plans for the coup remain secret.

The coup must succeed quickly, or it is unlikely to succeed at all. If some units move ahead of schedule, they may unwittingly tip off the government. Key government officials will be able to escape and rally loyalist forces. In a standoff, support for the coup-makers is likely to melt away. Thus, the coup-makers must arrest, assassinate, or isolate all officials and political leaders who could rally opposition to the takeover. The coup leaders or their representatives must appear on the mass media early to announce the success of the coup. Key government buildings, the transportation system, communications, and the media must be in the coup-makers' control. When they occupy such a dominant tactical position, the coup-makers can forestall a government counterattack. The government's remaining leaders will be few and out of contact with the public and one another. Pro-government supporters will be confused and demoralized. And waverers in the armed forces, who might have supported the government, will be outflanked. They will rarely risk a civil war within the armed forces to try to save a government whose fate has already been sealed. In essence, the coup, when executed with speed and precision, presents the country with a fait accompli. The full-dress coup just described can work even when the armed forces are badly divided, and senior officers are undecided or opposed to the coup.

Consequences

Coups often have long-term effects even when they do not achieve their intended objectives. A country's first coup is likely to alter the political situation permanently. In this respect, coups are like potato chips: it's difficult to stop with just one. A coup is a clear indication that the armed forces or military factions are willing to become overt political actors. Once this signal has been given, other political actors have to take them into account in ways that were unnecessary before. The armed forces may appear as an adversary to some and a potential ally to others. The military's control of brute force often becomes the trump card in the country's politics. The armed forces may find it virtually impossible to extricate themselves from politics even if they want to. And a round robin of military governments, civilian fronts for military factions, and weak civilian governments largely independent of the armed forces ensues. Military factions and coups against military-run governments can proliferate. In the worst circumstances, coups become matters of naked self-interest as military officers develop a taste for political power and its perks. Ideology, religion, and ethnic loyalties become mere pretext for rationalizing unvarnished power grabs. At other times, the situation is more complicated. Military factions ally themselves with civilians, or civilian extremists "knock on the barracks' door" to invite a coup that they believe will be in their political interest. What often develops is a dictatorship–democracy cycle in which military coups remove elected governments and establish military-dominated governments in their place. These military governments themselves yield power sooner or later to elected civilian governments, but the underlying problems that typify praetorianism and led to the coup in the first place remain. As a consequence a new coup eventually occurs, and the cycle continues. The next section details the dynamics of this cycle.

The dictatorship–democracy cycle

Democracies have been quite common in the developing world, but often these democracies are weak and subject to breakdown. Democracy often appeals to the middle class, but in the developing world the middle class is generally limited in size and relatively weak. Moreover, in the developing world the political culture often has strong authoritarian elements, and political institutions frequently lack the capacity to meet demands placed upon them. It is unsurprising then that democracy in the developing world has appeal, but democracy itself is rarely fully consolidated. By the same token, alternative regimes are also relatively difficult to consolidate as well. As a result, many countries suffer from a dictatorship–democracy cycle. Pakistan, Turkey, Nigeria, and many Latin American countries, among others, have had numerous military interventions followed by periods of relatively democratic rule. Once in the cycle, both military and political actors are seemingly trapped because of the limited range of choices available to them. Weak democracies newly reestablished remain weak and are inadequate to resolve the problems they face. The state is inefficient; political institutions are prone to deadlock, and a variety of political actors are members of the semi-loyal opposition.

Why civilians appeal to the armed forces

The conditions underlying praetorianism of themselves do not fully account for why specific coups occur. The objectives and strategic options available to political actors, however, flesh out the picture. Praetorian conditions affect how political actors calculate. The semi-loyal opposition is likely to resort to actual violence. And even democratic political actors are likely to resort to posturing and threats. Thus, politics in fragile democracies can often resemble the game of "chicken." The account that follows is a variation of Cohen's analysis of coups found in the Introduction (see also Cohen 1994). (The presentation below is not a proper game theoretic presentation since, among other things, it does not include a single objective payoff matrix. However, it does focus on strategic calculations.) "Chicken" is a staple of both game theory and popular culture. In the chicken game, two drivers (usually teenagers) speed toward one another on a narrow road. The object of the game is to force the other driver to swerve aside. The winner receives the reputation for daring and dominance within the group. If both swerve there are no winners. If neither swerves, there are only losers. To win the game outright, a driver must make a credible bluff – or not be bluffing – and his opponent must turn aside.

Like the game of chicken, praetorian politics includes bluffing and occasional disasters as violence leads to political breakdown, coups, and sometimes mass upheavals. The making of threats and bluffs is not the issue. Even in consolidated democracies, politics involves threats as well as bargaining when a political deadlock occurs although the threats are normally relatively mild and do not involve violence. Threats are, in fact, a normal part of politics, and they can even promote final agreement. When violence and political fragility are a part of the mix, however, the political calculus changes. An altered version of the game of chicken illustrates the dynamics of coup-prone praetorian politics. Call this revised version "political chicken." Unlike real-life chicken, the players of political chicken are political actors, and there are four players, not merely two. Each vehicle is directed by a team of two, an extremist and a moderate, who share a general aim but disagree on how far and how ruthlessly this aim can or should be advanced. This revision of the chicken game reflects the fact that political confrontations characterized as simple two-sided polarization are often more complex. While part of the political leadership may support an extreme position, others, including the mass of the population, is often much more moderate (cf. Bermeo 2003). In the real world, political coalitions (represented by our two-player teams) often include extremists and moderates. The hallmark of extremists is their willingness to use violence. Their commitment to any democratic system is conditional at best. The extremist member of one team may be leftists (or radical ethnic nationalists) seeking major changes in the system; on the other team, the extremist counterpart would be rightists (or members of the majority nationality) seeking to preserve the status quo at virtually any cost or even to strengthen their dominant position. The other member of each team/coalition is moderate in its aims. Moderates (the government and loyal opposition) are committed to democracy as well as their own specific policy goals. Conceivably the pro-democratic moderates within both teams/coalitions could compromise on divisive issues and work to maintain the democratic system. In an established democracy, this is the likely outcome. Compromise entails little cost, and failure to compromise often entails greater costs. But praetorianism and political chicken are played by a different set of rules. While the rule of law and democratic stability buffer the consequences of political decisions, praetorianism promotes all-or-nothing outcomes. Even if a moderate wants to break with its extremist partner, the political cost may be too high to do so. How can moderates disarm their own extremist allies while the opposition remains armed?

The moderate's optimal strategy is to bluff to extract maximum concessions from the other side. But the moderate does not want to actually carry through on the bluff if it seems clear that the other side is intent on carrying through on theirs. The moderate's highest priority is to avoid a crash. The "crash" in this case is the total breakdown of democracy. In contrast, the moderate's extremist partner is sure the other side is bluffing. Moreover, the extremist is confident that even if a crash actually does occur, their own vehicle is sturdy enough compared to others that they will escape with minor injuries at worst. In other words, the extremist puts different values on swerving and crashing than does the moderate partner. Furthermore, the extremist partner has the final say. The extremist can exercise the option of using violence without the explicit consent of the moderate. Since extremists have not been disarmed either physically or psychologically, they have capacity to engage in all-out violence on their own. Thus, the moderate must convince the extremist before a crash occurs that the extremist evaluation of the situation is incorrect and that swerving at the last minute is really a better strategy. Too often moderates fail.

Latin America, especially during the 1960s and 1970s, serves as a good illustration of how this dynamic actually materializes. Relatively developed and with a history of democratic reversals, Latin America in that era was divided over the issue of political reform. Although many of the countries of the region had attained significant levels of industrialization, the region, as a whole, had some of the most unequal divisions of wealth in the world. In most countries, the old, landed, upper class had retained power by sharing it, but by sharing it only on a narrow basis. The industrial and commercial elite received seats at the table. A portion of the growing middle class also received some of the fruits of economic progress. These groups, "the right," were generally in favor of the status quo. However, deep resentment and a desire for profound change remained among other sectors, such as the urban working class and rural landless. The political element of these sectors, "the left," took up the cause of change. The left and the right were each divided into moderate and extremist camps. Moderates were willing to compromise to accommodate the other side while still securing part of their own side's goals. The extremists were not.

The extremist camp on the left was inspired by the success of the Cuban Revolution. The Cuban revolutionaries and their would-be imitators claimed to have made a "revolution in the revolution." That is, they claimed to have discovered a new strategy, Cuban-style guerrilla war that would allow the left to take power across the continent. Since they believed they could always begin a guerrilla war and that they would win it, the extremist left took a dim view of compromise with the right (Debray 1967). On the other hand, moderates on the left were far less certain that the means favored by the extremists were workable or appropriate, and they were willing to work with moderate rightists to reform the system. Thus, leftwing moderates proposed substantial reforms, and they hoped to win concessions from the moderate right. They made land reform, long languishing on the political agenda, a priority. They proposed making the political system more equitable, and mooted the expansion of government programs in education, healthcare, and social development. Moderate reformers and their allies in the United States argued that their reforms were required to head off Cuban-style revolutions in the hemisphere by alleviating the underlying causes that might lead to revolution. In short, the threat of revolution was useful in making the moderate right and the United States government recognize that substantial reform was imperative.

Meanwhile, hard-line rightists argued that the real threat was any change in the status quo. Reform was not desirable, either in itself or as a means of preventing revolutionary violence. Revolutionary violence had to be countered directly and forcefully not by making compromises with the left, but by a willingness to use military means against those who posed a threat to the system. Movement in the direction of reform would not undercut the extremist left; it would only prompt them to make more demands. The extreme right also believed they could rely on their own countries' armed forces and on the United States, and thus in any violent confrontation, they were likely to prevail. After all, the armed forces generally could be counted on to defend the status quo against any extremist attempt to overturn it. The United States, from the initial victory of the Cuban Revolution, had sent ambiguous messages at best. While the US had sponsored the Alliance for Progress, a mammoth aid and reform program, it had also begun to rearm and retrain the region's militaries to counter a potential Cuban-style revolution. Most compellingly, history had shown the United States was willing to back or even sponsor pro-US right-wing coups.

For differing reasons, hardliners on the right and left each felt confident that the breakdown of normal politics would not be to their disadvantage. Although both the moderate left and the moderate right were willing to strike a compromise, they had to gain the backing of their coalition as a whole. Thus, the strategy of the extremists in both camps was to undermine the possibility for compromise. The credibility, self-confidence, and influence of the extremist component of both camps undercut the moderates. As the extremists strove to polarize the situation with threats, mass protests, and acts of violence, the credibility of the moderates suffered. Eventually the efforts at compromise gave way. Violent confrontations and coups d'etat followed. The extremists on the left had believed that revolutionary ideals were destined to triumph. They thought that the Cuban Revolution had demonstrated the effectiveness of a new strategy and tactics that would guarantee this victory. They were wrong. Only one left-wing movement actually succeeded in taking power by revolutionary means – the Sandinistas of Nicaragua in 1979. Instead, left-wing extremists and their right-wing antagonists helped provoke yet another swing toward dictatorship in Latin America. A coup occurred in Ecuador in 1963 and set the stage for a series of coups that put all but five countries in the region under military governments by 1973. And one of these five was communist Cuba itself. Even two countries that most experts believed were safely democratic, Chile and Uruguay, fell under the sway of military regimes. In short, institutions for crafting political compromises were in place, but the strategies adopted by important political actors – the extreme left and the extreme right – made them unwilling to use them.

While the example above refers to Latin American and ideological left/right, moderate/extremist divisions, the same sort of logic also applies to secular/fundamentalist, sectarian, and ethnic divisions as well. Extremists often hold moderates hostage and provoke a breakdown. Pro-government hardliners often quash reform because they consider the moderates who support it naïve. Even when the armed forces are initially on the sideline, they may feel themselves compelled to intervene on one side or the other. Outside of Latin America, the Turkish military has done so three times in the past decades to preserve its version of secularism and the Turkish state. Turkey has faced problems of ideological and religious extremist as well as ethnic nationalism. The Pakistani military has intervened repeatedly in the face of partisan, religious, and social strife, and it has used its interventions to further its own interests. The Nigerian armed forces first became embroiled in politics that were beset by ethnic and religious divisions.

Why the armed forces cannot consolidate power

If pro-democratic civilians cannot consolidate democracy, the armed forces often find themselves similarly hamstrung in trying to consolidate an alternative system. This has led various countries' armed forces to follow different patterns of intervention. Eric Nordlinger divides the types of military interveners into three basic sorts (Nordlinger 1977: 22–4, 112–17). The **moderator military** shies away from exercising governmental power directly; it prefers to exercise power by setting limits on what civilians may do. Coups are used primarily as threats to keep civilian governments in line, but the threat may have to be actually carried out. Moderator militaries are essentially oriented to the defense of the status quo. Their interventions lead to short-duration **emergency governments/regimes of exception** – at most. The duty of such emergency governments is to reestablish the proper political balance that was upset by the crisis provoked by the coup. Moderator militaries sometimes evolve into the second sort of military intervener, the **guardian military**. Although from time to time guardian militaries may intervene via a military coup and form governments directly controlled by the armed forces, their major interest is to supervise the manner in which politics is conducted. They exercise an often subtle but always pervasive influence on politics. And military officers often assume governmental posts not compatible with objective civilian control. In short, guardian militaries are content to remain largely in the background for extended periods provided military interests are protected. They often permit a degree of political competition. When in charge of governments directly, they groom civilian successors who will rule in the military's interest. The third sort of military intervener is the **ruler military**. When the armed forces assume this role both their goals and the duration of the rule is much more extensive. They may even attempt to remain in charge of the government indefinitely. Ruler militaries, in effect, seek a fundamental change in regime and may even attempt to mobilize society from above.

When the armed forces assume a moderator posture, one coup often leads to another. Although there are strong authoritarian elements in the political culture and institutional overload occurred, there is no consensus to replace elected civilian regimes with something else. Thus, the armed forces have to justify their intervention as an emergency response to a crisis and by citing of their constitutional duty to defend the state. These circumstances and rationalizations themselves give rise to limits on the duration and scope of military rule. Thus, regimes of exception can take only limited steps in reshaping politics, and they cannot remain in power indefinitely. Certain parties may be outlawed, certain politicians banned, but the status quo ante will, in its essence, be restored. Regimes of exception lack the political capital to do much more.

A coup d'etat that produces a government of this sort may provide a launching pad for a general to become president under the restored legal order. Yet, he serves as president because, just like any other politician, he has been chosen by constitutional political procedures, not because his colleagues in the armed forces have selected him. In this sort of situation, the armed forces cannot serve as a substitute for a political party or a permanent adjunct to it. The armed forces' overt political role is exercised only intermittently. Military governments last for a limited term. And the armed forces intervene in political disputes when civilians cannot solve problems or some civilian political actor threatens to step beyond the pale of what the armed forces consider permissible. What emerges is something like this. Under democratic rule the extremist, semi-loyal political actors eventually gain the upper hand. This provokes a military intervention, but pro-democracy political actors as well as institutionalists in the armed forces are unwilling to see a military government continue for long. Thus, the armed forces sooner or later turn power over to civilians, setting the stage for the next iteration of a four-player chicken game.

It might seem reasonable to expect a stable outcome at some point. This does happen. However, many countries resemble the dynamic describe here. The armed forces are unable to consolidate a regime of their liking because of the legitimacy issue. While the armed forces have variously used nationalism, anti-communism, and at times even socialism to buttress their regimes ideologically, the appeal of democracy often remains potent. The dictatorship–democracy cycle is clearly a manifestation of praetorianism. Political actors strong, clever, or unscrupulous enough are able to change the basic legal rules governing political competition and force other actors to adhere to the new rules. But only provisionally! The new legal rules are binding not because all major political actors sincerely accept them, but because the dominant political actors are able to back them up by force. In short, each regime (democracy or military government) has its own disloyal or semi-loyal opposition. When the regime changes, loyalists and the disloyal opposition change positions (and strategies).

The dictatorship–democracy cycle persists when, to gain any sort of credibility or general support, the armed forces must profess their adherence to democratic principles even when they replace a duly elected government with a military junta. This profession, whether sincere or insincere, sets up a ticking clock. Since the armed forces proclaim that they overthrew an elected government to preserve the nation and democracy, they must eventually acquiesce to the reestablishment of a democratic government. Democratic or other opponents of the military government generally can use this lack of long-term legitimacy to undermine the effectiveness of the government. The claim also provides an opening for opponents of military government within the armed forces to pressure the leadership to return the country to the old democratic status quo. In short, the version of praetorianism manifested in the dictatorship–democracy cycle has an unwritten (psychological) rule: major actors must profess their adherence to democratic norms whether they sincerely mean it or not. Disobey the rule, and lose political credibility.

However, even when they are formally out of power, the armed forces threaten democracy. The laws – the legitimacy of democratic principles and the constitutional system – are too weak to enforce obedience on the armed forces and restrict them to exercising their professional competencies. And the involvement of the armed forces in politics often erodes their professionalism. By the standard of Machiavelli cited above, the state lacks both good arms and good laws. We now turn to two concrete instances of the dictatorship–democracy cycle: Nigeria and Pakistan.

CASE STUDY: NIGERIA

Nigeria represents a clear example of the dictatorship–democracy cycle. The country has had three periods of democratic government and numerous military coups, many directed against military governments. Nigerian military regimes have often made the pretense of preparing for a return to democracy even when they were unprepared to actually carry out that promise. The ethnic issue rather than class is one of the fundamental keys to Nigerian politics. Moderates and extremist have often pursued similar ethnic goals. The armed forces have been divided along ethnic lines as well. Nigeria's problems are not unique in Africa. Nigeria is a typical product of the 1885–6 Congress of Berlin that established the boundaries of European colonies in Africa. These boundaries were established on the basis of the interests and convenience of European powers and overlooked historical, cultural, and ethnic factors that would have helped produce better integrated states and societies. As a result of the Congress, Great Britain received control over territories that later became the independent state of Nigeria. Nigeria is a patchwork of ethnic groups, speaking over 500 languages and dialects, but there are three major ethnic divisions that have shaped politics throughout the independence era (see Map 7.2). The Hausa-Fulani in the semi-arid North are predominantly Muslim and had had well-established kingdoms for a considerable period before Europeans subdued them. The southern peoples, the Yoruba in the Southwest and the Ibo in the Southeast, have had a different history. They largely practice Christianity and traditional religions. The Yoruba kingdom was beset by civil wars shortly before the advent of colonial rule, and the Ibo had only a loose form of political organization above the village level. The British, following the typical colonial practice of divide-and-rule, found the Hausa-Fulani resistant to colonial blandishment and instead attracted the Ibo in much greater numbers into the civil service and the military.

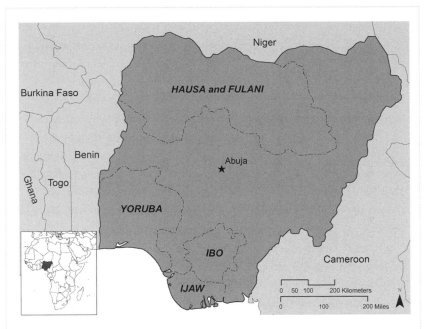

Map 7.2 Nigeria's major ethnic divisions
Source: Environmental Systems Research Institute (ESRI) map data. CIA

The Nigerian army was raised and trained in the traditions of the British army. Yet, this background proved insufficient to keep the Nigerian army under civilian control. The social and political conditions of Nigeria are quite different from those of modern Britain. Britain is a consolidated liberal democracy. Nigeria is a developing country, and it attained independence only in 1960. Neither the national question nor the role of the state in the economy had been settled. Politics follows ethnic lines, and the officer corps itself was fully Africanized only after independence. Thus, promotions were rapid during the first years of independence, and most high-ranking officers were new to their responsibilities. After independence, both civilian and military politics began to take on a winner-take-all character. Institutions were weak, and a civic culture was unknown among most of the poorly educated population new to the realities of democratic governance.

The so-called "First Republic," the constitution under which Nigeria governed itself from 1960 to 1966, followed the Westminster (i.e., British) model. It was a parliamentary system with representatives chosen by an SMD/PE formula. However, in a departure from the mother country's practice, Nigeria was a federal system with three, later four, regions. In each of these regions, one of the major three ethnic groups dominated. Each of the dominant regional parties allied itself with parties based on ethnic minorities within the other regions. This created a situation in which ethnically based governments and ethnically based oppositions dominated politics at the federal and regional levels. The first government formed after independence was a coalition in which northerners predominated. Developmental projects and an affirmative action plan put into effect by the new government were meant to redress regional and ethnic imbalances. This meant that the lion's share of developmental projects went to the North. It also entailed the hiring of less qualified northerners in preference to more qualified southerners for government jobs. A census scheduled for 1962 fueled hopes in the South that a new count of the population would redress the balance of power in their favor. The project was highly charged politically, and once the project was put into effect, evidence of fraud proliferated. The South refused to accept the results, and a new census was held the following year. After adjudication in the courts, a final figure was accepted that gave the North the majority. Meanwhile politics in the Western Region (the Southwestern part of the country dominated by the Yoruba) began to break down. The central government used its emergency powers to intervene. The regional premier was removed from office, tried and convicted of a treasonable felony. His deputy took over, forming a new party that split the political leadership of the region. Among the results was the creation of a new region, the Midwest.

The chaos that grew out of the general elections of 1964 demonstrated the inability of federal election authorities to keep order and assure that the process would be fair and free. The army was mobilized in an attempt to bring some order into the process. When the results were tabulated, the Northern People's Congress (NPC) gained sufficient seats in the national legislature to form a government on its own. During the election, the Western Region had been the most violent as political parties attempted to intimidate the voters and their opponents. Thus, a new election was called for the Western Region in 1965. But despite renewed violence the federal government failed to invoke its emergency powers to keep order. Nigeria's experiment with democracy was on the verge of miscarrying. And in January 1966, the military intervened. A failed coup led by Ibo officers, who then dominated the armed forces, seemed to many an attempt to return power to the South, specifically the Ibo ethnic group. Although the coup collapsed, the chaos left the commander-in-chief of the army, Major General Johnson Aguiyi Ironsi, in charge of the government. Ironsi seemed inclined to follow the same general policies that the coup-makers had backed. A number of senior Northern politicians had been killed in the coup, and Ironsi took no steps to punish the perpetrators.

In addition Ironsi undertook the centralization of government power, abolishing the regions and concentrating power in the central government. To northerners this seemed to be a move by the more developed South to place power in its own hands.

A counter-coup in July 1966 by northern officers restored the old regional status quo. Ironsi and most high-ranking Ibo officers were killed in the operation. The ethnic complexion of the army high command shifted. The Ironsi government had, to the minds of the coup-makers, demonstrated a strong regional bias. They, on the other hand, sought a regional balance. Lieutenant Colonel (later General) Yakubu Gowon, a Christian from the ethnically diverse middle belt, became the head of the government. He represented an ethnic/religious/regional compromise that would become common in Nigeria. Gowon reestablished the federal system, but a variety of developments embittered Nigerian politics further. Not only were Ibos purged from the officer corps, but a pogrom directed against them began in the Northern Region as well. The government of the Eastern Region responded testily. Ibos, forced out of power at the federal level and left unprotected in their own country outside of the Eastern Region, began to dream of independent statehood. This dream seemed all the more plausible because Nigeria's oil wealth which was just beginning to have a major economic impact was located primarily in the Eastern Region. On May 30, 1967, the Eastern Region declared independence as the independent state of Biafra, and a devastating thirty-month civil war ensued. On January 12, 1970, Biafra surrendered unconditionally.

Gowon initiated a technique of rule that commentators have dubbed a "permanent transition." Most of Nigeria's military rulers presented themselves as institutionalists, eager to return the country to democracy once the proper foundations were laid for the transition. The difficulty was that only two ever lived up to that pledge, and most attempted to prolong the process so as to keep themselves and the armed forces in power indefinitely. The Gowon government initiated a nine-part transition program that was supposed to return the government to civilian rule in 1976. A wide variety of nation and state-building measures were undertaken. Yet, power remained centered in Gowon's hands and those of the regional governors whom he appointed from the armed forces. General Gowon was overthrown in a coup in mid-1975. Eventually a new military government emerged under General Olusegun Obasanjo in early 1976. Obasanjo actually followed through on a transition that returned power to civilian hands in October 1979.

From 1979 to 1983, Nigeria was under the Second Republic, a new constitution that borrowed freely from the presidential system practiced in the United States. The president and a bicameral legislature were each separately elected. The two houses of the legislature had equal power. Under the new constitution federalism was retained. The number of states (which had replaced the old regions) increased to nineteen at first, and continued to increase thereafter since constitutional provisions made it relatively easy for local ethnic majorities to form their own states. To assure a national rather than a regional or ethnic focus, the new constitution adopted a number of novel provisions. To win the presidency a candidate had to win a plurality of the national vote in a direct popular election, but he also had to win at least 25 percent of the vote in two-thirds of the states. Similar provisions applied to the election of state governors. Political parties were prohibited from using religious, regional, and ethnic names and symbols. A balanced representation of ethnic groups in the cabinet, bureaucracy, administrative agencies, and the armed forces was established. New parties were formed. Phased elections began at the local level, then proceeded to the state, and finally to the federal level. Former politicians were prohibited from running, and, thus, a new political class was created from the ground up.

Plate 7.1 Retired General Olusegun Obasanjo as civilian president in 2005. Photo by José Cruz/ABr.

Despite its founders' intentions, the Second Republic reproduced the same North–South political divide that had so troubled the First. The northern-based National Party of Nigeria (NPN) had succeeded the NPC. Its nominee, Shehu Shagari, won the election of 1979, but the results were contested because he had failed to carry 25 percent of the vote in the required number of states. As president his problems continued to mount. After the end of the civil war, Nigeria had become one of the world's leading oil exporters. Shagari's government was at first buoyed by high oil prices. The state appeared to have plenty of revenue to meet a variety of developmental needs. In fact, oil-earnings funded state-sponsored industrial projects that among other things made Nigeria a producer of automobiles. Oil revenues and the over-valued national currency, the naira, supported cheap food imports. While this helped pacify urban-dwellers, the country's export agriculture as well as local food production suffered. Most serious of all, the oil boom promoted corruption. Nigeria was a soft state, unable to administer its laws and regulations efficiently, but it had undertaken vast projects in which direct spending by the state or state contracts offered lucrative opportunities for graft. It was not surprising that officials took advantage of them.

In the early 1980s oil prices began to collapse, and Nigeria, which had borrowed from international lenders on the strength of a seemingly inexhaustible revenue-generating capacity, found itself in difficult straits. The "floating" interests rates on the loans the government had taken out rose along with international interest rates generally. The 1983 election was a contentious affair even by Nigerian standards. The government was steeped in corruption and the economy faced serious problems. Shagari was re-nominated by his party. Violence and election fraud were substantial. According to the official results, Shagari won by a landslide and, along with him, a host of other NPN politicians. The reported results lacked credibility. On December 31, 1983, General Muhammad Buhari overthrew the Second Republic and established yet another military government.

The end of the Shagari government was welcomed by many. The military promised to root out civilian corruption and put an end to political divisiveness. In fact, Buhari's military government made a great effort to ferret out and punish corrupt officials from the Shagari government. Stories of theft from the state on a monumental scale became public. Buhari established tight security controls and tried to bring order out of the economic chaos that plagued the country. Still, the economy continued to flounder. In 1985 Buhari was replaced in another military coup by General

Ibrahim Babangida. Babangida at first seemed to be an energetic reformer eager to find an end to the troubles that beset the country's politics and reestablish democracy. He put into motion another multi-stage transition process much like the one implemented by Obasanjo in the late 1970s. Fulfillment of the multi-year time table was delayed repeatedly. The pretexts at first seemed plausible. However, Babangida's postponements became more and more controversial, and his intervention in the transition process became more and more heavy handed. Finally, in 1993 Babangida could delay no longer. The presidential election was finally held, and with a still incomplete vote count, Chief Mashood Abiola, a Yoruba Muslim, seemed to be the clear winner. It was at that point, on June 12, 1993, that Babangida closed down the transition process again, claiming new presidential elections would have to be held. After that, Babangida did not last long himself. Widespread opposition forced him to cede the presidency to Ernest Shonekan, a businessman. Shonekan was supposed to prepare for new elections early the coming year.

However, in November 1993 General Sani Abacha, the defense minister, overthrew Shonekan and established yet another military government. Babangida had lost credibility, and it did not take long for Abacha to lose credibility as well. Abacha had no intention of letting Chief Abiola assume the presidency or of actually calling new elections. Abiola was arrested after a series of efforts to pressure the military government to recognize his mandate. Abacha then began the now shop-worn drill of a multi-stage transition process, beginning once again with new party-formation. Abacha ruled with a heavy hand stifling political dissent. The economy continued to decline. Corruption was rampant. Rights violations were flagrant, but Abacha was able to ride out the mild measures taken against him by the major powers. By mid-1998, he had mooted the proposal of a presidential election in which he himself would be the only candidate. His rule, however, came to an end when he died in June 1998 of a reported heart attack.

A time of political uncertainty ensued as his successor, Abdulsalami Abubakar, took over. Abubakar was an unknown quantity, and to make matters worse Chief Abiola died suddenly while still in detention. Many wanted a quick transition. Abubakar in fact initially promised to adhere to his predecessor's October election date, but that was an unrealistic target. Political parties were in disarray. Abacha's promised October election was premised on him being the only candidate. Abubakar postponed the elections but only by some five months. Long-drawn-out transition processes had lost their credibility. Reorganization of parties and three separate elections proceeded in rapid order. The presidential election was held on February 28, 1999. Olusegun Obasanjo, the only other general besides Abubakar to return power to civilians, won; this time he became president as a civilian. The transition at last proceeded undisturbed by the political ambition of the military president and the officer corps. Obasanjo was reelected president four years later, and in 2007 retired after his two constitutionally allowed terms. The transition, however, was contested. Obasanjo had been unable to change the constitution to permit another reelection and his hand-picked successor, Umaru Yar'Adua, won controversial elections marred by violence and credible charges of fraud. Even after the return of democracy, the country continued to be plagued by massive corruption and undue military influence in politics.

The Nigerian case represents a classic instance of military "emergency" intervention that leads to permanent military influence. The first coup and first counter-coup had definite ethnic overtones. Extremists on all sides overwhelmed the influence of moderates. But the post-Second Republic period of military rule saw interventions of an even more questionable sort. Once in power, the officer corps developed an interest in staying in power. While earlier coup-makers could present themselves as frustrated institutionalists wishing to stay out of politics but forced to intervene by the press of circumstances, latter coup-makers could not make that argument believable. Military governments had provided senior officers with an opportunity to profit both legally and illegally from the governmental posts they held. Most military coups in Nigeria were against military, not civilian, governments. If praetorianism is to be outgrown, the nightmare of military rule has to produce political learning by all sectors. Nigeria's military moved from a moderator to a guardian role, repeatedly claiming rather unconvincingly that they were preparing the groundwork for a return to democracy. In fact, they became another illustration of the dictatorship–democracy cycle.

CASE STUDY: PAKISTAN

Pakistan serves as a second illustration of the dictatorship–democracy cycle. Its more than sixty years of independent political life has been difficult. Formed out of British India in 1947 at the insistence of the Muslim League, the country suffered from a number of political handicaps from the start. The formation of the country was a wrenching experience. With the partition of formerly British India, millions of non-Muslims left soon-to-be

Pakistan while millions of Muslims fled India to take up residence in Muslim Pakistan. The resulting inter-communal violence killed hundreds of thousands. The new country suffered from another problem: it was divided into two noncontiguous halves. The larger in terms of population was located in the Muslim-majority area of Bengal. A thousand miles to the west stood the territorially and administratively more important western part. The two parts of the country had had no previous history of being under the same government except that of the Mogul Empire and the British raj. In both cases, however, the regions were part of a larger, more religiously diverse imperial system. Though nominally a democracy from 1947 to 1958, from 1971 to 1977, and from 1988 to 1999, the democratic regime was dominated by the class of large landowners and operated under tutelage of the bureaucratic and military elite. Neither civilian nor military governments proved capable of solving the country's underlying social, economic, and political problems. Civilian politicians often sought alliances with the armed forces to help bring down their civilian adversaries.

Pakistan is, and was meant to be, a religiously homogeneous society. At present it is 97 percent Muslim. But Pakistan's religious homogeneity was insufficient to overcome other divisions. As originally configured, the majority Bengalis far outnumbered the minority population in the West. The fact that the united country's bureaucratic and political elite came from the West and granted little autonomy to Bengal was a cause of dissatisfaction and ultimately led to secession in 1971. Still, even the ethnic divisions in the West are significant. While the country is predominantly Muslim, divisions exist between Sunnis and Shiites. The Sunnis outnumber Shiites by four to one. This sectarian division has proven serious. At times, it has led to violence provoked by extremists on both sides.

From 1947 to 1958, Pakistan was governed by a nominally democratic government although parliamentary elections were never held. The country functioned under two iterations of a constituent assembly that was established to devise a frame of government that would resolve the differences between the new nation's competing groups, but such fundamental issues as regional or provincial autonomy, land reform, and the final shape of the constitutional system were never resolved. In the absence of a definitive resolution of these questions, the civilian and military bureaucracies took effective charge. Pakistan had inherited by far the smaller share of the old administrative apparatus that British India had bequeathed to its successor states. Most of the military officers and civil servants that acceded to Pakistan were of middle rank and below.

However, this did not stop them from becoming the dominant force in the new political system. Until 1956, the chief executive was the governor general, a post originally held by Muhammad Ali Jinnah, the charismatic head of the Muslim League. But Jinnah died in 1948, and the political influence of the Muslim League eroded. In 1956, a new assembly promulgated Pakistan's first constitution, but later that year, the president abrogated the document and dismissed the assembly. He was aided by the army's first indigenous commander-in-chief, General Ayub Khan. In 1958 Khan decided to dismiss the president, and the military took over direct rule.

The military regime under Ayub Khan immediately outlawed political party activity and sharply clamped down on dissent. However, the general promised a quick return to democratic rule. In 1962, a new constitution was promulgated that created a presidential system. Khan assumed the presidency. The independently elected chief executive possessed significant decree powers, was able to dominate the legislature, and was safe from impeachment. The president had control over the budget and possessed the right to proclaim a state of emergency and suspend civil liberties. In 1962 Ayub Khan eased some of the strictures of the state of emergency. He used the new constitution to civilianize his rule. Four opposition parties united to oppose Ayub Khan in the 1965 presidential elections. They demonstrated considerable support, taking over a third of the electoral college vote. Opposition to the government was catalyzed by a number of issues. Pakistan had lost its second war with India in 1965, provoking the opposition to criticize Ayub Khan for his "unnecessary concessions" in the cease-fire agreement. The politicians and people of East Pakistan too were becoming increasingly restive about their lack of representation in the Ayub Khan government. Sheikh Mujibur Rahman ("Mujib"), head of the Awami League in East Pakistan, called for economic and political autonomy for East Pakistan. Meanwhile, Zulfikar Ali Bhutto, the leader of the Pakistan People's Party (PPP) and a former foreign minister, called for revolution. Additional troubles ensued. By 1968, the country's lack of economic advance provoked political outbreaks. What started as an attempt by the regime to celebrate a "decade of development" ended in widespread protests. By 1969 Ayub Khan was also losing the confidence of his fellow generals. In March, he resigned, and General Yahya Khan, the army commander-in-chief, became president. He promised elections to a new national assembly that would form a government and write a constitution, but failed to concede important points to the opposition.

Elections were held in December 1970 according to new rules. Unlike previous elections that had given the West equal weight with the more populous East, the new system was based on the principle of one-person-one-vote that gave the East predominance. The Awami League won virtually every seat in the East, giving it the majority of seats necessary to form the government. It had campaigned on the League's basic platform calling for substantial autonomy. Bhutto's and the PPP's electioneering was based on Islam, democracy, and socialism. They carried a substantial majority in West Pakistan. The Awami leader proceeded to form a government, and at least initially Yahya Khan seemed to recognize his right to do so. However, Bhutto and the PPP were intransigent, saying that the country contained two majorities; they were unwilling to let Mujib dominate the new government. On March 1, 1971, Yahya Khan dissolved the cabinet and declared that the opening of the new national assembly would be postponed indefinitely. The reaction was cataclysmic. A civic strike began, and the authorities responded with repression. The Awami League was outlawed, and Sheik Mujib was arrested.

A civil war followed as East Pakistan declared independence. Militias in the new state were joined by some eastern military units, but the army was able to gain control of most of the country rapidly. A quarter of a million refugees fled to India early in the offensive. Within six months their numbers had swollen to 10 million. The Indian parliament voiced its solidarity with the people of East Bengal, and the stage was set for another India–Pakistan war. Once full-scale hostilities actually started, Indian forces defeated the Pakistani army in Bengal in two weeks. Mismatched in the best of times, the Pakistani military in the East was cut off from its strategic reserves. East Pakistan became the independent state of Bangladesh. In (West) Pakistan the military government collapsed. Zulfikar Ali Bhutto came to power. Bhutto had a charismatic personality and ran a highly personalistic government. His PPP had promised wide-ranging social and economic reform, a parliamentary government, and the resolution of the role of Islam in the country. In practice, Bhutto was unable or unwilling to deliver to any serious degree. The 1973 constitution, while formally providing for a parliamentary system, prevented the removal of the prime minister by the legislature, a key feature of any truly parliamentary regime. And while the constitution was also nominally federal, Bhutto dismissed provincial governments when he found it convenient to do so.

The country's defeat in war had given the new prime minister the opportunity to blame the crisis on the military, and it also provided him a pretext to purge the officer corps. Some fourteen thousand officers were removed. In addition, Bhutto established a paramilitary force independent of the armed forces over which he was able to exercise a significant degree of personal control. Bhutto's pledge of socialism led to the nationalization of the banks and other large firms. Moreover, the prime minister appeared to be following through with his threats to break the power of the wealthiest families in the country and redistribute land. This expectation was never realized. Under his rule, the old economic elite continued to dominate the country. Politically Bhutto drew more power to his own hands, retaining restrictions on the press and other civil liberties. And although he began his term by initiating a reform of the civil service, the patrimonialism inherent in the bureaucracy and the entire political system continued apace. His policy in dealing with the ethnic rebellion in Baluchistan was heavy-handed. Elections in March 1977 prompted an outpouring of opposition activity. Although the government allowed for a fairly free campaign, the threat of repressive measures always loomed in the background. The official results showed Bhutto and the PPP winning the election handily, but they were not accepted as reliable by the opposition. Fearing an outbreak of violence against his continued rule, Bhutto suspended some civil liberties. Negotiations between Bhutto and the opposition broke down. In July, he was deposed by a military coup.

When he came to power, General Zia ul Haq promised early elections as had Ayub Khan twenty years earlier. As was the case with his predecessor, he did not deliver on his promise. A martial law regime followed. Bhutto was tried for murder and executed in April 1979. Zia had disposed of a political rival, but he had not put an end to opposition to military rule. The Movement to Restore Democracy was formed in 1981, and Zia's actions were challenged both politically and in the courts. When the courts held that his institutional decrees had gone beyond what the constitution would permit, he forced the judges to resign, reinstating only those who swore an oath to support his contested decrees. Zia attempted to make Islamic law the norm in Pakistan. He established Sharia (Islamic law) courts, and he later introduced Islamic punishments for crimes. These efforts helped stir up sectarian opposition. As de facto president, Zia restructured the executive. The president was to be indirectly elected and have the power to dismiss the prime minister as well as the national and provincial legislatures.

Zia's preferred formula was to use nonparty elections to fill representative bodies. At the same time he struck up alliances with some of the executed prime minister's old opponents. Local bodies were filled according to the nonparty formula in 1981. A referendum in 1984 asked the people whether they approved of the president's Islamization policy. He interpreted the 98 percent affirmative vote as a vote for his continued rule. In 1985 a national assembly was elected, again by a nonparty vote. Zia lifted martial law with the proviso that his alterations of the constitution be accepted. Zia's attempt to use elected authorities to institutionalize his rule did not always prosper, however. His prime minister failed to pass an Islamization bill and failed to block a bill that legalized political parties once more. In May 1988 Zia dissolved the national and provincial assemblies, and called new elections. A month before the elections were to be held, Zia died in a plane crash. The reported cause was sabotage.

Although Zia had passed from the scene, the system he helped create lived after him. The prime minister continued to serve at the pleasure of the president, and the president himself was often informally under the thumb of the armed forces' chief-of-staff. The prime minister was dismissed in 1990 and again in 1996. Both times, the prime minister, Benazir Bhutto, Zulfikar's daughter, was dismissed by the president at the military's behest. It was not until November 1997 that the balance of power between the three officials shifted. On the strength of his January 1997 election landslide, Nawaz Sharif of the Pakistan Muslim League confronted the president and the newly established, ten-member military advisory council. The issue was a presidential veto of a law making appeals of contempt rulings easier. The president and his council resigned. As is typical in Pakistani politics the issues were personal rather than institutional. Sharif showed no desire to reinforce the rule of law. His majority passed legislation setting up a parallel judicial body to enforce their tough anti-terrorist measures.

Stung by political setbacks the armed forces were quiescent until October 1999, when the chief-of-staff, General Pervez Musharraf, seized power after Sharif attempted to remove him. Upon assuming power, Musharraf promised to reform the state and return the country to civilian rule, but he set no timetable. He later had the ex-prime minister put on trial for corruption. In June 2001, Musharraf declared himself president and indicated he would remain in that office even after legislative elections were held. Thus, with the 1999 coup, Pakistan initiated yet another iteration of the dictatorship–democracy cycle. And Musharraf too followed the process of civilianizing the regime under his continued presidency, making use of restricted parliamentary and regional elections. Yet, no more than the Nigerian military, have Pakistan's armed forces been unable to consolidate their position. Expedients of partial democratization, civilianizing a military president, and attempting to institutionalize Islamic law have all failed to establish the military role of

Plate 7.2 General Pervez Musharraf serving as president, 2007.

directing the government as legitimate. In 2007 demonstrations led by lawyers protested Musharraf's heavy-handed, politically driven reorganization of the judiciary. And late that year, the assassination of Benazir Bhutto, who had returned to Pakistan to contest the controversial parliamentary elections to be held in January 2008, put Pakistani politics into even more turmoil. Although legislative elections were held in early 2008, Musharraf resigned as president, and Bhutto's widower, Asif Ali Zardari, was chosen in his place; Pakistan remains in flux. It has yet to escape the dictatorship–democracy cycle.

Conclusion

Coups d'etat often occur because the society's elite, especially the armed forces, fears revolution or chaos, whether or not that fear is well founded. Usually it is not. Revolutions rarely succeed without a serious case of state failure. When one key element of the state, the military, is in good order at least in terms of being more powerful than any domestic armed opposition, it is difficult for revolutionaries to seize power. Instead, coups d'etat are more likely. When the government lacks legitimacy, when the nonmilitary elements of the state fail to carry out some of their key functions well, when the government is hamstrung and unable to act in the face of what appears to be revolutionary violence, the military is unlikely to remain passive. Unwilling to cede control to revolutionaries, allow disorder to grow, or permit the government to follow what they believe are unwise policies, the armed forces are likely to intervene instead. Military intervention can easily become a habit, and it can easily be used for other purposes than a legitimate national emergency. If the armed forces believe their institutional interests are threatened or if a particular military leader sees intervention as in his interest, the armed forces may well seize power. Such interventions are easier the second and third time. The dictatorship–democracy cycle thus created is often difficult to break. However, not all interventionist militaries become ensnared in such a cycle. The next chapter discusses efforts by some guardian and ruler militaries to break or avoid that cycle on their own terms, some with apparent success.

Questions for further consideration

1. What sorts of political crisis would have to occur for the military to become an overt political actor in countries like Canada, the United States, the United Kingdom, or other consolidated democracies that you are familiar with?

2. How do the armed forces differ from other parts of the state bureaucracy? How do they differ from other interest groups? How are they the same?

3. In developed democracies, how do the armed forces attempt to influence policies that affect them, such as budgets, personnel issues, retirement, etc.? What other sorts of influence can they often exercise in developing countries? Why?

4. What would some indicators of an impending coup be? Using Lexus-Nexus, Google, or another search engine find instances of such indicators. For instances some time in the past, what was the outcome?

5. Using reference resources, explore why the Soviet coup of 1991 failed and the Thai coup of 2006 succeeded.

6. Why would a military sometimes move from moderator-type interventions to those more typical of a guardian role?

7. What do the cases of military intervention in Nigeria and Pakistan have in common? How are they different?

Further reading

Samuel P. Huntington, *The Soldier and the State: The Theory and Practice of Civil–Military Relations*. New York: Random House, 1964. The classic study of modern civil–military relations and objective control of the military.

Jimmy D. Kandeh, *Coups from Below: Armed Subalterns and State Power in West Africa*. New York: Palgrave Macmillan, 2004. A discussion of coups led by junior officers and noncommissioned officers, overall an anomaly but common in West Africa.

Edward Luttwak, *Coup d'Etat: A Practical Handbook*. Cambridge, MA: Harvard University Press, 1979 [1968]. A detailed discussion of full-dress coups.

Eric A. Nordlinger, *Soldiers in Politics: Military Coups and Governments*. Englewood Cliffs, NJ: Prentice-Hall, 1977. Outlines the various types of military government and the nature of the officer corps.

Claude E. Welch, Jr., *No Farewell to Arms? Military Disengagement from Politics in Africa and Latin America*. Boulder, CO: Westview Press, 1987. Discusses how the armed forces retain political influence even when they retreat from exercising direct political control.

8 Military regimes

A man can build himself a throne of bayonets, but he cannot sit on it.
(Boris Yeltsin, Russian President, 1991–9)

In this chapter

The discussion of civil–military relations begun in the previous chapter continues. The chapter uses a structural–functional approach to explain why the armed forces has a difficult time consolidating long-term rule relying on armed forces' institutions and norms alone. Then, the chapter proceeds with a neo-institutional overview of two types of military-dominated regimes. The first, the party–military model, is based on an alliance of near equals: a revolutionary party and the armed forces. The party is substantially more than a mere facade for military rule, and its revolutionary aims are a serious part of the regime's program, at least initially. In the second type of regime, the military plays a guardian role. It has overall control of the government but cedes part of the day-to-day decision-making to its civilian allies. Elections that are far from fully fair and free are often permitted. Nonetheless, the armed forces have the final say over political decisions and retain an institutional presence in key areas of the state and the political arena. Case studies of Iraq, Chile, and Indonesia illustrate how the various types of political systems discussed in the chapter developed.

Introduction

For much of modern history, civilian control of the armed forces was the norm. Through the first half of the twentieth century, when military leaders seized permanent power, they regularly shed their military uniforms and assumed the civilian title of "president" or "king." In addition, these former military leaders took steps to keep the armed forces themselves out of politics, acting much as a chief executive of civilian origins might. In short, although the armed forces might serve as a stepping-stone to power, they rarely ruled directly themselves for any extended period of time. Rulers of military origin seemed to recognize that seizing power – building a throne of bayonets – would be the easy part. Ruling for an extended period as a military leader – actually sitting on such a throne – would be quite difficult. This difficulty is illustrated by the dictatorship–democracy cycle discussed in the last chapter. Nonetheless, in more recent times, some militaries in the developing world have felt the need to maintain military guidance over the political system and the necessity of ensconcing the armed forces and military officers in critical positions of state administration and the economy. Sometimes building explicitly on the experiences of the Soviet Union and Turkey from earlier in the twentieth century, they have experimented with new sorts of military regimes that did not involve direct rule by military officers as the key mechanism of control. These efforts have met with mixed success. The current chapter discusses three examples of these general approaches: Iraq, Indonesia, and Chile.

Military regimes and the requisites for continuity

Military regimes require the same basic requisites to achieve continuity as other regimes do: legitimacy, governmental efficacy, state effectiveness, and a loyal and competent armed force. Although they are perfectly capable of suppressing disorder and are often willing to strengthen state institutions to enhance their effectiveness, the armed forces lack legitimacy and the institutional capacity to make effective governmental decisions and produce consensus. What Nordlinger calls "moderator" militaries (see Chapter 7, 295) overcome these inherent problems by avoiding long-term governance. The legitimacy of their emergency rule rests on the legitimacy of the old status quo and on the public's belief that it was really under threat. Even if significant mass or elite political actors reject the legitimacy of emergency rule, the military government only needs to keep them in check for a limited period. The semi-loyal or disloyal opposition to military rule does not need to be co-opted, destroyed, or permanently suppressed. The armed forces' government does not need to craft new and convincing ideological foundations to underpin a new regime, nor does it have to develop efficacious political institutions to integrate all relevant political actors into the system. The self-imposed mission of the moderator military is minor repair of the status quo, not a complete system overhaul. In contrast, militaries that intend to remain in power indefinitely venture into uncharted territory administratively, politically, and ideologically. Regardless of the causes that led to the armed forces' seizure of power, militaries that engage in long-term rule have a strong tendency to become politicized. Unlike war, politics is

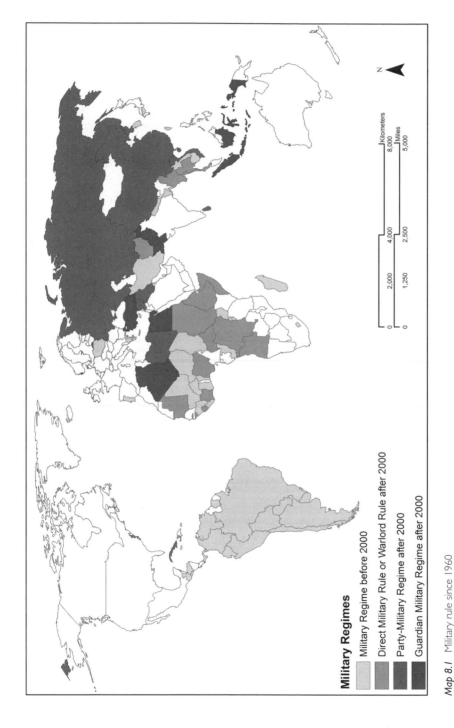

Map 8.1 Military rule since 1960

Source: Environmental Systems Research Institute (ESRI) map data. Data: O'Kane (1987); Siddiqa (2007); Department of State Background Notes

rarely an endeavor amenable to a technocratic style of management. Factions develop and must be placated or marginalized. Deals must be struck and incompatible ends reconciled. As they evolve, military regimes often come to look more political and less military, and the armed forces themselves come to look and behave like a political party.

There are several ways of attempting to finesse the problems associated by long-term military rule. One is the creation of a party–military regime. This sort of regime, in effect, subcontracts the important political functions to a pro-regime political party that shares power with the armed forces in a one-party state. Communist states followed this model. In the contemporary period a variety of states in the Middle East do. This model provides for a mobilization regime whose mission is to transform the social and economic landscape. An alternative model is essentially conservative in nature. It aims at regularizing control by a guardian military. As in the party–military model, the armed forces are not the overt governors; civilian politicians are. Yet, the armed forces retain a potent veto power over civilian policies and personnel as well as critical roles in the state and economy. Armed forces in Latin America made serious efforts to create guardian regimes in the 1960s and 1970s, but were forced to scale back their efforts since. In Asia, guardian regimes were more successful in both the areas of economic development and political control. But even there, guardian militaries have met with serious reversals. Defenders of liberal democracy should not be complacent, however. The mechanisms of day-to-day military influence described in the last chapter and the potential for coups d'etat remain largely intact.

Party–military regimes

A party-military regime is one way in which the military can assume a dominant role in the political system without the political instability that generally characterizes praetorianism. The **party-military regime** is an authoritarian regime based on an alliance of near equals. In this alliance a strong revolutionary party shares rule with the armed forces (Perlmutter 1981: 51–62). The party provides the regime's political cadres, the lion's share of civil servants, and the legitimizing ideology. The armed forces provide a key means of social mobilization and control and receive a disproportionate influence in policy-making. This sort of regime differs ideologically from short-term military rule. When the military assumes a moderator role and rules briefly, it generally has conservative objectives. The armed forces intervene via a "veto" coup (Huntington 1968: 222–4) to prevent the government for doing something with which they disagree or to force the government to prevent change from below. A real revolution is something the armed forces wish to avoid at virtually any cost. They fear rebellion from below and are suspicious of radical ideologies that seem to threaten the unity of the nation. In contrast, in party–military regimes, the faction of the armed forces that makes the coup sees itself as a revolutionary vanguard, much as a civilian revolutionary party might. Hence, upon taking power, they proclaim a revolution aimed at real political and social change, not the preservation of the status quo. The leading example of the regimes under consideration exist in Syria, Egypt under Gamal Abdel Nasser, Iraq (before 2003), and communist countries. Earlier versions espoused the ideology of pan-Arab nationalism and socialism.

Origins

Party–military regimes typically have their roots in revolutionary movements. In communist states, revolution is the reason for the party's existence. And in leading communist states, such as the Soviet Union, China, Vietnam, and Cuba, real revolutions from below occurred. This was not the case in most other instances where party–military regimes emerged. Burma's regime under Ne Win (1962–88) and intermittent Latin American examples emerged out of military coups. Muslim states, which represent the other key instances of the party–military type, had their origins in coups as well except in the case of Algeria. Be that as it may, the coup-makers who established party–military regimes had revolutionary aspirations.

In the communist world, the regime's armed forces grew up in close association with the communist party and often played a key role in the seizure of power. In Russia, the Red Guards, the party's militia, seized power from the Provisional Government and successfully fought a civil war to consolidate power. As its numbers expanded in the process, military commanders were overseen by political commissars, who were responsible for assuring that military commanders, sometimes of questionable loyalty, followed the party's dictates. The Red Guards became the Red Army, and after the Battle of Stalingrad at the height of the Second World War, the Soviet Army. In the process, the officer corps gained greater professional autonomy and status (gold braid and traditional insignia of rank were reintroduced). But the importance of the armed forces within the Soviet system remained undiminished. Large military budgets, the appointment of a uniformed officer as minister of defense, prominent positions for senior officers within the politburo and central committee guaranteed that influence. Along with the highly militarized interior ministry forces, the Soviet military was a bulwark against internal rebellion.

The Soviet model became the norm for civil–military relations in other communist states.

In China and Vietnam, where the Communist Party seized power by means of protracted people's wars (see Chapter 5), the military was intimately involved in the process of popular mobilization from the very beginning of the revolution. And during the Great Proletarian Culture Revolution in the 1960s, a period of intra-party political struggle, the Chinese military, the People's Liberation Army (PLA), played a pivotal role. It assumed key administrative and political functions and the party and government bureaucracy were temporarily sidelined. Since the late 1970s, the PLA has played a role more typical of communist militaries elsewhere although it continues to have important economic functions, managing its own firms in the defense and other industrial sectors. Cuba is the case in which the military preceded formation of the ruling party. Fidel Castro's guerrillas established the Communist Party of Cuba *after* they achieved the revolution. The old-line communists, who existed before Castro's seizure of power, were only one element of it.

The Middle East during the 1950s and 1960s was a seedbed for non-communist party–military regimes, and illustrates how organizations other than revolutionary parties can acquire a revolutionary vocation. The era was a time of great optimism in the developing world as a whole. All across the globe, peoples, long subject to a foreign yoke, were gaining their independence. And it seemed that political independence carried with it the possibility of a broader and more fundamental form of emancipation. New nationalist and socialist governments promised not only greater economic growth and national power, but also a more equitable distribution of wealth and a broad sharing of political power. These aspirations waxed strong in the Muslim world too. Much of the Arab world had attained formal independence in an earlier era, but regimes there had failed to live up to the latter-day radical aspirations that swept the region during the cold war. Many of these regimes were monarchies established by the French and British to be reliable partners for securing French and British interests. Some, such as the Saud family in Saudi Arabia, were native to the regions they governed. Others, such as Farouk in Egypt and the Hashimites in Jordan, Syria, and Iraq, were transplanted from outside. But in either case, they relied on traditional notions of loyalty and authority. They built networks relying on allies among the traditional elite even when, in some instances, the regime itself also included parliamentary or quasi-parliamentary institutions. The traditional elite was composed of tribal and clan leaders, as well as religious leaders of various sorts, and had deep-seated local roots. These elites had retained their influence under both Ottoman rule and later

European tutelage. They were the leaders recognized by a majority of the population, which still remained largely rural and traditional. Most political actors who had reason to be dissatisfied with the regime were relatively weak. The traditional middle class was largely composed of bazaar merchants, who had long dominated commerce. Neither the traditional middle class nor the working class was sufficiently large, nor was the peasantry well organized to serve as a decisive force for political change. Military officers often represented a disproportionately large and influential part of the modern middle class compared to more developed parts of the world. Thus, elements within the armed forces took upon themselves the role of revolutionary vanguard (Halpern 1965: 41–118, 251–80).

In the 1950s and 1960s, Arab nationalist sentiments flourished. Arab nationalism followed the general pattern of revolutionary nationalism described in Chapter 6. Specifically, Arab nationalism identified the Arab nation, defined primarily in terms of language and culture, as the true community to which individuals ought to feel loyalty. Arab nationalism saw the existing monarchies that ruled the region under European tutelage as backward and self-serving, propped up by foreigners, and subservient to foreign interests. These relatively new states, especially those in Mesopotamia and the Arabian Peninsula, were artificial creations. Their boundaries were established by the European powers, and their ruling families came to power because they were protégés of these same powers. It is no wonder that these monarchies repressed aspirations for true self-rule. They were corrupt and incapable of speaking for the interest of their own people. The Arab nation, the new ideology declared, ought to sweep aside these throwbacks to the past and lackeys of foreign imperialism.

The new regime would unite the Arab peoples transcending the artificial boundaries created largely by foreigners. It would be socialist and egalitarian. It would liberate its people from the slavery of poverty, ignorance, and political domination. It would establish a community that would transcend class. It would promote economic development, true democracy, and emancipation. Many, though certainly not all, of the advocates of Arab nationalism saw the vanguard party as essential. In a society in transition, the party would play a pivotal role in mobilizing people for the process of social change. Old ways of thinking and doing things would have to be transformed. The party would be a necessary vehicle through which the people could promote their interests and keep a check on governmental corruption.

In some countries, a civilian-dominated revolutionary movement, such as the Baathist Party, actually took root. But even where civilian organizations existed, they found it difficult to act independently of military support. As a consequence of the weakness of their civilian counterparts, radical movements within the armed forces often became more important than civilian radical movements. Arab nationalism had a special attraction for middle and lower-ranking officers – colonels down to lieutenants. They were reflex nationalists. Opportunities were passing their country by, and the chief villain for the lack of progress seemed to these officers to be the government of the day. These radical officers saw the monarchies in power, which were in league with imperial powers, as insufficiently nationalistic and progressive if not outright traitors to the national cause. By default these military movements often became the revolutionary vanguard within their countries. Middle and lower-level officers were likely to be sympathetic to the idea of revolution. Most were not part of the elite either by birth or by social attainment. Rather, they were often individuals of lower-middle-class origins, and they understood what life was really like for the masses of their countrymen. They had not yet reached the upper echelons of the officer corps, where both age and circumstance might have made them more satisfied with the status quo. Moreover, educated officers, much more than the masses of the population, were keenly aware of how politics affected national welfare. Much more than the masses of the population, they had a theoretical explanation for the causes of and solutions to the national malaise. And, most importantly, they were in a better position than almost anyone else to take up arms against the government and overthrow it.

Thus, the armed forces – or more accurately factions within them – aligned themselves against rulers and other privileged elites, especially the traditional sectors, whom they saw as blocking both social progress and national power. These military radicals did more than plot among themselves; they took direct action. A series of military coups began in Syria in 1949, culminating in a radical coup in 1954. In 1952, in Egypt the Free Officers Movement seized power. The monarchy fell in Iraq in 1958, and in Libya in 1969. In need of allies and a political base beyond the military, progressives in the armed forces often allied themselves with other political actors seeking revolutionary change. The oldest revolutionary nationalist party in the Middle East was the Baathist Party that held its first congress in 1947, although the movement and its ideology preceded the congress by several decades. The Baathists would be mimicked later by other parties and movements in the Arab world. These radical national socialist groupings remained key political actors in the region for much of the later half of the twentieth century.

Figure 8.1 Propaganda poster of Gamal Abdel Nasser.

The "revolution"

The coups that brought revolutionary militaries to power are classified as "breakthrough coups." A **breakthrough coup** heralds a fundamental change in the country's underlying political dynamics whether or not it immediately succeeds in overthrowing the existing regime (Huntington 1968: 205–7). After a successful coup, the new revolutionary military governments justified the seizure of power and the new government by appealing to radical nationalist or Islamist principles and aspiring to revolutionary change. However, this rapid road to power turns out to weaken the coup's prospects for revolutionary change in the end. The armed forces have a difficult time in building institutions to consolidate the revolution. A true revolution needs mass support to consolidate its victory. Radical change is never a quick, easy, or painless process. No real revolution – regardless of how the revolutionaries seize power – can succeed in effectuating the fundamental changes it aims at without mobilizing society behind it. A conventional revolution's third phase, where the radicals seize control and attempt to remake society in an entirely new pattern, is fully possible only because the radicals can rely on the support of a mass base. The power they have in the streets undermines more moderate leaders in the government. Although the radicals' "reign of terror and virtue" never lives up to their highest expectations, many things do change. Mass enthusiasm leads spontaneously to new organizations and a transformation of political culture. The creative third phase – sometimes quite a long one – precedes the inevitable retrenchment and loss of dynamism of the revolution's fourth phase. New institutions, however imperfect, are often the result.

In civilian-led revolutions, mass mobilization precedes the seizure of power. Wars of national liberation against colonial powers, prolonged insurgencies or civil wars against oppressive governments, mass demonstrations and protests bring an end to the old regime. At the same time they serve to build psychological and organizational links between revolutionary leaders and their constituents, and they create the organization and élan required to transform society radically. In short, civilian revolutionary vanguards have to mobilize mass support to overthrow the old regime since mobilizing the mass of the population is the only way for the vanguard to gain sufficient force to overthrow the old regime in the first place. In contrast to civilian-led revolutions, regimes established by a coup d'etat come about because of military force majeure. The "revolutionary" coup can enter a revolutionary third phase quite quickly, and almost as quickly it seems to experience a fourth-phase Thermidorean reaction. The coup's leaders do not lay the groundwork for a true revolution. The overthrow of the old regime is often widely popular, but the process of seizing power does not of itself entail the mobilization of society. It does not provide a true mass base. Inertia is the enemy. Revolutionary officers often realize their need for civilian allies if they were to accomplish their purposes. They need a revolutionary civilian party and mass organizations that will organize society behind the policy of the revolutionary government. They need sustained mass effort to truly shake off old habits and lay to rest old institutions.

Unsurprisingly, radical parties or their surrogates are a necessary part of the military-led revolutionary regime. The Baath Party eventually played a prominent role in the military regimes of Syria and Iraq. In Egypt, which was the most populous Arab state as well as the Arab state with the greatest prestige, Gamal Abdel Nasser came to power in the early 1950s as the result of a coup led by revolutionary-minded officers. Instead of allying itself with an existing party, Nasser's Revolutionary Command Council created a new party of its own, the Liberation Rally. In the 1960s Muammar Qaddafi came to power in Libya and developed his own version of Arab radicalism, establishing what officially is a *nonparty* state. In fact, the Libyan regime styles itself a *Jamahiriya* (a state of the masses). However, in a real sense, the supposedly revolutionary mass parties created in such a manner were virtually stillborn. They were forged not in the heat of a life-or-death revolutionary crisis, but on the basis of orders from above. Mass movements may develop organizations, but the revolutionary officers who lead the new regimes find it difficult to reverse the process and have organizations engender mass movements. Political mobilization is limited (Perlmutter 1974: 106–6, 127–9; Linz 2000: 170–1).

The failure to produce a pan-Arab state illustrates the problem. The creation of a pan-Arab state was an important goal of Arab nationalism. Despite several attempts, efforts to create a "United Arab Republic" foundered. The one that came closest to success was undertaken by one of the most charismatic leaders of his era. Gamal Abdel Nasser's personal appeal was region-wide. He was, in fact, able to create a short-lived version of a "United Arab Republic," composed of Syria and Egypt, but the union collapsed despite the fact that Arab unity had such appeal that its separate state members retained the name even after the entity fragmented. Pan-Arab ideology, agreements made between national leaders, organizational fixes, and even Nasser's charismatic appeal were insufficient to overcome local and factional rivalries and the inertia of the status quo.

Consequences

Some party–military regimes have been able to carry out a wide range of social and economic reforms along socialist lines in the fields of land reform, education, and public health. They expanded the state and provided jobs for the educated classes. Despite their achievements, these regimes do not fully live up to their goals. Although the ideology of Arab nationalism had considerable appeal, real political and social mobilization was difficult to engender and sustain. The leaders of these regimes were either unable to find adequate vehicles for mobilizing the masses or were unwilling to countenance a mobilization process that might escape their control. Consequently, the party, far from being either a mass party or a true vanguard party with a mass influence through associated mass organizations, frequently devolves into a large but much less ideologically potent organization. Those in politics or the state administration find it worth their while to join and participate. Ordinary people rarely see membership doing much to advance their own interests. Mass rallies eventually become contrived affairs, lacking the spontaneity and enthusiasm expected of such political exercises. The party simply becomes a permanent bureaucratic fixture of political life. Nor does the state come close to the ideal of participatory and ethical administration invoked as part of the rationale for making the revolution. The would-be revolutionary state, like its monarchist or nationalist predecessor, is today riddled with corruption and inefficiency. It is a weak but repressive state. Libya, in theory, had adopted a somewhat different political pattern. Local assemblies are supposed to replace the party and the mechanism through which the people's will is expressed and implemented. Yet despite the absence of an official vanguard party, popular consultation there too is more show than substance. All these regimes are failed mobilization regimes, having failed in the tasks of political mobilization and radical social change (cf. Perlmutter 1974).

One of the few branches of the state that normally operates with a degree of efficiency is the security service. By and large, the general public is not the major threat. The denial of the right to organize politically, and the state's ownership, control, or intimidation of the mass media allows the regime to keep the public in check. If riots or uprisings do occur, they can be quickly and brutally suppressed. Real threats are more likely to come from secretive radical groups or from within the armed forces themselves than from mass movements. For example, in Egypt during the 1980s and 1990s, the major threat to the regime came from Islamist groups that used political violence against the government, Coptic Christians, and foreign tourists. The government pulled no punches in dealing with them, engaging in wholesale arrests, torture, and summary trials. There did not appear to be a serious possibility of a military coup against the government. However, in less institutionalized and more personalized regimes, such as those of Iraq, Syria, and Libya, coups and assassination attempts from within the regime's own power structure have been a constant worry. Hence, the security services have had to be constantly on guard. And the leader had to be on guard against the security services as well. No one could be trusted completely.

As party–military regimes age, it is typical for the leader to draw power into the hands of his own clan or trusted associates, establishing personal loyalty as the most important criterion for service in the top echelons of the government, state administration, military, and security services. The more the top cadre of officials is associated with the leader, the more likely it is that they will stand or fall with him. Hence, no one must be allowed to build an independent power base. These tactics of securing one's rule have been used since at least the time of the tyrants of ancient Greece.

In sum, party–military regimes in the Muslim world and beyond have lost their revolutionary zeal. In fact, Egypt's party–military regime ended in the mid-1970s when President Anwar Sadat replaced the single mass-based Arab Socialist Union with competing ideological movements within the organization's successor. In Algeria, the regime party, the National Liberation Front, succumbed to the dominance of the armed forces even earlier. In 1965, three years after the country achieved independence, the military deposed the first president, Ahmed Ben Bella, demonstrating the military's predominance in the system. Both regimes today fall within the guardian type.

The future

The contemporary world has changed considerably from the one that gave rise to revolutionary oriented party–military regimes in the past. Communism has disappeared as a major revolutionary force, and the regional secular ideologies of socialism, nationalism, and pan-Arabism have been largely discredited as well. In their place, Islamism became the ideological foundation for revolution. Although internal politics have changed, sometimes dramatically, social conditions often mirror those of the earlier epoch. The middle class and middle-class political movements remained weak. Thus, in the last two decades of the twentieth century, radical Islamist movements formed alliances with elements of the armed forces as had their Pan-Arabist predecessors. Specifically in Sudan, military factions have allied themselves with Islamist movements in an attempt to establish an Islamic state. Just as the older revolutionary military regimes resembled truly revolutionary regimes of the same period, so too some military factions today find inspiration and allies in the Islamist movement.

Although its Arab nationalist version of the revolutionary party–military regime has lost its dynamism, military radicalism in the Muslim world today is assuming new forms. As some radical Islamists have attempted to cultivate members of the armed forces in order to use a coup as a means of seizing power, military regimes themselves have attempted to burnish their Islamic credentials in order to shore up their eroding legitimacy. This alliance is the natural outgrowth of the popular appeal of the Islamist explanation for these societies' contemporary problems. The logic of a military–Islamist alliance parallels that of the military–Pan-Arab alliance of earlier decades. The sentiments sweeping their societies as a whole also affect military officers. Civilian radicals are often looking for support that will allow them to put their ideas into practice anywhere they can find it. While the earlier alliance between the armed forces and pan-Arabists seems to have played itself out, a military–Islamist alliance may still be in its incipient stages. More pro-Islamist military coups and more Islamist military regimes are a possibility.

CASE STUDY: IRAQ

The history of modern Iraq illustrates a dynamic common in the Muslim world. A corrupt monarchy is threatened by the appeal of Arab nationalism and revolution, but civilian movements are unable to overthrow the regime or rule without military support. The military, in turn, considers itself the vanguard of a new order and co-opts civilians into the ruling coalition once the monarchy is overthrown. This coalition, while it radically transforms society, is unable to build a stable constitutional system. Thus, violence continues to play a pivotal role in politics, and military and political power coalesce.

Iraq is in the heart of Mesopotamia, one of the cradles of ancient civilization, but the country did not assume its current political form until after the First World War when it was carved out of the defeated Ottoman Empire. Shiite Arab Muslims comprise 60 percent of the population, but they have long been politically subordinate to Sunni Arabs who were patronized by the Ottomans. The Kurds are a significant non-Arab Sunni Muslim ethnic group that has periodically sought independence. They are about as numerous as the Sunni Arabs. The birth of Iraq as a sovereign state followed the pattern typical of much of the Middle East. It was largely a foreign creation.

Although Iraq is a relatively new state, the area has an ancient and rich history. From AD 750 to 1258, Baghdad was the capital of the Islamic world under the Abbasid dynasty. Even after political dominance passed elsewhere, Baghdad and the surrounding territory of Mesopotamia were the prizes contested by the Ottoman Empire centered in modern Turkey and the Persian Safavid Empire based in present-day Iran. The Ottomans appealed to the Sunnis for support while the Safavids did the same with the Shiites, thus deepening an already serious sectarian rift. By 1638 Baghdad was firmly in Ottoman hands. However, the struggle with the Safavids had weakened the government's ability to exercise firm control over Mesopotamia and allowed for a good deal of migration and warfare between tribal confederations in the region.

The multinational Ottoman Empire used Islam as a primary instrument for legitimizing its rule, at least among its predominantly Muslim subjects. The Turkish Sultan served not only as religious leader of his own direct subjects, but was defender of Muslims worldwide. In the early nineteenth century, however, the multinational character of the empire was challenged by the Egyptian revolt and attempts by Greeks and other European peoples, who were predominantly Christian, to free themselves from the Turkish yoke. But nationalism did not make much of an impression on the Arab portion of the empire in the nineteenth century. It was not until 1908 when the "Young Turks" took over the government, that things began to change significantly. The Young Turks wanted to transform the Ottoman Empire into a modern nation-state based on European models. They began Turkification of the Arabs, sparking resentment and planting the seeds for a broader revolt. The Young Arab movement was founded, and it put its headquarters in Basra in southern Iraq.

The First World War provided the first real opportunity for the Arab peoples to establish their own independent states. The Arabs revolted against the Ottomans during the war, and they were assisted by the British. British motives were far from altruistic. The Arab revolt advanced British war aims by creating civil war within the territory of one of its major enemies. At war's end the Ottomans were shorn of all their Arab and most of their non-Turkish territories, but the newly freed Arab people did not achieve full independence. While the revolt was based on the appeal of Arab nationalism, nationalism was a relatively new idea in the Arab world. And political disunity remained. This disunity, coupled with the traditional character of much of the region, allowed foreign powers, primarily Britain and France, to dominate regional politics after the First World War. Desirous of controlling the region's oil and recognizing its strategic proximity to the Suez Canal, the two European powers divided the Arab Middle East between them. The British assumed responsibility for most of the southern part of the region, encompassing the Arabian Peninsula, Trans-Jordan (Jordan), Palestine, and Iraq.

Attempts to impose British rule in Iraq led to a revolt in 1920, the "Great Iraqi Revolution" that united usually mutually hostile groups, Shiites, Sunnis, and Kurds, against the foreign enemy. The revolt was violently suppressed by the British occupiers, and the 1921 Cairo Conference produced a compromise of sorts. It provided for an indigenous Iraqi army and recognized an Iraqi government, but it also imposed certain limits upon the new Iraq. The government was supposed to yield to British interests. Faisal, of the Hashemite clan from what is now Saudi Arabia, was chosen to be the country's king. The British believed his nationalist credentials were sufficient to win his acceptance, but they also believed that he would remain weak enough to need their continued support. The British were at least partly successful. Yet, the British maneuver would undermine the new Iraq. Faisal, a non-Iraqi who came from the Arabian Peninsula, was never able to secure legitimacy, and as a leader of the Arab revolt against the Turks, he felt betrayed by the entire process. Nationalists opposed the Cairo Treaty without real effect. In 1932, Iraq was recognized as a sovereign state; its boundaries were fixed, and it was admitted to the League of Nations.

The new state of Iraq continued to be riven by a variety of divisions, many of them based on traditional loyalties. The country was split between Arabs and Kurds. The Kurds inhabited the major oil-producing region in the North and the city of Mosul. After the collapse of the Ottoman Empire, they had sought independence, but it had been denied them by the victorious allied powers. Thus, a restive Kurdish minority remained in the newly established states of Turkey, Syria, and Iran, as well as Iraq. The Kurds were to be a perennial source of friction within each of these countries and often served as a pressure point that a rival state could use to extract concessions. The Iranian government has armed and supported Iraqi Kurds at various times in the modern history of Iraq as a negotiating tactic. Thus, the Iraqi government, controlled by the majority Arabs, had to face a restive minority. At the same time, the Arab majority itself was split between Sunnis and Shiites. The division was ancient and had considerable political significance. It too had been manipulated by outsides for their own advantage. The division between settled townspeople and the tribal peoples and their traditional rulers, sheikhs, was another sensitive area. For the settled population, restricting tribal ownership rights and migratory practices was a necessary part of the country's modernization and served the modernized sector's interests. The sheikhs resisted such moves. In the 1930s, the accelerated pace of privatization of land ownership, the modernization of the state and the army, swung the balance against traditional claims. Ideologically as well, the country was seriously divided with ardent nationalists opposed to the very institution of the monarchy. In 1933 Faisal was succeeded by his son, Ghazi, an ardent Arab nationalist. Two coups in the mid-1930s set the stage for long-term military involvement in politics. Each left the king on the throne, but placed effective power in the hands of a political–military coalition that sought to advance the country along lines of the coalition's own choosing. In 1939, Ghazi was killed in an automobile crash. He was succeeded by his infant son Faisal II, and Amir Abd al Ilah was made regent.

Pan-Arabist sentiment had been growing in the army throughout the 1930s, and a Free Officers Movement was formed. The Second World War again made Iraq pivotal in world politics as German and Italian forces in

North Africa placed British interests in the region under severe threat. A military coup in 1941 put a nationalist civilian government in power and deposed the monarchy. But British intervention by means of the Arab Legion of Trans-Jordan removed the government and restored the regent to power. In the 1950s, a variety of factors set the stage for the monarchy's eventual overthrow. Increased revenue from oil had produced increased corruption. Moreover, the government had taken a foreign policy course that put it at odds with the Pan-Arab movement. It had joined the pro-US, British-supported Baghdad Pact in 1955. It had supported the French, British, and Israeli invasion of the Egyptian Sinai in 1956. In 1958 it had supported unification with Jordan, in opposition to the United Arab Republic of Egypt and Syria that was sponsored by Egypt's popular president, Gamal Abdel Nasser. In July 1958 fearing an anti-western revolt in Lebanon might spread to Jordan, King Hussein asked Iraq for assistance. That request triggered a coup d'etat led by Brigadier Abd al Karim Qasim and Colonel Abd as Salaam Arif. The Hashemite monarchy passed into history.

The new Iraqi Republic, however, was far from stable. Old ethnic and religious tensions remained, and along with them the divisions between military and civilian politicians grew in prominence. The coup-makers' proclamation of a revolution was greeted with widespread support. The king and other members of the royal family and the government were killed. Qasim and Arif eventually split. Arif backed by the Baath Party favored unification with Syria while Qasim opposed it. Qasim, who was Arif's senior in rank and backed by the communists, eventually removed his rival. Qasim's government undertook a policy of land reform, breaking the traditional power structure in the countryside, and the government nationalized the country's oil wealth. In 1961 it laid claim to Kuwait, provoking hostile reaction from the British and their regional allies. Domestically, Qasim faced difficulties on a number of fronts. The Baathists and officers of the armed forces in sympathy with them opposed him. Increasingly, Qasim had to rely on the communists. Eventually he even authorized the formation of a popular militia under their control, the People's Resistance Force. Still, he considered the communists unreliable, and the alliance with them became an on-again off-again affair. In addition, Qasim was unable to pacify the Kurds, who rose in revolt. After having staved off a number of coups and assassination attempts, in February 1963, Qasim was finally overthrown. The coup against Qasim had been orchestrated by the Baath Party, and the party controlled the new regime. It moved quickly to establish a one-party state. Arif was made president, but the Baath Party exercised the real power. The party itself was small with only about one-thousand members, not ideologically cohesive, and divided by factional disputes. At the time, its support was weak in the officer corps. In part to compensate for that, it formed its own party militia. In consonance with pan-Arabist principles, Iraq negotiated to form a United Arab Republic (UAR) along with Egypt (Gamal Abdel Nasser) and Syria.

In the meantime, Arif as president maneuvered to replace Baathists in the government with Nasserites. The Baath was removed from power in November 1963. Arif also worked closely with Nasserites in the military to build support for joining the UAR formed with Egypt and Syria in 1966. To that end, in 1964 a one-party state was formed under the direction of the Iraqi Socialist Union, a name that mimicked that of its Egyptian counterpart. Nasserite policies of nationalization of industry were carried out as well. However, by 1965 Arif's ardor for joining the UAR had cooled, and he began to remove Nasserites from positions of influence. That same year he appointed the first civilian prime minister since the 1958 coup, Abd Rahman Bazzaz. The new prime minister advocated political liberalization, autonomy for the Kurds, and the lessening of the political influence of the armed forces. In 1966, President Arif was killed in a helicopter crash and replaced by his brother, Major General Abd ar Rahman Arif. The regime continued on the course that the late president had set for a while. Opposing Bazzaz's proposed deal with the Kurds and fearing loss of its privileges, the officer corps pressed the new president to dismiss the prime minister. He complied and took over the office himself in May 1967. The regime continued in a weakened state until Arif was overthrown in mid-1968 by army officers unaffiliated with the Baath Party. In the political maneuvering that followed, however, the Baath Party was able to force out the coup-makers and gain control of the government in alliance with sympathetic officers.

The Baath Party of 1968 was much better organized than the Baath of 1963 when it had been easily removed from power. Three of the five members of the party's Revolutionary Command Council were Takritis; two of whom were closely related to one another. Key positions in the government also went to Takritis. Though he was not originally the senior-most of the clique, Saddam Hussein, eventually became the dominant figure. In 1979 he consolidated his control of the party and the government by assuming the general-secretaryship of the party and presidency of the government. With a military power base, the Baath Party could compel obedience. Political deal-making became restricted to a smaller and smaller clique. A consummate intriguer, Hussein had risen to power as a dark horse. Once in power, however, he was far from reserved, purging party, state, and army of potential challengers. Since the Qasim coup of 1958, it had become apparent that the Baath Party could not govern without the support of the armed forces, and the armed forces could not govern without the political apparatus provided by the party. In the post-1968 era, they ruled together. The military and the party had found one another. And Saddam Hussein had found them both. Under military and Baathist governments the country had been economically and socially modernized to a significant extent on the basis of oil wealth, but the militarization of politics and politicization of the armed forces brought stability only at a price. It undermined the proper functioning of both institutions. The armed forces' professional competence was diminished, and the ability of the party to build a meaningful consensus was damaged as well. Despite the absence of coups, politics under Saddam became a brutal affair.

Hussein was a man whose ambitions were wider than Iraq. He took the opportunity in 1980 to attack Iran when it was in the throes of internal violence spawned by its Islamic Revolution. His military leadership, however, was far from sure-handed. The campaign, poorly planned and poorly executed, failed to deliver a quick knockout blow to Iranian forces, and the war dragged on for most of the decade. The manner in which Iraq fought the war was instructive about the nature of the regime. While the Iranians frequently used the strategy of mass human-wave assaults, relying on their forces' enthusiasm for the revolution, the Iraqis were careful to conserve the lives of their soldiers. Even the plan for the initial assault seems to have been influenced by the regime's fear that the loss of any significant piece of national territory might cause the regime an irreparable loss of prestige. Instead of focusing on the southern front and the key oil Iranian oil center of Abadan, Iraqi forces were spread too evenly across the entire front. The necessary mass was lacking at the critical point. The war dragged on until 1988 and ended with the survival of the regime and the retention of Iraq's original territory. The regime had weathered a fierce Iranian counteroffensive, and portrayed its mere survival as a great victory.

In his 1990 invasion of Kuwait, Hussein again demonstrated the scope of his ambitions. The Iraqi claim to Kuwait had been raised almost three decades before by Qasim, but Hussein's invasion actually put the tiny but fantastically oil-rich emirate in Iraqi hands. However, Hussein had miscalculated both international reaction and the ability of the hastily assembled coalition's forces to crush his own. The invasion resulted in a broadly based United Nations-sanctioned coalition. Coalition forces under the leadership of the United States quickly retook Kuwait the following year. Iraq was forced to sign various disarmament agreements, and UN sanctions were imposed when Iraq failed to comply fully with them. Hussein's setbacks did not dull, and perhaps even enhanced, his hubris. He built a cult of personality around himself, constructed dozens of presidential palaces for his use, and tried to raise his stature regionally to the level of Gamal Abdel Nasser. He was quick to exploit not only pan-Arabism but also Islamic sentiment when it suited his interests. His capacity to survive, however, seemed more dependent on the sort of skills typical of tyrants of any age: cunning, willingness to use terror, and an ability to prevent the rise of any sort of united opposition to his rule.

The political evolution of Iraq demonstrates the political limitations of both the armed forces and single parties as rulers and modernizers. Until the period of the war with Iran, the Baathist regime had used its oil wealth to modernize the country and to benefit its people. Yet, the regime's military misadventures and international reaction to them showed that it was prone to serious political misjudgments. The success of the regime in consolidating power provided its adversaries with few ways in which to apply leverage to change the government. Legal opposition was not permitted. The illegal opposition was fragmented. The ethnic and sectarian groups that opposed governments in the past, the Shiites and the Kurds, did not cooperate with one another. The Kurds, in fact, were frequently divided against themselves, one faction occasionally making common cause with the Iraqi government, which both professed to oppose. Ideological splinter groups cooperated poorly with one another and lacked any substantial base of support within the country. The invasion of Kuwait proved a turning point. The country remained under United Nations sanctions for more than a decade and was diplomatically isolated. Worse still, the sanctions imposed on Iraq destroyed the middle class and imposed immense human suffering. Yet, the regime remained secure. Saddam Hussein was in little danger of losing power until he was finally removed by the United States' invasion of 2003.

Guardian military regimes

The guardian military regime is the second type of military-dominated regime that can achieve a degree of political stability. A **guardian military regime** is an authoritarian military-dominated political system in which ultimate political authority rests with the armed forces, but the day-to-day operation of the government is often in the hands of civilians or civilians play a significant role in government and administration.

Guardian regimes allow elections and limited political competition. In a guardian regime, as one analyst aptly puts it, the military rules, but it does not govern (Cook 2007: 33, 69). This does not imply that the armed forces take no role in state administration. Quite the reverse is often the case. Sometimes a military officer, retired or on active duty, serves as president. And guardian militaries can administer state-owned industries, serve in posts that would be typically held by civilians, and possess trusts and retirement funds that profit from state contracts. And senior military officers can always hold a civilian president, prime minister, or cabinet official accountable for governmental failures or interference with military prerogatives. The military as an institution is one-step removed from the totality of day-to-day governmental operations, and, unlike the government, is not accountable even nominally to the public.

Guardian regimes allow for elections in which the public is given a degree of control over the government. But the range of electoral choice offered the public is constrained. Elections are not fully fair and free. Potential opposition parties are not able to organize at will or campaign effectively since the use of the media and public rallies are subject to regime-imposed limits. Once voting has begun, the electoral process itself is controlled by the regime with insufficient guarantees that votes will be accurately tallied and reported. Still, the electoral process is more than a complete charade, and citizens and the opposition have to decide between abstention, which means no influence, and the limited influence that comes from participating in elections with biased rules and biased judges. Many guardian regimes can best be classified as "semi-authoritarian" since the arbitrary power of the government is mitigated by limited electoral competition. In effect, the pro-regime party or parties are junior partners of the armed forces, and these parties are often created by the military itself.

The guardian regime gives the armed forces numerous advantages that compensate for the limits it allows to be placed on its power. First, it provides the military with civilian allies beyond those that can be gained by officers' personal connections and political patronage. Regime parties can co-opt talented individuals, mobilize the public behind the regime, and provide a worthwhile vehicle for assessing public attitudes. In short, a pro-regime party will have many of the attributes of political parties anywhere. Second, with a civilian party as an integral part of the regime, the military as an institution gains what might be called "plausible deniability." Like a sovereign who appoints and dismisses a prime minister and a government at his or her own pleasure, the armed forces can hold the civilian government accountable when unpopular policies cause an otherwise uncontainable public backlash. The military gains breathing space. It is the civilian government at which the public anger is likely to be directed, not the armed forces. Third, the existence of elections and civilian officials gives the regime an aura of legitimacy. The regime, in some sense or other, is a matter of consent. It is "democratic" if only in a very limited sense of the word. Finally and most importantly, a guardian regime protects the military's core interests. These interests may be ideological: the military's commitment to national security as the armed forces envision it, or the armed forces' commitment to modernization and modern principles, again as they themselves envision them. In addition the economic and administrative interests of the armed forces can be secured: its control of key aspects of state administration, the preservation and advancement of military economic enterprises, and the guarantee of military salary, perks, and opportunities for retired officers. In short, sacrificing a degree of day-to-day power is worthwhile for the armed forces.

The armed forces' guardian role can be institutionalized in a variety of ways. Not all of them are equally important for every guardian regime. The basic principle underlying civil–military relations in guardian regimes is that the military should preserve complete autonomy while penetrating civilian political and governmental institutions. In short, contrary to the expectations of a party–military regime, control and influence flow only one way. At the highest levels of government, the constitution can provide for a National Security Council. This body should not be confused with the National Security Council found within the Executive Office of the President of the United States. The **national security council (NSC)** in guardian regimes is a joint civilian–military body composed of senior officials who are to give advice to or who must approve the proposals of the chief executive. The military members do not have to outnumber civilians for the council to register the military's views and pressure the civilian government to act accordingly. Matters of national defense, foreign policy, internal security, including banning of organizations, typically fall within the NSC's purview. In addition, the armed forces can be given reserved seats in the legislature, which allows the military to voice its views in the political arena as well. Military membership in and influence over pro-regime parties provides yet another avenue to voice military view. In the administrative realm, the armed forces' proper domain is widely defined. The military's position in the state bureaucracy both in terms of institutions it completely controls or appointments to normally civilian posts places the armed forces in a position to defend its interests as policies are actually put into execution. The role of military intelligence, usually directed at the military establishments of foreign states, includes branches directed to domestic intelligence – the investigation, disruption, and arrest of "subversives." Should these ordinary methods of controlling politics fail, the armed forces can dismiss the government, suspend the constitution, or declare emergency rule.

In sum, guardian militaries are able to have many of the advantages of direct military governance with few of the disadvantages. But the successful consolidation of a guardian regime requires building institutions. This cannot be accomplished overnight or in any political culture. Where civilian control of the military, democracy, and the rule of law are strong, the rise of a guardian military is unlikely. Where institutions of civilian oversight in the executive branch, the legislature, and civil society are strong, military pretensions to be the sole authoritative spokesman for the national interest are likely to be nipped in the bud. But in many parts of the developing world, these conditions do not obtain.

How guardian regimes arise

Guardian regimes evolve in a variety of ways. The institutions of a guardian military regime were developed in Pakistan under Zia ul-Haq and Pervez Musharraf (Siddiqa 2007: 83–111; Chapter 7). Elsewhere in the Muslim world, Egypt and Algeria's regimes currently follow the guardian pattern (Cook 2007). Until recently Turkey's did as well. Egypt and Algeria started as party–military regimes. But as a half century passed, both became status-quo oriented and risk averse. And in this respect it has come to resemble many of the other guardian regimes whose origins are quite different. While military governments have been common in Africa, few have advanced to the point of crafting the sort of stable institutions typical of guardian regimes. In Latin American and Asia, on the other hand, the armed forces made systematic efforts to consolidate guardian regimes. It is to these two regions that we now turn.

The attempt to create guardian military regimes in Latin America

Latin America represents perhaps the clearest and most easily documented case of the gradual evolution of the military from a moderator to a guardian role. In the midst of the cold war, many of the region's armed forces assumed the position of rulers in order to create new guardian regimes. These efforts misfired but have consequences felt to this day. The process began as early as the 1950s. Military journals, courses and lectures in military schools, and public speeches by senior officers gave witness to the intellectual ferment. Eventually the military in many countries developed a new doctrine (i.e., an officially promulgated set of concepts, organizations, and procedures) for expanding the armed forces role – the **national security doctrine (NSD)**. Moderator militaries return power to civilians in a matter of months or a few years. This had been the typical Latin American pattern for much of its history. Yet, during the last several decades of the twentieth century, new-style ruler militaries based on the NSD decided to remain in power much longer to change the nature of the political, economic, and social order. They asserted that their ultimate aim was to establish democratic stability and break the dictatorship–democracy cycle described in the last chapter (Stepan 1971). The form of "democracy" that the armed forces had in mind was not liberal democracy as previously practiced in Latin America and elsewhere. Perhaps the most sobering description of the ultimate goal comes from Chile's military dictator, Augusto Pinochet. Pinochet described the Chilean project as leading to an "authoritarian" or "protected" democracy (Pinochet 1977: 13). Civil and political liberties that citizens traditionally enjoyed under a liberal democratic regime were to be curtailed – permanently. The armed forces' role in domestic intelligence gathering and internal security policy-making would also be permanently increased. Establishing this new version of democracy was meant to justify prolonged military rules while the NSD provided an outline of the armed forces' new missions.

The National Security Doctrine

Part social science and part ideology, the NSD dates back to the 1950s. After the Cuban revolution, and even in the years immediately preceding it, Latin American armies had begun to reconsider their role. A parallel reconsideration had also begun during this period in the United States, which had begun to rethink the nature and purposes of its hemispheric military aid program. The fruit of this rethinking was the National Security Doctrine or rather a set of such doctrines developed by the armed forces of the United States (US Army 1974) and various regional militaries. As propounded in operations manuals, articles in military journals, and official statements, the doctrine held that developing countries were vulnerable to revolution because of a number of structural failings. First, the economy was insufficiently developed. While many developing countries had made considerable strides toward economic modernization, more was required. With high rates of population growth, a backward peasant sector, and an economic policy that seemed to be faltering, dramatic changes were needed. The second persistent problem was the fact that society itself was underdeveloped. Again, though strides had been made, levels of illiteracy were too high; the average level of schooling was too low, and basic healthcare and housing had been neglected. The third ongoing problem was the political system. The state was unresponsive and inefficient. Its often-extensive bureaucracy was underpaid and frequently under-worked. The state habitually interfered with development as much as it promoted it. Patrimonial practices were rife. Political parties were often undisciplined, unresponsive, and corrupt. Interest groups were frequently narrow in their orientation and uncompromising in their demands. General strikes, work stoppages of various sorts, withholding of goods from market, and similar measures meant to protest government policies were frequent tactics used by both masses and elites alike. The media often were either shamelessly subservient to government interests or scurrilously provocative. Intolerance, corruption, and inefficiency prevailed. Politicians tended to pursue narrow sectoral interests instead of the well-being of the nation. The constitutional structure of the government was in need of basic reform to increase efficiency and stability. Without these basic changes in political structures, the government would continue to be corrupt and prone to deadlock.

All these problems made countries liable to political instability. Revolutionary parties could mobilize people on the basis of their legitimate grievances. Short-term military intervention that arrested radical leaders and banned organizations that promoted violence had only a limited effect. As long as the underlying conditions remained the same, they would give rise to radical leaders and movements. This long-term problem required systemic, long-term solutions. And it was the duty of the armed forces to take the lead in implementing them. The overload hypothesis for explaining coups outlined in the last chapter followed the pattern: "social mobilization → … → political instability." The NSD formulated the problem in a similar fashion: "underdevelopment → popular unrest → revolution." Since the mission of the armed forces was to protect the state, the NSD implied that the military had a new mission – to address the causes of underdevelopment *and* stymie a revolution if it should occur. In short, while the overload thesis and social science generally saw military intervention as part of a complex of problems besetting developing countries, the NSD saw a certain type of military intervention as the solution.

The intervention did not on its face entail direct military rule, but it did provide a pretext for coups d'etat and long-term military rule. At minimum, the armed forces had to take on a new military mission – "internal defense and internal development." The new mission required the armed forces to undertake new roles and to transform traditional ones. These changes vastly increased military authority – and the potential for its abuse. The most benign of the new roles was military civic action. Civic action is really an expansion of the sort of the nation-building function that the armed forces had carried out previously, sometimes without explicitly recognizing it. Military organizations are modernization agents. As was noted in the last chapter, modern military forces, which require professional leadership, modernize and change the character of the officer corps, but modern military organizations affect the conscripted private soldier as well. In modernizing societies, many people may be rural, illiterate, and largely unfamiliar with the wider country that they inhabit. Military conscription moves the draftee forcefully into the modern world. He leaves his village, assumes new responsibilities in a modern, complex organization, and, if he does not already know how, may learn to read and write. These skills and the sense of belonging to a wider, national community modernize the outlook of the draftee or recruit. They move him from the traditional to the modern world. Hence, military organizations have a modernizing effect on the individual soldier and his family. Civic action is meant to expand the inherent nation-building role of the military by putting the armed forces to work on projects of value to the less developed sectors of society. Various military units have the equipment and skills that are often needed by rural villages or squatter settlements on the fringes of fast-growing conurbations. Medical units, engineers, and others can provide a variety of assistance: vaccinations and instruction in basic public health; aid in constructing village schools, wells, irrigation projects and other minor public works, and facilitating the development of local community organizations.

Military civic action helps address the problem of underdevelopment, but serving a development agent was not the military's primary mission, nor is it the primary reason for civic action. The armed forces' primary mission was national defense, and civic action was seen as simply a component of that more comprehensive mission. Traditionally, national defense entails combat with or deterrence of a conventionally armed foreign force, another state's army. However, the "security" in the national security doctrine referred specifically to *internal* security. The perceived threat was a rural insurgency such as that led by Fidel Castro in Cuba during the late 1950s and Mao Zedong in China during the 1920s, 1930s, and 1940s. And that particular focus not only altered the traditional roles of the armed forces, it set the stage for new military interventions of a sort unprecedented in the region. The role of fighting insurgents seems innocuous enough on its face. While fighting a foreign army normally entails the employment of large numbers of troops armed with modern weaponry, fighting a guerrilla enemy requires modest-sized forces – highly trained, light infantry, and the transport capability provided by helicopters to ferry them to regions of critical importance. Moreover, guerrillas usually operated in rural areas, away from major population centers. Thus, on its face it might seem that this change in the military's combat role would have little adverse effect on the civilian population. However, this was not the case. In fact, complementary changes in other military roles involved massive intervention in civilian life, and set the stage for military coups. The military's traditional roles involve more than direct combat; they include a host of combat support activities: intelligence, interdiction of enemy supply and reinforcements, denial of information, and attacks on the enemy's morale. In conventional war against a foreign army, the military gathered intelligence (i.e., information of military value), and cut off the enemy's troops in the field from their sources of supply and reinforcements. Intelligence gathering is a relatively straightforward matter involving the interrogation of prisoners of war and the use of technical means to try to observe the enemy's forces and predict his plans. Conventional strategy also entails the attacks upon the enemy's bases, his lines of transportation and communication, and his strategic reserves in his home country if possible.

In a counter-guerrilla strategy conventional intelligence gathering has little meaning, nor does the enemy possess the bases, lines of transportation and communication, or strategic resources directly comparable to an army fielded by a foreign state. The guerrilla gains supplies, recruits, and acquires information from the population. His strategic reserve is the political situation of the country itself and the popular organizations and popular hostility to the government that it bred. Hence, the military's customary combat-support functions had to be revamped, and when they were revamped, they frequently assumed a sinister and highly political aspect. If guerrillas are to be cut off from supplies, recruits and information, the population needed to be closely controlled by the police and military. Curfews have to be put in place, people's movement monitored, suspicious individuals questioned and detained. If the guerrilla is to be cut off from his strategic reserve, military intelligence has to infiltrate political, labor, church, civic, and professional, lest they serve as a recruiting ground for guerrilla forces and spread their propaganda. In short, military civic action is just one part of a larger effort to gain information and an entryway for its agents to infiltrate popular organizations and to spread pro-government propaganda.

Information was itself a weapon. In conventional wars military and economic data can provide critical clues about strengths and weakness; they are strictly controlled. In the sort of counter-revolutionary war envisioned by the NSD, the mass media themselves were seen as instruments of war. Censorship had to be instituted to insure that information that would undermine the government's efforts did not become public. The media had to be enlisted to put the best face possible on events and the actions of the armed forces. In other words, political information and open political discussion became targets. The NSD provided both the context and the pretext for military coups in many Latin American countries and elsewhere during the 1960s and 1970s. Latin American armed forces were influenced by the thinking of their own theorists, by that of others in the region, and by military training and exchange programs with the United States. Outside of the region, the United States also had an influence on the armed forces of South Vietnam, Thailand, and Pakistan. Large numbers of officers from Southeast Asia were trained in the United States during the Vietnam-war era from the mid-1960s to mid-1970s. For instance, General Zia ul-Haq, Pakistan's military dictator from 1977 to 1988, was a graduate of the United States Army's Command and General Staff College.

The NSD's evaluation of the threat faced by Latin American countries was unduly alarmist, but this perception of a substantial threat was widespread, nonetheless. Almost all relevant political actors believed that a "revolution in the revolution" (Debray 1967) was in the offing. Leftist radicals boasted they had a virtually sure-fire method of seizing power via Cuban-style guerrilla war. Most other sectors feared they were right. Fidel Castro's seizure of power had indeed sent a scare through the entire region, but later and more balanced analysis found that the Cuban Revolution had not found a new, better method for mounting a revolution. Rather, Cuba was, in large measure, a special case. The NSD, however, asserts that early corrective measures were better than massive responses later on. Thus, fearing the worst, the Brazilian military, a key developer of the NSD, overthrew leftist President João Goulart in 1964. A dozen other militaries in the region followed suit, in their own countries, within a decade.

Making the country safe for "democracy"

Once in power, militaries guided by the NSD sought to correct what they saw as the deficiencies of earlier democratic regimes. These deficiencies were problems typical of developing nations. But while the armed forces' description of the problems was generally accepted, their ideas about how to correct them were not. While professing to support democratic principles, the military downplayed true democracy. Politicians and political parties especially had to be put in their place. Civil liberties had to be curtailed on a permanent basis. Order and discipline had to be brought into the state administration. To do this, the powers of the chief executive had to be strengthened and the power of the legislature had to be weakened. The NSD-guided military often sought a permanent role for itself in the councils of the executive branch and seats in the legislature. Most Latin American military regimes created a National Security Council dominated by military officers who were supposed to advise the chief executive in times of national crisis. The military often sought to reconstruct the party system since they saw the party system itself as the source of many political problems that went far beyond the political vices of a few parties and party politicians. Thus, Brazil's military government tried to reshape the country's chaotic multiparty system into a two-party system, with a dominant pro-executive, pro-military party, and a loyal opposition party, destined by the rules that the military put in place to find itself a permanent runner-up. Pinochet in Chile wanted to minimize the role of parties altogether, making the president essentially above party.

Consequences

The NSD project of restructuring yielded mixed results at best. When the armed forces finally retreated from power, very little had changed. Military governments were no better at inducing economic and social progress than their civilian counterparts. Party structures and many of the admittedly corrupt practices associated with them were more resilient than the military had imagined. Political problems did not lend themselves to technocratic solutions the armed forces often sought to impose. Protracted periods of military rule produced a backlash across the region both among civilians as well as among sectors of the armed forces. While some officers became enmeshed in political and governmental administration, others became increasingly worried about the deterioration of professional standards that occurred when the armed forces assumed day-to-day governmental responsibilities. Institutionalists were also concerned about the civilian backlash that military rule provoked. Disputes between institutionalists and interventionists sharpened. Although intelligence officers generally resisted transferring power back to civilians, officers of other branches often saw such a transfer as the only way to preserve the integrity of the institution (Stepan 1988: 3–54). The systematic effort to produce guardian military regimes failed. The malaise that the prolonged period of military rule produced set the stage for the democratization movement described in the next chapter. Still, although the guardian role of the military has been discredited, the NSD focus on internal security and development lives on in the region's armed forces. And the "war on terror" and increase in crime could well invite a new expansion of the armed forces into areas of administration properly under civilian control. These dangers are not limited to Latin America alone.

CASE STUDY: CHILE

For decades Chile seemed to be one of the Latin American countries least likely to be subject to a military coup. It had been relatively prosperous and peaceful for decades in comparison to much of the rest of the region. From the turbulent 1930s until the 1970s, Chile had avoided the dictatorship–democracy cycle so common in the region. The Chilean armed forces seemed to be obedient to civilian authority and determined to retain a narrow view of their professional mission. Yet, in the 1970s things changed dramatically. The armed forces assumed a ruler role and sought to implement a series of changes to the nation's economy, society, and political system that would have resulted in a permanent guardian regime. The stage was set for a change in 1969 when Salvador Allende, the candidate of the Socialist Party of Chile and a united left alliance, was elected president. Allende received considerably less than a majority of the popular vote but was the plurality winner. The result was confirmed by the national legislature on the president-elect's promise to abide by the constitution. This promise proved difficult to keep. Allende headed a radical alliance that was composed of parties and factions of disparate political views. The more moderate, although they wanted to see radical social and economic change, were tactically cautious and wanted to work as much as they could within the Chilean constitutional system. Among these were the Communist Party of Chile (PCCh) and factions of Allende's own Socialist Party. Other factions that supported the government but were not officially members of it wanted a rapid implementation of people's power and had no intention of respecting the procedures of the established order.

Allende's victory was a shock not only to many Chileans but to the government of the United States as well. Unlike most of Allende's domestic opponents, the United States was unwilling to accept the election results. Working with Allende's opponents within Chile, the US government attempted to block his accession to power by a variety of means. In one incident, the armed forces' chief-of-staff was killed in a botched kidnapping attempt that was, in part, the work of the US Central Intelligence Agency (CIA). The general was a target because he was an unquestioned institutionalist who supported the peaceful accession of Allende to power. Although it was not clear until several years later, there were a group of senior officers in the armed forces who favored an interventionist position. They had come to the notion made explicit by the NSD that internal subversion was the greatest single military threat to Latin America generally and Chile specifically. Chief among the interventionist officers was General Augusto Pinochet, a former military professor of geopolitics.

Pinochet's writings on power, the need for a strong state, and international competition dovetailed nicely with core NSD concerns about political stability and national development.

When Allende finally took office, there was something of an initial honeymoon as the economy grew. Everyone's worst fears seemed to have been unjustified. However, within a year Allende's administration was beset by continual crises. Businessmen refused to reinvest fearing nationalization or outright confiscation of their property, and the economy collapsed. Extremists both inside and outside the ruling coalition began to seize factories, farms, and even organized within military units hoping to spur a revolution. President Allende was reluctant to intervene, remembering how a socialist president in the 1930s had ignominiously sold out his fellow radicals. Legislature–executive relations were turbulent. The opposition controlled the legislature and blocked the government's measures. In response Allende and the cabinet chose to rule by executive decrees of dubious constitutionality. Cabinet ministers were repeatedly removed from office by "no confidence" votes in the legislature only to see them reinstalled in different cabinet posts. During his last year in office, confronted by growing unrests and a collapsing economy, Allende invited military officers into his cabinet in an attempt to stabilize the situation.

It was not enough. On September 11, 1973, the armed forces staged a coup, and Allende, besieged in the presidential palace, committed suicide. The moderate opposition, led by the Christian Democrats who had headed the reformist administration that preceded Allende, believed that the armed forces would immediately return power to civilians. They were disappointed. Instead, the military decided to govern directly through a military junta composed of the commanders of the army, navy, air force, and paramilitary police. The junta called a political recess and forbade political activity even by politicians favorable to the governing junta. The civilian executive and the legislature were disbanded and remained so until the end of the military government in 1990. As part of the coup and its immediate aftermath, the armed forces rounded up leftists and other "subversives" en masse. Hundreds were summarily executed without trial and without official public notice of what had happened to them. These "disappeared" eventually become a national scandal and an international cause célèbre. After the initial purge, the junta established a national security service (DINA) to carry out repression. Military officers were appointed to official posts at central and local governments. Labor unions and other associations were forbidden to carry out many of their normal activities.

The armed forces could impose order, but they proved unable to make the economy grow. The economic malaise that had set in under the socialist government continued. In 1975, beset by continued deterioration in the economy, the junta decided to embark on a new course. It adopted a neo-liberal free-market economic policy. The "Chicago boys," economists recently trained at the University of Chicago and confirmed believers in the radical free-market views popular there, became the core of the military government's economic team. With some policy adjustments due to near financial collapse, the free-market approach became the hallmark of the Chilean military regime, setting it apart from other Latin American military governments. At about this same time, the army commander, General Augusto Pinochet, emerged as the leading figure of the military junta.

The ongoing political repression, however, began to provoke increased international and domestic criticism, and the armed forces began to feel the need for a public display of support for the government and its policies. Thus, in 1978 the junta called a national referendum ostensibly to respond to international criticism. Voters were presented with a choice between patriotically supporting the government in its stand against international interference or rejecting the military government's principled position. The "yes" vote of support was under an image of the Chilean flag, and the "no" vote under the black flag of anarchy. The government granted the opposition little broadcast time to campaign. Unsurprisingly, the "yes" vote won by a landslide. As the years of military rule wore on, Pinochet argued that the armed forces needed to remain in power so as to establish the proper economic, social, and political groundwork for a return to democracy. But when democracy returned it would not be the much-flawed variety that had failed the country in the early 1970s. Institutions would have to be remolded, and the country would become an "authoritarian democracy" – a government with a strong, nonparty executive, powerful security services, and weak political parties. Popularly based interest groups would have their power restricted. Labor unions, for example, would be organized at the level of the firm, and would not be able to form powerful federations.

In 1980 to regularize its rule and prepare the way for the eventual choice of a docile group of civilian politicians, the junta prepared a constitution that provided for both transitional and a permanent structures of government. In the transitional period, Pinochet would become president and the junta would serve as a legislative body. The permanent structure established a strong presidency, limited political parties, and installed retired military officers as ex-officio members of the Senate. Legislative procedures were established to favor the minority conservative parties. The president could not remove the heads of the armed services. And a national security council was established. The constitution was ratified by a referendum the same year with procedures not much improved from the 1978 referendum. Despite the passage of the new constitution, violent and peaceful dissent continued. The military regime's leading ideologue and leader of its constitutional convention was assassinated by leftwing extremists. And moderates continued to organize under the protection of the Catholic church. The economic crash of 1982 shook the confidence of the government and its economic team and led to mass protests. The military regime, however, was able to make adjustments. The Chicago boys were replaced by leaders with better connections to the business community, and a conservative civilian was appointed to head negotiations with the opposition. The government's strategy of temporizing worked, and the transitional structure remained in place until 1990 as the opposition agreed to abide by the transition mechanisms specified by the 1980 constitution. Under its own ground rules, the regime lost a plebiscite in 1988 and then a contested presidential election in 1989. The new civilian government is still partially bound by the restrictions in the 1980 constitution.

Chile's military regime represents a classic case of the NSD-driven military rule. The leadership of the armed forces decided early on to establish a long-term guardian regime. They expanded the role of the armed forces in the fashion prescribed by the NSD. Although the regime had no active insurgency to fight, DINA, the intelligence service, became one of its key instruments, and military officers assumed responsibilities of civilian administrators or subjected them to close supervision. The economy was remodeled. So too were private associations and political institutions. Even the transfer of power to civilians in 1990 followed the forms prescribed by the military-sanctioned constitution of 1980. At least initially, it appeared that the armed forces had gained much of what they wanted from the seventeen-year period of military rule: the left was demobilized, the economy grew, and politicians felt themselves bound by many of the decisions that had been made under military tutelage. Furthermore, at least initially, the prestige of the armed forces remained fairly high. Only gradually did the entrenched position of the armed forces begin to erode. The posts of non-elected senators were abolished. The president regained the right to dismiss the heads of the armed services. Leading human rights violators from the military regime began to be brought to trial. And senior military leaders began to affirm their belief in civilian control of the armed forces. By 2006 the aged Pinochet himself was under a cloud both for human rights violations and financial corruption. Only his death the following year assured that he would escape prison.

The rise of guardian militaries in Asia

While Latin American militaries took generations to move from a moderator to a guardian role, often Asian armed forces assumed a guardian role with a single coup. When Asian armed forces seized power, they were able to move quickly from protestations that military rule would last a relatively short time to advocating and establishing a permanent military-dominated regime. Asian military governments were often established without the NSD's ritualistic genuflections in the direction of democracy and without the elaborate justification in military doctrine provided by the NSD. Highly nationalistic and security conscious, Asian militaries developed their own nationalist ideology justifying an ongoing and predominant share of power for the military (cf. Brooker 1995: 158–69, 181–93). Such military regimes ruled in South Korea from 1961 to 1988, Indonesia from 1965 to 1998, Thailand for much of the post-Second World War era, and in Pakistan. As the fall of some of these regimes illustrates, however, aspiring to a guardian role and actually consolidating the institutions that assure it are two different matters.

These regimes were a reaction – albeit an overreaction – to some real problems. Developing countries in Asia as elsewhere, especially in the immediate post-World War II era, often spawned a variety of radical groups. Ideological radicals – communists or other extremist parties – often had significant appeal among organized labor and peasants hungry for land. In populous, far-flung countries such as Indonesia with its island archipelago stretching three thousand miles and even much smaller countries like Burma, ethnic separatists demanded independence or seemed poised to take it. The political status of minorities continues to be an issue throughout much of Asia even today (see Table 8.1). Governments that permitted a modicum of pluralism and civil liberties on the basis of principle or mere inefficiency had allowed these groups to take root and grow. Rarely were these groups in any position to seize power although in some cases their more extreme elements were more than ready to make the attempt should the opportunity occur. Often foreign threats were more than negligible. For example, South Korea faced a serious security threat from North Korea, and Pakistan faced a threat from India. Military officers were concerned with the trajectory of

Table 8.1   Politically significant ethnic groups in Asia

Country	Minorities
Afghanistan	4 ethnic minorities, no majority group
Bangladesh	2 ethnic minority, one religious minority
Bhutan	1 ethnic minority
Burma	6 ethnic minorities
Cambodia	Vietnamese minority
China	3 ethnic minorities
India	9 ethnic or religious minorities
Indonesia	3 ethnic minorities
Pakistan	6 ethnic or religious minorities
Philippines	2 ethnic minorities
Singapore	Malay minority
South Korea	1 ethnic minority
Sri Lanka	Tamil minority
Taiwan	2 ethnic minorities
Thailand	3 ethnic minorities
Vietnam	2 ethnic minorities

Source: Minorities at Risk Project, University of Maryland. "Political significance is determined by the following two criteria: the group collectively suffers, or benefits from, systematic discriminatory treatment vis-à-vis other groups in a society. The group is the basis for political mobilization and collective action in defense or promotion of its self-defined interests"

political development in their countries. In short, military rulers in Asia have been driven by traditional military concerns about national power, national security, and law and order more than ideological conceptions of progress and social change. Consequently, military regimes' primary focus was national security, political stability, and economic growth.

The coup that brought the armed forces to power often had a variety of pretexts. Dismal economic performance and political unrest often provided the backdrop. Concerns over foreign security threats in South Korea in 1961 and an aborted communist coup in Indonesia in 1965 also helped induce military takeovers in these countries. The coup-makers feared radical change initiated from below. The civilian governments that became the targets of military coups could be radical, moderate, or conservative. They became vulnerable because of their inability to address real or perceived problems that the armed forces regarded as serious. Most critically, the government was inclined to compromise with ideological radicals or ethnic minorities whom the military regards as a threat to national security. Even if it was not in the process of striking a deal with these groups, the armed forces saw the government as insufficiently forceful in dealing with them. Haunted by the specter of revolution or secession, the military intervened to take charge of events it believed were spinning out of control. The defenders of the coup argued that only the

armed forces had the authority and force sufficient to grapple successfully
with the crisis at hand. The emergency merely set the stage for guardian
military regimes.

More than anything else, these regimes developed
via a kind of slippery-slope process that began when a national emergency,
real or imagined, gave military leaders the opportunity to seize power.
The support or indifference of friendly foreign governments, especially the
United States, often helped give the coup-makers the necessary breathing
space and even temporary legitimacy. The coup-makers in these states did
not possess a clear ideological vision, nor did they see themselves as leading
a social revolution as the occasional Latin American NSD and all Middle
Eastern military regimes did. Rather, they were more concerned about
preserving many important elements of the status quo and repressing
popular unrest. The consolidation of long-term rule was normally the
work of the military strongman responsible for the coup. The principal
coup-maker sometimes proposed only an emergency government based
on a national consensus that included a return to civilian rule. However,
as events progressed it became clear he was unwilling to relinquish
real power. And as the regime evolved, the influence of the military
as an institution grew. Even when there was a purported willingness
to return power to civilians, the lack of effective civilian participation in
the government and the limited ability of civilians to mobilize opposition
to the regime from the society at large led to a gradual hardening of its
structure. In other words, with popular loyalties uncertain and different
principles of authority playing a role within the country, the armed
forces could seize power with little prospect of widespread resistance or
the use of legal sanctions against them. Once the armed forces overthrew
the existing civilian government, they moved to establish a new regime
more conducive to the national good as they saw it. The military justified
its rule by appealing to the theme of national reconstruction, national
renewal, or national salvation – conservative notions that stressed the
need to overcome class, ethnic, or local divisions, and to increase national
power against outside military threats. When civil society did not prove
strong enough or was too divided to prevent a slide to a more permanent
authoritarian system, the ad hoc emergency government developed
into a permanent one with a written constitution meant to render
the influence of the armed forces and the security services permanent.

With the establishment of new military-dominated institutions, the
prospects for a return to democratic rule became more and more remote.
Instead of handing power back to civilians, the military president used
a nominally civilian political party as a method of legitimizing his
continuance in power. Limited political competition might be tolerated,

but the leader never subjected himself to a fair and free election. The military played the predominant political role in the political system and often established a single-party state. A civilian political party or movement was almost always a necessary accouterment of regimes of this sort. A party controlled by the military provided the aura of popular participation and consent as well as giving the military links to the civilian elite. Yet, the party remained a creature of the armed forces, and it was meant to carry out their bidding. In sum, the evolution from emergency to permanent rule was normally not driven by ideology.

At their best, these military regimes could defend themselves by appealing to the nineteenth-century positivist slogan, "order and progress." However, results were mixed. Order was often imposed by repression. Although these regimes were intent upon economic modernization, only South Korean and Indonesian military governments could credibly claim real success in this area. Military regimes wanted the country to be prosperous, strong, and respected. They desired the state to be efficient and powerful. Yet, at the same time the regime's leaders were suspicious of democracy. They did not wish to see the development of independent political parties and interest groups. Consequently, they are also suspicious of various sorts of uncontrolled social mobilization, and the development of labor unions, peasant associations, and other forms of popular organization had to occur only under regime tutelage, if it was permitted to occur at all. These states, like party–military and NSD regimes, placed emphasis on security. Domestic intelligence services and the security services, generally, played an important role in maintaining the regime in power.

As a matter of course, military officers were often appointed to positions usually held by civilians from the highest to the lowest levels of administration, and the armed forces normally gained explicit representation in the legislature where legislatures are permitted to exist. Hence, the militarization of politics and the state administration became a natural byproduct of these regimes. The national security concerns of the armed forces drove policy-making and policy-implementation. The regime saw itself and the nation as under constant threat. Military conceptions of national security, patriotism, and frequently the communist threat, were prominent both in the media and in education. States of emergency were frequent or permanent, allowing the suspension of political rights and civil liberties. The national and military intelligence services were subject to few legal or practical limitations. Censorship – formal and informal – was a pervasive practice. Human rights abuses abounded. In effect, these regimes were national security states – i.e., regimes in which the overarching concern for security against domestic and foreign subversion or overt military threats shapes politics and policy decisively.

The winding down of the cold war and growing international support for democracy movements during the 1980s put pressure on military regimes to change, just as similar pressures influenced the behavior of authoritarian states elsewhere. When conditions turn against them, authoritarian regimes can be undermined as much by their success as well as their failure. In Korea, a prolonged period of prosperity helped raise the fortunes and aspirations of the middle class. While military governments disappeared from Latin America in the 1990s, in Asia several military governments have continued or reemerged. The record is decidedly mixed. Despite its economic success, the Korean regime disappeared in 1987. The guardian regime also collapsed in Indonesia a decade later. In Pakistan, after yet another interlude of elected government, the armed forces again seized control in 1999. Even elsewhere the establishment of civilian rule has not entailed the institution of effective civilian control over the armed forces. As with many NSD militaries, old habits die hard. Military role-expansion still remains both a reality and a threat. A return to open military rule, as happened in the case of Thailand in 2006, cannot be discounted in other Asian countries.

CASE STUDY: INDONESIA

For thirty-two years until 1998, Indonesia was under the control of a guardian military regime headed by the military strongman, General Raden Suharto. The government engaged in the process of building the nation, state, and economy. The regime saw itself as under pressure from both foreign and domestic forces. Internally ethnic separatism and, early on, an ideological challenge from the communist party provided the pretext for the coup and continued military government. The Indonesian armed forces developed the concept of a "dual role" as part of their doctrine. The military saw itself not only as the guarantor of the country's territorial sovereignty but also as an important element in the state's administrative structure, the key political decision-maker, and political mobilizer. Indonesia is a large and ethnically diverse nation. Many of the islands comprising the widely dispersed and culturally diverse Indonesian archipelago were rich prizes in the early phases of European colonization. Although the Portuguese gained the first footholds, it was ultimately the Dutch who came to dominate most of what is present-day Indonesia. The independent government like its colonial predecessor faced the problem of governing a far-flung territory, many parts of which were remote from its Javanese core. In fact, the western half of New Guinea was not incorporated into independent Indonesia until 1963. And Indonesia continued to make claims on the British territory in Borneo and Portuguese East Timor even after that.

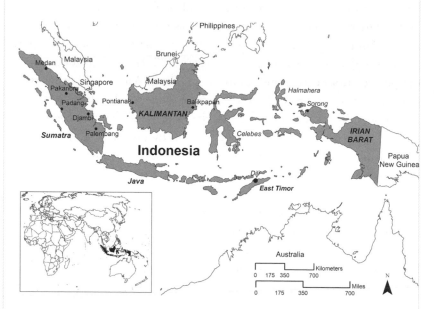

Map 8.2 Indonesia
Source: Environmental Systems Research Institute (ESRI) map data

The immediate path toward independence began during the Second World War when Indonesia was occupied by the Japanese. On Java, the main island, the occupation provided the political space for independence movements and others to organize. Indonesians participated in both government and the military. In March 1945, as the war wound down, the Japanese organized local independence committees to take over after occupation ceased. Indonesia proclaimed its independence in 1945 shortly after the surrender of Japanese forces ending the Second World War. A provisional constitution gave the chief executive broad powers. The Dutch, however, refused to recognize the country's independence, and a four-year national liberation war ensued. It was not until 1955 that the first general elections were held. Ahmed Sukarno, a radical civilian politician, was elected president. A new constitution established a parliamentary system and was based on Pancasila, an otherwise secular ideology that stressed belief in one God. But this was insufficient for some of the country's Muslims, who comprise nearly 90 percent of the population. Some of them wished to see a stronger official role for Islam.

Sukarno became an internationally recognized leader of the Non-aligned Movement that garnered considerable support from ex-colonial nations. Yet, at home the conflict among a multiplicity of parties weakened his government. Islamic groups, the Communist Party (PKI) dominated by the Chinese minority, and the armed forces were at odds with one another. Ethnic and religious tensions were also destabilizing. The Chinese minority made up the lion's share of the business class and bred resentment. Religious cleavages among majority Muslims and minority Hindus and Christians also caused concern. Economic problems further undermined the authority of the government. To strengthen his hand in dealing with the opposition, Sukarno revived articles of the original provisional constitution and imposed a "guided democracy" in 1959. This move toward authoritarianism was fairly typical of what governments of other ex-colonial countries were doing at the time. A bit later, Sukarno formed an informal alliance with the Indonesian Communist Party (PKI). Making use of its mass base; the PKI attempted to mobilize broad support for the regime. Sukarno's alliance with the PKI displeased many military officers. The president's lack of success internationally did not please the military either. From 1963 to 1965 Sukarno led a confrontation with Malaysia over claims to (formerly British) Borneo, but he was forced to back down.

In 1965 in what appeared to be an aborted PKI coup, six generals were killed. In response General Suharto immediately led a violent counterattack against the communists. In the fighting and the repression that followed, up to half a million communists and communist sympathizers were killed. Suharto went on to use the coup as a pretext to advance military influence. Sukarno was gradually eased to the political margins as the army strengthened its control of the country. Finally in 1967 a provisional assembly removed Sukarno from power and made General Suharto president. In 1968 the assembly granted Suharto a full five-year term. The assembly was made a permanent part of the new system, and it continued to grant Suharto regular five-year extensions of this mandate until 1998. Suharto proceeded to militarize the government.

The "New Order" regime officially provided for the dual role for the military in 1965. In this dual role, the armed forces were charged with traditional national defense responsibilities, and in addition military officers also served in other governmental posts in the state administration. The armed forces were seen as possessing the competence, patriotism, and loyalty necessary to develop the country under difficult circumstances. The origins of this dual role go back to the war for independence during which the guerrilla resistance exercised both military and governmental functions.

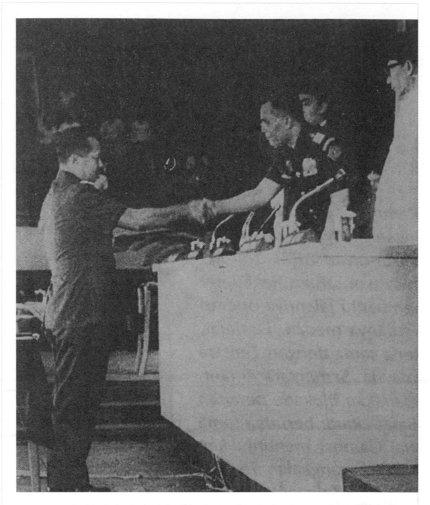

Plate 8.1   General Suharto accepting the presidency in 1967.

The constitution reserved a specific number of seats in the assembly for the armed forces. And the military was used to organize political support for the regime. Golkar, a pro-regime movement, served as the mechanism for controlling politics. While other parties were not outlawed, the rules of the game legal and otherwise were rigged to make certain that Golkar would dominate the system. The predecessor of Golkar had been established by the armed forces during the Sukarno regime as a makeweight against the communists. It was an umbrella organization for trade and profession-based groups. In the earlier period it had not been very effective, but in its latter-day version it was much enhanced. As the regime progressed, Golkar became personally responsible to Suharto and began to form mass organizations in addition to the functionally based groups. Other political parties were forced to amalgamate. Political competition was strictly limited. In 1985 all legal political parties were forced to accept the principles of Pancasila, and the government insisted that Muslim parties open their ranks to non-Muslims. The attack on Islamic identity provoked a backlash, but the government was more than willing to clamp down on open opposition as the situation required.

Indonesia's far-flung archipelago provided both threats and opportunities. The fall of the Portuguese dictatorship in 1974 led to a grant of independence to the country's remaining colonies including East Timor. Against the wishes of the locals, the Indonesian government took the opportunity to make good on its old claim and seized the formerly Portuguese part of the island. The seizure led to an ongoing insurgency. The central government continued to be faced with other ethnic nationalist insurgencies on various islands, occasionally exacerbated by inter-religious conflict. The economy under Suharto was run by economic technocrats and crony capitalists. The so-called "Berkeley Mafia," economists who had received their Ph.D.s from the University of California, helped correct the high government debt, inflation, and erratic statism of the Sukarno era. During much of the 1970s, Indonesia also profited from the surging increase in oil prices. This again gave the edge to advocates of state-led development; later stagnation in oil prices in the mid-1980s helped the pendulum swing back toward greater reliance on private investment. Through it all, Suharto's family and associates profited mightily from state contracts, concessions, and control of the banking system. Indonesia's economy grew sufficiently through most of the Suharto period for the country to be dubbed one of the new "Asian tigers." Yet, the general's version of crony capitalism led to widespread disaffection.

In 1997 most Southeast Asian nations as well as South Korea suffered from an international financial panic. Foreigners had been eager to invest in the Asian tigers to profit from these economies' rapid growth. But all was not well in many of these countries. Exuberance had led to real estate and investment bubbles. Asset prices had skyrocketed and currencies had become overvalued. Specifically, an overvalued exchange rate of the Thai baht that the central bank of Thailand was not able to maintain led to a run on the bank. Soon other countries in the region were caught in the panic as well. Investors pulled out their capital, currencies inflated, and economies crashed. Indonesia was no exception. Suharto bowed to the inevitable and signed a humiliating structural adjustment agreement with the International Monetary Fund (IMF). The agreement forced the government to regularize government finances and open the economy. In the wake of the 1997 Asian financial crisis, massive unemployment and popular protests, the assembly elected Suharto's handpicked successor as president in his place. But bowing to continued popular pressure, the assembly later rewrote the election laws and called new elections.

Non-Golkar parties now dominated the new assembly. In 1998 the military's dual role was officially abolished and a "New Paradigm" put into place that removed the armed forces from overt involvement in politics. Nonetheless, the de facto power of the armed forces remains significant, and the army and security forces often get their own way in trying to quell separatist rebellions and growing inter-communal violence. Successful prosecutions for human rights violations and Suharto-era corruption have been few. In 2006 a retired general was elected president.

Conclusion

The guardian military and party–army regimes discussed in this chapter have similarities that separate them as a group from short-term moderator militaries. They also have considerable differences among themselves especially in regard to their aims (see Table 8.2). Countries with weak states, political systems that cannot effectively solve problems, and weak civil societies are vulnerable to praetorianism of one sort or another. Episodes of emergency rule by the armed forces (operating as moderators) are a potential consequence of these weaknesses. The regimes discussed in this chapter represent another possible outcome. Where military leaders can discredit almost the entire civilian political class and choose to involve the armed forces as an institution in government and state administration, long-term military regimes can emerge. Such regimes change the nature of the political system by ensconcing the armed forces in positions of

Table 8.2 Comparison of regimes

Military regime type/ characteristics	Moderator military	Party-military	Guardian military
Long-term	No	Yes	Yes
Ideology	Conservative	Radical/revolutionary	Usually conservative
Military involved in day-to-day administration	No	Yes	Yes
Formalized presidential succession	No	Formal procedure often not followed in practice	Usually

power normally reserved for civilians and change the way the state is administered and political decisions are made. In addition they require an ideological justification for their rule beyond the pretext of responding to an immediate national emergency.

The brightest dividing line among military regimes is between armed forces that intervene with a revolutionary aim (i.e., those that work to establish a party–military regime) and all the rest. The armed forces in revolutionary party–military regimes take revolutionary change seriously and see themselves as political vanguards. Guardian militaries are generally status quo oriented and seek to forcefully demobilize groups and movements within society likely to effectively press for change. In fact, their aims in this regard are similar to those of most moderator militaries.

While some guardian militaries have been relatively successful in economic terms, most have had a mixed record even by their own standards. Only infrequently have NSD and other conservative regimes produced the order and progress at which they aimed, especially when it comes to engendering a pro-regime political consensus. Nor have revolutionary military governments produced the sort of radical transformations that they have sought. Today the middle class of many countries has been much less willing to tolerate military rule than they once were. Some countries have also seen the strengthening of institutionalist factions within the armed forces who seek to return the armed forces to their traditional foreign defense mission. In short, political learning has occurred after prolonged experiments in military involvement in politics. The progress has been uneven, however. The next chapter takes up the topic of this political learning and the democratization movement that brought change to both military-dominated regimes and authoritarian civilian systems. Chapter 13 will again take up the issue of how authoritarians, including military authoritarians, have been able to hang on in the face of pressure for democratization.

Questions for further consideration

1　Why do civilians with revolutionary aspirations sometimes seek military allies? What, if anything, has changed in this regard since the 1950s and 1960s?

2　What sorts of motives lead military officers to attempt to remold the political system so that the armed forces can play an institutionalized guardian role?

3　What are the basic points of contrast between party–military regimes and guardian military regimes? Why have the former occurred in the Middle

East and in countries that have had a communist revolution but been rare elsewhere?

4   The guardian regime in Indonesia did not survive the resignation of its first president, but the guardian regime in Egypt has had three different presidents. What might account for the Egyptian regime's greater durability?

5   Visit the Stockholm International Peace Research Institute (SIPRI) website at http://www.sipri.org/. How many countries with military regimes rank among states with a high level of military expenditure in terms of its percentage of Gross Domestic Product (GDP)? What helps account for this?

6   Once ensconced in power, why might the armed forces and individual military officers be reluctant to give it up?

Further reading

Steven A. Cook, *Ruling But Not Governing: The Military and Political Development in Egypt, Algeria, and Turkey*. Baltimore, MD: Johns Hopkins University Press, 2007. A detailed account of the theory and practice of guardian militaries focusing on the countries listed in the title.

Amos Perlmutter, *Egypt: The Praetorian State*. New Brunswick, NJ: Transaction Books, 1974. An account of the early years of Egypt's military regime that exercised significant influence in the Middle East for decades.

—— *Modern Authoritarianism: A Comparative Institutional Analysis*. New Haven, CT: Yale University Press, 1981. Chapter 8 has a classic analysis of various types of military regimes although Perlmutter's terminology differs from that used in this chapter.

Eric Rouleau, "Turkey's Dream of Democracy." *Foreign Affairs*, 79, 6 (2000), 100–14. A short description of Turkey's guardian military, how its National Security Council works, as well as the pressures and inducements from the European Union that have since eased the armed forces away from their guardian role.

Ayesha Siddiqa, *Military Inc.: Inside Pakistan's Military Economy*. London: Pluto Press, 2007. The book is a detailed analysis of the Pakistani military's core economic interests and how it has attempted to institutionalize its guardian role. Chapter 1 provides a theoretical description of guardian militaries and how they compare to other military institutions. Siddiqa uses the term "parent-guardian" for this text's "guardian."

Alfred C. Stepan, *The Military in Politics: Changing Patterns in Brazil*. Princeton, NJ: Princeton University Press, 1971. The classic description of the rise of the National Security Doctrine and the "new professionalism" that set the stage for attempts to institutionalize a guardian military in various Latin American countries.

Democratization in the noncommunist world

[I]t seems beyond a doubt that rulers cannot maintain their authority unless they are legitimated, and that they are legitimated by belief-systems … Where the claim of the ruler to authority is out of kilter with the prevalent belief-systems of the society, he must either "change his plea," that is, make himself acceptable in terms of that belief-system, or else de-legitimize himself and fall. The belief-systems are stronger than the ruling authorities because it is by their virtue that the rulers rule.

(F.E. Finer, *The History of Government*, 1997)

In this chapter

We consider a unique type of breakdown that beset authoritarian regimes in the last several decades of the twentieth century and continues today – democratization. Like revolution, democratization in the contemporary era commonly involves mass protests, but unlike revolutionary regime change, it rarely entails substantial mass violence. In the last several decades of the twentieth century a confluence of forces – the exhaustion of the communist economic and political model, the growth in the saliency of human rights, the rise of the middle class in many countries, and supportive international actors – helped stimulate pressure for democracy in both developed and developing countries across the globe. This chapter explores the dynamics of the process in noncommunist countries. It illustrates three sorts of contemporary democratization by means of three different case studies: Argentina, Taiwan, and South Africa.

Introduction

In 1991, Samuel Huntington published *The Third Wave: Democratization in the Late Twentieth Century* (Huntington 1991). The thesis he put forward has been broadly accepted. It stated that democracy had advanced in fits and starts throughout modern world history. There have been three great movements or waves of democratization as more and more authoritarian regimes were replaced by democracies. The first of these waves occurred from 1828 to 1926; the second wave lasted from 1943 to 1962, and the latest of these waves began in the mid-1970s. Each of the first two democratic waves had been followed by an anti-democratic reverse wave as countries reverted to undemocratic rule. Nonetheless, reversals never equaled advances. Some new democracies remained even after the reverse wave had spent itself. Moreover, when failed democracies reemerged again during the next democratic wave, they were less likely to fail a second time even when a general reversal of democracy occurred. "Third-wave" democratization has occurred in Europe, Asia, Africa, and Latin America against almost the full range of authoritarian regimes. Traditional monarchies, single-party states, military governments, and personalistic dictatorships have all found themselves under stress. As a result of this pressure, democratic transitions occurred that were forced, planned by the authoritarian regime itself, or negotiated. There have been rollbacks and stalemates as well as outright victories for democratic forces. In some places the struggle seems to have barely begun. Yet, in grand historical terms, democratic political actors globally met with unprecedented success, and democratization has not yet run its course. This chapter explores some of the major features of democratization movements in noncommunist states, leaving the democratization in communist states to the next chapter. This chapter examines both the underlying and proximate causes for the movement's success, some of the strategies democratic political actors have used to promote the democratization process, and the task of democratic consolidation, as well as three case studies that illustrate different patterns of democratization. The analysis begins with a discussion of how authoritarian regimes were ripe for democratization in the first place.

The breakdown of authoritarian regimes

Regimes break down because they cannot successfully accommodate change. Changes can come from within and from without, and they can include new technologies, new actors, and new ideologies. Regimes fail when they suffer weak legitimacy, state ineffectiveness, military incompetence or disloyalty, and the inability of government to address

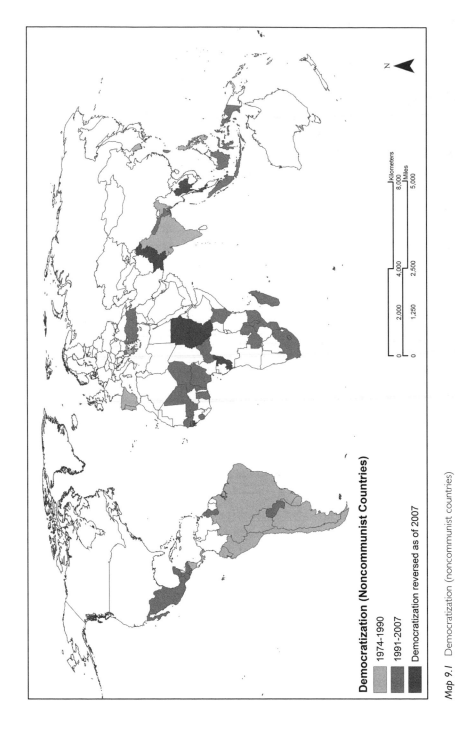

Map 9.1 Democratization (noncommunist countries)

Source: Environmental Systems Research Institute (ESRI) map data. Data: Huntington (1991); Doorenspeleet (2005); Polity IV; Department of State Background Notes

pressing new problems. When breakdowns occur, regimes usually suffer from serious failures in many of these areas, and weaknesses in one area only serve to compound weaknesses in others. This was indeed the case with authoritarian regimes in the late twentieth century.

The loss of legitimacy

The quote from Finer at the beginning of the chapter suggests one key cause of authoritarian-regime breakdown – authoritarian regimes lost legitimacy even in the eyes of many of their leaders and former adherents. Many leftwing authoritarians, like the communists, discussed in detail in the next chapter, failed to provide the material benefits they had so lavishly promised their peoples. It is not hard to understand why such regimes, having over-promised and under-delivered for decades, should have lost their ideological credibility. However, even those rightwing authoritarian regimes that were quite successful in economic terms saw an implosion of their legitimacy as well. In effect, both success and failure undermined rightwing authoritarians. When they failed, they lost credibility, and even when they succeeded, the alarmist premises upon which they were based were, nonetheless, shown to be false. Rightwing authoritarianism, such as that of NSD and other guardian military regimes discussed in the last chapter, was often based upon anticommunism and a pessimistic assessment of democracy's ability to defend property and existing authority. Through much of the twentieth century, rightwing authoritarians had been concerned about the "decline of the West." The decline of the West vis-à-vis leftist – especially communist – powers seemed all too evident even after the democratic third wave had begun. In fact, a decade into the process, the political sea change was not readily apparent even to the political scientist who coined the term "third wave" (Huntington 1984). The failure to recognize what was happening at the time can easily be explained. In the mid-1970s the United States, the world's leading anticommunist power, withdrew from Vietnam, allowing the country to fall to communists who were fighting a latter-day version of a war of national liberation.

Not only did the US lose the war in Vietnam; it did so in a way that discredited the very notion of democracy it claimed to be defending. The South Vietnamese regime that fell to the communists was a thinly disguised military dictatorship. Its American patrons had never been able to cultivate a truly democratic or nationalistic alternative to communist-sponsored nationalism in the country. Moreover, the manner in which the United States itself had fought the war often called into question the principles of human rights and the rule of law that it held most dear. By the end of the decade, anti-western radicalism seemed to be on the march. Radical nationalist regimes had been established in former Portuguese colonies in Africa, and the Soviet Union had invaded Afghanistan to support a local communist dictator. The United States made only what appeared to be weak and ineffective ripostes. Commentators spoke of the "Vietnam syndrome," a psychological and political condition that debilitated the US, making it unable to act even in the face of its ever more apparent international decline (cf. Cline 1975). Even the events that would become the turning point looked like a disaster in the making. Long-standing rightwing dictatorships fell in both Portugal and Spain, and it appeared that radical leftist regimes would take their place. Leftwing military officers held sway in Portugal, and a welter of groups among whom honest democrats seemed to be in the clear minority contended over Spain. Meanwhile in the rest of Western Europe, democratic since the end of the Second World War, communist parties, long-powerful minorities in several key countries, were on the march. They adopted tactics and principles that were characterized as "Euro-communist." As Chapter 4 noted, Euro-communism abandoned some of the key elements of Marxism–Leninism – the dictatorship of the proletariat, loyalty to the Soviet Union, and even democratic centralism – to make itself more palatable to Western European electorates. However, alarmists in the West believed this change was only tactical and that these communist parties still constituted disloyal oppositions who would revert to their original ideologies when it proved convenient.

As a result of the 1973 Arab oil boycott, the price of petroleum had increased fivefold. Economically, capitalist economies in North America, Europe, and Japan were suffering from high unemployment, high inflation, and recession, a combination of ills for which traditional economic remedies seemed to provide no ready solution. Although many developing nations were even worse off, liberal democracy seemed to be losing its ability to address the serious problems that their societies faced. Meanwhile, Soviet oil supplies and the favorable prices at which oil was sold to their allies cushioned the communist world from the disastrous economic effects of high oil prices. The apparent crisis in western foreign and domestic policy only confirmed what rightwing authoritarians had believed all along: although the United States and other liberal democracies were under assault by communists and associated radicals, they were too weak and internally divided to take decisive action against the threat. Rightwing authoritarians, however, believed that they had the formula. Actually, there were multiple formulas, sometimes radically different from one another, but all of them largely abandoned human rights, the rule of law, and the democratic process.

The pessimists about democracy and the West generally were wrong, although it would take until the 1980s, at least, for underlying trends to become apparent. It was not the West but the radical left that was critically wounded. Globally things had changed in a variety of ways during the three decades of the cold war. By the mid-1970s, the Soviet Union and other communist states had lost their ideological and economic dynamism. Radical regimes in the developing world that had imitated various elements of the Soviet economic and political model were suffering from the revolution of rising expectations. The regimes that grew out of liberation movements in Africa had frequently deteriorated into one-party or personalistic dictatorships; they had failed to live up to their promise. Many were sustained only by repression, popular apathy, and support from external powers. Their economic success and ability to withstand demands for substantial change were even more limited than was the motherland of socialism's.

Once the long-term results of state socialism became apparent, the decline of communism had a direct and indirect contagion effect on rightwing authoritarian regimes. In Latin America, military dictatorships found that their principal enemy, whose threat they had used to justify repression, had disappeared. The radical left in the region had changed its colors. The demise of "real existing socialism" as the communist system was called deprived leftists of a working model. The radical left could no longer say that when they took power they would establish Soviet-style socialism purged of its defects. Soviet-style socialism had been revealed to be a system characterized primarily by defects. People's democracy too appeared less benign the closer one came to it. Many leftist exiles spent a decade or more in Soviet satellite states. While these radicals were grateful for refuge, they were far less favorably impressed by the quality of the regimes that offered it. In short, the radical left was ready to move from semi-loyal to loyal opposition once a credible democracy – however flawed – was established. The ideological collapse of communism deprived the authoritarian right of an opposition whose presence it could use to rally pro-democratic alarmists and allow the armed forces to present themselves as the saviors of democracy rather than its destroyers (Castañeda 1993: 241–7, *passim*).

This dynamic of "no enemy, no pretext for military rule" deprived Latin American military regimes of what moral authority they had had. They had seized power promising a return to democracy, and they were the most vulnerable; but most rightwing regimes also suffered from an inability to establish their legitimacy on independent grounds. Stable rule in the long run seemed to depend on a commitment to something more positive than *anti*-communism and the prospect of international or separatist threats.

Lack of governmental efficacy and state effectiveness

Ideological weakness was only one element of a set of interlocking problems. Authoritarian regimes either failed to provide economic opportunities for educated members of their societies, or, having provided these opportunities, they failed to satisfy the political demands of groups they had empowered economically. In short, in the course of their development, authoritarian regimes faced new political actors or old political actors, newly empowered, whose demands they could not easily accommodate under their authoritarian rubric. Most leftwing authoritarians, like their communist counterparts, failed to deliver adequate economic growth to provide opportunities for their growing populations. Twenty or thirty years after full independence, ex-colonies, with their rapid population growth rates, were predominately young. The younger generation had no direct memory of the colonial era and the sacrifices required to end it. The leaders of the independence struggle had settled into comfortable positions that gave them disproportionate power and prerogatives compared to the rest of the population. The young, some quite well educated, were often unemployed or underemployed. For them, the glories of the independence struggle and the new society that was supposed to transcend the divisions and injustices of the past held little allure. Dissident politicians joined youth and members of the middle class as actors newly enabled by changing international conditions.

Rightwing authoritarian regimes often found themselves in a similar situation. They tended to disenfranchise large sectors of the population, politically and often economically as well. Most rightwing regimes followed an economic policy called "state capitalism." Under **state capitalism** the state plays a major role in the economy, allocating credit, investing in favored industries and firms, protecting local producers against foreign competition, and even establishing state firms in areas such as communications, steel and chemical production, and other areas requiring large-scale investment that the private sector cannot generate. One key factor distinguishes state capitalism from socialism. State capitalism pays little or no attention to social equity. An illustration of the attitude underlying this policy comes from a general under the Brazilian military regime. When asked how the country was doing, he reputedly responded that the country was doing fine, but the people weren't. Failure to provide for the people's welfare fed popular frustration.

Many in the middle class came to oppose authoritarianism even when they had benefited from it economically. Middle-class democratic activism developed in Korea and Taiwan, which were authoritarian states, Singapore, a semi-authoritarian state, and Hong Kong, a British colony under close metropolitan control until 1997. In all these so-called "Asian tigers" with the exception of Hong Kong, it was state capitalism that produced sustained and rapid economic growth. Their economic success had led to the creation of an economically empowered middle class. And the growth of this new middle class put the continuity of the authoritarian regime at risk.

In sum, authoritarian regimes that failed to produce sufficient economic growth stirred opposition. Their weak legitimacy gave them few options other than raising the level of repression or easing themselves out of power. Regimes whose economic policy had met with success encountered a different problem. A growing economy had produced an enlarged middle class and increased the size and self-confidence of the working class. The expansion of higher education too provided a reservoir of anti-regime activists. Thus, economically successful regimes faced persistent demands for greater political inclusion.

External actors and external support for democratic ideas

Third-wave democratization was a global phenomenon that allowed democrats in one country to support democrats in others both directly and indirectly. Modern communications between countries created opportunities for political learning. Advocates of democracy could copy from successes attained by democracy movements elsewhere. Dissidents found allies among civic organizations in democratic societies. Countries in established democracies made the protection of human rights part of their foreign policy. The international media focused on incidents of repression and undercut authoritarian governments' pretensions that they were really democratic and possessed widespread popular support. In short, by the 1970s civil society had become international in a variety of important ways. As a consequence, the political elites within authoritarian states began to argue among themselves about the appropriate strategy to use in the face of new and unexpected demands from hitherto quiescent oppositions.

From the very first the European Economic Community (EEC) – the lineal predecessor of today's European Union (EU) – had systematically supported pro-democracy forces in Spain and Portugal. When in 1974 a group of radical army officers overthrew the neo-fascist government of Portugal and set the country on a radical course, the EEC became a force for stability and democracy. EEC aid and advice bolstered pro-democracy activism among students, political organizers, trade unionists, and the middle class. It helped set both transitions on a more moderate and democratic course by holding out eventual EEC membership to these countries once they had established fully democratic political systems. This promise was fulfilled in 1986 when both Spain and Portugal became part of the organization. Human rights arrived on the international agenda just as many post-colonial regimes and Marxism–Leninism were beginning to falter. Thus, authoritarianism's detractors at home were now joined by an array of outside forces. International Nongovernmental Organizations (NGOs), such as Amnesty International, Human Rights Watch, and many religiously affiliated groups, were eager to work with civil–society associations. Government-sponsored foundations could provide aid and advice to help inchoate political opposition parties. Election monitors and the international media shed often-unwelcome light on the authoritarian government's manipulations of their own media and elections. Democracies put the compliance of authoritarian regimes' previous human rights commitments on the diplomatic agenda. In 1990, France changed its policy. Long a patron of its ex-colonies' authoritarian rulers, France promoted national conferences in African countries between the governments and oppositions.

By the 1970s the role of the Catholic Church, an international actor par excellence, had changed as well. Throughout the nineteenth and much of the twentieth century, the Catholic Church had been the bulwark of rightwing authoritarianism. In previous eras the church had condemned liberalism, equal rights, and religious toleration, and it was often supportive of rightwing movements opposed to democracy. This posture gradually changed, and by the Second Vatican Council in the 1960s, the church officially espoused human rights, democracy, and freedom of conscience. This reversal had practical consequences. It deprived rightwing authoritarians in countries with large Catholic populations of important psychological support. The rulers of these countries had often relied on the implicit (or even explicit) endorsement of the church to buttress their otherwise dubious legitimacy. The church also provided important forms of direct aid to the democrats: the use of church property, training, public advocacy for those suffering human rights abuses, and an important voice in favor of democracy. While rightist governments could arrest or attack individual churchmen and women, they could not directly confront the church itself. The Catholic Church also played a pro-democratic role in communist countries, especially Poland, where nationalism traditionally had a Catholic religious coloration.

Summary

By the mid-1970s authoritarian regimes began to find themselves under increasing pressure. Many of them had claimed to represent the wave of the future, but their varying revolutionary and counter-revolutionary claims had generally been shown to be hollow. In practical matters too, they had failed to craft policies that met the needs of much of their populations. These disaffected sectors found spokesmen in the shape of individual dissidents and dissident organizations, and movements for democratic change developed. These movements received support from private organizations and governments abroad. Under these pressures, many authoritarian systems began to crack. Their ruling elite often lacked an effective strategy to counter an increasingly potent disloyal or semi-loyal opposition. What ensued was a political struggle that was in several key ways historically unique.

The politics of regime transition

The first democratic wave from 1828 to 1926 lasted almost a century and involved the sorts of evolutionary and violent developments described in Chapter 2 and profited from the anti-authoritarian aftereffects of the First World War. The second wave from 1943 to 1963 was much more compressed. It was in part the consequence of the Axis defeat in the Second World War and the resulting triumph of democracy and human rights. It was much broader in its impact than the first wave, but perhaps less deep. Decolonization struggles and United States' influence in the western hemisphere were part of the story, but most of these gains in the developing world did not last. The third wave has been both broad and deep and has features that set it apart from previous waves as well as the sorts of breakdowns we have encountered in earlier chapters. Countries that became democratic in the third wave had not suffered defeat in war. While democratic forces were supported by external actions, democratization was driven primarily by an internal dynamic.

Third-wave democratization shares some fundamental similarities with the two sorts of regime breakdown (revolutions and coups) that we have examined earlier, but differs from both (see Table 9.1). Revolutions occur when a counter-elite, a revolutionary vanguard, links up with a radical

Table 9.1 Revolutions, coups, democratization

	Revolution	Coup d'etat	Third-wave democratization
Mass movement	Yes	No	Yes
Violence	Yes	Yes (limited)	No
Involves negotiation	No	No	Yes
Results when successful	Regime change	Regime change (in some instances)	Regime change

mass movement to overthrow a regime debilitated by massive failures in a variety of areas. In contrast, coups occur, when a sector of the armed forces, often linked to other elements of the ruling elite, decide to overthrow a government that has failed, either in objective terms or simply in the eyes of the coup-makers. Regimes that suffer successful coups d'etat also suffer from debilitating weakness although the presence of a mass movement seeking radical change is not necessarily one of them. While it is true that third-wave democratization most frequently involved mass movements for change, as do revolutions, these movements rarely engaged in the sort of violence typical of almost every true revolution. Like coups, democratization has been, at least in part, an intra-elite affair (O'Donnell *et al.* 1986, Anderson 1999). The ruling elite has usually acceded, albeit often under considerable pressure, to substantial regime changes through negotiation. The phenomenon of mass movements coupled with elite negotiation is worth exploring further since it has been so common and promises to be used in the future.

Another version of "political chicken"

Some of the principal dynamics underlying the struggle for democracy can be captured by a version of "chicken" similar to the one described in Chapter 7. (Again, this version takes liberties with the game theory format, stressing how various players view the likelihood of outcomes.) In the earlier version, a divided left and a divided right faced one another in a weak democracy. Neither the moderate right nor the moderate left could afford to abandon their extremist partners because of the advantage the threat of force gave them. As a result, the extremists on both sides wound up controlling the outcome. A "crash" occurred as democracy was overthrown and rightist hardliners controlled policy under a newly established authoritarian regime. In contrast the democratization struggle begins under a weak authoritarian regime. The regime is weak because of loss of legitimacy or manifest policy failures. In the current rendition of the chicken game, the two sides negotiate the terms of regime change. The "crash" is large-scale escalation of anti-regime violence and regime-directed repression that makes an agreement or peaceful democratic change impossible.

Again the two sides are divided. As pro-democracy movements grew up in their midst, the ruling elite in authoritarian regimes developed visible fissures between authoritarian hardliners and accommodationists. The first group desires to preserve the regime despite the cost; the latter have much more limited objectives. The hardliners doubt any compromise with the opposition is really feasible. They see the political actors they confront as fundamentally the same as they faced earlier, before the establishment of the authoritarian regime. Repression is the authoritarian hardliners preferred strategy. They calculate that the gain from repression is well worth its possible cost. The moderates/accommodationists, on the other hand, see things differently. Their minimum objectives do not include the preservation of the authoritarian system in all its rigor. They are willing to liberalize – i.e., open up public space to allow greater freedom of the press, place controls on the intelligence and security services, allow for the formation of truly independent political parties (cf. Huntington 1991: 121–4).

The moderates among the authoritarians may also be willing to democratize – allow for fair and free elections, apportion the legislature so that it reflects population and is less gerrymandered to support authoritarian interests. However, the moderates want to protect private property and established social hierarchies, and to prevent legal prosecutions of corruption or human rights abuses committed under the authoritarian regime. These, of course, are minimum objectives, not starting points for negotiation. The authoritarians control the means of repression and can crush most demonstrations. In addition, they hold legal power, but lack the moral authority that normally undergirds it. In actual practice, the authoritarian elites (especially the hardliners) usually had at best only modest mass support. This meant that party officials, high-ranking members of the government, and senior military officers spoke for themselves and for relatively few beyond their own ranks, despite their posturing. Unless the democratic camp overplayed its hand, members of the regime found it difficult to animate a broader grouping of pro-regime forces. Hence, the debate between hardliners and moderates is essentially an intramural affair within a fairly select group of high-ranking figures.

The democratic camp is divided as well. It includes moderates willing to bargain and hardliners who seek to further the democracy movement's maximum objectives – the immediate establishment of full electoral democracy and punishment of key figures from the authoritarian regime for their crimes, and for some even the complete transformation of society. In other words, the democrats all wish to change the regime substantially, but one faction prefers negotiation and compromise and is willing, nominally at least, to play the role of semi-loyal opposition that can be bought off by sufficient government concessions. In contrast, the radical faction among the democrats believes that negotiation is futile and that the regime only negotiates for purposes of stalling and dividing its opponents. The radicals argue for a broad front *and* direct action – that is, strikes, protests, and escalation of demands that can force the regime's hand. They are a disloyal opposition. The radicals believe that a

Figure 9.1 "Where are they?" A demonstration in Santiago, Chile, commemorates those "disappeared" (illegally executed) in the Chilean coup of September 11, 1973. Photo by Uri Rosenheck.

brokered transition will involve insufficient concessions to make compromise worthwhile. The radicals are often the old radical left that preceded the imposition of the authoritarian regime, or its political heirs.

The struggle for democracy is, in large part, a matter of inter-elite bargaining between the regime's leaders and well-established leaders of the democratic opposition. Moderates on both sides generally seek a pacted or brokered transition that allows for a new democratic regime to be established by peaceful means that achieves its side's minimum objectives. Thus, while radicals and hardliners posture and bluff (and sometimes engage in open acts of violence too), the moderates assume a negotiating posture. Again, as in the pre-coup version of chicken, the extremists on each side, who are willing to risk a crash, strengthen their side's bargaining position – at least up to a point. Each side in the negotiation must assess the political strength and actual objectives of the other. Neither is willing to give way until they are assured that they have extracted the maximum possible from their opponent. A host of unknowns impinged upon the process. Are the moderates actually willing to give in to the rejectionists on their side of the table, end negotiations, and return politics to the streets? How strong is the other side? Will the government be able to count on popular passivity if it ratchets up repression? Can the democratic opposition marshal sufficient popular enthusiasm to make the country ungovernable? Will increased pressure lead to a palace coup and more pliable negotiators on the government side or the reverse? Psychology, perception, and the timing of political moves play such large roles in this process that one leading transition expert compared political transitions to actors performing a play before an audience (Whitehead 2002: 36–64).

Outcomes

More often than not, once a strong democratization movement was underway, a crash did not occur. Particular outcomes depended on the strength, canniness, and luck of both sides, as well as external factors. Although the general international situation was favorable for the democrats' success, certain countries received more outside attention and support than others. The influence of the moderates became more pronounced as the influence of hardline authoritarians and radical leftists willing to use violence to obtain their objectives diminished. The democrats were more likely to get their way if they clearly had mass support. A unified front among the authoritarians, most likely when a single dictator had dominated the regime, tended to strengthen its hand, and allowed the regime freedom of maneuver to split the oppositions.

By the 1990s momentum was clearly with the democratic camp. By one count, some forty-seven countries became democratic from 1989 to 2001. The socioeconomic, geographic, and demographic profiles of many of these new democracies varied considerably from those that had become democracies in the previous decade and one-half. Had earlier patterns persisted, many of the latter group would not have become democratic (Doorenspleet 2005: 51, 170). Given the much more limited number of new democracies in this decade, it would seem that the heyday of democratization has passed.

Outcomes of the democratization process varied. Huntington classifies them under three broad categories: transformation, replacement, and "transplacement" (Huntington 1991: 124-63). On one extreme, **transformation**, the authoritarian regime is able to impose a settlement of its own choosing. Negotiations with the democrats may be fitful or largely symbolic if they occur at all. The authoritarian government gains close to its maximum objectives because, in the final analysis, it has the de facto power to impose a settlement. At the other end of the spectrum is **replacement**, the regime in essence collapses and is replaced by one established by the democrats. Even in this scenario, negotiations can occur, but here the shoe is on the other foot. The democrats have the upper hand in terms of power. The legal power of the government comes to count for very little. The authoritarian regime, for example, might pass an amnesty law, but the democratic government that replaces it will not respect it. In situations where the resources of the authoritarian government and the democratic opposition are more evenly balanced, negotiations are serious and much more than symbolic, and **transplacement** occurs. The pacts struck by negotiators are of critical importance since they do in fact shape the regime that emerges after the transition. This third sort of transition is explicitly "brokered" – i.e., official representatives of the government and opposition groups sign a negotiated agreement that governs the transition process and places some limits on its results. Alternately, the agreement amounts to a tacit understanding between the outgoing authoritarian government and major opposition actors about the rules of the newly emerging democratic system.

This section explores three different instances of democratization from three different geographical locales: Latin America, East Asia, and Africa. These cases also involve three different sorts of authoritarian governments: ruler military, a one-party regime, and a racist authoritarian government operating behind a democratic facade. Although a small sample, these cases illustrate the breadth of third-wave democratizations.

CASE STUDY: ARGENTINA: REPLACEMENT

For much of the twentieth century, Argentina held great attraction for pessimists. It showed how a country rich and developed even by western European standards could become the poster-child of the democracy–dictatorship cycle. From the 1950s until the 1990s, powerful political forces placed high demands upon a political system that seemed incapable of satisfying them. Chief among these forces were the military, on the one hand, and the Peronist party–labor alliance, on the other.

The mutual antagonism of these two groupings helped define the period. Political confrontation was made worse by the decline of Argentina's economy, and the country's continued economic failures also set in motion an overall decline in its morale and its international standing. Argentina's exports of grain and beef had made it one of the world's ten wealthiest nations before the First World War. But by 1980, the country was in the grips of a prolonged economic slide. Its perennially high inflation, low Gross Domestic Product (GDP) growth, and its uncompetitive Import Substitution Industrialization (ISI) incubated industrial sector made the economy lethargic at the best of times (see Chapter 7).

The armed forces of Argentina were among the most professional on the continent, but that did not prevent them from intervening in politics. The democracy–dictatorship cycle had already begun in the first part of the twentieth century in the era preceding the emergence of the military–Peronist division. In 1930 the military overthrew an elected civilian president from the middle-class Radical Party because senior officers believed he was politicizing the armed forces. The armed forces would be embroiled in politics for the next half century. The key military figure during that period was Juan Domingo Perón. Then Colonel Perón rose to the position of labor minister under a military government in the mid-1940s. His and his wife's patronage of the labor movement served him well. When Perón was removed from office and arrested by his colleagues, workers demonstrated and forced his release. In 1946 he was elected president of the country. Perón used the country's foreign currency reserves to nationalize many foreign-owned businesses thus expanding the state. Pro-labor laws and regulations increased the number of holidays, raised pay, and enhanced labor rights. He squeezed as much revenue as he could out of the agricultural export sector in a variety of ways. He even attempted to establish Peronism as the official ideology of the nation and the armed forces. A populist, he was careless of constitutional niceties. By 1955 Argentina's growing economic problems and the increasing strength of the forces arrayed against him led to a coup and his twenty-year exile.

The armed forces managed to remove Perón from the presidency, but they could not destroy his influence or the power of the movement he represented. The only way to keep Peronists out of office was to exclude them from the political process. Thus, the exclusion of the Peronist Party from elections became one of the bedrock objectives of the armed forces. There emerged a classic praetorian situation. While the military was able to veto any opening to the Peronists, the Peronists were able to prevent any civilian or military government hostile to their interests from consolidating power. The country was polarized between Peronists and the armed forces. Moderate political parties with a substantial base in the middle class could not bridge the gap. They were unable to attract sufficient working-class votes to defeat the Peronists in an open electoral contest. And governments elected under restrictive rules imposed by the military were generally hostages of either the military or the electorally excluded Peronists, and they were unable to placate the one without arousing the active opposition of the other. If they backed the armed forces' anti-Peronism, they were subject to protests and general strikes by the labor movement. If they decided to prepare the way for the return of Perón or his party to active politics, they faced the likelihood of a coup. In three decades, the country had five elected presidents, but none of them finished his term (O'Donnell 1979).

In 1966 General Juan Carlos Onganía overthrew the civilian government. His regime lasted until 1970. Formerly an institutionalist committed to keeping the armed forces out of politics, the general was now committed to the project of transforming society from above. Proclaiming an "Argentine revolution," he closed down the political parties and intervened in the universities. The regime claimed it would ultimately bring about "true democracy" and "social peace." Onganía appointed a technocrat as economics minister. The new minister lowered tariffs, attempted to attract foreign investment, and undertook measures to contain inflation. The plan, by and large, seemed to be working. In May 1969, however, a revolt erupted in the city of Córdoba. The economy there was languishing, and students, who formed the nucleus of the rebels, had serious grievances against the government. Their universities were intervened, and state subsidies had been cut. Auto workers participated as well, angered by sharp cutbacks that had occurred in previous years of the economic plan. The outburst in Córdoba was followed by outbreaks elsewhere. The economics minister was fired. Matters grew worse. As the 1970s began both the social peace and the economic plan were under severe threat. A variety of radical groups were increasingly resorting to violence. Onganía was forced out of office. As his successor, General Roberto Levingston assumed the presidency in mid-1970, the situation continued to worsen. Nine months later, General Alejandro Lanusse became president. After trying to placate the unions, he and the dominant faction in the armed forces decided to lay the groundwork for returning civilians to power once more. They did so with Argentina facing economic collapse and escalating political violence.

A Peronist stand-in won the presidency, and eventually Juan Perón himself assumed the office. The return of Perón to the country and his election as president were greeted by almost universal relief. The armed forces had demonstrated their incapacity to solve the country's problems. Non-Peronist politicians had also revealed their ineffectiveness, and their election to the presidency was only possible because of the exclusion of the Peronists. However, Perón too was ill-equipped to meet the problems or to fulfill the expectations that greeted him upon his return to office. Old and infirm, he lacked the physical stamina the political situation required. Perhaps even worse, the Peronist movement had never been able to coalesce into a unified, disciplined, political party that could serve as an instrument for Juan Perón or anyone else to use in resolving the political crisis. Yet, Argentina's problems – 40 percent inflation, a stagnant economy, political polarization, and steadily mounting political violence – required a Perón of mythical stature. Perón died less than a year after resuming the presidency. The presidency of Isabel Perón, his widow, who had been elected as her husband's running mate, provided the denouement to the Perón era. Beset by mounting problems that only worsened after the death of Juan Perón, the administration sank into ineffectiveness and inaction. The armed forces only needed to bide their time until another coup was greeted by a general sense of relief.

After the 1975 coup the military began a period of what they boasted would lead to national reconstruction, and it attempted both economic reform and national pacification. The results of both efforts were horrendous. The armed forces' "dirty war" defeated the terrorist threat, but only at the cost of widespread human rights abuses, including at least ten thousand and possibly as many as thirty thousand extra-judicial executions. As the scale of the abuses became known, groups such as the Mothers of the Plaza del Mayo organized ongoing mass protests. The economy initially grew, then collapsed. It registered negative growth in 1981 and 1982 in excess of 6 percent while inflation skyrocketed into the triple-digit level. To make matters worse, the extensive loans that the government had taken out during the 1970s were falling due, and the country faced a staggering debt burden. Within the military itself serious fissures had developed. After four years of military rule and an apparently regularized transition from one military administration to another, the new President, General Roberto Viola, was ousted from office and succeeded by the mastermind of the maneuver, General Leopoldo Galtieri, the army chief-of-staff. Galtieri apparently harbored ambitions of becoming president again after a transition to civilian rule. Yet he was unable to exercise effective control over the other service chiefs or even dominate the army. The military factionalism typical of Argentina through most of the century was, if anything, more intense during the Galtieri government than it had been previously.

The final blow that brought down the military regime was essentially a self-inflicted one, the Falklands/Malvinas War. The war was fought to secure the small island group off the coast of Argentina that the country had long claimed and which had been occupied by the British for nearly two centuries. The initial stages of the conflict were a case study in tactical finesse and strategic miscalculation. In the end, Argentina lost the islands, one of the most important ships in its fleet, and most of its modern military aircraft. Tens of thousands of its troops were captured. What had promised to be a quick and popular national crusade calculated to unify the country behind the military government turned into a military and political disaster. The war set the armed services at one another's throats and galvanized public opinion behind the demand for the immediate return to civilian rule. In the aftermath of the Falklands/Malvinas War, Galtieri and the three service chiefs were forced to resign, and a caretaker president, a retired general, was appointed. Concerned about possible prosecutions of military personnel as a result of the dirty war against terrorism in the late 1970s, the military attempted to pass a self-amnesty law, only to see the measure later rescinded by civilians. The negotiations between the armed forces and the democratic opposition largely favored the democrats who could mobilize widespread opposition against the discredited military. Although groups within the military pressured for the continuance of the military regime, elections were held and a new president inaugurated in late 1983.

The newly elected Alfonsín government had a number of advantages over its civilian predecessors, in part, stemming from the collapse of the previous military regime. The new government could rely on a general willingness among almost all sectors to give the incoming administration a decent opportunity to prove itself. The military, half of whose high command had been replaced, lacked the cohesion and morale to threaten the government seriously, at least in the short run. And Raúl Alfonsín, a member of the middle-class Radical Civic Union, had won a majority of the vote in an open presidential contest. He had done the unprecedented. He had defeated a Peronist presidential candidate in a free and honest election. Hence, Alfonsín was hostage to neither the Peronists nor the anti-Peronist military. Yet problems with both the military and the economy got beyond his control. While Raúl Alfonsín wanted to rein in the armed forces, he was, nonetheless, cautious about angering an institution that had been so politically powerful in the past. After several years trying to get the armed forces to punish those most responsible for the massive human rights abuses of the previous military regime, the Alfonsín government was forced to take action itself. The human rights trials for previous junta members, however, pleased few. Human rights advocates and relatives of the "disappeared" (those who had been extra-judicially executed by the armed forces) took direct action in the courts. The armed forces resisted, sometimes violently. The president's attempts to reshape and modernize the armed forces were met by resistance as well. The officer corps came to regard military reform as just another part of a plot to destroy the armed forces. By the end of his term of office, Alfonsín had faced three military revolts. Yet in terms of military restructuring, he had made some progress. He had overseen the enactment of a new military code and cut the military budget; he had laid the groundwork for eventually bringing the armed forces under civilian control.

The problems with the armed forces were not the only major difficulties Alfonsín faced. An economic plan meant to stop inflation and promote economic growth backfired. By early 1989 it was clear that the Radicals were so unpopular, a Peronist would win the election. The only question was who. In the event, Carlos Saúl Menem, the governor of La Rioja province, won both the Peronist primary and the general election. An unreconstructed Peronist as governor, spending freely and seemingly unconcerned about the long-term economic consequences, he changed his stripes upon assuming the presidency. After trying a variety of other measures, the new government established that most radical of anti-inflation mechanisms, a currency board. The currency board prevented the government from expanding the money supply and so put an institutional brake on inflation. That plus privatization, liberalization of trade and investment as well as the loosening of many internal economic regulations placed him in a mold that was virtually the complete opposite of his hero, Juan Perón. So too did his dealings with the armed forces. Perón had tried to use the military to support his political program. Menem was willing to support their autonomy and more. He acceded to their demands for the pardon for human rights violators. Imprisoned junta members were freed. As part of his bid for national reconciliation, some leftist prisoners were freed as well. Eventually, only a handful of military prisoners still languished in prison. This did not completely end the troubles, and when one of the long-standing leaders of the military rebels inspired a coup, Menem reacted harshly against him and the coup participants. A further amnesty of earlier military rebels followed. By the end of the 1990s, the only military officers still in prison were those who had participated in the anti-Menem coup. By 1998, civilian judges, on their own initiative, were beginning to bring cases against senior officers once more. But by this time, the political climate had changed. The armed forces were quiescent.

The 1976–83 military regime was a watershed. The armed forces tried radical solutions for economic problems, violent solutions for the problem of dissent, and a military solution for the nagging foreign policy problem posed by the Malvinas/Falklands Islands. They failed on all fronts. Recurring protests strengthened the hand of democratic politicians who wanted constitutional government reestablished. The Alfonsín government, though it provoked military revolts from middle-grade and lower-ranking officers, was able to secure the obedience of the high command, regardless of its lack of enthusiasm for the government's program. Menem, aided by the success of his economic program, tried to mend fences with the armed forces despite his Peronist roots. The 1990 coup attempt turned out to be the last gasp of full-scale military obstructionism. Discredited as a potential government, the armed forces were content to define their professional interests narrowly. Increasing military integration with former rivals, Brazil and Chile, and involvement in United Nations' peacekeeping operations have given the Argentine armed forces a more conventional and apolitical focus. By the 1999 presidential inauguration, three presidential terms had passed without a coup – a modern Argentine record.

CASE STUDY: TAIWAN: TRANSFORMATION

The political evolution of Taiwan provides an example of an authoritarian regime transforming itself. An unpopular, essentially "foreign" ruling class opened its ranks and changed the rules of the political game to allow for democratic contestation of its rule. There was popular pressure to do so, to be sure, but leaders of the regime acted earlier than they would have had to to secure the continuance of their influence and a peaceful transition.

Contemporary Taiwanese political history is intimately linked with the history of the rest of China since Taiwan's long-time ruling elite migrated from there in 1949. Modern Chinese history begins with the 1911 overthrow of the Chinese emperor inspired by nationalist theorist and activist, Sun Yatsen. Sun's initial efforts to liberate China foundered in the face of superior power exercised by remnants of the old regime known as warlords and foreign powers that controlled much of China as officially recognized zones of influence. It was not until after the formation of the Communist International (Comintern) in 1918 that the picture began to change. Sun's nationalist revolutionaries accepted advice and direct assistance from the Comintern. Sun's reformed party, now known as the Guomintang, KMT, or Nationalist Party, took on the classic pattern of any Marxist–Leninist political party, adopting party rules and structures recommended by its Comintern advisers. However, the KMT was not a true communist party despite its organizational principles. Simultaneously, the Comintern was advising the newly formed Chinese Communist Party (CCP) and promoted an alliance between its two protégés. Since both the CCP and the KMT needed a military force in order to suppress the warlords, form a strong central government, and deal effectively with the foreign powers occupying China, the Comintern provided military aid and advice as well. Shortly after the KMT's first convention in 1924, Sun Yatsen died. He was replaced by General Jiang Kaishek, one of the new military leaders groomed in the joint KMT–CCP military academy. Cooperation between the KMT and the communists continued for several years. Their most successful joint endeavor was the "Northern Expedition," which saw Jiang's army, supported by communist activists in the enemy's rear, liberate Hankow, Shanghai, and Nanking from warlord control. However, by 1927 Jiang had broken with the CCP, and a new civil war ensued. This war between communists and Nationalists was waged, off and on, for more than two decades. Finally, in 1949, Jiang Kaishek and his Republic of China government were forced off the mainland, and fled to Taiwan, a former Japanese colony recently restored to China at the end of the Second World War.

During the civil war against the communists and the war against Japan (1937–45), the KMT had changed its character. It had ceased to be a group of idealistic revolutionaries and become the party of power. The KMT had made its peace with various warlords, and the party itself had become dominated by conservative military and business interests. Its commitment to the social and economic status quo had undermined its capacity to govern. Its communist adversaries had adopted the strategy of protracted people's war. The CCP was able to champion the peasantry against the landlords while the KMT found itself allied with the landlords against the peasantry. The Nationalists' social conservatism did not serve them well. The vast mass of the population of the country was composed of peasants, and most of them had little use for the KMT. Nonetheless, the party seemed unwilling or unable to change. When the Republic of China (ROC), as Jiang's regime was known, assumed control of Taiwan at the end of the Second World War, it behaved virtually as an occupation force. The local Taiwanese felt greater kinship with the departing Japanese than they did with the mainland Nationalists. In 1947 an uprising occurred against the KMT, and it was brutally suppressed. In 1949, when Taipei became the Republic of China's capital, Taiwan was in the odd situation of having two governments over its territory. Taiwan was the only remaining province under the control of the ROC, but the Nationalists insisted on keeping the national legislature and the rest of the national government in place. In fact, no new national legislative elections were held until the early 1990s, leaving legislators originally chosen in 1947 in place for almost half a century. For much of its rule the KMT and the ROC government were virtually alien forces on the island. The leadership of the party, the executive branch, and the government were mainlanders. Provincial and local elections were held, but the KMT allowed them to be neither fair nor free.

Only gradually in the 1980s did the KMT begin to change politically, but before that, the government had undertaken a set of far-reaching economic reforms. In 1949, Taiwan's economic and social conditions were not that different from the rest of China. Local landlords, whose control of the land gave them both economic power and social prestige, dominated a largely peasant population. On the mainland the KMT had been the party of the status quo, but the party had learned its lesson from losing the civil war. On Taiwan, it undertook a land reform program, forcing landlords to accept government bonds or shares in partially privatized state firms as in exchange for their land. Such a reform had been politically impossible for the KMT on the mainland. There the landlords were well connected with the Nationalist Party. However, that was not the case on Taiwan. The KMT political elite and the local economic elite were distinct. The economic reform programs – land reform, partial privatization, and industrial protection – proved successful. They boosted industry and provided the peasantry with land and the opportunity for rural development. The successful implementation of reforms provided a launching pad for Taiwan's spectacular growth from the 1960s into the twenty-first century.

Political reform, though delayed, eventually followed as well. Jiang Kaishek died in 1975, and the presidency of the Republic of China passed to his son, Jiang Chingkuo. A new political dynasty seemed to be emerging within the mainland-dominated party and government. But the younger Jiang recognized that the political formula of mainlanders dominating locals was not viable in the long run. He continued and accelerated the indigenization of the KMT, recruiting native Taiwanese and advancing them in the party's leadership structure. At the same time, political life was liberalized. In 1987, Jiang Chingkuo died. Later that same year, the state of emergency, an outgrowth of the civil war, was lifted. Leadership of the KMT passed into the hands of Lee Tenghui, a Taiwanese who had been groomed for a leadership role by the younger Jiang.

Plate 9.1 Taiwan's democracy alive and well in 2006. Peaceful protestors demand the president's resignation.

Opposition parties found it easier to organize and attract votes. The Democratic Progress Party (DPP) became an outspoken advocate for local Taiwanese interests. The holdover national legislature with members first elected in 1947 was eventually disbanded. In 1991, multi-party elections for the new national legislature were held. The KMT maintained control, but the DPP established itself as the major opposition force. The first contested, presidential elections took place in 1996. Lee Tenghui won, and was returned to the presidency. Under Lee's leadership the mainland faction of the KMT was marginalized. A number of ex-KMT mainlanders have formed their own political party. In presidential elections in 2000, the DPP candidate, Chen Shui-bian, won. The Guomintang continues to own important media outlets and other private businesses. Nonetheless, the regime-directed democratization process has gone far, and the former opposition has elected its own two-term president. The Republic of China has unequivocally ceased to be a one-party state.

CASE STUDY: SOUTH AFRICA: TRANSPLACEMENT AND PACTED TRANSITION

South Africa was one of the outcaste regimes of the late twentieth century – and for good reason! A white minority held the native African majority in check, granting them no political rights and denying them many basic human rights as well. The system that the regime established was known as "**apartheid**," and it was nominally to provide for the separate and equitable development of all ethnic groups. In reality it served as a legal mechanism for repression instead. The legal principle underlying the system assigned each ethnic group a "homeland," with whites, barely 10 percent of the population, accorded full rights in the vast majority of the country's territory. Native African peoples, group by group, were each assigned to territorially defined homelands, each with its own supposedly independent government. "Coloreds" (people of mixed race) and Indians (people whose parents and grandparents had emigrated to South Africa from then British-controlled greater India) were accorded lesser status than whites and faced restrictions. However, they were considered citizens of South Africa proper even though they could only buy homes in certain neighborhoods and towns segregated for their use.

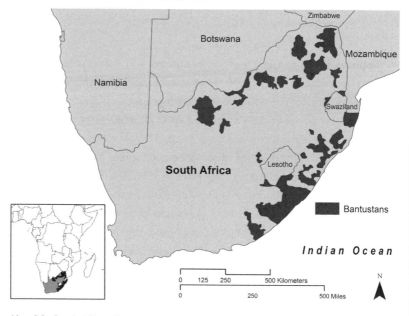

Map 9.2 South African Bantustans
Source: Environmental Systems Research Institute (ESRI) map data. CIA

The separate legal status of native Africans was the key to the government's systematic discrimination against them. They were legally foreigners outside their nominal home countries. Thus, they could not own property or settle permanently in white-controlled areas of South Africa. Their temporary residency and foreign status meant that they were subject to the sorts of controls that would be offensive when applied to citizens even in the eyes of most authoritarian governments. The homelands or Bantustans were small, impoverished territories with which most supposed citizens had had no real connection before they were created. African homelands were completely surrounded by South Africa and had no viable method of sustaining their nominal populations. The vast majority of breadwinners were compelled to work in South Africa proper under the terms set by the South African government and their employers. This extreme version of the "divide and rule" strategy was the brainchild of the Nationalist Party. The Nationalists had controlled the government for over four decades previous to black majority rule. Their base of support was the Afrikaner population, descendants of Dutch, French, and German immigrants who had reached South Africa centuries before. With a distinct culture and language, their true homeland was, in fact, South Africa; they were no longer simply European settlers. Afrikaners constituted a majority of the white population. They had been conquered and subordinated to British rule at the end of the nineteenth century when Great Britain along with other European powers had taken a renewed interest in Africa as a target for colonization. As self-rule under British tutelage was transformed into independence, the Afrikaners gained the upper hand politically against their white counterparts of English descent. While the English were generally more liberal than Afrikaners, there was little support for outright majority rule among whites, who were the only ones granted the right to vote.

While the South African government defended apartheid as reasonable and fair, most of the world saw through the legal subterfuge. International condemnation was followed by international boycotts. The Security Council of the United Nations was prevented from imposing a legally binding embargo only by the threat of a veto by the United States. But even the United States participated in part via various measures passed in the 1980s. The boycott forced the South African government to import oil and other essential commodities at premium prices sufficient to compensate embargo violators for their risk. In addition the government undertook programs to produce ersatz oil as the Germans had done during the Second World War using highly technical and uneconomic methods to make the essential commodity. The embargo obviously had an effect, but circling the wagons and fighting off attackers had been part of Afrikaner culture from frontier days. Historically Afrikaners had been embattled, and Afrikaners had an array of institutions to support them besides the Nationalist Party. The Broderbund was a semi-secret organization that overlapped with the Afrikaner elite. The Dutch Reformed Church was so much a part of the establishment that it was sometimes referred to as the "Nationalist Party at prayer." And Afrikaner hardliners could easily portray major African-backed organizations as a disloyal opposition bent on the destruction of the Afrikaner race and western civilization.

The major African organization was the African National Congress (ANC), which was, in fact, a multiracial grouping of South Africans of all races, but it was the black Africans that predominated. Linked with the ANC was the Communist Party of South Africa (CPSA). Under the rules of the ANC, communists were allowed to have dual membership as members of the ANC proper and also through the official position of the party in the ANC's governing structure. Also affiliated with the ANC was the Confederations of South African Trade Unions (COSATU), which had a strong position among black laborers in essential industries such as mining and metalworking. Even more horrifying to Afrikaners were the "black consciousness" and black supremacy movements, such as the Pan-African Congress (PAC), that believed the ANC was too moderate in its positions. The ANC and the PAC were outlawed in 1960 after protests and a massacre of the black population in Sharpeville, a black township near Johannesburg. Thereafter the organizations operated from exile, sponsoring a largely ineffective guerrilla war. Suspected ANC militants and members of other radical organizations were regularly arrested by the authorities. Assassination and torture were common practices. In conducting its guerrilla war, the ANC, in turn, found it easier to hit "soft" civilian targets rather than strictly military ones. Attacks on theaters and shopping centers, however, only confirmed Afrikaners' beliefs that the ANC was a barbaric organization that could not be negotiated with.

In the mid-1970s, the strategic situation of white South Africa had taken a turn for the worse. The Portuguese withdrew from their colonies worldwide, leaving neighboring Angola and Mozambique in the hands of black former guerrillas. A civil war ensued in Angola as the three national liberation factions had a violent falling out. The South Africans, ever the practitioners of "divide and rule," backed one of them both indirectly and with the incursion of their own military forces. The Soviet Union backed the official government. Cuban troops entered the fray as military advisers and combatants on the government's side. Several years later, the British government negotiated a settlement that brought black majority rule to the former Southern Rhodesia, now Zimbabwe. The Afrikaners looked more embattled than ever.

Despite the gathering threats early in the decade, the 1980s eventually saw a turn for the better. The United States and the Soviet Union negotiated an agreement that, among other things, called for a Cuban withdrawal. Despite the fact that the civil war continued, the Cubans left. In actual practice, Zimbabwe under a black-majority government appeared rather unthreatening once the white government was forced out. Entrenched rights for whites in the constitution protected their privileged position and kept the country economically viable. And the country's black government took no action that seriously threatened white rule in South Africa directly. Internally things were beginning to change as well. Economic sanctions had a serious effect on the country's long-term growth prospects, and elements of the ruling elite began to recalculate apartheid's economic, psychological, and moral costs. Spokesmen for the Dutch Reformed Church began to criticize the injustice of apartheid. The Broderbund itself was divided. Moderates within the Nationalist Party began to assume leadership positions. Things changed dramatically when W.F. de Klerk became prime minister in 1989. De Klerk decided to pursue a policy that would establish social peace in place of an ongoing if low-intensity civil war and bring South Africa back into the world community.

A key part of de Klerk's strategy was the legalization of the ANC and the PAC as well as the freeing of Nelson Mandela, an ANC activist who had been jailed for over two decades. Mandela was well recognized internationally, and many had campaigned for his release. The freeing of Mandela set the stage for a complex series of negotiations over the shape of the future South Africa. De Klerk and most moderate whites would have preferred entrenched property and political rights for the white population as whites in Zimbabwe received, even if they were only temporary. This sort of arrangement could well entail a guaranteed minimum representation of whites in the legislature, a representation large enough to prevent constitutional revisions that undermined their basic interests. In addition de Klerk and the whites generally preferred a highly decentralized structure of government since it seemed clear that the ANC was likely to control the national government. The white minority's best hope for retaining a modicum of real power would likely be on the local level.

Negotiations were far from simple. White extremists outside the government and inside the government's own security service did their best to complicate the process. The Inkatha Freedom Party had always been a fly in the ointment of black-African unity. Inkatha, dominated by the Zulu ethnic group, shared some aims with the white minority. They too wanted a federal system that would assure them significant local power. They also wanted some sort of effective mechanism to prevent a single-party government at national level. This was difficult to do given the fact that any electoral system that was democratic would likely yield an ANC majority in the legislature. As negotiations preceded, provocateurs from the security services set about instigating black-on-black massacres involving supporters of the ANC and Inkatha. The security service's strategy was simple. If Africans showed themselves unable to operate in a civilized manner, maybe the white community and the government would come to their senses and break off negotiations or at least take a hardline posture. Extremists on the African side also saw negotiations as a sell out. Whites – even Afrikaners whose roots went back centuries – were colonial interlopers on a black continent. They should be forced out. As it was, the hardliners on neither side were able to scuttle the negotiations.

The agreement that was reached included a transitional government and constitutional package that was to be ratified by a popular plebiscite. The shape of the package was more favorable to the black majority than Zimbabwe's had been. There were no entrenched rights and the system was federal but without the local government powers that whites and Inkatha had wanted. The transitional government was to have a short duration with black majority rule beginning quickly. The prickly issue about what to do with the human rights violators of the old regime remained for the new government to solve.

In an attempt to smooth ruffled features, when Nelson Mandela was elected president in the first black-majority elections in 1994, he offered a coalition government to Inkatha and the Nationalists. Inkatha rejected the offer and the Nationalists later withdrew, finding their influence within the cabinet limited. The human rights issue was handled by a Truth and Reconciliation Commission, a feature of some other transitions as well. The commission, headed by Anglican Archbishop Desmond Tutu, operated under a set of rules meant to purge the country of pent-up desire for revenge on the part of Africans and long-standing denial on the part of many whites. Those who confessed in detail to their crimes would be granted an automatic pardon; those who refused to cooperate would still be subject to prosecution.

As with other countries where the transitions to democracy have come to a more or less successful close, problems remain. Most members of the

African majority have made only slow economic progress although the
progress of the small African middle and upper classes has been dramatic.
Old resentments die hard as do old stereotypes. The black majority
wonders why whites have it so much better and when they themselves will
benefit. The white minority often ascribes the economic advancement of
Africans as the result of personal connections and racial bias. The Afrikaner
minority, many of whom were privileged economically only in comparison
to the Africans, wait. The ANC possesses unchallenged political dominance.
Still, the prime ministry has been transferred peacefully to Mandela's
successor, Thabo Mbeki. And the elections scheduled for 2009, although
embittered by intra-ANC feuding and Mbeki's forced resignation, are likely
to adhere to democratic standards as have those in the recent past.
Overall, the likelihood of political breakdown seems to be diminishing. In
South Africa the democratic consolidation
has begun.

Summary

Of the three transitions discussed here, Argentina's fits the pattern of a
simple replacement. The outgoing military government was unable to
secure most of its main objectives. Military hardliners were
outmaneuvered by democrats and by moderates within their own ranks.
Moderate democrats dominated the pro-democracy coalition. Alfonsín
himself was a moderate. He pressed the military to change, but did not
force the pace. He achieved only limited results. The Taiwanese transition,
in contrast to Argentina's, was one dominated by the KMT government.
The regime saw the handwriting on the wall, and made the changes
necessary to preserve for itself a competitive – even dominant – position
in the reformed system. In South Africa, the Nationalist government
initiated the democratization process, but was not able to control it.
South Africa is an example of a truly brokered transition.

Regardless of type, no political transition involving long-standing
injustices and deep-seated fears can be completely satisfactory.
Democratization involves significant change, but it is not revolution
where one party forces its solutions on all the others. Deals have to be
made, and maximum objectives have to be set aside if negotiations are to
have a democratic and peaceful outcome. Even where the democrats have
the upper hand, a clear outcome is far from assured. Even after democratic
transitions, the old political actors may still remain and possess significant
power. The Argentine armed forces retained enough power to disrupt the

political process for almost a decade. The KMT remains the dominant party in Taiwan although splits within the party can keep it from power. Rightwing nationalists occasionally engaged in political violence in South Africa. And the dramatic business of pro-democratic regime change to be successful must be followed by the humdrum business of democratic consolidation.

Problems of democratic consolidation

Democracy is subject to reversal. As Huntington noted, the previous two democratic waves were followed by reverse waves when authoritarianism was reestablished in many new democracies. Unless institutional, economic, and societal changes occur after the transition to democratic rule, the democratic character of the new system is likely to erode and democracy itself may even be overthrown. It goes almost without saying that democracy depends upon the sort of political and governmental institutions described in Chapter 4. Yet, institution-building is a more subtle and challenging task than merely drafting constitutions, statutes, and party charters. The legal element is important, but even more critical is the underlying human element embodied in attitudes, practices, and expectations. This means that underlying problems of the state and economy need to be fixed, and the social and political infrastructure necessary for a successful democracy constructed. In short, the authoritarian legacy needs to be overcome if democracy is to be consolidated, i.e., made secure against possible reversal. Many democracies face the task of consolidation, including many of those that were democratic prior to democracy's third wave.

Assuring fair and free elections

Many new democracies have had little prior experience with fully democratic government. Fair and free elections require the establishment and policing of voting lists, the promulgation of rules for forming political parties, and enrolling parties and their candidates on the ballot. Candidates must be able to gain access to the media to publicize their views. The media themselves must be sufficiently diverse and independent so that they can serve as watchdogs able to criticize the government and investigate political and other public malfeasance. On election day the polls themselves must be watched at voting time. Precautions must be taken to assure that votes are honestly tabulated. All these are largely procedural matters. Once parties and interest groups realize they have a vested interest in doing so, they will provide poll watchers themselves. The opposition needs to assure that the electoral process is fair and free. In short, policing elections is a matter of informed self-interest.

Securing the rule of law

Establishing the rule of law is a more complex and subtle process than monitoring elections and safeguarding party competition. Supporting the rule of law is a matter of self-interest, but it is a matter of enlightened self-interest. The majority – the general public – must recognize that tolerance and fairness are preeminent virtues. This recognition is not always easy to come by in societies that have not been governed according to the rule of law in the past. The importance of a historical foundation is striking. Most consolidated democracies have had the rule of law for a considerable period. In most of them, the struggle for constitutionalism and the rule of law preceded the struggle for democracy.

In most new democracies, however, the rule of law had not been well entrenched before democracy was established. Rather, the judiciary remained under the thumb of autocratic governments and the privileged few, making the courts the instruments of a narrow elite. The lack of historical experience has undercut attempts to establish liberal legal institutions in new democracies. Moreover, these institutions are not easily transplanted. They require adequate financial support, training of personnel, and the elimination of practices inimical to the defense of individual rights. Corruption and cumbersome procedures impede fair access to the courts. Public attitudes – political culture – are also of critical importance. If the general public and the judges, themselves, do not really expect judges to be independent of the parties and leaders who control the government, they are unlikely to become so. The rule of law is a fragile growth that needs to be nourished over time.

Building state effectiveness

Developing countries in the process of democratic consolidation often have "soft" states. Some states are weak by design. They carry out only minimal functions because the government of the day and the founders of the state intend them to do little more. These weak states protect life and property, resolve disputes between private parties, establish and maintain a stable currency, and provide the rudiments of elementary education, transportation, and public health. States that are weak by design, but efficient in terms of what they do, are termed "**minimal states**." In contrast, **soft states** are weak in the sense of being inefficient and incapable of executing their assigned tasks effectively. And they may lack the moral authority to carry out their functions effectively. A soft state is one that aspires to many of the functions of the modern welfare state but suffers from a serious lack of capacity: inadequate staffing, inadequate training of staff, budgets that are too small, and an overly ambitious policy agenda to carry out. Most importantly, soft states have limited moral authority. The modern state assumes not only a professional bureaucracy but also a citizenry that recognizes the state's moral authority. However, many people in developing countries, where new democracies abound, view the state as the enemy.

Large-scale corruption often flourishes in soft states. Since the state's administrative personnel are usually poorly paid and poorly trained, political and economic elites face few effective administrative and judicial checks. Those with money and connections are able to defend their interests even when these interests run clearly contrary to the dictates of the law and constitution. Elites are often able to manipulate the procedures of law that are supposed to give everyone an equal hearing and chance to receive justice. State offices and contracts can be used to aid cronies of the powerful and buy support. Cronyism and corruption can also undermine the judiciary and the rule of law. When this occurs, legal judgments and orders can be purchased, criminal penalties avoided, and the judiciary can be used as a political tool of the ruling clique. In short, patrimonialism can flourish in a soft state and void the rational-bureaucratic norms of the rule of law that are essential for a consolidated liberal democracy.

Establishing civilian control of the armed forces

As part of the state, the armed forces may also suffer from the failure to live up to the standards one might expect from a modern institution, let alone one functioning in a liberal democracy. In successful contemporary states, the armed forces are professionally competent and loyal to the constitution. Hence, they are also loyal to the government of the day that has been established according to recognized constitutional procedures. The ethnic, regional, religious, or class background of military officers plays only a minor role in assuring their obedience to their civilian superiors or securing them promotions. However, in countries where military budgets are inadequate or spent unwisely, where training facilities are poor, and where norms of professionalism are a rather new imposition, the armed forces will suffer from many of the same pathologies as the civilian bureaucracy. While formally adhering to professional and constitutional norms, they will seek more effective ways to advance their careers, protect their families, and promote the interests of the institution to which they belong.

In addition, the armed forces' domestic intelligence apparatus may have a chilling effect on the political process, or information it gathers can be used to blackmail and undermine civilian political authorities. Lack of proper outside scrutiny can allow bribery to become a political tool of the armed forces as well. The greater the involvement of the military in the domestic policing and security function, the greater will be the danger. In short, even in countries that have been subject to military rule, the return of democratic government does not of itself solve the underlying problems of the military and security forces. The one sector of the state apparatus that works well, even in soft states, is often that which is responsible for political repression. But it works well in the sense of authoritarian norms and objectives. Democratic consolidation requires it be brought under control.

Establishing civilian control of the military is a complex matter. It entails the cultivation of civilian experts on military affairs who can advise the executive branch, the legislature, and the public at large. In addition, civil authorities must have the desire to ferret out information and the perseverance to assure that the armed forces stay within the laws and their budget. This is no mean task when the military has become accustomed to operate autonomously. The declaration of domestic political emergencies and the use of military force to quell them can create special dangers. The armed forces locally or even nationally might be tempted to take the law into its own hands. Emergencies have provided a ready pretext for coups d'etat. Often an additional problem impinges on the government in newly established democracies – the need to defend the rule of law and hold perpetrators of egregious human rights violations to account. This can be highly sensitive politically and full accountability may be prevented by a formal or informal transition pact. Still, it is hard to entrench the rule of law if past abuses go completely unpunished and the perpetrators remain defiant and unrepentant.

Building social capital

Democracies work because citizens organize themselves into civic associations, interest groups, and political parties. They generally united with people like themselves to attain their common objectives. They are driven by what Alexis de Tocqueville called "self-interest rightly understood" (see Chapter 3). Authoritarian regimes promote a mentality of obedience and intolerance. Authoritarians see independent social organizations as a danger to the regime. In countries where democracy is not yet consolidated, the persistence of attitudes and habits that run counter to democratic citizenship is common. In addition, interest groups, civic associations, and political parties that do exist are often co-opted into a patron–client network. Local nongovernmental organizations (NGOs), international NGOs, and official government aid organizations have recognized the problem of developing social capital. They have organized and funded community health projects, agricultural cooperatives, women's and youth groups, community organizations, and a host of other grassroots associations to promote the capacity of citizens in new democracies to recognize their own interest and the collective good and act systematically to realize it. It is a long-term educational process of empowerment that involves considerably more than "book learning."

Economic efficiency and social equity

Problems of economic efficiency and social equity are a leitmotif of modern politics – even in its authoritarian versions. Communism often managed to achieve a modicum of social equity. Basic education and healthcare was provided to everyone; so too was old-age assistance. However, communist economies were, by and large, inefficient. And when communism ended, so too did the social protections provided by the regime, leaving post-communist systems the task of attaining both economic efficiency and social equity. Other authoritarian systems that are under consideration here were much more of a mixed bag. Rightwing state capitalist economies sometimes produced favorable economic results. The trickle-down effect sometimes benefited the middle and lower classes, but many of these economic systems were failures, and even some relative successes failed to produce significant trickle down. This meant that newly installed democracies face the task typical of modern governments of increasing the wealth of their countries and making sure all important social actors and their constituencies were basically satisfied. Lack of equity creates problems beyond the existence of injustice; it can weaken the quality of democracy itself since wealth can be translated into political power. There seems to be no single foolproof formula for bringing about rapid growth with equity. Politicians and commentators have put forward both the modern welfare state as well as the minimal state as models. Democratic consolidation may depend on the ability of the new democracies to satisfy the economic aspirations of their citizens. The record since the 1990s has been mixed. Few countries with inefficient, inequitable economies have managed to find the solutions to these problems.

Summary

Some of the same political actors that helped further the transition to democracy have remained involved in the effort to consolidate it. Political parties, NGOs (both domestic and international), as well as foreign governments and multilateral organizations have all remained active in the process. The task of democratic consolidation has many levels from building governmental and administrative structures, developing and strengthening political parties, and promoting the growth of civil society. None of these tasks is ever really finished, but new democracies and newly reestablished democracies are especially vulnerable to overthrow and backsliding in a more piecemeal fashion. Among the policy community that supports democratization, both policy choices and priorities often remain contentious. Yet, the interest in consolidating democracy continues to be widespread.

Conclusion

Third-wave democratization is now some three decades old. There should be little surprise that participants and observers now understand its parameters fairly well – even if largely intuitively. In the early years of democratization, some authoritarian elites thought that limited liberalization or limited democratization would do the trick and allow them to retain power. They believed that the old regime could be modified at the margins and survive. Many were disappointed. Regime-led transitions often worked best when the dominant elites from the old regime realized that the "jig was up." In Finer's words, they realized that they had to "change their plea." The leadership of the KMT democratized systematically and survived, its economic power intact and its political power still significant. With brokered and opposition-dominated transitions, the results can be more favorable to the democrats, but favorable outcomes cannot be guaranteed. In the Argentine transition, democrats had the upper hand, but elements of the armed forces remained spoilers after the transfer to democracy. They were able to frustrate and then block prosecutions for human-rights violations of historical proportions for more than a decade. Today some third-wave democracies are consolidated, but in many others, the process of consolidating it is a continuing task. Sometimes erstwhile beneficiaries of the old regime remain players, even if semi-loyal ones, but regardless of the political lineups, the need to build democratic institutions, strengthen civil society, and solve the problem of economic growth with equity is ongoing. In other countries, democratization has barely begun. Ruling elites have learned how to stall or sidetrack the process. Thus a variety of authoritarian and semi-authoritarian regimes continue to exist. They are the topic of Chapters 11 and 12, but, first, Chapter 10 turns to democratization of communist regimes.

Questions for further consideration

1 What might explain the fact that democratization comes in waves?
2 There were some revolutionary upheavals during prior waves of democratization. What might account for their largely being absent today?
3 Compare and contrast democratization in Argentina, Taiwan, and South Africa. What sorts of factors strengthened and weakened authoritarians and democrats in each case?
4 The rate of democratization has been lower in the first decade of the 2000s than earlier. What might account for this decline?
5 Some countries have had previous experience with democracy prior to a period of authoritarian government. In such cases, when democracy returns, it is likely to be more stable that in newly democratic countries with no significant prior experience with democracy. What explains this?
6 Why is the consolidation of democracy likely to be a long-term process? Why might some countries find it difficult to establish democracy in the first place, let alone consolidate it?

Further reading

Lisa Anderson (ed.), *Transitions to Democracy*. New York: Columbia University Press, 1999. An anthology with articles by some of the leading scholars in the field of democratization going back to 1969.

Larry Diamond, *Developing Democracy: Toward Consolidation*. Baltimore, MD: Johns Hopkins University Press, 1999. Discussion of the issue of democratic consolidation.

Larry Diamond and Leonardo Molino (eds), *Assessing the Quality of Democracy*. Baltimore, MD: Johns Hopkins University Press, 2005. Discusses issues of democratic consolidation and provides comparative case studies.

Samuel P. Huntington, *The Third Wave: Democratization in the Late Twentieth Century*. Norman, OK: University of Oklahoma Press, 1991. Probably the best single volume on third-wave democratization.

Guillermo O'Donnell, Philippe C. Schmitter, and Laurence Whitehead
(eds), *Transitions from Authoritarian Rule: Prospects for Democracy*.
Baltimore, MD: Johns Hopkins University Press, 1986. Contains case
studies from the range of countries experiencing democratization.
Part IV summarizes the dynamics of the process and gives advice to
democrats.

10 Democratization and economic reform in the communist world

Anyone who believes that the worker can be lulled by fine revolutionary phrases is mistaken ... If no concern is shown for the growth of material and spiritual riches, the people will listen today, they will listen tomorrow, and then they may say: "Why do you promise us everything in the future? You are talking, so to speak, about life beyond the grave. The priest has already told us about this."

(Nikita Khrushchev)

In this chapter

The discussion of contemporary democratization continues, focusing on the communist and post-communist worlds. The collapse of communism as a distinct ideological, political, and economic system in open competition with liberal democracy and capitalism has profoundly shaped the contemporary era. This chapter explores how and why communism collapsed in Europe and how communist parties in Asia and Cuba have been able to retain their political dominance by adopting some key elements of capitalist economics. Post-communist regimes range from nearly consolidated democracies, on the one hand, to authoritarian regimes, on the other. The chapter includes case studies on the Soviet Union and the People's Republic of China. The chapter addresses the structural–functional weakness of these and communist systems generally as well as the strategic choices of key political actors and the political economy of the post-state socialist era.

Introduction

Perhaps much more than he realized, Khrushchev was right! When Khrushchev spoke, communism in the Soviet Union had been making material advances for decades, and the Soviet leader was confident that that progress would continue. Yet, it was in the Khrushchev era (1953–64) that the decline in Soviet economic prowess began, and that decline lasted for decades. In the face of this persistent failure in state effectiveness, communist rule could not maintain its legitimacy either. However, as was the case with other political breakdowns, a third factor was needed to bring European communism to an end – governmental inefficacy. European communist states made political decisions that backfired. In attempting to reinvigorate communism both politically and economically and bring it closer to its ideals, Mikhail Gorbachev, the leader of the Soviet Union from 1985 until 1991, prepared the way for European communism's collapse. Just how pivotal governmental decisions were to the fall of European communism can be seen from the contrasting experience of communist regimes outside Europe. Although Asian communist states and communist Cuba suffered from many of the same difficulties as the Soviet Union and its European allies, these non-European communist regimes followed a different political path. In Cuba and Asian communist states, the party was able to maintain its monopoly on political power. Instead of coupling economic reform with democratization, they pursued economic reform alone and in a much more cautious way than did the USSR. Thus, while they reshaped their economies significantly, they retained their grip on political power.

This chapter begins with an investigation of the crisis that faced communists and many leftwing radicals in the last quarter of the twentieth century. It continues with a case study on the Soviet Union and an analysis of the democratization process in communist Europe. Next, the chapter takes a look at communist regimes that survived. A case study of the People's Republic of China (PRC) examines the most successful survivor. And the chapter concludes with a short discussion of reform in other Asian regimes and Cuba.

The breakdown of communist regimes

The breakdown of communist regimes had two underlying elements: weakening legitimacy and growing state (specifically economic) ineffectiveness. There was a growing doubt about the communist party's ability to live up to its own moral ideal. This legitimacy crisis helped provoke opposition within society and divided the ruling elite.

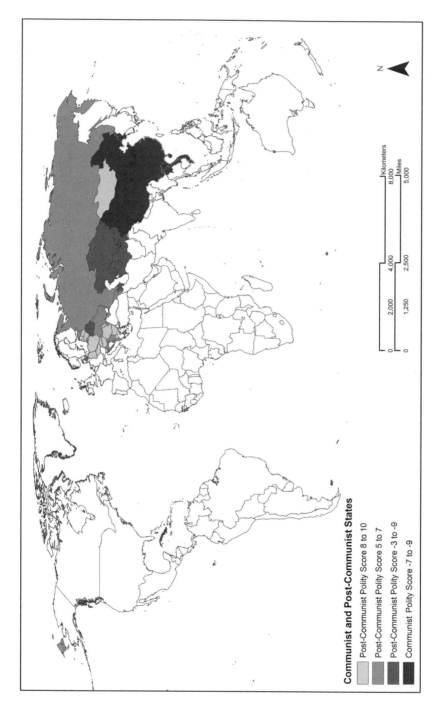

Communist and Post-Communist States

- Post-Communist Polity Score 8 to 10
- Post-Communist Polity Score 5 to 7
- Post-Communist Polity Score -3 to -9
- Communist Polity Score -7 to -9

Map 10.1 Communist and post-communist states (2004)

Source: Environmental Systems Research Institute (ESRI) map data. Data: Polity IV

Note: Polity IV ratings range from +10 (most democratic) to −10 (most authoritarian)

The international prestige of democracy and external support strengthened democratic dissents at the same time as the regime was beginning to falter. A second element that facilitated breakdown was the growing realization that state socialism was an inefficient way of managing an economy.

Communism's legitimacy crisis

Communist regimes eventually came to suffer from two legitimacy problems. First, they had not attained their revolutionary goals. And second, at least in some cases, they were insufficiently nationalist. The second problem was particularly important for most European communist states other than the Soviet Union and for certain national groups within the Soviet Union itself. The nature and limits of the second problem are easy to understand. As a revolutionary party, communists saw themselves as a vanguard enthusiastically backed by a mass movement, and when revolutions were home grown this was largely the case. However, most European communists had come to power with the aid of Soviet troops, and the resulting communist regimes always felt it necessary to cleave closely to the Soviet line even though in many cases these nations were historic enemies of Russia. When Hungary in 1956 and Czechoslovakia in 1968 failed to follow the Soviet line, they provoked a Soviet invasion and Soviet imposition of a more compliant local communist government. For much of the general public, the forced alliance with the Soviet Union rankled.

Yet, even states where the communist revolution was home grown experienced a legitimacy problem. By the decade of the 1970s, many living under communist rule and some communist party members themselves were developing serious reservations about Marxism–Leninism, the principle that gave communist rule its moral authority. Marxism–Leninism was not simply a general notion or sentiment but an elaborate ideology embodied in a seven-hundred-plus page political catechism (Kuusinen *et al.* 1963). Karl Marx had argued that the communist revolution would usher in a new era, an era in which all the political and social problems of the past would disappear. Human beings would be emancipated once and for all. Full communism would bring about an age of abundance, where each could have what he needed and wanted. The state – the means of coercion – would disappear. Even the burdensome nature of work would disappear. Machinery would replace the drudgery of much human effort, and human beings would be immensely more productive than they had been in the past. Individuals would not be compelled to work by force or necessity. Their work would be voluntary and liberating. As members of the community, each would control his or her own production (Marx 1977: 168–71).

This seemingly utopian hope did not disappear with Marx's death. Even as other Marxists at the turn of the last century began to discount it, Lenin kept it alive and made it a fundamental point of difference between his and other Marxist movements. Nor did the hope disappear from later communist pronouncements. The Program of the CPSU [Communist Party of the Soviet Union] of 1961 assured its readers, under communism, human beings would "harmoniously combine spiritual wealth, moral purity and a perfect physique" (CPSU 1961: 109). Convinced communists held that their beliefs and expectations were entirely scientific, but it is not surprising that noncommunist commentators readily describe such beliefs as millennialist and quasi-religious. Their realization would constitute, almost literally, a new heaven and a new earth.

Millennialism had important implications. The prospect of supreme achievement calls for supreme effort. Neither Marx nor latter-day communists believed the revolution would immediately result in full communism. Human beings and their material environment would have to be transformed first. Communism and the "new communist man" would have to be built. That was what state socialism and people's democracy (the communist version of one-party rule) were all about. In the Soviet Union, the building of communism required a civil war (death toll, three million); agricultural collectivization (death toll, seven million); purges (death toll, five million); and the Great Patriotic War (World War II) that killed another twenty million Soviet citizens. In addition, a succession of economic five-year plans stressed heavy industry and military production and downplayed the production of consumer goods. The Soviet Union became a totalitarian system that attempted to reach into every facet of Soviet life and to eliminate opposition, whether open or covert. The sacrifices the Soviet people were forced to endure were justified in the name of the glorious future that awaited both the Soviet Union and the world.

According to communist ideology, both the future and the methods selected to bring it about were matters of scientific precision. Communists declared that Marxism–Leninism was a scientific enterprise. Marx had predicted the fall of capitalism on the basis of the laws that governed its development. Others added to the list of scientific truths. Lenin had reaffirmed Marx's predictions, extending Marxist economic analysis to turn-of-the-century colonialism. In addition to supporting Marx's claims to scientific objectivity, Lenin had added another important element to scientific Marxism with his concept of the vanguard party. After the failure of revolutionary efforts immediately after the First World War,

Stalin's theory of "Socialism in one Country," affirming that the prerequisites for full communism could be built in Russia without the help of more advanced industrial states, was added to communist dogma. In every case, these basic theories as well as the policy choices made by the CPSU were supposedly grounded on an objective scientific understanding of the workings of society, the economy, and history. Those who refused to recognize this were either ignorant or biased. The communist worldview was the one correct one. All others were a product of "false consciousness."

This extreme view of the correctness and objectivity of communist theory and practice was difficult to sustain. To do so, communists resorted to a number of self-deceptions. First, they maintained a pre-twentieth-century view of what constituted science. The philosophy of science most widely accepted in the contemporary era holds that science is not so much a body of conclusions as a methodology. To be counted as scientific, statements have to be capable of falsification – i.e., we would have to know what sort of empirical test or what sort of observable evidence would lead us to reject the theory. (There is no empirical *verification* of a theory – proving a theory true – since there is always a variety of possible explanations other than the theory being tested that could account for the outcome of a test.) As theories continually survive tests that could have falsified them they gain a stronger and stronger standing as scientifically "corroborated." Some theories achieve such strong corroboration that they are virtually unassailable in practice, but they never become dogmatic absolutes. They are always dependent on evidence (Popper 2002: 10, 17–18).

Communists did not adhere to this contemporary view of science. The foundations of science for them included not only a method, but substantive understandings of the facts as well. For example, communists saw materialism (the belief that all things are matter or created from matter) as scientifically correct. Thus, they saw any religion or any explanation of reality that includes references to spirit or soul as unscientific and in error. Contemporary philosophers of science can only shrug their shoulders at this view of things. The theory of materialism is an assertion not susceptible to empirical testing. It has no scientific standing. For the contemporary philosophy of science, natural science investigates the material world, not because matter is the only thing that exists, but because matter, in its various forms, is the subject of the natural sciences. In other words, according to the contemporary interpretation, Marxism–Leninism was a "science" only for its adherents.

Many of the specific predictions of communist ideology also resisted falsification and would be regarded as unscientific according to the contemporary understanding of the philosophy of science. Marx, Lenin, and other communists rarely gave dates for their predictions. Their predictions were almost always of the "in the long run" variety, so that there was no way to declare them false because they failed to materialize within a specified timeframe. Thus, if the First World War, the Great Depression, and the Second World War (each seen at the time as capitalism's final crisis) all failed to usher in the global end of capitalism, these events did not falsify the theory since the theory never had made such specific predictions in the first place. However, regardless of its scientific standing or lack of it, the credibility of communist theory was severely tested by events as the twentieth century wore on. Soviet communism was delegitimized because of its continued tendency to over-promise and under-deliver. In short, communism and Khrushchev as leader of the Soviet Union during a critical period fell into the trap that he himself elaborated in the epigraph.

It is hard to read Marx and Lenin without feeling their revolutionary enthusiasm and sensing an unspoken hope that communism was just around the corner. Marx argued that as capitalism develops, its irrationalities become more and more manifest and its crises become deeper and more frequent. Lenin anticipated that the Russian Revolution would be the spark that would set off world revolution. He believed that worker control of factories would come about once the revolution had begun. Stalin's Great Socialist Offensive in the late 1920s inspired a mass mobilization of human and natural resources to modernize the country dramatically. But full communism never arrived. People became cynical. As noted in Chapter 5, Soviet jokes captured this malaise. One of these took the form of an apocryphal story from the era of long-serving CPSU General Secretary Leonid Brezhnev. In the story, set a few years after he assumed the leadership of the party, Brezhnev is trying to impress his mother by showing her that he has indeed "made it big." He takes her to his luxury apartment in the Kremlin and shows her around. He shows her his servants, his private garage with a fleet of luxury automobiles. She says nothing. Brezhnev tries again. He takes his mother to his dacha outside of Moscow. No country cottage this but another luxurious domicile, again with servants always at the ready. His mother still says nothing. Exasperated, Brezhnev flies her to his hunting lodge in the Ural Mountains, a retreat resplendently provided with all the creature comforts and servants anyone could possibly want. Again Brezhnev's mother makes no response. Finally, at wit's end Brezhnev turns to his mother and demands a response: "Mama, what do you think?" The old lady looks at him pensively and responds: "Well, Leonid, this is all very nice, but what if the Reds [communists] come back?" (Smith 1976: 48). The point of the joke is simple: the Soviet Union did not live up to its principles.

At the same time that Marxism–Leninism's prestige waned, that of liberal democracy grew. As early as 1948, the Soviet Union had voted for the United Nations Universal Declaration of Human Rights. Communist states declared themselves to be "people's democracies," recognizing the legitimacy of the democratic ideal though certainly not the way that ideal was implemented in liberal democracies. There were largely perfunctory gestures. The Soviet Union could ignore the democratic principles to which it had given nominal support. There was no specific indication in the declaration of how they were to be implemented. At the same time, the Soviet Union could credibly claim that it did better in guaranteeing certain basic economic and social rights, such as the right to a job, a decent income, and health care, than did many of its capitalist counterparts. More critically, there was no international enforcement mechanism. Thus, the Soviet government also felt free to sign the universal declaration as well as a variety of other such conventions that were negotiated in the decades following. The official recognition of democracy and rights actually contradicted the theoretical analysis of rights that usually typified Marxism. Karl Marx and later thinkers had seen rights as a capitalist creation, guaranteeing a worthless, merely formal equality of workers with their capitalist masters. Social and economic institutions were what mattered. Rights and democratic procedures meant nothing. Soviet leaders would later regret their blithe accession to these rights conventions.

New political actors and ideological change

In 1975, the process of pro-forma support for democratic norms went a step further. The Soviet Union, along with its Warsaw Pact allies, the United States-led North Atlantic Treaty Organization (NATO) members, and a number of European neutrals signed the Helsinki Accords. This agreement had three basic parts: military confidence-building measures meant to limit the possibility of a Warsaw Pact–NATO conflict starting by accident; cultural and economic exchanges, and yet another agreement to respect basic human rights. Hardliners in the United States saw the agreement as a dangerous step that would lead to the weakening of NATO and its replacement by a toothless international body in which the Soviet Union wielded a veto. Moreover, the accords provided for the sort of economic exchanges the Soviet Union then sought to compensate for its growing technological weakness.

To hardliners in the United States – and to those in the Soviet Union as well – the human rights provisions seemed worthless at best: another unenforceable declaration valuable only for Soviet propaganda. Yet it did not work out that way. Helsinki watch groups formed in signatory countries including the USSR. Composed of private citizens, these groups monitored Soviet compliance and criticized noncompliance openly. When the Soviet groups were shut down and their leading members arrested, western journalists, government officials, and groups operating elsewhere took up the cause. Reporting on rights violations was extensive. The welfare of detainees became a matter of public concern in the West. Western government officials began to give a high priority to airing rights complaints when they met their Soviet counterparts. Thus, the Helsinki Agreement helped set the stage for a pro-democracy movement within the Soviet Union.

There had been a generational change in communist countries as well. Communism was not a complete failure. The Soviet Union had made significant progress in living standards of what had prevailed under the tsars. However, by the 1970s Soviet achievements in standards of living and social justice that had excited their parents and grandparents no longer seemed so impressive to the younger generation. Soviet youth measured their country by different standards, those prevailing in the West, not those derived from Russian history, and the USSR clearly came up wanting. If anything, this dissatisfaction was more common among the Soviet Union's allies than in the USSR proper. The citizens of communist East Germany especially could easily compare their standards of living with their brethren in liberal democratic West Germany. Some dissidents were not so young. Even privileged members of the establishment became outspoken critics of the regime. Perhaps the leading representative of this group was Andrei Sakharov, a nuclear physicist who was dubbed "the father of the Soviet H-bomb." Although Sakharov was sent into internal exile and prevented from communicating freely with the outside world, his prominence meant that his plight received widespread news coverage outside the communist world, coverage that helped to further undermine the moral authority of the Soviet regime. Early in the 1980s, a labor-based movement aided by the Catholic Church with its new Polish pope and dissident intellectuals sprang up to challenge the communist regime in Poland. Similar movements would emerge later in the decade in other Soviet-bloc states in Europe.

State ineffectiveness: the crisis in state socialist economic planning

During the early cold war period, state socialism appeared to be the key to rapid economic growth with equity. Socialism as practiced by the Soviet Union, the first and most economically powerful socialist state, became a model for other ruling communist parties. Even states not sympathetic to

Table 10.1   Soviet economic performance

Decade/growth	Gross domestic product (%)	Investment (% of GDP)	Return on investment (%)
1950s	10	20	23
1960s	7	25	5
1970s	5	28	1
1980s	2	30	0

Source: World Bank (1996): 2–3

communist ideology adopted Soviet state-socialist methods in whole or in part. But by the 1970s the Soviet Union was in economic trouble. Rates of economic growth that had been spectacular during the 1950s had become anemic. Table 10.1 illustrates the growing problem. Some Central European communist states had already begun to experiment however tentatively with economic reform. By the end of the 1970s, the People's Republic of China too had come to recognize that reform was essential. As it turned out, the Soviet Union's earlier economic dynamism had been an aberration. The socialist system could produce dynamic rates of growth in the early phases of industrialization when a country was blessed with ample human and natural resources. However, state socialism was ill suited to an advanced industrial economy or the task of conserving scarce resources. At the same time, its highly bureaucratized structure meant that state socialism was difficult to change in the best of circumstances. And since the politically powerful benefited from it, it was difficult to form a coalition in support of substantial change in the socialist economic system

State socialism had two basic principles. The first was that all productive property was to be owned by the state. All mines, factories, apartments, utilities, communications and transportation systems were in public hands. In almost every case, most agricultural land too was, in effect, owned by the state although in many cases it was nominally the collective property of those who worked it. The second principle of state socialism was reliance upon central planning to match resources to needs. Planning was the province of the state planning agency, and the typical planning period was five years. The state planning agency not only produced a five-year plan, but the agency updated it annually, via one-year plans throughout the five-year period. Thus, the step-by-step process of implementing the plan could be revised annually to account for shortfalls of over-fulfillment of targets. It was centralized planning above all that was supposed to overcome what communists saw as the irrationality and anarchy of capitalist production. It was the planning system that lay at the heart of state socialism's problems.

State socialism was good at mobilizing large quantities of untapped resources – both human and natural – and applying known technologies to the basic tasks of economic development. The Soviet Union was able to generate vast amounts of hydroelectric power, to explore for and exploit easily accessible oil reserves, to build a steel and chemical industry, and to establish a vast railway network. The country's vast resources and low level of development help account for the rapid rate of growth in the initial decades of state socialism there. However, even as early as the 1960s, Soviet economists were concerned about the ability of unreformed state socialist methods to generate high rates of growth in the future. Their worries were well founded. Nonetheless, the Soviet leadership was unwilling or unable to address fundamental problems with the system. These problems affected state socialist systems in a variety of different cultural environments and levels of economic development (Smith 1976: 285–319).

Misinformation

The rationality of the state-socialist model depended on the planners having accurate information about the resources actually available. By and large, this information had to be obtained from enterprises that actually controlled those resources. But reporting was rarely accurate. The greater the resources reported, the higher would be the quota placed on the enterprise. Thus, it was in the enterprise manager's interest to shade his reports, understating what he really had, at least to the degree that he could disguise his own under-reporting. This tendency was not restricted to one or two individuals; it was one of the perverse incentives embedded in the system itself. Since planners allocating quotas were aware of this, they compensated, but not in any scientific or rational way. They guessed and simply raised the quota to a level that would be unreasonable if the reports they had received had really been accurate.

Misallocation of resources

In market systems, producers' goods in high demand will rise in price, and only those able to put them to profitable and productive use will be able to buy them. Consumers ultimately have a decisive influence over production by buying or not buying certain products, based on their quality and price. Firms whose products do not sell either change them or go out of business. In short, in a market system, pricing and consumer choices send signals to producers about what to produce. But neither pricing nor consumer choice functioned under state socialism the way they do in market systems. Prices were administratively determined. Resources were allocated to firms and goods to retail outlets by administrative fiat. The ability of a retail outlet to actually sell its merchandise played no significant role in allocating resources. There were no alternative goods available to consumers besides those that were provided by the state. In a state-socialist system there was no reality check that allowed planners to determine if the prices they assigned matched the preferences of consumers, nor could they determine if their allocation of resources among firms was efficient or not. Even the use of profit as a measure of efficiency in such a system was highly artificial. Profit would be ultimately determined by the administratively set prices of raw materials and finished products. Thus, it could not serve as an effective measure of efficiency, as it does in a market system.

Bias against consumers

State socialism focused on investment since investment would build the material base for full communism. Yet, this bias in favor of investment did not promote efficiency. Steel, chemicals, transportation equipment, machine tools were churned out, whether or not they could be put to efficient use. Resources were wasted because under state socialism waste entailed few penalties for those responsible for it. There were few or no adverse consequences for managers who produced shoddy products or polluted the environment. There were few or no rewards for satisfying consumers and preserving the environment. A plant would stay in operation, whether or not the goods it produced were ultimately sold. In addition, the state socialist pricing system undervalued spare parts and repair services. As a consequence, shortages of consumer goods were endemic. Their quality was poor. And consumers were forced to take what they could get. In the Soviet Union, if a line formed in front of a shop, the standard practice for consumers was to queue up. The goods available were probably in short supply, and even if she had enough herself, the impromptu shopper could trade her purchases with neighbors for things she did need. State socialist practices were justified by the slogans of building for the future and establishing the material base for full communism. Yet, in reality investment practices were wasteful in the extreme, and penalized consumers to no real purpose.

Black markets

State socialism encouraged black markets on a variety of levels. Consumers, denied desirable products on which to spend their income, bought what they could when they could get it from sources legal and illegal. Yet, more significant to the overall inefficiencies of the system was the black market in producers' goods. Under state socialism, the primary control the planners exercised over the firm was the quota. If the firm failed to make its quota, heads would roll regardless of how legally and morally impeccable the behavior of the director and his subordinates had been. If the quota had been met, few questions would be asked. A famous incident reported in the *Moscow News* in the mid-1960s illustrates this point. The director of a collective farm had over-fulfilled his meat-production quota to the extent that it gained him awards and recognition across the entire Soviet Union. A year or two later, however, the hero-director was unable to meet the quota assigned. In fact, he failed miserably. An investigation ensued. It turned out that the man had slaughtered his breeding stock! Rarely, however, was breaking the rules so self-defeating, so foolish, and so easily discovered after the fact. More typically, managers kept excess stocks of whatever goods they could lay their hands on even though the excess was supposed to be returned to the system. Managers hoarded because they knew that their suppliers are unreliable, and the failure of a supplier to deliver parts or raw materials, did not excuse the manager's own failure to make his quota. Thus, spare stocks were critical for career success. In a pinch, the manager could swap his excess of commodities he did not need for commodities he did, even if this swap had to be multi-sided, involving three, four, or even more enterprises. All this was, of course, illegal. However, no one in the know had the incentive to report it. If the plant manager's head rolled, the head of the chief party official at the plant was likely to roll also. Planners knew the practice was common, but had little incentive to interfere since it overcame some inherent inefficiencies in the state socialist system.

Inflexibility

Perhaps the most important defect of the state socialist system was its inability to develop and adopt new technologies. Invention and innovation cannot be foreordained on the basis of rigid five-year plans. Only in a mere handful of areas, did the technology of even the most advanced state-socialist economies manage to remain on the cutting edge. More common was the attempt to acquire technology from abroad. *Reverse engineering* was a common practice in the Soviet Union. It involved purchasing a product on the open market in a foreign country, then having engineers work backward, designing a process to produce that product. Thus, the country could acquire new technology by purchasing even a single copy of a new product. Such methods, while inexpensive in the short run, tended to lead to long-term inefficiencies. If a country really wanted new technology, not simply the end product but also the means to produce it, it could acquire a *turnkey plant*. Such an acquisition was an expensive proposition, however. The new owner had to sign a contract with the company that produced the product and pay for the building of an entire plant to produce it, but in the end the new owner would have not only *a* way of producing the product but also *the* way that the original innovator itself had used. Yet, without the ability to innovate and update, the turnkey plant would quickly become outdated.

Consequences

As the Soviet Union began to run out of easily extractible resources and its rate of population growth declined, it was unable to maintain anything like the dynamic growth it had enjoyed in earlier decades. This problem was only compounded by the fact that the Soviet Union by the 1960s had already industrialized and needed to develop more sophisticated and rapidly evolving technologies. By the 1980s, the country faced the prospects of inevitable long-term decline. Other communist regimes found themselves in even more difficult straits. Lacking the natural resource base of the Soviet Union, China could not apply state socialist methods with anything like the Soviet's initial success. The state socialist model had run up against its limits. It could produce a few key commodities, such as military goods, because it paid little attention to efficiency, only to final results. But it lacked the ability to develop and apply sophisticated technologies across the board, or to satisfy the demands of middle-class consumers. As the Soviet Union faltered economically, so too did other states that followed a similar economic formula.

CASE STUDY: THE COLLAPSE OF THE SOVIET UNION

Virtually all communist regimes felt the effects of communism's legitimacy crisis and the inefficiencies of state socialism, but the history of the last decade of the Soviet Union illustrates that other factors were critical for the collapse. In the Soviet Union and European communist states, the ruling elite could not agree upon and implement an effective reform policy. Nor were they able to steel themselves sufficiently to engage in wholesale repression sufficient to crush pro-democracy movements. This failure in governmental efficacy is the key element that helps explain why communism collapsed in some places but not in others. Once consolidated, communism usually offered little scope to the opposition. Opponents had to choose between "voice" and "exit." However, trying to voice one's views within the system and move it in the direction of reform seemed a hopeless project. The mass media, as well as professional, civic, and social organizations, existed under party supervision. Even churches were closely monitored so as to curtail dissent. There were few ways to amplify one's individual voice. One of the few, a method that was used extensively in the Soviet Union, was samizdat or self-publishing – i.e., typing with carbons one's own or another's work one wished to circulate. The strategy of "exit" seemed no threat to the system either. Eventually communist regimes, as with other authoritarian governments, were willing to grant political exile to particularly troublesome and prominent dissidents. They might speak against the regime while abroad, but their effect at home would be minimal. Exile also had the effect of lessening the publicity they could attract. Once free of the danger of state oppression, the exiled dissident drew correspondingly less attention from the international media or human rights activists. Although communist states were increasingly delegitimized, the repressive apparatus in these states was in good working order.

However, the pro-democracy dissidents gained traction because the idea that both Soviet economic and political practice had to be reformed gained a following among the ruling elite. In the Soviet Union, the government itself provided the opportunity for semi-loyal or disloyal oppositions to organize, all the time thinking that it was reforming communist practice, moving communism back to its first principles, and building support for a reformed communist regime. Mikhail Gorbachev, the General Secretary of the CPSU, even forced this same role on the more reluctant of his European protégés. Communist reformers seemed genuinely perplexed when they discovered that the public at large did not share their ideals. Realists in other communist countries knew better, and did not embark on a process that would lead to democratization, putting an end to party rule.

Gorbachev and the need to reform

The Soviet Union's problems had been evident for at least a decade, but it was not until Mikhail Gorbachev became General Secretary in 1985 that the CPSU came to address them seriously. When Gorbachev was chosen as General Secretary, he was a relatively young fifty-four. His three predecessors who had died in office were decades older, and the long illnesses that ultimately brought them down were originally described as "colds." They and their senior colleagues were with considerable accuracy labeled a "gerontocracy" – a government by the old. Meanwhile, as the leadership had aged and become more set in its ways, dissatisfaction with the system had grown. While no officially recognized opposition was in view, dissent grew beneath the surface and the dissatisfied were a potential constituency to be mobilized by those seeking radical alteration in the system. Gorbachev, young and dynamic, was eager to address the problems that he believed undermined the long-term viability of the Soviet Union and communist party rule (Kotkin 2001). His efforts backfired. Their failure, though perhaps not the extent of their failure, was predictable, since Gorbachev's reform efforts ran squarely against characteristics deeply ingrained in the Soviet system. Those who would lose power and influence could be counted on to resist his reforms. They had a variety of mechanisms at their disposal.

When Gorbachev assumed office, the USSR was not facing an immediate crisis. Economic growth rates were still positive. Dissidents were not able to mount a popular mass campaign against the regime. Centrifugal tendencies among ethnic minorities were still held in check. Internationally, the pro-Soviet military alliance, the Warsaw Pact, was functioning, and the Soviets had allies in Cuba, Vietnam, Afghanistan, Angola, and Ethiopia. The Soviet Union was at the high point of its military power. In short, there was no pressing need for hasty emergency measures although serious problems were percolating beneath the surface. The economy had lost its dynamism. Rates of growth had been in long-term decline since the 1960s, and, if the pattern continued, it did not take a great deal of foresight to predict a real economic crisis within the next several decades. State socialism could not meet the challenges of rapid technological advance and the increasing cost of extracting natural resources, once the cheap and easily exploitable resources had been largely exhausted. The inability of the leadership to make significant reforms in the state socialist system had its roots in the Soviet political system. The real power structure of the USSR had assumed a form typical of late-communism. Well-established interests had representatives in the collective leadership. The collective leadership itself made most decisions by consensus. The head of the Politburo, after all, was a figure who was a first among equals according to the party rules themselves. The Brezhnev period (1964–83) had reinforced the practice of consensus building as a precondition for dramatic policy initiatives. This formula was a recipe for preserving the status quo.

Reforming the economy

Gorbachev, however, decided to break with the status quo. This meant changing the rules and incentives built into the economy. Almost immediately upon assuming office, the new general secretary began calling for economic reform. The first measures that he imposed were standard state socialist fare: reorganizing the troubled agricultural sector and imposing labor discipline. But soon economic restructuring (**perestroika**) began to take on a wider, less traditional, meaning. Gorbachev began to argue that elements of capitalism should be introduced into the Soviet Union to improve sectors that had traditionally performed poorly.

He further argued that the role of central planners should be restricted, and that aspects of the free market ought to be introduced. The general secretary also realized that successful reform would entail the shifting of economic priorities away from defense production, which consumed a disproportionate share of Soviet economic resources. During the cold war, the Soviet Union and the United States had engaged in a worldwide rivalry, each fielding huge military establishments that included strategic weapons able to destroy the other many times over. Soviet policy since the mid-1970s had supported pro-Soviet regimes in Ethiopia, Afghanistan, and Angola that consumed inordinate quantities of military materiel. Furthermore, Soviet direct engagement in the Afghan war had damaged the USSR's international prestige. Domestic reform, thus, required a change in foreign policy to make the cut in the military budget safe in terms of the country's security and prestige. As a consequence, Gorbachev undertook far-ranging negotiations with the United States to substantially reduce military forces: strategic arms, intermediate range missiles, and conventional forces in Europe.

Gorbachev's evolving political strategy

As Gorbachev's economic reforms were met with resistance from conservatives within the leadership, he was forced to try to marginalize and then remove them. Eventually, Gorbachev was compelled to seek basic changes in the political order itself, changes that undermined the system that had been in place since the time of Khrushchev. Gorbachev's first political move was to change the composition of the Politburo, Central Committee, and the so-called power ministries – defense, interior, and foreign affairs. The hardline foreign minister, Andrei Gromyko, for example, was hived off into the then largely ceremonial position of state president. Appointing new people to office was a time-honored tactic going back to Stalin and made more humane in its consequences during the post-totalitarian period. A new leader could best cement his position by surrounding himself with like-minded colleagues who owed him something. On a slightly less traditional level, Gorbachev called for openness (**glasnost**). The term and the practice were actually staples of communist practice. The public had always been encouraged to engage in the process of criticism and self-criticism, but only in strictly circumscribed ways.

The party, the party line, and high-level party and government leaders were supposed to be immune from such criticism. Only lower-level functionaries who were not adhering to the line were open to public criticism. Gorbachev's call, however, opened the floodgates of criticism of personalities, policies, and principles hitherto exempt from such attack, whether the new general secretary actually intended it or not. The genie was out of the bottle. And, regardless of his real intentions, Gorbachev found such criticism useful for undermining his colleagues who opposed his designs for radical reform. Nonetheless, opposition to his schemes continued from within the party. Especially at key union republic (regional) posts, party and government leaders were able to short-circuit the general secretary's reform efforts. Stymied by his party colleagues, Gorbachev was forced to change the political rules radically and breathe life into the governmental system known as "people's democracy."

The Soviet Union had the quintessential facade constitution. The constitution served a largely symbolic purpose. Real decisions were made behind the scenes by the party elite. The government was to implement the policy line established by the party, and the legislature was to demonstrate popular support for those policies by automatically ratifying the government's and the party's proposals. Traditionally, voting was important simply as a show of civic support for the party and as a way of educating the public about the party's program, but it did not decide policy. Elections in people's democracies were noncompetitive except in rare instances at the lowest levels. There were normally only as many candidates nominated as there were seats available in the legislature. Moreover, ballots were normally constructed in such a way that if the voter wished to vote for the authorized slate or individual, all he or she needed to do was to put the ballot in the ballot box. Voters did not need to go to the voting booth unless they cared to vote against the party-sanctioned slate or individual. Such mechanisms rarely produced any unexpected results although, in theory, a failure of a candidate to receive a majority of votes cast would require another election. In well-run communist regimes, such negative results simply did not happen. During the heyday of the Soviet system, voter turnout was high. 98–9 percent was the norm since voting was mandatory, and enterprise directors, government-office heads, and others made it their job to see that their employees voted. Since virtually every voter was a state employee or pensioner, it made no sense for any of them to fail to vote and risk retaliation. Not only was turnout high, the winning candidates regularly received similarly high percentages of the vote. Again, only incorrigible mavericks would be likely to risk retaliation by actually making use of their right to mark their ballots in secret.

Legislatures in people's democracies were as powerless as the electorate. They only met intermittently, often only for one or two weeks a year. Elected legislators were in a position similar to delegates in party congresses (see Chapter 5); they did not have much capacity to modify or reject the proposals of the leadership – in the case of the legislature, the prime minister and council of ministers. Hence, once again, effective power gravitated into the hands of the few. The country's president, the prime minister, the cabinet ministers (normally called members of the council of ministers in communist regimes), top civil servants, and military officers were all members of the party. Ordinary legislators did not need to be although their nomination is subject to party review. They had no significant policy-making role to play in any event. In sum, as elsewhere in the communist world, an interlocking directorate of party and state officials had held real power within the Soviet system. Senior members of the government, at national and sub-national levels, senior military officers, and intelligence officials were all likely to be members of the party's central committee. Sometimes the head of the party, the party's general secretary, also served as prime minister or state president. At the very highest level, members of the politburo, the top dozen or so party leaders, were normally important ministers in the government, powerful officials from the party secretariat (central bureaucracy), or key party officials at the regional level. Informal elite consensus determined policy. The actions of official legal institutions simply announced, implemented, and rallied support for that consensus.

It was this system that Gorbachev wanted to change by revising the constitution, calling competitive elections, and directing the official committees that approved candidates to ensure there were multi-candidate races. In 1989, competitive elections were held for the new Soviet legislature, the Congress of People's Deputies. Gorbachev himself was chosen as state president, an office now endowed with real power. Many party officials suffered defeat, yielding a more representative legislature than the old Supreme Soviet, the former Soviet legislature, had been. That same year, Gorbachev proposed changes in party rules that would restrict the ability of long-term incumbents in republic party leadership posts to retain their offices. Further, he wished to open the party up, drawing in new members and fresh blood. Yet, the reform of the party faltered and failed to dislodge the old guard, even though changes to the state constitution were largely successful.

Consequences

Gorbachev-era reforms promoted economic dislocations and political disintegration. Planners and ministries resisted their impending loss of power. When new rules freed substantial amounts of production from quotas, planners imposed mandatory contracts in their place. Collective enterprises that had been encouraged to run restaurants and other consumer-oriented services were denied licenses and supplies to carry on their business. Firms that earned hard currency by sales abroad found their earnings forcibly transferred into ruble accounts, preventing them from buying on the international market in return. As one wag put it, Gorbachev's policy of a gradual transfer to capitalism was like a gradual transfer from left-side-of-the-road driving to right-side driving by having half of the drivers change their practices while the other half did not. The results were similar. Soviet economic production began to fall precipitously. Such a fall was, perhaps, to be expected given the difficult nature of the transition the country was attempting, but the Soviet Union's economy never recovered. Russia and most of the USSR's successor states were not able to record positive growth even a decade after the transition first began.

During the era of democratization, the Soviet Union itself began to unravel. The USSR was nominally a federal system even allowing union republics, of which there were fifteen in 1989, the putative right to secede. The nominal federalism of the constitution, however, was always counteracted by the centralization of party rule. Federalism had allowed for certain concessions to ethnic groups that were in the majority in their areas. The largest and most significant of these were those of the fifteen union republics. Education, broadcasting, publishing, and government business could be carried on in the predominant national language as well as Russian. And the union republic bore the name of the majority nationality: Russian, Ukrainian, Uzbek, Lithuanian, etc. Federalism also provided a power base for regional leaders. The Soviet-era slogan, "national in form, socialist in content," summed up the nature of the compromise. Still, many national groups chaffed under the strictures imposed by the USSR. Most notable were the Baltic republics of Latvia, Estonia, and Lithuania, which had been independent from the collapse of the tsarist empire until they were forcibly incorporated into the Soviet Union in 1940, and Armenia and Georgia in the Caucasus.

The loss of the regime's legitimacy and Gorbachev's policy of democratization allowed ethnic nationalists to come to the fore. They did so in a number of republics, earliest and most persistently in Lithuania.

Lithuanian nationalists, supported by the local communist party, asserted their constitutional right to secession and threatened to secede on their own if they were denied permission by the Soviet Union to do so.

By 1990 ethnic nationalists had gained strength in other union republics as well. Gorbachev temporized, arguing that, though there is a constitutional right to secede, that right had to be implemented via appropriate legislation. The legislation was not forthcoming, but for the remainder of the USSR's existence, the promised new union treaty remained a festering and divisive issue.

Throughout 1991 the multiple crises continued to deepen until hardliners took Gorbachev prisoner while he was on vacation in the Crimea on August 19. The coup was amateurish from start to finish and quickly collapsed. What remained of the moral authority of the CPSU quickly disintegrated, and Gorbachev himself banned the organization. The abortive coup sounded the death knell of the Soviet Union. Nationalist politicians and simple opportunists seized the opportunity to create an independent state power base for themselves in the union republics. The Baltic states unilaterally seceded followed by the remainder of the other fifteen republics, including the Russian Republic, governed by the popularly elected Boris Yeltsin (see Map 10.2). In December 1991, a president without a country, Mikhail Gorbachev left the Kremlin. His attempt to reform the system started a democratization process he could not manage.

Plate 10.1 Continuity or change? A traditionally styled set of Matriochka nesting dolls shows key Russian leaders over the past centuries. From largest to smallest: Yeltsin, Gorbachev, Brezhnev, Khrushchev, Stalin, Lenin, Nicholas II, Catherine the Great, Peter the Great, and Ivan the Terrible.

Even the leaders of the failed August 1991 coup who had tried to turn the clock back had not proclaimed that their aim was to save socialism or

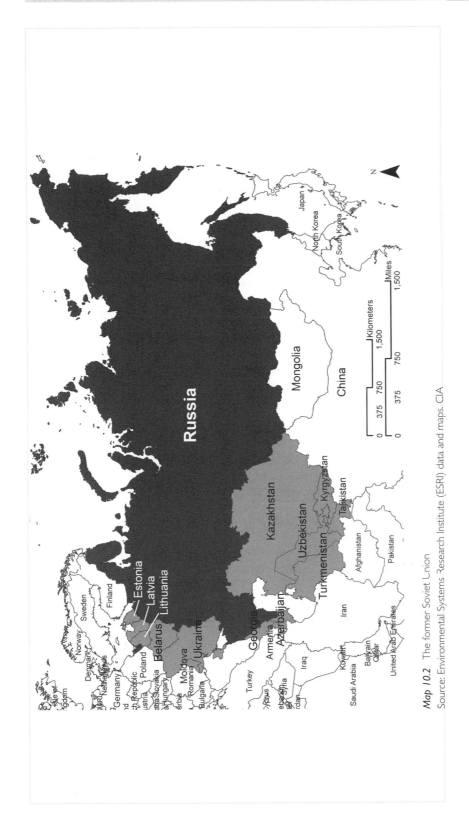

Map 10.2 The former Soviet Union

Source: Environmental Systems Research Institute (ESRI) data and maps. CIA

defend communist principles. Rather, they said that they had seized power to save the country – to preserve the nation. It was an appeal to nationalism that seemed to echo Stalin's appeals during the Second World War for Russians and the Russian Orthodox Church to resist German occupation. But in 1991 even that appeal did not work. The country was already fragmenting along ethnic lines. In December 1991, the Soviet Union officially came to an end. Fifteen separate sovereign states emerged. Although the various regimes that emerged used a variety of means to try and legitimize themselves, none attempted a straightforward appeal to Marxism–Leninism. That ship had already sailed.

Democratization in the Soviet bloc

European communist regimes outside the Soviet Union were initially much more subject to pressures for democratization than the USSR had been. Central European communists governed societies that had had previous experience with democratic government, however brief and flawed. So too had the Soviet Baltic republics of Latvia, Estonia, and Lithuania. Populations there not only had democratic but also nationalist aspirations since most of these regimes had been imposed with the help of the Soviet Army at the end of the Second World War. Many communist governments there were eager for reform long before the third-wave democratization began. Poland and Hungary had seen reform communists come to power in the 1950s. But these moves had been reversed. Czechoslovakia too had seen reform communists deposed by a Soviet invasion in 1968. And during the 1980s Central European communist regimes had experimented with reform even before Gorbachev became general secretary of the CPSU. In fact, state contracts with collective entities especially in the area of consumer services were pioneered there. Poland's Solidarity movement, composed of workers, intellectuals, and churchmen, had engaged in on-and-off confrontation and negotiations with the martial law government.

Formerly, hardline communists in Central Europe could rely on the USSR to block reform. This automatic Soviet support had evaporated by 1989, when a serious crisis developed in Communist East Germany – the German Democratic Republic (GDR). Hungary's opening of its border with Austria allowed East Germans to follow an exit strategy in massive numbers. Citizens of the GDR had long sought escape to the German Federal Republic (FRG) or West Germany, which granted automatic citizenship to anyone of German ethnicity regardless of prior citizenship.

In the early 1960s, a crisis had been averted when the Berlin Wall was hastily erected blocking what had been, until then, a primary escape route for East Germans seeking to flee to the West. The opening of the Austro-Hungarian border by the reformist communist regime in Hungary nearly three decades later allowed East Germans, who could travel freely through the communist bloc, to travel to Hungary, then to noncommunist Austria, and from there to West Germany. Thus, the German communist regime faced a serious crisis on the fortieth anniversary of its founding. Instead of following the policies of his predecessors, Gorbachev, the liberalizer, pressured the hardline GDR government to reform. The announcement by the GDR government that it was going to liberalize actually made the situation worse. Popular protests quickly got out of hand, and the government lacked the will and ability to stop them. Protesters tore down the Berlin Wall and with it both the symbol and the reality of communist power. The Czechs and other central Europeans needed little further encouragement. Popular protests throughout the bloc intensified. By the end of the year, communism in Central Europe had collapsed.

The defection of the Soviet Union had deprived bloc hardliners of critical support. The communist leadership could not unite on a policy of repression. With no meaningful threat of repression to brandish against the opposition, direct mass action, either actual or threatened, by pro-democracy movements carried the day. Radical democrats attained something close to their maximum objectives. Only Poland followed a truly pacted transition primarily because its agreement had been struck before communist rule had begun unraveling elsewhere in the bloc. But even there, the party was swept from power despite the advantages the procommunist gerrymandering of the Polish Senate had given them in the accords. Communist rulers in Cuba and Asia could only watch aghast and profit from the lessons learned from their counterparts' mistakes.

Problems of democratic consolidation

The exit of communists from power in Europe did not of itself ensure the development of a secure democracy. In fact, results were quite mixed (see Map 10.1). Today some Central European states are barely distinguishable from the long-time counterparts further west, except that they are usually considerably poorer on a per capita basis. In fact, in 2004 Poland, Hungary, the Czech Republic, Slovakia, Slovenia, Latvia, Estonia, and Lithuanian were admitted into the democratic rich-man's club – the European Union (EU). Other states such as Albania, most of the now independent states that once comprised Yugoslavia, and most states of the former Soviet Union have not fared so well. In many, former communists have assumed a nationalist mantle and continue to run their now-independent countries in a highly authoritarian fashion. The five countries of what was once Soviet Central Asia fall into this class. Some have energy resources and their proximity to the Middle East and Afghanistan makes them key allies in the US-led struggle against terrorism. This has induced the United States to wink at violations of human rights that it would have otherwise severely criticized. With little external pressure for change and the internal opposition repressed, peaceful democratic reform does not seem to be on the horizon. The states of the Balkans and the Caucasus region of the former Soviet Union are a mixed bag. In some, largely unreformed ex-communists are firmly in control. In others, democratic reformers contend with a range of ex-communists for control of the government and the advancement of democratic reform. Only one, the ex-Yugoslav Republic of Slovenia, has advanced to the status of a consolidated democracy. For some of these countries, the lack of oil and gas resources may be a blessing in disguise. So too may be the absence of an Islamist terrorist potential since the United States and the West are less likely to waive their principles and support authoritarians simply for geo-strategic reasons.

In post-communist states that have taken an authoritarian path, ex-communists have had a variety of advantages over the democratic opposition. Because ex-communists inherited a strong political organization – although almost universally the communist party was renamed – they had an advantage over their opponents after the regime transition occurred. And they were often able to dominate politics after communism officially ended. When people had no direct experience of organizing public affairs in a democratic fashion, undemocratic practices often became the norm. Ex-communists used nationalism to appeal to deeply held prejudices against minorities and rally support. In more traditional societies, leaders relied on members of their clan and personal alliances to rise to positions of leadership. In some states, new leaders were often unreformed or barely reformed ex-communists. It was not a matter of ideology. Marxism–Leninism quickly lost most of its elite and mass allegiance. Rather, these ex-communists were unconcerned about institutionalizing the rule of law and democratic norms of governance because putting these principles into practice would have limited their personal power. Communist regimes systematically manipulated the courts. In high profile and politically sensitive trials, courts followed the wishes of the ruling elite. In this tradition, post-communist states often come to practice "rule by law" rather than the "rule of law."

Governments use the law and the courts as a means of persecuting opponents, applying harsh procedures and penalties selectively. Friends of the government can expect impunity; its enemies can expect the full weight of the law to be used against them.

Civil society too suffers under severe handicaps. Civil society must be healthy if democratic governments are to really respond to the public's true wishes. However, communist rule either subverted institutions and practices useful for democracy or actually stymied their development in the first place. Communism often created suspicion and distrust, and undermined the foundations for the creation of voluntary associations. Under communism the regime had made it its business to demobilize society and destroy the groups that composed it. In their place, the party had built a network of "transmission belts" – that is, organizations similar to true civil society organizations that would echo the party line and monitor any potentially dissident behavior. Unions and professional associations were meant to advance the party line. For the citizen the state was often the enemy, and these nominally independent private groups were simply instrumentalities of the state.

In those post-communist states that followed an authoritarian pattern, political parties became vehicles for political strongmen. Sometimes, as was the case with Boris Yeltsin in Russia, the chief executive tried to place himself above party. In regimes that remain communist, little political reform has taken place at all. Leaders seemed to fear that even a partial political liberalization could quickly open a Pandora's box of problems. In regimes of this sort, even those that permitted opposition parties to exist, these parties were often weak to begin with, composed of a few activists with virtually no mass base. Often politics was reduced to a hunt for patronage and privilege. The ability of parties and politicians to represent their constituents even when elections take place is limited when partisan politics is reduced to place-seeking and providing personal favors for constituents.

Authoritarian oriented post-communist regimes have been particularly resistant to applying internationally accepted standards or accepting international aid and supervision to assure fair and free elections. Free and fair elections involve two basic sets of criteria: those dealing with political competition, and those that have to do with the process of voting and the tabulation of votes. Democratic elections must guarantee the right of the citizen to vote; there must be no fraudulent votes; votes themselves must be honestly counted; and the winners must be allowed to assume office. These requirements are largely technical in nature and deal with voting itself. They require the proper registration and identification of voters, the security of balloting procedures, the absence of intimidation and fraud at polling stations, and an accurate mechanism for tabulating votes. Outside technical assistance is often useful when states attempt their first free election. Outside monitors are also helpful. Ultimately, however, poll-watching and technical supervision must come from local sources if democracy is to be consolidated. The basic competitiveness and openness of the process is a critical, and often subtle, requirement. To meet this criterion, election campaigns must give candidates and parties a decent chance to get their message to the public. Barriers to the formation of political parties and the placing of candidates on the ballot must be aimed at facilitating the people's choice among intelligible alternatives. Candidates and parties must have access to the mass media. The governing party must not use its position to disadvantage its opponents in such a way as would undermine the evenhandedness of the process. In regimes with authoritarian proclivities, these standards have been more honored in the breach than the observance.

The mass media are one of the key elements of modern society. In democratic societies, the media must be free from the effective control of a single cohesive political elite. It must foster diversity of views to assure that the public has the chance to obtain the information it requires to make an informed choice about public affairs. It must stimulate discussion on topics other than those of the government's choosing. It must serve as a conduit for organizing and mobilizing the public. These tasks are not easily carried out in any society. And it is often extremely difficult in the political and economic environment that follows the fall of communism. The government necessarily plays a role in regulating the media. It taxes them. It assigns broadcast frequencies. It sometimes owns newspapers or broadcast companies. In some cases, it sells newsprint or authorizes its importation. It advertises. It issues press releases. Its courts try cases concerning libel. It regulates access to secret information. Any of these normal functions can be abused. Communist regimes, in fact, made it their business to abuse them since control of the media is critical to the maintenance of the regime. Pitfalls abound. Media may fall into the hands of wealthy "oligarchs" willing to sell their support to the ruling political elite for economic and political favors. The government may intimidate the opposition press. Even freelance gangsters, operating independently of any official instigation, can assassinate or threaten journalists and editors, silencing them directly and intimidating others.

In sum, democratization in the post-communist world is uneven and a work in progress. Countries that have been historically oriented toward the West and that have had experience with democracy in the past have made considerable progress in consolidating democracy. Those with the less fortunate historical legacy of a long period of communist rule or no real democratic experience have often become mired in authoritarian abuses of power.

Economic reform in post-communist states

The International Monetary fund (IMF), the European Bank for Reconstruction and Development (EBRD), and many governments have encouraged post-communist states to develop capitalist market economies. Increasingly, countries and multilateral organizations are discovering that the creation of properly functioning economic markets is no easy matter. It is one thing to deregulate and liberalize; it may be quite another to create the organizational infrastructure that makes modern capitalist economies work comprehensively. Post-communist states have struggled with the problem of creating the institutions that support markets, but other developing economies have run up against similar difficulties. These market-supporting institutions are easy to describe, but often hard to establish.

Private property

Privatizing has become one of the primary demands of economic reformers in formerly state-socialist (communist) economies as well as in many countries that had formerly followed a policy of state-led growth. Even where private ownership is the general principle underlying a country's economic model, equitable privatization of state firms that provides the state with immediate revenue, establishes the basis for effective competition and/or regulation, and does not shortchange the public is difficult. In post-communist states, the problem is doubly difficult because there is no functioning example close at hand of how stockholders, managers, labor, and the government are supposed to cooperate.

The problems besetting privatization in post-communist states are various. First of all, capitalism assumes a certain dispersion of economic power. Unless firms compete with one another, a true market cannot exist. Second, state ownership, as practiced under state socialism, led to huge inefficiencies. Managers (the *nomenklatura*) were patronage appointees of the communist party. They did not know how to negotiate contracts, market desirable products, or secure parts and raw materials from the least expensive sources. Their skills were political and bureaucratic: meeting quotas and securing additional aid as necessary. Removing such managers by putting production facilities in private hands seemed a necessary step for establishing capitalism. However, privatization – the sale of state assets to private individuals or firms – was beset by a number of difficulties. Privatization has often been unpopular both with politicians and the public, sometimes for very good reasons. In many cases, as with farmland in Russia, the process of privatization has hardly started. In other cases, privatization did occur, but corruption and insider deals were rampant. Either the old *nomenklatura* took over ownership of the firm by issuing stock and keeping most of it themselves, or privatization was a sweetheart deal between the government and its well-connected cronies. In either case, the efficiencies expected from private ownership often did not emerge. Some key institutions that allow modern capitalism to work efficiently were absent or dysfunctional in post-communist states.

The stock market

Most large-scale capitalist enterprises today are publicly held – i.e., owned by a large group of shareholders whose shares can be easily traded. Such indirect ownership serves a variety of functions. It allows stockholders to invest in companies without having to take personal responsibility for managing them or even selecting their management. It allows firms themselves to raise new capital by issuing new stock. As a result, it promotes the efficient organization of the economy since efficient firms and wise investors are rewarded while others languish or even fail. But these benefits cannot be obtained unless stock can be bought and sold knowledgeably and shareholders' rights are protected. These, in turn, require a transparent system for keeping firms' accounts, regulation of stock markets to assure fairness, and judicial mechanisms to enforce shareholders' rights. In modern capitalist economies, these practices have evolved over time. They can be adapted by new capitalist states if there is the political will to do so. However, their implementation requires an adequate code of corporate law as well as consistent oversight by legislatures, executives, and regulatory agencies. Communist states and post-communist states often lack the political will to provide such consistent implementation.

Banks

Banks exist in a wide variety of economic systems. They existed under state socialism. But the role of banks under state socialism was decidedly different from that of capitalist banks. Under state socialism credit was allocated according to the five-year and one-year plans. Banks did not

undertake an independent assessment of the financial risk entailed in
lending money to customers, nor could they set interest rates that take
risk into account. They simply functioned as one more cog in a
centrally directed economic machine. Under capitalism banks are the
intermediaries between savers and borrowers. They attract capital by
paying savers a desirable rate of interest. And they allocate capital
among those who want it, charging interest in return. They weigh the
risks of a loan against the returns to be expected from it. Successful
banks are successful because they carry out these functions well.
If a bank, like any other enterprise, loses money consistently, it will fail.
Unlike bankers under state socialism, capitalist bankers actually make
investment decisions. Capitalist banking presumes both a degree of
independence for banks, as well as oversight of banks by state regulatory
institutions. If banks are not basically free to choose their borrowers, loans
become political decisions made on behalf of the politically well
connected instead of economic decisions meant to yield a profit and
promote overall economic efficiency. Yet, independence goes
hand-in-hand with a certain degree of state supervision. The state sets
reserve requirements, insures savings, and prevents banks from engaging
in insider loans and undertaking undue risk. Banks function efficiently in
the proper sort of regulatory environment. Both bankers and regulators
need to be properly trained. In many post-communist states, bankers have
been unable to properly assess risks, and regulators have been unable to
properly supervise banks. This has led to inefficiencies. In other cases, the
results have been much worse. Savings programs and investments sold to
the public have, at times, been thinly disguised pyramid schemes rather
than real investment opportunities. Some banks, as parts of large
conglomerates, have provided so-called *"nomenklatura* capitalists" and
other insiders with a vehicle for stripping assets from their companies and
transferring them out of the country. State socialist banks must have their
entire ethos transformed, if they are to function efficiently within a
market economy.

Results of economic liberalization in socialist states

The attempt to move from state socialism to capitalism has followed a
variety of routes. The fall of communism in Europe presented the new
regimes with a difficult choice: rapid liberalization and quick change to
capitalism, which would maximize the short-term dislocation and pain; or
gradual transition, promising less pain, but also less gain until well into
the future. A number of Central European states followed the first, the
"big bang," approach, privatizing as quickly as possible and dismantling

most of the controls and cross-subsidies typical of the state socialist system. Other countries took a more limited approach, some almost avoiding reform entirely. According to World Bank studies, those economies that reformed fastest have recovered quickest from the shock of transition. Polish growth rates turned positive in 1992. Slovenia's and Romania's in 1993. The Czech Republic's and Hungary's became positive in 1993. And by 1994, the Baltic states, Moldova, and Slovakia had joined those that had turned the corner. The dual economies (partly state socialist, partly private) of the PRC and Vietnam continued to grow after partial liberalization. The PRC's growth rate for more than two decades has been one of the highest in the world (World Bank 1996: 172, *passim*). Russia and much of the former Soviet Union continued to founder economically until the rapid rise of oil and natural resources prices in the past several years. In summary, the introduction of capitalism and the market has had mixed results. For some Central European states and the former Soviet Union, weakness in political reform has matched weakness in economic reform.

CASE STUDY: THE PEOPLE'S REPUBLIC OF CHINA

The People's Republic of China (PRC) has been the most successful communist regime since the collapse of European communist rule more than a decade and a half ago. Faced with economic and political difficulties greater than those of the Soviet Union or its European satellites, the PRC has been able not only to survive but also to prosper. In addition, it has been able to retain the key elements of the old political system with minimal political liberalization and only vestigial democratization. While the legitimacy of Marxism–Leninism has deflated, the communist party has, nonetheless, managed to retain political control by incorporating new elements into the old ruling elite and privileged sectors of society. In short, it resolved its state effectiveness problem and built a new pro-regime coalition capable of making efficacious decisions. In its new iteration, it has relied on nationalism as much as communism to provide an ideological foundation for the regime's legitimacy. Most other communist survivors have adapted elements of Chinese policy into their own survival strategies. Reform in the PRC began in 1978, seven years before Gorbachev's appointment as General Secretary of the CPSU, with the rise to power of Deng Xiaoping, an official of the revolutionary generation. Deng was, in effect, China's anti-Gorbachev, a leader who would transform the system without destroying it. Deng had the delicate task of revitalizing the Chinese economy while maintaining the dominant position of the Chinese Communist Party (CCP). He succeeded.

Deng Xiaoping consolidates his position

Even before Deng could begin serious economic and political reforms, he had to establish his own authority to prepare the way for substantial policy change (Pye 1992: 328–68). At the same time he had to pay deference to the memory of his late predecessor and founder of the People's Republic, Mao Zedong. As a national hero, Mao could not be directly attacked. Yet, Deng had been purged several times under Mao, and his policies flew in the face of what Mao had been trying to accomplish. Deng addressed the task of asserting his authority on a number of levels. The first was to shift the blame for Mao's radicalism and the country's economic failings to the so-called "Gang of Four," headed by Mao's widow, Chiang Ching. The four had been leading figures during the Cultural Revolution of the 1960s, a period of turmoil during which Deng himself had been purged. Deng charged them with being responsible for much of the violence and injustice of the era, and they were eventually tried and imprisoned. Yet, Mao Zedong, in whose name the Cultural Revolution had been initiated, was only subject to mild criticism. Mao's theories were correct, and Mao himself was upright, the party line of Deng's era went. Although Mao occasionally did err, the true blame belonged primarily to others who committed serious crimes in his name.

Reforming the economy

Deng Xiaoping's economic program was one of gradual experimentation that took the country in an increasingly state-capitalist direction. Deng described the process as feeling for the steppingstones while wading across a river. In the late 1970s, he began his economic reforms by announcing goals apparently compatible with orthodox state-socialist principles. His "four modernizations" – agriculture, industry, science and technology, the military – were departures from the version of socialism espoused by Mao Zedong. Mao had promoted a policy of national self-reliance, limiting foreign trade, eschewing foreign investment, and using locally developed technologies and techniques almost exclusively. Deng radically altered this focus, seeking foreign trade and access to foreign technology. In response, foreign businessmen, like generations of their predecessors before them, once again saw China as a huge untapped market and flooded into the country to make their proposals.

Yet, industry was not the first priority for modernization. That honor fell to agriculture, and it was there that Deng Xiaoping took his most radical steps in the direction of reform. Communes, huge collective farms, had been the primary organizations in the Chinese countryside. And something like 80 percent of the Chinese population was rural. The communes were generally inefficient and unpopular. Guided by the principle of the "iron rice bowl," everyone received an equal share of what the commune produced. Though nominally a collective enterprise controlled by the workers, like collective farms in the USSR and elsewhere in the communist world, communes were actually under party and government control. The state set prices and production targets. All produce sold was sold to the state. Cadres – officials responsible to the government and party – managed the communes. And with no institutional check, these cadres often abused their power. The peasants, always desiring to own land and manage their own affairs, were denied the right to do either. Deng's changes in collective agriculture began cautiously enough. Various reforms allowed separate work groups to be rewarded according to how well they carried out their tasks, instead of receiving equal rewards along with everyone else regardless of performance. Under the "household responsibility system," peasants were given the opportunity to opt out of their normal arrangement with the commune to specialize in a particular service, such as transportation, that the collective required. Their new relationship would be covered by a contract. Any profit from the activity would accrue to the peasant. In addition, the prices of agricultural inputs and agricultural products sold to the state were changed in the peasants' favor. By the end of the 1980s, the commune itself had been abolished along with its associated production brigades. The commune was replaced by the township; the brigade by the village. And households held long-term leases on land. Only basic grains were covered by mandatory state contracts. Agricultural production boomed.

By the end of the 1980s, industry too had gone beyond the rather timid reforms of the early years of Deng's rule. The government permitted small privately owned or collectively owned enterprises. In addition, the government established certain Special Economic Zones (SEZs) in eastern China. Numbering four in 1979, these zones expanded to fourteen by the early 1990s. The regulations governing SEZs permitted enterprises that were jointly owned by foreign and state firms. These enterprises became one of the engines of the PRC's economic growth. Another important engine of growth was the quasi-public sector, consisting of firms owned by provincial and municipal governments. During the Deng years, many of these had been able to break the shackles of the state plan. They were managed more like private companies than state-socialist firms. They bought and sold, hired and fired, on the basis of profit. The one major sector of the economy that continued to be managed along state-socialist lines, the official state sector, remained a drag on Chinese economic progress and a potential time bomb that was difficult to defuse.

Chinese economic progress since the Deng era has been substantial, but the economic system is still in flux and harbors substantial trouble spots (see Bergsten *et al.* 2006). The state portion of the dual economy in many cases provides subsidized inputs to well-connected quasi-public firms and private enterprises. In addition, it provides what is, in effect, social insurance to a large portion of the population. The PRC is without any real national healthcare, unemployment compensation, housing assistance, or pension system. As is the usual case under state socialism, firms provide these services to their employees. Failing state firms have been caught in a bind. If they are to become profitable, state firms must cut their costs. They cannot compete with private and quasi-public firms if they lack the managerial flexibility those firms have and are forced to bear costs that those other firms do not.

From a macroeconomic perspective, the bankruptcy of enterprises whose reformation looks hopeless, mass firings in others, and the abandonment of the state firms' welfare functions make eminent sense. However, from the point of view of social policy, it would be a disaster, putting hundreds of millions of people literally out on the street with no reasonable hope of employment or support. But the longer radical reform of the state sector is delayed, the greater will be the drain on state finances and the greater the risk of a collapse of the financial system that supports state firms. Other problems also exist. Business success in China often depends on connections. The rule of law is weak. The ability to influence regulators, obtain inputs at knockdown prices, and secure the necessary permissions are more important than a mastery of existing laws and regulations. This situation has increased opportunities for official corruption since well-connected party and government officials, and their sons and daughters, are the necessary gatekeepers to decision-makers. Western businessmen especially have complained, but those who know how to work the system have been able to survive and prosper. The prevalence of corruption, however, can lead to an increase in popular cynicism. The growing inequality of the distribution of wealth has only added to the process.

In the rural sector, too, all is not well. Although the condition of China's rural population has improved since reforms began, the peasantry still suffers from arbitrary impositions made by those in authority. The party has been careful to allow only limited political liberalization. By the end of the 1990s, village leaders were elected, but elections had not been extended to any higher level. Moreover, the fairness and freedom of the process in these local elections have been subject to question. Cadres still are able to exercise considerable influence. Thus, while the mandatory contracts peasants are forced to sign over only a limited share of what they produce, taxes and fees have often increased. Appointed officials, unaccountable to the people whom they are supposed to serve, are the ones who impose these extra charges. In addition, Chinese agriculture also remains inefficient by global standards. However, the consolidation of plots would require outright ownership of land, instead of long-term leases, and the resulting consolidations would probably displace additional people to the cities.

China's dual economy (partly state owned, partly private) is at least partly insulated from foreign economic shocks. It weathered the financial crisis that struck much of Southeast Asia and Korea in 1997 and 1998. China's currency, the yuan, is not freely exchangeable on international markets. The country has massive reserves of foreign currency. Money is not free to enter and leave the country as its holders wish. Foreigners can legally own only a limited amount of stock in Chinese enterprises. As the 1997–8 crisis hit, the PRC's authorities congratulated themselves for the durability of their less-than-up-to-date financial system. Yet, over the years this too has begun to change as China has begun to open its financial markets.

Maintaining the rule of the party

Although the PRC is officially a state based on Marxism–Leninism and Mao Zedong thought, these ideologies can no longer provide a real moral foundation for the regime. Instead, the country's economic and scientific achievements, and Chinese nationalism, partially fill the psychological void. But national pride alone cannot adequately ground the rule of the party. Formal and informal institutional arrangements have been the key to securing party rule. The party has experimented with constitutional changes, but without any major effect. Local officials have often subverted elections, and the promised reforms have stagnated. Although China's national legislature, the National People's Congress, has shown some independence, by the turn of the twenty-first century, it was not up to the task the PRC's written constitution assigns it.

The key to the regime's stability lies outside the parameters of its official written constitution. The leadership of the Communist Party of China (PCC) has taken steps to assure that the sort of challenge to party rule that developed in the Soviet Union during the Gorbachev years will not develop in China. The party has reinforced the principle of collective leadership, and it has introduced a new feature, the orderly and voluntary retirement of senior officials. Retirees are replaced by their junior protégés while, at the same time, the seniors often monitor and continue to mentor them. Like all Communist states, the PRC possesses no formal definitive way of resolving disputes within the leadership. Yet the transfer of power from Deng to Jiang Zemin was peaceful and orderly. The party successfully managed what could have become a succession crisis as Deng Xiaoping's health waned. The cohesion of the collective leadership of the party has remained fairly high. The transfer of power from Jiang's generation to the next in 2002 went according to plan in both the state and party (*Journal of Democracy* 2003: 5–81). Nothing remotely approximating the leadership struggles of the Cultural Revolution of the 1960s (see Chapter 5) with its massive purges and public disorder has appeared on the horizon.

Party membership remains desirable for the young, not because of the party's moral authority but because party connections provide a ready avenue for personal advancement. Thus, in an odd twist, careerism has been transformed from a vice to a virtue. By 2002, party membership was open to capitalists! And the party officially changed its rules in accordance with the "three represents." Instead of representing just the proletariat and the peasantry, the party now speaks for the "most advanced productivity and culture in China as well as the fundamental interests of the maximal majority of the Chinese people" (*China View* 2003). The organs of repression remain under full party control. And there is no toleration of effective dissent. Ethnic nationalism is beyond the pale. The PRC is a unitary state, and the constitution, even in theory, provides no right of secession. Minorities who dominate the populations of Tibet and western China have been suppressed. There is no policy of *glasnost* or openness. Dissidents are kept within strict limits.

The Tiananmen crisis in 1989, when hundreds of thousands gathered in Beijing's main square demanding democracy, led to a crackdown. The then party chairman and a moderate, Zhao Ziyang, who had argued for dialogue, was purged. He had been handpicked by Deng Xiaoping himself, but even Deng turned against him. In 1999, as the fiftieth anniversary of the PRC's founding and the tenth anniversary of Tiananmen approached, authorities were meticulous in rounding up dissidents, in an apparent

attempt to forestall any problems. The party has been as certain as it can that no challengers can mobilize a mass base. Communications (including the Internet) are monitored, censored, and blocked. No independent organization that might oppose the party is allowed to mature.
Only regime-controlled labor unions are permitted. Independent Protestant churches, the Catholic church affiliated with Rome, and the Fulan Gong, a quasi-religious grouping, have been persecuted. Exile and imprisonment have been meted out liberally to dissidents. In short, the CCP retains its political dominance, but it is not the same organization that won a long and bitter revolutionary war in 1949. Its exclusivity remains, but its moral authority and ideological fervor have dissipated. It is no longer the party of peasants, workers, and guerrilla fighters. It is the party of state functionaries and the well connected. Ideological commitment is a thing of the past.

Summary

Economic reform began in the PRC almost a decade before it started in the Soviet Union. Compared to the Soviet Union, China's partial economic liberalization plus its political orthodoxy has been a stunning success.
The PRC's rate of economic growth in Gross National Product (GNP) per capita was 7.8 percent, from the mid-1980s to the mid-1990s. (Since then the averages have been even higher.) This was the very period during which the Soviet Union and its successor states were suffering precipitous declines in GNP. Although the regime did face one serious political challenge during the Tiananmen Square protests of 1989, it managed to survive with its political power intact. In essence, it was the PRC that served as the test bed for similar policies adopted by other surviving communist regimes. The stability of the PRC rests on three pillars: the regime's economic success, repression, and the ability of the party to serve all major elite interests. Neither party leaders, nor business people, nor increasingly technocratic officials see radical change as being in their interest. Foreign governments and multinational corporations (MNCs) see China as an attractive market and a manufacturing center from which to export goods back to their home countries. Unlike the Soviet Union and its European allies, China has largely managed to successfully blunt foreign governmental pressure to liberalize. The policy of partial economic liberalization coupled with strict political control has had a stabilizing effect on the PRC.
The Chinese Communist Party never allowed the reform process to get out of hand. Economic reforms were incremental although cumulatively they have altered the shape of the Chinese economy significantly and

Plate 10.2 China under construction. Shenzhen, China in 2004. Photo by Rüdiger Meier.

produced world-class rates of economic growth. The party was even more cautious about political reform than it was about economic reform. It never allowed mass movements the political space to grow in strength and challenge the regime effectively. The party leadership was remarkably unified, and when fissures did emerge, the hardliners purged the accommodationists to retain control of the reform process. The process of reform added to rather than challenged hitherto privileged sectors. The greatly enlarged economy allowed more individuals to share in its benefits. Chinese cadres (the equivalent to Soviet *apparatchiks* and *nomenklatura*) did not lose power or influence. Instead, members of a new business and professional class with good connections to the political establishment gained significant economic benefits. Still, the proletariat and peasantry, in whose name the revolution took place in the first place, have largely been left out. Rural and urban unemployment remain a problem. The restructuring of state firms has meant more and more pensioners have lost support. The rule of law, seen as attractive for business, has been far from fully implemented, and local cadres are still able to wield abusive power over the population. Authorities normally quash popular protests rather than addressing the underlying complaints. Thus, China continues to be stable not because it has arrived at a new consensus about the moral basis of the government, but because the party has strengthened its hand economically and politically and has been careful to deal with popular unrest promptly and decisively.

"Reform" in other non-European communist states

During their heyday communist parties could rely on their ideology to provide moral authority and state socialism to provide both economic resources as well as methods of social control. The collapse of the Soviet Union constituted a watershed in the history of all communist states. It made clear that, to survive, these states would have to contend with the ideological deflation of Marxism–Leninism and the lack of economic efficiency of state socialism. In addition, each has had to survive in its own particular national and international environment.

The dissolution of the Soviet Union marked a clear end to that earlier epoch. Once the Soviet communist party had begun to liberalize, pressure for full democratization was not far behind. By liberalizing politically, the USSR and European communist states had opened the floodgates of opposition. Asian communist leaders and the communist rulers of Cuba had ample opportunity to learn from the experiences of the Soviet and Central European comrades. They have avoided the pitfalls that destroyed their European counterparts, and they have strictly limited political liberalization and democratization. Just as China has, they have been forced to rely increasingly on nationalism to fill the ideological void left by the communist ideology's loss of credibility. Just as China has, they have had to experiment with economic policy. Ill-considered or too rapid economic reform could lead to an economic or political breakdown. Among surviving communist regimes, the leading role of the party remains substantially unchanged. At the same time, since the survivors faced economic problems that beset all state socialist systems, they decided to carefully modify economic policies gradually. They have allowed only limited economic liberalization and controlled trade with the outside world in such a way as to maximize economic growth. In short, other surviving communist regimes have followed a set of policies similar to those of the PRC, but none with the degree of success or the range of innovation that has been typical of China. Although none has had the economic attraction for foreigners that China has had, each has recognized the need for foreign technology and investment.

The least innovative survivor has been North Korea, which retained a totalitarian political system and was extremely cautious in its economic openings. Yet, even the reclusive North Koreans have cautiously expanded their economic ties with South Korea. The South, while generally welcoming the prospect of unification, is perfectly willing to see any culmination of the process delayed indefinitely. The cost of national unification of communist East Germany with West Germany has been an object lesson for the South Koreans. The economic gap between the communist and capitalist parts of Germany was much smaller than the corresponding gap between the two Koreas, and the population of the communist half much smaller than the capitalist. Still, the attempt to fully integrate the two Germanys has been a significant economic drag for over a decade.

Cuba too has followed a slightly different formula from that of the PRC, reforming less economically and relying on the personal charisma of its supreme leader, Fidel Castro. Internationally, Cuba has had to contend with the ongoing United States economic embargo. The communist island has relied on the tourism industry, financed, in large measure, by foreign investment. The country has also been aided by money exiles in the US who send to family members still in Cuba. The dollars eventually find their way into the coffers of the central bank, which can use them to finance the country's foreign-trade deficit. Internally, the government has been unwilling to liberalize to any significant degree. It has had a history of cautious economic liberalization followed by a renewed tightening of economic controls. However, with the retirement of Fidel Castro from the presidency in 2008 and accession of his brother, Raúl, to power, economic reforms accelerated.

In short, China has blazed the trail that other surviving communist regimes have followed at least partially. Nonetheless, today each communist regime is largely on its own. The days of socialist internationalism have long since passed. Only the threats posed by North Korea's nuclear weapons/capacity coupled with the parlous state of its economy might succeed in attracting concessionary trade arrangements and aid from the PRC to stave off a regional disaster. But North Korea is the exception. Communist regimes remain subject to both internal and external pressures, but, for the time being at least, they seem to have found a political and economic formula that allows for continued party rule.

Surviving communist regimes have learned to govern without the overarching appeal of communist ideology and a mobilized mass base among the workers and peasants that originally propelled them to power. The ruling elites of these regimes have recognized a fundamental fact: the first rule for insuring regime continuity is to avoid governmental crises in the first place. The economy should advance. The state should be efficient, and corruption must not be allowed to seriously undermine that efficiency. The military and security forces should be loyal and competent. And perhaps most importantly, individuals who might become leaders of opposition movements co-opted. Those that cannot be co-opted should be suppressed. Thus, governmental crises will be less likely to arise. If they do, the government will have the necessary resources to surmount them. The surviving communist regimes seem to implicitly recognize several important principles. If they are to confront pressures for change successfully on an ongoing basis, they must do so from a position of strength. The ruling elite itself must be unified and have the will to use force. They must have at least a semblance of popular support. And the counter-elite must be weak and disunited, and its ability to mobilize a mass following limited. If they cannot rely on the underlying legitimacy of the regime, they must at least have a cadre of leaders and influential members of the society who support them.

In sum, as with revolution, democratization does not happen automatically, nor does it work its results uncontrollably like some sort of blind force of nature. Revolution and democratization are the cumulative result of individual decisions, clever or foolish. And if their triumph is the result of strategic choices made by key political actors, then that triumph might be postponed by choices of other key political actors – perhaps postponed indefinitely. During the third wave, democrats have ousted authoritarians because they were able both to negotiate with factions of the ruling elites and to judiciously threaten mass action against recalcitrant members of the old regime. In Europe communists lost out because they were divided among themselves. Surviving communist regimes have taken steps to make sure that capacity of democrats to mobilize and negotiate remains strictly limited or nonexistent. At the same time they have taken steps to unify the ruling elite and judiciously expand its constituency.

Conclusion

In the last two decades of the twentieth century, communist regimes faced a multifaceted crisis. Economic performance lagged. And along with it, communism's ability to fulfill its promises and maintain its legitimacy flagged as well. Pro-democracy movements developed in a variety of communist states further pressuring governments for fundamental change. The communist regime that was least affected was that of North Korea. The Korean exception aside, all regimes were forced to make substantial changes that reshaped considerably the politics of the communist world and had substantial spillover effects for radical leftwing movements generally. Various European communist states undertook the most profound changes in the system, coupling radical economic reform with political democratization. Initially a laggard in the process, the Soviet Union pushed its European allies forward faster than most of them wished as the 1980s wore on. Cuba and Asian communist regimes made few political changes and democratized not at all. Most did, however, experiment with substantial economic reform, abandoning state-socialist orthodoxy. The crisis that communist regimes underwent eventually produced three disparate sets of regimes. Most Central European ex-communist states (including the three Baltic former Soviet states) have become full-fledged liberal democracies and market economies. Asian communist states and Cuba have retained party rule and reformed the economy, most bringing in many elements of capitalist-style management, foreign investment, and foreign trade. (North Korea stands out as the laggard here.) A third group of regimes composed of most of the states of the former Soviet Union and much of the former Yugoslavia find themselves in a kind of halfway house, neither completely authoritarian nor fully democratic. Some in the last group have been subject to democratization movements when fraudulent elections led to widespread protests and the eventual resignation of the government. In short, communism has not fully passed from the scene. Both its legacy and its reality live on.

Questions for further consideration

1 Discuss the problems communist regimes faced since the mid-1970s in terms of legitimacy, state effectiveness, and governmental efficacy. How did different regimes handle them differently?

2 What sorts of problems beset state socialism? Why were complete privatization and the complete opening of markets not effective solutions?

3 Why were central European countries most likely to become consolidated democracies? What general lessons might be drawn from this fact?

4 Is the People's Republic of China on the road to democratization? Defend your answer.

5 Is communism as a political system likely to occur in new countries? Why or why not?

6 What problems of democratization and creating a market economy are unique to former communist states? How do you think these problems might be addressed?

Further reading

C. Fred Bergsten, Bates Gill, Nicholas R. Lardy, and Deck Mitchell, *China: The Balance Sheet*. New York: Public Affairs, 2006. A discussion of Chinese economic policies and their consequences.

Stephen Kotkin, *Armageddon Averted: The Soviet Collapse, 1970–2000*. Oxford: Oxford University Press, 2001. An analysis of the Gorbachev era.

Hedrick Smith, *The Russians*. New York: Ballantine Books, 1976.
A readable, detailed account of the Soviet Union's political culture and economic system at the height of the Brezhnev era by a leading American journalist.

World Bank. *The World Development Report 1996: From Plan to Market*. Oxford, England: Oxford University Press, 1996. An analysis of the problems of trying to establish a capitalist economy in former state socialist states.

The politics of contemporary patrimonial rule

Tyranny pays regard to no common interest unless for the sake of its private benefit, and the aim of tyranny is what is pleasant … Money is the aim of tyrants … A tyrant's [bodyguard consists] of mercenaries.

(Aristotle)

In this chapter

We explore the topic of patrimonialism – politics based primarily on family ties, personal loyalty, and patronage. Regimes that follow this style of rule fall into two basic categories, which are considered in turn. One sort is modernizing autocracy – a traditionally legitimized and organized regime with some modern features and aspirations to modernize. This type of patrimonialism softens the naked self-interest that often typifies personalistic rule by a respect for tradition. The second sort of contemporary patrimonial rule, neo-patrimonialism, however, entails few checks. Neo-patrimonialism exists in regimes that are formally modern, respecting the rule of law and adhering to the principles of bureaucratic rationality in theory. But in practice these regimes ignore such standards and are actually governed on the basis of personal connections and patronage. The chapter includes a case study of both a modernizing autocracy, Saudi Arabia, and one of the most extreme examples of neo-patrimonial regimes, Zaire under Mobutu Sese Seku (1965–97). Using a structural–functional and neo-institutional approach, the chapter shows how patrimonial methods can animate both traditional and modern structures.

Introduction

Patrimonialism is probably as old as government itself. **Patrimonialism** as a system of government makes the legitimacy of the regime depend upon the subject's personal loyalty to the ruler. The subject trades loyalty for personal benefits. Patrimonial regimes make little distinction between the private interest of the ruler and the ruler's public functions. The private purse of the ruler and the public treasury are frequently interchangeable. Moreover, the principles that apply to the ruler apply, with necessary changes, to subordinates as well. They too use their offices to advance their self-interest. In the contemporary world patrimonial regimes appear in many ways to be throwbacks to the practices of the past. Most modern regimes base their legitimacy on universal principles rather than particularistic loyalties. And they embody the principle of bureaucratic rationality. Patrimonial regimes do neither. Bureaucratic rationality distinguishes between the interest of the officeholder and the public responsibilities of the office. Patrimonial regimes either do not recognize or subvert this principle. To remain stable, today's patrimonial rulers must avoid the practices of ancient tyrants and restrain their own and their followers' avarice lest they meet a typical tyrant's end – assassination or revolt.

Contemporary patrimonial regimes come in two basic forms. One is traditional in its structure; the other is nominally modern and democratic. The first encompasses all tradition-based governments in which the monarch has either absolute power or considerable power. (Constitutional monarchies, such as that of Great Britain, where the queen's powers are almost entirely ceremonial, are not under consideration here.) Absolute monarchs – traditional autocrats – are virtually unchecked although some quite powerful monarchs do, in fact, face some limits placed on their powers by constitutions or elected assemblies. Traditional authoritarian regimes of this sort have much in common with many European monarchies of the nineteenth century. During that period many hereditary rulers in Europe had considerable power, and they and their supporters had to decide whether to accommodate or attempt to fend off popular demands for a share of political power. The same choice often faces traditional authoritarian governments today.

The second sort of patrimonial regime is more properly denominated **"neo-patrimonial."** "Patrimonial" because the practice resembles the patrimonialism found in traditional regimes; "neo" (new) because patrimonialism occurs within a nominally modern system, where such practices are supposed to be illegal. Many modern regimes have elements reminiscent of patrimonialism – personal and family connections as well as self-interest can sometimes trump the public good and proper respect for rules and procedures. However, most modern regimes recognize this as corruption and attempt to punish it. But under neo-patrimonialism corruption is the system, and it is rarely punished. The most extreme type of neo-patrimonialism is termed "**sultanism**" or "**neo-sultanism**." Under neo-sultanistic systems, institutions are weak and dependent upon the will of a single individual. The rule of law and bureaucratic rationality disappear almost totally as operative principles. When the ruler is removed from the scene, apparently autonomous, self-sustaining institutions, such as the political branches of the government, the armed forces, and much of the bureaucracy may collapse as well (Chehabi 1998: 3–48). Both traditional authoritarian and neo-sultanistic regimes place the ruler's personal interest and personal loyalty to him above all else. In doing so they risk falling victim to the vices Aristotle ascribed to tyranny. After considering the challenges both these types of systems face, this chapter investigates each of them separately in more detail.

Breakdown and continuity in patrimonial and neo-patrimonial systems

Regimes that are either patrimonial or neo-patrimonial in nature rest on personal or family connections. This personalism both helps legitimize the regime and pervades governmental, state, and military structures. On a variety of levels such reliance can put the system in peril. In traditional societies the legitimacy of the ruler's status was based on personal loyalty founded on the historical status of a particular family; in neo-patrimonial systems loyalties are more personal and less familial. Loyalty – and legitimacy – cannot be taken for granted. Even in the traditional societies of medieval Europe, loyalty had to be reinforced by the exchange of oaths, and the continual conferring of benefits was also necessary since subordinates could often find a pretext to break their oaths. To function effectively, patrimonial legitimacy must be constantly cultivated. The same is true for neo-patrimonial systems.

Modern times place traditional notions of loyalty and legitimacy under further stress. Actual or potential political actors are likely to be much more numerous than in earlier ages and have available to them ideas about alternative forms of legitimation. In short, the disloyal and semi-loyal opposition may be founded on principles and not just a set of loyalties competing with that of the ruler. Personalism in state and military administration is also problematic at best in modern times. Appointments based on personal loyalty may preclude rebellion, but it is no guarantee of effectiveness in either the civil bureaucracy or the officer

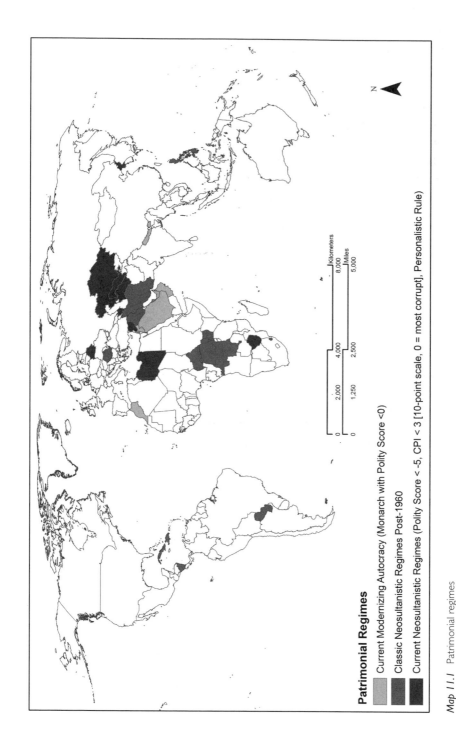

Map 11.1 Patrimonial regimes

Source: Environmental Systems Research Institute (ESRI) map data. Data: Polity IV; Chehabi and Linz (1998); Transparency International; Department of State Background Notes

Note: Polity IV ratings range from +10 (most democratic) to −10 (most authoritarian)

Patrimonial Regimes

Current Modernizing Autocracy (Monarch with Polity Score <0)

Classic Neosultanistic Regimes Post-1960

Current Neosultanistic Regimes (Polity Score < -5, CPI < 3 [10-point scale, 0 = most corrupt], Personalistic Rule)

corps of the armed forces. Even governmental efficacy can come under stress. Freed of the immediate need to secure advice or consent, single authoritarian leaders often make mistakes. Even the most deft of rulers can begin to lose their touch as they age. This makes succession crises a staple of personalistic system unless hereditary succession has been firmly established, and occasionally even then the system may be convulsed by plotting and political maneuvering. It is not surprising that in the modern era patrimonial systems can only survive in societies that are still in many ways very traditional and the neo-patrimonial systems take root in societies with not much more than a surface veneer of modernity.

Modernizing autocracies

When all else fails, people rely on personal connections – friends, family, those owing them personal obligations – to get them through. Because of this, patrimonial regimes are among the oldest on record and among the most diverse. Throughout history, emperors, kings, chiefs, and headmen ruled because their subordinates owed them loyalty. They, in exchange for this loyalty, provided some sort of tangible benefit – protection, wealth, or a share in political power. In most countries, kings who wield real power or even absolute power have been consigned to the history books. However, in a few countries at least, they are very much alive and well. These are traditional authoritarian regimes. Although the actual power of the ruler varies, these regimes here will be called "**modernizing autocracies**." In generic terms, an autocracy is any absolute government in which power is vested in one individual. In the specific sense that the term is used here, an **autocracy** is a *traditional* government vested with absolute or nearly absolute power whose subjects are personally loyal to the sovereign on the basis of his or her traditional right to rule.

A *modernizing* autocracy is an autocracy in which the government is attempting limited modernization of its military and state structures. All contemporary autocrats have attempted to modernize to a limited degree, since without at least some modernization their states and armed forces would be ineffective. The modernizing autocracies of specific concern here are Morocco, Jordan, Saudi Arabia, the United Arab Emirates (UAE), and other small Persian Gulf states, Swaziland, Nepal, Bhutan, and Brunei. Some of these regimes, Jordan and Morocco for example, are sometimes classified as "constitutional monarchies" as was Iran under the Shah (see Chapter 6). Yet, even though their autocratic character is somewhat circumscribed, in most instances they resemble autocracies under stress rather than true constitutional systems where a separation of powers and well-accepted balance of authority gives a variety of political actors a nearly equal share of legal power.

Traditional authority as an eroding asset

While they do not seem to be about to disappear entirely from the world stage, modernizing autocracies, once prolific, have today been reduced to a relative handful of countries. In contrast, at the turn of the twentieth century, some of the largest states in terms of population and territory were modernizing autocrats. A number of them represented proud and much admired civilizations. China, the Russian Empire, and the Ottoman Empire were all modernizing autocracies. At the beginning of the twenty-first century, most modernizing autocracies would be ignored were it not for the oil resources some of them possess. They have only a modest population individually and even collectively. Most of these monarchies actually owe their existence to European imperialism. Many blessed with the advantages of abundant oil resources have become traditional monarchy/welfare states. In short, if modernizing autocracies were biological entities, today we would declare them an endangered species. What happened?

Much of the story has to do with loss of legitimacy. An autocrat can claim the right to rule by inheritance or on his selection by a small group of electors. In either case the autocracy's practices and traditions are hallowed by time. It was the sanction of tradition that gave autocracy its staying power in the past. The ruling elites in an autocracy strove to maintain the sanctity of the traditional order lest would-be reformers or revolutionaries mobilized the population against them. The sanctity of the past is often a matter of inertia. Traditional people find it difficult to image a world without their traditional autocratic ruler simply because they have no experience or knowledge of any other political order. A dramatic illustration of this can be found in *Dr. Zhivago,* a 1968 Academy Award-winning film set in the period of the Russian Revolution. In one scene, a communist agitator announces to a group of already mutinous soldiers that the tsar has been overthrown. One of the soldiers, who appears to be an old peasant drafted into the army as Russia's military disasters mounted, asks the agitator a question. "Who's the new tsar then?" he wants to know. The agitator is somewhat taken aback at the man's failure to grasp the situation. "There is no tsar!" he tells him. The old peasant soldier is incredulous: "No tsar ..." The old soldier's incredulity is understandable. Tsarist Russia was a society in the process of modernization, but the old soldier was clearly a traditional man. That is not to say that he was a traditionalist ideologue, preferring the tsarist

autocracy to other forms of government on theoretical grounds.
He was not. He had apparently not even thought of such questions before.
The structure of political rule did not seem to him to be a matter of
human choice. There had always been a tsar. There would always be a tsar,
just like the sun always rose in the East and set in the West. It is just this
sort of psychological outlook, this restricted and non-ideological
worldview, that once made traditional regimes so stable. But such a
worldview has faced increasing practical and technological challenges.

The need for modernization: sowing seeds of opposition

By the end of the nineteenth century, most of the autocracies had become
modernizing autocracies (cf. Lewis 1995: 286–311; Halpern 1965:
41–112). Failure to modernize would have meant collapse. Modern
military organizations were capable of defeating pre-modern armed forces.
This advantage had first emerged in the 1500s with the rise of European
powers on the world stage. The advantages possessed by Europeans were
considerable: fully rigged sailing ships, instruments of navigation,
personal firearms, and mobile cannon. These technologies gave the states
that possessed them the ability to project their power around the world.
However, until the nineteenth century, the advantages conferred by
modern technology were not overwhelming. When faced by a
well-organized government capable of defending its interests, more
modern imperialist states sometimes were forced to give way.
For example, as we saw in Chapter 2, traditional Japan managed to defend
itself for two hundred and fifty years. However, by the mid-nineteenth
century, powers wedded to traditional technologies could no longer hold
out against modern powers. Improvements in propulsion (i.e., the
introduction of steam power), artillery, firearms, and communications
enhanced the already great advantages that modern powers had. So too did
the introduction of railroads, iron ships, and improved systems for
stabilizing naval artillery. If a country was to remain independent and a
regime was to survive, military modernization was essential.

Military modernization, however, entails more than the purchase of a
few modern cannon and other pieces of up-to-date military hardware.
Military modernization requires the change of the entire military system
and those elements of the society that support it. The traditional military
elite – be they European knights, Japanese Samurai, or Chinese military
Mandarins – were not trained to handle modern weapons personally, nor
were they trained to manage modern military forces. Military
modernization entails the training of specialists and professionals for a
new-model officer corps. The alternate strategy of relying on mercenaries

or foreigner officers is, at best, a stopgap measure. Military modernization requires the modernization of the state administration too. Traditional methods of military pay and recruitment do not suffice. Traditional organizations were often based on high status individuals who received land in exchange for the duty and privilege of doing military service. These leaders, in turn, often raised additional troops from among their own personal retainers. Most often, only smaller full-time forces were actually paid in cash. In a modern military, officers and regular troops need to be paid, housed, fed and equipped by the central government. Modern military equipment is expensive and subject to constant obsolescence.

Taxes need to be collected, and traditional methods of raising revenue, such as tax farming and relying on the local elite to collect revenue and forward a share to the central government, are unreliable and inefficient. Only a modern rule-based bureaucracy presiding over a cash economy will suffice. And, as with military modernization, administrative modernization involves a host of indirect changes. Bureaucrats are members of the educated middle class. Schools and universities have to be built, or students have to be sent abroad to get their education if future bureaucrats are to be adequately educated. The development of a cash economy requires that commercial agriculture displace subsistence production. This, in turn, requires investment and results in the displacement of a considerable segment of the rural population, as larger, more efficient commercial farms replace subsistence plots. Some of the newly dispossessed may move to the cities, while others remain unemployed in rural areas.

Unemployment is both a problem and an opportunity. Industrialization is an essential part of economic modernization. The development of modern machine manufacturing is the hallmark of capitalism. It led to immense increases in wealth. Late modernizers also find it in their interest to develop an industrial base. Light manufacturing, such as clothing and textiles, frequently begin the industrialization process, but for a variety of reasons many governments want to push the process further. From the perspective of military security, a manufacturing base capable of producing military equipment is highly desirable. Self-sufficiency in military production may be impossible, but the manufacture of light arms, spare parts, and light vehicles is of great value in itself. The greater the degree of self-sufficiency the country possesses, the less it will be subject to pressure from foreign powers that supply its military materiel. The government may even be tempted to subsidize military production and the steel, chemical, and engineering industries needed to support it

By modernizing, an autocracy is better equipped to withstand the sort of military and diplomatic pressures that foreign powers can bring to bear against it. But, for all that, it continues to be under stress. The new source of stress is primarily internal, created by the modernization process itself. The new middle and working classes have a view of the world that differs from their peasant forefathers. They have jobs in a modern sector of the economy. The middle class is educated and accustomed to employment that requires them to make decisions and gives them some control over their activities. More and more people need to be educated as jobs in the modern economy become more important, so the size of the middle and working classes grows. People are urban and literate. They seek new sources of information. The mass media develop. Universities and the media are potentially sources of instability. Both these institutions disseminate ideas and information that can undermine the legitimacy of the existing political order. Students, whose intellectual horizons have expanded, find themselves faced with a society whose limits are much more confining than they expect. Young and less averse to risk than their elders, students can provide both radical ideas and the sort of mass support necessary for radical action. Many of them may come to see the old regime as a block to their personal advancement and national progress.

The working class too is a group that is likely to be out of step with the old regime and the ruling elite. While not advantaged as other political actors, workers can often put pressure on the authorities. There is strength in numbers and strength in organization. The urban working class has, or at least can have, both. Even the character of the rural population has changed from what it was under a purely traditional society. The commercialization of agriculture creates a large group of rural landless. Seasonal laborers, unemployed for extended periods, often come to resemble the working class of the cities more than the small independent peasant proprietors. Even the traditional elite finds itself in an altered situation. They frequently face new challenges from the rising business class. The commercialization of agriculture, and the modernization of the state administration and the armed forces, compel the elite to adapt. They cannot rely on the traditional sources of wealth and power alone. They must change with the times economically and politically. A section of the traditional elite may resist change, sometimes violently.

In sum, modernization opens up a Pandora's box of changes. And these changes can give rise to opposition to the regime's policies and the regime itself. Once modernization is well under way, it is impossible for the regime to manage public affairs in the way it had done in the past. The middle class, the working class – urban and rural – the armed forces emerge as potentially significant political actors. Fewer and fewer people are in the position of the old Russian soldier, unable to even imagine a

form of government and society other than the traditional one under
an autocrat.

Political actors: government and opposition

The privileged sectors in a modernizing autocracy (the government and its
major beneficiaries) include the monarch and the traditional sectors
associated with him – i.e., traditional secular leaders and the religious
establishment. They, by and large, share a common aim to enhance the
authority of tradition so as to preserve their privileges and to exclude
other groups from a meaningful share of political power. Even autocrats
who wish to promote liberalization and democratization need to manage
the process. Modernizing autocrats often have to oversee an ongoing
policy debate among their advisers and close supporters. It is a debate that
has echoes in the country at large. Since Western European imperial states
first began the era of overseas expansion, the societies they invaded
economically and militarily have had to make a choice about their own
cultures and practices: should they adopt the ways of the outsiders or not?
Opinion split. Traditionalists argue that tradition needed to be reinforced
not abandoned. Foreign innovations should be adopted only sparingly if
at all. Reform for them means returning to the golden age of the past.
In contrast, modernizers argue for more or less wholesale adoption of
modern ways – military, economic, educational, and social. Modernizers
see tradition as largely a dead weight holding the society back. In the
nineteenth century these debates raged in the Russian, Chinese, and
Ottoman empires. Today they continue in the remaining modernizing
autocracies.

The less privileged sectors include the middle classes, the rural
population, as well as the working and lower classes in the urban
population. These groups constitute a potential opposition whose
orientation can range from loyalty to outright disloyalty. The less
privileged sectors sometimes mirror the traditionalist–modernist split
found among the privileged and the autocrat's senior advisers. Today's
modernizing autocracies in Muslim countries face both Islamists and
democrats. The former are traditionalist, and the latter are modernizers.
Outside of the Islamic world, the semi-loyal or disloyal ideological
opposition in question is composed primarily of democrats. Islamists hope
to mobilize the disaffected, both the youth and the devout middle class
behind their movement. Democrats also hope to mobilize the disaffected.
And they too recognized the importance of the middle class, historically a
principal bearer of democratic ideology. Ethnic separatists and radical
leftists are sometimes part of the opposition's ideological mix.

The armed forces are a source of potential opponents as well, and their position is pivotal since they control the instruments of violence that can either defend or overthrow the regime. By their very nature, they are uniquely cohesive. They possess the tight discipline and a hierarchical command structure that other institutions lack. As noted in Chapter 7, the armed forces are patriotic, nationalistic, even jingoistic. They are concerned, above all, with national power. They are a quintessentially modern institution in a modernizing society. Since many of the members of the officer corps are likely to be drawn from the middle class, these officers may see the modernizing autocracy as insufficiently modern. Officers can easily come to feel that the autocrat and the traditional elite are more concerned with continuing their monopoly on power than they are about truly modernizing and protecting the country. In this respect, the autocracy can appear to be a roadblock to modernization, and the armed forces the vanguard of a new society, especially where the working and middle classes are not very politically active (see Chapter 8). It is not surprising, then, that radical ideologies can take root among junior officers, and grow in influence as these officers reach middle rank.
In addition, outside actors – foreign governments and important foreign economic interests – can play a key role in maintaining or undermining modernizing autocracies. Although modernizing autocracies have been among the states most in need of foreign patronage and support, this support is a double-edged sword. It can be a source of aid and diplomatic help, but it can also give rise to popular resentment against the autocrat and his government.

Modernizing autocrats have had to face a basic choice similar to that faced by many European monarchs in the nineteenth century
(see Chapter 2). They can resist the tides of change as did the Bourbons of France, or they can accommodate change by liberalizing and democratizing slowly and eventually cede meaningful political power to others as did the Hanovers/Windsors of Great Britain. The delaying strategy is played out with some of the same tactics as the resistance strategy although with less vigor and a greater willingness to retreat in the face of escalating opposition. If followed to its logical conclusion, the accommodationist strategy leads to the emergence of a new regime, one in which the former autocrat becomes a largely ceremonial figure. But an accommodationist strategy can be even more disastrous as the last chapter demonstrated in the case of communist regimes. In the contemporary era, even partial liberalization or limited democratization can be extremely dangerous. These reforms can unleash forces that are difficult to control. The disaffected are likely to organize once they are given the opportunity to do so. A counter-elite can emerge to lead the incipient mass movement

and challenge the regime. Faced with unprecedented challenges, the ruling elite itself can fracture, leading to indecision on contradictory, self-defeating actions. In addition, some autocrats have to deal with constitutional restraints imposed by constituent assemblies, by the autocrat's own concession in the face of popular pressure, or by foreign powers when the regime was first initiated. These autocrats have the option of playing a rollback strategy, i.e., they can attempt to expand their power and to limit the institutional checks on their power.

Maintaining or clawing back autocratic power

Regardless of the overall strategy they follow, modernizing autocrats have been able to employ a variety of tactics to enhance their power and to control forces likely to undermine their power and that of their close personal supporters. These measures (Maghraoui 2002; Seznec 2002; Herb 2002; Brumberg 2002) are aimed at limiting the political and social effects that are the byproducts of the modernization process.

Limiting civil liberties

Complete or nearly complete freedom of speech, press, and association in regard to political issues is rare outside of established liberal democracies. More often than not, governments regard the mass media, education, and private associations as potentially dangerous and subject them to close scrutiny and regulation. These restrictions can be used to buttress the autocracy's power. The media can be licensed and censored; the government can prescribe curricula at schools and universities. Freedom of association can be restricted. All these restrictions, which seem unwarranted in liberal democracies, are normal in many other regimes. Further, modernizing autocracies can and often do mandate courses in the regime's ideology or religion for everyone, and they frequently discourage the development of disciplines, such as the social sciences, that are likely, by their nature, to breed social and political criticism. Instead, the state is likely to favor science, engineering, business, and technical curricula over the humanities and social sciences. Even students the state sponsors for study abroad are likely to find their options restricted by their own government.

The state frequently subjects the press and the broadcast media to censorship. While the regime may target political criticism most of all, materials that threaten public morals are also commonly part of the censor's mandate. This gives the government censor the aura of high (albeit Puritanical) moral purpose. In the final analysis, however, just like other authoritarian regimes, modernizing autocracies often need to employ harsher methods of repression than mere censorship to keep potentially subversive forces. A strong domestic intelligence service, not subject to judicial check, often plays an important role. The intelligence service routinely infiltrates a variety of groups thought to represent a subversive threat. The regime often outlaws some or all political parties, reserves the right to use preventive detention against those it considers dangerous, and engages in torture.

Controlling political participation

The restrictions placed on civil liberties in modernizing autocracies are normally considerable, and violations of basic human rights can sometimes be egregious, but modernizing autocrats have more than merely negative sanctions in their political repertoire. Autocrats are free to use a variety of devices to enhance their legitimacy by creating the appearance of popular consent and allow the dissatisfied to vent their spleen relatively harmlessly. Public expression of grievances when kept within strict bounds is preferable to having the dissatisfied organize clandestinely where their activity is harder to track. Traditional autocracies – whether modernizing or not – often have mechanisms whereby the autocrat himself can meet and consult with the people and the elite. Such consultations can be used to provide an aura of popular support and legitimacy, and reinforce traditional political norms. The monarch, as the focal point of the regime and the person to whom his subjects are personally loyal, can hear his subjects' problems, pledge his assistance, and deflect criticism from his own person and the system to lower-level functionaries.

Elected assemblies can also serve a similar purpose. However, in the case of an assembly, the connection between the monarch and his subjects is more institutionalized and is mediated through the assembly's formal structures. Assemblies take various forms. The least consequential is an assembly of notables that serves as an advisory body and is appointed by the monarch himself. Such consultative bodies have little or no independent influence beyond that of their individual members. Since they are not elected, they lack the ability to really represent society's interests. Moreover, the monarch has little incentive to appoint people who are likely to disagree with him. Thus, consultative assemblies do little to defuse any existing popular pressure for a more direct role in the government.

Elected representative assemblies have greater stature than consultative bodies appointed by the monarch, but the autocrat can often place significant restrictions on them. Elections to such assemblies are frequently manipulated to serve the ruler's interest. Generally, these manipulations aim at minimizing the representation of modern political parties that are liable to be critical of the absolutist system and at maximizing the representation of traditionalists. There are a number of ways these aims can be achieved. The most direct is the prohibition of party identification on the electoral ballot coupled with a prohibition on partisan campaigning. The exclusion of parties advantages local notables, who are often traditionalists. Coming from prominent families with a considerable stake in the system, such men are likely to adhere to ideologies and policies friendly to the political and social status quo. The voter, largely ignorant of the partisan and ideological orientation of candidates, often votes for the candidate he knows. Yet even when parties labor under restrictions that limit party identification or specifically partisan campaigning, they sometimes discover and evolve useful counter-maneuvers themselves. The reputation of some candidates may be sufficiently widespread that lack of party identification may not matter. But for most voters and most candidates, some way of identifying the candidate's stand is critical. Sometimes a subterfuge is possible. Candidates of a single party or group of parties may be able to campaign as members of loose associations and so provide the voters with an alternate way of identifying their members' ideological and policy orientation.

Even if they cannot totally suppress political parties, modernizing autocrats have other means to prevent partisan politicians from actually assuming effective control of representative assemblies. The most straightforward of these is to have the monarch appoint a certain number of assembly members himself. In addition, seats can be reserved for members of the traditional elite or elected officially recognized professional groups. More subtle methods are also available. The Single Nontransferable Vote (SNTV: see Chapter 4) is likely to promote support for traditional notables. Small districts can promote patronage politics. The over-representation of certain elements of the population can be further assured by the apportionment of districts. Rural areas are more likely to support traditionalists, and the autocrat can easily make them the beneficiaries of malapportionment. Women are at times excluded from the franchise altogether. So too are resident aliens, even those who have been born in the country or hold essential state jobs. In sum, modernizing autocrats can craft popular assemblies along lines that will make them little threat to the regime.

Even a representative assembly that by and large reflects the interests and ideological perspectives of the country at large is unlikely to be much of a direct threat to a modernizing autocrat's power unless important members of the assembly are able to mobilize support within the society at large to press for substantive change. Monarchs can play the game of divide-and-rule, co-opting some of the opposition and isolating others (Lust-Okar 2005). Representative assemblies often exist at the autocrat's pleasure. He delegates to them whatever powers they have. Even when a written constitution limits the monarch's power, he may use his right to dissolve the assembly (without calling new elections) to enhance his power. Moreover, whether they function under written constitutions or not, assemblies rarely have the right to appoint key members of the government in defiance of the monarch's wishes. This is true even when the assembly has powers over legislation and minor ministries. In other words, the prime minister, the ministers of defense, interior (police), foreign affairs, and economics customarily must have the confidence of the monarch.

This monarchical control of appointments, coupled with the right to dissolve assemblies, gives the supposedly constitutional monarch instruments to make himself a true autocrat. Should the effective power to appoint and remove key ministers slip from the autocrat's hands, however, the regime would be well on the way to becoming a constitutional monarchy, with a head of state of limited powers. But, of the modernizing autocrats who lost power in the second half of the twentieth century – the kings of Syria, Egypt, Iraq, Libya, Bhutan, and Nepal, and the Shah of Iran – only two, the kings of Bhutan and Nepal, became constitutional monarchs. The remainder were overthrown outright, most often by the armed forces. Thus, in comparison to risks from other quarters, popular assemblies appear to be a manageable threat to autocratic regimes.

Cultivating traditional sectors

As we have noted, modernizing autocrats have to balance pressures for modernization against the need to maintain key traditional aspects of the regime. Modernizing the traditional elite itself is one important way to effect this sort of balance. Members of the royal family and the aristocracy can become modern military officers, businessmen, and technocrats in the government service. Although their personal ambitions may conflict with each other, they all have a vested interest in the preservation of the regime. As such, they are much more reliable than commoners, whose ultimate political sympathies may be open to question. Traditional institutions and peoples are another source of strength. The urban population and those working in the most modern sectors of the rural economy are likely to evaluate the government by pragmatic standards. If the regime delivers the benefits of security and prosperity, they will usually support it. In effect, the more modern sectors of society are likely to evaluate the regime in the same way that modern liberal-democratic electorates evaluate governments – on the basis of a largely utilitarian calculus. More traditional people, on the other hand, are more likely to be loyal to the regime for reasons of sentiment and belief. The political popularity of the Hashemite monarchs in Jordan, for example, rests on the monarchy's Bedouin subjects, not their Palestinian urban and village population.

Wearing a nationalist mantel

As modernization advances, traditionalism can become a diminishing asset, and the regime may need to rely on more modern public appeals than on more traditional ones. Nationalism is normally a card played by an autocratic regime's opponents, sometimes with devastating results. The Free Officers who overthrew the monarchies of Egypt and Iraq argued that the old regime had failed to fulfill the people's national aspirations. Nationalism has often been a stumbling block for other Arab monarchies as well. The Hashemites in Jordan have frequently found themselves on the wrong side of the nationalistic aspiration of their Palestinian subjects. While Jordan's kings have often sought accommodation with western governments and Israel, the Palestinians of Jordan have usually taken a more intransigent position. The Persian Gulf monarchies too have often been seen as insufficiently committed to popular pan-Arab projects. This need not be the case. King Hassan II's "Green March" into the former Spanish Sahara during the 1970s and his position that the territory is by right Morocco's played well at home. And during the 1990s, even the Gulf monarchies learned from experience. Despite their reliance on Western military support, they showed a decided reluctance to follow the lead of western powers, especially the United States. In the confrontation between the US and Iraq, these states' peoples often sympathized with the Iraqis. And this was a sympathy that their governments could ill afford to ignore.

Managing the military

Modernizing autocrats have generally attempted to reinforce and build upon long-established norms of social organization and personal loyalty to secure their rule. Their control of the armed forces is based on the same principle. The armed forces and their leaders are drawn from politically reliable classes as much as possible. Princes of the blood normally constitute a reliable recruitment pool especially for senior officers. They have too much at risk to lead a coup against the monarchy. Rural and tribal peoples with a traditional connection to the monarch, rather than urban dwellers, provide a suitable recruitment pool for the troops. In Jordan, for example, the Bedouins rather than the Palestinians serve as the primary base of the army. In Brunei the sultan uses an elite force of

Gurkhas, foreign soldiers recruited on an individual basis from Nepal, to help guard himself against potential coups. The military's personal loyalty to the sovereign is often reinforced by his role in personally directing the armed forces.

In addition, other measures can be used to prevent military conspiracies. The army may be divided into two separate forces organized and equipped differently and subject to different chains of command as in Saudi Arabia. Or senior officers may be forced to receive the monarch's personal permission to hold meetings with one another, as was the case under the Shah's regime in Iran. At one time some of the small Persian Gulf states with minuscule armed forces, had officers seconded to them from the United Kingdom. These officers could be expected to follow the policies of their government that saw the monarchy as a de facto protectorate. In short, autocrats rarely regard military professionalism and patriotism alone as sufficient guarantees for military loyalty and obedience. History shows their caution in this matter is warranted.

Distributing oil income (if it's available)

Most of the modernizing autocrats of the Persian Gulf have possessed an advantage that many of their defunct counterparts lacked – oil. Oil is not of itself a "silver bullet" for the political problems facing modernizing autocrats or any developing country's government. The attempt to exploit the wealth derived from oil can lead to serious problems, such as corruption and overly ambitious development projects. States with large populations, such as Nigeria and Mexico, have often found oil as much a curse as a blessing. Yet, the oil states of the Gulf and Brunei have relatively small populations. The oil booms of the 1970s and the current decade gave them the opportunity not only to lavish money on industrial, infrastructure, and military projects, but it allowed them the luxury of expanding their welfare states. They could do all this without borrowing. In fact, many ran a substantial budget surplus, giving them a financial cushion for the future. Such states have been termed "**rentier states**" since they live off the revenue ("rents") from their oil instead of taxing their own people. While the imposition of taxes has often led to demands for representative government from the people taxed, rentier states are positioned to avoid this dynamic (Zakaria 2003: 73–6). However, oil revenue may not be an adequate hedge for rentier states indefinitely. The damage caused by the 1991 Iraq war drew down Kuwait's accumulated savings substantially while Saudi Arabia's disappeared entirely. And the fall in oil prices during most of the 1980s and 1990s put pressure on government budgets of other Persian Gulf states as well. By the end of the twentieth century, the ability even of the small Gulf oil monarchies to

457

maintain their levels of government-supported employment, development spending and welfare benefits came under severe stress. Things have eased considerably because of the oil price boom that began in 2004. Yet even that may not give Saudi Arabia the economic cushion it enjoyed in the 1970s, given the large increase in the kingdom's population over the past several decades.

Using religion as legitimizing factor

Autocrats can use religion to underpin their authority. Today's remaining modernizing Muslim autocrats have avoided the difficulties the last Shah of Iran and his father created for themselves with their militantly secular approach to modernization. In fact, most of the remaining modernizing autocrats have leaned in the other direction. Yet, since Islam does not explicitly sanction monarchy, and its standards of social justice may be difficult for any regime to meet, Islamic autocrats normally prefer to stress the purely social norms of Islam rather than other elements. And Islamic monarchies normally enforce religious norms, often quite strictly. The conservative interpretation and strict enforcement of sexual and other social norms reinforces the regime's legitimacy in the minds of its traditionalist supporters. Even with partial modernization, the Persian Gulf monarchies have generally managed to keep their societies isolated from many outside influences. Except in a few cases, the presence of foreigners is limited. The open display of western life-styles is prohibited. Publications and broadcasts are strictly censored. And, of course, the open practice of religions other than Islam, not to mention proselytization, is forbidden.

Such religious conservatism, however, gives rise to two sorts of opposition. Liberals, on the one hand, often argue that the government places undue restrictions on women, limiting their rights before the law, as well as their right to employment, travel, and free movement. Traditionalists, on the other hand, often see the regimes as hypocritical. Many of the wealthy members of the elite are known for their un-Islamic life-styles that they practice discretely inside their palaces and more openly outside the country. Such charges of moral decadence are especially telling against the Saudi elite. The Saud family rose to the top in the new country, in part, because of its adherence to the Wahhabi sect of Sunni Islam, a sect known for its severe moral strictures. And the kingdom holds the two holiest sites of the Muslim religion. In sum, religion seems an almost essential support for modernizing autocracies in Muslim countries, but the autocrat must strike a delicate balance between traditionalists and modernizers inside his inner circle and without. As modernization continues, this balancing may become ever more difficult.

Students are likely to continue to study abroad. Members of the middle class will continue to travel. Modern communications and the Internet will make inroads and present alternatives to traditional practices. Emphasizing religious fundamentalism may help undermine the appeal of liberal critics. But reliance on religious traditionalism to legitimize the regime may, at the same time, legitimize Islamist critiques of the regime itself.

Placating and manipulating foreign patrons

In addition to their other advantages, the remaining modernizing autocrats have generally played their geopolitical cards skillfully. Morocco, Brunei, and Bhutan find themselves in locations fairly remote from key flashpoints involving the major powers. Morocco's friendship with the United States, Brunei's with the United Kingdom, and the Himalayan kingdom of Bhutan's general willingness to accede to Indian leadership in critical matters have rendered their international situation relatively secure. The more turbulent situation in the Persian Gulf has led the modernizing autocrats there to follow a more complex foreign policy. The importance of the region's oil has given them a trump card. Although the United States specifically and western powers generally have often been critical of authoritarian governments elsewhere, the Gulf monarchies have largely escaped such official criticism. The United States has been much more concerned with access to oil, the defense of Israel, and the political stability of the region than with cultivating the growth of democracy there.

The Persian Gulf monarchies have been able to nationalize foreign oil holdings and to secure defense guarantees. Especially since the war against Iraq in 1991, they have gained access to some of the West's most advanced weaponry. At the same time, these states have been careful about associating themselves too closely with the United States and its allies. They restrict the numbers and location of foreign troops. They regulate how foreign forces that are based on their soil can be used. US-promoted defense cooperation among the Gulf monarchies has been less than successful. In short, these states have been careful about their own national, Arab, and Islamic identities. The Gulf monarchies, especially Saudi Arabia, have made use of its wealth to reward friends, to punish enemies, and to win over wavering states. Even in the heyday of Pan-Arabism in the 1960s, Saudi contributions were used as an effective lever of Saudi influence. Today's remaining modernizing autocrats find themselves in an essentially defensive position internationally. Yet, their political skill and the extensive resources that many of them possess have given them a fairly strong position.

Practicing patrimonialism astutely

Of the non-repressive tactics available to the autocrat, probably the most important is patrimonialism astutely practiced. Above all, he must avoid looking like the ancient tyrants described by Aristotle, self-serving rapacious rulers surrounded by equally self-interested and corrupt supporters. Since autocracy rests on a traditional foundation, the distinction between the person of the monarch and the monarch as an officer of the state is blurred. This blurring allows the modernizing autocrat to balance the need for modernization against the need to preserve the traditional foundations of his own authority. He is thus often free to determine what, if any, representative assembly exists. He can bend with the wind, yielding to political pressure for a popular assembly, but refusing to grant it substantial powers on a permanent basis. Even where a written constitution provides the monarch with less flexibility, he can use his substantial powers to his own advantage, appointing and cashiering officials as its suits his interests, timing his moves so as to provoke as little popular opposition as possible. Since most important offices are in the monarch's gift, he controls both important sources of patronage and, directly or indirectly, most of the resources of the state. Import licenses and government contracts can be lucrative sources of wealth. The monarch can use these as a means of cementing the loyalty of the elite. Appointments to the officer corps are another area critical to the survival of the regime. The autocrat can use his control over the armed forces to assure himself of its loyalty.

Above all, autocrats should take care of the interests of the members of his extended royal family. If satisfied, these princes can buttress the regime. If dissatisfied or indifferent, they will provide the autocrat and the regime little effective support (Herb 1999). At the same time, the modernizing autocrat cannot let patrimonialism get out of hand. Concerns about loyalty cannot be allowed to completely overbalance the need for competence and efficiency. The economic difficulties that beset Iran during the late 1970s illustrate the sort of problems that can arise from the failure to find a proper balance. The regime's overly ambitious industrialization schemes and its lavish spending on the celebration of the monarchy and the personal luxuries of the royal family backfired. Although the military remained under the shah's control and there was little dissatisfaction among the elite, the regime was overthrown by a revolt from below. In the two decades that followed, the smaller monarchies of the Persian Gulf have not been subject to the same sort of difficulties. Their higher Gross Domestic Product (GDP) per capita has put them in a more favorable position than any of the large-population oil states. But even the oil-generated wealth of the Gulf monarchies has its limit, as noted above. In such a situation, it may be more difficult to strike the proper balance between the major beneficiaries of the regime rewarded by the regime's patrimonial largess and the interests of the general public.

Summary

In the short run, none of today's modernizing autocrats face the sort of revolutionary ferment that toppled the shah's regime in Iran. Nonetheless, there are grounds for concern over the long term. Financial strains, official corruption, inefficiency, the growth of the middle class, and the revolutionary appeal of Islamist politics collectively represent a significant threat. Many of the regimes have experimented cautiously with power-sharing. Few, however, have made anything like a full commitment to develop a modern constitutional system, subjecting the government to popular control or establishing meaningful protection for individual rights. It remains an open question what will become of such constitutional experiments as do exist. There are several possibilities. Pressures on these regimes may worsen and lead to a revolt from below (as in Iran) or provoke a coup (as in Iraq, Syria, and Egypt). On the other hand, political maneuvers may give the autocrats an indefinite lease on life, allowing them to balance traditional and modernizing forces successfully well into the future. A middle-range possibility also exists. These regimes might carry out the experiments with constitutional development seriously and successfully. In the last case, we might expect to see the evolution of modern constitutional monarchies. By sacrificing their right to rule, royal families, like some of their predecessors outside the Islamic world, might retain their right to reign. However, there are few precedents for such developments in recent times.

CASE STUDY: SAUDI ARABIA

Saudi Arabia is a modernizing autocracy. In fact, it is the most important modernizing autocracy at the turn of the twenty-first century. The country is located in a region that had been long cut off from the modern world, but the second half of the twentieth century faced Saudi Arabia with the need to adapt. The major supplier of oil on the international market throughout much of the post-World War II period, Saudi Arabia could not remain in isolation. It was buffeted by the currents of modern Arab nationalism, by the Arab–Israeli conflict, and by the cold war. As an important state in one of the most unstable regions of the contemporary world, it had to modernize as a defensive measure if for no other reason. While the monarchy had to face challenges from Arab radicals during the cold war, as the cold war ebbed, a new threat emerged – political Islam. The regime's moral corruption and alliances came under question. The challenges faced by the regime are typical of those faced by other modernizing autocracies. Yet, because of the country's importance, they have received greater attention from the outside world.

The modern state of Saudi Arabia lies astride the most holy and most important historical sites of Islamic history, Mecca and Medina. By the time the Prophet Muhammad died in AD 632, he ruled most of the Arab nation from his capital at Medina. The caliphs, who inherited his secular power, continued to rule from Medina for several decades. But some thirty years after Muhammad's death, the capital was moved to Damascus in Syria. The ability of the caliphs in Damascus and later Baghdad to impose their control over Arabia varied through time. The caliph was supposed to provide protection to those making the Hajj, the annual pilgrimage to the holy sites, but often local rulers were able to exercise their own claims to provide such protection. As at the time of the Prophet's birth, politics in Arabia continued to be dominated by clan and tribal interests. In 1258 the last Abbasid caliph was killed when Baghdad fell to the Mongols. The fourteenth century saw the rise of a new power, the Ottoman Turks. Converted to Islam, the Ottomans eventually conquered an empire that included the Balkans, Anatolia, Mesopotamia, Egypt and North Africa, and much of the Arabian Peninsula. The Ottoman Sultan became the new caliph.

The Ottoman Empire remained multinational until early in the twentieth century when Turkish nationalists attempted to promote its Turkish identity. Although it was marginalized politically early in the history of Islam, Arabia remained an important religious center. Thus, the character of the regime that controls the two holy sites continues to be important not only to the people of the country itself but also to the rest of the Islamic world. It was not by chance that the Saud dynasty rose to power in the newly formed state after the First World War. The family was known for its support of the Wahhabi sect, one of the strictest in all Islam. Muhammad ibn Abd al Wahhab, who lived in the eighteenth century, came from Uyaynah, an oasis in southern Najd near the present-day capital of Riyadh in the central part of the peninsula. A religious scholar and student of Islamic law, he led a movement that tried to purify Islam of practices that he believed were contrary to the teachings of the Prophet. He focused on the religious principle that there was only one God and thus opposed saint veneration and religious ceremonies that had become common in Islam.

These practices, he argued, were reversions to paganism. God is one.
He does not share his power with anyone. Abd al Wahhab was opposed by
the Shiite communities in the area, who had come to support many of the
practices that Abd al Wahhab opposed. After his efforts elsewhere did not
bear fruit, he sought support from other local leaders in his home region.
And the Al Saud family was willing to provide it.

The al Saud family had had its origins in the 1500s, in the same general
area in which Abd al Wahhab was to rise to prominence. The al Saud were
traditional tribal leaders, possessing the sort of vague authority that went
with that position. In 1744 Muhammad ibn Saud and Muhammad ibn Abd al
Wahhab swore an oath to form and govern a state by traditional Muslim
practices. This link with the new religious movement provided the al Saud
with a moral basis upon which to extend their authority. Saud began to lead
expeditions in the neighboring towns to wipe out the practices against
which Abd al Wahhab preached. By 1765 when he died, Muhammad ibn
Saud had spread his own and Wahhabi authority over most of the Najd
region in central Arabia. His son took over his mission, extending his
authority into Sunni towns in the Hijaz in the Northwest of the peninsula,
including Mecca and Medina, in 1803. This brought them into conflict with
the Ottomans. The Ottoman Empire had been in serious decline for several
centuries, but as the leading representative of Islam, the sultan could not
allow the holiest shrines of Islam to escape his control. Beset by internal
weakness, he deputized his lieutenant, the governor of Egypt, Muhammad
Ali, to put down the revolt. Egyptian forces defeated the al Saud in 1818. Ali
reestablished the authority of the Sharifs in the region, which they had
ruled since the tenth century. This brought an end to the first Saudi state.

A rebuilding process began. In their old heartland, the al Saud extended
their authority, by military campaigns, treaties, and the shrewd use of
Wahhabism. Campaigns were conducted according to the rules of Islamic
law, and tribute to the al Saud was rendered accordingly. By 1905 Abd al
Aziz had begun the process of reestablishing the al Saud to their earlier
position of dominance by his capture of the Najd. He was recognized by the
Ottomans and, in turn, recognized the sultan as his overlord. Abd al Aziz
continued to expand his control, relying on a system of alliances and a
radical Wahhabi movement, the Ikhwan, that provided many of his shock
troops. The Sharifs, who continued to control the Hijaz with the holy places
of Mecca and Medina, opposed Abd al Aziz in the West. They were allied
with the British who encouraged them to revolt against the Ottomans
during the First World War. The British were interested in propping up a
number of local rulers along the Persian Gulf coast; they wished to prevent

the rise of a single Arab state. A series of mistakes by the Sharifs after 1919, however, put them at a disadvantage and lost them British support. Abd al Aziz took control of the Hijaz in 1924. This put him in position to consolidate his control over what became modern-day Saudi Arabia.

Plate 11.1   Faisal bin abd al Aziz al Saud, son of the founder of modern Saudi Arabia and king from 1964 until he was assassinated in 1975.

Abd al Aziz was able to manage and control a number of disparate forces that were either opposed or unsupportive of his attempts to build a modern state in the peninsula. He outmaneuvered the British and defeated the Hashemite Sharifs. Abd al Aziz, however, was careful in dealing with his defeated enemies. Members of the Hashemite family were allowed to stay and prosper in the Hijaz. He also arranged for intermarriages with the Rashidi family whom he had defeated in the process of extending his control into the northern part of the peninsula. He was careful to cement his relations with tribal leaders, whose aid he had counted on in extending his influence. He had to deal with the radical Wahhabi differently. They opposed the use of any technology unknown at the time of the Prophet and along with it the creation of a modern state. By popular consultation across his domain and by persuading religious teachers (*ulama*), who originally opposed his project for the creation of a modern state, he managed to gain their support to disband the radicals' military forces. By the 1930s, the discovery of oil in Saudi Arabia provided the new kingdom with a financial windfall. The wealth generated by oil provided a financial resource the ruling family could use to cement its support among the disparate elements of the kingdom. It would become an essential element in Saudi domestic politics. By the time Abd al Aziz died in 1953, the kingdom had been consolidated.

Abd al Aziz's son, Saud, had been named crown prince by a long-established process of family consultation. With the death of his father, he assumed the throne. Saud had been profligate with his own personal resources before he became king, and he was so with the resources of the state thereafter. His tendency to appoint his younger sons to ministerial posts instead of more competent, older family members angered others in the family. Wasteful projects proliferated while development and education languished. Popular dissatisfaction also grew as people became aware of the dual culture developing in the country. The elite, who at one time lived little differently from commoners, had become wealthy and displayed the fact conspicuously. Saud also tried to limit the influence of modern and western ideas in the country. Members of the elite and the middle class who studied abroad were forbidden to study political science, law, and similar subjects. Saud's social conservatism made his support of Gamel Abdel Nasser and Egypt puzzling. While both leaders supported the liberation of Arab peoples from foreign oppression, Nasser was a socialist and an anti-monarchist. Other members of the Saudi elite feared that the presence of large numbers of Egyptian advisers in Saudi Arabia would spread dangerous ideas.

In November 1964 the *ulama* issued a fatwa deposing Saud and making Faisal king. As king, Faisal followed policies that he had initiated during two earlier periods, one as virtual regent for Saud and the other as his prime minister. Faisal was a pious Muslim and a modernizing autocrat par excellence. He attempted to govern with the openness and magnanimity of a traditional tribal leader while modernizing the country economically and administratively. He invested in primary schools, vocational schools, and universities. A school for girls was opened although it was put under religious control. The armed forces were modernized. He permitted the introduction of television in the kingdom. He supported the Arab side in the 1967 and 1973 wars with Israel. And with the oil boycott of 1973, Saudi Arabia became the dominant power in the Organization of Petroleum Exporting Countries (OPEC). The oil boom that followed provided the kingdom with financial reserves of $150 billion.

When Faisal was assassinated in 1975, power passed to Crown Prince Khalid. Under King Khalid (1975–82) and King Fahd (1982–2005), the regime continued its modernization process while at the same time attempting to reconcile modernization with traditionalist critics.

These critics became especially important in 1979, when a group of rebels seized control of the Grand Mosque in Mecca. The diatribes against the Saudi monarchy followed the same line as had those of the recently victorious revolutionaries in Iran. The seizure sent shockwaves through the kingdom. After receiving a religious dispensation to use force to retake the shrine, the military, aided by French Special Forces, took over two weeks to complete the operation. All the surviving rebels were eventually executed, but the revolt was an object lesson about the dangers the regime faced from Islamic radicals. The government became increasingly cautious in both its foreign and domestic policies. During the crisis, the king had made promises of major reforms, but never fulfilled them. Instead, controls over society were tightened. Meanwhile, military modernization proceeded full pace. The armed forces were expanded and purchased some of the most modern military equipment available from the West. The National Guard, the successor of the old tribal militias and Islamic radical forces that had played an essential role in the formation of the kingdom during the early part of the century, was modernized as well. The regime, thus, continued to play a policy of using the divisions within the armed forces to help solidify its control. The tribal-based National Guard continued to be regarded as the regime's internal security force.

Saudi Arabia has been an ally of the United States since 1945 when Abd al Aziz met with President Franklin Roosevelt on a US warship in the Persian Gulf. The US gained access to Saudi oil in exchange for promoting the security of the country and the dynasty. This relationship has not been without its difficulties, however. The Iraqi invasion of Kuwait, in August 1991, presented the regime with a dilemma. If it remained passive, Iraq could threaten the security of Saudi Arabia itself, but if the regime supported a western-led coalition in pushing Iraqi forces out of Kuwait, it would open itself up to conservative and pan-Arab criticism. The regime could not sit on the fence; without Saudi Arabia as a staging area, any coalition attempt to attack Iraqi forces in Kuwait would have been impossible. The government supported the coalition efforts, and, fortunately for the monarchy, the coalition victory came relatively swiftly. However, the long-range prospects for the country's security did not improve. Plans, sponsored by the United States, for a multinational Arab force to be stationed in the kingdom to help provide security came to nothing. So too did efforts to increase the US presence, if only by way of adding to the pre-positioned US military equipment in the kingdom, that would facilitate rapid emergency deployment of US forces in a crisis.

Real political reform has been minimal. In February 1992, the king issued decrees providing for the semblance of a constitution. He appointed a consultative council to advise him on the governance of the kingdom, and some powers were to be devolved to regional governments. Yet, these changes were of no great significance. Not only was the council appointed by the king, its powers were only advisory, and it could be dismissed at will. The governorships were filled with members of the royal family or tribal loyalists. The royal family continued to intermarry with tribal and business elites. The media remained under government control. And important positions in the administration remained in the family or under its control. The regime continued to support a strict interpretation of Islamic law, and began to violate homes to make sure that Islamic norms were being adhered to. The regime used its patronage or denial of patronage to certain groups as a method of controlling them. The *ulama*, critical for the legitimacy of the regime and patronized by the state and the royal family, remain largely under their control. The various segments of the business community and the middle class benefited from their connections with the royal family and profit from state contracts, access to government employment, and inside information. The various regions were treated differently. The Shiite East found itself shortchanged as did the Southwest.

The fall of oil prices that began in the mid-1980s placed significant pressure on the kingdom. By the end of the 1990s, its foreign reserves had virtually disappeared. The fall in oil revenue forced a cutback in foreign employment, which had skyrocketed since the oil boom that began in the early 1970s. The decline in revenue also meant the regime's ability to buy support by the lavish distribution of jobs, state contracts, and social benefits also had to be curtailed. The change in the government's financial situation only served to exacerbate the opposition that had grown up despite the regime's efforts to forestall it. Those who felt they had not benefited sufficiently from the country's oil wealth as well as those who had received favorable treatment found reason to oppose the government. The motivation for the have-nots is obvious. Relative deprivation played a considerable role. However, even those groups who had access to state resources came to recognize their own distinct interest and were empowered by their success to demand more. Demands against the regime became more public, violating the norm that political discussion was to remain a private matter. While demands for liberal constitutional and administrative reform played a role, the most persistent demands came from religious conservatives. Groups based inside and outside the kingdom, most notably al Qaeda, continued to oppose the government; in 1995 United States military barracks in Riyadh came under terrorist attack, and in 2004 the country suffered terrorist attacks again.

At the turn of the twenty-first century, the modernizing autocracy of Saudi Arabia continued to face the dilemmas of modernization. Political changes were modest. In 2005 the regime held all-male elections for one-half of the seats on municipal councils (the other half are appointed). Islamist candidates endorsed by the religious establishment did well. In short, the regime continued to govern by its well-established methods. The intelligence services remained large and pervasive; surveillance and censorship of private communications were widespread. The regime has not moved significantly in the direction of constitutionalism and the rule of law. As one scholar put it, Saudi Arabia has followed the "paradigm of monarchy as a family business" (Herb 1999: 21). At the same time criticism of the principle of autocratic government was becoming more widely and more clearly voiced. Neither liberals nor religious conservatives found the formula for ruling particularly attractive. Still, as the holder of one-fourth of the world's oil reserves, the regime possesses a tremendous asset. It is able to insulate itself from the criticism of allies, who have pushed other governments much less authoritarian to liberalize. Furthermore, it is able, given Saudi oil's low cost of exploitation, to drive other exporters out of the market by lowering prices and selling as much oil as it needs to meet its financial targets. But, if modernization is an inexorable process, oil, the regime's ace in the hole, may not be able to save it indefinitely.

Neo-sultanistic regimes

Neo-patrimonialism, i.e., politics based on largely unchecked personal power and patronage in a nominally modern system, is common in the developing world. Sultanism is its most extreme variant. **Sultanistic** or **neo-sultanistic** regimes are nominally modern regimes in which all the effective governmental power resides in the hands of a single dictator and where constitutional and other limits upon his power are essentially nominal. In a truly neo-sultanistic regime, all the offices and institutions of government depend upon the ruler. When he is removed from power, the government collapses, and even the state may be threatened (Chehabi and Linz 1998: 10). Neo-sultanistic regimes conform to the essentials of Aristotle's tyranny. They are kleptocracies (i.e., regimes based on theft) since the dictator feels little scruple about using state power to increase his personal wealth and the wealth of his principal subordinates. In fact, the loyalty of the dictator's principal subordinates is guaranteed, in large measure, by his willingness to allow them to despoil the state along with him. The dictator is normally satisfied with the docility of the general public and other political leaders. In short, other political actors are allowed to exist provided they play a clearly subordinate role and follow strategies designed not to challenge the dictator in any substantial respect. However, political opposition that steps beyond the narrow pale it is allowed faces repression.

Neo-sultanism is an "ideal type," a standard or model used to explain how politics works but not meant to be an exact description of any actual regime. Some regimes come quite close to adhering to this standard. The Duvalier dictatorship in Haiti, which collapsed in the mid-1980s, and the Mobutu dictatorship in Zaire, which ended in 1997 (see the case study), fit this pattern quite closely. Other regimes such as Stroessner's in Paraguay (1954 to 1989) fit the pattern closely but did not suffer institutional collapse when the dictator was removed. Still other regimes in the developing world are rife with corruption and systematically violate the rule of law although their leaders may not be able to exercise full-fledged sultanistic control. Nonetheless, neo-sultanism is a useful concept since it describes a set of vices common to a significant number of contemporary political systems.

How neo-sultanism arises

From a modernization perspective, neo-sultanistic regimes represent instances of arrested development just like modernizing autocracies. Neo-sultanism is most likely to arise where the modern economy is an enclave within a largely traditional social and economic fabric. Countries with a small but economically significant export sector provide sufficient revenue to modernize some elements of the state. A military establishment can be armed and trained. The rudiments of a modern state organization can be established. A modern-looking judiciary and legislature can be provided for. Yet, in such a modernizing society where the truly modern sector remains small, much of the society remains traditional by default. A small middle class, a dependent or impoverished peasant sector, a lack of social capital characterize these societies. In these situations access to state revenues can become an important prize for the political elite. And the contest to acquire that prize may assume a winner-take-all character where the winner becomes a neo-sultanistic ruler. Neo-sultanistic regimes can arise where praetorianism prevails.

In fact, neo-sultanistic regimes often have their immediate origin in coups. In short, partial modernization, clever but unprincipled political leadership, and an international political environment auspicious for the cultivation of such local leaders can promote the rise and continuance of neo-sultanistic regimes.

Techniques of neo-sultanistic rule

Like their traditional authoritarian counterparts, neo-sultanistic regimes rely on personal connections, patronage, and loyalty based more on payoffs than principle. Neo-sultanistic regimes, however, are modern at least in form. The leader does not pretend to be a traditional ruler although he makes extensive use of some of the techniques reminiscent of traditional rulers: patronage-based politics, the exaggerated importance of personal loyalty to the ruler, and the downplaying of modern norms of bureaucratic rationality and the rule of law. Some neo-sultanistic regimes establish the office of "president for life," but such legalistic mechanisms are not an essential part of neo-sultanistic systems. Many of these systems, in fact, resemble modern liberal democracies in their official constitutional structures, but they are facade democracies. The constitution serves a ceremonial rather than an effective function. The constitution and the procedures it describes legitimize the role of the leader as being the chosen representative of the nation and by right holding office and exercising extensive powers. However, the real business of politics goes on behind the constitutional facade. Deals are cut; opponents are bought off or repressed; elections are fraudulently conducted. As a consequence of their modern – even democratic – pretensions neo-sultanistic rulers can use some but not all of the techniques their truly traditional counterparts employ.

Personalism

Any sultanistic regime, be it a traditional one or one that is neo-sultanistic, is rooted in the authority of the ruler and his ability to control individuals and institutions. While it is rare for the ruler to convincingly portray himself as a heroic figure, he can often successfully pose as paternalistically interested in the personal welfare of his subjects. He is the patron, the godfather, the source of all patronage. Regardless of truth or falsity of the picture of the leader as a wise and benevolent father-figure, he must in actuality head a patronage network of virtually universal reach. It is this network that allows him to co-opt potential opponents and cement the loyalty of his associates and his subjects. The ruler's personal authority and his ability to confer or withhold benefits are one of the keys to the system.

Controlling governmental institutions

If personalism is to prevail, the neo-sultanistic leader must render the courts, the bureaucracy, and the armed forces subservient to his will. Under neo-sultanism, the legislature's role too is largely ceremonial. The legislature possesses no effective power or real will to serve as a check upon the executive. The leader's ability to dispose of the revenues and resources of the state largely as he pleases provides him with the ability to subvert the other institutions of government. Members of supposedly autonomous institutions can be bought off so that their legal independence becomes largely a charade. In a society with weak institutions and limited social capital, many politicians are willing to play a subordinate role in the patronage game. If they should fail to do so, the ruler has harsher weapons in his arsenal. In sum, by being able to buy off or coerce potential opponents, the neo-sultanistic ruler can maintain himself in power despite the nominal democratic and liberal elements of the system that promote rotation in office, and he can ignore the rule of law.

A regime party and ideology

Neo-sultanistic rulers often find it convenient to establish a subservient political party and personality-focused ideology that supports the position of the leader, or they may make use of a party or ideology already in place. Whatever its origin, the regime party does not assume the status of old-style totalitarian parties. It lacks that degree of institutionalization and the sort of mass base typical of totalitarian parties. The regime party serves as an instrument for the neo-sultanistic ruler. No more than the institutions of government can it represent an independent force within the system. Under the sultanistic style of rule, it is simply another part of the patronage network and another vehicle for exercising political control. It is essentially a cadre party even if it seems to pretend to a more expansive role. Neo-sultanistic rulers may find an ideological defense of the regime and its policies useful although ideology is not a major underlying principle or legitimizing element in neo-sultanistic systems. The ideologies of sultanistic regimes, when they have them, can vary widely. These ideologies are not notable for their cogency or logical consistency. They are unlikely to be taken seriously outside of the country or often even within it. These ideologies may contain religious elements or appeals to leftwing or fascist-like principles. A common thread is nationalism and adulation of the leader. In short, the official legitimizing principles of the regime – including democracy, cold-war anti-communism, or nationalism – are merely formalistic, inspiring little popular enthusiasm.

The armed forces

Neo-sultanistic rulers have to pay close attention to the armed forces since the military and security forces play a considerable role in maintaining them in power. Under a truly neo-sultanism, the military is not sufficiently institutionalized to play a role independent of the figure who leads it. The leader takes steps to assure that it will never develop this independent institutional perspective or the ability to act upon it. The dictator must also insure that no one in the armed forces is able to amass the power or popularity that can threaten his rule. Positions in the officer corps are positions of privilege. The ruler supervises appointments in more than a perfunctory manner since he must assure officers are personally loyal and beholden to him. Thus, ordinary rules about professionalism, the nonpolitical character of the military, and promotion based on time in rank and merit are regularly ignored, as are rules requiring retirement. However, the neo-sultanistic ruler must assure himself that the armed forces are not only loyal but have the technical capability to defend the regime. This can lead to the classic dilemma of loyalty versus competence. Since the neo-sultanistic dictator cannot be satisfied with objective civilian control (see Chapter 7), the problem may require creative solutions. To resolve it, some rulers have made use of elite forces personally responsible to themselves or irregular forces capable of repression and serving as a counterweight to the official military.

Foreign support

Foreign political actors also play a role in buttressing neo-sultanistic regimes. Foreign corporations can provide the capital necessary to develop the country's economic resources; foreign governments can assist with aid and training for the armed forces and diplomatic support and political cover. It is often useful for dictators to appear to be democrats. Most sultanistic dictatorships have a facade constitution providing the trappings of democracy. The praise and cultivation by powerful foreign governments can give this pretense of democracy badly needed credibility. In the extreme, foreign powers may provide military forces to suppress revolts against the regime. In return, foreign patrons receive access to valuable economic resources, a strategic ally, and stability within a region where instability is perceived as threatening their interests. There has been a quite obvious shift of where foreigners have been willing to support sultanistic regimes over the past several decades. During the cold war, the United States was especially concerned about leftist movements in Latin America and access to minerals in Africa. During the current era with terrorism and energy availability in the forefront, the regimes in places such as Central Asia where both of these concerns are critical are likely to receive uncritical support.

The durability of neo-sultanistic regimes

Increasingly since the 1980s, neo-sultanistic dictators have found it necessary to fight off pressure to democratize or liberalize. This pressure has come both from internal and external sources when their foreign patrons turned against them. To fend off such pressure, dictators have put forward a variety of largely sham reforms. They have tried to stack national conferences intended to promote a transition with pro-regime elements. They have agreed to elections and then attempted to subvert the electoral process. They have played a "divide and rule" strategy, attempting to buy off one portion of the opposition while intimidating the other. The weakness of civil society is a key to the dictator's strength.

Neo-sultanistic regimes are inherently fragile because of their lack of moral purpose. Despite the political skill of its leading figure, both ancient tyrannies and modern neo-sultanistic regimes have been subject to a variety of mishaps. Since so much depends on the dictator's personal control, as the dictator ages, his principal subordinates may become restive. Personal rivalries or greed can spiral out of control, and the dictator's ability to control politics may falter. The coup that brought Stroessner's rule to an end was generated by this sort of crisis. If the society is sufficiently developed, as Paraguay was in 1989, when a personalistic dictator leaves or is forced from the scene, democratization may ensue. Loosening neo-sultanistic controls too much or applying them too stringently can also result in a regime-ending crisis. The society itself may find neo-sultanistic rule unacceptable and rise up against the dictator at some point as happened against Ferdinand Marcos of the Philippines in 1986.

A sultanistic dictatorship survived for over forty years in Nicaragua under the Somozas and Haiti under the Duvaliers. The sultanistic dictator, Trujillo, ruled the Dominican Republic for decades, and his counterpart, Batista, controlled Cuba for much of the 1950s. For nearly two decades, Ferdinand Marcos dominated the Philippines in a sultanistic style until he was deposed in 1986. In post-independence Africa, a number of these regimes arose. The most notorious and long-lived of them was that of Mobutu Sese Seku in Zaire (1965–97). Sultanistic dictators may be replaced by other dictators of the same type. In Nicaragua and Haiti, son succeeded father. In Zaire, a popular rebellion replaced Mobutu with a successor who ruled in essentially the same style.

But revolutions, popular revolts, and foreign pressure can lead to a real political transition. This has happened in the Philippines and Nicaragua. However, the conditions that allowed for the rise of a neo-sultanistic dictator, in the first place, often endure and permit the rise of another neo-sultanistic dictator or another authoritarian or semi-authoritarian form of government. Democratic transitions are always subject to reversal. Today parts of the former Soviet Union in Central Asia and the Caucasus and parts of Africa have suffered from forms of rule that closely resemble the sultanistic ideal type.

In sum, neo-sultanistic regimes cannot survive in societies that have attained a significant degree of modernization. The institutional checks provided by professional and apolitical armed forces, a modern bureaucracy, and the judiciary establish a barrier to a would-be dictator's use of sultanistic techniques. And in societies that are economically developed and possess a large middle class, the attempt to use such techniques would, sooner or later, produce large-scale resistance. However, neo-sultanistic dictatorships can survive in societies that are not sufficiently modern to generate the necessary institutional or societal resistance to the abuse of power typical of this form of government. Societies where traditional norms and patrimonial linkages are strong, and whose allies or neighbors tolerate or encourage such dictatorships, provide breeding grounds for sultanistic dictators.

Neo-sultanism and the emergence of failed states

Once any regime is undermined, actual breakdown may take a variety of specific routes. A coup d'etat may remove the leader. So too can revolutionary movements. And as society matures, neo-sultanistic rulers may find themselves subject to pressures for democratization. These breakdowns have been the topics of previous chapters. One form of breakdown that neo-sultanistic rule is susceptible to has not been discussed thus far – state failure. Foreign invasion, civil war, secession, and insurgency can all produce state failure by depriving the state of the personnel, resources, and legitimacy it needs to function effectively (Rotberg 2004: 1–93). While other forms of government besides neo-sultanism can suffer state failure, neo-sultanistic regimes may be particularly prone to this sort of breakdown. Sultanism entails corruption and inefficiency. Such patrimonialism run rampant can undermine the foundations of the state itself, leading the administration of the country to collapse. Law and order, public services, economic activity, education, and the healthcare system break down. In short, the collapse of a sultanistic regime can lead to the same consequences as defeat and enemy occupation after a major war. Yet, given the proper circumstances, a modern society defeated in war can rebuild itself, using the skills of the population. Even with the state and its military temporarily destroyed, a modern society is, in the words of the noted Scottish geographer, Halford MacKinder, a "going concern" (MacKinder 1962: 8–10). It can often reconstitute itself in short order. However, state failure normally occurs in fragile societies that are only partly modern, where the GDP, education, social capital, and modern economic skills are limited to begin with. State failure not only disrupts the governmental services basic to a civilized life; it also destroys the society's capacity to carry them out. Skills are lost, loyalty and trust are subverted, and the basic ethos necessary for good government and good citizenship is undermined.

Recently, failed states emerged in Africa during the 1990s. The presidents of Zaire/Congo, Somalia, and Liberia had pushed the corruption typical of the sultanistic regimes beyond sustainable limits. During the cold war period, their superpower patrons had provided the necessary financial and military support to sustain neo-sultanistic regimes in a number of countries, despite the growing difficulties these regimes experienced. But the end of the cold war saw Russia/the Soviet Union unable to support overseas commitments of any appreciable cost, and the United States, now without a rival, was unwilling to sustain the existing system or compel real reform. As a neo-sultanistic government begins to collapse, outsiders – governments in the region or private criminal organizations – may aid local insurgents who exercise de facto control parts of the country containing valuable assets. Diamonds have proven an attraction, but so too has the eventual exploitation of other mineral resources. Although they have not been neo-sultanistic, states in other areas have suffered failure or near failure during the 1990s: Afghanistan under the Taliban and Cambodia after extended and brutal wars. Many other weak states under rapacious or incompetent rulers could easily slide into the pathology.

The process of state failure can be accelerated by war, drought, and famine. In fact, famines themselves are a symptom rather than a primary cause of state failure. As the research of Amatyra Sen (Sen 1981) has shown, functioning public administrations and governments concerned with the problems of its people can prevent famines. In modern times, famine is a political disaster brought about by incompetent administration or unconcerned governments. The natural problems leading to it only provide the opportunity for the political failure. The symptoms of state failure are stark: the breakdown of the cash economy because of such rapid inflation that the national currency loses its capacity to serve as a medium of exchange; the breakdown of public order and a wholesale increase in crime; loss of control of national territory to internal insurgents, foreign armies, or both. Most troubling, the armed forces themselves turn on the population, using the weapons to take what they please by force. The process of state failure does not occur overnight, it is a rot that attacks state institutions and the public faith in them that may take decades. But the fall of the regime, when and if it occurs, may be dramatic.

State failure often leads to the growth of warlordism. **Warlords** are leaders commanding sufficient formal or informal military forces and personal adherents to partially fill the void left by the collapsing state administration. They impose order and protect those individuals and property that they choose to protect. Warlords may be clan, ideological, religious, or simply criminal leaders, but the primary basis of their authority is force. They cannot provide even the minimal requisites for a minimal state. Lacking an established body of law or a neutral method to resolve disputes, their rule is by definition predatory. Warlords may profit from protecting an economy that would be illegal under the rules of any law-abiding state: production and transportation of drugs, smuggling, and the illicit extraction of natural resources. Once a state has collapsed and warlords have taken over, a concerted international effort may be required to reestablish it.

CASE STUDY: ZAIRE

If any country deserves the sympathy of the outside world for the injustices heaped upon it during the nineteenth and twentieth centuries, it is Zaire (currently the Democratic Republic of the Congo). Its colonial experience was among the harshest and most tragic. Its independence-era government was among the world's worst. Efforts of the world community to correct problems that outsiders had been instrumental in causing were fitful at best. Zaire from 1965 to 1997 was ruled by Mobutu Sese Seku, a former sergeant-major in the Belgian army in the Congo, who took over the country via a coup d'etat and ruled it as his personal fief for over thirty years. Zaire represents a classic case of neo-sultanistic rule. The Zairean experience also illustrates the sort of processes that undermine the state and lead to state failure. States fail not by accident but as the result of systematic abuse and negligence. Zaire is large and diverse, making it difficult to administer in the best of circumstances. It is in terms of territory the largest country in sub-Saharan Africa, approximately the size of the United States east of the Mississippi River. Its 40 million people belong to 250 ethnic groups and speak 250 different languages. Zaire is poor.

In 1997 when the Mobutu regime collapsed, the economy ranked 115th out of 123 countries in terms of GNP (Gross National Product) per capita. Its GNP per capita was an estimated $790.

Map 11.2 Zaire
Source: Environmental Systems Research Institute (ESRI) map data. CIA

The economy of independent Zaire, as in colonial times, was largely based on the export of primary products such as copper, cobalt, diamonds, and coffee. The mineral wealth especially attracted foreign investment. Zaire, however, remained poor, and the mismanagement of the Mobutu government made it poorer still. From 1965 to 1990 the economy consistently lost ground. During that period, GNP actually declined at an annual rate of 2.2 percent. The Mobutu government conducted 6 monetary reforms and launched 2 new currencies in its 32 years in office. Typical of the sort of hyper-inflation that Zaireans had to endure was the fate of "New Zaire," the currency unit that replaced the "Zaire" in late 1993. When it was first issued, the new currency traded at 10 to the dollar. Yet by the time Mobutu fell in 1997, the New Zaire was trading at 100,000 to the dollar, having lost 99.99 percent of its value in 4 years.

The colonial predecessor of modern Zaire, the Congo Free State, was established by the Congress of Berlin (1884–5) as the personal domain of King Leopold II of Belgium. Under the king's rule, the colony was subject to war, regimentation, and repression. Colonial authorities collected rubber and ivory by force and violence, at times using local chiefs to impose their exactions, then dismissing them when they resisted. Revolts were violently suppressed. The king's personal power was not checked until 1908 when the government of Belgium annexed the colony outright because of the horrendous abuses that occurred under Leopold's rule (Hochschild 1998).

While the most outrageous practices of the colonial administration of the king were eventually curtailed somewhat, forced labor continued and the local population enjoyed few rights. The hand of the colonial administration was heavy. By independence some ten thousand European administrators directed the state. The power of the military and foreign corporations was immense. Belgium did little to prepare the country for independence. Most Africans were kept under tribal law, and only an educated few were given the modern legal status that European settlers in the colony enjoyed. The Belgians established little in the way of local government. Not until 1957, three years before independence, were Africans given the right to vote for local government councils and a limited share in running their own affairs. But by that time, these limited rights proved unsatisfactory. A national awakening had occurred, and the decolonization movement had swept across Africa. And the Belgian Congo could not escape United Nations' (UN) scrutiny. The Congo, however, was poorly prepared to administer its own affairs. The number of college graduates remained a mere handful. No native Congolese held officer rank in the Belgian Congo's military forces. There had been no appreciable effort to establish local Congolese institutions that could ease the administrative problems inherent in the transition from foreign rule to independence. And, worst of all, the newly independent Congo became caught up in cold war politics.

In January 1960 a roundtable conference laid the groundwork for independence, and national elections were held in May. As a consequence of these elections, Patrice Lumumba, whose party won the largest number of votes, became prime minister. Lumumba was a leftist, distrusted by the West, especially the United States. After the official beginning of independence on June 30, events developed quickly. In July the army mutinied against its European officers. The rebellion spread to the provinces of Katanga and Équateur. Within a matter of days, Joseph-Désiré Mobutu (later Mobutu Sese Seku) was made chief-of-staff and the officer corps was Africanized. National unity itself was threatened when Moïse Tsambe declared mineral-rich Katanga an independent state. The Belgians stepped in to suppress the rebellion, and the central government requested UN assistance. The first UN troops arrived on July 15. Meanwhile a rupture occurred between Prime Minister Lumumba and

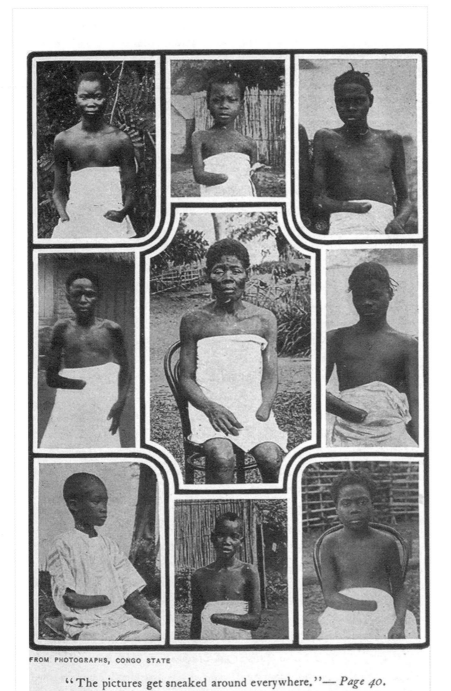

FROM PHOTOGRAPHS, CONGO STATE

"The pictures get sneaked around everywhere."— *Page 40.*

Plate 11.2 Atrocities in the Congo under King Leopold of Belgium. Source: *King Leopold's Soliloquy*, 1905.

the President, Joseph Kasavubu. Kasavubu dismissed Lumumba and appointed a new government. The change solved little. By mid-September Mobutu, as chief-of-staff, was in effective, if temporary, charge of the government. It was only a first step in his consolidation of power. Over the next five years, a complex series of power struggles ensued. Patrice Lumumba was assassinated; Katangese succession was finally suppressed, and in November of 1965 Mobutu seized the presidency by means of a coup d'etat.

Mobutu established a neo-sultanistic regime, using the state and its ability to control the country's wealth to feather his own nest. For over three decades, Mobutu successfully played off against each other the international and domestic interests that might have moved to unseat him. During the entire cold war period, his position was buttressed by Zaire's strategic importance. Zaire was situated in the heart of southern Africa and was a storehouse of strategic minerals. The region was of critical importance to the United States and western powers for both economic and military reasons. Southern Africa was a major producer of such militarily important minerals as cobalt, platinum, and manganese, whose only other major commercial source was the Soviet Union. The US-supported assassination of Lumumba and the rise of Mobutu to power provided the United States, France, and Belgium with a reliable ally in a region that became increasingly unstable as the cold war progressed. By the mid-1970s Mobutu's usefulness was further enhanced by the establishment of radical Marxist regimes in nearby Angola and Mozambique, regimes supported by the Soviet Union. During the same period neighboring Southern Rhodesia, under the name Zimbabwe, had its independence recognized and an African government established. Soviet influence seemed to be on the march, and the inherent instability of the region was even more evident. Mobutu was needed as an ally more than ever.

The strategic importance of Mobutu's regime insulated him from the sort of pressure to which other governments were often subjected. As the financial condition of the government became more and more desperate, Zaire, like many other governments similarly circumstanced, had to rely on the International Monetary Fund (IMF) for assistance. But while the fund normally imposed and enforced stringent requirements for financial and economic reform on member states receiving its assistance, Zaire managed to avoid fulfilling the most burdensome IMF exactions and instead received relatively favorable treatment. Suspicions rose that the US and France had helped shape policy since the two countries had a great deal of influence over IMF policy and its day-to-day management.

Mobutu was equally skillful in handling domestic forces. He played the nationalist card and established Mobutuism as the official national ideology, in the process developing a personality cult for himself. Mobutuist ideology included three principles: nationalism, revolution, and authenticity. The first principle was directed against regionalism and tribalism. The second, revolution, was not as radical as it sounded. It amounted to essentially a third-way approach somewhere between capitalism and communism. Such approaches proliferated in the cold-war era. Authenticity accounted for the change the country's name from Congo to Zaire, as well as other name changes. The old European names of provinces and cities were replaced by African ones. People too were forced to take African instead of European or Christian names. Mobutu, himself, dropped Joseph-Désiré and assumed Sese Seku Nkuku waza Banga, or "all-conquering warrior who goes from triumph to triumph." In light of the supposed Zairean tradition that the people should not have two chiefs, an official one-party state was created.

Mobutuism provided a pretext for the nationalization of foreign firms and the official abolition of opposition parties, but it was Mobutu's mastery of the techniques of neo-patrimonial rule that accounted for his ability to keep potential domestic opponents at bay for over three decades. Mobutu knew how to distribute the spoils of office to win the personal loyalty of some, and how to use force to intimidate others. The expropriation of foreign-owned assets provided an opportunity for Mobutu and his cronies to profit handsomely. Expropriation did not drive away foreign investment since foreigners were anxious to profit from Zaire's mineral wealth. Thus, Mobutu and his state were able to issue licenses and control the royalties from foreign firms exploiting the country's vast trove of natural resources. In 1993 Mobutu was estimated to have a personal fortune worth $5 billion. He was not loath to let his loyalists profit either. A dozen or so intimates benefited mightily. In addition, President Mobutu developed a 10,000-man-strong cadre of administrators who were personally loyal to him. He saw to it that administrative posts were rotated among this group so that each have a chance to hold a position where perks, legal and illegal, were more lucrative. The military remained poorly trained and disorganized. This not only allowed state funds to be siphoned off to other uses; it assured Mobutu that the armed forces would be unable to act effectively against him. Elite units, however, were well trained, mostly by Israelis, and they were drawn primarily from Mobutu's own Équateur province. So too were the vast majority of the high command and defense ministry officials.

Commanders of individual units were to be personally loyal to the president, and Mobutu sought to deal with each directly rather than follow a typical hierarchical command structure. The apparatus for controlling the civilian population consisted of a variety of paramilitary and intelligence services. As with the military, Mobutu sought to control each of these services directly. They all had individual access to the president and had, like most other branches of the government, a reputation for corruption and systematic human rights violations. Over three decades, the regime faced a variety of local rebellions and protests, but it remained capable of putting them down, sometimes with foreign assistance until almost the end of its tenure. By 1990, however, Zaire had reached a crisis. As statistics on inflation and the fall of GNP demonstrate, Mobutu's rule produced a steady decline in the productivity of the economy. Similar decay had affected the state apparatus and the lives of the people. Public services were erratic or nonexistent. Lower-level functionaries were not paid on time or with any currency of real value. Infrastructure had rotted away, and the very enterprises that provided export earnings had slowed down their activities or closed. Most dramatically, the international situation had changed. The cold war had ended. Cuban troops that had aided the Angolan government were gone. France, long a leading patron of Zaire and other French-speaking African states, had begun to change its African policy.

Since its involvement in the continent, France had followed a policy of realpolitik, serving the narrow national interests of France regardless of the consequences for human rights or democracy in Africa. Following this line, the French found Mobutu and similar dictators perfectly acceptable custodians of French interests. However, by 1990 the French view had shifted. Just as democracy and human rights had become important foreign policy issues for other states in dealing with other parts of the world, France decided to apply these principles to Africa as well. With the end of the cold war, the forces of democracy seemed to be on the ascent. Hence, the French encouraged their African protégés, many of them also presidents-for-life like Mobutu, to hold national conferences where the government and opposition could negotiate reforms to liberalize and democratize their systems of government. With France, the US, and Belgium conditioning their continued assistance to the country on the calling of a national conference, Zaire was under pressure to change.

Yet, even though he was faced by both external and internal pressure for democratization, Mobutu played his hand skillfully. He convened a national conference in early 1991, but instead of negotiating a democratic transition, he relied on a strategy of negotiation and force to stay in power. Only one-third of the delegates were representatives of opposition political parties. Mobutu followed a policy of obstructionism as well as divide and rule. The process dragged on for several years. Against a background of popular protests and riots both by the population as well as government troops, two separate governments emerged. One approved by the national conference and headed by an ex-Mobutu interior minister, Etienne Tshisekedi, as prime minister, and the other, led by another opposition politician, was appointed by and responsible to Mobutu himself. Mobutu was successful in depriving the Tshisekedi government of its foreign support. The US distrusted the prime minister because of his background. France was willing to negotiate a compromise choice as prime minister to resolve the differences between Mobutu and Tshisekedi. With the internal opposition divided and foreign powers unwilling to increase pressure against him, Mobutu remained in power and in command of the state machine.

The final crisis that brought Mobutu down was related to international events. The mid-1994 genocide against Tutsis in neighboring Rwanda led to a pro-Tutsi reaction from other countries in the region. These countries backed Tutsi exiles in their bid to overthrow the Hutu-dominated government. A Tutsi-dominated government was set up in Rwanda, and Hutu extremists who had led the genocide fled. Many of them found their way into eastern Zaire. There they established secure bases and planned to continue their struggle. Although the new Rwandan government protested, the Zairean government seemed both unwilling and unable to take action. The presence of a new group of Hutu in Zaire only exacerbated tensions on its eastern frontier. Both native Zairean Tutsis, who had been in the country since before independence, as well as later arrivals had long been the target of hostility from other groups in the population. The presence of Hutu refugees and an increased availability of guns only worsened the problem.

In August 1996 a wave of violence against Zairean Tutsis began. When the Tutsis in Zaire, supported by their Rwandan brethren, revolted, Mobutu played the nationalist/ethnic card. Anti-Tutsi feeling was further inflamed when the Rwandan army invaded eastern Zaire and destroyed Hutu enclaves, forcing the refugees either to flee deeper in Zaire or to return home. At this point Mobutu lost control of much of the eastern part of the country, but the collapse of the state seemed to be of only regional significance since ethnic Tutsis were unlikely to rouse the support of the country's other groups. However, the situation quickly changed when

Laurent Kabila, an opponent of Mobutu since the 1960s, joined the rebellion on October 8. Kabila had long led an apparently moribund insurgency in Shaba province. He became the figure around whom the rebels could rally. Zaire's army collapsed. Citizens had more to fear from the fleeing Zairean forces, which raped and looted as they retreated, than they had from anyone else. Despite the size of the country, the difficulties of the terrain, and the dismal state of the transportation system, the rebels advanced with remarkable speed. The civil war was over by May 1997. The state and its army's capacity to defend it had been hollowed out. Mobutu fled the country and died shortly thereafter.

Throughout his four years in office, Laurent Kabila was a disappointment. The state functioned no better than it had during Mobutu's last years, which is to say virtually not at all. Both his victory in the civil war and his effort to suppress rebellions against his own rule depended heavily on foreign troops. Murdered in early 2001 by one of his own bodyguards, Kabila was succeeded by his son, Joseph. Zaire, renamed the Democratic Republic of Congo by the elder Kabila, remains an internationally recognized "sovereign" state, but lacks any effectively functioning state structure. Rebellions contained by foreign forces have not been suppressed completely. This outcome is not surprising. In many ways, Laurent Kabila, though a leftist, seemed to be cut from the same cloth as Mobutu in that he appeared to be more interested in personalized power than institution-building. Even though the younger Kabila was elected president in his own right in 2006, he has yet to take firm command and rebuild the capacity of the Congolese state. In any event, the process of state-(re)building in Congo is likely to be a difficult one. While the personnel of the old state have not completely disappeared, the state's morale, sense of probity, and capacity have substantially eroded. The causes of this have their roots as far back as the colonial era, but the neo-patrimonialism of Mobutu Sese Seku and his cannibalization of the state for the benefit of himself and his cronies has been the most important and most immediate cause.

Conclusion

Contemporary patrimonial rulers, whether traditional or nontraditional, buck modern trends that put primacy on ideology and bureaucratic rationality. They use a variety of tactics to hold onto power. They combine co-optation with repression. Yet, if they are to consolidate their position, they have to avoid the worst excesses associated with patrimonial rule, the sort of excesses that Aristotle warned against when he described tyranny. Most tyrants – the analogue of modern personalistic patrimonial rule in classical Greek antiquity – lived on borrowed time. Today's patrimonial rulers are shrewder than ancient tyrants in a variety of ways. While ancient tyrants flaunted their arbitrary power, most modern patrimonial rulers have assumed a paternalistic posture in an effort to acquire some semblance of moral legitimacy. Furthermore, they have often engaged in stop-and-go tactics of liberalization or negotiation to divide the opposition.

In addition, patrimonial regimes in Muslim countries threatened by Islamic revolution have implemented Islamic law as the law of the state to inoculate themselves against Islamism. They have given financial aid and recognition to Islamic leaders and institutions. They have incorporated Islam into education and other state-sponsored activities. But as with the use of liberalization in dealing with the democratic opposition, these concessions are not meant to truly empower the Islamist opposition lest they develop the moral authority and physical power to start a revolution and actually overthrow the regime. In sum, building a regime on the basis of self-interest plus personal and familial connections is still a live option today in some countries. Patrimonialism may not have the moral or ideological appeal of democracy and the rule of law generally or of political Islam in the Muslim world, but they are a continuing, if limited, element of politics in many regimes. The patrimonial regimes that have survived and even prospered into the twenty-first century have made good use of these apparently moribund practices to form an elite and pro-regime coalition capable of resisting fundamental change.

Questions for further consideration

1   Compare and contrast the failures and successes of modernizing autocracies and neo-sultanistic states. Which are likely to be more stable in the long term? Why?
2   Some natural-resource-rich developing countries experience the "resource curse" as did Zaire – resource wealth led to large-scale corruption and political decay. How have the modernizing autocracies discussed in this chapter managed to avoid this problem?
3   What do you think the best long-term strategy for modernizing autocracies should be – repression or accommodation? Why?
4   Why are failed states difficult to rebuild? What sorts of efforts might be necessary to rebuild them?

5 When is neo-sultanism potentially an attractive strategy for ruling today? What would lead to the expansion or contraction of the number of rulers who might find it attractive?

6 During the cold war patrimonial regimes could rely on support from the West, especially the United States, because they were anti-communist. What resources do such regimes have today for gaining foreign support?

Further reading

Jason Brownlee, William B. Quandt, Abdeslam M. Maghraoui, Jean-François Seznec, Michael Herb, Jillian Schwedler, and Danniel Brumberg, "Democratization in the Arab World?," *Journal of Democracy*, 11, 4 (2002), 5–68. A useful series of essays on the Middle East.

H.E. Chehabi and Juan J. Linz (eds), *Sultanistic Regimes*. Baltimore, MD: Johns Hopkins University Press, 1998. Provides both the theory and case studies of neo-sultanistic regimes.

Michael Herb, *All in the Family: Absolutism, Revolution, and Democracy in the Middle Eastern Monarchies*. New York: State University of New York Press, 1999. Argues that keeping fellow members of the ruling family onboard is the key to survival in Middle Eastern modernizing autocracies.

Ellen Lust-Okar, *Structuring Conflict in the Arab World: Incumbents, Opponents, and Institutions*. Cambridge: Cambridge University Press, 2005. Analyzes the divide-and-rule strategy of Middle Eastern modernizing autocracies and other authoritarian states in the region.

12 Hybrid regimes

I do not think that it is possible to combine several principles in the same government, so as at the same time to maintain freedom, and really to oppose them to one another ... Accurately speaking there is no such thing as a mixed government.

(Alexis de Tocqueville, *Democracy in America*, 1835)

In this chapter

We consider a puzzle: why have regimes that are neither fully consolidated democracies nor fully consolidated authoritarian systems survived in great numbers into the twenty-first century? More importantly, why are many of them stable? This persistence of stable intermediate or hybrid types of regimes (or mixed governments as ancient and medieval commentators would have called them) illustrates the limits of the structural–functional approach. Structural functionalism predicts gradual consolidation or collapse. It tells us what sorts of requisites are needed for regime continuity. When these requisites are present, it is unlikely a regime will break down quickly since the political, economic, and social environment provide backup mechanisms to correct for specific failures and mistakes. But functional requisites are only part of the picture. Thus, this chapter focuses on the techniques and strategies followed by political elites in contemporary hybrid systems, a focus influenced by rational choice and game theory. The chapter includes cases drawn from Latin America and Russia.

Introduction

What Tocqueville termed "mixed governments" are today called "**hybrid regimes**." The mixed governments Tocqueville knew relied on such features as hereditary executives with significant powers and popularly elected assemblies to balance constitutionally contrary principles of legitimacy. Contemporary hybrid regimes also balance competing principles, but they do so in a different way. They have constitutions that are nominally democratic, but these constitutions do not guarantee fully in practice what they promise in theory. Depending on how seriously they fail to implement the basic requirements of democratic governance, these regimes may be classified as either "**semi-authoritarian**" – seriously in violation of democratic norms – or "**semi-democratic**" – failing to live up to democratic norms but approximating democratic practices in many respects. But for either variety the problem is the same: how can contrary principles coexist in the same regime in a stable fashion?

Both nineteenth-century mixed governments and twenty-first-century hybrid regimes survive despite their own internal logic and in spite of the fact that they seem to be running against a democratic tide. As many do today, Tocqueville saw democracy as the wave of the future, and he believed that in the clash of principles within mixed or hybrid regimes democracy would win out in the end. However, contrary to such democratic expectations, today many countries find themselves in a state in between democracy and authoritarianism where both democratic and authoritarian principles seem to be in play. Such regimes either fail to guarantee true political competition and an effective and universal right to vote, or they do not protect basic civil rights and civil liberties. It is tempting to say along with Tocqueville that hybrid regimes are somehow in the process of becoming democracies. But the data do not seem to support this claim. While it is true that some countries in this in-between status have experienced improvement in their adherence to democratic standards, others have seen deterioration. Still other countries have oscillated between improvement and deterioration or have remained stuck in a middle position. And some of these regimes seem quite stable (Carothers 2002).

The nature of hybrid regimes

Of the two competing principles of hybrid regimes, one (democracy) is formally proclaimed and not fully practiced while the other (authoritarianism) is actually practiced albeit by underhanded means. Officeholders, even when regularly elected, are not fully accountable to the public, and constitutional protections are neither wholly respected by the executive nor adequately enforced by the courts. However, unlike the ostensible constitutions of communist and some other authoritarian systems that exist solely for ceremonial purposes, the constitutions of even semi-authoritarian regimes are not totally nugatory. They do or can mean something. Semi-authoritarian rulers have to take internal rivals and at times the formal procedures of gaining, retaining, and exercising power seriously. The opposition, while weak, is not powerless. More than that;

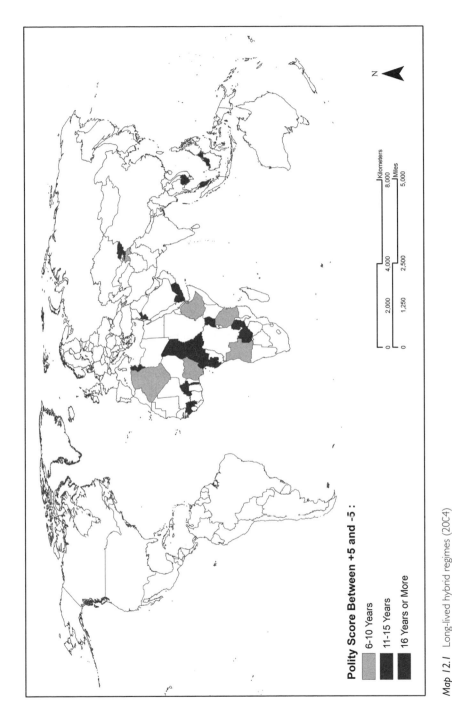

Polity Score Between +5 and -5 :

6-10 Years

11-15 Years

16 Years or More

Map 12.1 Long-lived hybrid regimes (20C4)

Source: Environmental Systems Research Institute (ESRI) map data. Data: Polity IV

Note: Polity IV ratings range from +10 (most democratic) to −10 (most authoritarian)

the ruling elite itself feels obliged to adhere to democratic norms on many occasions, usually violating them openly only when it has to do so to retain power. Thus, these regimes conduct elections although they are less than fully fair and free, and odds are stacked against the opposition. But they are not so unfair that the opposition feels it should automatically refuse to participate.

Varieties of hybrid regimes

Hybrid regimes are usually classified as "partly free" by Freedom House (Freedom House 2008) because they fail to meet certain standards of democratic governance. One standard, the political rights standard, includes the right of all citizens to vote and have the vote fairly counted, the right to form political parties and compete in elections, and the effective control of the people's representatives over public policy. The other standard, the civil liberties and civil rights standard, includes the right to the integrity of one's person and property; the right to associate freely in religious, labor, professional, cultural, community, and educational organizations; the right to speak out and publish freely, the right to protest peacefully and petition the government; and the guarantee of all legally established rights via an independent judiciary and the rule of law. Regimes can fail to fully meet either one or both of these sets of standards. Fareed Zakaria has labeled democracies that effectively implement the principle of majority rule (i.e., guarantee *political* rights) but seriously fail to protect minority and individual rights as "illiberal democracies" (Zakaria 2003). They are also called "electoral democracies." In contrast, other regimes fail in the opposite way. They are considerably less than fully democratic in terms of the political rights they grant to their subjects, but they protect many of the personal rights that fall within the category of civil liberties. These "liberal autocracies," traditional authoritarian regimes that have accommodated demands to liberalize, existed in the nineteenth century, and, in retrospect, were way stations on the road to full democratic development. A third sort of regime falls short in both categories. They are sometimes referred to as "electoral authoritarianism" (e.g., Schedler 2006). In short, hybrid regimes fail to institutionalize their nominal principles adequately, and in the worst cases, political development has taken a deviant path (Ottaway 2003).

Although most hybrid regimes are nominal liberal democracies, they can assume other forms as well. For example Iran's theocratic (especially from 1997 to 2004) mixed democratic and theocratic principles, and Jordan's is a monarchy. Guardian military regimes can also fall within these parameters as well. Hybrid regimes also exist in a variety of geopolitical regions. In some post-communist states, former communist leaders and parties have been able to adopt a democratic facade while retaining effective power and excluding real opposition. Rulers of many African states have been able to avoid real democratization by buying time, negotiating with the opposition, foreign donors, and foreign governments but changing as little as possible. In Asia Malaysia and Singapore stand out as examples of longstanding hybrid regimes; they have taken steps to stifle the opposition and undermine the rule of law for decades. Some 1990s-era hybrid regimes in Latin America have already disappeared although some of more recent vintage remain viable. The economic performance of hybrid regimes has varied widely as well. Some, such as Singapore and Malaysia, have been among the most successful economies in the world. Others, such as Azerbaijan and Zambia, are in a state of decay. Still others occupy a middle position. Despite their differences, hybrid regimes frequently share some common characteristics. They most often preside over societies riven by class or ethnic divisions, and where interclass or inter-communal violence has actually occurred or seems likely. These societies are also likely to have had a tradition of authoritarian – or worse totalitarian – government along with weak institutions (Ottaway 2003: 14–23).

Accounting for continuity

Continuity is not automatic. It depends upon legitimacy, state effectiveness, governmental efficacy, and effective and obedient armed forces. Advanced democracies are stable as were traditional authoritarian regimes for centuries, and communist and other one-party dictatorships through much of the twentieth century. Each of these systems was able to rely on broadly accepted legitimizing principles, state organizations that were effective in their eras, governmental structures that produced efficacious decisions that addressed problems that could threaten regime survival, and armed forces that loyally defended the regime. Furthermore, even regimes with weak legitimacy have survived in the contemporary world. Bucking democratic trends is not unprecedented (see Chapters 10 and 11). However, hybrid regimes are different. Some of their key practices are at odds with the nominal principles of their constitutions, and at least some citizens are likely to take these principles seriously. Occasionally, outrage over the violation of democratic standards may inflame virtually the whole of society. Governing in such systems has some of the aspects of a balancing act. To maintain their position rulers must act with guile and skill.

In this respect, hybrid regimes resemble aerodynamically unstable highly advanced aircraft. Like contemporary semi-authoritarian and semi-democratic regimes, stability is not built into the system. Instead these modern aircraft remain safely airborne because of computer-assisted, fly-by-wire avionics. These clever devices constantly adjust the plane's flight-control surfaces to compensate for the craft's inherent tendency to move erratically with even minute changes in temperature and air pressure and quickly crash. The aircraft do not crash because the computerized systems make adjustments faster and with greater precision than human beings would be able to. By the laws of aerodynamics, the airframe is highly unstable (i.e., crash-prone), but the aircraft as a whole, in actual practice, is actually quite stable. Proper corrective maneuvers taken in time can compensate for defects that would otherwise destabilize a system – be that system a physical system, such as an aircraft, or a political system.

Rulers do not need to resort to the kinds of high-tech apparatus found in sophisticated aircraft. While computers aid advanced aircraft, ruling elites in "unstable" systems rely on what they have learned from the experience of their successful and unsuccessful counterparts. The regime can continue largely as before if elites can trim their strategies in a timely fashion. In short, like flying an inherently unstable airframe, regime survival involves the rulers' willingness and ability to adjust, sometimes on short notice, as the situation requires it. To make these adjustments successfully they need to have a repertoire of tactics and techniques at their disposal. So long as neither democracy nor authoritarianism is consolidated, these in-between systems are in permanent flux. Though particular regimes may remain relatively stable, the continuity of none of them is guaranteed since, unlike computing and aerodynamics, politics is more art than science.

Fending off democratization

Hybrid regimes survive as partly authoritarian by swimming against the democratic third wave that began in the mid-1970s in Europe and eventually spread across the globe. The popularity of democracy forces hybrid regimes to adopt periodic elections as the official means of selecting the government's leadership, but democratic pressures, unmatched by the proper local conditions, have been insufficient to consolidate democracy fully. Just as hybrid regimes are in an in-between state in terms of politics, they are often in the same sort of condition economically and socially as well. They generally are weakly institutionalized and have political cultures not fully conducive to democracy. Often the societies governed by hybrid regimes are sharply divided along religious, ethnic, or class line. These conditions provide an opening for political actors with an authoritarian inclination to rule undemocratically. Such political actors have a battery of techniques to stack the political deck in their favor. However, these techniques differ substantially from those of neo-sultanistic or other authoritarian regimes, since institutions, while weak, and political culture, while not truly democratic, count for something. Leaders of hybrid regimes can use authoritarian tactics but they cannot apply them in too heavy-handed a fashion. Their key objective is to dominate the electoral process so as to manage domestic and international political actors pressuring for full democratization. Many of the techniques that hybrid regimes employ are also used in consolidated democracies. What makes hybrid regimes' use of them different is that these questionable tactics are not adequately restrained by legal or popular checks, and they are only available to pro-regime elites.

Electoral manipulation

Any political system, no matter how liberal and democratic it is, has to have rules for determining who can vote and run for office, how parties are formed and officially registered, and how popular votes are to be translated into seats won. In addition, voting districts have to be set and polling places established. As we saw in Chapter 4, the devil's in the detail. Every choice of rules benefits some potential competitors and disadvantages others. What separates hybrid regimes from their democratic counterparts is their ability to take advantage of the rule-setting process unfairly and brazenly while proclaiming its rules are really just and fair. Compounding this legal chicanery is the regime's ability and willingness to use illegal methods when legal manipulations fail.

Legal manipulations are legion. Hybrid regimes regularly disqualify opposition parties and candidates. They may outlaw opposition parties altogether, force the opposition to run on a single ticket, or induce it to divide into a myriad of small factions to weaken it, depending on what seems most conducive to the ruling party's success. Electoral districts may be malapportioned so as to dilute the vote of the opposition by denying districts in which it is strong a fair share of representatives. Permits to hold rallies and demonstrations can be withheld. The regime may curtail the opposition's access to the state-owned media while the government makes use of state media to the maximum extent possible. The ruling party also has innumerable ways of illegally thwarting the opposition. Police or pro-government gangs may break up opposition meetings and intimidate opposition candidates and supporters. Voting rolls can be manipulated so that "ghost voters" (names, not people) can cast ballots for the ruling party. "Flying voters" can travel from place to place and vote many times for the government. Ballot boxes can be stuffed with pro-government votes even before voters arrive at the polls. And just as pro-government voters may vote many times, opposition voters may be prevented from voting at all. Their names may disappear from the official rolls; they may be forcefully kept from the polls by the police or pro-regime thugs; their ballots may be lost after they are cast, and opposition votes may not be honestly tallied. In the end, government officials may refuse to release the final count and require a new election or a runoff. All the while, the government may prevent neutral local or international observers from watching the process close at hand and blowing the whistle on regime-engineered fraud (Schedler 2002: 44–5).

Controlling civil society

In the contemporary era, it is rare for a country to have a middle and working class so small and inert that civic associations such as labor unions, professional associations, business groups, community groups do not exist. And countries controlled by hybrid regimes are typically not at the lowest level of economic and social development. Civic associations, sometimes very active ones, do exist. And the opposition is likely to form political parties. Such civic and political groups constitute the principal challenge to the continuity hybrid regimes. Regime breakdown from below – be it revolution or democratization – depends in part upon the development of mass movements. But mass movements require leadership if they are not to be stillborn or their efforts at change chaotic. Thus, one of the tactics of maintaining power is preventing semi-loyal or disloyal elites from linking up with the dissatisfied mass of the population. Although ruling elites can rarely prevent the emergence of such organizations entirely, they can retain their dominance by managing and neutering civic organizations.

Hybrid regimes, in effect, allow partial freedom of association, but they do not allow associations to have full rights to organize and compete politically. Regimes either deny civic associations rights to participate in the political process, or they grant such rights only in the formal sense while at the same time limiting their access to the mass media. In addition, regimes can harass associations' efforts to organize and voice their opinions via mass demonstrations and other similar means. The ruling elite may also sponsor its own nongovernmental organizations (NGOs) and tame opposition parties – i.e., organizations that present no

fundamental break with the regime and are often infiltrated by
pro-regime elements. As Chapter 9 pointed out, international NGOs
supporting human rights, free elections, women's and children's rights
can serve as important allies for the opposition in the democratization
process. Thus, hybrid regimes often try to curtail their influence or
eliminate it entirely. Foreign contributions to political campaigns can be
outlawed. So too can foreign contributions to local NGOs. Those
foreigners associated with NGOs can be expelled from the country
(Ottaway 2003: 18–19). Russia has taken the restrictions a step further by
applying them to religious denominations other than the Russian
Orthodox Church as well.

Patronage and corruption

Neo-patrimonialism is often rife in hybrid regimes. Of course, personal
connections and IOUs are important in almost every human context.
They are the grease that allows the political and social machine to work
more effectively. In hybrid regimes, however, personal connections and
patronage cease to facilitate what otherwise might be a democratic
political process and instead supplant that process and override the rule of
law on a routine basis. Connections are the primary determinant for the
distribution of public funds. In the worst cases, semi-authoritarian
regimes resemble neo-sultanistic dictatorships described in the previous
chapter. When government contracts, state-funded loans, commercial
privileges, and protection are essentially in the leader's or ruling party's
gift, the government can use it to develop and maintain support among
the social and economic elite. Patronage on a much smaller scale can also
be useful in building popular support.

In situations where ordinary citizens cannot expect efficient and fair
treatment by state agencies or due process from the courts, they often
come to rely on what connections they have. Subservience to the local
political boss may seem a small price to pay to gain help from state
authorities. In fact, for many, personal loyalty to a patron may be part of
the fabric of everyday life. Getting a job, borrowing money, or getting aid
in an emergency may involve cultivating the support of a well-off member
of the local community by doing his bidding and showing respect in
ordinary circumstances. Ordinary people are likely to feel themselves
ill-informed and willing to accept the "guidance" of a benefactor about
how they and their family ought to vote or whom they ought to support
politically.

Such patron–client networks organize politics and society in a manner
that helps weaken civil society. Citizens come to rely on their limited

connections with more politically important people instead of their own capacity to form organizations and work with their peers. Patron–client politics is retail politics. It is biased in favor of the elite. Clients purchase access to state services that should be guaranteed as a matter of right at the price of their votes and political loyalty. In contrast, modern liberal democratic politics is wholesale politics. Independent citizens organize to support their common interests and vote for candidates and parties on the basis of judgments about policies. They support public policies that suit their interest and further their conception of the public good.

Patron–client politics, in contrast, allows the elite to channel popular energies in ways useful to their own interests. When politics assumes such a form, the clients often become shock troops in political struggles against the opposition. The use of patronage is especially important at election time when the delivery of benefits to an individual or community can be directly associated with the beneficence of the ruling party. At the same time, individuals and communities that support the opposition can be put on notice that their access to government services is under threat.

Using and abusing the media

Hybrid regimes cannot control the media in the ways that totalitarian or fully authoritarian states regularly do. They often have to contend with an outspoken or even rancorous opposition press. But, in modern times, incumbency confers inherent advantages to the governing party even in functioning democracies. What incumbents do is news because they are part of the government. What the members of the opposition do may or may not be news, depending on their personal prominence and their political prospects. Incumbents in much of the world have additional advantages not normally available to their counterparts in well-established democracies, which have more effective checks on the abuse of power. The government issues broadcast licenses and licenses to print publications; it can force media that support the opposition to cease operations. The government can prosecute for seditious libel. It often controls access to newsprint. It can censor the media. It can plant news stories and even fund nominally independent media outlets. The presence or absence of advertising from state-owned firms can make or break a publisher or broadcaster financially. Bribery, and, failing that, intimidation and outright violence can be used to assure favorable coverage and to control unwanted publicity. Confronted by the pressures the leader and his supporters can bring to bear, journalists, editors, publishers, and broadcasters may well decide that discretion is the better part of valor, or at least safer and more profitable.

Playing on fears and divisions

Hybrid regimes often rule societies rift by ethnic, religious, or class divisions. Often the memories of intercommunal, interclass, or political violence are fresh. Even economically successful countries such as Singapore and Malaysia have experienced intense ethnic- and class-based rivalries. The majority, fearing that ceding real power to the minority may undercut its own ability progress, clings to the ruling party that proclaims itself a defender of its interests. At the same time, elites representing the minority fear an even worse situation should extremists from the majority group actually take power. Thus, minority politicians strike the best deal they can with the ruling party rather than challenging it. Fear of political violence too, such as Islamist terrorists in Egypt or radical leftists in Peru, helped rally the mass of the population behind the government. Such political–psychological dynamics help the ruling elite keep opposition of various stripes in check. Even the democratic opposition – political leaders as well as parties – constitute a semi-loyal opposition from the government's perspective since it wishes to see the democratic norms of the constitution actually put into practice. Intercommunal fears both help divide the democratic opposition and delegitimize it in the eyes of the population. Popular fear of political violence by leftists or Islamists can further disorient the democratic opposition and justify their political marginalization via highhanded regulations or their outright repression. Feeling itself under threat, the population is more likely to rally around the authorities.

Political parties

Some hybrid regimes have pro-regime political parties that are not very effective or none at all. Others that have taken care to develop and maintain pro-regime political parties have often fared better than those that have neglected them. Proper use of pro-regime parties can help mobilize support from the population and resolve differences among competing factions of the elite. Both of the functions are important. Popular opinion counts for something, and the elite cannot govern in crass independence of it. In a parallel fashion, various members of the political elite have the possibility of cultivating a power base independent of the top leader and his immediate coterie. In such instances, disputes over policy or power can lead to a political crisis or even regime breakdown. An example of such a situation occurred in the Philippines in the mid-1980s. The rule of Ferdinand Marcos had many of the hallmarks of neo-sultanism, and Marcos seemed unable to develop more sophisticated and nuanced techniques. Specifically, he did not effectively develop and cultivate a political party that might have helped him overcome or co-opted competitors. In contrast, Mahathir Muhammad, Marcos's counterpart in Malaysia, was able to rely on the United Malay National Organization (UMNO) to contain and buy off competitors on a variety of occasions (Brownlee 2007: 30–5, 210–11).

Enhancing and using "constitutional" executive powers

National emergencies, legitimate or contrived, provide excellent pretext for suppressing the opposition. The use of "emergency power" is not of itself an abuse. Even most democratic constitutions explicitly or implicitly allow for the declaration of states of emergency that permit the suspension of civil liberties and due process guarantees. However, emergency can enhance the powers of the security services (i.e., elements of law enforcement and intelligence charged with protecting the security of the state) by permitting surveillance, disruption, and arrest of the opposition. The declaration of a state of emergency may limit the checks the judiciary is able to impose on the executive and security services. It is not unheard of for declaration of one state of emergency to follow another or a state of emergency to be prolonged indefinitely, but even without such a legal pretext, the political police and domestic intelligence services often cannot be effectively checked by a judiciary that is already weak and penetrated by the chief executive politically. Abuse of emergency power and other executive authority in nominal democracies has a long history. Nineteenth-century Latin America's supposedly democratic constitutions were so prone to such abuse of power that one scholar, reversing a popular slogan, has labeled them the "constitution of tyranny" (Loveman 1993).

In fact, presidential systems, such as those of Latin America, provide excellent seedbeds for overweening executives and abuse of power that is often required to check the opposition when hybrid regimes are hard pressed. Presidential systems, by their nature, make the chief executive independent of the legislature. Often presidential systems provide the chief executive with considerable constitutional powers to effect his will despite opposition from the legislature. Even without the power to issue decrees, declare emergencies, or force rapid legislative considerations of his proposals, the chief executive in a presidential system often has the capacity to personalize political issues. The legislature is many; he is one. With the capacity to speak with a single voice against a sometimes-cacophonous legislature, the executive can often reshape and personalize political debate. Where opposition parties are weak and amorphous, as they often are in hybrid regimes, presidents can dominate the system. Personalities are often easier to understand and may be a more attractive focus for political campaigns than the technical details of party programs. Candidates with strong personalities, especially incumbent presidents, can claim they are the embodiment of what the nation needs and what the people want. The more amorphous the coalition against him, the greater is the incumbent's advantage. However, parliamentary systems too are capable of supporting a dominant executive and executive abuse of power. The prime ministers of Singapore and Malaysia have relied on their ability to dominate the ruling party and, along with it, the legislative assembly. Using this control they have often behaved in a manner typical of strong presidents, restricting the rights of the opposition, politicizing the courts, and building up a strong personalistic base of support. Malaysia for instance has never let the emergency powers that were authorized in response to a legitimately threatening communist insurgency in the 1950s lapse.

Gaining support from the military and security services

Liberal–democratic constitutionalism assumes that the armed forces will be professional and apolitical. Military officers are promoted on the basis of their professional competence, not their political connections. The business of soldiers is national defense in the narrow definition of the term. Politics should be left to the politicians. Yet, in many countries, apolitical professionalism is not the norm. In addition, the security services – the paramilitary police, militarized units of the interior ministry common in post-communist states, and domestic intelligence agencies – often play a critical role. The role of these forces is the internal security of the state. It is their business to protect against and ferret out subversion. In countries with a recent communist or authoritarian past, their conception of what constitutes internal subversion is likely to be unduly broad by democratic standards. The alliance between the political elite, on the one hand, and the armed forces and security services, on the other, is often easy to fashion.

States with poorly trained armed forces and an imperfectly professionalized officer corps, such as those in Africa, constitute another challenge and opportunity for hybrid regimes. Poorly paid armed forces may give rise to rebellions from below (Kandeh 2004). More typical coups from the officer corps also pose a threat. In fact, coups in support of democracy, such as Mali's coup of 1991, are not unknown. Hybrid regimes in such circumstances have two basic alternatives. They can take good care of the armed forces, making sure they have no professional or economic motive to overthrow the government. And they can gain the support of a foreign military patron. The presence of foreign military bases or even the implicit threat of foreign military intervention on behalf of the government should a military rebellion occur can keep a potentially restive military in check. Historically, the French have been willing to play this role in Africa (Clark 2006: 129–33).

Manipulating foreign support

Foreigners are important in other ways as well. Foreign political actors, especially democratic governments and multilateral agencies, have played a major role in democracy's third wave. Yet, many leaders of hybrid regimes have learned how to resist their blandishments and in fact turned aside the pro-democratic pressures. Properly managed, foreign governments can provide critical support through a variety of means. Foreign firms and governments are often satisfied if the government maintains a "good business climate" – i.e., enforces policies that make foreign direct investment (FDI) safe and profitable. As with oil monarchies discussed in the last chapter, the local rulers are not simply the stooges of foreigners, however. They may be able to extract considerable concessions from foreigners and considerable revenue from imposing taxes and royalties on FDI. Foreign governments have provided diplomatic support, economic and military aid, and even soldiers to suppress a rebellion against their local protégés.

Foreign governments may see hybrid regimes as strategic allies. This was true during the period of the cold war. During the cold war, the Soviet Union backed those rulers that leaned in its direction, labeling them "progressive." In contrast, the United States spoke of its friendly dictators as representatives of the "free world." The ideological divisions of the cold war have largely passed, but individual states and multilateral organizations have remained less than consistent in promoting human rights and democratic values. And the "war on terror" has helped promote its own crop of less than democratic governments that serve as key allies for the United States in Central Asia and elsewhere. An increasingly economically assertive People's Republic of China has been adamant in decoupling economic relations from human rights and democracy. Thus, hybrid regimes have little to fear from Chinese pressure and may find economic relations with China a buffer against pressures to democratize from other states. In addition, democratic governments may engage in wishful thinking, assuming that if non-democratic governments accept foreign investment, open their markets, and move in the direction of capitalism, democratic progress cannot be far behind. There is little evidence to support this hope.

Summary

Hybrid regimes are no accident. Leaders have learned how to control the institutions upon which power depends and override institutional and societal checks. They have developed the skills to outmaneuver their opponents. And they have built networks so as to gain a significant measure of popular support. Further, the international community has often tolerated and even honored governments run in a less than democratic manner, ranging from the mildly corrupt to the egregiously despotic. Rule based on the skill and cunning of an individual leader has a limit of course: no one can live forever. Yet, in some cases, the transition from one leader to another may be relatively smooth, even planned and engineered by the outgoing incumbent. And even when such planned transfers are not the case, conditions may allow the same style of rule to continue. Sometimes, however, public outrage over stolen elections, corruption, or government brutality has provoked a true change in the system.

The post-communist world

Post-communist regimes fall into a variety of classes. Many of the formerly communist states of Central Europe outside the Balkans, plus the formerly Soviet Baltic republics of Estonia, Latvia, and Lithuania, have made considerable strides toward the consolidation of liberal democracy. Most of these have had a number of fair and free elections, have transferred power from one party or coalition to another by peaceful means, and have implemented the rudiments of the rule of law. In most of the former Soviet Union, however, liberal democracy remains, at best, highly imperfect. The independent states of the former Yugoslavia too have experienced periods of semi-authoritarian rule. Torn by ethnic rivalries, these states have provided poor ground for the development of democracy in the first place.

Twelve of the fifteen successor states of the former Soviet Union have had extremely difficult political transitions. The requisites for consolidating liberal democracy and capitalism in post-communist states as laid out in Chapter 10 were hard to meet. In many of former Soviet states, semi-authoritarian regimes have come to hold sway, and the political opposition along with the rule of law is severely constrained. The reasons behind these developments are not hard to fathom. Most of the states of the former Soviet Union have had no modern experience of independent statehood. Nor have they had any experience with democracy or liberalism. The imperial government, until its overthrow in 1917, was an autocracy. Throughout much of the nineteenth century, Russia had tried to modernize the state albeit fitfully and without complete success. Its territorial components were imperfectly integrated with one another. Various parts of the empire had been attached to its Russian core at various times. Belarus and Ukraine had been integral parts of the empire for centuries.

The states of the Caucasus region and those of Central Asia were nineteenth-century additions to the tsar's domain, but they too had not been independent states before Russia acquired them. Their Russianization was limited. Provided elites swore allegiance to the tsar and were able to speak Russian, little more was required. The mass of the population retained their traditional way of life and their traditional languages and religions. In short, the "Tsar of all the Russias" presided over a multinational empire that was continental in scale. Neither his government nor his subjects had fully entered the modern world. Further, the farther into its southern or eastern periphery its peoples were, the less likely they were to be deeply affected by imperial Russia's growing contacts with the modern world. Change was limited. As far as the non-Russian peoples were concerned, both Russianization and modernization accelerated. Yet, for seventy years of Soviet rule, many of the same authority structures remained in place, only in communist garb. The national question had been a problem for the Communist Party of the Soviet Union (CPSU) when it was first formed, and it remained so until the end. Before the revolution, Lenin had attacked the tsarist government's nationalities policy and called for the self-determination of peoples. In practice, the application of that principle tore the old tsarist empire apart.

Lenin and his Bolsheviks could not reintegrate the empire by persuasion. Nationalism proved stronger than proletarian internationalism, and much of the territory of the old Russian Empire had to be reacquired by force. The Soviet Union represented a compromise between Great Russian and local nationalisms. "National in form; socialist in content" became the maxim. Non-Russian peoples were to be granted cultural rights, provided communist principles commanded the state and society. The use of the Russian language was encouraged, and Russians were encouraged to migrate to non-Russian republics. Still, only in a few were the locals in danger of becoming outnumbered by the new immigrants. And when independence occurred, the Russian minority, as well as other ethnic minorities often gerrymandered in the new states when they had been union republics of the Soviet Union, appeared as threats.

Nor had the Soviet period modernized and democratized the behavior of the political elite. The central leadership of the CPSU had been quite happy to allow communists with deep roots in their republics to govern them under Moscow's supervision. In short, local political clans that relied on traditional patronage networks continued to flourish. At the same time, the modernization process under state socialism did little or nothing to provide the groundwork for a modern liberal democratic state or a capitalistic market economy. The regime established its own patron–client networks. State socialism evolved a network of *apparatchiki* (functionaries in the party's "apparatus" or bureaucracy) and *nomenklatura* (party appointees holding positions in the state and the economy).

State socialism had provided a poor foundation for the building of a modern market economy. State socialist norms were supposed to promote the rational allocation of resources, but this allocation of resources was focused on a few basic goals – production of military materiel and the support of the industrial base necessary to manufacture it. Even so, the standard was effectiveness, not efficiency in the market sense of the term. Cost was no object so long as quotas were met, and the objectives of the state and its five-year plans were attained. Even the rules promulgated by the government made little difference. The important thing was to meet the quota. If that was achieved, lesser failures could be tolerated. People's democracy assured that the state was accountable to the party leadership, not the general public. The rule of law counted for little. Seventy years of communist development left the former Soviet Union with a large and largely unusable industrial base. Too much had been invested in heavy industry. The former Soviet Union possessed excess steel-making capacity at a time when the world as a whole was awash with excess steel capacity. Its technology was backward. Its distribution system was archaic. The *apparatchiki* and *nomenklatura* were accustomed to manipulating the system for their own advantage. The public prior to the revolution had been generally passive.

Development in the post-Soviet period often took place behind a democratic and capitalist facade, behind which authoritarian practices continued to function. After the forced economic and political mobilization of the Soviet period, the general public was disgruntled, suspicious, and, once again, often passive. The collapse of communism led to a political transition, but, in many instances, it was a transition with few genuinely democratic features. The rule of law and public accountability were not consolidated. Presidents often used their formal and informal political powers to shape policy to their liking without adequate checks. In these situations, legislatures counted for relatively little. Elections for the chief executive were seldom completely fair or free. The incumbent president usually possessed an unfair advantage over his opponents. Presidential control of or influence over the media and the electoral system, the absence of a sufficient number of poll-watchers, foreign or domestic, frequently allowed incumbents to dispatch their opponents with relative ease. Sometimes, even mass disaffection from the incumbent, as measured by opinion polls, failed to materialize in a pro-opposition vote at election time. Incumbents were continually able to wrong-foot the opposition. Real reform was stymied. However, the inherent advantages of incumbents did not guarantee a seamless transition between communist rule and post-communist hybrid rule. In Ukraine, Moldova, and Belarus authoritarian incumbents lost to authoritarian competitors (Way 2006: 167–8).

Policy-making and implementation has been a morass. Privatization, where it occurred, was likely to benefit only the well connected. Although Russia chose to privatize state industries rapidly, in many other parts of the former Soviet Union, attempts at privatization were limited and the old *nomenklatura* often remained in charge. Even in Russia, privatization benefited insiders, often allowing those who managed state property to assume ownership over the newly privatized firms they had once managed for the state. Authoritarian practices seem to come naturally to most politicians in the former Soviet Union. And the anti-liberal, anti-pluralist, and anti-market ideology and practices of the Soviet period did little to prepare the way for a more modern and successful society. Many of the states of the former Soviet Union are still in a state of transition economically and politically. But it is a state of transition that could become virtually permanent. The hybrid regimes there have tended to sacrifice long-term goals for short-term gains. Leaders succeed, but societies merely endure.

CASE STUDY: RUSSIA

The case of the Russian Republic under the presidency of Boris Yeltsin illustrates in concrete terms the way hybrid regimes often function in the former Soviet Union. If anything Russia is more democratic than many other former Soviet states. But its democracy was, as Michael McFaul puts it, only an "electoral democracy" (McFaul 2001). The political rights standard was formally respected, but fair competition and civil liberties were curtailed. As with many other hybrid states, its political traditions were authoritarian and totalitarian. It was in the throes of economic restructuring and suffered from extreme divisions of wealth. Ethnic minorities challenged the authority of the central government. Still, the story of Russia under Yeltsin's rule from 1991 to 1999 was also one of missed opportunities. In 1991, during the final phase of the Soviet Union's collapse, Boris Yeltsin had been a popular hero as he helped face down the coup-makers who had kidnapped Soviet President Mikhail Gorbachev. The aim of the coup had been to roll back the clock or at least to stop the process of decay that was eroding the control of the party and threatening the stability of the Soviet system. But by the time of the coup, the Soviet Union had already been mortally weakened on a variety of levels. Its legitimacy was open to question. Its state was crippled and ineffective. And its governmental processes had become dysfunctional. After the coup failed, Yeltsin used his stature to help bring about the breakup of the Soviet Union itself. Several other republics had also been eager to break away even before the coup, and they seized the chance for independence. As the political control of the center decayed, opportunists even in the republics previously loyal to the Soviet system changed their garb from communism to nationalism. In the end all fifteen union republics, the constituent parts of the Soviet Union, seceded.

Yeltsin's rule in Russia, the major successor state to emerge from the Soviet Union's collapse, was personalistic, and he largely ignored the opportunity to consolidate democracy. Because he had been elected to the post of Russian president and was assured of popular support for a time, Yeltsin had the opportunity to engage in a wholesale political reform. Russia had been organized and its president elected as a constituent and subordinate part of the old Soviet Union, and a new election and a new constitution seemed appropriate and could have set the stage for a rapidly paced process of democratic consolidation. Instead, Yeltsin temporized. A constitutional commission was appointed to revise the old document, but there appeared to be little sense of urgency even though the existing government was an interim affair. Yeltsin himself chose not to call new elections although he certainly would have won them hands down. Nor did he choose to form a new political party to rally support behind political and economic reform. Instead, he remained above party, appointing and dismissing ministers, but largely blaming them for mistakes or for unpopular policies. In essence, by design or negligence, the democratization of Russia proceeded at a snail's pace. Conflicts soon developed between Yeltsin and the legislature demonstrating too late the wisdom of calling new elections for an interim Russian government immediately after the failed coup and collapse of the Soviet Union. By the time the situation had reached a crisis point in October 1993, Yeltsin was no longer the unequivocal popular hero he once had been. He was forced to manipulate the system to stay in office rather than democratizing it.

Under Yeltsin, the condition of the Russian economy went from bad to worse. In fairness, this could not be attributed to Yeltsin alone.

Reform efforts during the final years of the Gorbachev government had sent the economy reeling. Even radical reformers, whom Yeltsin backed, at least in part, admitted that economic reform would lead to a decline in Gross Domestic Product (GDP) for at least some period of time. The Russian economy, after all, was badly in need of what reformers called a "structural adjustment." The fall in GDP that had begun with Gorbachev was not just a cyclical problem that could be cured automatically with time. The industrial plant of Russia, its mines, its oil and gas fields, and its infrastructure were badly out of date and poorly managed. The accounting system was ludicrous. Few other than the firm's managers actually knew what was going on. And even if they did, they could rarely assess the firm's real potential. Nor did banks function to assess economic risks and potentials, and make loans to firms whose promise justified it. They still functioned as just another control mechanism of the old state socialist system. The country was also lacking so-called "human capital." While the Soviet Union had done a good job of producing engineers, scientists, and mathematicians, it had done a poor job of training people with managerial competence. The people who were running the economy had been brought up with the old bureaucratic Soviet mindset. Their task was to make their quota. The development of new products, the acquisition of new markets, and new sources of supply was not something that fitted comfortably within the state socialist framework. It was not surprising that attempts at reform led to further collapse of GDP even though the informal (or gray) economy, activities outside of official government purview, continued to grow.

Regardless of who was actually to blame or how much of the economy's decline was inevitable, Boris Yeltsin as president lost popularity. Fiddle as he would with his economic team and rail against the legislature and the head of the central bank for their unwillingness to back tough reform measures, he could not escape political responsibility. Thus, by the time the president and parliament confronted one another, in almost open civil war, Yeltsin could no longer rely on the reflex support of the general public. His attempt to remain above the political fray and govern without becoming a party leader had, in actuality, backfired. When Yeltsin attempted to dissolve the parliament in September 1993, its members refused to leave. He was forced to rely on the support of Pavel Grachev, the chief-of-staff of the armed forces, and attacked the parliament building with tanks, forcibly dismissing legislators who had called for his removal, by means of a popular rebellion if necessary. A new constitution supported by Yeltsin was ratified in a referendum in December. Yet, the triumph of hardline nationalists and communists in the simultaneous parliamentary election illustrated the weakness of Yeltsin's support.

Yeltsin was able to remain in charge, because of an imbalance between the powers of the president and the legislature, as prescribed by the new constitution. The appointment of the prime minister remained largely within his hands, since a nomination, once refused by the Duma, the lower house of the legislature, could be resubmitted. Refusal of the nomination by the Duma a third time would result in new elections for the Duma but not the president. The president alone controlled the ministries, especially the powerful ones – the defense, foreign, and interior ministries. Possibly even more significant than the president's formal powers over the legislature was his ability to control legislative perquisites – cars, apartments, etc. This and the volatility of public opinion often led the legislature to grumble but ultimately toe the line on Yeltsin's appointments. It was better to keep a seat in the Duma along with its perquisites than to face the voters anew. The imbalance between the president and the legislature was serious enough, but additional features of the Russian system added to its anti-democratic character. Russia as with other post-communist states has had to face the issue of privatization. If privatization were not to occur, the country ran a serious risk of continuing to suffer from the same economic rot that had affected the economy during the last decades of official state socialism. Old managers, old organizations, and old habits would remain in place. Loss-making enterprises would continue to receive a state subsidy indefinitely, and no meaningful structural adjustment would occur. The radical reformers, who managed to gain important though shifting influence with the president, argued for shock therapy, bringing the government budget quickly into balance, strictly limiting the central bank's monetary emissions, and privatizing state firms as rapidly as possible.

The seesaw struggle between Yeltsin and the reformers, on one side, and the legislature, on the other, over the budget and the money supply had persisted through the early 1990s. However, by the middle of the decade, the sound-money advocates had largely won the day. The central bank and the relevant ministries were largely under their control. In the mid-1990s, privatization began in earnest. The strategy of the reformers was to undertake and complete the process as quickly as possible. Creeping privatization had begun before, but few of the firms sold provided much attraction for investors. They were large loss-making industrial enterprises with excess employees and old technology. The privatization process had frequently put a de facto controlling interest into the hands of the ex-*nomenklatura*, who continued to manage them. Few outsiders were willing to invest, when a variety of practices prevented any effective stockholder control or oversight. The firms privatized during the crash process, however, were more attractive: natural resource companies, media firms, and banks. But it was various groups of insiders well connected with Yeltsin and his inner circle who snapped them up. While this put large portions of the economy in private hands, it did not create conditions for economic growth. The new Russian tycoons that emerged from the crash privatization used their wealth and influence to increase their own power and to do battle with one another over the sweetheart privatization of additional state companies. The conglomerates each controlled lucrative natural resources holdings. These were the only products that Russia could export on a competitive basis, and provided Russia with most of its hard currency earnings. They were clearly revenue producers, but the profits generated from them were not reinvested in such a way so as to produce growth and modernization in the country's sickly industrial and agricultural sectors. The banking arms of the conglomerates were poorly regulated and served as a source of funds for the conglomerate's other activities. The media arms provided the tycoons with a way to support or pressure the government as the interest of each tycoon required.

Yeltsin's influence over the state-owned media and the ability of the privately owned media controlled by his political allies helped give him a decided advantage in terms of publicity in the 1996 presidential election. In that contest he came from an early showing of single digits in the public opinion polls to a victory in the runoff. Yeltsin's opponents seemed to lack the killer instinct, and rumors circulated that they had been bought off and voter tabulations fudged. A complicated set of maneuvers continued under Yeltsin's second presidency, pitting the tycoons against one another and against various Yeltsin advisors and ministers, in a struggle for the political and economic advantage.

The economic segment of Russia's new elite in some ways resembled the "robber barons" of the United States one hundred years before, with an element of the 1920s mafia thrown in for good measure. They were willing to bribe politicians, campaign shamelessly for their own interests, and, if the situation required it, engage in violence against their opponents. But the analogy with the robber barons is inexact. The up-and-coming industrial elite in the United States had contributed mightily to the advancement of the American economy: steel mills and railroads were built, and the oil industry expanded at a breakneck pace. The new Russian tycoons did little more than gain control of natural resources, already largely developed, and sell them on established international markets.

Much of the wealth the tycoons earned found its way out of the country. Moreover, the violence and corruption were all too real. The economic policy followed by the government produced a variety of crony capitalism. The country lacked a number of essential requirements that might have led to western-style capitalism: the rule of law, secure property rights, public auditing of companies, clear lines of authority between national and regional governments, effectively applied bankruptcy laws, clear and well enforced tax codes, and effective legislative oversight.

Efforts to establish these requisites for market capitalism proceeded only fitfully. At the same time, reformers promoted a tight monetary policy in an effort to control inflation and make firms more efficient. In tandem with this policy, they liberalized trade and investment and arranged loans from the International Monetary Fund (IMF) and other private, governmental, and multilateral international lenders. These reform priorities led to a mix of policies that did little to prevent the growth of *nomenklatura* capitalism (dominated by insiders) and the largely predatory conglomerates that came to exercise not only economic but political power, as well. As with other economies under stress and lacking many requisites of an efficient capitalist market or adequate regulation, those with influence and wealth discovered the means to profit via financial transactions that provided few benefits for the real economy.

Yeltsin thus presided over a ramshackle political and economic system that he could not fully control. The state of his health for much of his first and all of his second term compounded the difficulties he faced. So too did the political strategy he had chosen after the collapse of the Soviet Union. A leader who placed himself above party, he looked more like the old tsar wishing to retain as much authority in his own hands as possible but failing to accept political responsibility for the failures of his ministers. As he traveled through the country during the 1996 campaign, he held court like a traditional personalistic leader, acting as if the national treasury were under his personal control. He regularly promised to solve the problems brought to him by the people at each campaign stop, and made promises for each locality's particular needs.

In addition to all the other problems Russia faced, ethnic separatists challenged the unity of the new Russian Federation. In Chechnya, a region in the Caucasus, an insurgency gained de facto independence for the republic for a time, defeating a large-scale Russian expedition to recapture the region in 1996. It was not until the fall of 1999, a renewed military push reestablished central government control. The 1999 offensive took place after terrorist bombings in major Russian cities set the stage for more forceful central government action. Terrorist actions inside and outside Chechnya continued even after Russian occupation was established. Moreover, the Chechens were not alone among ethnic minorities seeking either full independence or significantly greater autonomy within the federation. Other republics within the Caucasus region were flashpoints for protest and violent conflict as well. Regional leaders outside the Caucasus began to exercise significant powers over tax revenue, the economy, and, in some cases, even the terms of service of conscripts drafted from their regions.

All these developments took place at a time when the government was attempting to limit the budget deficit and when the state was crippled by inefficiency and corruption. The political style that Yeltsin had chosen to adopt succeeded if success is measured by the leader staying in power. By that standard, Yeltsin's second presidency was a limited success, but even from this perspective, it seemed to be at best a holding operation. While he remained president, the ability to make policy slipped from his hands. His ministers and associates plus the leading tycoons schemed and maneuvered, like the ministers and cronies of an incompetent and aging absolute monarch. Yeltsin left office via a surprise resignation on December 31, 1999, that prepared the way for his appointed prime minister, Vladimir Putin, to assume the presidency and run as an incumbent.

Plate 12.1 Personalistic rule continues. The billboard from the 2007 legislative elections reads, "Moscow votes for Putin."

Putin took control of the patronage network and quarrelling political entourage that had surrounded Yeltsin and won the March 2000 elections easily. With the increase in oil prices, the economy grew under the new president's watch.

Putin's leadership was more consistent and successful than that of the ailing and alcoholic Yeltsin, but Putin departed little from the authoritarian style of his predecessor. The opposition, including liberals and democrats, was marginalized. Putin strengthened government control of the media, outlawed foreign support for local NGOs, and cracked down on businessmen opposed to his government. In 2000 central control of regional governments was strengthened with the establishment of seven federal districts whose heads were presidential appointees charged with coordinating administration. A presidential decree in 2007 established that seats in the lower house of the national legislature, the state Duma, be elected by proportional representation with a 7 percent threshold necessary to secure any seats at all. As a result, the faction-ridden democratic opposition disappeared from the Duma after the elections in December of that year. Putin's former associates in state intelligence became key figures in the new governing elite. Although he decided to retire from the presidency after the two terms the constitution mandated, he designated a protégé, Dmitry Medvedev, who many viewed as his creature, as his successor and announced plans to serve as prime minister. Medvedev won the March 2008 elections handily. Putin will thus remain in power, turning the constitutionally weaker office of prime minister into an effective power base.

Populism in Latin America

Latin American **populism** is a method of governing that stresses the charisma of the leader, the unity of the leader with the people of the nation, economic change, and a carelessness concerning democratic norms. When political opposition and the rule of law pose checks to the populist leader and his government, they are seen as illicit by populist movements. Hence, populist governments fit the definition of hybrid regimes when they stray too far from democratic norms. Populist leaders govern under democratic forms but are willing to violate democratic principles when it suits their interests. The partially institutionalized nature of politics and partially democratic political cultures common in the region lend themselves to this type of politics. Leftwing populists had had a field day from the 1930s through the 1950s. They had appealed to a political base composed largely of the poorer classes, but most had tried to build a multi-class alliance behind their projects for economic growth and redistribution. However, their style of leadership eventually succumbed.

Beginning with the 1960s Latin America underwent a number of stages of political evolution that stressed institutions rather than the personalistic style that was an essential element of populism. Democratic reformers in the earlier part of the period had stressed party-building, state-building, and political reform. Military governments that overthrew many of these democracies declared their intention to reform political, economic, and social institutions as well. However, as the 1980s progressed, military governments were pressured out of office, and the region faced a set of economic problems similar to, but generally much less serious than, those of former communist states. These new conditions would provide a fresh opportunity for the use of populist techniques, although most of those using them would more commonly pursue rightwing economic policies rather than the leftwing policies of their predecessors.

Most Latin American countries had followed a state-directed path to economic development under both civilian and military governments, but by the 1980s, the model was exhausted. State regulation had led to inefficiencies and corruption. Lax monetary policy had led to hyperinflation with some countries suffering inflation in excess of 100 percent per month for extended periods. The economy seemed in need of wholesale reform. A number of countries, most notably Peru, Argentina, and Brazil, had experimented with novel, so-called "heterodox" methods of reform, but they had found them to be costly failures. The economic crises that beset Latin America during the 1980s, when the region's GDP per capita actually fell, did more than damage the region's economies and its people's welfare; it had promoted the de-institutionalization of politics. This de-institutionalization had, in fact, begun under the military governments that had controlled many countries for over a decade. Although many of these governments had aspired to build new institutions, they in actuality were more effective in undermining old ones. For example, the military government had tried often successfully to demobilize the political community, especially the left. Leftwing political parties were often outlawed. Many of their leaders were arrested and executed. Political recesses, when all political activity was forbidden, were often prolonged. The media were censored. Military officials intervened in trade unions. Sometimes labor legislation was substantially changed to limit trade-union activism. Military regimes were largely successful in destroying or demobilizing the radical left.

When civilian rule returned, much of the radicalism and many of the radical organizations had disappeared. While civil society – the churches, civic associations, and the media – received a new lease of life and were in effect strengthened by their resistance to military rule, political parties were not. The sterility of the old political parties and their formulas was further demonstrated by the economic crises of the 1980s and early 1990s. In many countries, the public was looking for a way out of their economic difficulties and the old parties and personalities seemed unable to provide it. As the 1990s began, many countries seemed willing to try more orthodox methods that involved deregulation of the economy, a strict monetary policy, and the liberalization of trade and investment. This willingness provided an opening for a new rightwing version of populism, what a noted political scientist christened "delegative democracy" (O'Donnell n.d.). This did not imply that Latin America was ready to embark along the authoritarian path again. Few leaders were willing to return outright to an authoritarian past, but there appeared to be no consensus about constitutional arrangements and political leadership. Or if there was a consensus, it was a negative one. In opinion poll after opinion poll, politicians as a group, as well as political parties and the legislature, did poorly.

In was into this environment that the new politicians who practiced delegative democracy entered. These leaders claimed to represent the will of the people, but like their leftwing populist predecessors of mid-century they tended to ignore constitutional rules that specified how the people's will should be legally determined. They practiced old-fashioned pork-barrel politics and developed a personal relationship by means of frequent public appearances and associating themselves with local public works projects and other patronage schemes.

CASE STUDY: PERU

Alberto Fujimori, President of Peru from 1990 to 2000, demonstrated a leadership style that has wide appeal in the region; it illustrates the perennial appeal of personalism and the ability of personalistic leaders to override institutional constraints (Levitsy 1999). In 1990 when he first ran for office, Fujimori presented himself as a non-politician in a society where the established political parties had been discredited. The failure of the country's two major political parties to control a violent leftwing insurgency or to solve the economic problems that reached crisis proportions in the 1980s had undercut all established politicians and parties. In the 1990 elections, two citizen-based reform movements took shape.

One was headed by the Nobel prize-winning novelist Mario Vargas Llosa, who openly promised economic shock therapy: quickly cutting popular subsidies, balancing the budget by cutting social services, deregulation, and the privatization of state-owned firms. The other movement, strongly supported by some Christian evangelicals, called itself Change-90 and backed the rector of a state agricultural university, Alberto Fujimori, for president. Though a relative unknown at the beginning of the campaign, Fujimori emerged as the leading candidate of the anti-Vargas Llosa forces, and he defeated the novelist in the presidential runoff election. The winning candidate presented himself as the representative of popular forces including the largely disenfranchised Amerindian population.

While on the campaign trail, Fujimori had opposed the shock policies Vargas Llosa advocated. However, after the election Fujimori underwent a conversion. But Fujimori lacked the power to put the neo-liberal policies he had come to favor into practice. The multi-party legislature where the president did not have a clear majority objected. In 1992 budget battles had become particularly heated. By 1992 the insurgency that had become a serious problem under his predecessor had grown significantly, as well. Car bombs were exploding in the capital, and the insurgents were threatening to begin the final phase of the war that they claimed would bring them victory. This did not seem an idle threat. Insurgents were intimidating the courts, and those caught and imprisoned actually controlled the wings of the prison in which they were housed. In response, Fujimori led a "self-coup." With the support of the military, he dismissed the legislature and the courts, and declared he would rule by decree. Military tribunals took over the trial of accused insurgents, and using summary procedures they convicted large numbers of them. The governance of the prisons was tightened. The armed forces and security services intensified their campaign against the insurgents. Within six months of the self-coup, the leader of the largest and most violent insurgent group was captured, eventually tried, and convicted of treason. On the economic front, unhampered by the legislature Fujimori was able to formulate a budget and liberalize by decree. Foreign and domestic pressure, however, forced him to call a new constituent assembly to draft a new constitution. The assembly was dominated by his loyalists, and the document produced provided for a strong executive, and as Fujimori had wished, for one immediate re-election of a sitting president contrary to the previous constitution. Fujimori's style of leadership included frequent trips around metropolitan Lima and the hinterland to open schools, clinics, and other public works. He liked to take credit personally both for these projects as well as for the pacification of the country and the end of economic chaos. With the opposition still fragmented and the public generally satisfied with the virtually complete victory over the insurgents as well as progress in the economy, Fujimori was elected to a second term in 1995.

It soon became clear that, despite the constitutional revision, Fujimori did not consider two terms sufficient. He pressured the judiciary to declare that his election in 1995 was his first term since his previous term had begun under the auspices of the previous constitution. However, by 1998 his popularity had plummeted and opposition movements seemed intent on finding some way to block a second re-election. But the judiciary, dominated by presidential loyalists, allowed him to run again. Fujimori won reelection in 2000, a victory that the opposition protested. Although Fujimori was re-inaugurated, public opposition was sufficiently intense that the Organization of American States (OAS) was called upon to mediate the controversy. Only months after Fujimori began his third term, a scandal broke that led to his resignation and exile. A videotape of the country's de facto intelligence chief and Fujimori's political fixer, Vladimiro Montesinos, bribing a legislator to switch to Fujimori's party was made public. The tape was only one of thousands of such "Valdivideos" that quickly came to light showing the shadowy Montesinos bribing politicians, businessmen, and other public figures. Meant to blackmail the others involved, the tapes sounded the political death knell for Montesinos and his patron. Fujimori was forced to resign, and new elections were called. The winner was the leading candidate who had opposed Fujimori a year earlier.

Plate 12.2 Alberto Fujimori (left) with OAS Secretary General César Gaviria during negotiations over the contested 2000 elections.

Fujimori's style of leadership was heedless of the principle of the rule of law. A guerrilla war and widespread political violence set the stage for use of authoritarian measures. In addition, the backing of the armed forces and security services allowed a presidential interruption of constitutional rule. Even after the ratification of the new constitution, military influence in the government remained strong. Fujimori's ability to intimidate the media and divide the opposition was considerable. Perhaps most importantly, throughout the 1990s, Peruvian political parties never regained their balance from the disasters that befell them in the 1980s. They were never able to present clear, detailed, and persuasive alternatives to the government's policies. Nor were they able to field a set of attractive candidates sufficiently popular to overcome Fujimori and the collection of movements linked to him. In short, the parties were not able to counter effectively the nebulous system of personalities and loosely organized movements that had displaced them. De-institutionalization had been significant.

Prospects for populism

Contemporary populism or delegative democracy is a form of personalistic, semi-authoritarian rule that arises in times of crisis in societies where democracy is recognized as legitimate, but where the constitutional system that is supposed to institutionalize it is weak. Populism can emerge when there is popular yearning for a strong hand at the tiller, popular willingness to try radical policies, and a leader able to claim a democratic mandate while ignoring constitutional checks on his power. The ability of democracies to transcend to populism depends on a variety of factors. Chief among them is the maturity and development of civil society, the resiliency of political and governmental institutions, and the passing of the sort of crises that gave rise to populist tendencies in the first place.

Although Fujimori was forced to leave office, populism remains a risk in Latin America when weakly institutionalized democracies come under stress, and where strong leaders strike a culturally responsive cord. Hugo Chávez, inaugurated President of Venezuela in 1999, and Lucio Gutiérrez, who was President of Ecuador from 2003 to 2005, represent this trend. Both men were former unsuccessful coup leaders who entered civilian politics. Both took a leftist position in the campaigns. Both, as military men, seemed to be the classic "man-on-horseback," a type which seemed only a decade before to be a dying breed in the region.

Chávez's persona and style has resonated beyond Venezuela. In Bolivia in 2005, another populist leftist, Evo Morales, won the presidency and his party also took control of the lower house of the legislature. Morales, an Amerindian, the first to win the country's presidency, began efforts to revise the constitution and move the country in the direction of "twenty-first-century socialism" – a term coined by Hugo Chávez. The regional governments in the richer, whiter, eastern part of the country resisted. A year after Morales's election, a leftist, US-trained economist, Rafael Correa, won the presidency of Ecuador, another country with a large, marginalized Amerindian population. He too invoked the twenty-first-century socialist slogan and sought Chávez's aid. Meanwhile in Nicaragua, an old-line radical socialist from the 1980s, who had been opposed militarily by the United States during his first government, Daniel Ortega, won the presidency again. In the new century, with rightwing populist delegative democracy now passé, more traditional looking leftwing populism seemed once again on the march. The economic injustice, weak institutions, and rising frustration of hitherto excluded classes have helped fuel its rise. The fate of these movements and whether they will result in entrenched hybrid regimes remains an open question.

Hybrid regimes in other parts of the world

Other parts of the world besides Latin America and former communist states have partly free regimes. Africa has seen perhaps more than its share. African regimes have arisen in slightly different circumstances from those described above. African states have a British, French, or Belgian colonial heritage. If anything, state structures and the sense of nationalism are weaker there than in ex-colonial states elsewhere. Most African states govern multi-ethnic societies where the focus of most people's loyalties is familial and local rather than national. In many cases African states started independence as nominal liberal democracies, but the essence of democratic governance never emerged or quickly collapsed. In the worst instances, neo-sultanistic regimes, such as that of Mobutu Sese Seku in Zaire described in the last chapter, took control. In other African states one-party regimes based on revolutionary ideologies were established. With the advent of African democratization in the early 1990s, the governance of many of these states improved, but far too many remain mired in the partly free category where democratic norms are advertised but less than fully respected.

Hybrid systems have emerged in Asia as well. In fact, Asia presents two examples of successful hybrid systems – Singapore and Malaysia. Both of these countries were originally part of the same British colony and thus share the same colonial heritage and some of the same advantages and problems. Both countries are multi-ethnic societies in which Malays, Chinese, and Indians are the major ethnic groups. However, in Singapore the Chinese predominate while in Malaysia Malays do. The countries gained independence during the 1960s, an era when the threat of communism was taken quite seriously in Southeast Asia. In fact, Malaysia fought a decade-long insurgency against the communists that began while the country was still under British colonial rule. Emergency-era laws remain on the books long after serious threats have passed.

Unlike most of their African counterparts, Singapore and Malaysia inherited effective bureaucratic structures and stronger governmental institutions. Fear of communal violence helped promote robust governments in which the majority nationality predominated but where significant protection was extended to the minority. Strong political leaders were the order of the day. Lee Kuan Yew served as prime minister in Singapore from 1959 to 1990, and continued to play an important role thereafter. Eventually, his son became prime minister. In Malaysia Mahathir Muhammad was prime minister from 1981 to 2003. As important as their strong personalities were, each helped fashion a ruling party that came to dominate the politics of their respective countries. In Singapore, the People's Action Party (PAP) has governed the country since 1959. It has managed to reduce the opposition to a token number of seats in parliament. In Malaysia the communally-based United Malays National Organization (UMNO), which Mahathir headed, has ruled the country since independence, sometimes in coalition with other parties. In both countries the rule of law and basic civil liberties are curtailed, and the ruling party gives itself considerable advantages in regulations surrounding such things as press freedom, freedom of assembly, the financing of political campaigns. In addition, the UMNO has used public policy and political patronage to cultivate its political base among the Malay majority. Given the restrictions under which the opposition labors, the ruling parties appear to be genuinely popular.

This popularity can be accounted for, in part, by the governments' overall economic success. Both Singapore and Malaysia have been successful developmental states. They are numbered among the "Asian tigers," the economies that have outstripped all others in economic growth for decades. Singapore's performance has been the most dramatic. Its 2006 GDP per capita was $33,500. Malaysia, a larger and much more rural country, has also made strides. Its GDP per capita for the same year was nearly $13,500 (IMF 2007). Chinese family-based firms have provided engines for economic growth in both countries as they have elsewhere throughout the region. In addition, foreign investors have found both Malaysia and Singapore attractive. Overall, challenges to these countries' semi-authoritarian rule have been muted. In sum, Malaysia and Singapore are among the Asian states that Francis Fukuyama calls "empires of deference" (Fukuyama 1992: 235–44), non-democratic regimes that have successfully bucked democratic trends and appear both prosperous and stable.

Conclusion

When Tocqueville wrote in the 1830s, he was taking a long view of history. His thesis about the inevitability of democracy was based on his analysis of history that went back to the year 1100. Thus, advocates of the inevitability thesis, like Tocqueville, might still claim that, regardless of experience of the durability of hybrid regimes over the past several decades, democracy will triumph in the long run. Yet, for the indefinite future, hybrid regimes are likely to be a staple of comparative politics. Democratic forms and democratic principles have wide resonance, but in many countries democracy lacks the institutional and societal basis likely to provide for its flourishing. Ruling elites often lack the will to follow democratic norms, respect pluralism, and abide by the rule of law. Elements of the opposition may be uncommitted to democracy as well. Society may be riven by deep divisions based on class or ethnicity. With limits on the media and on rights of association, speech, and assembly, the mass of society may be generally sympathetic to the regime, largely demobilized, or open only to clandestine and radical organization.

Semi-authoritarian systems maintain the barest of democratic facades. While they may be subject to sudden collapse, those who rule them are often adept at keeping the opposition far from the levers of power and denying it any effective legal way to compete for power. Corruption is often rampant. In contrast, semi-democracies, even those in which the rates of corruption are high, are highly imperfect democracies. Admittedly, all actual democracies are imperfect. Elections can be less than fully fair and free as established politicians and special interests take unfair advantage of their positions. The rule of law can sometimes run amok. But semi-democratic regimes suffer from more serious failures to live up to liberal democratic principles. They are political systems where an individual leader or sequence of leaders is able to subvert democratic principles for an extended period because of underlying institutional weaknesses. The least authoritarian of semi-democratic regimes are those in which a legitimately elected leader partially subverts the rule of law and democratic procedures for a time. Once he leaves or is forced out, the democratic institutions retain the capacity for the system to right itself.

In sum, hybrid regimes constitute a mixed bag. Some are more open and closer to democracy than others. In certain countries, backsliding from the norms of democracy has proven only temporary. And, as with high-tech fly-by-wire aircraft, stability is not built into these systems. Stability is the by-product of the way the system is managed. In the physical world, electronics are notoriously finicky and failure prone when subjected to extraordinarily high doses of electromagnetic radiation. In the political world regimes, when they are subject to intense economic, military, or even natural shocks, may be failure prone as well. In fact, rulers of hybrid regimes have been suddenly forced from power in Georgia, Ukraine, and Kyrgyzstan in 2003, 2004, and 2005, respectively, by pro-democracy mass movements. The long-term continuity of all hybrid regimes is by no means guaranteed.

Questions for further consideration

1 Why might the strategies for hybrid rule be attractive to ruling elites in certain political environments? Why might democratic strategies and programs of democratic consolidation seem risky?

2 What risks do proponents of democracy face in semi-authoritarian regimes? What handicaps do they labor under?

3 Russia has remained mired in practices that are less than democratic at best. What effect is this likely to have on neighboring countries where it has considerable influence?

4 Many western powers and organizations have been committed to the spread of democracy. In what ways is their role necessarily limited? How can semi-authoritarian rulers react to limit pressure for democracy from outside the country?

5 Consider the case studies in this chapter. How can internal threats to national security strengthen the hand of semi-authoritarian rulers? What role can serious economic problems play?

6 Singapore and Malaysia have been economic success stories. What sorts of reason could account for lack of a democratization drive by a growing middle class?

Further reading

Jason Brownlee, *Authoritarianism in an Age of Democracy*. Cambridge, England: Cambridge University Press, 2007. A study of Egypt, Iran, Malaysia, and the Philippines and the successful and not so successful use of techniques for creating stable semi-authoritarian rule.

Thomas Carothers, "The End of the Transition Paradigm," *Journal of Democracy*, 13, 1 (2002), 5–21. Attacks the prevalent notion that democracy is inevitable, arguing that partly free governments can survive for extended periods.

Freedom House, *Freedom in the World,* http://www.freedomhouse.org/template.cfm?page=15. The Freedom House website provides overall scores and country analyses.

Marina Ottaway, *Democracy Challenged: The Rise of Semi-Authoritarianism*. Washington, DC: The Carnegie Endowment for International Peace, 2003. The theory of semi-authoritarianism plus a variety of case studies.

Polity IV, *Polity IV Country Reports,* http://www.cidcm.umd.edu/polity/country_reports. The website provides not only country reports but downloadable data sets.

Andreas Schedler (ed.), *Electoral Authoritarianism: The Dynamics of Unfree Competition*. Boulder, CO: Lynne Rienner, 2006. An anthology of articles discussing hybrid regimes in various regions and analyses of the techniques they use.

Fareed Zakaria, *The Future of Freedom: Illiberal Democracy at Home and Abroad*. New York: W.W. Norton, 2003. Argues that electoral democracy that guarantees majority rule often does not effectively secure individual or minority rights.

New political
actors and new
ideologies in the
postmodern era

Change is inevitable in a progressive country. Change is constant.
(Robert Peel, British statesman, 1867)

In this chapter

We investigate recent trends in political culture and political economy that
are helping to reshape the character of politics in the contemporary world.
These trends are associated with the development of postindustrial society
in the West and globalization – the increasing interlinking of economies,
cultures, and peoples around the world. These changes include the erosion
of old class identities, immigration, the increased importance of women as
a self-conscious political group, the formation of political movements
representing indigenous peoples, the increased influence of multilateral
economics institutions, as well as significant demographic changes across
and within countries. Some of these changes have a direct effect on politics
and public policy; the influence of others is more subtle and cumulative.
But all are likely to have a considerable, if not entirely predictable, effect
on politics in the long run.

Introduction

If "modern" means "new," the term "postmodern" can seem a bit odd. Yet
"modern" in the historical sense has a more specific meaning. It refers to a
society with the type of attributes that developed during the modern era
outlined in Chapter 2: a society based on rationality and a functional

division of labor, a society that places a high value on science and material accumulation, a society in which the equality of all citizens and equal rights play a major role. Modern society, which had been developing since the end of the Middle Ages, eventually became industrial society. Industrialization took off in the nineteenth century. In the mid-twentieth century the economic power of states was measured in tons of steel produced annually and the density of the railroad network. As a result of modernization capitalism and the productive forces it unleashed produced new political actors – the middle class and the industrial working class. The numerical dominance of these two classes brought predictability into democratic politics once prosperity became general.

But industrial society did not stand still. Today no one would determine how advanced a nation's economy was by focusing on steel production or its rail network as analysts would have fifty years ago. Robotics, telecommunications, computer software have become some of the hallmarks of an economy's sophistication. In short, the most advanced and wealthy economies produce knowledge and provide services, and the production of things has fallen into second place. They have moved into a "postindustrial" phase. This change has had profound effects both on people's lives and on the nature of politics in postindustrial societies. Not only have the most advanced societies become postindustrial; they have also become postmodern. Values have changed, and political actors unknown or marginalized throughout much of the modern era have emerged. Peel's reference to progress and his focus on country (the nation-state) have a quaint sound to them. They are nineteenth-century – they are "modern." The postmodern era has begun to take a different attitude toward material progress, and globalization has reshaped and diminished the role of the nation-state. New values and new political actors have begun to emerge.

Contemporaneously with the development of the postmodern era has come globalization. **Globalization**, in the broad sense of the term, is the strengthening of ties between countries. It involves the movement, exchange, and intermingling of goods and services, peoples, technologies, ideas, and cultures across all of the world's inhabited continents. Globalization had its beginnings in the European Age of Discovery and the colonization that followed hard upon it, but globalization has become more pronounced than ever in the last half of the twentieth century. Computers, inexpensive means of electronic communication (telephones, radio, television, the Internet), containerized shipping, increased international trade and investment, relatively inexpensive air transport, migration, the development and multiplication of international forums such as the United Nations, the Organization of American States, and the

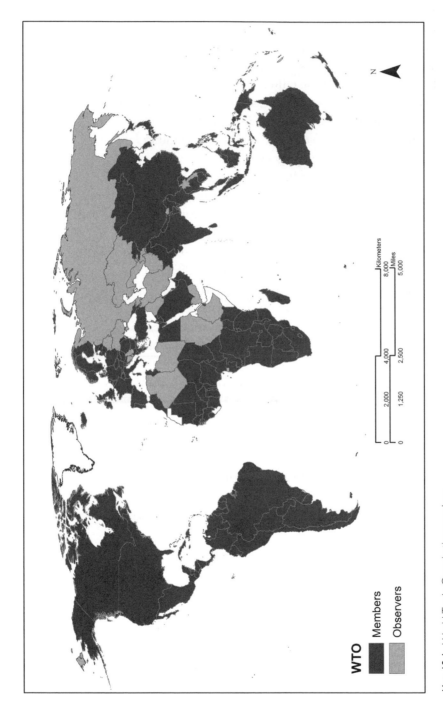

Map 13.1 World Trade Organization members

Source: Environmental Systems Research Institute (ESRI) map data. Data: World Trade Organization

Asian Pacific Economic Cooperation forum have all accelerated an already intense process. Globalization has allowed actors, ideologies, and technologies from outside a country's borders to have a sometimes profound influence on its domestic politics. This chapter examines some of the changes in values as well as the emergence of new political actors and the evolution of older ones that postmodernism and globalization have helped usher in; its aim is to provide information and analysis for assessing the likely trajectory of future developments.

The postmodern era

Postmodernism is both a sociological fact and a theoretical approach to the world. **Postmodern theory** (common today in the fields of literature and philosophy) is skeptical of the modern project. It is an intellectual attempt to explain and defend, among other things, identity politics (see below). Postmodernism rejects universal principles, abstract formal standards of judgment, and even modern science. It is critical of modernity's universalism, individualism, and achievement-oriented standards. The postmodern approach argues for traditional sources of community and knowledge. To cite a specific example, *modern* feminists are likely to argue than men and women are fundamentally the same while *postmodern* feminists are more likely to stress the irreducible differences between the sexes and claim a special and different status for women. Postmodernism also defends the unique and irreducible value of different cultures and communities based on ethnicity and race. Postmodernists see modern social structures, legal formulas, political programs, and political parties as inadequate. Postmodern theory's appeal rests in large measure on the fact that it accords well with many features of contemporary society.

Postmodern values

Economies changed markedly in the mid to late twentieth century. As economies have changed, so too has the structure of the labor force and the values people hold. Many people began to think about life less in terms of traditional loyalties and the acquisition of material necessities of life and more in terms of their own personal satisfaction. In the mid-twentieth century, unionized production jobs provided the bulk of well-paying positions in the economy. As people moved from the countryside to the city, and they and their children eventually prospered, they nonetheless remained focused on issues of economic security. The rise of the postindustrial service economy changed that. Blue-collar jobs and unionization declined. More people found themselves in non-industrial jobs, not the low-paying agricultural or personal service jobs of decades past but relatively highly paid professional positions in finance, medicine, education, engineering, and design. With more money, people began to consider other needs as well. Hence, the rise of postindustrial society has gone hand in hand with the rise of postmodern values.

Scholars have studied value issues by means of cross-national surveys, asking the same basic questions to respondents in a variety of nations and computing the results. These scholars have classified postmodern values into two basic complexes. The first set is "secular-rational" values as opposed to traditional values. Those who hold traditional values say that religion, family, and country are important in their lives. Patriotism, respect for parental authority, and religious belief and observance are important. On the other hand, the holders of secular-rationalist values lay stress on the opposite principles. By and large, as societies become more prosperous, they become more secular-rational in their values. But some countries buck the trend. The United States while advanced economically is as traditional in its outlook as many less economically developed countries.

The other complex of values is that of "self-expression" as opposed to survival values. As we have just alluded, people who have barely enough resources to get by or where their command of these resources seems to remain insecure, are likely to be concerned with their and their family's basic economic needs. When such needs can, in large measure, be taken for granted, people are more likely to focus on other requirements for a fully human existence. At a certain point, desire for leisure can displace the need for extra income: an afternoon off may be more important than an extra hundred dollars in the bank. A job that is interesting and gives a person more autonomy may be more important than a job that pays somewhat more but is highly regimented, dangerous, or dirty. Society as a whole may come to recognize that parks, clean air and water, and aesthetically pleasing surroundings are more important than an extra fraction of a percent of economic growth. In short, the ability to do what one wants and develop one's talents is more highly valued than an extra increment of wealth (Inglehart 1997).

Identity politics

Postmodern society and postmodern attitudes have also provided space for identity politics. In traditional societies, a person's status was largely determined by ascription – he or she was born into a social status. Modernity puts forth a different ideal – status should be the result

of achievement. All should start equal although they may not necessarily
end so. Individuals by talent and hard work should have the right to
achieve their own status. Implicit in the modern ideal is individualism
and the freedom to make one's own individual choices regardless of what
any group, other than one a person freely chooses to belong to, wants.
In short, group membership is instrumental, a means to an end. A person
belongs to a group because it serves his or her individual goals. Loyalty to
the group is provisional.

Of course, the importance of loyalty to a group one is born into has
never completely disappeared even in the most modern of societies.
Nor have even the most modern and open of societies truly lived up to the
principle that universal standards of achievement ought to be applied
universally and even-handedly to everyone. Gender, racial, ethnic, and
religious biases continue to play an important role in modern society.
Inherited characteristics and inherited group membership matter in terms
of how an individual is treated. Still, modern standards argue that such
biases are illicit and ought to be abolished. All human beings are equal
and ought to be treated the same way. Today these views have come under
serious challenge. The development of postmodern values has gone hand
in hand with another development that appears in some ways to be almost
its polar opposite – **identity politics**. Identity politics is politics based on
traditional ascribed or biological differences such as race, ethnicity,
gender, sexual orientation, and religion. All of these groups, religion
excepted, are based on a status inherited from birth that cannot be
changed. In effect, identity politics represents a return to more traditional
and particularistic notions.

Forcing an identity upon someone, differentiating people on the
basis of inherited characteristics, can stigmatize and debilitate. It is, in
fact, often meant to serve as a basis for making invidious discriminations.
Hence modern ideologies of the center and left usually label such
identifications as unjust, and the people that freely accept them as
backward or bigoted. However, the phenomenon of identity politics is
something altogether different. People who practice identity politics
embrace their ascriptive identities, be they based on race, ethnicity,
gender, sexual orientation, or religion. They see such self-identification
as positive. It can give an identity, belonging, and a sense of place and
purpose in an otherwise chaotic world. Identity politics breaks with the
modern project of basing politics on class and economic interest, and
rooting community on individual consent. In both developing and
developed societies, the modern project has broken down, or at least
failed to live up to the more utopian hopes that many of its progenitors
entertained. Both modern politics and modern technology seem to have

run up against their limits. Identity politics seeks to recognize or create true communities of interest and demands recognition for these groups as real communities not just a random collection of individuals.

Some consequences

Both postmodern values and identity politics have come to shape politics in many countries in both the economically developed and less developed worlds. They are likely to shape it more profoundly in the future. Postmodern values undermine well-established political actors and their strategies. As blue-collar workers become less numerous, the influence of labor unions has declined. Labor, socialist, and social democratic parties that have relied on working men and women as their core constituents and stress issues of economic security as their rallying cry may have to rethink how to compete effectively for votes with parties of the center and right. Problems faced by the parties of the left just begin here. For many, issues of economic security have not gone away. For some, in fact, they have become even more salient. Growing unemployment, the gradual decline of the welfare state, and feelings of hostility toward immigrants have made rightist parties more attractive to many former constituents of leftwing parties. The center and rightwing parties can drive a wedge between immigrants and the working class – two groups that orthodox leftists imagine would be natural allies. Attempts by the left to "modernize" the welfare state by cutting back on its benefits hardly reinforce blue-collar voters' traditional loyalties to the left.

At the same time, the traditional left may have new and increasingly stronger political competitors on the left as well. Identity politics replaces or dilutes the importance of class. So too do other non-economic left issues. "Green" or pro-environment politics arose in the 1970s and, along with it, political parties whose primary focus was on environmental issues. These parties are generally leftwing in their orientation, but their policies and constituencies are different from those of the traditional left. Green voters are more likely to be middle-class professionals than the traditional socialist voter. They are more likely to focus on issues of self-expression rather than economic security. The very sort of industrial development that greens may wish to avoid may be considered almost literally the bread and butter of traditional labor. It's not surprising that the past several decades have seen a collapse of the left toward the political center. Socialists advocating state ownership of the means of production have been on the defensive. Social democrats, in favor of the welfare state though not necessarily state ownership, have often promoted privatization of state-owned assets. Even the traditional advocates of the welfare state have often not defended its programs vigorously, concerned that the aging of the population makes the full range of welfare benefits unsustainable in the long run.

Many other modern or modern-sounding political projects have also run into serious difficulties as well. Attempts to modernize the developing world have often failed to live up to expectations. It is no wonder that younger generations would seek to recapture a lost but still remembered past, and that they would be receptive to political activists stressing ethnicity and religion as the foundation of the good life and political order. The Islamic world has been more than receptive to such appeals in the past several decades. The collapse of communism, a modern project par excellence, has opened the way for ethnically based identity politics in many post-communist states. The rise of ethnic nationalism in the former Soviet Union helped fill the void left by the debunking of the old Marxist–Leninist certainties about the eventual creation of a workers' paradise. Yugoslavia too was subject to this loss of political faith with some of the same results. Former communists became ethno-religious nationalists, ripping apart the older federal union into its constituent parts, and then fighting wars, both international and civil, to try to create ethnically homogeneous states. Ethnic nationalists flourished in other Central European states as well although avoiding most of the sort of violence that occurred in Yugoslavia. By the turn of the twenty-first century, these conflicts have been dampened down somewhat. Many Central Europeans seem to be committed to the European Union (EU) project of greater economic, political, and cultural integration of Europe's peoples. The EU's successes since the 1950s have given that project an attractiveness and credibility it is hard for ethnic-nationalist politicians to compete with. But ethnic nationalism is far from dead, especially in economically troubled and repressive states.

In the EU proper as well, the EU's thoroughly modern project is not without its opponents. The disappearance of the nation-state or at least the weakening of its traditional legal sovereignty is decried by so-called "Euro-skeptics." Euro-skeptics fear the loss of national sovereignty to an increasingly remote and dictatorial European bureaucracy unresponsive to both European peoples and national governments. Of the major members of the EU, the British have been the most consistently outspoken about these fears. Identity politics is perhaps more evident within the EU's member states than it is in the political disputes that occur between member governments. Although it is among the most modern parts of the world, the continent has also experienced some of the strongest backlash against modernity. The postmodern dissatisfaction with modernity's supposed rootlessness and lack of meaning has stimulated both neo-traditional movements and anti-traditional ones. These movements are not only in conflict with modernity but also with one another.

The continent's growing number of Muslims has increasingly sought to reinforce and gain legal recognition for their religious identity. But the recognition of Islam flies in the face of the continent's largely secular culture, its largely Christian history, and the remaining legal recognition of Christianity still retained by some states. Even for many moderate Muslims, the sort of recognition homosexuals and others demand for their lifestyle stands in opposition to the moral norms many Muslims accept and expect the law to recognize and enforce. A highly visible instance of this conflict occurred in 2002 in The Netherlands. Pim Fortuyn, a gay-rights activist, campaigned against extending recognition and protection to the Islamic community in the country in part because of its traditionally repressive attitudes not only toward gays but also toward women and those seeking free expression and making untraditional lifestyle choices. He personally gained 14 percent of the vote in national legislative elections, and his party became the second-largest party in parliament in May after his assassination (*New York Times* 2002). Nor is ethnic nationalism dead in the EU. Violent nationalists still exist in the Basque country and Corsica, carrying out bombings and assassinations in Spain and France. Northern Ireland, a part of the United Kingdom (UK) where political violence is of recent memory, could slide back into the abyss. The political conflict between Walloons and Flemish in Belgium and Scots and English could yet lead to secession.

In sum, identity politics as postmodern values have undermined the class-based, economically focused politics typical of modern industrialized societies. The new fault lines they have revealed may be less easily paved over than the old. Politics about the division of economic spoils is susceptible to compromise in a way that identity-based conflict is not. A dollar or a pound can be divided a hundred ways, but it is not always so easy to see how disputes over recognition, pride, and status can be so easily resolved. In less economically developed societies, identity politics could be more destabilizing still, since it points to major failures in the regime's policies and suggests an alternate principle of legitimacy.

New political actors

The change in traditional values and social structures has served to bring new political actors to the fore. Neither of the groups discussed in this section is new in the sense of having been physically absent from society. Quite the reverse! However, they are new in the sense of people newly empowered. The rise of women and indigenous peoples as political actors is a multifaceted story involving the decay of old political and social structures and the emerging sense of consciousness of being members of a group with similar interests and a need for collective action. In short, each of these groups had the potential for being significant political actors for quite some time, but that potential has only begun to be realized in relatively recent years. The incorporation of women and indigenous peoples in the broader movement for the recognition of human rights illustrates how the modern concept of rights has evolved to incorporate aspects of postmodern identity politics.

Women

"Women hold up half the sky," as the Chinese proverb has it. Since the 1950s the importance of women's roles has become increasingly evident. Women have advanced their rights in strictly legal terms although not everywhere and not without meeting resistance. Perhaps even more important, governments, international aid agencies, and others have begun to recognize the practical importance of women in society, politics, and the economy as well (UNIFEM 2005). Largely unheralded until quite recently, women have played a significant role in economic development that has been poorly recognized both in law and in the academic literature. For instance, agricultural aid workers, usually men themselves, were accustomed to talking to men assuming that since men legally owned the land, it was they who would adopt the improved techniques and seeds the workers had to offer. Yet, the situation in reality was quite different. In Africa it is often women who work the fields and make the decisions on what to plant and how to plant it. Their involvement and interest in the outcome was often much more intense than that of their husbands. For the men, if the crop yielded a surplus to sell, they would have more money to spend. For the women, feeding the family and providing for any surplus was a real and pressing concern. Persuading the women, as it turned out, was often more critical to getting new techniques adopted than persuading the men.

Women also play an important role in other areas of development. Again, until recently, this role has been little noticed or supported. The World Bank and regional development banks give developmental loans often for massive projects. Private banks lend to businesses and individuals to enable them to invest. But most people in developing nations fall below the threshold that warrants consideration for even the smallest private-sector bank loans. Poor but enterprising people in both rural and urban areas who need only the equivalent of several hundred dollars to invest in a sewing machine or another simple piece of equipment used to have the local moneylender as virtually their sole recourse. Today development agencies and private foundations have recognized the importance of micro-lending for economic development and improving the standard of living for people in the developing world. Credit cooperatives have emerged with some capital and guidance provided by outside agencies but with local people making the decisions. Women often play the dominant role in many of these loan-granting cooperatives. Loans are of negligible size to most people in the developed world, but they can have an appreciable cumulative effect economically and develop society's social capital as well.

Women's control of their own affairs has had a positive effect on limiting population growth. Experts have long recognized that successful attempts to limit the rate of population growth are associated with two factors: the availability of birth control and a rise in a family's or a society's standard of living. People with growing incomes and growing aspirations are less likely to regard children as an economic asset or the birth of children as an uncontrollable natural fact. Wealthier families normally have fewer children than the poor, but this association poses a "chicken and egg" sort of problem. Once wealthy, people have fewer children and invest more time and money in each child. This, in turn, improves the child's chance to survive and prosper, and to acquire a good education. But often the choice of having fewer children must precede the family's accumulation of wealth. Why and how do poor families decide to stop having children after the birth of the third or fourth child? The answer again resides with women. When medical personnel counsel women directly, when women do not need the permission of their husbands to use birth control, they decide to have fewer children. This should not come as a surprise. In almost every society, it is women who are tasked with the primary childcare burden. It is women who can best see the effect additional children have on the overall well-being of the family. When men do not have a major role in raising the children, they can afford to be less concerned about the sort of burdens additional children represent. And having a big family is often a sign of male potency and a mark of prestige. Unsurprisingly, in countries where women have been the prime movers in making decisions about family size, the rate of population growth and the resultant press upon natural resources and public services slows. Across much of Latin America and parts of Asia this has begun to occur.

Women have also started to assume control of their own affairs in other ways. Increasingly women have been able to enter public service and the military. Women's police stations have opened in Brazil, where female officers are responsible for acting upon family and sexual violence. The presence of female heads of government is no longer a rarity. In the developed world, affirmative action has aided the advancement of women. In a few western societies, women politicians outnumber men. In industrialized societies, strict gender roles have begun to blur. The female empowerment index (Map 13.2) is a rough indicator of current progress. It attempts to measure women's position relative to men in the areas of income, professional status, and political influence.

The situation is far from uniformly hopeful. In even the most progressive societies, much remains to be accomplished to achieve full gender equality. Crimes against women are often treated more leniently than those against men, just as crimes against minorities are often less harshly punished than those against members of the majority population. In societies governed by more traditional norms, the gap between genders is even greater. In parts of Africa, female circumcision is common. The use of female infanticide and the selective abortion of female fetuses have led to an imbalance of males in China, India, and South Korea. In many developing societies, girls receive less care and less education than boys. The reasons for this are varied. Males often have the traditional obligation of caring for their aged parents while women care for their husband's parents. If the extended family is all one has to rely on in old age, girls are an economic burden with little long-term payoff. In other societies the family of the bride must pay a costly dowry to the groom's family. And again, this norm makes girls a burden.

Often, traditional norms limit women's sphere of activity to the home, and educating girls seems a senseless endeavor. Yet, it is literate and educated women who are likely to take childbearing decisions into their own hands with or without the knowledge of their husbands. Educating girls makes them more resourceful, enterprising, and autonomous in general. Both developing and developed nations have seen the increased participation of women in politics. The importance of education, childcare, and healthcare – so-called "women's issues" – in the United States is no accident. While the percentage of women in leadership positions lags far behind their share of the general population in most countries, they have made dramatic strides in many others. In several Nordic countries women have reached near parity among the political class. And although women's organizations and issues vary by region and even country, women's issues and their demands for voice and authority are not likely to disappear.

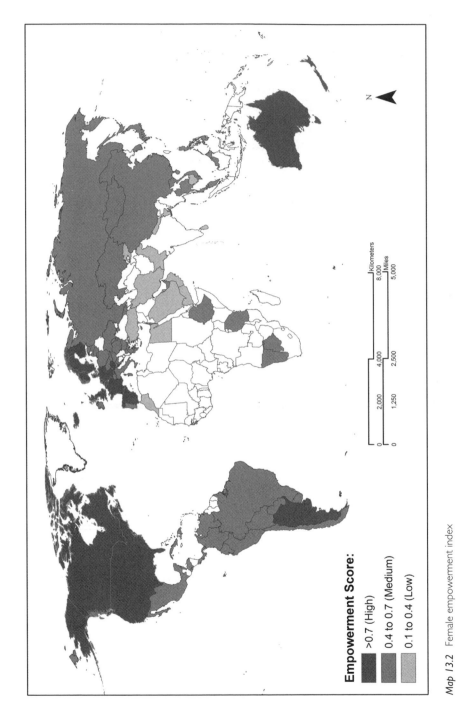

Map 13.2 Female empowerment index

Source: Environmental Systems Research Institute (ESRI) map data. Data: UNDP

Note: The empowerment score is based on a composite of female to male ratios of seats in the national legislature, senior government officials and managers, professional and technical workers, and the ratio of female to male earned income

Empowerment Score:

>0.7 (High)

0.4 to 0.7 (Medium)

0.1 to 0.4 (Low)

Indigenous peoples

The principle of self-determination of peoples made gains throughout the twentieth century. The dam broke after the Second World War when the colonial peoples of Africa and Asia won their independence. Yet, only recently have the rights of indigenous peoples come onto the political agenda. Native Americans in the western hemisphere, the Maori in New Zealand, and the aboriginal people of Australia are among these indigenous or "first peoples" who have been pushed aside by European settlement. But first peoples – those who had settled the land – have been pushed aside by others than Europeans. In parts of Africa and Asia minority races have been pushed aside and marginalized by the now numerically dominant group. Nearly fifty countries, including the United States, China, Russia, and most of Latin America, have indigenous minorities. Since the 1990s, indigenous peoples have achieved greater visibility for their plight if nothing else, and nation and international movements, as well as international conferences, have sought ways of correcting long-standing injustices. Control of the land itself, the rights to use existing natural resources (such as guaranteeing hunting and fishing rights), intellectual property rights to the genome of unique flora and fauna are among the salient issues that need to be addressed. Governments, majority populations, and corporations both domestic and foreign have frequently run roughshod over the rights of the indigenous population in many parts of the globe (Minorities at Risk 2005).

In Canada and Australia indigenous peoples have achieved signal legal victories recognizing their land claims. In a scattering of Latin American states, native peoples have secured legal recognition of their cultures and languages, a not insignificant victory when it guarantees that judicial and other governmental matters can be conducted in their own language instead of Spanish. But significant challenges remain there and elsewhere. The land indigenous peoples have been forced to occupy, once considered remote and uneconomic, is now often coveted for its oil, gas, and mineral reserves, as well as for its ranching and farming potential. This puts indigenous peoples in a position often more difficult than before, since powerful multinational corporations (MNCs) backed by national governments see significant profits to be made. Only occasionally has there been a silver lining to the cloud as was the case when some of the native peoples of Ecuador were able to sue the Chevron Texaco Corporation in US courts (Forero 2003). Indigenous peoples are often a small minority within existing populations, which weakens their political leverage even in a democratic context. Yet, in certain Central and South American countries, indigenous peoples constitute a majority or large minority of the population. Historically, they have been excluded politically and remained largely passive in the face of dominant political actors, at best co-opted within patron–client networks. Nonetheless, where indigenous people's numbers are significant, their political mobilization can have a significant effect on politics. In Ecuador this has just begun to happen. In 2002, a coalition, in which Amerindians played a major role, elected an insurgent ex-military officer as president. In 2006 Bolivian Amerindians elected one of their own as president of the country. Other countries in the region have yet to move to this point.

Summary

Neither women nor indigenous peoples have fully actualized their potential power or adequately vindicated their rights. The effective disenfranchisement they continue to face is emblematic of the sort of problems other groups face as well. Sometimes these groups are minorities who find their position undercut by dominant majority populations. For example, the Tibetans and Uighars of western China find themselves effectively disenfranchised by an authoritarian government dominated by the Han Chinese. In democracies, too, minorities can find themselves at risk as is clear from US experience and the experiences of Muslims in Hindu India. However, the changing domestic and international political climate may yet provide opportunities for these groups to develop as effective political actors.

Globalization

Contemporary domestic politics is not only affected by postmodernism; it is heavily and specifically influenced by a key aspect of the postmodern era – globalization. Globalization has shaped politics on a variety of fronts: economic, cultural, and demographic. It has to a significant degree broken down the barriers between purely domestic and purely international politics. As we have already seen in a variety of contexts, international actors sometimes have a profound effect on domestic politics. Ideologies and new technologies often originate abroad as well. However, the contributions of globalization to domestic political development have been unique in the scope and rapidity of their effects.

Globalization and international politics

Under today's version of globalization, the international system itself is at once more integrated, and its interconnections are more numerous and diverse than earlier. Globalization today is different from foreign influence and foreign intervention of the past. In earlier epochs imperial powers attempted to retain a monopoly on trade with their colonies. To do this, they excluded competitors from their colonial markets and secured for themselves the exclusive right to the resources of the colony. This was part of a general policy of managing trade so that the country – and its national treasury – would maximize their cash revenue and was originally known as mercantilism. Mercantilists saw trade as essentially a zero-sum game – you sold, you won; you bought, you lost – since anything you purchased abroad sent gold or silver out of the country while exports brought gold and silver in. This perspective, today also known as "economic nationalism," has hardheaded common sense about it. Modern states, after all, need wealth to fight wars. But this approach to foreign policy also encouraged war by making "favorable trade relations" an important diplomatic and military objective. Thus, states would conquer territory to create empires or browbeat weaker states into allowing them to have unequal access to their markets (Allen 1991a).

Today's globalization has generated new sorts of political actors – nongovernmental organizations (NGOs), multilateral organizations, and transnational corporations (TNCs), i.e., global companies with no particular national base. The global system is more a web of economic and cultural relationships than a set of competing imperial hierarchies as it often was in past eras. Pressures and influence travel in multiple directions through the global system. Contemporary versions of economic nationalism are alive and well, but countries now are forced to operate within a legal network that limits states' economic policies. International organizations both governmental and nongovernmental have an effect on domestic politics. Contemporary migration has reversed the old pattern of migrants moving from more to less developed countries. Even more than under colonialism, influence is not a one-way street. The less powerful influence the more powerful as well as being influenced by them.

In the contemporary world, forms of power other than military force have become critical. Direct aid as well as favorable trade relationships can be methods of influence. Embargoes on trade and other sanctions can serve as means of coercion. "Soft power" – the attractiveness of a country's form of government, its ideas, and its popular and high culture – is important as well. Contemporary international law is more balanced than was international law in the heyday of imperialism. Human rights law provides a moral check at least on the exercise of raw force. NGOs, such as Amnesty International, have acted independently of governments to support these values and influence other countries' domestic politics.

Other NGOs such as Doctors without Borders and the Friends Service Committee provide humanitarian assistance. Governments too have provided an array of human rights and relief efforts, providing aid and advice, and making human rights an important part of their diplomacy. In short, contemporary international politics sometimes promotes democracy and the protection of weaker parties.

Yet, the record on the whole is mixed at best. The globalized world is certainly not one of simple benevolence and equality. Power politics on the international level continues. Countries with the reality or even the promise of natural resource wealth can attract powerful foreign patrons. Oil-producing states with repressive governments have often attracted such support. Countries seen as strategically important allies have received support regardless of the morality and legality of their conduct. Economic and military aid as well as the prestige conferred by association with a major international power has helped political elites and individual leaders pressured by popular forces pressing for change. In the cold-war era, anti-communist dictators received such assistance. Currently, under the rubric of the "war on terror," a new contingent of dictatorial governments has obtained similar support. For example, as a result of the war on terror, the United States has befriended the dictator of Uzbekistan, Islam Karimov, and other leaders with questionable democratic credentials at best.

As in the past, great powers, states with influence throughout their region and beyond, have been able to exercise considerable indirect control over weaker states. They have secured for themselves, their military forces, and their corporations legally recognized rights by treaty and other formal agreements. In addition, dominant countries' informal influence has often been extensive. Their diplomatic representatives may pull political strings behind the scenes. Close liaison between military and intelligence personnel may make the agencies of the dependent state seem like adjuncts to the dominant power. Politicians and others in the weaker state may actively seek the advice and support of one of the great powers. Such practices do not entail an official loss of sovereignty although they may occasionally bear a striking similarity to indirect colonial rule. Despite their continued influence, the role of the great powers today is far different from the outright colonization of the nineteenth and early twentieth centuries.

The globalization of culture

Contemporary globalization has made foreign firms and foreign governments considerably more than bit players on many countries'

domestic political and economic stage and consequently on their
cultural stage as well. English has become the major international
language of diplomacy, commerce, science, and tourism. For many
countries, globalization has meant westernization or even
Americanization. United States' news networks, restaurants, fast-food
outlets, films, music, and banks are everywhere. In many cases, they
spread values alien to the local culture. While this clash of cultures is the
leitmotif of much of world history, it is, nonetheless, a potentially
destabilizing element that changes the nature of politics in many
countries. Foreign influence has bred resentment as often as not expressed
in cultural or religious terms. Even Europeans have reacted against the
influence of US-made films, television programs, and fast food. There and
elsewhere governments, individuals, and groups have attempted to limit
American influence, not always with great success. "Jihad versus
McWorld," as one commentator (Barber 1995) terms it, is an underlying
theme of global politics.

Yet, globalization of culture is not exclusively a one-way street
whereby richer countries penetrate poorer. Latin American and especially
Brazilian *telenovelas* (soap operas) are widely exported. India's "Bollywood"
makes more films than America's Hollywood and distributes them
globally. Tourism and other mechanisms have cultivated a taste for
what had been hitherto foreign and exotic among the economically well
off. Music, art, and cuisine of developing countries pervade the
economically developed. A variety of sports have become globalized.
Football (soccer in the United States) has become the world's most
important sport. The sport's quadrennial World Cup is one of the most
followed events in the world. Basketball has spread globally as well.
Cricket has become a favorite throughout the former British Empire.
Cultures have also gone regional. Al Jeezera, the pan-Arab television news
network, and its imitators have allowed the Arab-speaking world to see its
region and the world at large through a different lens. They have made
modern standard Arabic a dialect that is actually increasing, replacing
local dialects. Similar influences have promoted the intermingling of
European cultures. In 2005 Latin Americans began exploring their own
regional news network.

In sum, culture is a form of soft power. It provides a door through
which diplomatic and economic influence can enter. Beyond that, it can
build bridges and nurture a sense of community broader than the
nation-state, but it can also create expectations and standards of
comparison that promote a sense of injustice and outrage. In short, it can
undermine or buttress a regime's legitimacy and provide instruments to
strengthen loyal, disloyal, or semi-loyal oppositions.

Immigration

While the spread of western influence has often traveled along commercial avenues, much of the cultural influence of developing countries has been the result of migration. The movement of peoples is as old as the human race, but that movement has taken on different characteristics in each age. Immigration (whether it is international or internal) has a number of general features. It is, first of all, a push/pull phenomenon. Lack of opportunities at home compels immigrants to leave; at the same time opportunities elsewhere beckon. Second, immigrants frequently aspire to return to their birthplace once they have acquired sufficient wealth, but in many cases they cannot or later are not willing to do so. In the nineteenth century, Europe and parts of Asia sent immigrants to the New World. Europeans settled in Australia and New Zealand. Immigrants from then British India settled in Africa and the Caribbean. Even before the nineteenth century, Chinese immigrants had settled throughout much of Asia. Immigrants provided labor, skills, and sometimes capital to their new homelands. However, immigration often entailed disruption and conflict. The late twentieth and early twenty-first centuries are no different.

Europe has been one of the focuses of recent immigration. The nineteenth and early twentieth centuries saw a populous Europe send millions of immigrants to the much less populated countries of the New World. Most people in the United States are well aware of how this immigration reshaped the demographic profile of their own country. Often they are less aware of the fact that the same wave of immigration helped reshape much of the rest of the western hemisphere as well. Italians, Germans, and Irish settled in South and Central America too, as did lesser numbers of Chinese, Japanese, and South Asians. Yet, for Europe at least, the immigration flow has now reversed. The old continent is more the recipient of migrants than the source of them. Immigration into Europe presages a change in politics there, and immigration has, in fact, changed it already. Immigration into Europe began in the decade after the Second World War when the continent suffered from a labor shortage and other parts of the world had a labor surplus. The imperial or ex-imperial powers, Britain and France, for example, granted certain of the colonial subjects the right to settle in the mother country. Other countries such as Germany with no overseas colonial empire since the First World War admitted millions of Turks to meet its labor shortage. Doors were also open to immigrants fleeing persecution back home. Even when policies promoting immigration changed in the face of growing unemployment, close family members were often allowed the continued right of immigration. As was

the case with much nineteenth-century immigration, the expectation
that immigrants would return to their home countries after a relatively
brief period turned out to be ill-founded. Many migrants not only stayed;
they later brought their families as well. Thus, they have contributed
indirectly to the unemployment problem that besets many European
economies.

The immigration phenomenon has broader consequences as well. Many
of these consequences are the result of the continent's inexperience with
being a host to immigrants. European societies have nothing equivalent to
the "melting pot" myth of the United States. Americans like to think of
themselves as a nation of immigrants where everyone becomes quickly
integrated into the society. While this conception is inaccurate, it has
some basis in fact. The sheer scale of immigration that began in the
nineteenth century forced the United States to recognize diversity in
religion and culture, however reluctantly. It also provided an environment
where the sons and daughters of immigrants, if not the immigrants
themselves, learned English. Maybe most important, citizenship could be
gained by "soil" (being born in the country) or by voluntary transfer of
allegiance. In contrast, until rather recently, Germany had strict laws
determining citizenship by "blood." This meant that individuals of
German ethnic extraction could automatically gain German citizenship
even though their family had not lived in Germany for centuries, while
ethnic Turks born in Germany were not German citizens regardless of
their knowledge of the language and their intention to remain in the
country. France, while it does not impose the test of blood to gain French
citizenship, has stressed cultural unity. It has established legal protections
for diversity based on the historical rather than the recent diversity of
France. For example, the French state recognizes and supports Catholic
practices in the field of education, but denies such support and
recognition to Islam.

Europe's lack of recognition of outsiders is largely the result of its
history. In many cases it is accurate – or nearly accurate – to speak of
European countries as nation-states. Nationality in the ethnographic and
cultural sense often coincides with the legal boundaries of the state. Even
in clearly multinational states such as Belgium, each national group has a
consciousness of its own identity and a jealousy about its identity being
maintained and officially protected. These national identities are deeply
rooted historically. This situation makes it difficult to accommodate new
additions to the ethnic and cultural mix gracefully. Accommodation may
be doubly difficult when immigrants themselves resist integration into
the historically dominant culture. This political/cultural clash appears
especially serious given the underlying demographics. The native

population of most advanced industrial societies is destined to shrink, sometimes drastically. The number of births per woman of childbearing age is below the replacement rate. On the other hand, immigrant populations generally are reproducing at considerably above the replacement rate. And they are likely to do so for a generation or two. Hence, the native population needs immigrants and their children to support the economy and the welfare state as the native-born population ages. But immigration constitutes a cultural shock.

Contemporary immigration not only affects Europe but other areas of the developed world as well. The United States had relatively little immigration in the mid-twentieth century, but it began receiving new waves of immigrants again by the end of the twentieth century. Latin Americans and Asians, hitherto much more thinly represented in the general population, constitute the lion's share of the new immigrants. Japan, a culturally and ethnically close-knit society, has its Korean minority. Although the minority population is not large, Japan finds it difficult to deal with them equitably. Australia too, long a country settled primarily by Europeans, found itself with a large recently admitted Asian community, much to the shock of nativists.

Urbanization

Urbanization is not a new phenomenon, nor is it uniquely connected with globalization, but it has been accelerated by the globalization process. Urbanization is an almost inescapable part of modernization. In Europe it occurred as commerce grew and capitalism developed. In countries that industrialized later even in a limited way, urbanization was at least in part an offshoot of the local economy's connection with the world economy. The more agriculture becomes commercialized and the greater the importance of the international market, the more small cultivators are forced off the land. Just as this was the case in early periods of industrialization, it is also the case today as free trade in agricultural products has increased. Small cultivators often have a hard time competing with imported food especially when foreign producers are heavily subsidized. Some of those displaced migrate to the developed world, but often the destination is their own nation's cities even though employment opportunities there are limited. The pressure of urbanization was made worse by overall rapid population growth. The growth of population was a seemingly inexorable process. Basic methods of disease prevention and sanitation have spread from the advanced industrialized countries to other parts of the world. Life expectancy in poorer countries has skyrocketed, but the birthrates remained high till quite recently. Thus the population grew at an unprecedented rate.

Plate 13.1 Results of rapid urbanization. A street in a squatter settlement in Asunción, Paraguay, 2005.

Just as industrialized countries face the cultural and economic problem of incorporating foreign immigrants, less industrialized countries face the even more pressing problem of accommodating poorly supported municipal services to an influx of new rural migrants. Often they succeed in doing so only in a limited fashion or virtually not at all. Rapid urbanization and population growth has complicated the problems of governance for countries with weak states, governments of questionable legitimacy, and societies with limited economic resources. Rapid urbanization and population growth have served to further undercut both legitimacy and state effectiveness. They have confronted governments with festering problems they have been ill-prepared to address in an efficacious manner. Urbanites are more likely to be aware of what's happening in their own country and the world at large even when their awareness is based on misconceptions. It is easier for urban dwellers to organize and communicate with one another. In short, in the developing world urbanization has compounded problems that can set the stage for political breakdown.

The emergence of today's globalized economy: the rise and fall of the Bretton Woods system

Economic integration is perhaps the most important and most hotly debated feature of contemporary globalization. The origins of contemporary economic integration can be traced to the aftermath of the Second World War. When leading policy-makers of the allied powers met in 1944 in Bretton Woods in New Hampshire to plan the economic structure of the post-war world, they firmly rejected the more extreme forms of economic nationalism. Economic nationalism, be it full-blown mercantilism or more limited protection of domestic markets, had long been an element of most states' policies, but the Second World War convinced almost everyone that economic nationalism had to be tempered or it risked bringing on yet another world war. This realization led to the establishment of treaties and multilateral institutions to promote trade and investment and to help regulate the world economy. It was out of these arrangements that contemporary globalization developed (Krugman and Obstfeld 1997: 237–42, 549–63).

The importance of international trade

The promotion of international trade was one of the post-war planners' key policy objectives. They believed that international trade could increase prosperity, promote development, and render armed conflict less likely if it was done under the aegis of free markets. Post-war planners based their position in part on economic liberalism – the theory of capitalist economics developed by advocates of free markets during the Industrial Revolution. These liberal analyses as modified by later thinking became the basis of the new international economic system. Economic liberalism rejected mercantilism and economic nationalism that had promoted monopolies and exclusions. Economic liberalism held that economic nationalism was wrongheaded. Liberalism believed that free trade was sound policy for an individual state even when other states did not reciprocate. If trade were truly free and uncoerced, trade was a positive-sum game. Each side would be a winner. Unless each party values what the other has more than what it itself possesses, no free exchange is possible. Once the trade takes place, each is better off by its own evaluation. Economic liberals viewed a fixation on money flowing into the country as mistaken. Money is simply a store of value, and it has value only because you can purchase things with it. While earning and saving money is prudent, one saves and invests only to be able to consume in the future.

In short, mercantilism's focus on achieving a trade surplus (and the resulting accumulation of gold and silver) was irrational. It turned money, a mere instrument, into an absolute good. All that is necessary is for a country to be able to pay for what it buys and not fall hopelessly into debt because of frivolous expenditures. In other words the liberal recommendation was at root simple. Buy the goods that are cheapest and best regardless of where they are made. Sell to the people who will buy your products. When the value of imports equals the value of exports there will be no problem. If imports exceed exports the imbalance will ultimately produce counter-pressures. Excess demand for foreign goods will drive the prices of locally produced goods down, thus increasing demand for locally produced goods. This happens not because government controls the movement of specie (gold and silver), but because it does not do so (Allen 1991b). Thus, there is a tendency for exports to balance imports, or more accurately, for a country's overall international transactions to balance. In other words, in theory at least free markets are self-correcting. Accordingly, in the final analysis empires drain revenue; they do not generate it. If a government protects property, balances its budget, and establishes a sound currency, in the end economically all will be well.

Yet, few countries when liberal trade theory was first developed or even now take the theory as their sole guide. Most states' economic policy is a mixture of economic nationalism and liberal free trade. Countries and interests within them negotiate to gain favorable access to markets. Few governments believe they can be so blasé as to allow wealthy and important firms, or whole economic sectors to fail and the workers they employ to become suddenly redundant just because things may work out for the better in the long run. Furthermore, firms and workers act politically to protect their vested interests, and regardless of their commitment to liberal trade theory, governments cannot afford to ignore them. In the international arena, national power often depends upon having an advanced industrial economy, not simply a prosperous one. In short, the current trading system and individual states' policies are a mixture of free trade and economic nationalism (Gilpin 1987: 131–262).

In addition, although theory held free trade in currencies should correct imbalances in trade, the practice often produced different results. In the real world, governments were apt to act on the basis of a short-term perception of their interest. Experience showed that a government sometimes chooses to decrease the value of its currency. This was intended to stimulate exports and get the country out of economic trouble. Such devaluations can set off a chain reaction. And when a large number of states adopt this "beggar-thy-neighbor" policy of intentionally devaluing their currencies or erecting tariff and other barriers to trade, no one benefits and the world economy is apt to spin out of control. The post-war planners recognized that new mechanisms were needed to prevent such problems.

Managing the global economy: multilateral institutions

To overcome the problems they anticipated, post-war planners provided for new mechanisms in the form of three new multilateral institutions. **Multilateral institutions** are international organizations to which states belong. In some, each state has an equal vote. In others, the vote of the state is in proportion to its financial contribution to the organization. The **World Trade Organization** (WTO) – originally the General Agreement on Tariffs and Trade (GATT) – exists to promote trade by facilitating the writing and enforcement of trade agreements among its members. The **International Monetary Fund** (IMF) was established to police currency exchange rates. Although liberal theory saw the free exchange of currency as part of a free trade system, in the aftermath of the Second World War, economic planners believed fixed exchange rates were a better policy choice for the international economy. Fixed exchange rates would insure predictability and encourage long-term international contracts. Thus, for a quarter century the IMF policed a post-war financial system based on fixed currency exchange rates. Currencies were pegged against the US dollar, and the United States pledged to buy back dollars from other governments at the rate of $35 for one ounce of gold. States agreed to get the IMF's approval before changing their exchange rates. The third major postwar institution, the International Bank for Reconstruction and Development (the **World Bank**), was meant to provide money for rebuilding war-torn countries after the Second World War and providing development loans to poorer countries thereafter. Its major focus was on **project loans**, i.e., lending extended to a country on a case-by-case basis given the viability of a particular investment (such as a dam or highway system) and its likelihood of contributing to the country's overall development.

The GATT/WTO, the IMF, and the World Bank were part of an essentially liberal structure that would promote generally free trade as opposed to closed trading zones controlled by imperial powers. At the same time, they assumed that states would defend their interests, and trade agreements would require the consent of every participating state. This partial free trade arrangement worked well enough after the Second World War for Japan to abandon its imperial ambitions and prosper mightily even though she had no colonies or any official zones of influence. The GATT has gone through seven negotiating rounds that have lowered barriers to trade, not only tariffs but so-called non-tariff barriers – such as quotas and product quality regulations – as well.

For nearly four decades after the Second World War, Bretton Woods-model capitalism was only one of three different economic models that competed with one another on the global stage. The capitalist model stressed private property, free trade, and free markets. It saw the multilateral institutions as key promoters and regulators of international economic integration. Its practitioners were among the most prosperous and successful countries in the world. But capitalism was far from unchallenged. Communism provided a second radical alternative model to post-war capitalism. Domestically communist states relied on government ownership of the means of production and centralized state planning for the entire economy down to virtually the smallest detail. Communist states, by and large, rejected international markets and multilateral institutions in which capitalist states were the leading members. Instead, communist states arranged large-scale state-to-state barter agreements among themselves. Communist trade with capitalist states was limited.

Most developing countries followed a third model that was a hybrid of the other two. Some favored policies of state-led growth that consciously borrowed from both the capitalist and communist models. Almost all tried to mimic some of the policies that early industrializing countries, such as the United States, Germany, and Japan, had followed. The early industrializing countries had protected their local market and fostered the growth of national industry by direct and indirect subsidies. This was the so-called "infant industries" policy. Later, developing countries substituted local manufactures for imports, and the policy was frequently termed **import substitution industrialization (ISI)**. ISI states generally did not reject multilateral institutions, but instead sought to reform them along lines that would be friendlier to their own interests, seeking large grants and loans under favorable terms, technology transfers, and entry into developed countries' markets on a preferential basis. For decades the World Bank and later regional development banks that followed the same pattern were receptive to this argument as were leading economists and policy-makers in developed capitalist countries.

The collapse of the Bretton Woods system

As it turned out, the post-war system did not endure. The economic shape of the world began to change decisively in the 1970s. The first major change was a breakdown of the system for assuring stable currency-exchange rates. The fixed currency-rate regime fell apart when the United States revoked its pledge to support the dollar in 1971. Despite numerous attempts to reconstruct the old system, exchange rates came to be determined largely by market forces. The new system of market-determined exchange rates put constraints upon countries whose economies are relatively small and whose currencies are not widely used. The United States, Japan, the UK, and the twelve European nations who all use the euro as their currency have the luxury of large economies. Furthermore many nations' central banks hold dollars, yen, and euros as reserves.

This revised system gives the major economic powers a decided financial advantage that smaller economies do not have. For example, the United States runs large governmental budget deficits as well as trade deficits. But because the US economy is large and relatively strong, and the dollar is widely held, the United States can easily borrow from foreigners at reasonable rates of interest. To a certain extent the United State does not have to earn dollars; it prints them. Of course, it cannot run larger and larger trade and fiscal deficits indefinitely, or foreigners would begin to lose confidence. They would then refuse to loan the US government money and sell dollars and dollar-denominated assets. However, in the meantime the United States has a wide margin for error. The margin for error for smaller economies, especially those of developing countries, is considerably less. They have to borrow internationally in dollars – not their own currency. Their central banks, the financial clearing houses run by their governments, have to maintain adequate reserves of dollars so that foreigners who wish to repatriate their profits can easily do so. Without the guarantee of being able to take money back home, foreigners would not have invested in the first place. In addition, if the local currency loses its value or appears to be about to lose its value, foreigners will pull out, or they will demand a high rate of interest to compensate for the possibility of losing money by holding the local currency.

The second major shock to the international economy was a series of oil price rises during the 1970s that increased petroleum's price five-fold in inflation-adjusted terms. This increase affected prices beyond oil itself. Products made from petroleum such as agricultural chemicals and plastics increased in price; so too did transportation, heating, and cooling. The oil shock sent even the industrial democracies into a period of high inflation, high unemployment, and recession. In most cases, developing countries that were not oil-exporters received an even worse shock. As a result of the twin shocks of the 1970s, economic growth has been slower and more erratic for most countries and the global economy as a whole ever since.

The third major shock to the international economy was the debt crisis that emerged in the early 1980s. It was connected to the oil crisis. The 1970s had seen a transfer of hundreds of billions of dollars from oil importers to oil-exporting countries. Oil-exporting states with small populations found themselves with a surplus of income, which they invested in the major privately owned international banks. Awash with cash, the banks, in turn, made loans to countries at historically low real rates of interest (the rate of interest when the effects of inflation are factored out). The governments of many oil importers and even some high-population oil exporters took the opportunity to borrow "cheap money." Most hoped to invest it in ISI projects that would have a substantial economic benefit. But the borrowers had not been able to lock in low interest rates. Short-term loans needed to be rolled over repeatedly under new terms, and long-term loans were at floating rates of interest.

The debt crisis began in 1982 when Mexico announced it would not be able to pay its debts, in large part, because of a staggering increase in interest payments. Mexico's interest rate problem was an indirect result of the United States Federal Reserve and other wealthy countries' central banks deciding to raise the interest rates they charged to historically high levels. The central banks were interested in putting an end to high inflation at home, but the decision had the side-effect of increasing the interest rates paid by Mexico and other debtor countries. The prospect of default loomed for many other developing countries as well. They too had borrowed heavily in the 1970s when interest rates had been low, and they now found themselves unable to repay those debts. The 1980s debt crisis spelled the doom of the ISI model, and sent the debtors, cap in hand, looking for some sort of debt relief.

Despite the oil-induced shocks to major capitalist powers, by the 1980s the capitalist model of international integration had clearly gained the upper hand. Communist-style state socialism had declined and then collapsed. In addition, most states that followed ISI policies also began to run into substantial problems of which the debt crisis was only one symptom. The most successful countries – South Korea, Taiwan, Hong Kong, and Singapore – had actually been able to graduate into exporting manufactured goods like their successful predecessors. They were largely unaffected by the crisis. They had sufficient foreign revenue to service their foreign debt. These exporting countries were able to balance the imperatives of economic nationalism with the liberal demands of the current international trading system. Many other countries that followed the policy of state-led growth ran into difficulties and never graduated from ISI to exporting. Thus, they were unable to earn the foreign exchange necessary to pay their debts. And problems with repaying foreign loans made them amenable to moving more clearly in a capitalist direction. The IMF and later the World Bank were to play an important role in forcing this change.

Neo-liberalism and the Washington consensus

The capitalist version of international economic governance that came into vogue in the 1980s was significantly different from what the post-war planners had originally envisioned. In their early history, the multilateral institutions were guided by a Keynesian approach. In fact, the British economist John Maynard Keynes was one of the leading architects of these institutions. Keynes was concerned with promoting trade and limiting the influence of economic nationalism, but he stressed the role of the state in regulating the domestic economy and stimulating growth. He believed that the IMF ought to promote fixed exchange rates and limit the role of currency markets. The Keynesian approach was tolerant of or even friendly to ISI. Neo-liberalism, which became the leading economic doctrine as a result of the crises of the 1970s and 1980s, is far different. In fact, neo-liberalism is an updated version of a pre-Keynesian approach – economic liberalism. While Keynes had adapted liberalism by moving in the direction of state-led growth, neo-liberalism moved back in the opposite direction. It added to basic liberal ideas the promotion of international financial markets and strengthening of multilateral organizations to settle international trade and financial disputes.

Neo-liberalism, contrary to Keynesianism, stressed both free trade and a strictly limited governmental role in even the domestic economy. Neo-liberalism came to dominate the thinking of economists and treasury ministries in many of the world's economic powers. By the 1980s the IMF and the World Bank (Stiglitz 2002: 11–16), both of which have their headquarters in Washington, DC, promoted a set of neo-liberal policies that would become known as the **Washington consensus** (Box 13.1), designed to satisfy foreign financial markets and return debtor countries to financial health. The new approach promotes foreign investment and has laid the groundwork for new financial and business networks. Neo-liberalism, as with economic liberalism before it, argues that its preferred policies create a win–win situation. Governments need to promote economic growth, and investment is the key factor in promoting growth. The state invests when it builds roads, schools, and the infrastructure required for other public services. Sometimes the state invests in other ways as well, building such things as dams, steel mills, highways, railroads, and airports. When the state invests, it uses its power to collect taxes or requisition labor and property. However, neo-liberalism argues most investment should be private rather than public since private management is likely to be more efficient than public.

BOX 13.1
THE WASHINGTON CONSENSUS

Overview

The term "Washington consensus" was coined by economist John
Williamson. In 1994, Williamson described the consensus as embracing the
following elements.

- **Fiscal discipline** Budget deficits should be small enough to be financed
  without inflation. This means a deficit of no more than 2 percent of
  Gross Domestic Product (GDP).
- **Public expenditure priorities** Public expenditure should focus on
  primary health and education as well as infrastructure. (Investment in
  state firms, pensions, subsidies, and higher education should be curtailed.)
- **Tax reform** Governments should broaden the tax base – i.e., cut
  exemptions – and lower marginal tax rates. Tax administration should be
  improved.
- **Financial liberalization** The ultimate objective is market-determined
  interest rates. Preferential interest rates available to some groups but not
  others should be abolished.
- **Exchange rates** Exchange rates should be unified. No special access
  to foreign exchange for any interest group. Exchange rates should be
  managed so that they maintain a level sufficient to encourage
  nontraditional exports. This competitive level should be maintained.
- **Trade liberalization** Quotas and other quantitative trade restrictions
  should be replaced by tariffs. Tariffs should be progressively lowered until
  they reach a uniform level of 10 to 20 percent.
- **Foreign direct investment** Barriers to the entry of foreign firms
  should be abolished. They should compete with domestic firms on a
  level playing field.
- **Privatization** The state should sell state-owned firms.
- **Deregulation** The government should abolish restrictions on new
  firms entering the market or limiting their competitiveness. All
  regulations must be justified on bona fide grounds of health, safety,
  prudent financial regulation, or similar grounds.
- **Private property** Property rights should be secured at reasonable
  cost. Formal property rights protection should be extended to the
  informal economy (i.e., small-scale producers and merchants not
  currently possessing formal property rights).

Source: Williamson 1994: 26–8.

Private investment, in turn, should include both domestic as well as foreign capital. The successful recruitment of both sorts of investors involves a variety of investor-friendly initiatives: deregulation, balanced budgets, low uniform taxes, privatization, and a reduced role for the state generally. Among these are measures assuring the relatively free flow of capital both into and out of the country. Since the 1980s, the IMF and even the World Bank have promoted their preferred policies by making structural adjustment loans. Unlike project loans, **structural adjustment loans** focus on a country's economic policies as a whole – the tax, regulatory, fiscal, etc., policies just mentioned. The country's government signs a **letter of intent** setting out targets that the government pledges to meet in these economic areas. Thus, IMF loans embody the principle of **conditionality** – the loan is delivered in installments as the country successfully meets its targets. Often countries require loans in the tens of billions of dollars, which the IMF did not supply directly, at least not in the 1980s. However, the signing of an agreement with the IMF gives private international banks a signal that the country is on its way to financial good health and that it is once again safe to loan it money. Thus, an IMF loan is frequently an unofficial prerequisite for additional private lending.

Consequences

Neo-liberalism and the Washington consensus have helped change the face of international and domestic economics. The conditions in letters of intent typically require a national budget surplus to assure creditors that governments will be able to pay back new loans. Budget cuts, investor-friendly taxes on consumers, and the deregulation of foreign trade and the domestic economy are also the order of the day. At times, the IMF will even insist that rate increases be allowed for foreign-owned utilities if a loan is to be considered, as they did with Argentina in 2003. Thus, the IMF and increasingly the World Bank have come to serve as a kind of economic-policy police. As a result of IMF impositions and other multilateral measures, such as WTO trade rules, countries have been forced to relinquish de facto control of their own economies.

Neo-liberal policies have also altered both the quantity and type of foreign investment. Foreign investment occurs in three basic ways. One is loans. Foreign governments, privately owned foreign banks, and multilateral institutions loan money to both governments and private firms. The terms of the loan and the dates by which principal and interest have to be repaid are established by contract. Beyond the terms of the contract, the foreign investor's control over and stake in the local economy are limited. Prior to the 1980s, financial regulation in the developing world made loans the primary means for foreigners to invest there. As the IMF forced countries to liberalize their international financial rules, the importance of loans as a source of foreign investment declined and other means of foreign investment gained enhanced importance. The second major source of foreign investment is portfolio investment – investment in stocks, bonds, other financial instruments, and currency. IMF-sponsored policies opened up these markets, often highly regulated previously, to foreign investors. This has allowed both investors with a long-term focus as well as those interested in quick profits and a quick turnaround on their money to enter a developing country's financial markets. The third method by which capital enters a country is foreign direct investment (FDI). FDI occurs when investors bring foreign currency into a country to buy land, factories, mines, or other physical assets by buying out existing owners, or when they open new enterprises themselves. Capital invested through FDI is not very mobile. Investors own physical assets that they would have to sell to remove their funds from the country. In the past, governments have often subjected FDI to significant levels of regulation in an attempt to preserve control of their own economy and its "strategic industries." Under the neo-liberal formula these regulations must disappear.

For countries with the least effective states, the state and fiscal reform prescribed by the Washington consensus has cut inflation and generated modest economic growth, at least in some cases. However, opponents of the Washington consensus argue that the results of following its policy prescriptions have been unfair for a variety of reasons (Stiglitz 2002). First, economic liberalization as prescribed by the Washington consensus has often undercut the quality of life for much of the population in developing countries. Liberalization means a cutback in state services, education, medical care, pensions, and salaries of state employees. Liberalization makes new goods and improved services available but only for those wealthy enough to afford to pay for them. This can be especially difficult for the poor since cuts often target subsidies on food and transportation. State services that remain may also deteriorate in quality because of required budget reductions. Privatization of state monopolies can also be a problem. A state that cannot manage an industry efficiently is unlikely to be able to regulate it effectively. Thus, state monopolies that are often inefficient and patronage-ridden are replaced by private monopolies that are profit-driven and inadequately regulated. At best Washington consensus policies lower inflation, balance the budget, stabilize exchange-rate fluctuations, and promote modest growth. However, the economic growth these policies have promoted is far below that of the pre-debt crisis era (Chang 2008: 24–6).

Second, neo-liberal financial liberalization has led to financial volatility that has undermined various developing economies since the early 1990s. Much portfolio investment is highly mobile. Stocks, bonds, currency, and other financial assets can often be easily bought and sold. Contemporary electronically linked financial markets make this process easier than ever. In the past, developing countries had often limited or slowed down such transactions through a variety of means. The Washington consensus, however, supports the completely free movement of capital. And the IMF uses its influence to have governments remove all forms of capital controls even those meant to staunch massive and sudden movements of speculative capital. Speculation or arbitrage seeks quick profits through massive investment and equally quick and massive disinvestment. Arbitrageurs anticipate small price changes in certain assets in a relatively short period of time. The secret to their making a profit is first to guess correctly, second to invest massive amounts of money in local markets at precisely the right time, and third to turn that investment around quickly, selling very soon after they buy. In 1994, when its financial house had appeared to be in order, investors suddenly became aware that Mexico's peso was in fact overvalued, i.e., the central bank lacked the dollar reserves to pay off those who might wish to convert pesos to dollars. A panic ensued as everyone who could rushed to exchange pesos for dollars while the supply of dollars lasted and the old exchange rate still held. Similar situations developed in Thailand, Indonesia, Malaysia, and South Korea in 1997, in Russia and Brazil in 1998, and Argentina in 2001.

Third, some citizens of developing countries and even some sectors of economically developed countries find the neo-liberal model unbalanced. Under the neo-liberal model, FDI and foreign trade have taken on a new aspect previously not much in evidence. WTO trade rules have been the leading cause in this regard although they have worked hand in hand with IMF-sponsored easing of rules on foreign investment. WTO rules make it harder for countries to protect their domestic markets against foreign-produced goods. Thus, freer trade plus easier foreign investment has allowed companies to move domestic production abroad. Multinational corporations (MNCs) still acquire factories to manufacture products for sale in the countries where the factories are located. But today these firms often seek offshore export platforms – factories intended to manufacture goods for export back to the firm's home country or to other industrialized countries whose production costs make building industrial plants there unattractive. Increasingly, MNCs can also use foreign contractors to manufacture the products for them instead of manufacturing them themselves. Firms such as Nike and its network of contractors manufacture products in Asia and sell them in North America and Europe. In fact, such out-sourcing is not restricted to manufacturing, but can include services, such as software engineering, accounting, and customer relations. Thus, global trade is no longer conducted primarily by national firms competing with one another but by transnational firms and networks each seeking the lowest production costs. This out-sourcing first of high-paying manufacturing jobs and then even higher-paying white-collar jobs has produced a backlash in countries such as the United States. Opponents argue that a policy of "exporting jobs" is unsustainable in the long run. Workers in advanced industrial countries cannot effectively compete with those in other countries where the cost of living and wages are dramatically lower.

In sum, today's global economic patterns are considerably different from those of both the recent and more distant past. First, while regional trading blocs exist, the vast colonial empires of the early twentieth century have disappeared. Imperial control has been replaced by an economic order managed through multilateral organizations. National interest still plays an important role in trade policy, but national interest has to be mediated through the IMF and the WTO. Those who dislike the arrangement speak of a de facto loss of national sovereignty; those who look on it favorably are more likely to label the new arrangements "pooled sovereignty" since the new order has been established by international agreements acceded to by each member state. Second, as multilateral organizations have come into their own as regulators of the global economic system, their underlying policy has shifted decisively away from Keynesianism toward neo-liberalism.

Plate 13.2 Anti-WTO protest in Hong Kong in 2005.

The new economic order has come to promote the liberal state and undermine the welfare state. Third, international trade is more important than in the past and has taken on a novel character. Today trade between regions and countries is often trade between different arms of the same MNC, not competing companies from different countries.

Conclusion

Change, to cite Peel, is a constant. Just as Peel would have had a hard time imagining the details of the postmodern world, people today can at best make educated guesses about the shape of the future. Still, postmodern values, identity politics, and the rise of newly emergent political actors are likely to remain important and even increase in importance. So too is globalization and the institutional actors critical to it. In the contemporary world, international influences play an important role in domestic politics. The economy, culture, and even many people's families have become increasingly globalized. Unsurprisingly, governments and domestic political actors face opportunities and constraints from the international environment. Outright imperialism has passed from the scene, but its aftereffects live on. Developing countries, most of whom are ex-colonies, find themselves caught between the traditional and modern worlds. Not fully modern, they cannot go back to an era when they existed in splendid isolation from modernizing countries on far-distant continents. Rather, they are forced to wrestle with a host of economic, political, and social problems bequeathed to them by history. International law has changed since the first stirrings of globalization. One nation can no longer conquer another and officially incorporate it into an empire. But indirect control and the exercise of soft power by outsiders can affect a government's ability to control its own territory and people.

Along with the change in the legal framework, the contemporary world has also seen the rise of novel political actors and institutions on the international level. Transnational NGOs and multilateral institutions, such as the IMF and WTO, are important parts of the contemporary political landscape in almost every country in the world. International law and practice has raised human rights to a new level of visibility. Perhaps now more than ever, international economic pressures influence countries' domestic politics. Through much of the cold-war period, countries and ruling elites could play off the United States against the Soviet Union, gaining aid and freedom to maneuver politically since each of the then super powers was anxious to win allies. Today one economic system reigns supreme. Countries wishing to break ranks with the Washington consensus often find themselves without significant international support. Instead, they find international pressures and popular forces at home working at cross-purposes. This is sometime the case even in advanced industrialized countries where the opportunities globalization provides to MNCs sometimes works against the interests of the home-country employees and governments. Immigration has affected the warp and woof of many countries' domestic politics in the developed world. Countries that have been unaccustomed to large-scale foreign immigration find themselves the new home of migrants, who may not want to assimilate. At the same time that this clash of cultures occurs, the aging of the indigenous population of many industrialized countries seems to make immigration an economic necessity. Today no nation is an island in the figurative sense even though some may be so in the literal geographic sense.

Questions for further consideration

1　Consider the range of party ideologies discussed in Chapter 4. How are voters with postmodern values likely to regard each of them? How might parties adapt to these new voters?

2　How is immigration affecting politics in developed democracies where it is occurring on a large scale? What could promote integration? What could promote polarization?

3　Women's political and social roles have been changing. How is this likely to affect politics in the developed world? In the developing world?

4　Where indigenous groups are a large percentage of society, how might they be able to influence the political process? Where they are a relatively small percentage, how might they?

5　What sorts of issues does massive urbanization raise for developing countries? What are the risks in not addressing these issues effectively?

6　What effects has globalization had on the developing and developed worlds? What sorts of coalitions domestically are likely to form in support of it or against it?

Further reading

Benjamin R. Barber, *Jihad versus McWorld: How Globalism and Tribalism Are Reshaping the World*. New York: Ballantine Books, 1995. Analyzes the culture clash between traditional, modern, and postmodern values generated by globalization.

Elizabeth Croll, *Endangered Daughters: Discrimination and Development in Asia*. New York: Routledge, 2000. Analysis of discrimination against females as manifested in the lower female birth and survival rate and its consequences.

Joseph M. Grieco and G. John Ikenberry, *State Power and World Markets: The International Political Economy*. New York: W.W. Norton, 2002. Short introduction to contemporary international economics.

Ronald Inglehart, *Modernization and Postmodernization: Cultural, Economic, and Political Change in 43 Societies*. Princeton, NJ: Princeton University Press, 1997.

United Nations Development Fund for Women, *Progress of the World's Women 2000: UNIFEM Biennial Report*, http://www.unifem.undp.org/ progressww/2000/, and *Progress of the World's Women 2002*, http://www. unifem.undp.org/resources/progressv2/. Extensive review of women's issues.

14 The future of democracy

It's hard to make predictions, especially about the future.

(Source unknown)

In this chapter

We examine democracy's global prospects. To many in the developed world and developing world as well, democracy seems to be a just and potentially stable political system to which peoples universally aspire. But this belief has provoked debate on both counts. Democracy may not be universally applicable to all societies. And democracy may fail to promote social justice or individual and minority. The chapter treats each of these issues in turn.

Introduction

For good reason, democracy is the major theme of four chapters of this book and at least a secondary theme in most of the remainder. Third-wave democratization has put other forms of government at risk. Communism has collapsed as an ideological system and many leftwing and rightwing dictatorships have been undermined and collapsed as well. Yet numerous authoritarian governments – some of them governing quite important countries – continue to soldier on. Similarly, many semi-democracies and semi-authoritarian regimes have remained stubbornly resistant to full democratization. Moreover, the quality of democratic governance is an ongoing issue not only for new democracies but for established democracies as well. Many democracies, especially in the developing world, have been unable to promote the sort of general prosperity that has been instrumental in ensuring the stability of liberal democracy in the developed world. They have either failed to develop policies that promote rapid economic growth or failed to arrive at a social bargain that ensures an equitable distribution of resources. Thus, democracy's exportability, durability, and quality remain issues for debate. This chapter takes up these issues.

Is democracy durable and transportable?

In some ways the future of liberal democracy has never looked brighter. From its inception democracy has had to endure a variety of attacks – sometimes physical, sometimes ideological, sometimes both. During some eras, it virtually disappeared as a functioning political system altogether. Given that history, the 1990s were especially heady times. Communism collapsed in the Soviet Union and Central Europe. Along with it, the physical threat to democracy largely vanished. No anti-democratic regime now marshals the economic or military power that would make it a serious threat to the dominance of democracy within the international system. Democracy has swept through Latin America. Long-standing authoritarian regimes in South Korea and Taiwan democratized. And a wave of democratic transitions began in Africa. In 1991 Samuel Huntington noted that, between 1973 and 1990, the percentage of democratic regimes (out of all regimes) nearly doubled (Huntington 1991: 26). There seemed to be good grounds for optimism about democracy's future. It seemed to be taking root where its consolidation or even its emergence was virtually unprecedented. Yet the inevitability of democracy or even its likelihood for many countries was contested. Six years later this democratic optimism was contested even by Huntington himself (Huntington 1996).

The inevitability of democracy thesis

The belief that democracy is inevitable is not new. Revolutionaries in Europe and America over two hundred years ago often advanced that belief. The latest version of the inevitability thesis made its appearance in the 1990s. As the Soviet Union collapsed, *The End of History and the Last Man* by Francis Fukuyama (Fukuyama 1992) appeared on the best-seller lists. Fukuyama argued that with the collapse of communism, history had in principle ended. All major theoretical issues about government and economics had been resolved. Politics, even war, would certainly continue, but the basic principles that human beings had argued and fought about for so long had been resolved. No one could hope to resurrect the state-socialist system no matter how much they might wish to do so. No one could re-establish the legitimacy of people's democracy and the vanguard party. History had demonstrated the implausibility of such

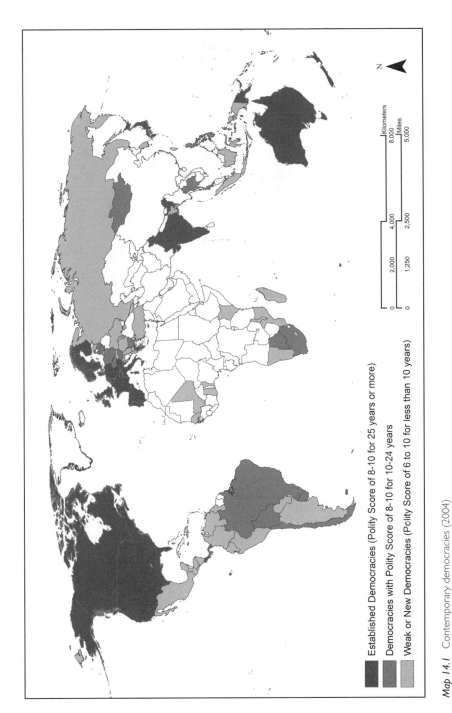

Map 14.1 Contemporary democracies (2004)

Source: Environmental Systems Research Institute (ESRI) map data. Data: Polity IV

Note: Polity IV ratings range from +10 (most democratic) to −10 (most authoritarian)

Plate 14.1 Francis Fukuyama. By permission.

notions as it had tested and discarded so many other economic and political systems in ages past. The only viable form of regime in the modern world was liberal democracy. The only viable economic system was capitalism. Fukuyama is often portrayed as a naive triumphalist, championing western dominance of the world. But many of his critics seemed to have missed his point. At its root the end-of-history thesis is not an invitation to complacency. Fukuyama had argued that the basic questions about human liberation were resolved, not that all was right with the world. He, in fact, speculated that some societies might be doomed, for the foreseeable future, to backwardness and authoritarianism.

Fukuyama based his analysis on the philosophy of Georg Wilhelm Friedrich Hegel, the same philosophy that had inspired Karl Marx. Hegel's philosophy of history was grounded on the notion that human freedom is the end or goal of history. Human beings have purposes. Their purpose, in generic terms, is to get what they want – to determine their own destiny, to be free. Since human beings are rational, they consciously or unconsciously learn from the past. Thus, history was a progressive phenomenon. Human beings would continue to struggle individually and collectively until they had achieved the freedom that allowed each to determine their own future. If one or a few alone attained such freedom, the result would be unstable. Others, equally human and equally desirous of emancipation, would struggle to attain freedom for themselves.

Thus, a form of government that made only one or a few free would ultimately be undermined and overthrown. In the long run, sometimes the very long run, any regime that systematically denied freedom to anyone was unstable. The only inherently stable form of government would be one in which the freedom of all was recognized. Once such a government had been fully established and each understood their position within it, that form of government would be stable. Since no one could gain greater rights and recognition without threatening the rights of others, all would resist the unjust attempts of the one or the few to overthrow the system (Hegel 1956). Hegel's account of humanity's progress toward freedom was stated in the most abstract terms that seemed to invite more concrete elaboration.

Fukuyama's thesis was only one attempt to put political flesh on the theoretical bones Hegel had laid out. The controversy over what Hegel meant or how Hegel's principles should be applied arose much earlier. Shortly after his death, Hegelians had divided between right and left, and each into its own sub-factions. Karl Marx had formed one of the latter. Marx's contribution to the debate was to make economic emancipation the key to human emancipation. If the productive power of human beings could be increased sufficiently to meet the requirements for everyone's full human development and if property relations could be changed so that all had equal access to what all produced, human emancipation would be assured. The final liberation of all human beings would occur under a form of society Marx called communism. Lenin gave Marx's theory a new twist by making the communist party the vanguard (or overseer) of the final stages of the historical process that led to communism. Other later writers gave Hegel a liberal-democratic interpretation. For Alexander Kojève, writing in the post-World War II era, human emancipation meant liberal democracy and the welfare state. Under such a system, human beings had political rights and economic security. The system itself was stable. It had mastered the vagaries of the natural environment and provided its citizens with effective control over their own destinies. Enlightened administrators governed under the overall control of the majority. The rights of all were protected, and everyone's interest was recognized. In principle, history was complete when Napoleon defeated the Prussians at the Battle of Jena in 1806. But it was not fully complete until the formation of the European Community (Fukuyama 1992: 66–7).

Fukuyama, however, thought that history had lasted a little longer. For much of the twentieth century, the issue of which system – communism or liberal democracy – would triumph was an open question. For decades, state socialism seemed to provide the basis for rapid economic development. People's democracy too had considerable legitimacy.

It was not until the 1970s that state socialism began to lose its credibility and people's democracy its moral authority. Given this loss of effectiveness and legitimacy, the collapse of communism seemed foreordained. Although when and how communism would collapse could not be accurately foretold before the actual events, the fact that it could not deliver what any system ultimately had to deliver to remain stable meant it would inevitably lose out in the economic, ideological, and diplomatic competition with liberal democracy. At least that was how things often appeared in retrospect. The Hegel/Kojève/Fukuyama view is rationalist. It assumes human beings as such are capable of critical thought. It also assumes that stable political systems are grounded on consent. A system whose subjects view it as oppressive and that rests on principles that they consider fraudulent is unstable. Repression and continued good luck are required to maintain it. In the long run such regimes, even if they survive, cannot flourish.

Fukuyama saw current challenges to liberal democracy as theoretically inconsequential. Present-day authoritarians present no systematic challenge to liberal democratic principles. They constitute only a practical challenge in military, diplomatic, and sometimes economic terms. Unlike communism or fascism, they represent no alternative system. Because their heavy-handed control of society discourages the sort of intellectual, scientific, and economic activity that leads to self-sustaining economic progress, the capacities of their states and economies are essentially derivative, even parasitical. They rely upon scientific and technological developments elsewhere to support their capacity to pose a military challenge. To repeat, events continue, sometimes very serious and threatening events, but history has stopped. The overarching questions about legitimacy, constitutionalism, and economic structure – the substantive questions about human freedom that is the goal of history – have been answered.

Fukuyama's version of the end-of-history thesis leaves open a great many questions. Both capitalism and liberal democracy are capable of many variants. Economists and policy-makers argue about the best mix of economic policies. Should liberal democracies establish or continue to support welfare states, or should they move in the direction of the minimal state? The end of history has not foreclosed this debate. Should constitutional reform move in the direction of a parliamentary or presidential system? A majoritarian or consensus system? Federalism or unitary government? The end of history has not rendered these issues moot either. In short, although history has ended, details that are quite important to all of us remain to be resolved, and there appears to be no definitive resolution in sight. One might go further and argue that no definitive resolution is possible. The future developments in technology or science cannot be predicted. Nor can ecological or demographic change be predicted or controlled with any degree of certainty. Questions about policy as well as about administrative and governmental structures still remain in play. Only the question of the purpose of government and politics, and the basic norms political structures must adhere to, have been settled. Countries that have not adopted some version of liberal democracy and capitalism are not predetermined to do so. But their failure to adopt them will lead to internal instability and, possibly, international instability. Liberal democracies may well have to be on their guard for problems created by such historical throwbacks.

Democracy: a western cultural peculiarity

Critics have challenged the rationalism and universalism inherent in the end-of-history argument. Hegel and all of his disciples, Fukuyama included, stress the rational character of human history and social organization. Hegelians, the critics assert, fail to give sufficient weight to the non-rational element in human affairs. Societies are governed by habit and emotion that often have little to do with rational analysis. The rationality that all human beings share may be insufficient to overcome the particularity of their attachments and their own self-interest. Human beings' common rationality may turn out to be more instrumental than moral. Maybe the ends proposed by liberals – securing individual rights – are not universally acceptable to rational people. Worshiping God in a particular manner and compelling others to do so may be an alternative end. Maybe the nation and its prestige can be an overriding end, an end that supersedes the protection of individual rights or even precludes their recognition. Maybe a prosperous authoritarian welfare state would satisfy those living under it. Why should theoretical issues matter under such a system? In short, critics have taken issue with the root assumptions of the end-of-history argument. And if these assumptions are wrong, the argument collapses.

In 1996, Samuel Huntington, the author of *The Third Wave*, published another book, *The Clash of Civilizations: Remaking of World Order* that seemed to take issue not only with Fukuyama but also with the ideas he himself had entertained earlier about a rising tide of democracy. In *Clash*, Huntington asserted that the world was divided into a number of civilizational zones whose core political values were incommensurate with one another. Huntington identified seven or eight contemporary civilizations: the Sinic (Chinese), Japanese, Hindu, Islamic, Orthodox, western, Latin American, and African. He hedged on Africa, since

North Africa is Islamic as is a considerable portion of Africa south of the Sahara. European imperialism has also had a considerable influence on the region. These factors and the diversity among Africans themselves render its classification as a separate civilization open to doubt. Civilizations, Huntington argued, were based on deep-seated rather than superficial traits. If civilizations are important, they serve as bases for feeling oneself a member of one community rather than another. They ground moral, social, and political norms. Thus, even though two groups may be influenced by consumerism, follow the same fads, and enjoy the same popular media, these two groups do not necessarily share the same civilization. "The central elements of any culture or civilization," Huntington wrote, "are language and religion." On this score, the notion that we inhabit a universal civilization that embodies liberal-democratic norms vanishes (Huntington 1996: 59).

Neither English, the lingua franca of contemporary western civilization, nor Christianity comes anywhere close to being universal. Moreover, the revival of Islam, Hinduism, and, more recently, Orthodoxy, points in the direction of a clash of civilizations rather than their unification. International events provide evidence that bears this out. The Islamic world's tendency to rally around the banner of Islam, at least emotionally, in times of international crises is well known. The Orthodox – Russians, Serbs, Greeks, and others – also tend to support each other in opposition to other civilizations. The fault-lines of international politics, Huntington found, were becoming increasingly civilizational. So too are the divisions of domestic politics. In places like Bosnia, Yugoslavia, Turkey, differences over religion matter. Furthermore, linguistic and religious differences are not going to erode rapidly. While *The Clash of Civilizations* was specifically about international affairs and not domestic political transformations, it had clear negative implications for the advance of democracy and the stability of democracies where they had been recently established.

A number of contemporary semi-authoritarian leaders have made the argument that traditional authoritarian values ought to be preserved because they promote the sort of society that is more desirable than what evolves under full democracy. Lee Kuan Yew, the former prime minister of Singapore, has argued that what he calls "Asian values" are superior to Western liberal-democratic values. His position has been echoed by other political leaders and intellectuals in Japan and other Asian countries (cf. Zakaria 1994). Democracy brings many undesirable features along with it. Democracy's stress on individual rights tends to downplay the importance of the community and individual responsibility. The freedom of the press can lower the standards of public discourse and permit the

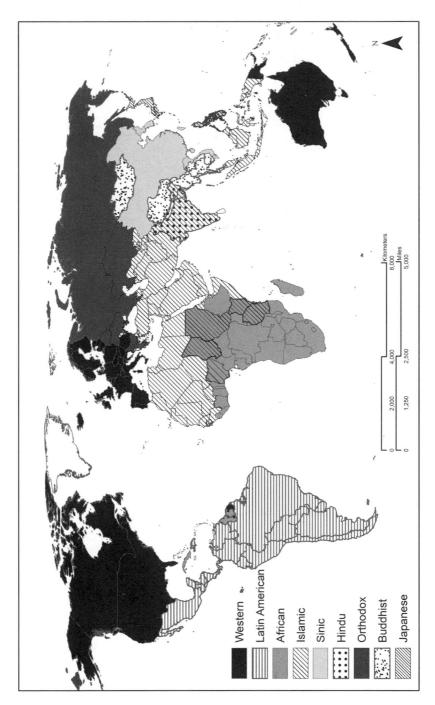

Map 14.2 Civilizations of the contemporary world according to Samuel Huntington

Source: Environmental Systems Research Institute (ESRI) map data. Data: Huntington (1996)

Western
Latin American
African
Islamic
Sinic
Hindu
Orthodox
Buddhist
Japanese

Plate 14.2 Lee Kuan Yew (center) and Singapore's ambassador to the US meet with US Defense Secretary Cohen, 2000.

publication and circulation of pornography. Individualism erodes the family, promotes selfishness, and even encourages crime. A good society ought to promote responsibility, family and social cohesion, the obedience to law, and the respect for authority. Such a society can be both prosperous and orderly. It can obtain the virtues of modernization without its associated vices.

In keeping with these notions, the government of Singapore has found ways to curtail democracy and promote the sort of orderly society that leaders such as Lee advocate without rejecting democracy or the rule of law outright. A series of electoral regulations makes Singapore essentially a one-party state. The opposition finds it difficult to field candidates, to campaign, or to criticize the government. It is not primarily a matter of physical intimidation. Laws, regulations, and court decision have largely neutered the opposition. The media's rights to publish and broadcast are also curtailed by the application of libel laws that protect officials from criticism. A variety of laws regulating public conduct have been strictly enforced. Singapore's courts authorize the death penalty with considerable frequency, considering the country's small population and low crime rate. Yet Singapore is an orderly and prosperous society. Despite the sort of social divisions between Chinese, Malays, and Hindus that have led to violence elsewhere in the region, the city has maintained social and political peace. Without a natural resource base, Singapore has become an economically developed country with a rate of growth that is the envy of most countries in the world.

In effect, Lee's argument implies that modernization, westernization, and democratization are separable. A regime can choose to modernize its economy and administration without unintentionally promoting individualism and other democratic values. The Asian-values thesis is supported by the prosperity and stability that Singapore has enjoyed for a prolonged period. A small city-state with a competent bureaucracy and prosperous economy, Singapore's mixture of democracy and authoritarianism may, in fact, be durable. Singapore's semi-authoritarianism delivers the goods: wealth and personal security. Moreover, it does so in a way that is generally efficient. Although a plutocratic elite dominates the system, this elite helps produce real wealth that does, in fact, trickle down. The ruling party of neighboring Malaysia and several other countries in Southeast Asia have also espoused the Asian-values position, even though their achievements are much more limited.

Summary

The dispute between Hegel/Kojève/Fukuyama and Huntington/Lee is at its root about the necessary effects of modernization. The end-of-history thesis predicts that authoritarian regimes and anti-capitalistic economic systems will be dead-ends. Alternative systems cannot match the stability of liberal democracy or the economic capacity of capitalism. The end-of-history thesis further argues that authoritarian systems are inherently unstable. The greater their level of social and economic development, the greater their instability. Liberal democracy, on the other hand, constitutes a stable end point of the developmental process, and a reversion to other forms cannot produce any overall benefits. In short, modernization and democratization are inseparable in the long run. In contrast, the Huntington/Lee position implies that modernization can lead to stable and successful forms of authoritarianism or semi-authoritarianism and that the development of liberal democracy outside the West and Latin America will be difficult at best. Modernization and democratization are distinct. Liberal democracy is a development peculiar to the West, and its exportability is limited.

Does liberal democracy promote social justice?

We noted in Chapter 2 that stable liberal democracies in the West and Japan have at their foundation a social bargain that guarantees a modicum of equity in the division of wealth and opportunities. This bargain rendered moot the fears of many nineteenth-century liberals that the impoverished majority would encroach upon the wealth and rights of the rich minority once majority rule had been fully established. As the twenty-first century dawns, many of the poor of the developing world, even in democracies, face an economic situation similar to that of their counterparts in the industrializing world of the nineteenth century. Bereft of opportunities to secure even a basic level of education, adequate employment, and the physical necessities for their families, they live in desperation. At the same time, nothing like what nineteenth-century liberals feared appears in prospect. The position of the wealthy is so politically secure that demands for social justice remain unanswered. Widespread poverty is not the only problem these liberal democracies face. Liberal democracies in the developing world are often insufficiently liberal. They do not protect basic civil rights and civil liberties. The rule of law is not adequately implemented or respected. In short, democracy often suffers a quality problem with two distinct aspects. Elections are held and people vote, but the majority remains impoverished and dissatisfied, and basic rights are inadequately protected.

The problem of "hard" democracies

Since the nineteenth century, the left has agonized and agitated about the quality of democracy. Radicals believed that political democracy, by itself, was inadequate. They demanded social democracy. Hence, early Marxists called themselves "social democrats" to dramatize their difference with the so-called "bourgeois" democrats, who believed that formal political democracy was sufficient. In Europe the split between political democrats and social democrats eventually became a policy issue to be resolved by democratic means within democratic institutions rather than a conflict between those who favored and those who opposed revolution. Most developed countries have established welfare states – legal frameworks that secure to their citizens the right to education or training, unemployment compensation, pensions, and health care. The United States is among the least generous of these developed-world welfare states. And, in fact, Americans usually refuse to use the term "welfare" to refer to the major programs that characterize the modern welfare state – Social Security, Medicare, and unemployment compensation. Nonetheless, regardless of the terminology these programs constitute the heart of the social bargain that defines the scope of state activity and underpins the legitimacy of modern, liberal-democratic regimes in the United States and elsewhere in the developed world. In many new democracies, however, the issue of social democracy lives on.

Latin Americans have a name for liberal democracies that limit basic liberties and provide few or no welfare services. They call them *democraduras*. The name is a play on words. In Spanish the word for dictatorship is *dictadura*; and the word for democracy is *democrácia*. *Dura* is also the word for hard while *blanda* is the word for soft. As transitions from military authoritarian regimes began, military governments liberalized, loosening the restraints they had placed upon political activity. Commentators began to refer to these late-period military governments as *dicta-blandas* – "soft dictatorships." By the same token, the democracies established by the transitions were often dubbed *democra-duras* – "hard democracies" because they retained some of the features of the old military authoritarian regimes. Economic restructuring that often ran counter to the interests of the middle and lower classes that had begun during the military regime continued. Programs, such as subsidies for food and transportation, have been eliminated or drastically curtailed. The left has been politically demobilized. An elite consensus favors policies that squeezed the lower class economically and promised the trickling down of benefits only in the long run. It was not surprising that many complained that these "hard democracies" fail to meet popular expectations. The hard-democracy phenomenon is not restricted to Latin America. And it is, in part, the byproduct of the Washington consensus promoted by important multilateral institutions, the International Monetary Fund (IMF) and the World Bank and others as we saw in Chapter 13.

Implementation of the Washington consensus requires structural adjustment – the systematic deregulation of the domestic economy as well as of foreign trade and investment, budget balancing via reductions in popular programs and increases in regressive taxes, and privatization of state-owned industries. Advocates of structural adjustment believe that it would produce not only rapid economic growth but also general prosperity that will benefit almost everyone. Many developing countries are heavily indebted to private foreign banks and the multilateral institutions already. Given the pivotal role of the IMF and its principle of conditionality, these countries often have little choice but to accept the IMF's policy directives. Thus, structural adjustment loans have become a device to pressure elected governments to accept policies many of their constituents adamantly opposed. Such loans were granted to provide a financial cushion that would compensate the government for lost revenue and the need for short-term relief programs, until the benefits of the economic adjustment take hold.

The politics of structural adjustment

The stated purpose of structural adjustment seems benign enough: the creation of a more prosperous and eventually a more equitable, society. Yet, the actual workings of structural adjustment programs caused serious hardship and created political difficulties. Letters of intent signed by the government laying down the terms of the loan specify such things as the size of the government budget deficit and which government-spending programs are to be cut and by how much. The failure to meet a target is usually followed by the refusal of the IMF to deliver the next scheduled installment of the loan. The pressure imposed by such externally sponsored economic programs sets off internal political struggles. Each domestic interest group is concerned about shielding itself from the adverse immediate effects of the program and capitalizing, if it can, on the short-term gains it offers. This struggle takes place within the confines of a political and administrative environment that by this time the reader can easily appreciate. Post-communist and developing societies suffer from political, constitutional, and administrative defects that often lead to bias, inefficiency, and corruption in the state and government. The mass of the population often has difficulty articulating its interests and having its interests adequately protected by the government. Patrimonialism, with its attendant nepotism, cronyism, and general corruption, often prevails. Elite interests, both corporate and personal, are likely to win out. The losers are likely to get the hindmost. Thus, the winners and losers in the politics of structural adjustment are generally predictable.

The immediate losers are state employees and beneficiaries of government social and educational programs. Streamlining the government often entails cutting the number of employees. Holding the line on wages paid to government workers is a relatively easy way of reducing the budget deficit. In times of even moderate inflation, simply refusing to grant wage adjustments can cut the wage burden. Employees of state-owned corporations also often stand to lose. Whether the enterprises are privatized or simply rationalized by the state, cuts in employment are to be expected. The fact that the number of employees is often inflated for political purposes makes state employment an especially attractive target for economic reformers. Teachers and medical personnel employed by the state are likely to feel the pinch as well despite the fact that the Washington consensus holds such state functions are critical for development. Although these groups are often unionized and able to protest, they rarely have the political clout to reshape adjustments along the lines they would prefer. Cutting the deficit normally takes precedence over other aims that require additional spending. State pensioners are also likely to suffer. Pension funds in the developing world are usually poorly managed. In post-communist states, they are virtually nonexistent. Thus, pension payments in large measure come out of current expenditure, and, again, cutting the deficit takes priority over almost everything else. Even the armed forces, an elite interest that often controlled the previous regime in new democracies, may find itself on the short end of structural readjustment. Military equipment and salaries seem largely superfluous expenditures in parts of the developing world that face no substantial military threat. The armed forces, however, are normally better connected than other groups whose budgetary resources are in jeopardy. Consequently, they often escape the worst strictures of structural adjustment.

Those interests that do well are those who serve to profit from privatization, liberalization, and the reduction of the fiscal deficit. This includes some, but by no means all, business interests. The more a firm or enterprise depends on international trade, the more its products and services are competitive and marketable internationally, the more it is likely to profit from structural readjustment. Developing-country governments previous to structural adjustment often regarded such enterprises and their activities as "cash cows" to be used to support the budget and as a source of income transfers. Hence, agricultural exporters are likely to be advantaged as are multinational corporations (MNCs) and their affiliates both foreign and domestically owned. Privatization, one of the central recommendations of the Washington consensus, opens other opportunities for profit. State firms in developing and post-communist countries are often inefficient and patronage-ridden. Privatization is designed to put a quick end to those problems. Moreover, the sale of state-owned enterprises and the leasing of airports, ports, and other facilities to private firms can generate revenue much needed by the government if it is to bring the budget into balance.

In practice, however, privatization entails political and administrative pitfalls. The policy objectives of privatization are increased efficiency, better provision of services at equitable cost, and revenue for the state. These objectives are likely to come into conflict with each other. If the state sells a utility (and many state firms fall within this category), it risks replacing a public monopoly with a private one. But the weaker the regulatory regime the state promises bidders, the higher the bids are likely to be. In the best of circumstances privatization creates problems, and developing and ex-communist countries are not likely to be in the best of circumstances. A weak state, inadequate guarantees for the rule of law, and the ingrained practice of political and business cronyism place additional strains on the privatization process. Insider bidding is likely to occur. If it does, both the state and the public that use the service are short changed. The politics of structural adjustment is essentially an elite-driven process. The international financial and business community and the governments of powerful and wealthy countries have set the general parameters of the way the international economic system works. Their ability to do so rests both on their current economic power as well as the failures of previous economic regimes in debtor countries. The legacy of state socialism and of the developing-world welfare state seems to offer no practical option for new democracies but to deal with the IMF, World Bank, and the global economic powers. They and other global economic actors control the incentives and disincentives. These sorts of arrangements may not seem fair to developing countries, whose governments often want forgiveness of existing debt without strings attached, plus additional grants and technology transfers. These were, in fact, the very proposals floated by the developing countries when they called for a "new economic order" in the 1970s. They received little support then, and today the developing world is in an even weaker bargaining position.

International politics may seem unfair, but domestic politics is often even more skewed. Plans for divesting the state of responsibilities are fairly easy to execute. Measures to replace old programs are not always so effective. Programs targeted to the poor may replace general subsidies on such services as transportation and basic foodstuffs, but they are difficult to carry out effectively in a weak state. Those groups that are best organized and most well connected are likely to win out. Even unionized state employees have more clout than people who work in what is known as the informal sector, i.e., in jobs that are unprotected by unions or government regulations. Politics often degenerates into a struggle between elite interests and those mass interests that are best organized. State employees are often more concerned with saving their own jobs than expanding employment and services to those below the poverty line. In this contest between the privileged and the not-so-privileged, the unprivileged sit on the sidelines. For almost two decades, the political left has been unable to form a coalition sufficiently broad to be able to stop or redirect the structural adjustment process. At the same time, the reformers have had little success in giving structural adjustment a humane face. The lack of a social bargain undercuts the legitimacy of hard democracies and presages problems in the long run.

Possible consequences

Hard democracies can survive in a number of ways. Under one scenario, the public would simply become apathetic, believing nothing can be done. People might simply refuse to vote and not bother to protest, either individually or en masse. The growth of apathy would preserve hard democracies and keep them hard. Governments would grow more responsive to foreign or narrow domestic interests rather than to the mass of their own citizens. Governments and commentators would come to measure policy success in terms that would have little to do with popular welfare or social justice. Such a democracy would be harsh in its policies, but it would not require wide-scale repression to sustain it. A second scenario is perhaps even more troubling. If the public, in fact, begins to protest, governments may react with repression. Political mobilization raises the specter of a return to authoritarianism. But since outright dictatorship is out of favor in most parts of the world, the international community could well react against it; thus, this scenario simply foresees hard democracies getting even harder. States of emergency and the suspension of civil liberties would be defended on supposedly democratic grounds. Political leaders might well believe that they have no other policy alternatives than the very ones they are following. They would quash dissent in the name of democracy. These two scenarios foresee hard democracy ceasing to be a transitory stage in the process of democratic deepening and consolidation. Rather, hard democracies would become a regime type. The process of debate and the consideration of policy alternatives would be carefully manipulated. Domestic intelligence services would be strengthened. Riot control police would be reinforced and frequently used. The process need not be sudden. A semi-authoritarian system could become completely stable. This process could happen almost imperceptibly. Many fear the process is already under way.

A third more hopeful scenario is also possible. The structural adjustment policies meant to produce a general prosperity may, indeed, begin to work. It is often easier to control inflation than to generate economic growth. It is often easier to raise GDP than it is to generate employment. Yet, in the interim politicians may find ways to soften the harsher aspects of these policies, cut corruption, and actually expand basic health care and education. Structural adjustments may deliver the promised benefits over time although, as the twenty-first century begins, this question still remains open. Chile, which began its program in the mid-1970s, took two decades to see tangible results. However, political coalitions, that might reshape policies and make them more equitable, will not emerge automatically. The behavior of politicians, interest groups, and global economic actors bears watching. A fourth scenario is also possible. It is, in reality, a radicalization of the third. This last scenario foresees the rise of social movements that demand both political democracy and economic justice. If it were to succeed in its goals, such a movement would have to combine sustained popular support, technical expertise, and the acquiescence of powerful international actors. Such movements would probably also have to ally themselves with progressives in developed countries who are also critical of the way the IMF and other multilateral institutions conduct their business (cf. Stiglitz 2002).

Does democracy protect liberty?

Throughout this text, the terms "liberal" and "democracy" have usually been linked, but the reader well knows that this has not always been the case historically. Democracy etymologically means rule by the people. Its etymology indicates nothing about individual rights. Indeed, ancient democracies were illiberal in theory and often in practice. They recognized no limits on their powers, overseeing matters of religion and personal conduct that we today would regard as far beyond the proper scope of any government. The nineteenth century too saw a clear distinction between liberalism and democracy. Liberalism recognized the primacy of each individual's rights. Liberals argued that the purpose of government – any government – was to protect these rights. Nineteenth-century liberals often feared that democracy would lead to majority tyranny. The development of liberal democracy and the welfare state put an end to those fears in industrially developed countries by accommodating the interests of the rich and the needs of the poor. But the issue of illiberal democracy has not died in the developing world.

Contemporary critics, such as Fareed Zakaria (Zakaria 2003: 13–161), have pointed out concrete instances of how elections alone fail to guarantee respect for constitutionalism and the rule of law. The regimes we identified as "populist" in Chapter 12 are among those that fall into this category. In theory, these regimes have constitutions, sometimes long-established constitutions, and a history of elections under such constitutions. However, in actual practice constitutionalism and the rule of law are weak. Economic emergencies sometimes coupled with internal war have provided the pretext for strong personalistic rule that runs roughshod over constitutional guarantees. This practice becomes even more dangerous when it is actually supported by the public. The style of leadership and even the constitutions established in many post-communist societies fall into this same sort of pattern. Leaders may simply be following traditional patterns of personalism and patrimonial rule. In some instances, they gain the active support of the majority on other grounds besides. Ultra-nationalism, ethnic hatred, or religious chauvinism often has strong appeal in societies facing many-faceted political, economic, and social crises. Elections alone provide inadequate safeguards for minorities threatened by indignant majorities and extremist governments willing to take sometimes-murderous measures in the majority's name. The danger of violation of minority rights is real. The pogrom carried out by the elected Hutu government against Tutsis in Rwanda, in which hundreds of thousands died, stands as a cautionary tale worth remembering. Given the danger of illiberal democracy, commentators like Zakaria have warned that the West ought to be cautious about pushing the electoral formula further. Better, they say, to work for the liberalization and establishment of the rule of law in new transitional regimes than to try to advance electoral solutions that may make governments even less willing or able to follow the rule of law than they were before. As Zakaria points out, liberal guarantees were put into place before democratization occurred in countries that are now stable liberal democracies.

Yet, Zakaria's advice to governments and others to put issues of the rule of law first and promotion of democratic elections second is open to question (Plattner 1999; Carothers 2007). Downplaying the importance of elections and guarantees for party competition is likely to have perverse results. Nonparty regimes have a bad track record in regard to both democracy and liberal rights. James Madison's remark over two hundred years ago that minority rule is no real solution to the problem of majority tyranny is pertinent. Madison argued that checks and balances, federalism and other devices could prevent a homogeneous, self-interested majority from running roughshod over the rights of the minority. Following an essentially Madisonian rationale, Arend Lijphart (Lijphart 1999) has made detailed proposals on how to craft consensual as opposed to majoritarian governments. The trick is to make use of democratic constitutional devices known in Madison's day along with those of more recent vintage, such as electoral systems that encourage direct representation of minorities, to protect minority interests and encourage the rule of law. While illiberal democracy is a legitimate concern, the solution to the problem is not some sort of liberal authoritarianism where the minority rules the majority. To use Madison's language, from a slightly different context, it would be a "remedy ... worse than the disease" (Madison 1961: 58). An adequately democratic constitution that is frequently ignored in practice may be better than a non-democratic one. Civil society and the political opposition may eventually be able to breathe life into what seems to be a moribund document or they may demand the establishment of constitutional guarantees. Illiberal democracy, in short, may become less illiberal and more democratic as time goes on. The pre-twentieth-century European pattern of liberalism first, then democracy, seems to have few twenty-first-century analogues. In sum, while Zakaria's proposed solution to the problem of illiberal democracy may not be workable, the problem itself is quite real.

By way of a conclusion

The issues concerning democracy's future – its improvement, as well as its exportability to and durability in social environments where it has not flourished in the past – do not have cut and dried answers. Thoughtful commentators, such as those whose views are reviewed here, disagree among themselves. The study of comparative politics is, like politics itself, an ongoing endeavor. Nonetheless, comparative politics can contribute to the resolution of the political issues raised in this chapter. It provides the necessary intellectual context in which the future of democracy (and other contemporary regimes) can be fruitfully discussed. It not only examines alternatives for establishing just and durable regimes or reforming regimes; it also explores strategies by which such changes can be brought about. And even though comparative politics is an academic discipline practiced by a host of specialists, it is also accessible to ordinary citizens. Even students at the beginning level can acquire the requisite sophistication to vote intelligently and contribute meaningfully to public discussion of these and other important political matters.

Questions for further consideration

1 Who sees political culture playing a stronger role, Fukuyama or Huntington? Explain.

2 Go to the Freedom House website (www.freedomhouse.org). Are "Free," "Partly Free," and "Not Free" countries clustered in various regions? What might account for this? What might a proponent of Huntington's thesis make of it? How might a defender of Fukuyama's position respond?

3 Go to the United Nations Developmental Program (UNDP) website (www.undp.org). How does the UNDP define human development? What are its components? What sorts of social and economic policies could address deficiencies in these indicators? How might improvements in these areas help cement a social bargain in developing democracies?

4 Does Freedom House measure qualitative issues concerning democracy? Does the United Nations Developmental Program? Explain.

5 Is democracy necessary for high levels of human development? Compare UNDP index scores with Freedom House rankings. What sorts of states show the greatest discrepancy? What might account for this?

Further reading

Francis Fukuyama, *The End of History and the Last Man*. New York: Free Press, 1992. Argues that democracy and capitalism are universal values and the only way to build stable and just societies.

Samuel P. Huntington, *The Clash of Civilizations: Remaking of World Order*. New York: Simon and Schuster, 1996. A detailed but largely implicit argument against the end-of-history thesis.

Joseph E. Stiglitz, *Globalization and Its Discontents*. New York: W.W. Norton, 2002. A Nobel Prize-winning economist critiques the Washington consensus.

Fareed Zakaria, *The Future of Freedom: Illiberal Democracy at Home and Abroad*. New York: W.W. Norton, 2003. Discussion of the dangers of illiberal democracy.

Glossary

absolute deprivation the condition of living at the level of bare subsistence.

absolutism a system of government in which the rulers are legally or morally unlimited in the exercise of their power.

accommodation a strategy of political actors in power to give in to some demands for political change so as to preserve the basic features of the regime. Or a strategy of those outside the ruling elite of going along with the demands of the ruling elite so as to preserve their own status and privileges.

accountability the liberal-democratic principle that citizens must have the ability to reward and punish officeholders and parties for good or bad conduct and successful or unsuccessful policies.

agency problem see **principal–agent problem**.

alternative vote (AV) a version of the single-member district/majority election (SMD/ME) electoral system. Also known as "instant runoff."

apartheid in white-ruled South Africa, a policy of strict racial separation that deprived native Africans of any rights in most of the country.

authoritarianism a regime that severely restricts personal liberties or the rights of the public to participate in politics, or an attitude that values such restrictions.

breakthrough coup a coup that sets the stage for profound changes in the political system.

bureaucratic rationality the modern, rule-bound principle of state administration that distinguishes the personal interests of the

administrator or bureaucrat from the public interest of the state.

cadre party a political party with a small, weak, or nonexistent central organization to manage party affairs and help determine policy.

capital for Marxists especially, productive property and monetary wealth coupled with the ability of using one to acquire the other.

capitalism for Marxists especially, an economic system that protects and stimulates the growth of capital.

catch-all party a political party with many of the same organizational principles as mass parties but with a multi-class base and less sharp ideological focus.

Christian democracy a political ideology inspired by Catholic social teaching that combines conservatism in morality with a commitment to economic, social, and political reform.

civic culture a political culture in which participation in politics is instrumental and rational; i.e., it is oriented toward the achievement of specific goals. A civic culture includes tolerance and respect for the right to dissent.

civil–military bargain see **objective civilian control**.

civil–military relations the official and unofficial relationship between the civilian government and the armed forces. Civil–military relations include the aspects of civilian control of the military via oversight, budget, appointments, prescribing of rules for military governance, and employment (or the lack of such rules).

civil society the assemblage of organizations that stands between the state and political organizations, on the one hand, and the individual citizen and family, on the other.

closed-list PR see **party list**.

coercive capacity the ability of the state to enforce its rules and defend its territory, especially through military force.

colonialism the practice of establishing sovereign control over other states or unorganized territories without the consent of the subject population. Also known as "imperialism."

communists also Marxist–Leninists, a radical revolutionary movement led by a vanguard party that sought to overthrow capitalism and ultimately establish a worker-run utopia in which all repressive institutions such as police and prisons "wither away" on a global basis.

comparative politics the branch of political science that studies the domestic politics and political institutions of political systems around the globe.

concurrent powers in a federal system of government, powers shared by both the central and lower level of government.

conditionality see **structural adjustment loan**.

confederalism a constitutional system of central–local government relations in which the local governments are sovereign.

confidence vote in a parliamentary system, a vote by the legislature to determine whether or not the government (prime minister and cabinet) will remain in office.

consciousness especially "working-class consciousness," for Marxists, direct experience coupled with the theoretical understanding of that experience. Communists stress theoretical understanding over direct experience.

consensus government a governmental structure that protects minority participation and minority rights via a bill of rights and electoral or legislative procedures that require minority consent to policies that are particularly important

to minority interests. Also called "consociational government."

conservatism a political ideology stressing traditional norms, a strong state, caution about change, and defense of the status quo.

consociational see **consensus government**.

constitutionalism the principle that established rules in the basic law (constitution) restrict what officeholders may do and determine who has the right to hold office. (Compare **facade constitution**.)

coup d'etat the seizure or attempted seizure of governmental power by a small armed group, usually from the state's own military.

democratic centralism the principles by which the communist party governs itself, nominally democratic but in practice highly authoritarian and centralized.

democratization expanding the franchise and the rights of effective political participation, or (re-)establishing a democracy after a period of authoritarian rule.

determinism the belief that absolute causal laws govern events in nature, human society, and individual conduct. Chance and choice are only matters of appearance.

dialectic for Marxists, the belief that history advances by a series of struggles between classes in "contradiction" (i.e., conflict) with one another. At any stage, the conflict can be resolved only by the victory of the oppressed class.

dictatorship of the proletariat the communist idea that the communist party has to rule in an absolute and unchecked manner for a time after a communist revolution in order to destroy the enemies of the working class completely.

direct rule a policy by which an imperial power puts its own functionaries in place in the administration of a colony. (Compare **indirect rule**.)

disloyal opposition those opposed not only to the government of the day and its policies but to the regime itself.

dissolution of parliament in parliamentary government, calling new legislative elections before they are required by law or the constitution.

dual power in revolutions or pre-revolutionary circumstances, a situation where effective power is shared by formal governmental institutions and mass movements contending for power with the government.

economic determinism for Marxists, the theory that economic factors account for political, cultural, and social systems and their breakdown.

electoral democracy a political system that follows the principle of majority rule but curtails the rights of the minority to organize and speak out effectively.

electoral system the legal formula used to determine who is elected to office on the basis of votes cast.

elite an individual or select group that exercises a disproportionate share of political power.

emergency government a short-duration military government. Also called "regime of exception."

ethnic nationalism nationalism whose focus of loyalty is a subgroup within a state.

exit an opposition strategy within an authoritarian political system in which opponents simply refuse to participate or physically leave the country. This may induce the regime to reform.

facade constitution a written constitution that appears to serve the purposes of constitutionalism but exists largely for ceremonial purposes. It does not effectively limit the powers of those in power or prescribe the way people actually gain office. (Compare **constitutionalism**.)

fact a discrete bit of information or data. A fact is a piece of evidence the existence of which can, in principle, be verified by all knowledgeable observers. (Compare **theory**.)

failed state a political system unable to carry out the basic functions of government, such as maintaining law and order, and protecting the state's territorial integrity.

fair and free elections elections conducted in such a manner that the political opposition is free to organize and campaign for office. Among other things, the opposition must be given access to the mass media. All citizens must have the right to vote without burdensome requirements. Voting must be honestly conducted, and votes accurately counted and expeditiously reported.

fascism an extreme authoritarian ideology that stresses national greatness, the role of force, intolerance toward adversaries, and the creation of a new order based on a mythical past.

federalism a constitutional system of central–local government relations in which sovereignty is shared but in which the most important powers and the right to settle disputes over shared powers belong to the central government. Federalism can be "dual federalism" where lower levels of government have autonomous tax or court systems, and conflict between levels of government has often been the norm. Or federalism can assume the form of "cooperative federalism" where institutions are more integrated, and lower levels of government essentially fill in the details and administer federal policy.

finding an analysis of facts acquired systematically by appropriate methods.

form of government see **regime**.

game theory a branch of mathematics that developed during the mid-twentieth century and later adopted by students of comparative politics, among others. Game theory is a highly systematic approach to the sometimes-complex interrelationships between individual choices and payoffs when players compete with one another or when they try to cooperate but cannot coordinate their actions.

glasnost a typical Soviet device of openness or publicity meant to buttress communist party rule. It was given a radical twist by Mikhail Gorbachev (1986–91) in an effort to build support for his policy changes.

globalization the strengthening of ties between countries worldwide, including the movement, exchange, and intermingling of goods and services, peoples, technologies, ideas, and cultures.

governmental efficacy the ability of those in office to address serious issues confronting the regime in an effective manner.

Greens a political party that originated in the counterculture movement of the 1960s and rejected capitalism, conventional politics, and the pollution and social dislocations of the modern industrial age. By the 1980s the Greens had become a center-left, pro-environment grouping.

guardian military regime a military-dominated political system in which ultimate political authority rests with the armed forces, but the day-to-day operation of the government is in the hands of civilians or where civilians play a significant role in government and administration.

head of government the partisan official who holds effective executive power.

head of state the executive official who has the highest rank within the governmental system but no or little effective executive power. The head of state role is largely ceremonial. In presidential systems the head of state and head of government are the same person.

hybrid regime see **semi-authoritarian/semi-democratic regime.**

hypothesis a prediction of events or statement about causal relationships to be confirmed or falsified by evidence.

identity politics ideologies and political associations based on the positive acceptance and assertion of an inherited status such as race, ethnicity, religion, gender, or sexual orientation.

ideology a comprehensive and relatively coherent set of political ideas that describe the proper purposes and methods of government, evaluate institutions and policies, and serve to mobilize a mass following for the purpose of political action.

illiberal democracy a term coined by Fareed Zakaria to indicate an electoral democracy that provides for majority rule but did not protect individual and minority rights or the rule of law.

import substitution industrialization (ISI) an economic policy popular in many developing countries in the post-Second World War era; it stresses protection of national industries and frequently government investment in the economy.

indirect rule a policy by which an imperial power allows traditional local authorities to remain in place to administer a colony subject to overall imperial control.

industrial policy a set of governmental decisions that channels state subsidies, tax benefits, and research grants into economic growth areas, and cushions industries and their employees who are hard hit by economic change.

institution a long-standing pattern of behavior that has a strong normative component. Members of institutions not only can be expected to conform to these established patterns; as members, they are morally obliged to do so as well.

institutionalism the approach to comparative politics that focuses on the *formal legal rules* that direct how the government, the various parts of it, and related entities such as political parties, are supposed to work. (Compare **neo-institutionalism.**)

institutionalist a military officer who believes that the armed forces ought to obey their political superiors and refrain from initiating or threatening coups.

institutionalization the capacity of governmental and state institutions to carry out their basic functions.

interest group corporatism the practice within some liberal democracies of large business associations, labor federations, and government leaders getting together to resolve major policy issues. (Compare **state corporatism.**)

interest group pluralism the practice in some liberal democracies of interest groups competing with one another to influence government policy, each trying to get its own way.

intergovernmental relations especially in federal or confederal systems, the politics and policies involving the highest level of government interaction with lower levels.

International Monetary Fund (IMF) a global multilateral organization established to help regulate currency exchange rates of member countries. Since the 1980s it has promoted neo-liberal policies.

interventionist a military officer who believes that the armed forces have a duty to intervene in politics at least under certain conditions.

Islamist an adherent to political Islam (Islamism), which tries to bring religious solutions to political problems. Some, but not all, strands of the movement are revolutionary.

judicial review review of executive action by a court of law to determine if it is legal. Also, review by a court of law of legislation to determine if it is constitutional.

legal–rational authority a system in which state functionaries apply laws and rules made by superior authorities and have at most strictly limited discretion in applying such rules.

legitimacy the moral authority to rule a country, as recognized by the citizens of that country. In comparative politics legitimacy is a psychological factor supporting a regime and those who hold office within it.

letter of intent see **structural adjustment loan.**

liberal democracy the modern system of representative government that embodies the principle of majority rule while protecting individual (liberal) rights.

liberal rights security of person and property, freedom of religion, assembly, speech, press, and the right to criminal due process.

liberal state a state that respects the rule of law and guarantees basic liberal rights as well as providing for a free market and a money supply but having few other economic functions beyond these. Also called a "minimal state."

liberalization expanding the rights of citizens in the areas of freedom of conscience, speech, press, association, and criminal due process, and strengthening the rule of law.

loyal opposition those who oppose the government of the day and its policies, but are loyal to the regime.

majoritarianism the principle that the popular majority ought to determine all policies regardless of minority rights and interests.

mass actor a group that possesses political power because of its numbers.

mass party a political party based on a commitment to principle and deriving much of its strength from a mass membership, whose interests and point of view the party represents. Mass parties are class based.

materialism a philosophical theory espoused by such thinkers as Thomas Hobbes and Karl Marx that held that matter was the only thing in the universe.

method a systematic way of acquiring facts to test hypotheses or theories.

minimal state see **liberal state.**

moderator military armed forces that usually refrain from exercising governmental power directly, but will intervene via a coup d'etat and rule for a short duration thereafter.

modernizing autocracy a traditional monarchical government vested with absolute or nearly absolute power which is attempting limited modernization of its military and state structures, and its economy.

multilateral institution see **multilateral organization.**

multilateral organization a formally organized international body composed of representatives of national governments with either specialized or general focus. Also known as "multilateral institution."

multiparty system a system of government where no single party can dominate the legislature and where a coalition of parties is required to choose a chief executive.

nation a broadly based community that has the ultimate claim to its members' loyalty and which aspires to complete or partial self-government.

national liberation the process of freeing of subject peoples from foreign, often colonial, rule. Sometimes this process involves "wars of national liberation," which are often conducted as protracted people's wars.

national liberation front a group of leaders or parties seeking to end colonial rule over their country.

nationalism loyalty to one's nation; the belief that one's nation ought to achieve its rightful position in the world. (See also **ethnic nationalism** and **pan-nationalism**.)

national security council in guardian military regimes, a joint civilian–military body composed of senior officials who are to give advice to or approve the proposals of the chief executive.

national security doctrine a military doctrine (i.e., an officially promulgated set of concepts, organizations, and procedures) that expands the armed forces' role from the mission to defense against external threats to the defense against internal subversion as well as to the economic, social, and political development of the country.

neo-colonialism direct economic but only indirect political control by a powerful foreign country over a dependent country (often its ex-colony).

neo-institutionalism the approach to comparative politics that looks at the informal rules that govern institutions, their historical development, and the political strategies followed by members of these institutions.

neo-liberalism a set of policies based on classical economic liberal (free-market) principles stressing trade liberalization, balanced government budgets, financial liberalization, deregulation, privatization of state-owned firms, and currency and central bank reforms.

neo-patrimonialism the practice of patrimonialism within a state that is nominally modern and which is supposed to be governed by the norms of bureaucratic rationality. (See **patrimonialism**.)

neo-sultanism an extreme form of neo-patrimonialism.

new left a group of movements or parties prominent during the 1960s and 1970s that adhered to an anti-statist and participatory vision of democracy and economic reform.

no confidence vote see **confidence vote**.

objective civilian control (of the armed forces) a system of civil–military relations in which the civilian government grants the armed forces significant professional autonomy in exchange for control over decisions concerning war and peace, military budgets, senior level appointments, and other military policies that have a critical impact on the government and the public. Also called the "civil–military bargain."

old regime the system of government that immediately preceded a revolution.

pan-nationalism nationalism whose focus of loyalty is a group that extends beyond the boundaries of a single state.

parochial political culture political culture in which the individual has no specific political role or role expectations; its focus is local. Individuals have local ties and associations, but these are not overtly political.

parliamentary government a system of executive–legislative relations in which the legislature (parliament) chooses and removes the chief executive (prime minister).

participant political culture a political culture in which citizens taking an active role in shaping the outcomes of the political process is seen as a good in itself.

party list in a PR electoral system, a party's list of candidates running for seats in the legislature. The list can be a "closed list" where a candidate's place on the list determines whether the candidate is elected. Or the list can be an "open list" where popular votes for a specific candidate help determine whether that candidate is elected.

party-military regime an authoritarian military dominated regime based on an alliance of near equals. In this alliance a strong revolutionary party shares rule with the armed forces.

patrimonialism the approach to state administration that stresses kinship, friendship, and personal connections. Political office is seen as a benefit conferred upon the officeholder, and little distinction is drawn between the officeholder's public function and private interest. In the strict sense, a state is patrimonial when patrimonial principles are explicitly recognized as being proper and legitimate. (Compare **neo-patrimonialism**.)

patron–client relationship a relationship in which a high-status, more powerful, and wealthier individual or family (the patron) forms an association with weaker, lower-status, and poorer individuals and families (the clients), trading limited benefits for loyalty. Also known as "clientelism."

perestroika the process of economic restructuring undertaken in the Soviet Union by Mikhail Gorbachev (1985–91).

personalism the practice of basing authority primarily on the person of a ruler or leader rather than the formal office he or she holds.

pluralism the existence and toleration of many diverse and competing groups, such as political parties, interests groups, churches, and other private associations.

political actor an individual or formally or informally organized group that exercises or contends for political power.

political culture the set of basic political attitudes that characterize a country's population or one of its subgroups.

political economy the approach to comparative politics that examines both a country's overall economic policies and the set of interests that back them.

political mobilization an increase in political participation either via the institutions of government or by mass demonstrations, strikes, and similar means to force government to change from the outside.

political party an organization whose purpose is to run and elect candidates to office on the basis of some common set of principles or policy commitments.

political power the ability of one person or group to impose its will on another via political means such as law, the police, and military force.

political socialization the branch of comparative politics that examines the formal and informal mechanisms by which political culture is inculcated.

political system see **regime**.

polyarchy a term used by Robert Dahl in place of "liberal democracy." The term highlights the fact that the general public selects its rulers from a variety of competing political elites and does not rule directly.

populism especially in Latin America, a style of rule that stresses the leader's direct connection to the people and downplays institutions and democratic norms. Populism tends to arise in times of economic change or stress.

postmodernism a theoretical approach that rejects universal principles, abstract formal standards of judgment, and even modern science; also attitudes and ideologies typical of post-industrial society in the West that focus on self-realization rather than economic security.

praetorianism the political condition in which brute force and the threat of force are substituted for negotiation, persuasion, and law.

presidentialism a system of executive/legislative relations in which the executive and legislature are chosen independently of one another by direct or indirect popular election. Also known as "separation of powers."

principal–agent problem in a situation in which an individual or group (a "principal") delegates to someone else (an "agent") the authority to do something in the principal's name. The principal must devise effective methods of assuring the agent acts in the principal's interest. (Also known as the "agency problem.")

principal contradiction see **dialectic**.

project loan the sort of loan typically extended by the World Bank, that provided financing for a specific project or projects on the basis of their economic viability. (Compare **structural adjustment loan**.)

proletarian internationalism the communist principle that all workers and working-class parties ought to support one another regardless of the national interest of their country. In practice, the principle meant unquestioning support for the foreign policy of the Soviet Union.

propaganda of the deed terrorist violence or an effective demonstration of power by a revolutionary vanguard.

proportional representation (PR) an electoral system that assigns seats in a legislative body according to the percentage of the overall vote each party wins. Commonly PR assigns seats district by district in multi-seat districts. (See also **party list**.)

protracted people's war a form of twentieth-century revolutionary struggle that reverses the normal pattern of seizure of power in the capital followed by national consolidation. In a protracted people's war, revolutionaries mobilize political and eventually military support in the countryside only challenging the old regime in its traditional power centers after years or even decades of development.

rational choice the approach to comparative politics that stresses how political actors calculate the best use of resources to attain their political ends, carefully weighing options and likely outcomes.

reaction a nineteenth-century ideology that championed the old monarchical status quo against democratic change. Unlike conservatism, it argued reform was unnecessary.

realpolitik especially in international relations, the belief that politics is solely or primarily about power and that leaders do a disservice to their states if they make judgments on the basis of moral considerations.

rebellion mass political violence directed at the overthrow of an established regime.

regime a system of government that has sufficient moral authority and physical power to secure its continuance even as individual leaders leave office. Also called "form of government" and "political system."

relative deprivation the *perceived* discrepancy between what individuals think they can attain and what they believe they are entitled to.

rentier state a state that is funded on the basis of revenue ("rents") from oil or other natural resources instead of income from taxes on its own people.

replacement democratization in which an authoritarian regime in essence collapses and is replaced by one established by the democrats.

repression the use of force to suppress political actors who demand change.

responsiveness the liberal democratic principle that the elected representatives are the agents of the voters that elected them.

revisionists a group of turn-of-the-twentieth-century Marxists who argued that Marx's economic laws were incorrect and that Marxism could be reconciled with a liberal democratic regime.

revolution a rebellion, with its attendant mass violence, whose leaders and much of their mass following hold ideologies that prescribe what sort of new regime ought to be created on the ruins of the old.

revolution of rising expectations a phenomenon that occurs within modernizing societies. The experience of rapid change leads to the dramatic growth in the sense of relative deprivation and popular pressure for the government to deliver the benefits the population feels it is due.

revolutionary dictatorship of the proletariat and the peasantry for communists, an interim phase after the revolution and before the full dictatorship of the proletariat that may occur in some communist revolutions.

ruler military armed forces that assume direct control of the government for extended periods.

semi-authoritarian/semi-democratic regime any one of a variety of political systems that possess a nominally democratic constitution but fall significantly short of full democratic rights of participation or protections for civil liberties.

semi-loyal opposition those willing to abide by the rules of the regime *within limits*. If the government tolerates or actually threatens to do certain things of which it disapproves, the semi-loyal opposition will move to outright disloyalty and seek to overthrow the government.

separation of powers see **presidentialism**.

shareholder capitalism the set of basic economic policies typical of the United States and the United Kingdom that stresses economic freedom, markets, and the ability of corporations to make decisions in the best interest of their shareholders regardless of the wider social consequences.

single-member district/majority election an electoral system in which one candidate is elected in each district by a majority of votes. Requires a runoff if no candidate achieves a majority on the first round.

single-member district/plurality election or "first past the post," an electoral system in which one representative is elected in each district, the plurality vote winner in each district taking the seat.

single transferable vote (STV) an electoral system that resembles open-list proportional representation.

social capital the skills and habits of civic participation necessary for a well-functioning democracy.

social contract a collective agreement among individuals to live together under a government.

According to thinkers who subscribe to the idea of the social contract, no government can be legitimate without a prior explicit or implicit social contract.

social democracy in the nineteenth century, a radical Marxist ideology that aimed at revolution and the establishment of a communist society; in the contemporary era, a moderate leftist ideology supporting liberal democracy and the welfare state.

social frustration the collective dissatisfaction with the way society is run and with those that run it.

social market a set of economic policies that provides for worker seats on corporate boards of directors, an extensive welfare state, and political bargaining typical of interest-group corporatism.

social mobility the ability to change, especially improve, one's social and economic status.

social mobilization the change from traditional to modern attitudes.

socialist state a communist state that follows the economic model of state socialism.

soft state a term coined by Swedish sociologist Gunnar Myrdal to indicate a weak state in the developing world whose weakness was the result of corruption, neo-patrimonialism, and the lack of a civic consciousness.

stakeholder capitalism the set of economic policies practiced by many western European countries that limits the rights of corporations and their shareholders in order to protect others with economic and social stakes in corporate decisions, such as workers, local communities, and the country at large.

state an organized political entity that possesses territory, population/citizens, and a government that has sovereignty – the ultimate legal say about what goes on in its territory. Also, the permanent part of the governmental administration responsible for implementing the decisions of the policy-making part of the government.

state capacity state effectiveness and coercive capacity.

state capitalism a system of economic management sometimes adopted by rightwing regimes. It stresses the role of the state in fostering the growth of industry as well as founding and running major state firms. Unlike western socialism, which it otherwise resembles, it does not include the aims of social equity or the welfare state.

state corporatism the practice in some authoritarian regimes of asserting top-down control of official, labor unions, peasant associations, professional associations, and similar entities while excluding all unofficial entities from any meaningful share of power. (Compare **interest group corporatism**.)

state effectiveness the ability of the permanent administrative apparatus of the government to impose law and order, acquire sufficient resources to implement policy, and protect and cultivate the resource base upon which the state draws.

state of nature in social contract theory, the condition that exists before the formation of a social contract.

state socialism the economic system typical of communist states before the 1980s. It was based on state ownership of all productive property and centralized state planning in place of markets.

structural adjustment loan a loan from the IMF or World Bank meant to promote change in a country's economic policies along neo-liberal lines. The country's government signs a "letter of intent" setting out targets that the government pledges to meet. The loan agreement embodies the principle of "conditionality" – the loan is delivered in installments as the country successfully meets its targets.

structural functionalism the approach to comparative politics that considers political systems in the broadest sense: the formal and informal structures that comprise a political system and the functions these structures must carry out for the system to survive.

subject political culture a political culture that stresses the duty of the citizen to obey state authorities unquestioningly and is intolerant of dissent.

subjective civilian control (of the armed forces) a system of civil–military relations in which the civilian governmental and military elites come from the same class

sultanism an extreme form of patrimonialism practiced in some traditional societies.

surplus value for Marxists, profit earned by capital.

taxi party an extreme form of cadre party that is very small and whose leaders frequently switch from one party to another.

technocrats individuals who hold high governmental positions because of their technical training and professional experience outside of politics. Technocrats are distinguished from politicians who rise to high office via a political career.

theory a generalization or set of generalizations that define basic terms and propose explanations of how the world or a part of it works. (Compare **fact**.)

third way an approach to politics that seeks to combine elements of liberal democracy, capitalism, and state socialism especially in the third world during the mid-twentieth century, or an approach taken by contemporary leftwing parties that downplays the importance of government ownership of productive property or the welfare state.

third world a term used for developing countries in the cold war era. The first world was the capitalist democracies, and the second world was comprised of communist states.

totalitarianism a regime that severely restricts personal freedom, denies effective political participation to its citizens, violates the rule of law, and forcibly mobilizes them behind the regime's project to transform society.

traditional authority a form of legitimacy resting on long-established political practices or the sense that these practices are the will of God.

transformation democratization in which the authoritarian regime is able to impose a settlement of its own choosing.

transparency the liberal-democratic principle that requires the public to be aware of what their agents are doing. Hence, secrecy must be minimized, corruption prevented, and the public must be able to easily understand who was responsible for making a decision.

transplacement democratization in which the resources of the authoritarian government and the democratic opposition are evenly balanced, and negotiations are instrumental in producing a compromise transition to democracy.

tutelary democracy in the developing world, a semi-democratic or semi-authoritarian system justified by its leaders as being a necessary preparation for full democracy.

two-party system a political system in which two large parties are dominant, and one of them almost always controls a majority of the legislature and the chief executive.

unitary government a constitutional system of central–local government relations in which the central government is sovereign.

vanguard an organized revolutionary group contending for power.

vanguard party a political party based on selective membership criteria, tight discipline, a utopian ideology, and top-down decision-making.

voice an opposition strategy within authoritarian systems that seeks to advocate for change either

publicly or within the ruling councils and thereby induce or force substantial reform.

warlord a leader commanding sufficient formal or informal military force and personal adherents to partially fill the void left by the collapsing state administration in a failed state.

Washington consensus de facto agreement on basic policy recommendations for developing countries between the World Bank and International Monetary Fund, both of which are headquartered in Washington, DC. These recommendations promote neo-liberal reforms. (See **neo-liberalism**.)

welfare state a liberal state that provides economic and social rights to education, income, health care, and state-supported retirement to all its citizens.

(western) socialism the economic system in which the state owns utilities and major industries that are strategically important for the development of the economy and attempts to further social equity through the welfare state.

World Bank a global multilateral institution established after the Second World War to promote reconstruction and development. The bank's official name is the International Bank for Reconstruction and Development.

World Trade Organization (WTO) formerly the General Agreement on Tariffs and Trade (GATT), a global multilateral organization to promote trade by facilitating the writing and enforcement of trade agreements among its members.

References

Allen, W. (1991a) "Mercantilism," in J. Eatwell, M. Millgate, and P. Newman (eds), *The New Palgrave: The World of Economics*, New York: W.W. Norton.

—— (1991b) "Specie-flow Mechanism," in J. Eatwell, M. Millgate, and P. Newman (eds), *The New Palgrave: The World of Economics*, New York: W.W. Norton.

Almond, G. and Verba, S. (1963) *The Civic Culture: Political Attitudes and Democracy in Five Nations*, Princeton, NJ: Princeton University Press.

Almond, G., Appleby, R.S., and Sivan, E. (2003) *Strong Religion: The Rise of Fundamentalism around the World*, Chicago: University of Chicago Press.

Anderson, B. (1983) *Imagined Communities: Reflections on the Origin and Spread of Nationalism*, London: Verso.

Anderson, L. (ed.) (1999) *Transitions to Democracy*, New York: Columbia University Press.

Apter, D.E. (1996) "Comparative Politics, Old and New," in R. Goodin and H.D. Klingemann (eds), *A New Handbook of Political Science*, Oxford: Oxford University Press.

Aristotle (1926) *Nicomachean Ethics*, trans. H. Rackham, London: William Heinemann Ltd.

—— (1932) *Politics*, London: William Heinemann Ltd.

Banfield, E. (1958) *The Moral Basis of a Backward Society*, Glencoe, IL: The Free Press.

Baradat, L. (2003) *Political Ideologies: Their Origins and Impact*, Upper Saddle River, NJ: Prentice-Hall.

Barber, B. (1995) *Jihad versus McWorld: How Globalism and Tribalism Are Reshaping the World*, New York: Ballantine Books

Bentham, J. (1948) *The Principles of Morals and Legislation*, New York: Hafner.

Bergsten, C.F., Gill, B., Lardy, N., and Mitchell, D. (2006) *China: The Balance Sheet*, New York: Public Affairs.

Bermeo, N. (2003) *Ordinary People in Extraordinary Times: The Citizenry and the Breakdown of Democracy*, Princeton, NJ: Princeton University Press.

Bernstein, E. (1963) *Evolutionary Socialism*, trans. Edith C. Harvey, New York: Schocken Books.

Bloc, M. (1961) *Feudal Society*, trans. L.A. Manyon, Chicago: University of Chicago Press.

Boix, C. and Stokes, S. ((2007) *The Oxford Handbook of Comparative Politics*, Oxford: Oxford University Press.

Brinton, C. (1965) *The Anatomy of Revolution*, New York: Random House.

Brooker, P. (1995) *Twentieth-century Dictatorships: The Ideological One-party States*, New York: New York University Press.

Brownlee, J. (2007) *Authoritarianism in an Age of Democracy*, Cambridge, England: Cambridge University Press.

Brownlee, J., Quandt, W., Maghraoui, A., Seznec, J.-F., Herb, M., Schwedler, J., and Brumberg, D. (2002) "Democratization in the Arab World?," *Journal of Democracy*, 11, 4: 5–68.

Brumberg, D. (2002) "The Trap of Liberalized Autocracy," *Journal of Democracy*, 11, 4: 56–68.

Burke, E. (1774) "Speech to the Electors of Bristol," Online. Availabe HTTP: http://www.econlib.org/library/LFBooks/Burke/brkSWv4c1.html (accessed May 2, 2008).

——(n.d.) *Reflections on the Revolution in France*, New Rochelle, NY: Arlington House.

Calleo, D. (2001) *Rethinking Europe's Future*, Princeton, NJ: Princeton University Press.

Cardoso, F.H. and Faletto, E. (1979) *Dependency and Development in Latin America*, trans. M. Mattingly Urquidi, Berkeley, CA: University of California Press.

Carothers, T. (2002) "The End of the Transition Paradigm," *Journal of Democracy*, 13, 1: 5–21.

—— (2007) "The 'Sequencing' Fallacy," *Journal of Democracy*, 18, 1: 12–27.

Castañeda, J. (1993) *Utopia Unarmed: The Latin American Left After the Cold War*, New York: Knopf.

Challand, G. (1978) *Revolutions in the Third World*, New York: Penguin.

Chang, H.-J. (2008) *Bad Samaritans: The Myth of Free Trade and the Secret History of Capitalism*, New York: Bloomsburg Press.

Chasteen, J.C. (2006) *Born of Blood and Fire: A Concise History of Latin America*, 2nd edn, New York: W.W. Norton.

Chehabi, H.E. and Linz, J. (eds) (1998) *Sultanistic Regimes*, Baltimore, MD: Johns Hopkins University Press.

China View (2003) "'Three Represents' is Marxism for Contemporary China: Official," Online. Available HTTP: http://news.xinhuanet.com/english/2003-09/24/content_1095983.htm (accessed April 1, 2006).

Chirot, D. (1994) *How Societies Change*, Thousand Oaks, CA: Sage.

REFERENCES

Churchill, W. (1996) "Speech in London, November 10, 1942," in A. Jay (ed), *The Oxford Dictionary of Political Quotations*, Oxford: Oxford University Press.

Clapham, C. (2004) "The Global–Local Politics of State Decay," in R. Rotberg (ed.), *When States Fail: Causes and Consequences*, Princeton, NJ: Princeton University Press.

Clark, J. (2006) "Armed Arbiters: When Does the Military Step into the Electoral Arena?," in A. Schedler (ed.), *Electoral Authoritarianism: The Dynamics of Unfree Competition*, Boulder, CO: Lynne Rienner.

Cline, R. (1975) *World Power Assessment: A Calculus of Strategic Drift*, Washington, DC: Center for Strategic and International Studies.

Cohen, Y. (1994) *Radicals, Reformers, and Reactionaries: The Prisoner's Dilemma and the Collapse of Democracy in Latin America*, Chicago: University of Chicago Press.

Colburn, F. (1994) *The Vogue of Revolution in Poor Countries*, Princeton, NJ: Princeton University Press.

Communist Party of the Soviet Union (1961) *Programme of the Communist Party of the Soviet Union*, Moscow: Foreign Languages Publishing House.

Cook, C. and Walker, W. (2001) *Facts on File World Political Almanac: From 1945 to the Present*, 4th edn, New York: Checkmark Books.

Cook, S. (2007) *Ruling But Not Governing: The Military and Political Development in Egypt, Algeria, and Turkey*, Baltimore, MD: Johns Hopkins University Press.

Cornell, V. (1999) "Fruit of the Tree of Knowledge: The Relationship between Faith and Practice in Islam," in J. Espositio (ed.), *The Oxford History of Islam*, Oxford: Oxford University Press.

Croll, E. (2000). *Endangered Daughters: Discrimination and Development in Asia*, New York: Routledge.

Dahl, R. (1971) *Polyarchy: Participation and Opposition*, New Haven, CT: Yale University Press.

Davies, J. (1962) "Towards a Theory of Revolution," *American Sociological Review*, 27, 1: 5–19.

Debray, R. (1967) *Revolution in the Revolution? Armed Struggle and Political Struggle in Latin America*, New York: Grove Press.

Diamond, J. (1997) *Guns, Germs, and Steel: The Fates of Human Societies*, New York: W.W. Norton.

Diamond, L. (1999) *Developing Democracy: Toward Consolidation*, Baltimore, MD: Johns Hopkins University Press.

Diamond, L. and Molino, L. (eds) (2005) *Assessing the Quality of Democracy*, Baltimore, MD: Johns Hopkins University Press.

Doorenspleet, R. (2005) *Democratic Transitions: Exploring the Structural Sources of the Fourth Wave*, Boulder, CO: Lynne Rienner Publishers.

Dore, R., Lazonick, W., and O'Sullivan, M. (1999) "Varieties of Capitalism in the Twentieth Century," *Oxford Review of Economic Policy*, 15, 4: 102–20.

Dryzek, J. and Holmes, L. (2002) *Post-communist Democratization: Political Discourses across Thirteen Countries*, Cambridge: Cambridge University Press.

Elazar, D. (1987) *Exploring Federalism*, Tuscaloosa, AL: University of Alabama Press.

Engels, F, (1969) "Introduction (1895)," in K. Marx, *The Class Struggles in France, 1849–1850, Selected Works*, 1, Moscow: Progress Publishers. Online. Available HTTP: http://www.marxists.org/archive/marx/works/1895/03/06.htm (accessed May 3, 2008).

Esmein, J. (1973) *The Chinese Cultural Revolutions*, New York: Anchor.

Fainsod, M. (1967) *How Russia Is Ruled*, Cambridge, MA: Harvard University Press.

Fanon, F. (1963) *The Wretched of the Earth*, New York: Grove Press.

Farrell, D. (2001) *Electoral Systems: A Comparative Introduction*, New York: Palgrave.

Finer, F.E. (1962) *The Man on Horseback: The Role of the Military in Politics,* New York: Frederick A. Praeger.

—— (1997) *The History of Government*, Oxford: Oxford University Press.

Forero, J. (2003) "Texaco Goes on Trial in Ecuador Pollution Case," *New York Times*, October 23, 2003. Online. Available HTTP: http://select.nytimes.com/search/restricted/ article?res=F70610F93C550C708EDDA90994DB404482 (accessed May 3, 2008).

Freedom House http://www.freedomhouse.org/.

—— (2008) *Freedom in the World*. Online. Available HTTP: http://www.freedomhouse.org/template.cfm?page=15.

Friedrich, C. and Brzezinski, Z. (1965) *Totalitarian Dictatorship and Autocracy*, 2nd edn, Cambridge, MA: Harvard University Press.

Fukuyama, F. (1992) *The End of History and the Last Man*, New York: Free Press.

—— (2004) *State-building: Governance and World Order in the Twenty-first Century*, Ithaca, NY: Cornell University Press.

Fuller, G. (2003) *The Future of Political Islam*, New York: Palgrave.

Geddes, B. (1999) "What Do We Know about Democratization after Twenty Years?" in N. Polsby (ed.), *Annual Review of Political Science*, 2: 115–44.

Gerges, F. (2005) *The Far Enemy: Why Jihad Went Global*, Cambridge: Cambridge University Press.

Gilpin, R. (1987) *The Political Economy of International Relations*, Princeton, NJ: Princeton University Press.

REFERENCES

Grieco, J. and Ikenberry, G.J. (2002) *State Power and World Markets: The International Political Economy*, New York: W.W. Norton.

Gurr, T.R. (1970) *Why Men Rebel*, Princeton, NJ: Princeton University Press.

Hadenius, A. and Teorell, J. (2007) "Pathways from Authoritarianism," *Journal of Democracy*, 18, 1: 143–56.

Halpern, M. (1965) *Politics of Social Change in the Middle East and North Africa*, Princeton, NJ: Princeton University Press.

Headrick, D. (1981) *The Tools of Empire: Technology and European Imperialism in the Nineteenth Century*, Oxford: Oxford University Press.

Hegel, G.W.F. (1956) *The Philosophy of History*, trans. J. Sibree, New York: Dover.

Herb, M. (1999) *All in the Family: Absolutism, Revolution, and Democracy in the Middle Eastern Monarchies*, New York: State University of New York Press.

—— (2002) "Emirs and Parliaments in the Gulf," *Journal of Democracy*, 11, 4: 41–7.

Hirschman, A. (1970) *Exit, Voice, and Loyalty: Responses to Decline in Firms, Organizations, and States*, Boston, MA: Harvard University Press.

Hobbes, T. (1950) *Leviathan*, New York: E.P. Dutton.

Hochschild, A. (1998) *King Leopold's Ghost: A Story of Greed, Terror, and Heroism in Colonial Africa*, New York: Houghton Mifflin.

Hollis, M. (1994) *The Philosophy of Social Science: An Introduction*, Cambridge: Cambridge University Press.

Homans, G. (1967) *The Nature of Social Science*, New York: Harcourt, Brace and World.

Hoover, K. (1988) *The Elements of Social Scientific Thinking*, 4th edn, New York: St. Martin's Press.

Hueglin, T. and Fenna, A. (2006) *Comparative Federalism*, Toronto: Broadview Press.

Huntington, S. (1964) *The Soldier and the State: The Theory and Practice of Civil–Military Relations*, New York: Random House.

—— (1968) *Political Order in Changing Societies*, New Haven, CT: Yale University Press.

—— (1984) "Will More Countries Become Democratic?," *Political Science Quarterly*, 99: 193–218.

—— (1991) *The Third Wave: Democratization in the Late Twentieth Century*, Norman, OK: University of Oklahoma Press.

—— (1996) *The Clash of Civilizations: Remaking of World Order*, New York: Simon and Schuster.

Inglehart, R. (1997) *Modernization and Postmodernization: Cultural, Economic, and Political Change in 43 Societies*, Princeton, NJ: Princeton University Press.

Inglehart, R. and Norris, P. (2003) *Rising Tide: Gender Equality and Cultural Change around the World*, Cambridge: Cambridge University Press.

International Monetary Fund (IMF) (2007) *Data and Statistics*. Online. Available HTTP: http://www.imf.org/external/pubs/ft/weo/2007/02/weodata/weoselgr.aspx (accessed May 3, 2008).

Jefferson, T. (1944) "First Inaugural Address," in A. Koch and W. Peden (eds), *The Life and Selected Writings of Thomas Jefferson*, New York: Modern Library.

Journal of Democracy (2003) "China's Changing of the Guard," 14, 1: 5–81.

Kandeh, J. (2004) *Coups from Below: Armed Subalterns and State Power in West Africa*, New York: Palgrave Macmillan.

Karatnycky, A. (1998) *Freedom in the World: The Annual Survey of Political Rights and Civil Liberties 1997–1998*, New Brunswick: Transaction Publishers.

Kasfir, N. (2004) "Domestic Anarchy, Security Dilemmas, and Violent Predation: Causes of Failure," in R. Rotberg (ed.), *When States Fail: Causes and Consequences*, Princeton, NJ: Princeton University Press.

Kepel, G. (2002) *Jihad: The Trial of Political Islam*, trans. A. Roberts, Cambridge, MA: Harvard University Press.

—— (2004) *The War for Muslim Minds*, Cambridge, MA: Harvard University Press.

Kotkin, S. (2001) *Armageddon Averted: The Soviet Collapse, 1970–2000*, Oxford: Oxford University Press.

Krouwel, A. (2006) "Party Models," in R. Katz and W. Crotty (eds), *Handbook of Party Politics*, London: Sage Publications.

Krugman, P. and Obstfeld, M. (1997) *International Economics: Theory and Policy*, 4th edn, Reading, MS: Addison-Wesley.

Kuusinen, O.V., Arbatov, Y.A., Belyakov, A.S., Vygodsky, S.L., Mileikovsky, A.G., and Sheidin, L.M. (1963) *Fundamentals of Marxism–Leninism: Manual*, 2nd edn, trans. C. Dutt, Moscow: Foreign Languages Publishing House.

Lasswell, H. (1936) *Politics: Who Gets What, When, How*, New York: McGraw-Hill.

Lenin, V.I. (1902) *What Is To Be Done?: Burning Questions of Our Movement*, trans. J. Fineberg and G. Hanna. Online. Available HTTP: http://www.marxists.org/archive/lenin/works/1901/witbd/ (accessed May 2, 2008).

—— (1935) *Two Tactics of Social Democracy in the Democratic Revolution*, New York: International Publishers.

—— (n.d.) *Imperialism: The Highest Stage of Capitalism*, Moscow: Foreign Languages Publishing House.

—— (1965) *The State and Revolution*, Moscow: Progress Publishers.

REFERENCES

Levitsky, S. (1999) "Fujimori and Post-party Politics in Peru," *Journal of Democracy*, 10, 3: 78–92.

Lewis, B. (1995) *The Middle East: A Brief History of the Last 2,000 Years*, New York: Simon and Schuster.

—— (2002) *What Went Wrong? The Clash Between Islam and Modernity in the Middle East*, New York: HarperCollins.

Lijphart, A. (1999) *Patterns of Democracy: Government Forms and Performance in Thirty-six Countries*, New Haven, CT: Yale University Press.

Linz, J. (1978) *The Breakdown of Democratic Regimes: Crisis, Breakdown and Reequilibration*, Baltimore, MD: Johns Hopkins University Press.

—— (2000) *Totalitarian and Authoritarian Regimes*, Boulder, CO: Lynne Rienner.

Linz, J. and Valenzuela, A. (eds) (1994) *The Failure of Presidential Democracy*, Baltimore, MD: Johns Hopkins University Press.

Lipset, S.M. (1959) *Political Man: The Social Bases of Politics*, Garden City, NY: Doubleday.

Locke, J. (1963) *Second Treatise (Of Civil Government)*, in P. Laslett (ed.), *Two Treatises of Government*, New York: New American Library.

Loveman, B. (1993) *The Constitution of Tyranny: Regimes of Exception in Spanish America*, Pittsburgh: University of Pittsburgh Press.

Lust-Okar, E. (2005) *Structuring Conflict in the Arab World: Incumbents, Opponents, and Institutions*, Cambridge: Cambridge University Press.

Luttwak, E. (1979 [1968]) *Coup d'Etat: A Practical Handbook*, Cambridge, MA: Harvard University Press.

Machiavelli, N. (1940) *The Prince*, in *The Prince and the Discourses*, New York: The Modern Library.

MacKinder, H. (1962) *Democratic Ideas and Reality*, New York: Norton and Co.

Madison, J. (1961) *The Federalist Papers*, Jacob E. Cooke (ed.), Middletown, CT: Wesleyan University Press.

Maghraoui, A. (2002) "Depoliticization in Morocco," *Journal of Democracy*, 11, 4: 24–32.

Mair, P (1996). "Comparative Politics: An Overview," in R. Goodin and H.D. Klingemann (eds), *A New Handbook of Political Science*, Oxford: Oxford University Press.

Mao Zedong (1962) "Strategic Problems of China's Revolutionary War," in A. Fremantle (ed.), *Mao Tse-Tung: An Anthology of His Writings*, New York: Mentor Books.

Marx, K. (1965) *Capital*, 1, Moscow: Progress Publishers.

—— (1969) *Theses on Feuerbach*, 11, in *Marx/Engels, Selected Works*, 1, Moscow: Progress Publishers. Online. Available HTTP: http://www.marxists.org/archive/marx/works/1845/theses/theses.htm#018 (accessed May 3, 2008).

—— (1970), *Critique of the Gotha Program,* in *Marx/Engels, Selected Works*, 3, Moscow: Progress Publishers. Online. Available HTTP: http://www.marxists.org/archive/marx/works/1875/gotha/ch01.htm (accessed on May 3, 2008).

—— (1977) *Critique of the Gotha Program*, in D. McLellan (ed.), *Karl Marx: Selected Writings*, Oxford: Oxford University Press.

—— (1977) *The German Ideology*, in D. McLellan (ed.), *Karl Marx: Selected Writings*, Oxford: Oxford University Press.

Marx, K. and Engels, F. (1977) "The Communist Manifesto," in D. McLellan (ed.), *Karl Marx: Selected Writings*, Oxford: Oxford University Press.

McFaul, M. (2001) "A Mixed Record, An Uncertain Future," *Journal of Democracy*, 12, 4: 87–94.

Meyer, K. (2003) *The Dust of Empire: The Race for Mastery in the Asian Heartland*, New York: Public Affairs.

Mill, J.S. (1958) *Considerations on Representative Government*, New York: Bobbs-Merrill.

Minorities at Risk Project (2005) College Park, MD: Center for International Development and Conflict Management. Online. Available HTTP: http://www.cidcm.umd.edu/mar/ (accessed January 4, 2008).

Molavi, A. (2003) "The Disenchantment," *The Wilson Quarterly*, 27, 1: 48–52.

Moore, B. (1993) *Social Origins of Dictatorship and Democracy: Lord and Peasant in the Making of the Modern World*, Boston, MA: Beacon Press.

Myrdal, G. (1968) *Asian Drama: An Inquiry into the Poverty of Nations*, New York: Pantheon.

New York Times (2002) "The Netherlands: A Million Votes for a Dead Man." Online. Available HTTP: http://query.nytimes.com/gst/fullpage. html?res=9B00E7D91038F931A15756C0A9649C8B63 (accessed May 3, 2008).

Nkrumah, K. (1965) *Neo-colonialism: The Highest Stage of Imperialism*, London: Thomas Nelson and Sons.

Nordlinger, E. (1977) *Soldiers in Politics: Military Coups and Governments*, Englewood Cliffs, NJ: Prentice-Hall.

O'Donnell, G. (1979) *Modernization and Bureaucratic-Authoritarianism: Studies in South American Politics*, Berkeley, CA: Institute of International Studies.

—— (n.d.) *Delegative Democracy?*, Notre Dame, IN: Helen Kellogg Institute for International Studies Working Paper. Online. Available HTTP: http://kellogg.nd.edu/publications/workingpapers/WPS/172.pdf (accessed May 3, 2008).

O'Donnell, G., Schmitter, P., and Whitehead, L. (eds) (1986) *Transitions from Authoritarian Rule: Prospects for Democracy*, Baltimore, MD: Johns Hopkins University Press.

REFERENCES

O'Kane, R. (1987) *The Likelihood of Coups*, Brookfield, VT: Gower Publishing Co.

Ottaway, M. (2003) *Democracy Challenged: The Rise of Semi-Authoritarianism*, Washington, DC: The Carnegie Endowment for International Peace.

Ottaway, M. and Choucair-Vizoso, J. (eds) (2008) *Beyond the Façade: Political Reform in the Arab World*, Washington, DC: The Carnegie Endowment for International Peace.

Paine, T. (1961) *The Rights of Man*, New York: Doubleday.

Pape, R. (2005) *Dying to Win: The Strategic Logic of Suicide Terrorism*, New York: Random House.

Pei, M., Nathan, A., Gilley, B., Dickson, B., Wang, S., Yang, L., Chen, A., Xiao, G., and He, Q. (2003) "China's Changing of the Guard," *Journal of Democracy*, 14, 1: 5–81.

Perlmutter, A. (1974) *Egypt: The Praetorian State*, New Brunswick, NJ: Transaction Books.

—— (1981) *Modern Authoritarianism: A Comparative Institutional Analysis*, New Haven, CT: Yale University Press.

Pinochet, A. (1977) *The New Institutional System in Chile*, Santiago, Chile.

Plattner, M. (1999) "From Liberalism to Liberal Democracy," *Journal of Democracy*, 10, 3: 121–34.

Polity IV. *Polity IV Country Reports*. Online. Available HTTP: http://www.cidcm.umd.edu/polity/country_reports/.

Polk, W. (2007) *Violent Politics: A History of Insurgency, Terrorism and Guerrilla War, from the American Revolution to Iraq*, New York: HarperCollins.

Popper, K. (2002) *The Logic of Scientific Discovery*, London: Routledge Classics.

Prebisch, R. (1950) *The Economic Development of Latin America and its Principal Problems*, New York: United Nations.

Przeworski, A., Alvaarez, M., Cheibub, J., and Limongi, F. (1996) "What Makes Democracies Endure?," *Journal of Democracy*, 7, 1: 39–55.

Putnam, R. (2000) *Bowling Alone: The Collapse and Revival of American Community*, New York: Simon and Schuster.

Putnam, R., Leonardi, R., and Nanetti, R. (1993) *Making Democracy Work: Civic Traditions in Modern Italy*, Princeton, NJ: Princeton University Press.

Pye, L. (1992) *China: An Introduction*, 4th edn, New York: HarperCollins.

Qutb, S. (n.d.) *Milestones*. Online. Available HTTP: http://www.youngmuslims.ca/online_library/books/milestones/hold/index_2.asp (accessed May 3, 2008).

Rhodes, R.A.W., Binder, S., and Rockman, B. (eds) (2006) *The Oxford Handbook of Political Institutions*, Oxford: Oxford University Press.

Rotberg, R. (2004) "The Failure and Collapse of Nation-states: Breakdown, Prevention, and Repair," in R. Rotberg (ed.), *When States Fail: Causes and Consequences*, Princeton, NJ: Princeton University Press.

—— (ed.) (2004) *When States Fail: Causes and Consequences*, Princeton, NJ: Princeton University Press.

Rouleau, E. (2000) "Turkey's Dream of Democracy," *Foreign Affairs*, 79, 6: 100–14.

Rustow, D. (1999) "Transitions to Democracy: Toward a Dynamic Model," in L. Anderson (ed.), *Transitions to Democracy*, New York: Columbia University Press.

Sakakibara, E. (1995) "The End of Progressivism," *Foreign Affairs*, 74, 5: 8–14.

Sartori, G. (1997) *Comparative Constitutional Engineering: An Inquiry into Structures, Incentives and Outcomes*, 2nd edn, New York: New York University Press.

Schedler, A. (2002) "The Menu of Manipulation," *Journal of Deomcracy*, 13, 2: 36–50.

—— (ed.) (2006) *Electoral Authoritarianism: The Dynamics of Unfree Competition*, Boulder, CO: Lynne Rienner.

Schumpeter, J. (1975) [1947] *Capitalism, Socialism, and Democracy*, 2nd edn, New York: Harper.

Sen, A. (1981) *Poverty and Famines: An Essay on Entitlement and Deprivation*, Oxford: Clarendon Press.

—— (1999) *Development as Freedom*, New York: Alfred A. Knopf.

Seznec, J.F. (2002) "Stirrings in Saudi Arabia," *Journal of Democracy*, 11, 4: 33–40.

Shugart, M. (2006) "Comparative Legislative–Executive Relations," in R.A.W. Rhodes, S. Binder, and B. Rockman (eds), *The Oxford Handbook of Political Institutions*, Oxford: Oxford University Press.

Siddiqa, A. (2007) *Military Inc.: Inside Pakistan's Military Economy*, London: Pluto Press.

Siegle, J. and Weinstein, M. (2005) *The Democracy Advantage: How Democracies Promote Prosperity and Peace*, New York: Routledge.

Sigmund, P. (ed.) (1972) *The Ideologies of Developing Nations*, New York: Praeger Publishers.

Skocpol, T. (1979) *States and Social Revolutions: A Comparative Analysis of France, Russia, and China*, Cambridge: Cambridge University Press.

Smith, A. (n.d.) *The Wealth of Nations*, New Rochelle, NY: Arlington House.

Smith, H. (1976) *The Russians*, New York: Ballantine Books.

Smith, W. (1982) *European Imperialism in the Nineteenth and Twentieth Centuries*, Chicago: Nelson-Hall.

REFERENCES

Soudriette, R. and Ellis, A. (2006) "Electoral Systems Today: A Global
Snapshot," *Journal of Democracy*, 17, 2: 78–88.

Stepan, A. (1971) *The Military in Politics: Changing Patterns in Brazil*,
Princeton, NJ: Princeton University Press.

—— (1988) *Rethinking Military Politics: Brazil and the Southern Cone*,
Princeton, NJ: Princeton University Press.

Stiglitz, J. (2002) *Globalization and Its Discontents*, New York: W.W. Norton.

Susser, B. (1992) *Approaches to the Study of Politics*, New York: Macmillan.

Tilly, C. (1978) *From Mobilization to Revolution*, Menlo Park, CA:
Addison-Wesley.

Tocqueville, A. de (n.d.) [1835] *Democracy in America*, trans. H. Reeve,
New Rochelle, NY: Arlington House.

United Nations Development Fund for Women (UNIFEM) (2005) *Progress of
the World's Women 2005*. Online. Available HTTP:
http://www.unifem.org/resources/item_detail.php?ProductID=48/
(accessed May 3, 2008)

United Nations Developmental Program (UNDP) (2007/8) *Human
Development Report*. Online. Available HTTP:
http://hdr.undp.org/en/reports/global/hdr2007–2008/ (accessed
May 3, 2008).

US Army (1974) FM [Field Manual] 100–20: *Low Intensity Conflict*,
Washington, DC: Department of the Army.

Watts, R. (1999) *Comparing Federal Systems*, 2nd edn, Montreal:
McGill-Queen's University Press.

Way, L. (2006) "Authoritarian Failure: How Does State Weakness Strengthen
Electoral Competition?," in A. Schedler (ed.), *Electoral Authoritarianism:
The Dynamics of Unfree Competition*, Boulder, CO: Lynne Rienner.

Waylen, G. (1996) *Gender in Third World Politics*, Boulder, CO: Lynne
Rienner Publishers.

Weber, M. (1964) *The Theory of Social and Economic Organization*, New York:
The Free Press.

Welch, C. (1987) *No Farewell to Arms? Military Disengagement from Politics in
Africa and Latin America*, Boulder, CO: Westview Press.

Whitehead, L. (2002) *Democratization: Theory and Experience*, Oxford: Oxford
University Press.

Wiarda, H. (1981) *Corporatism and Latin American Development*, Boulder,
CO: Westview Press.

Williamson, J. (1994) "In Search of a Manual for Technopols," in
J. Williamson (ed.), *The Political Economy of Policy Reform*, Washington,
DC: Institute for International Economics.

Wilson, W. (2002) *Constitutional Government in the United States*,
New Brunswick: Transaction Publishers.

World Bank (1996) *The World Development Report 1996: From Plan to Market*, Oxford: Oxford University Press.

Zakaria, F. (1994) "Culture is Destiny: A Conversation with Lee Kuan Yew," *Foreign Affairs*, 73, 2: 109–26.

—— (2003) *The Future of Freedom: Illiberal Democracy at Home and Abroad*, New York: W.W. Norton.

Index

Note: *italic* page numbers denote references to plates/figures/maps/tables.